THE FAMILY IN LAW

The Family in Law by Archana Parashar and Francesca Dominello provides a jurisprudential analysis of current family law, connecting doctrinal discourse with sociological, historical and economic analyses of the institution of the family.

The law's reliance upon the nuclear family ideology is central to the book's discourse, and provides the framework for in-depth analysis of the key areas of family law – marriage, divorce, children and property matters, as well as the legal regulation of abortion, assisted reproductive technologies, child protection and adoption.

The book is written for Australian legal actors whether students, academics or professionals. Readers are encouraged to question current frameworks, critique well-known cases and make informed conclusions about what changes could be made to engender a fairer and more equitable society.

In developing doctrinal analysis within a theoretical framework, the approach of the book challenges the conventional boundaries of family law, giving all readers a solid foundation and well-rounded understanding of this area of law and how it functions in the wider social context.

Archana Parashar is an Associate Professor in Law at Macquarie University and an Adjunct Professor of Law at the National Academy of Legal Studies and Research, Hyderabad and National University of Advanced Legal Studies, Kerala.

Francesca Dominello is a Lionel Murphy Scholar and lecturer in Law at Macquarie University.

THE FAMILY IN LAW

Archana Parashar and Francesca Dominello

CAMBRIDGE
UNIVERSITY PRESS

CAMBRIDGE
UNIVERSITY PRESS

University Printing House, Cambridge CB2 8BS, United Kingdom

One Liberty Plaza, 20th Floor, New York, NY 10006, USA

477 Williamstown Road, Port Melbourne, VIC 3207, Australia

4843/24, 2nd Floor, Ansari Road, Daryaganj, Delhi – 110002, India

79 Anson Road, #06–04/06, Singapore 079906

Cambridge University Press is part of the University of Cambridge.

It furthers the University's mission by disseminating knowledge in the pursuit of education, learning and research at the highest international levels of excellence

www.cambridge.org
Information on this title: www.cambridge.org/9781107561793

© Cambridge University Press 2017

First published 2017

Cover designed by Tanya de Silva-McKay
Typeset by Integra Software Services Pvt Ltd
Printed in China by C & C Offset Printing Co. Ltd., February 2017

A catalogue record for this publication is available from the British Library

A Cataloguing-in-Publication entry is available from the catalogue of the National Library of Australia at www.nla.gov.au

ISBN 978-1-107-56179-3 Paperback

Additional resources for this publication at www.cambridge.edu.au/academic/familylaw

Cambridge University Press has no responsibility for the persistence or accuracy of URLs for external or third-party internet websites referred to in this publication and does not guarantee that any content on such websites is, or will remain, accurate or appropriate.

Please be aware that this publication may contain several variations of Aboriginal and Torres Strait Islander terms and spellings; no disrespect is intended. Please note that the terms 'Indigenous Australians' and 'Aboriginal and Torres Strait Islander peoples' may be used interchangeably in this publication.

CONTENTS

ACKNOWLEDGEMENTS

This book is a culmination of many years of conversations between us. We have developed our views by sounding out colleagues and students in our classes. However, this project is a joint venture in more ways than that and we acknowledge the inputs and encouragement of colleagues and well wishers over time. In particular we wish to thank the staff of Cambridge University Press for supporting the publication of this book. We are very grateful to former Commissioning Editors, David Jackson, for encouraging us to submit a book proposal, and Martina Edwards for overseeing the final stages of that process. We are particularly thankful to Lucy Russell and Emily Thomas for their patience and guidance during the process of writing this book. We are grateful to the anonymous reviewers for their comments on the various chapters and to Joy Window for proofreading all of those chapters.

Macquarie Law School provided a very conducive atmosphere for completing this project and among others we would like to thank our colleagues Natalie Klein and Lise Barry for their support. We also wish to acknowledge the financial assistance provided by the Faculty of Arts, Macquarie University, and the research assistance provided by Dilara Reznikas and Isabella Ryan.

It is only appropriate that this book on family law was made possible due to the support of our families and we acknowledge this most sincerely. Archana dedicates the book to her mother and father, and her husband Vasudevacharya; Francesca to the memory of her parents, Cesarina and Vincenzo; her husband, Michael; her sisters, Antonella and Marisa; her children, Edita and Orlando, and all her nieces and nephews. Together we dedicate the book to our friend and mentor, Tony Blackshield, and to the memory of our friend and colleague, Lucy Martin.

PREFACE

Family law is an area we can all claim to have a vested interest in because of the impact it can have on everyone in society. This book adopts a unique approach to the study of family law by locating the family as central to understanding the content of family law and its development. Approaching the study of family law in this way, we have used an interdisciplinary framework that draws on sociological, historical and economic analyses of the institution of the family. There are many difficulties in trying to move across disciplinary boundaries, but in focusing on what these discourses say about the nature of family our aim is to demonstrate how the law also has its own understanding of what constitutes a family. The different things these discourses say about the family provide a framework for critiquing law's treatment of the family and thereby contribute to achieving a fairer law.

This approach is also unique in developing a distinctly jurisprudential analysis of family law. If, as we contend, the law has its own idea of what is a family then it becomes more clearly apparent how the law is engaged in the construction of the legal meaning of 'the family'. Hence the title of the book – *The Family in Law*. In developing this jurisprudential understanding of family law we are guided by the precept that legal meaning is constructed knowledge. In jurisprudential terms this view challenges the dominant positivist conceptions of law, particularly the understanding that the law is ascertainable by a process of applying objective and neutral reasoning. Although positivism has many nuances and has been challenged extensively in various critical discourses, it is also true that it retains a hold on our collective legal imagination. Thus, while cutting edge legal discourses are usually critical in nature, mainstream legal discourses have remained mostly doctrinal. This is well illustrated in the divide that exists in legal scholarship between those academic journal articles that are interdisciplinary and theoretical in an expansive sense and legal textbooks that are largely, if not exclusively, doctrinal.

The prominence of the legal positivist mode of thinking is achieved by a number of strands coming together; that is, in common law jurisdictions the heavy emphasis on judicial interpretations as the source of legal meaning helps create the impression that it is possible to discover the true meaning of any law. The conceptual device of legal reasoning as a special kind of reasoning legitimises the authority of judges to provide objective interpretations of the law. Legal education that emphasises learning specific skills over theoretical analyses of the law complements this worldview. It follows that the dominant understanding of legal study as professional training makes engaging with critical or interdisciplinary analyses of the law an optional extra, a matter of personal preference.

Critical theoretical analyses of law thus remain on the periphery of legal scholarship, revered and ignored at the same time.

We wish to bridge the gap between critical and doctrinal analyses of the law but without getting lost in the technical jargons of these different ways of thinking. For example, we use Foucault's insight that discourse is constructed and extend it to demonstrate how legal discourse is formed at various sites. However, we intentionally avoid engaging in technical debates about different methods of discourse analysis or on the 'correct' way of interpreting Foucault's ideas. We have also chosen not to engage with the contemporary debates about legal positivism or critical legal thought. Our aim is to carve a path between the technical extremes of critical and doctrinal thought in order to demonstrate how legal meaning is constructed rather than discovered. The focus of the book is on family law and how the family is constructed in law, but the implications of what we are saying run deeper. In the broader context of law this approach has profound implications for all legal actors because it means accepting that we each have a role in the construction of legal knowledge through the way we express our own conceptions of law. This also means we share a responsibility in the content of law and whether it operates fairly in society.

The book provides an overview of the legal doctrine on the conventional key areas of family law – marriage formation, divorce, children and property matters. In the discussion of these areas we develop the central thesis of the book – that family law relies on the nuclear family construct as the norm against which all other family structures are measured. This conceptualisation continues to reproduce certain assumptions about the family in law; namely, that it is predominantly a private institution whose main function is to provide economic and emotional support for its members. As will be made evident, provisions for property settlement, child support, and the presumption of equal shared parental responsibility cumulatively function in a way that places the greater costs of family breakdown on the more vulnerable members of the family, in an attempt made by the state to avoid bearing these costs itself.

This approach is problematic for a number of reasons, particularly as it implicates family law in maintaining relations of inequality that exist in the family and in society more broadly. As the realities of gender inequality, discrimination and poverty persist in our society, this book is a timely contribution in considering the place of family law within the wider social context. In demonstrating the ideological function of current family law perpetuating the nuclear family as the dominant structure, our aim is to enable the reader to explore the possibilities of family law engendering a more fair and equitable society.

In developing the doctrinal analysis of family law within an interdisciplinary theoretical framework, the book challenges the conventional understanding often found in conventional family law texts (that family law merely reflects the assumptions made about the family in other disciplines), to explore how the law makes explicit choices in regulating family life and the values to be pursued in law. In each chapter these choices will be exposed through an examination of the way the law understands the family, constructs its own legal knowledge about the family, and how these legal assumptions impact those seeking relief in family related matters. In exposing the choices made in the field of family law, readers will be able to understand the law as a site for the construction of legal knowledge about the family. In exposing the different ways the concept of family can be understood, the reader will be able to consider and reflect on their own understanding of the family and begin to appreciate how they could make a valuable contribution to the construction of family law.

Archana Parashar and Francesca Dominello

TABLE OF CASES

TABLE OF STATUTES

STUDYING FAMILY LAW

1.1   Introduction to family law

Family law is a ubiquitous area of law. It is an area that touches all of our lives in a way probably not paralleled by any other area of law. If this statement seems startling, it may be because of the association we usually make between family law and dispute settlement. We wish to take this as the starting point of this book and argue that family law is more than a dispute settlement mechanism. It determines many of the legal aspects of our relationships with our parents, spouse or partner, and children. It thus has much wider implications and is a significant factor that shapes our conventional understandings of what is a family. It is the constitutive role of family law that makes it a subject that should be of interest to everyone, and not only to legal scholars and practitioners.

Once it is accepted that it is the legal discourse of family law that informs or influences the wider understandings of 'what is family', it is important for judges, the legal profession, policy-makers and family law scholars to also be aware of how their conceptualisations of 'family' have a bearing on how we as a society think about family and its regulation by the law. They are after all the people who are most actively engaged in the making of 'Family Law'. Our book aims to increase awareness of this function of family law and how the law is actively engaged in the construction of ideas about the family and familial relationships.

This is not the usual approach to the study of family law, or any other area of law for that matter. The positivist conception of law, especially the understanding of law as objective and value-neutral, continues to prevail in legal study. In this regard our book challenges this positivist view of legal knowledge by developing the understanding of law as constructed knowledge. As we analyse family law throughout the book, it will become apparent that it is necessary to emphasise that family law is not value-free, but invokes particular understandings of 'the family' that have corresponding effects on broader society. For that matter, it is also important not to simply assume that family law is merely reflecting social realities, and to the extent that it embodies norms through its construction of the family, it is important to identify what these are and how they impact on society.

The claim that 'legal knowledge is constructed knowledge' is not novel, but our emphasis is to uncover how family law functions to entrench a particular conception of 'the family'. In particular, and central to the thesis of the book, is the reliance of the law on the construct of the nuclear family, traditionally conforming to the marriage model and comprising a union between a man and a woman, and their dependent children.[1] This approach in law is supported by the 'conventional wisdom' found in sociology that '[i]n Australia, the nuclear form of the family has predominated throughout this century. As the dictionary of sociology tells us, the nuclear family is a small group composed of husband, wife and immature children which constitutes a unit apart from the rest of the community'.[2] This is despite the

---

1   Belinda Fehlberg and Juliet Behrens, *Australian Family Law: The Contemporary Context* (Oxford University Press, 2008) 145.
2   Peter McDonald, 'Extended Family in Australia: The Family Beyond the Household' (1992) 32 *Family Matters* 4.

evidence in the research which suggests that there are many different kinds of families in existence in Australian society.[3]

The law's reliance on the nuclear family construct as the norm against which all other family structures are measured continues to reproduce certain assumptions about the family in law – namely, that it is predominantly a private institution whose main function is to provide economic and emotional support for its members, who are defined by their affective and biological ties to one another. We aim to explore the legal effects of this construct on the individuals who find themselves in the family law system and the continuing effects of this construct on the relations between them and with the state, even after their familial relationships have broken down.

In developing our argument we will use an interdisciplinary framework. Thus, the book gives an overview of the legal doctrine relating to the conventional key areas of family law – marriage, divorce, children and property matters, and extends the coverage to the legal regulation of abortion, assisted reproductive technologies, child protection and adoption. However, in our analysis of these areas we will develop a jurisprudential analysis of family law that connects the sociological, historical and economic analyses of the institution of family and the doctrinal discourses of law. The nature of interdisciplinary studies is a contentious area but, rather than engage in that debate, we will explain our approach. It is common for the interdisciplinary study of law to invoke the concepts and emphases of other disciplines, be they sociology, economics or cultural studies. We will also draw on other disciplines in our analysis of family law, and extend our analysis primarily to aspects of the judicial method in the case law, in order to demonstrate how the construction of legal meaning takes place. In approaching family law in this way, our aim is twofold.

First, our broader aim is to critique the law by drawing on the relevant sociological, historical and economic literature on the family to demonstrate how family law functions in ways that preserve the nuclear family and continue to perpetuate heterosexual normativity, cultural bias, age, sex and class hierarchies, and the sexual division of labour within and outside the family. In identifying these ideological functions of family law in supporting the nuclear family, we will provide the foundation for readers to explore how Australian family law may engender a fairer and more equitable society. Our aim in this regard is to inspire readers to consider whether family law could be different in view of the different ways 'family' can be conceived.

Second, in critiquing the doctrinal analysis within an interdisciplinary theoretical framework, our more immediate aim is to challenge the conventional boundaries of family law as found in the main texts on family law in Australia. For example, our approach extends further than the understanding of family law as reflecting the assumptions made about the family in other disciplines and explores how the law makes explicit choices in regulating family life. In this way family law can be understood as a site in which knowledge about the family is constructed. In each chapter these choices will be exposed as we examine the way in which law understands the family, constructs its own legal knowledge about the

3   See generally David de Vaus, *Diversity and Change in Australian Families: Statistical Profiles* (AIFS, 2004); Robyn Hartley and Peter McDonald, 'The Many Faces of Families: Diversity Among Australian Families and its Implications' (1994) 37 *Family Matters* 6.

family and the values to be pursued in law, and how these legal assumptions affect those seeking relief in the various jurisdictions in Australia that deal with family-related matters. In exposing the choices made in the field, we aim to enable readers to understand how they could make their own valuable contribution to the area of family law through their research and scholarship.

We are not suggesting that family law is coherent and without any contradictions in its various aspects.[4] Nevertheless, our analysis of the various aspects of family law demonstrates how family law broadly constructs discourses about families in a way that hierarchies found in contemporary society are maintained rather than challenged.[5] Thus, our overall aim is to deepen awareness and understanding of this dynamic area of law by critically examining the assumptions about family relations that are present in the law, and also to demonstrate how the construction of legal meaning is an ongoing process and can therefore change. Judicial interpretations of the relevant legislation will be the main focus of our analysis, as they remain the authoritative pronouncements of the law. We all are involved in questioning or accepting these pronouncements and therefore share the responsibility for the construction of family law.

1.2   Structure of the book

The book is divided into 12 chapters. Each chapter provides an overview of the key provisions and case law relevant to each topic and analyses the legal developments within an interdisciplinary framework.

This chapter sets out the interdisciplinary framework for our study of family law. Chapter 2 examines the history of family law and provides an overview of the constitutional arrangements and institutional structures of family law. This includes coverage of the court system and alternative dispute resolution mechanisms, and the treatment of violence within the family law system. Chapter 3 focuses on the legal requirements for marriage, the legal regulation of non-married couples, and the same-sex marriage debate. Chapter 4 looks at the legal requirements for divorce and the regulation of violence in family law. Chapter 5 provides an overview of the legal treatment of family property in the event of relationship breakdown. Chapter 6 looks at spousal maintenance. Chapter 7 considers private ordering in family law property and maintenance proceedings and the status of financial agreements in family law. Chapter 8 examines the treatment of children in the family law system. It examines the concepts of childhood and parental responsibility, as well as the court process and alternative dispute resolution mechanisms used in child-related proceedings. The broad range of factors used in determining these disputes are covered, with particular focus on the treatment of violence and child abuse. Chapter 9 expands the scope of enquiry to examine how other factors, such as wishes of the child, parent relocation and Aboriginal and Torres Strait Islander culture, are treated

---

4   See John Dewar, 'The Normal Chaos of Family Law' (1998) 61(4) *Modern Law Review* 467.

5   The hierarchies of contemporary liberal market economies extend beyond gender, race and sexual differences. Rather than focus on the existence of such hierarchies, we shall focus on how family law helps maintain or challenge them.

in these cases. Chapter 10 is divided into two parts: the first provides an overview of child-maintenance and support provisions and child-maintenance agreements; the second broadens the scope of the study by examining the main themes arising in the chapters on financial relations and children in the context of social-welfare policy and law. Chapters 11 and 12 consider the legal regulation of family life in the broader contexts of abortion law and child-protection regimes; and adoption and reproductive technologies.

1.3   Methodology

The analysis of family law in these chapters relies on three interconnected concepts related to the family: the nuclear family, the sexual division of labour, and the public/private divide. Focusing on these concepts will help to develop understanding of how the legal regulation of the family promotes the heterosexual nuclear family as the norm; reinforces certain assumptions about the family, and the roles of men and women and their place in society; maintains the sexual division of labour in families and in the marketplace; and perpetuates the economic dependency of the more vulnerable members of families.[6]

An obvious response to the assertion that family law supports the nuclear family is the claim that this family is not the only one upheld in law. This is true and our overview of the range of sociological and philosophical theories of family will illustrate the influence in this area of law of the liberal conception of individualism, which emphasises individual autonomy and freedom in family formation. We also include a discussion of the influence of feminist discourse in raising awareness of violence and oppression in the family. But in accepting the influence of liberalism in the legal recognition of other family structures (like de facto relationships), or feminism in acknowledging violence in the family (especially in cases involving children), we maintain that family law continues to uphold the nuclear model as the norm.

In developing our theoretical framework, we argue that family law moves between conceptions of the nuclear family as a union between two autonomous and equal partners and as a union that generates dependencies. It thus uses the discourse of individual autonomy on the one hand, and paternalistic concern to protect more vulnerable family members, usually women and children, on the other. Whether this approach can provide a framework for the development of a fair and equitable family law will be explored throughout the book. Family law doctrine, when analysed within an interdisciplinary framework, will illuminate the choices that are made in family law about whether to promote autonomy or maintain dependency, and will provide a source for critique of the preference given to the nuclear family structure in view of the disadvantageous effects it can have for the more vulnerable family members.

---

6   For instance, family law tries to preserve the social and economic support families provide despite the breakdown of these relationships through, eg, property settlement, child support, and the presumption of equally shared parental responsibility. However, these legal provisions cumulatively function so that the more economically vulnerable members of the family are expected to bear the costs of family breakdown in the attempts of the law to contain these costs on the state. This assertion will be substantiated in the following chapters.

1.4   The relationship between the law and family

As mentioned above, the proposition around which this book is structured is that family law chooses one kind of family, the nuclear family, and privileges it as 'the family'. Two immediate questions arise – how does the law incorporate a particular notion of family, and why does it matter? Preliminary answers to these questions are that law does so by portraying itself as a value-neutral dispute resolution mechanism; and it matters because in the process family law functions to legitimise the hierarchies that exist in families and in broader society. But we can only begin to appreciate these questions and answers if we understand that legal knowledge is constructed rather than discovered. This helps explain why legal developments in the area of family law cannot be understood in isolation from the social, economic and political developments in the wider society, and implicates everyone engaged in the legal process in the construction of legal knowledge.

But is the nuclear family the only family? In the following sections we briefly discuss the existence of plural views of family; the choices made in law to adopt certain definitions of the family and not others; the reluctance in positivist thinking about law to acknowledge that such choices are made; and the possibility of making these choices visible by understanding the law as constructed knowledge.

1.4.1   What is a family?

Family law incorporates not only a conception of law but also a conception of family. It is therefore important to explore the concept of family. The institution of family has existed in different forms in all societies throughout history. In the European context, the conventional story is that the extended family has morphed into the modern nuclear family owing to various factors, most notably the transformation of feudal and agrarian societies into modern and industrialised societies. Historians and sociologists generally support this explanation for changes in the family in Europe. For example, Stone, a well-known family historian, argues that increasing industrialisation and urbanisation in Europe meant that the structure of family changed from an extended family to an affective unit comprising the husband and wife and their biological children.[7]

Without going into the details of these debates at this stage, it is worth noting that the legal regulation of the family has similarly transformed and family law has come to focus on the man and the woman and their children as its subjects. The history of family law usually tells a story of progressive development where the formerly patriarchal institution of marriage has been transformed into an egalitarian institution.[8] Moreover, it is now commonly

---

7   Lawrence Stone, 'The Rise of the Nuclear Family in Early Modern England; The Patriarchal Stage' in Charles Rosenberg (ed), *The Family in History* (University of Pennsylvania Press, 1975) 13.

8   Extensive literature exists on this issue, but for an introduction see Martha Minow, '"Forming Underneath Everything that Grows": Toward a History of Family Law' [1985] *Wisconsin Law Review* 819.

claimed that law accommodates a plurality of families and is at least trying to be non-discriminatory even if this is an aspiration rather than an achieved goal.[9]

In examining the question 'what is a family?', let us begin by asking ourselves how we understand an arrangement to be 'a family'. One answer that everyone can agree with is that there is a basic lack of agreement on the matter. White and Klein provide a brief introduction to the different ways in which we understand family and its importance.[10] They illustrate this diversity by asking: which of these is a family?[11]

- A husband and wife and their child.
- A single woman and her three children.
- A 52-year-old woman and her adoptive mother.
- A man, his daughter, and the daughter' son.
- An 84-year-old widow and her dog.
- Two lesbians in an intimate relationship with children from previous relationships.
- Two children, their divorced parents, the current partners of their divorced parents and children of step-parents from previous marriages.
- A child, his stepfather and the stepfather's wife subsequent to his divorce from the child's mother.
- Two adult male cousins living together.
- A childless husband and wife who live 1000 miles apart.
- A married couple, one son and his wife and the children of this latter couple, living together.
- Six adults and their 12 children all living together in a communal home.

How we determine if any of these are considered 'a family', whether it is explicitly informed by a philosophical position or a common sense understanding, invokes certain theoretical assumptions and it is necessary for us to be aware of them. In the laws related to families these assumptions set the aims and content of regulation.

Moreover, it is evident that when discussing 'the family' we are not necessarily talking about the same thing. McDonald claims, for example, that 'family' is often equated with 'household', but that is only one among many ways of conceptualising the family.[12] He explains that changing ideas, rather than structural changes, explain the morphing nature of family. It could be ideas about individual autonomy, romantic love and privacy that shape our views of what constitutes a family. He elaborates on this by presenting how other researchers may depict the family as a unit of cooperation and exchange. Another approach

---

9   Various examples that show how both family law principles and process attempt to accommodate family diversity can be found. For a positive review of family law principles on same-sex parenting, see generally Adiva Sifris, 'Gay and Lesbian Parenting: The Legislative Response' in Alan Hayes and Daryl Higgins (eds), *Families, Policy and the Law: Selected Essays on Contemporary Issues for Australia* (AIFS, 2014) 89. See also in the same publication (at 169) Helen Rhoades, 'Children, Families and the Law: A View of the Past with an Eye to the Future'.

10   James M White and David M Klein, *Family Theories* (Sage Publications, 3rd ed, 2008).

11   Ibid 20.

12   Peter McDonald, 'Extended Family in Australia: The Family Beyond the Household' (1992) (32) *Family Matters* 4; Sherry Saggers and Margaret Sims, 'Diversity: Beyond the Nuclear Family' in Marilyn Poole (ed), *Family: Changing Families, Changing Times* (Allen & Unwin, 2005) 66.

has been to reject the idea that there can be a definitive definition of 'family' and to accept that people define their own families according to relationship, purpose and activity, circumstances applying or perceived obligations.[13] Therefore, it is difficult to say that there is one definition of family or that there is any consensus on the aims the definition should fulfil. Thus, individuals may determine their own families according to societal or personal expectations, notions of reciprocity, the history of their relationship, and altruism. This is amply reflected in the contemporary literature as well as in the common understanding that a plurality of family relations exists and the nuclear family is no longer (if it ever was) the dominant norm.[14]

Even so, at the level of ideas and idealised morality the nuclear family maintains a stronghold. The image of the nuclear family constituted by an increasing emphasis on individual autonomy, romantic love, ties of affection between parents and children, and the protection of the privacy of the family by the state continues to permeate the popular consciousness. Thus, in spite of the sustained and varied challenges to this conception (particularly since the 1960s),[15] and the substantial body of research on the plurality of family forms that exist in western societies, the actual decline of the nuclear family as a norm, or even as an aspiration, has been rejected and declared to be a myth.

Bittman and Pixley explain that the significance of the claim that the decline of nuclear family is a myth can be better understood if we follow the argument that the effects of myth have little to do with the truth of the matter.[16] They rely on Luhmann's two types of expectations – cognitive and normative – to explain that normative expectations are not usually modified even when they are contradicted by events. For example, the belief in an equal partnership between husband and wife in marriage is not shaken by evidence that the domestic division of labour is not an equal division. So too, the contemporary discourses that claim that the nuclear family is in decline, and the postmodern arguments that claim that the family is being replaced by other arrangements, can be seen as normative expectations. The point Bittman and Pixley are making is that the available evidence does not support the claim that the nuclear family is in decline. In fact, they argue that the belief that we live in diverse family structures is not the reality, either empirically or as an idea. The nuclear family continues to be the dominant family form in contemporary life.

So while in the literature on the plural forms of family the nuclear family seems to have lost its monopolistic position, what is not so apparent in this literature is the powerful cultural pre-eminence that the nuclear family has in society. Therefore, the decline of nuclear family at the empirical level is different from the hold of this idea on our imagination. But even the empirical evidence of such a decline is problematic, because evidence does not necessarily support the claim that the nuclear family (traditionally contained within the institution of marriage) is in decline. Instead where there has been an apparent decline in the proportion of 'nuclear family' households (such as in Australia), this can be partly explained as resulting from increases in life expectancy and changes in fertility. Thus, any changes to

---

13   McDonald, above n 12.
14   See de Vaus, above n 3.
15   Michael Bittman, 'The Nuclear Family in the Twenty First Century' in Jake M Najmann and John S Western (eds), *A Sociology of Australian Society* (Macmillan, 3rd ed, 2000) 301.
16   Michael Bittman and Jocelyn Pixley, *The Double Life of the Family: Myth, Hope and Experience* (Allen & Unwin, 1997) 1–15.

family structure are not because the nuclear family form has become unpopular. Alternative household structures may be better explained by patterns of fertility, for example baby booms/declines, ageing of the population, and a combination of rising divorce rates and an increasing number of people who will never marry.[17] Moreover, cultural diversity among Australia's Aboriginal and Torres Strait Islander peoples and immigrant populations, as well as social trends, has resulted in more single-parent, step and blended, multiple household and same-sex families, but these families have not replaced the nuclear family as the norm, evidenced by how they have not been provided with the same degree of state assistance and recognition.[18]

1.4.2   The choices law makes in determining what is a family

This is an important issue for the law's conception of family.[19] There is no avoiding the task of choosing a conception of family or families that law works with. Even with respect to the nuclear family, how we theorise the family (in law) has repercussions for real people; for example, if the law assumes that the nuclear family has been replaced by an egalitarian partnership, it will take a certain shape – validate the reflexive choices view of family that could make the reality of the dependency that exists in families invisible in law. But if the law upholds the dependency model of family too much, this could be at the expense of facilitating choice in forming and ending our intimate relationships. We will examine this point further by examining the broad contours of family law.

1.4.2.1   The broad contours of family law

Family law is most commonly understood as the law that determines the creation and dissolution of marriages or marriage-like relationships. This area also governs the resolution of disputes about maintenance and property, as well as parenting and child-support disputes that can arise at the end of a relationship. However, it is less clear whether family law extends to the regulation of domestic violence, provision of childcare facilities or social-welfare benefits. Similarly, it is more difficult to answer whether the area extends to the right to abortion or the availability of latest assisted reproductive technologies, for example. In most of the mainstream legal discourse, family law is viewed as boundary marking. It is treated as a specific area of law concerned with the formation of marriage (or similar intimate relationship) and divorce and certain ancillary matters.

The laws and policies that may have an impact on intimate relationships while they remain intact are not usually included in the subject of family law. Indeed the law seems to operate on the assumption that while these relationships remain intact family law does not regulate them, and the parties (usually the adults involved) decide on their mutual roles and obligations free of any state interference. In the case of marriage, only when the marriage relationship ends does the law step in to make divorce orders. In regard to intimate relations

---

17   Ibid 4.
18   Saggers and Sims, above n 12, 87.
19   For a discussion of some salient issues, see Alan Hayes and Daryl Higgins (eds), *Families, Policy and the Law: Selected Essays on Contemporary Issues for Australia* (AIFS, 2014).

more generally, it is only when they break down and the partners cannot agree on how to settle their affairs that family law steps in to order their parenting arrangements and finances. The boundary-marking role of the law also depicts it as a value-free mechanism in so far as the law does not define what is a 'good' or an 'ideal' family. This apparent neutrality of family law legitimises it, but it needs to be examined closely.

The legal definitions of 'family' of necessity draw upon other disciplines. Furthermore, many interdisciplinary conceptions of family in turn point to the need to justify the particular contours of family law. However, a cursory acquaintance with family law reveals that it is mostly concerned with monogamous partners and parent–child relations. Moreover, the *Family Law Act 1975* (Cth) ('FLA') contains a specific provision addressed to the courts to consider the need to protect and preserve the institution of marriage.[20] Indeed, it would seem that every relationship is regulated according to the marriage model. The influence of the hetero-nuclear family construct is no more obvious than in the marriage provisions that exclude same-sex marriages.[21] The recent extension of the property provisions for married couples to de facto relationships also demonstrates the primacy of the marriage relationship in law.[22] However, if family law chooses the nuclear family and privileges it as the family to uphold and protect in law, this will have uneven consequences for different members of society. In particular, the family law provisions regulating divorce, property division and parenting of children interlink to reinforce the power disparity between men and women (and their children) in our contemporary society.[23] Similarly, the nuclear family upheld as the norm in family law can also work to the disadvantage of other sections of society, such as people of different sexualities or Aboriginal and Torres Strait Islander peoples, who may have different parenting practices.[24] Thus, the protection of alternative family structures is lacking in law. Therefore, it is essential for us to identify how the law legitimises these choices. These choices may be explained in the broader historical, sociopolitical and economic context in which the law operates. But in the legal context, the dominance of the positivist conception of law cannot be ignored.

The mainstream conception of law continues to be a positivist conception despite the fact that critical views about law and legal knowledge exist in abundance.[25] Among other

---

20   FLA s 43(1)(a).

21   In the *Marriage Act 1961* (Cth) s 5, '"marriage" means the union of a man and a woman to the exclusion of all others, voluntarily entered into for life'.

22   FLA pt VIIIAB.

23   See generally Bruce Smyth and Ruth Weston, 'Financial Living Standards after Divorce' (Research Paper No 23, AIFS, 2000).

24   For recent cases on same-sex parenting and the difficulties facing lesbian co-parents seeking parenting orders under the FLA, see *Flynn v Jaspar* [2008] FMCAfam 106; *Keaton v Aldridge* (2009) [2009] FMCAfam 92; *Snell v Bagley* [2009] FMCAfam 1144. See generally Jenni Millbank, 'The Limits of Functional Family: Lesbian Mother Litigation in the Era of the Eternal Biological Family' (2008) 22(2) *International Journal of Law, Policy and the Family* 149. In the context of disputes involving Aboriginal and Torres Strait Islander children, the weight a judge gives to the child's right to enjoy his or her own culture under the FLA does not have to be consistent with Aboriginal or Torres Strait Islander parenting practices: *Offer v Wayne* [2012] FMCAfam 912. For more information on Aboriginal and Torres Strait Islander child-rearing practices, see Secretariat of National Aboriginal and Islander Child Care, *Growing Up Our Way: Child Rearing Practices Matrix* (2014) <http://aboriginalchildrensday.com.au/wp-content/uploads/2014/05/Growing-up-our-way-.pdf>.

25   For an accessible analysis, see Margaret Davies, *Asking the Law Question* (Law Book Co, 3rd ed, 2008).

explanations for the continued dominance of the positivist view of law is that it makes it easier to think of law as objective and neutral. In the context of family law, the positivist conception of law helps justify the use of objective rules to decide disputes between former partners when they can no longer resolve their differences. These rules are supposed to fit the way we as a society organise our personal lives. However, family law does not simply reflect the existing societal arrangements. Nor is any other area of law doing this. Law is better understood as something that comes into existence through discursive practices; it does not already exist, waiting to be discovered and applied. As we develop our argument, our point will be to show that all legal thinkers need to be alert to their role in the discourse formation of family law.

1.4.2.2   What does family law do? What should it do?

We accept that families are considered essential for the emotional stability of individuals (if not for other reasons as well).[26] It thus becomes imperative to consider whether families can be created or regulated without perpetuating economic disadvantage and social oppression. The role of law in creating such a change or maintaining the status quo is significant and needs to be explored. This in turn raises the question of what family law does in regulating familial relations. More importantly, what should it be doing? That is, can family law be understood as a dispute resolution mechanism only? Further, should law maintain a stance of neutrality in the settlement of disputes and thereby maintain the dynamic that existed before relationship breakdown? Or should the law aim to create substantive justice at the end of the relationship and intervene in the interests of the more vulnerable family members? Moreover, all aspects of the legal system play a role and are interconnected. Thus, legal provisions, whether dealing with procedural and/or substantive aspects, have the potential to exacerbate power disparities or alleviate them.

If we accept that the nuclear family perpetuates social inequality, we then need to consider whether family law should reflect this. Or should family law aspire to create rules that embody a fair arrangement for everyone concerned? Our view is that the latter stance should be accepted, as everyone has a stake in the content of family law. We approach the analysis of family law on this basis. In the context of this area of law, this means examining the procedure and substance of the law. In family law, it is especially important to analyse the procedural shift from adversarial litigation to alternative dispute resolution methods, including conciliation and mediation. Whether these are the most appropriate means to alleviate some of the identified drawbacks of the legal system, especially for the more powerless sections of society, needs to be considered. More broadly, any analysis of family law needs to address the question of whether reform to the substantive law has the potential to transcend the inequities that exist between men, women and children, and for people of different sexualities, cultures and socioeconomic backgrounds in contemporary social arrangements. Once it is accepted that the creation of an egalitarian and fairer society through law reform is a desirable goal, we are required to have some acquaintance with theoretical ideas about family and society from disciplines other than law. Such a study of family law provides a good opportunity to illustrate the relationships between the law, society and the state, and insight on how family law could be different.

---

26   As explained by Linda Nicholson, *Gender and History: The Limits of Social Theory in the Age of the Family* (Columbia University Press, 1986) 136–7.

The liberal state transgresses the public/private divide to regulate personal relations under the rubric of family law and it should aspire to do so in a just and fair manner. However, the kind of family the law upholds is assumed to be the existing norm in society and, as indicated above, this has varying consequences for different people. Moreover, family law is conceptualised as only about intimate relations and children. For an assessment of whether the law's definition of family is good, bad or indifferent, it is essential to ask where these norms come from. Both empirical and theoretical explanations are available. Sociology is the discipline most concerned with the institution of family and has many theories to offer.[27]

However, there continues to be resistance to this approach. In terms of 'knowledge construction', the disciplinary boundaries are invoked to bring into doubt whether lawyers need to know sociological theories of the family or indeed any other disciplinary knowledge related to families. In legal scholarship, the debate persists about what constitutes legal proficiency, and the idea that lawyers are professionals who primarily require technical knowledge of legal doctrine tends to be the dominant viewpoint. Accordingly, at most, theory is considered relevant for legal scholars, while legal professionals are required to develop their legal skills. We cannot go into the details of these debates,[28] but wish to argue that theoretical understandings of law are equally relevant for professionals, practitioners and scholars.

For example, one of the basic concepts in the FLA is that, if necessary, the court can alter the property interests of the parties if it is 'just and equitable to make the order'.[29] The notion of what is 'just and equitable' requires interpretation. How this notion is understood may change depending on which source of disciplinary knowledge is used as the reference point. For example, lawyers representing their clients could argue that what is just and equitable should be informed by sociological and/or feminist scholarship. The judges in turn could rely on this knowledge, but its meaning could be constrained through the application of conventional methods of legal reasoning, which purport that the role of judges is to apply and not make the law. Thus, how the courts have previously interpreted the concept is important, and so too is the interpretation of lawyers advising their clients in these cases.

Furthermore, given that the parties are expected to resolve their disputes without coming to the court, a high proportion settle privately or with the help of mediators and/or lawyers. It is worth pondering where these experts get their ideas of what may be a 'just and equitable' distribution of resources. The judicial pronouncements may be a guide, but they have to be interpreted as they are not mathematical formulas. Thus, the question whether the shift to alternative dispute resolution methods is conducive to just and equitable outcomes becomes a significant issue. Viewed in this way everyone in the family law arena – the parties, the experts and the professionals – have a reason to inform themselves about what is 'just and equitable' in family law terms.

In the discussion below, we will examine the sociological theory of the nuclear family based in structural functionalism, as it will help to explicate how the nuclear family is legitimised in law. We acknowledge that structural functionalism is no longer the accepted

---

27   See White and Klein, above n 10, for a relatively recent survey of these theories.
28   For an introduction to this literature, see Sean Coyle, 'Two Concepts of Legal Analysis' in Sean Coyle and George Pavlakos, *Jurisprudence or Legal Science: A Debate About the Nature of Legal Theory* (Hart Publishing, 2005) 15.
29   FLA s 79(2). See details in Chapter 5.

wisdom within the discipline of sociology.[30] However, it is present in the legal discourse of the family in multiple ways and for that reason it is necessary to understand the theory in its original form. For example, the idea derived from structural functionalism that the family is necessary for the socialisation of children finds expression in family law in various ways, as we will illustrate in the following chapters.

Thus, the significance of the structural functional view of family is not that the law explicitly endorses it, but the extent to which this is the common sense understanding of family that surfaces in various ways in family law discourses. With this background context in mind, we next examine the three concepts of the family: the nuclear family, the sexual division of labour, and the distinction between public and private spheres of life. All three come together to explicate the contemporary contours of family law.

1.4.3 Concepts of the family in law

1.4.3.1 The concept of the nuclear family

The main issue we address in this section is how the nuclear family is supported in the wider literature and to what extent this knowledge is applied in family law. In modern societies it is not unusual to say that a family consists of a married couple (a husband and wife) and their biological children. It is a heterosexual, monogamous union that is considered necessary for the wellbeing of its members, especially children.[31] Moreover, it is the normal or universal family, with 'normal' meaning that it is inevitable because it is the natural state of being. There are various reasons why,[32] and in the following discussion we examine three explanations: the common sense or empirical claim that 'this is how everyone lives'; the biological claim that it is for the protection of vulnerable children, and therefore necessary for the survival of the human race; and the claim based on the functionality of family that it best meets the needs of broader society.[33] We elaborate on these claims in greater detail below.

It may come as a surprise that each of these justifications, all relating to the conception of family in modern times, continue to reflect to some degree Aristotle's view of the family. Aristotle, writing in 335–330 BC, argued that family is properly structured by gender. The husband, 'fitter for command', rules. According to Aristotle, the sexes express their excellences differently: 'the courage of a man is shown in commanding, of a woman in obeying'.[34] Through these complementary roles, marital good is promoted. It is also important at this point to note the influence of Christianity, some centuries later, in its formulation of the

---

30   For a concise analysis, see David Cheal, *Family and the State of Theory* (University of Toronto Press, 1991). See also White and Klein, above n 10, 53ff, claiming that the rise of neo-functional family theory is a significant contemporary development that makes structural functionalism very relevant.

31   There is extensive literature in this area, but for an introduction see Michael Anderson (ed), *The Sociology of the Family: Selected Readings* (Penguin, 2nd ed, 1980); see also David M Newman, *Families: A Sociological Perspective* (McGraw-Hill, 2009).

32   See the articles in Arlene S Skolnick and Jerome H Skolnick (eds), *Family in Transition* (Pearson Education, 17th ed, 2014).

33   We use selected authors to illustrate our argument and do not intend to provide an exhaustive survey of this scholarship.

34   *Politics*, ca. 330 BC, 1253b, 1259b, 1260a; *Nicomachean Ethics*, ca. 325 BC, 1160–62, extracted from Jonathan Barnes (ed), *The Complete Works of Aristotle: The Revised Oxford Translation* (Princeton University Press, 1999) vol 2.

'goods' of marriage to include fidelity and procreation – both seen as essential in ensuring paternal guidance for the children of the marriage.[35] And in more modern times, as we will see, the socialisation of children in the family has been treated as essential for preparing 'men' for good citizenship in the state.[36] Viewed in these ways, the family is perceived as necessary for ensuring the continuation not only of the human race through procreation, but also of society as a whole through the socialisation of children. And, as will become increasingly apparent, it continues to be a hierarchical structure, supported by gender differences and legitimised for the benefit of the child.

The classical formulation of the nuclear family as the normal family can be seen reflected in a celebrated book by Lasch.[37] In that book, Lasch argues that the family is where we retreat for solace and comfort from 'a heartless world' that exists outside the family. He defends the private family against radicals (politically left and feminist critics) and an ever-expanding state. He is critical of modern sociology of the family for focusing on the relationship between the partners rather than on the role of family in socialising children. In his view, it is evident in the way that the helping professions, the school and the peer group have taken over family functions and have invaded family and undermined it. He argues that a healthy family is important for personal and individual development. For this development, the tasks of caring for the young and teaching them discipline and love must be carried out within the family by parents along gender lines. Thus, he takes issue with feminist claims that the family is to blame for the economic oppression of women.[38] The remedy for removing the economic dependence of women in families lies in changing the work environment rather than the family, in his view. His response to the feminist critiques of marriage and the nuclear family is to make the work arrangements more humanised. In this regard he implies that the gendered divisions of family life should be better accommodated and reflected in the social economy, and not the other way around.

Another stream of thought depicting family as a biological necessity are the claims made in sociobiology. Briefly and somewhat simplistically, sociobiology claims that family is biologically necessary for human survival. Therefore, there is no point in trying to change it. The discontent of some with the family can be addressed within the family. This is illustrated well by Rossi in her argument that it is a central biological truth that the continuity of the human race requires reproduction and child rearing through the institution of family.[39] She argues that, while in earlier sociological literature this understanding was misconstrued because it depended on biological determinism, which assumes that women can perform these tasks, the more contemporary emphasis of sociology on variant forms of families based on individual choice undermines the role of women as mothers, and therefore is

35   John Finnis, 'The Good of Marriage and the Morality of Sexual Relations: Some Philosophical and Historical Observations' (1997) 42(1) *American Journal of Jurisprudence* 97, 105–6.

36   This understanding may also be attributed to Aristotle. See also Georg WF Hegel, 'Elements of the Philosophy of Right' in Allen W Wood (ed), *Cambridge Texts in the History of Political Thought* (Cambridge University Press, 1995) 211–13.

37   Christopher Lasch, *Haven in a Heartless World* (Basic Books, 1977) xiv–xvii, 37–43.

38   For an introduction to the feminist critique of the nuclear family, see Carole Pateman, *The Sexual Contract* (Polity Press, 1988).

39   Alice S Rossi, 'A Biosocial Perspective on Parenting' (1977) 106(2) *Daedalus* 1. For a critique of the assumptions in sociobiology, see Stephen J Gould, 'Sociobiology: The Art of Storytelling' (1978) 80 *New Scientist* 530.

also misplaced. This celebration of egalitarianism in the family ignores the fundamental biological fact that women are better suited than men to nurture their young. The demands for egalitarian relations between sexual partners expect women to adopt male behaviours. The fact that women's roles as nurturers were used in the past to disadvantage women is not reason enough to deny this biological fact. In her view, science has gone a long way towards rejecting biological determinism by acknowledging social sciences research, but the social sciences are afraid of acknowledging the relevance of biology lest they be accused of biological determinism.

The third view of the family that is important to our discussion is the sociological theory of structural functionalism. This theory advances the understanding that any major social institution should serve the interests of the individual as well as of the society in which that individual lives. In this sense, the function of family as an institution is to satisfy the needs of the individual and of the society as well.[40] Functionalism is a form of explanation rather than a set of substantive ideas.[41] The most well-known sociologist of this theoretical strand is Talcott Parsons.[42] His views about the nuclear family have been extensively critiqued and are no longer the dominant view in sociology, but it is also the case that his views have been very influential in normalising the idea of the nuclear family.[43] It is worthwhile to understand the building blocks of his views.

As Cheal explains, structural functionalism views family as an adaptive unit that mediates between the individual and society.[44] When the structure of society changes, the forms of family life change to create a fit between family and society. Thus, as western societies entered the period of modern industrialisation, families had to adapt to meet the needs of an industrial economy. The conjugal family evolved and took precedence in modern social life because it was the structure perceived to be the best equipped to meet the needs of the capitalist economy.

White and Klein explain that Parsons' perspective on families, described as functionalism, divides the social world into three systems:[45] the cultural system comprising shared symbols and meanings; the social system comprising organised social groups and institutions; and the personality system comprising specific generic types of personalities. Families are based on the social system that requires socialisation processes to integrate individuals into groups or societies. The basic/irreducible functions of family are primary socialisation of children in order for them to become members of society and the stabilisation of the adult personality for the adults to operate well in society. These two functions are interlinked, as a child can only be socialised into a society when the society is institutionalised and organised into expected role structures – that is, when the adults have received stability from such role structures as well.

Family contains four fundamental types of status roles, but the basic role structure of the family is the normal nuclear family. In such a family, the father in his actions is instrumentally

---

40   Cheal, above n 30, 3–6, 8–18.
41   White and Klein, above n 10, explain that in functional theory questions about why things exist are answered by how things exist or function. We are looking for a functional explanation every time we ask how something works, rather than asking why something exists.
42   Talcot Parsons and Robert F Bales, *Family, Socialization and Interaction Process* (Routledge, 1956).
43   See also White and Klein, above n 10, 53–5, for the view that Parson's views have found a new life in the ascendance of neo-functionalism.
44   Cheal, above n 30, 4.
45   This account is based on White and Klein, above n 10, 34–40.

oriented and he navigates the external world. The mother is expressively oriented and thus navigates relations between family members. In Parsons' theory, it is this role structure within the family that explains socialisation. The process of socialisation helps produce a social actor, who is involved in a system of relationship with others. The institutional structure of the family with its sets of binary relations enables the child to define him- or herself within the context of well-defined others. It is because of these relations that the child becomes adept at relationships within the family and in the outside world. The child acquires competence at social interaction (roles) within the family and then extends these skills to relationships outside the family such as school and work.

According to this theory, a family with a stay-at-home mother and breadwinner father best achieves the structural functional outcomes of well-adjusted individuals in a smoothly functioning society. This understanding of family and society has been critiqued extensively,[46] and in sociology structural functionalism is no longer the dominant theory. However, for our purposes it is important to understand the details of this theory because it is very often the case that these ideas about the roles of men and women in the family are upheld in law, but they are not in any formal sense based on structural functional ideas. To further explicate these roles, we now turn to the concept of sexual division of labour that underpins the theory of structural functionalism.

1.4.3.2   The sexual division of labour

Taking the assumptions underlining all three theories outlined in the previous section to the next level, they translate into, and legitimise, the production and maintenance of the sexual division of labour both in the home and outside of it. At the theoretical level the concept of the sexual division of labour, now more commonly described as 'gendered work', reflects gendered assumptions about men and women.[47] Men are worldly while women are homely. So understood, the sexual division of labour refers to men working to generate an income and women working in the home performing domestic and caregiving functions without economic return. Although this was never entirely true (especially for working-class women) and has become less true (for middle-class women), the concept of gendered work has not become obsolete. At a more practical level, it captures the different kinds of work performed by men and women in contemporary domestic and market arenas. Feminist analyses have shown that when women enter the paid labour market they are concentrated in industries that can be characterised as predominantly female. Moreover, same-sex segregation is present within specific occupations and firms.[48]

---

46   See, eg, Barry Thorne, 'Feminist Rethinking of the Family' in Barry Thorne and Marilyn Yalom (eds), *Rethinking the Family* (Longman, 1982); Pauline Boss et al (eds), *Sourcebook of Family Theories and Methods* (Plenum, 1993); Mark Poster, *Critical Theory of the Family* (Pluto Press, 1978) ch 7, 166–205. For an argument that the nature of families has changed owing to increased individualisation, see Ulrich Beck and Elisabeth Beck-Gernsheim, *Individualization: Institutionalized Individualism and its Social and Political Consequences* (Sage Publications, 2002).

47   Lee Chalmers, 'Gendered Work' in Alex C Michalos (ed), *Encyclopedia of Quality of Life and Well-Being Research* (Springer, 2014) 2472–5.

48   For an overview of the history of women's workforce participation in Australia, see Glenda Strachan, 'Still Working For the Man? Women's Employment Experiences in Australia Since 1950' (2010) 45(1) *Australian Journal of Social Issues* 117.

This is a vast area of study and has generated extensive literature.[49] We rely on an article by Curthoys as it illustrates all the relevant issues.[50] She analyses many theoretical explanations that rationalise this phenomenon on the basis of specific biological differences between men and women and their inherited ideologies and socialisation, and on the broader influences of human capital theory, labour market segmentation, employer discrimination and industrial organisation. She concludes that it is the capitalist economy that structures both distinctive productive relations and a distinctive kind of family household. In a capitalist economy, only part of the population is in direct wage employment and all others subsist in dependent relations. Thus, the work of personal caring remains largely within the household and is sustained through dependence on a wage earner. Women largely do private caring; men rarely choose, or are forced, to do this work and, as a result, men and women relate differently to the labour market, with women having a lower participation in it.

This lower participation of women in turn means that when they are in the labour market they command less remuneration than men. Once it is the case that men earn more than women, then a material and ideological base is laid for women to withdraw from the labour market to care for children (or other family members) when required. In conclusion, Curthoys argues that the division between men and women in the labour market is the product of a fundamental contradiction between the simultaneous existence of the capitalist relations of production and a family household structure. This contradiction manifests as the existence of the sexual division of labour informed by sexist ideologies about the roles of men and women in society. Writing in the 1980s, she envisaged that job segregation by sex would, in time, be undermined by several developments such as women's growing employment rates; closing the gap between male and female wages; closing the gap between male and female years of education; and the political influence of feminism. However, some three decades later we still live in a society where the sexual division of labour has not disappeared, and this requires an explanation.[51] The ideology of gender differences offers only part of the explanation.

These differences are housed within the private and public spheres of existence that further entrench and legitimise the sexual division of labour. One major consequence of the liberal conception of life is that the private sphere – the family – should be free of state/law regulation. This approach depends on the nuclear family as the 'natural' and therefore private family. In turn, this approach enables the sexual division of labour to appear to be a natural phenomenon, obscuring not only the effects of capitalism in its reproduction, but also how the sexual division of labour is institutionalised in part through family law. As noted above, family law concerns itself with private life and so its existence is explained and legitimised as facilitative only. As a legal category, family law gives the appearance that the law steps in only if the parties cannot resolve their disputes themselves. It thus has a boundary-marking function and is treated as though it is value-neutral. The ideology of family law is supposed to be one of giving freedom to the parties to organise their family lives

---

49   See, eg, the literature discussed in Scott Coltrane, 'Gender Theory and Household Labor' (2010) 63(11) *Sex Roles* 791.

50   Ann Curthoys, 'The Sexual Division of Labour: Theoretical Arguments' in Norma Grieve and Ailsa Burns (eds), *Australian Women: New Feminist Perspectives* (Oxford University Press, 1986) 319.

51   Peter McDonald, 'Social Reproduction: The Need for a New Social Contract' (2000) 48 *Growth* 33.

as they wish to do.[52] In this manner, family law normalises, rather than problematises, the public/private dichotomy.

1.4.3.3   The public/private dichotomy

The distinction between public and private spheres of life existed even in classical politics, but its adaptation in modern thought through liberalism is premised on very different assumptions and consequences. Nicholson makes a significant point that 'public' and 'private' are analytical categories; they are not natural, but have been constructed in theory and implemented in practice.[53] It follows that there is nothing natural about being able to demarcate family (private) from the economy or the state (public). The historical specificity of how these categories came into existence makes it possible to question the inevitable or natural separation of the political and personal.

Nicholson analyses Locke's theory and argues that while classical liberalism is a theory of the state, it is equally a theory of the family. However, its theory of family is patriarchal rather than egalitarian – a rather serious charge against liberals who think they are the champions of equality. The pre-modern conception of paternal political authority came to be replaced with the modern conception of authority of the state, but the older, patriarchal authority of the man was strengthened within the family. This was achieved to a large extent by drawing distinctions between the public and private spheres.

Similarly, even though contemporary ideas continue to separate the family from the economy, it is important to remember that both have a common origin in the structures of kinship. In pre-industrial society and in early modern times, the household was a productive and therefore an economic unit. The separation of family and economy is a cumulative effect of the changing meaning of productivity and reflects a more limited meaning of economic activity that refers to the production and exchange of commodities. The significance of acknowledging this separation as a historical development, and not a natural state of affairs, is that it affected women more than men. It is not surprising then that feminists have extensively critiqued the concepts of public and private, and questioned their characterisation as spheres of regulation and freedom respectively.[54] The following discussion relies on Poole's seminal work on the public and private sphere where he explains why the public and private spheres are conceptualised in a specific manner and thereby challenges the distinction between them.

Significantly, Poole finds that the two spheres are not separate, but are dependent on each other.[55] The liberal conception of the public sphere can happen only if there is a

---

52   We will illustrate this throughout the book and, as an example, mention here the assumptions of individual choice and freedom that inform no-fault divorce, the 'clean break' philosophy that underpins settlement of financial relations, and the presumption of shared parental responsibility that applies in child disputes. In our view, in the contemporary law none of these issues is a 'legal' issue, but all are treated more like private matters. Even at the end of relationships they can remain private matters to be settled by the parties in private agreements.

53   The following discussion is based on Linda Nicholson, *Gender and History: The Limits of Social Theory in the Age of the Family* (Columbia University Press, 1986) 106–28.

54   Feminists have asked 'what kind of freedom?' and 'whose freedom?'. Thus, domestic violence, rape within marriage, and child abuse and neglect have only gradually been subjected to law. For a collection of essays on the topic, see Hilde Lindemann Nelson (ed), *Feminism and Families* (Routledge, 1997).

55   The following discussion is based on Ross Poole, *Morality and Modernity* (Routledge, 1991) 46–50.

particular kind of private sphere. A liberal capitalist society requires this kind of private sphere for the market economy to be able to exist. This can be understood better if we first identify the assumptions on which explanations of how a market economy functions are built.

In capitalist economies, market exchange is a contractual economic activity between relative strangers for mutual benefit and profit maximisation. There is no place for sentiment or altruism and the market individual is considered to use reason as the guiding factor. Poole in his analysis draws on the political economic theory of Max Weber. According to Weber, rational activity is a necessary condition for the rationalisation of the processes of production, distribution and social organisation, and for these to work they need to be institutionally separated from the family, from the erotic and the emotional. Therefore, both the market and the bureaucracy operate 'without regard for persons' and on 'calculable rules'. The principle of calculable rules is of particular importance to the modern bureaucracy. It is achieved by a conceptual exclusion of the personal, the emotional and the domestic, and makes it possible for modern rationality to operate in the market and bureaucratic operations.

At this point, it is important for us to stop and question, as Poole does, whether a market-based economy could actually reproduce itself. If market actors are considered to act rationally in order to maximise their self-interest, it becomes difficult to suggest that they would produce children who would be like them and only interested in pursuing their own interests. Moreover, it does not seem to be rational behaviour to bring up children who may not be altruistic in turn and prepared to look after the parents. It is for this reason that theorists have always assumed the existence of a private sphere where life is organised according to a different set of values. This is the explanation for conceptualising the doctrine of separate spheres where life is divided into public and private, separate but unequal spheres of life. As mentioned above, in Weber's thought modern rationality is possible because the emotional mode of existence is excluded from the market processes of production, distribution and social organisation. The corollary to this conception is that the private sphere of domestic life becomes the rightful place for non-rational or emotional behaviours, and for this reason it is treated as the lesser member of the binary division.

This exclusion and subordination makes the modern public and private spheres possible. Furthermore, Poole argues that this distinction maps onto another distinction, that between male and female. In fact, it is more accurate to describe these as the constructs of masculinity and femininity. The public and private distinction gets associated with masculine and feminine values respectively. It is important to understand, however, that this mapping is not because women in fact inhabit the private sphere and men the public sphere, but because certain values get defined as masculine or feminine. Thus, the attributes required for the public arena of rationalised institutions of capitalist production, market exchange and bureaucratic administration are also characterised as masculine traits. By contrast, attributes required in the private and domestic sphere of family relations are characterised as feminine qualities. Women largely inhabit this sphere of domesticity and these feminine characteristics in turn make it difficult for them to enter public life. The point that gets lost in all this is that the concept of 'feminine' is a construct and is different from the qualities of females.

As we saw in the earlier justifications for the nuclear family as the natural family, the roles of men and women are clearly demarcated and, despite being complementary, they turn out to be hierarchical as well. This hierarchy needs to be explained; it will also help to analyse the contours of family law in later chapters. Feminists have utilised the concept of the sexual division of labour to explain how women's labour in both paid and unpaid work comes together and is normalised by reference to the concepts of public and private spheres.[56] The continuing effects of the public/private distinction can be seen in family law. On the one hand, the law treats the intact family as private, allowing the dependencies created by the sexual division of labour in caring for children to be distributed unevenly between men and women. On the other hand, when the relationship breaks down and enters the public realm, the dependencies that existed are obscured by the law applying a neutral stance in treating the parties as autonomous individuals existing on an equal footing with one another. In present times, this seems most evident in the application of the presumption of equally shared parental responsibility in cases involving disputes over the care arrangements for children at the end of a relationship.

However, not everyone may be convinced that the sexual division of labour is as problematic for women as it seems in the above discussion. One counter-argument to these critiques of sexual division of labour is that women are not a homogenous group or a mass of 'mindless zombies' who lack agency or are unable to make real choices.[57] Hakim's argument is an illustration of the strand of thought that explains women's presence in the private sphere as an effect of choices made by responsible adults. The suggestion is that different women make different life choices with some choosing to be home-centred with paid work as a secondary activity, while others choose to be career-oriented and place less emphasis on domestic considerations. The explanation for men and women occupying different roles in family and the economic sphere thus becomes a function of the choices women make.

But even if one accepts that women make choices about whether to work in or outside the home, or both, these choices reflect the gendered hierarchy of our contemporary society. These choices have to be made primarily by women because culturally they are available only to women. Moreover, the cost of choosing not engage in paid work is heavy in economic terms and in a capitalist society this does not equate with rational behaviour.[58] It thus is an inevitable conclusion that the choice explanation diverts attention from structural inequalities and converts a social issue into an individual problem.

An important element missing in the choice argument is that women make such choices because of their responsibilities for child bearing and rearing. Wage work is organised in a manner that makes it very difficult, if not impossible, for women to engage in such work and bring up children at the same time. We use the word 'women' intentionally as it is a cultural reality of our contemporary societies that care work is predominantly the responsibility of women.[59] Thus, women with children are the ones who are making choices about engaging

---

56   See, eg, essays in the following collections: Thorne and Yalom, above n 46; Susan Boyd (ed), *Challenging the Public/Private Divide: Feminism, Law, and Public Policy* (University of Toronto Press, 1997); Margaret Thornton (ed), *Public and Private: Feminist Legal Debates* (Oxford University Press, 1995).

57   The term used by Hakim in Catherine Hakim, 'The Sexual Division of Labour and Women's Heterogeneity' (1996) 47(1) *The British Journal of Sociology* 178.

58   See McDonald, above n 51, for the argument that women respond by restricting fertility. However, for the present book the more relevant issue is how the FLA facilitates this 'choice'.

59   See, eg, Nancy Folbre, *Valuing Children: Rethinking the Economics of the Family* (Harvard University Press, 2008) 121–38; see also Nancy Folbre 'Reforming Care' in Janet C Gornick and Marcia K Meyers (eds), *Gender Equality: Transforming Family Divisions of Labor* (Verso, 2009).

in wage work or domestic but unpaid work. This has damaging economic effects on their lives if their marriage or similar relationship ends.[60]

Family law plays a major role in maintaining this state of affairs by the way that it too endorses the idea that the organisation of family life is the product of making choices[61] and that the power to do so is equally available to both partners. In its design then, the law is facilitating the organisation of society through a family structure that endorses dependencies. This is the nuclear family of law. As we saw above, various thinkers explain the need for such a family but they make the common assumption that this arrangement will continue for the lifetime of the partners. Difficulties especially arise when the relationship between the two adults breaks down and both of them are expected to start afresh.

In the family law literature, the question that is not asked very often is whether it is a fair system of law that apportions the costs of bringing up children disproportionately between men and women.[62] One obvious reason for the lack of consideration of this issue reflects the choice argument that functions to make it a personal or a private issue. Furthermore, family law claims that it will compensate the primary carer, if need be, by dividing the property of the two spouses in a just and equitable manner when the relationship breaks down. Both of these are problematic arguments that do not address the structural issues arising from a gendered labour market that is shielded by the private family arrangement.

This returns us to the question we posed earlier: what is the aim of family law? One way of answering this question is to try to imagine a situation where no such body of law called family law exists. Two adult partners may be treated as independent contracting agents or as partners in a joint venture, rather than as a collection of individuals. Either way, dividing the available resources between the parties and determining their responsibilities for the children are required if their relationship breaks down. This leads us to the question: how may this be done fairly and what constitutes a just outcome?

1.5   Justice in the family

To start, it is important to point out that in liberal thought justice is a value that operates in the public sphere, and the implication is that it is not a relevant value in organising families. Thus (and building on the discussion in the previous sections), the nuclear family

---

60   This is evidenced in various studies of the effects of dissolution on women with children. See for an earlier example Peter McDonald, *Settling Up: Property and Income Distribution on Divorce in Australia* (AIFS, 1986); for a more recent assessment, see David de Vaus et al, 'The Economic Consequences of Divorce in Australia' (2014) 28(1) *International Journal of Law, Policy and the Family* 26.

61   These choices include when to enter into a marriage or marriage-like relationship, when to leave and whether to have children, how to bring them up and how to organise your finances in an ongoing relationship. At the end of a relationship, the autonomy to make choices is overridden primarily if the financially dependent partner will require social-welfare support. We illustrate this point in later chapters.

62   It is worth emphasising at this stage that the following discussion is not about the value of different kinds of work. The love, care and altruism that prevail in family relations are all valuable ways of being, but the point here is that family law does not concern itself with any of these issues. Instead it operates on an assumption of gender neutrality that does not adequately account for the social or cultural expectations around caregiving work.

construct relegates the family to the private sphere where familial relations are organised by the natural relations of affection and trust arising from the biological ties of mother and father to their offspring. Feminists have criticised these claims, arguing that abuse of women and children in the family and the financial inequalities between men and women that are produced by the sexual division of labour outweigh the virtues of love and affection in the family. Justice is an essential value that should apply to the family to protect the more vulnerable family members from the violence and exploitation that can, and does, occur in families.[63] In the discussion below, we analyse the concept of justice and how it could apply so that family and fairness exist together. Okin uses the public concept of justice to orient the regulation of relations between men and women in intimate relationships. Kymlicka extends this approach and through the concept of contracts explores justice in the family on other than gender grounds.

Okin, in an influential book, develops the argument that inequalities between men and women in families are a result of the unequal distribution of unpaid labour of the family or the caregiving work.[64] Okin argues that, rather than adopt an uncritical defence of the family for its promises of love and devotion, it is more important to rethink the family as a just institution. This is important not only for individual women, but also for social justice. She addresses two very different arguments that claim that family is beyond justice.[65]

For example, Sandel in his book *Liberalism and the Limits of Justice* argues that family is a unit where people have common rather than conflicting interests.[66] The relationships are organised around values of love and altruism and in that sense this institution operates with much nobler values than those of justice. Thus, justice is irrelevant to the family because when conflicts of interests arise or there is a scarcity of resources to be distributed, men are capable of protecting the interests of all of the members in the family unit. Sandel claims that values and interests of members coincide enough and, in more or less ideal family situations, spontaneous generosity and affection will prevail. Moreover, if members of a family start operating in accordance with principles of justice it will result in the loss of other nobler virtues. It is in this sense that family is beyond justice.

Okin responds to Sandel's argument by claiming that it is based on two faulty premises: first, that it misunderstands the idea of justice as the primary or first virtue; and, second, it idealises the family. She explains that justice as a primary virtue for social associations does not make justice the highest virtue, but it makes it the most essential virtue. The explanation for why it is the most essential virtue lies in addressing the second faulty premise of Sandel's argument that idealises the family. In the contemporary context the idea of

---

63   For a collection of essays, see Alison Diduck and Katherine O'Donovan (eds), *Feminist Perspectives on Family Law* (Routledge-Cavendish, 2006).

64   Susan Moller Okin, *Justice, Gender and the Family* (Basic Books, 1989). The following discussion draws especially on 25–34, 36–40.

65   They are present in two books: the first is Michael Sandel, *Liberalism and the Limits of Justice* (Cambridge University Press, 1982); and the second is Alan Bloom, *The Closing of the American Mind* (Simon & Schuster, 1988). Due to the constraints of space, we will not discuss Bloom's book. Briefly, Bloom claims that family is beyond justice because it is naturally hierarchical. Okin dismisses his arguments by pointing out that the problem with his account is that what nature is and how natural differences are ascertained are nowhere articulated. Also, if biology is destiny, how can we explain the interventions of modern medicine and other aspects of modern life?

66   Sandel, above n 65.

common interests in the family is flawed because it overlooks the social reality that there are times when interests do conflict – domestic violence may be an extreme but all too common example of that. Furthermore, the assessment of such arrangements would be dependent on whether, if wives asked for their fair share of the property, they would be entitled to it. If and when the 'common interests' assumption broke down, would the distribution of scarce resources be made on just principles?

Okin notes this is an important issue for contemporary families because no-fault divorce is usually the norm that applies in western legal systems. Furthermore, even in ongoing families the resources or social goods like time for paid work or leisure, access to finances and even physical security are unevenly distributed. Contemporary gender-structured families cannot only rely on the spirit of generosity of the dominant – usually male – head of the household, but also need to be just to improve the life chances of women and children in the family. Furthermore, Okin observes that justice is essential for families because they are the first schools of justice – this is where we learn to develop the sense of justice needed for public life.[67] Thus, there is no reason why family life cannot be based on the virtues of love and affection *and* justice. Families built on the virtues of love, intimacy, harmony and in accordance with justice are just. But if the family is not just, then despite the virtues of love and affection they are worse off.

Therefore Okin argues that an egalitarian family is not an absurd impossibility but necessary for a fair society. She suggests that, in order to protect the vulnerable members of the family in the short term, equal sharing of financial resources between the parties during marriage should be guaranteed by law. Both households should also enjoy the same standard of living in the event of marriage breakdown. In the long term, justice in the family requires the creation of a genderless society where men and women equally share the child-rearing responsibilities. Justice requires fathers to become more involved in child care and mothers more attached to the workforce. The result will be men and women sharing paid and unpaid work and child care equally.

However, once it is accepted that there is a place for justice in the family, further issues arise about what justice in the family would entail. Okin's argument addresses gender justice, but it is equally necessary to ask how we can ensure that various other differences, such as sexuality or race, are not used as bases for denying justice in family relations.

Kymlicka claims that Okin's thesis begs fundamental questions about who has the right to bear and care for children.[68] He asks: should *only* heterosexual couples have the right to care for children? In Kymlicka's view this is the crucial question that a theory of family justice must answer. Thus, before deciding how to distribute the costs of domestic labour, the theory of justice for the family would need to consider who has the right to form a family in the first place. Kymlicka points out that to assume that family justice is about fairness between mothers and fathers in bringing up their children is closing the possibility of asking the prior and more fundamental questions of who has the right to be a mother or father and why mothers and fathers have the right to bring up their biological children. At one level,

---

67   See also Susan Moller Okin, 'Political Liberalism, Justice and Gender' (1994) 105(1) *Ethics* 23.
68   Will Kymlicka, 'Rethinking the Family' (1991) 20(1) *Philosophy and Public Affairs* 77, 77, 82–97; he also discusses the implications of regulating families through the notion of contracts. For a seminal text discussing the implications of contract principles for gender equality, see Pateman, above n 38.

as Kymlicka observes, the answer to this question seems obvious, but it is a question that family theorists have not addressed.

It is important in our pursuit of sex equality to avoid entrenching other forms of discrimination and inequality. As Kymlicka makes clear in his criticisms of Okin, the creation of a gender-free society, through the promotion of shared childcare responsibilities between mothers and fathers, may support the idea of the nuclear family as providing the best environment for children, and thereby preclude those who do not fit this norm from caring for children. In this regard, it is important to acknowledge how nuclear family ideology has undermined other groupings in society, such as sole-parent families and same-sex couples. Indeed, deviance from the norm can lead to the introduction of extreme measures in the name of child protection. In Australia, a notable example is the negative impact of the state-sanctioned practice of forcibly removing Aboriginal and Torres Strait Islander children from their families and creating what is now commonly referred to as the Stolen Generations.[69]

In mainstream western societies, the care of children by their biological parents is generally considered to meet their best interests. Kymlicka acknowledges this in his critique of Okin's endorsement of that the idea that the responsibility for children lies with their biological parents.[70] He explains that this may be because the parents are able to procreate without third-party assistance. However, the increasing use of assisted reproductive technologies means that we are no longer bound by biology in forming a family. Biological ties between children and their parents could be broken down completely by the formation of contracts between individuals for the sale of genetic material with the intention of reproducing children. However, Okin and other liberals are reluctant to extend the principle of freedom of contract to human reproduction, in the interest of protecting the child. Okin makes an important distinction between men and women having a right to parent a child and exercising parental responsibility for a child. This responsibility can only be exercised as a trust for protecting the interests of children.

In his critique of Okin, Kymlicka shows that the liberal principle of freedom of contract when extended to families can create the possibility of markets in genetic material and reproductive services, and that, when applied to families, the trust principle leads to a possibility of parental licences and judicial control. He notes how liberals are reluctant to endorse either of these outcomes. Similarly, he notes how feminists have for the most part been reluctant to organise families on principles of contract, ostensibly because that would commodify reproduction and sex, which would be dehumanising and alienating for women and children.

But Kymlicka argues that, in theory and in practice, a less exacting standard applies to the heterosexual and monogamous family than to any other family arrangement. Our attitudes to polygamy, surrogacy, single mother and same-sex parenting all point to this conclusion as these are judged by more stringent standards than the monogamous, heterosexual family, which is assumed to be the rightful place for the rearing of children. Thus, according

---

69   Human Rights and Equal Opportunity Commission, *Bringing Them Home: Report of the National Inquiry into the Separation of Aboriginal and Torres Strait Islander Children from their Families* (1997) ('*Bringing Them Home*') <https://www.humanrights.gov.au/publications/bringing-them-home-report-1997>.

70   See also Finnis, above n 35.

to him, the difficult questions that a theory of 'just family' must address go beyond sex equality within the heterosexual and monogamous family.[71]

Therefore, the issues that lie at the core of what may constitute a just family law go beyond gender equality and encompass justice for families who do not conform to the nuclear family model. For now, this discussion brings us back to the central proposition of this book – that family law endorses and privileges the heterosexual, nuclear family over all other forms of family. It reproduces the gender hierarchy in families that is produced by the sexual division of labour, most noticeably in the rearing of children. The nuclear family in turn sets the norms of who can and cannot parent a child.

Any analysis of family law must be able to address these issues. The law's answer that family law is a neutral or value-free dispute resolution mechanism, therefore, does not provide an adequate explanation of the contours of family law. The discussion above alerts us to the need for an explicit articulation of the theoretical assumptions made about both family and law. Moreover, views about the nature of legal knowledge, its claim to objectivity and its construction all depend upon theoretical assumptions. Therefore, a theoretical study of family law is a necessity rather than a matter of choice.

1.6   Family law in theory

Cheal explains that there are at least two ways of describing theory.[72] In a narrow scientific sense, theory is a set of propositions related to what is observed. In a wider sense, theory or theoretical perspectives affect the process of theorising. This is because what constitutes valid social scientific knowledge is itself determined by such perspectives. They provide us with concepts and suggest the kinds of questions we should ask. Some issues thus become more important than others. The assumptions made in turn orient the ways of answering questions and in interpreting the observations made. This raises the question of whether value-neutral social science knowledge is possible. More specifically in regard to family theory, Cheal claims that social scientists of necessity draw upon discourses about family experiences that are a rich source of ideas. It is in this way that theories of family are extensions of lived social practices. Knowledge is affected by the conditions under which theorists work; these conditions in turn inform the assumptions they make about the nature of people, the nature of society, relations between individuals and society, and about what is a good society or a good person.

What is not acknowledged sufficiently in mainstream thinking is that these assumptions are matters of choice and therefore subject to debate. Feminists, for instance, have critiqued the mainstream sociology of family for not including women's perspectives in their accounts. The wider issue here is the nature of knowledge, or what counts as valid knowledge, in any discipline and how it is utilised by another discipline. Thus, in the sociology of the family a discernible trend has been to analyse changes in contemporary families as the phenomenon of individualisation.[73] This was a point made earlier with respect

---

71   See also David Archard, *The Family: A Liberal Defence* (Palgrave Macmillan, 2010).
72   Cheal, above n 30, 18–23.
73   For example, Anthony Giddens, *The Transformation of Intimacy: Sexuality, Love, and Eroticism in Modern Societies* (Stanford University Press, 1992); Beck and Beck-Gernsheim, above n 46; Carol Smart and Bren Neale, *Family Fragments?* (Polity Press, 1999).

to increased individual freedom and choice in the formation of families. For example, and in brief, it is argued by Beck that in western societies individualisation can be illustrated by many social phenomena, and he illustrates this with a social history of marriage.[74] Beck claims that we now organise our intimate relationships to suit our individual desires and preferences. Unlike earlier societies, family ties are now more a matter of choice and we decide how and when to create certain affinities. This logic supports the claim that we, as a society, now choose to live in many different kinds of relationships, including relationships formed without marriage, without children, single parenthood, same-sex relationships and even part-time relationships.[75] In contrast, feminist critiques explain how individualism is not available equally to men and women. Moreover, such an emphasis on individuality in sociological theory is not desirable as it leads to undervaluing obligations and duty.[76] If law were to adopt this discourse, family law would take a particular shape. Would it be desirable for the law to develop in this way?

To an extent, this idea of individualisation is already present in family law. But in our view the law takes an inconsistent approach. For instance, at the stage of divorce or break-down of a de facto relationship, the law assumes that it is assisting two equally independent people to move on. At this level, the past history of the parties, especially related to who was performing the primary caregiving role and its effects, is rendered legally irrelevant. Divorce law thus endorses the individualisation thesis that it is not the business of law to force two adults to stay together. In doing so, the law of divorce creates a disconnect between how social relations are organised and how family law sees the two individuals. It thus contributes to the undervaluing of the caregiving functions of women who undertake primary respon-sibilities for children.

Yet in its financial provisions, including property distribution and maintenance, the law acknowledges the dependencies created by the non-wage work of caregiving. However, such acknowledgement by the law is woefully inadequate as is evidenced by the fall in the standard of living for women with children at the end of a relationship. The question for legal theorists is: why does this continue to be the case? We argue that this outcome is a consequence of family law and related scholarship buying into the rhetoric of law that creates the aura (if not a promise) of a fair outcome for both partners if the marriage or marriage-like relationship ends. Another way of looking at this is to reiterate the question posed earlier: what is the aim of family law? It is not nearly enough to say that there is no single coherent aim of family law and that the law is merely reflecting reality or even the normal chaos of love.[77] We suggest that family law helps legitimise the existing gender hierarchies in society through the legal rhetoric of its promises that the end of the financial relationship will be 'just and equitable' for both parties and that 'the best interests of the child' will be protected.

74   Ulrich Beck, 'Losing the Traditional: Individualization and "Precarious Freedoms"' in Beck and Beck-Gernsheim, above n 46, 1, 8.
75   Beck and Beck-Gernsheim, above n 46, 98. Compare the discussion of Bittman and Pixley above.
76   See, eg, Baroness Ruth Deech, 'Divorce – A Disaster?' (2009) 39 Family Law 1048. See also Diana Mulinari and Kerstin Sandell, 'A Feminist Re-reading of Theories of Late Modernity: Beck, Giddens and the Location of Gender' (2009) 35(4) Critical Sociology 493.
77   Dewar, above n 4.

To understand these inconsistencies in the law, it is important to trace them to their social origins. The effects of gender divisions are inextricably linked to cultural expectations of what it means to have meaningful relationships. 'Family' can thus be understood as referring to the ideological expectations of relatedness, which includes issues of who should live together, share income and perform certain common tasks; and in that sense analysing family from a gender perspective is different from analysing household structures of co-residence arrangements of people.[78] Smart analyses this cultural meaning as the ideological enclosure of marriage. Among other things, how this ideology operates has to do with ideas of love, altruism and personal fulfilment.[79] The significance of this analysis for us is that family law supports this ideology at the stage a family relationship is formed and while it continues, but at the end of the very same relationship it adopts another stand – that family law is no more than a dispute resolution mechanism. That is, at the end of a relationship, law is a technical device for dispute resolution. It does not wish to know anything about messy emotions, sacrifices or altruism. It is there to help end the relationship between two autonomous individuals and enable them to move on in life.

In this process the ideological dimensions of gender differences are translated into technical tasks of dividing the available property and enabling the 'dependent' partner (usually the woman) to start being independent. This change of discourse from family being about love, affection and altruism to being about two autonomous individuals is central to understanding how family law is implicated in maintaining a gender hierarchical society. Furthermore, it is central in providing a theoretical explanation of how family law manages to appear to be value-neutral and, in treating both parties as equals, may even appear emancipatory for the financially weaker partner.

However, these ideas are not often found in the study of family law. The positivist views of knowledge and thus the conventions of theorising have increasingly been questioned by postmodern or postpositivist ways of theorising.[80] Notwithstanding that, in mainstream legal writing the positivist views are still the dominant way of understanding law. It is a particular feature of the common law to treat judicial pronouncements and interpretations of statutes as the core of legal doctrine. An enormous amount of effort in legal scholarship and education is directed at analysing legal doctrine.[81] One effect of this focus is that theoretical analyses of law are deemed less important than the legal doctrine. We are acutely aware that this is an over-generalisation, but what we wish to convey is that, since the conventions of the discipline of law put in doubt the relevance of theory, it becomes much harder to ask which theories should apply and why. This topic is very broad in scope and we can only mention

---

78   Greer L Fox and Velma M Murray, 'Gender and Families: Feminist Perspectives and Family Research' (2000) 62(4) *Journal of Marriage and the Family* 1160.

79   Carol Smart, *The Ties That Bind* (Routledge & Kegan Paul, 1984) 143–6.

80   In particular, we rely on the insights of Foucault about discourse formation and the power to classify some things as knowledge. See Michel Foucault, 'Truth and Power' in Michel Foucault, *Power/Knowledge: Selected Interviews and other Writings 1972–77* (Colin Gordan et al trans, Pantheon Books, 1980).

81   Most areas of law have textbooks or casebooks that are a collection of 'relevant' court decisions and accompanying commentary. For an analysis of this development, see David Sugarman, 'Legal Theory, the Common Law Mind and the Making of the Textbook Tradition' in William Twining (ed), *Legal Theory and Common Law* (Basil Blackwell, 1986) 26.

it here. The main issue, however, is that theory is used eclectically in legal education, leaving the positivist understandings of law largely unchallenged.[82] At the same time, cutting-edge legal scholarship is critical in its orientation, but this literature is not systematically integrated in legal education and thus the discourse of law in educational institutions remains predominantly positivist. The classical genre of legal texts is the casebook, and family law is no exception in this regard. Admittedly, this is an overly inclusive statement in so far as most family law texts include varying levels of sociological literature. However, the reasons why literature from other disciplines is used in these texts vary, and this is where our argument for studying and analysing family law in a theoretical manner becomes relevant. We argue that a theoretical understanding of family law is necessary to understand how law constructs knowledge about families and then proceeds to regulate them.

Therefore, we aim to critique legal doctrine in order to identify the ways that family law privileges the nuclear family. Family law scholarship is deemed more sociologically informed (and thus more enlightened) than many other areas of 'hard' law.[83] At the same time, family law invokes the standard legal conventions to legitimise itself as a neutral body of law. What is obscured in the process is that the discourse of family and of family law is formed and reformed regularly. Therefore, one of the main issues for legal scholarship on family law should be how the 'truths' of law are constructed and what may be the content of those truths. In line with Michel Foucault's understanding, we accept that discourse is not simply language or concepts or even an internally consistent set of ideas. Rather, discourse determines what can be said and thought within a discipline, and who can speak and is considered to have the authority to speak.[84] Thus, the importance of what the judges have to say about the law and concepts of legal reasoning intermesh to produce the dominant conception of legal knowledge. So too, how the scholarship analyses legal developments helps in constituting the truths of law.

Family law is not separate from its discourses and therefore it is relevant to examine how these discourses are formed, and what roles different institutions or individuals might play in their construction.[85] It is commonly accepted that discourse is not intentional in the sense that it is not simply produced by the knowing subject.[86] It must nevertheless be the case that all of us are involved in maintaining or constructing the discourse of law every time an idea is repeated and endorsed or challenged. Therefore, as students, researchers and teachers in the discipline, it is incumbent upon us to take seriously our responsibilities as institutionally endorsed speakers and be self-reflexive about what ideas about law we endorse or critique.

---

82   This is well illustrated in the survey of law school curricula in Richard Johnstone and Sumitra Vignaendra, *Learning Outcomes and Curriculum Development in Law: A Report Commissioned by the Australian Universities Teaching Committee (AUTC)* (Higher Education Group, 2003).

83   This can be easily illustrated by the contents of mainstream textbooks on family law. It is a recurring theme in these textbooks that family law is shaped by wider social institutions. However, with few exceptions, the analysis of legal provisions does not extend to a jurisprudential critique of legal knowledge.

84   Stephen Ball (ed), *Foucault and Education: Disciplines and Knowledge* (Routledge, 1990) 2.

85   The field of discourse analysis is wide, but not our main focus here. For an introduction, see Ruth Wodak and Michael Meyer (eds), *Methods of Critical Discourse Analysis* (Sage Publications, 2nd ed, 2009). We seek to avoid an overly technical use of discourse analysis, as our main aim is to identify how the legal doctrine retains an aura of objectivity.

86   Gavin Kendall and Gary Wickham, *Using Foucault's Methods* (Sage Publications, 1999) 42.

Briefly, the argument is that there is no such thing as bare facts or empirical reality, waiting to be discovered. All observations or empirical facts are conditioned by the perspectives of the observers; this is sometimes described as the theory dependence of observations.[87] Postmodern and post-structural writers have made it possible for everyone to recognise that all concepts employed in social sciences are derived from the common sense knowledge or value preferences of those theorising. The conventions of theorising which support the idea that acontextual and abstract theories can yield universally true answers are now suspect. This conception of law as constructed knowledge is present in legal scholarship, but is effectively marginalised.[88] Thus, while there is ample legal scholarship that uses such insights, it does not find its way into either the teaching of law or legal doctrine. As a result, the dominance of the positivist conception of knowledge in law is as yet unshaken. It is this confidence of legal thinkers that they can study, understand and apply law without having to necessarily acknowledge other discourses that can partly explain why family law is seen as problematic from the perspectives of both men and women. The same limitations inform the legislative moves and judicial interpretations in the area. There is not much systematic articulation or justification of why family law is the way it is. Unsurprisingly, there is not much scope for any systematic consideration of what family law should be doing.

We offer the following discussion in advancing our argument that law and legal knowledge are constituted knowledge like any other knowledge. The discourse of law is formed at many sites, but one of the primary sites is legal education. How law and legal theory are portrayed in legal education sets the foundations for how future professionals will conceptualise legal knowledge. Therefore, if the hegemony of positivist understanding of law is to be challenged, it ought to be challenged at the level of how law is taught and analysed. But more importantly a systematic theoretical framework could make the construction of ideas its primary focus.

The fundamental issue therefore is that family law (and other areas of law) cannot be understood in a stand-alone manner. The constitutive nature of legal discourse, if made the main focus of legal analysis, can explain the inevitable connections between law and society, but not as a simple reflection of each other. We contend that such a view of knowledge compels every one of us to admit that we all make choices about the categories of analysis, the issues and the way to analyse them (for example, promoting gender justice as opposed to the cost and time efficiency of the family law system). Thus, family law is far from being value-free and we cannot avoid our own perspectives informing how we choose to study or analyse it. This is not the same thing as saying that relativism is inevitable because every perspective is as good as any other perspective. Rather, the acknowledgement of a perspective makes it necessary for us to justify its adoption. This requires us to take responsibility for our views and be self-reflexive about them. Researchers and thinkers would have to make deliberate efforts to identify their own points of view and relate to others' points of view. The critiques of any perspective would not be foreclosed, but nor would it be credible to dismiss any view for being biased. Moreover, once it is possible to acknowledge that

---

87   See Davies, above n 25, 131. She refers to Anthony O'Hear, *Introduction to the Philosophy of Science* (Clarendon Press, 1989) ch 5 and Karl Popper, *The Logic of Scientific Discovery* (Unwin Hyman, 1959) 93–5.

88   See generally Archana Parashar, 'Re-Conceptualizing Regulation, Responsibility and Law' (2008) 8 *Macquarie Law Journal* 59.

knowledge is constituted in our practices, it must follow that responsibility for our ideas lies with us. It has the potential to fundamentally challenge the claimed neutrality of law and enable construction of ideas about a genuinely fair family law.

In conclusion, it follows from the above discussion that it is no longer possible to claim that family is a 'natural' institution. Any analysis of family law must uncover how it is constructed in discourses about the law and family. As we have argued, choices are always being made about what the state is doing with regard to the regulation of families. These choices affect everyone, and therefore it is incumbent upon all of us to aspire to the creation of just families in law. Whether we, for example, conceptualise families as loving relations or economic relations will lead to certain views on what shape family law should take in regulating family relationships.

FAMILY LAW AND ITS INSTITUTIONS

2.1   Introduction

The focus of this chapter is on the institutional framework of Australian family law. A brief background of Australian family law before Federation will lead into a discussion of the division of powers between the federal and State parliaments after the *Constitution* was adopted in 1901. The provisions in the *Constitution* that give power to the Commonwealth Parliament to make laws with respect to 'marriage' and 'divorce', and the *Marriage Act 1961* (Cth) ('MA') and the *Family Law Act 1975* (Cth) ('FLA') that were enacted with respect to these powers, are discussed to demonstrate the special status the relationship of marriage has in Australian law. Further, our discussion will show how this status has been reinforced by the High Court's interpretation of these powers in ways that have confined their scope to the making of laws on marriage as understood in nuclear family terms. The discussion of key High Court cases will provide the backdrop to understanding the limits of the constitutional arrangements. In a changing society, these decisions posed challenges to the efficiency of the system of Australian family law and over the last 30 years have led to a range of significant reforms to accommodate changing perceptions of family (notably, blended families and de facto relationships). As a result of these reforms, family law has increasingly regulated non-conventional relations like de facto and same-sex relationships. Our contention is that, despite these developments, the law continues to privilege the heterosexual nuclear family as the norm. This is most recently illustrated by the High Court upholding the challenge to the validity of the *Marriage Equality (Same Sex) Act 2013* (ACT) ('ACT Act').[1]

This narrow construction of family and family law has a number of consequences. A narrow construction of family law focused on the creation and dissolution of marriage or similar relationships leaves marginalised families out of the purview of family law. This narrow approach is facilitated by an abstract style of legal analysis that inadvertently supports the nuclear family model by ignoring the issue of how legal knowledge of what a family is constructed through the perspectives of law-makers. So too in constitutional legal analyses, conventions of interpretation create a distance between the law and its interpreters. The effect is that the consequences of judicial interpretation are not considered to be relevant as it is deemed to be an impartial process and not a matter of choice or intention.

The coverage of the institutional arrangements of Australian family law in this chapter also includes an overview of the various courts that have exercised jurisdiction in this area. The introduction of the Family Court of Australia ('FCA') and the more recent shift in the sharing of its responsibilities with other courts, like the former Federal Magistrates Court, now known as the Federal Circuit Court ('FCC'), will be analysed to examine the debate about whether a specialist court like the FCA is actually required. This will also permit us to examine the jurisprudential issue of whether family law can be conceptualised as a self-contained system or whether it requires an explicit integration within the wider legal system.

Considering the shift to 'non-court-based family services' in Australian family law (referred to as alternative dispute resolution or 'ADR' in this chapter), it also makes sense to provide an overview of these developments in this chapter.[2] A summary of the various ADR

---

1   *Commonwealth v Australian Capital Territory* (2013) 250 CLR 441.
2   FLA pts II–III. Under the FLA, provision is made for family counselling (pt II div 2); family dispute resolution (pt II div 3); arbitration (pt div 4); and family consultants (pt III).

mechanisms in place in the family law system and the debates on the effectiveness of ADR compared to litigation will also provide the background for the discussion of ADR mechanisms in subsequent chapters. This background will help illustrate the tensions that exist owing to different conceptions of the family, particularly the dependency model versus the model of individual autonomy. An overview of the changes to the legal response to violence in personal relationships in this context will be the focus of the discussion, providing the background for the more detailed discussion of the current ADR processes in later chapters.

The legal provisions analysed in this chapter include the constitutional arrangements and the referral of State powers to the Commonwealth. The scope of the marriage and divorce powers in s 51 of the *Constitution* is analysed by reference to key constitutional challenges to provisions of the MA and the FLA in the High Court. The chapter also gives an overview of the court system exercising jurisdiction in the field of family law. A general overview of the ADR provisions in the FLA is also provided. ADR in divorce, property and child-related proceedings will be examined in more depth in later chapters.

2.2   The family in Australian law – an overview

The starting point for the discussion in this chapter is s 51 of the *Constitution*, which grants legislative powers to the Commonwealth Parliament to:

> make laws for the peace, order, and good government of the Commonwealth with respect to …
>
> (xxi) marriage;
>
> (xxii) divorce and matrimonial causes; and in relation thereto, parental rights, and the custody and guardianship of infants …

For the following discussion, we shall refer to them as the 'marriage' and 'divorce' powers. The continuing legacy of the adoption of the *Constitution* in 1901 is that the area of 'family law' in Australia is defined by reference to these legislative powers in the *Constitution*. Thus, family law is conventionally described as law about these matters. Since these powers mention only the specific powers in regard to marriage and divorce, with a few other matters broadly described as matrimonial causes, the laws enacted are similarly contained.

So far in Australian legal history, Commonwealth laws made according to these powers uphold the notions of marriage and divorce as related mainly to a heterosexual and monogamous union. This position continues to reflect the understanding of marriage at the time of Federation. Quick and Garran, in *The Annotated Constitution of the Australian Commonwealth*, affirmed the English law definition of marriage as 'recognized throughout Christendom' to be 'the union between a man and a woman' and 'its essence is that it is (1) a voluntary union, (2) for life, (3) of one man and one woman, (4) to the exclusion of all others'.[3]

---

3   John Quick and Robert R Garran, *The Annotated Constitution of the Australian Commonwealth* (Angus & Robertson, 1901) 608, citing *Bethell v Hildyard* (1888) 38 Ch D 220.

As marriage has been treated as the foundation for the formation of 'law's family' a significant consequence has been the general inability of family law to consider many of the issues and concerns facing other families – such as Aboriginal and Torres Strait Islander families, migrant and refugee families, and same-sex and sole-parent families – that may arise owing to the uneven impact of political and socioeconomic forces on them. Other areas of study in the fields of, for example, criminal law, discrimination law, social security law, succession law and migration law may focus on law's treatment of socially disadvantaged groups, but their focus may not lend itself well to examining the effects of law on these family structures. Thus, a narrow construction of Australian family law that mainly focuses on marriage formation and divorce, the resolution of property disputes, and the parenting and maintenance of children when intimate relationships break down is not relevant to all family types and therefore cannot meet the needs of all families in society. The notion of the heterosexual monogamous marriage as the unarticulated basis of family law imposes that family model on everyone with the effect of marginalising already disadvantaged groups in society.

The conventional approach in family law is legitimised, in part, by the lack of theoretical debates about the law and its definition of family, making it difficult to critique the shape of the law in a principled manner. This problem is exacerbated by the confinement of 'family law' to the laws made pursuant to the powers under the *Constitution* that are, in turn, interpreted by the High Court in an a-contextual manner according to conventions of constitutional interpretation. This approach appears to be value-neutral, but, as we demonstrate below, works in ways to normalise the heterosexual marriage as the normative basis of Australian family law. A similar effect is evident in the shift from litigation to the private resolution of disputes in the family law jurisdiction.

The discussion below will show how these processes facilitate the informal incorporation of ideas about the normative family into the legal system. These outcomes happen despite the appearance that our family law is inclusive of different family forms and progressive in facilitating the resolution of disputes that arise within them. Indeed, they happen because of the assumptions that law-makers rely on as they determine the scope of family law.

The point made in Chapter 1, that constructions of 'family' are dependent on the perspective adopted by the author, bears repeating. Such different perspectives on the political and socioeconomic forces can and do shape ways of understanding the 'family'. This point can be demonstrated by comparing different accounts of the history of the family in Australia. Brown and Gilding give two very different accounts of how the Australian family developed in Australia.[4]

Brown begins his history of the Australian family by tracing the history of the nuclear family in Britain, which emerged from the effects of industrialisation. According to Brown, the Australian family followed in becoming a specialised social agency mainly concerned with the regulation of sexual relations and the socialisation of children. He identifies four interconnected elements that helped create the nuclear family form in Australia. First, there were the effects of the Industrial Revolution out of which (unlike in Europe) cohesive family life was able to grow and flourish. Second (and again unlike the class-based societies of the

---

4   Morven S Brown, 'Changing Functions of the Australian Family' in A P Elkin (ed), *Marriage and the Family in Australia* (Angus & Robertson, 1957) 82, especially 82–3, 87–99, which provide the basis for the following account; Michael Gilding, *The Making and Breaking of the Australian Family* (Allen & Unwin, 1991) 31–47.

United States and Britain), a shortage of women available to do domestic work meant that Australia developed as a relatively classless society and the dominant view across all of its sections was the need for a basic wage to support family life. Third, the shortage of women meant that women were in a superior position, not only in choosing marriage partners, but also in enjoying the material privileges that would come with marriage. The marriages formed were based on mutual respect and companionship.

According to Brown, marriages lasted because women were content to perform the roles of wives and mothers and had no desire to establish a life for themselves outside the home, while unmarried men preferred to engage in male bonding – mateship – rather than chase women. For Brown, male sexual repression was made all the more complete by the absence of prostitution in the Australian bush. Finally, Brown points to role of men in shaping the Australian nuclear family. The male head of the household was the ultimate authority figure in the family as well as the representative of the family in public. However, owing to women's status in the family, they could resist overt male domination in the family. In these ways, the nuclear family flourished in Australia with men and women assuming their complementary roles as husbands and wives, and was supported by external forces conducive to its development.

The idealised version of the history of the Australian family in Brown's account is consistent with the structural functional view of the family discussed in Chapter 1 in that it provides the best fit between the family and the economy. It is a view that prevailed for most of the 20th century as historians took for granted the idea that 'the Australian family was "born modern", nuclear and relatively isolated from kin and community networks'.[5] Gilding, writing over 30 years later, presents an entirely different version of Australian family life.[6] He challenges the conventional view that the rise of industrialisation and the nuclear family coincided. Unlike Brown's picture of family life, sprawling out into the suburbs as cohesive family units, Gilding describes the cramped life and destitution in the cities arising from economic pressures. Thus, while Brown portrays Australia as a classless society, Gilding's account of history suggests otherwise. He portrays the viability of the nuclear family as depending on the husband working. For working-class families this often meant the children working as well. But the nuclear family did not spare women from violence or desertion. Working-class women especially were financially compelled to stay with violent husbands. According to Gilding, approximately half of the wife murders in the 1880s were the result of spousal violence.

These two accounts of Australian families draw very different pictures because their points of view are different, showing how focusing on different factors can shape our understanding of the way that families are formed and function.

Similar observations can be made when Brown's account of early male and female relations in Australia is compared to Hamilton's account of these relations. Brown, writing in the 1950s, is oblivious to the impact that colonisation had on Aboriginal and Torres Strait Islander peoples and their kinship structures. He is writing at a time when historians were focused on the history of Australia's British heritage. At the time, the impact of British settlement and the contributions that Aboriginal and Torres Strait Islander peoples have made to Australia's history were largely ignored and seen as irrelevant to Australian history. Hamilton, writing

---

5   Gilding, above n 4, 31, citing Patricia Grimshaw, 'Women and Family in Australian History: A Reply to the Real Matilda' (1979) 18(72) *Historical Studies* 412, 415.

6   The following account is based on Gilding, above n 4, 31–3, 35–7.

in the 1980s, is writing at a time when historians are becoming increasingly interested in the interconnections between Australian and Aboriginal and Torres Strait Islander histories. Unlike Brown, who perpetuates cultural amnesia about the effects of colonisation on Aboriginal and Torres Strait Islander peoples, Hamilton explicitly engages in exposing the processes of colonisation, especially the impact on Aboriginal kinship structures in outback Australia.[7] Thus when Brown refers to the absence of women in the bush, he is focusing generally on relations between white women and white men. In contrast, Hamilton's focus on Aboriginal history in the Northern Territory exposes a very different story about the early Australian bush. Her study focuses on examining the failure of Christian missions in 'civilising' Aboriginal people in the early period of frontier violence against them. In identifying the factors that contributed to this failure, she reveals how the sexual violence and exploitation of Aboriginal women by white men drastically transformed Aboriginal family structures and their culture. Hamilton argues that in comparing early experiences of settlement in the Northern Territory through documents like the newspapers, official documents, missionary documents and pamphlets, and speaking to the contemporary Aboriginal community elders who recounted the stories as told by their parents or other kinfolk, there is a striking disparity between how Aboriginal people understood the domestic and sexual role of women, how the official records talked about them, and how the early pioneers were indifferent to the importance of Aboriginal women to them.

However, sexual relations between white men and Aboriginal women left visible and uncontestable signs in the form of venereal diseases and part-European children. The demand for sexual services from Aboriginal women was constant and had disastrous consequences that went beyond the merely physical. As a result of these practices, the reproduction of Aboriginal families and their societies was undermined as marriage, kinship, rights over ritual property, territory and knowledge could not withstand such long-term withdrawal of women and girls from traditional marriage arrangements. Thus, what could be described by Brown as womanless communities is explained by Hamilton as the denial of the history of sexual relations between European men and Aboriginal women. The effect of such sexual relations was to significantly transform Aboriginal societies by undermining family connections and ties to land.

The immediate issue here is not that one is a true account and the other is not, though in broader terms the account we accept to be true could have important implications for advancing reconciliation in Australia. Rather, the point of these comparisons is to demonstrate how the production of knowledge is determined in part by the authors' values and ideologies, the scope of their enquiries and the questions or issues they explore. These examples also show how the immediate historical context can also influence the conclusions writers make. If, as most postmodern writers explain, the truth of any social situation depends on one's viewpoint, it becomes relevant to identify the assumptions on which any argument is constructed.[8] However, as the above discussion shows, the assumptions we make may only become evident when differences in perspectives are compared.

---

7   Annette Hamilton, 'Bond-Slaves of Satan: Aboriginal Women and the Missionary Dilemma' in Margaret Jolly and Martha MacIntyre (eds), *Family and Gender in the Pacific* (Cambridge University Press, 1989) 236, 236–8, 251–8.

8   This is equally significant for empirical studies of the Australian family. There is an abundance of empirical data about the different kinds of families, but not nearly enough theoretical analyses of the ideological implications of framing issues in a particular manner. Australian Institute of Family Studies produces very useful research and we will use it extensively; see Australian Institute of Family Studies ('AIFS') <https://aifs.gov.au/publications> for the list of publications.

A similar claim can be made about law and it is an important claim to make, especially when certain consequences flow for actual families, depending on the perspective of the family adopted in law and policy. Therefore, in the case of family law it is important that the assumptions about the family that is the subject of legal regulation are articulated and justified. However, this emphasis is not part of the mainstream legal discourse of family or families. Instead primacy is given to following the standard method of legal reasoning. In the context of Australian constitutional law, it is standard High Court practice to determine the question of whether a law is a valid exercise of legislative power according to principles of constitutional interpretation. Moreover, in doing so the High Court does not consider the effects of its decisions on real families. These are considered to be political issues or issues of policy. The High Court is concerned only with determining whether a law is a valid exercise of power.

This compartmentalisation of law into different subject areas, and the conventional division of powers between different arms of government to make, interpret and administer laws, may be legitimised in legal terms as upholding the rule of law. But this allows the law to avoid facing up to its own exclusions. In the context of family law, the law's exclusions have the effect of maintaining the monogamous heterosexual union as the norm. Only by broadening the purview of study to include those family structures that deviate from the norm can we begin to critique the normalising power of the law and the hierarchies that it creates.

In this regard, it is important to acknowledge that, as laws are made with respect to the marriage or divorce powers, certain assumptions about the family are also being incorporated into these laws. In considering the validity of these laws, the judges on the High Court will also be relying on assumptions about the family or marriage. With these ideas in mind, in the following discussion we will address three interrelated issues: the historical context of Australian family law; the constitutional arrangements for making family laws in Australia; and the institutional structures involved in the administration of family law, which include courts with family law jurisdiction and the rise of ADR. In examining these issues we illustrate how the law perpetuates the heterosexual monogamous marriage in view of the three interrelated concepts of the family discussed in Chapter 1: the nuclear family, the sexual division of labour, and the private and public distinction.

2.3   Historical context of family law

The origins of Australian law can be traced to the common law in England. In the context of family law the English law maintained the Christian view of marriage: that it was a sacrament that was not dissoluble.[9] Moreover, being a religious matter, it was regulated by the church. Initially the remedies in ecclesiastical courts primarily related to declarations of the validity of a marriage. After the Reformation and the split between the Catholic and Protestant Churches, England severed ties with the Catholic Church and declared itself a Protestant

---

9   Discussed in detail in Chapter 4. For a brief history of the developments leading to divorce becoming legally permissible, see Roderick Phillips, *Putting Asunder: A History of Divorce in Western Society* (Cambridge University Press, 1988).

state. The most significant change for our present purposes was the creation of the law of divorce in Britain with the enactment of the *Matrimonial Causes Act 1857* (UK), which was duly adopted by the Australian colonies.[10]

The Commonwealth of Australia came into existence through the operation of the *Commonwealth of Australia Constitution Act 1900* (Imp). In that Act the UK Parliament gave legal effect to the *Constitution*, and decreed that the Australian colonies would be 'united' as the States of 'a Federal Commonwealth' on a date to be determined (which turned out to be 1 January 1901). Because the States are 'united', the national government has sovereign powers; but because it is a 'federal' Commonwealth, the States retain some of their powers as well. In other words, power is divided. Section 51 of the *Constitution* lists the law-making powers of the Commonwealth, including the powers relating to marriage and divorce. Any power not assigned to the Commonwealth remains with the States. If the Commonwealth does not have power to make a law, or has not exercised its power, or has made a law that allows the States to legislate concurrently, then the States have residual power to make laws in that area. A limited number of powers are vested exclusively in the Commonwealth, but most of the powers assigned to the Commonwealth can still be exercised by the States as well; that is, they can be exercised concurrently. This gives rise to a possibility that a State and the Commonwealth may both make laws in a way that gives rise to a conflict; but s 109 provides that whenever such a conflict arises the Commonwealth law will prevail. The Territories are controlled by the Commonwealth and under s 122 of the *Constitution* the Commonwealth has absolute power to legislate directly for them and to make whatever laws it likes. The Commonwealth has legislated to give the Australian Capital Territory and the Northern Territory some limited form of self-government. This legislation has a similar effect as s 109 of the *Constitution* in so far as a law of a Territory is ineffective to the extent of any inconsistency with a Commonwealth law.[11]

After Federation, the Commonwealth Parliament did not enact laws on marriage and divorce for some time. In 1959 it replaced the existing State laws relating to matrimonial causes with a single Commonwealth law by enacting the *Matrimonial Causes Act 1959* (Cth). This Act commenced operation on 1 February 1961 and replaced all existing State and Territory laws at the time.[12] The Commonwealth also enacted a separate *Marriage Act 1961* (Cth) ('MA'), which commenced operation on 1 September 1963. The *Family Law Act 1975* (Cth) ('FLA') replaced the *Matrimonial Causes Act 1959* (Cth) and continues in operation. The constitutional issues that arose from the enactment of the FLA are to a large extent comprehensible if it is kept in view that the *Matrimonial Causes Act 1959* (Cth) was primarily a divorce Act.[13] It provided for the resolution of property and parental disputes only as secondary or ancillary relief to proceedings for principal relief, such as the dissolution

---

10   For a general history of divorce in England, see Shepherd Braithwaite Kitchin, *A History of Divorce* (Chapman & Hall, 1912) 171–210. For an Australian historical account, see David Mayer Selby, 'Development of Divorce Law in Australia' (1966) 29 *The Modern Law Review* 473.

11   *Commonwealth v Australian Capital Territory* (2013) 250 CLR 441.

12   L V Harvey, 'Marriage Counselling and the Federal Divorce Law in Australia' (1964) 26(1) *Journal of Marriage and Family* 83 explains the difficulties that arose with different State divorce laws.

13   Anthony Dickey, *Family Law* (Thomson Reuters, 6th ed, 2014) 23.

of marriage.[14] The FLA, however, in addition to introducing a new law of divorce, also created new laws relating to the custody and guardianship of children, the maintenance of children and spouses, the declaration and alteration of the interests of spouses in property, and matrimonial injunctions. Significantly, it also permitted applications for relief to be made without instituting proceedings for divorce or other principal relief.[15] The Family Court of Australia was also created to administer the new Commonwealth family law. We will discuss this later, but for now we will examine key challenges to the constitutional validity of the MA and FLA in the High Court.

2.4   Constitutional law and the family

In this part we discuss how the constitutional grant of legislative power to the Commonwealth Parliament with respect to marriage and divorce has shaped the contours of family law. Various provisions in the MA and FLA were challenged on the basis that the Commonwealth Parliament lacked the legislative competence to make these laws. A brief study of the constitutional cases that have come before the High Court shows that interpretation usually reflects the complexities of the division of legislative authority between the Commonwealth and the States. The main issues that have arisen with respect to the MA and FLA have related mainly to whether various provisions were enacted as an exercise of the marriage power or the divorce power pursuant to s 51 of the *Constitution*.

With respect to the marriage power, the issues have related to its scope and whether it gives the Commonwealth power to legislate only for the formation of marriage in the MA, or also includes the regulation of the incidents of the relationship, including any children of the marriage. With respect to the FLA the issues have included whether the FLA can allow proceedings to be commenced in the absence of an application for principal relief; if yes, is such a law an exercise of power under the marriage or divorce power? A further question has been whether the law can affect the rights of third parties who are not the husband or wife.

In determining the scope of the Commonwealth's legislative authority, conventions of interpretation of the *Constitution* play a significant part. It is therefore necessary to ask

---

14   See s 5(1) of this Act: 'unless the contrary intention appears – "matrimonial cause" means – (a) proceedings for a decree of – (i) dissolution of marriage; (ii) nullity of marriage; (iii) judicial separation; (iv) restitution of conjugal rights; or (v) jactitation of marriage; ... (c) proceedings with respect to the maintenance of a party to the proceedings, settlements, damages in respect of adultery, the custody or guardianship of infant children of the marriage or the maintenance, welfare, advancement or education of children of the marriage, *being proceedings in relation to concurrent, pending or completed proceedings of a kind referred to in either of the last two preceding paragraphs*, including proceedings of such a kind pending at, or completed before, the commencement of this Act; (d) any other proceedings (including proceedings with respect to the enforcement of a decree, the service of process or costs) *in relation to concurrent, pending or completed proceedings of a kind referred to in any of the last three preceding paragraphs*, including proceedings of such a kind pending at, or completed before, the commencement of this Act ... ' (emphasis added).

15   FLA s 4(1): '"proceedings for principal relief" means proceedings under this Act of a kind referred to in paragraph (a) or (b) of the definition of matrimonial cause in this subsection' and '"matrimonial cause" means: (a) proceedings between the parties to a marriage, or by the parties to a marriage, for divorce or a decree of nullity or (b) proceedings for a declaration as to the validity of a marriage; or a divorce or the annulment of a marriage ... '.

whether they are simply rules of interpretation or have normative implications. This raises the issue of whether the chosen approach to interpretation is connected to substantive issues of fairness with respect to the family laws that are made. Another way of formulating this idea is that a theoretical understanding of the nature of interpretation is necessary to understand how law is constituted in a particular form. The determination of these issues has mainly depended on the scope of these powers. As we will see, intrinsic to their determination is the concept of 'marriage' and whether it has to be a heterosexual monogamous union.

2.4.1   The Constitution and the legislative authority of the Commonwealth Parliament

As noted at the outset of the chapter, s 51 of the *Constitution* grants legislative powers to the Commonwealth Parliament to make laws with respect to 'marriage' and 'divorce and matrimonial causes'. Over the years the High Court has had occasion to interpret these powers in various respects. There are various ways of analysing these decisions of the High Court and it is common for family law scholars to explain them as matters of constitutional interpretation arising within a federal system of government. However, in the discussion below, in order to reflect upon the conventions of interpretation that are used in these cases, we illustrate how the High Court, through its interpretation of these powers, is privileging the notion of the heterosexual nuclear family and undermining the interests of those whose family structures do not conform to this model. These interpretive choices reveal how judges participate in the creation of the discourse of the normal family.

In *Attorney-General (Vic) v Commonwealth* the High Court discussed the extent of the marriage power.[16] The Commonwealth Parliament in enacting Part VI of the MA provided for the legitimation of ex-nuptial children in cases where their parents were subsequently married, while also providing that the children of a void marriage would be considered legitimate in some circumstances.[17] The Victorian Attorney-General challenged the validity of the law on the basis that the Commonwealth Parliament had exceeded its legislative power with respect to 'marriage'. This raised the question of how far the Commonwealth could go in making laws under the marriage power.

The High Court upheld the validity of these provisions. A majority of the judges found that the 'marriage' power is not limited to making laws for the formation of marriage; it covers the status that marriage involves, including the mutual rights and duties between spouses. The majority also found that the Commonwealth Parliament had power to make laws with respect to the relationship between married partners and the children of their marriage.[18]

---

16   *Attorney-General (Vic) v Commonwealth* (1962) 107 CLR 529.

17   Sections 89–91 respectively declared an ex-nuptial child to be legitimate if the parents married subsequently; if the parents married in the country of father's domicile and that law did not extend similar recognition; and if at the time of intercourse at least one parent believed on reasonable grounds that the marriage was valid. Section 94 declared bigamy to be an offence.

18   Although there are different emphases in various judges' formulations, we will not go into those details here. See Lisa Young et al, *Family Law in Australia* (LexisNexis Butterworths, 8th ed, 2013) 139–44 for a detailed discussion.

In reaching these conclusions the Court rejected the argument of the Victorian Attorney-General that the Commonwealth was overriding State succession laws by making ex-nuptial children legitimate, enabling them to inherit property that they would not have been able to inherit under State laws. In his view, the Commonwealth law dealing with legitimation was not about marriage but about succession, which was within the power of the State to make laws. The High Court majority disagreed and held that the marriage power extends to the Commonwealth making laws for the legitimation of children. The majority observed that State parliaments, if they wished, could modify their succession laws and deny inheritance to such children.

From the perspective of a constitutional lawyer, the approach to interpretation of the marriage power in this case confirms the principle of constitutional interpretation that the powers conferred by s 51 are to be construed liberally in accordance to their terms and without any assumption that particular matters were 'reserved' to the States.[19] In upholding the legitimation provisions as a valid exercise of the marriage power, the High Court's conclusion was also consistent with the principle that there is no requirement for a law to be exclusively about one head of power or that a law be primarily or even substantially concerned with a grant of power.[20] The constitutional law emphases are perfectly legitimate; however, they also function to obscure how the Court's conclusions also construct the nuclear heterosexual family – the married couple and their biological children. In other words, no space exists for even articulating these ideas, as the High Court is doing what it is supposed to do.

The High Court had occasion to explore the scope of the marriage and divorce powers in the case of *Russell v Russell; Farrelly v Farrelly*.[21] This was the first time that the validity of provisions of the FLA was challenged. The High Court had to determine, among other things, the validity of provisions in the FLA that conferred jurisdiction on courts to make custody and maintenance orders and determine the property rights of spouses where no proceedings for principal relief had been commenced. The issue here was that if proceedings could be initiated without there being an application for primary relief, how could the Commonwealth justify these provisions of the FLA? Would they be characterised as laws with respect to the marriage power or the divorce power?

The technical argument related to the interpretation of the relationship between these powers and whether the scope of the divorce power to confer jurisdiction served to limit the scope of the marriage power so that it could not confer jurisdiction as well.[22]

---

19   James Crawford, 'The Constitution and the Environment' (1991) 13 *Sydney Law Review* 11, 14.
20   Ibid.
21   (1976) 134 CLR 495.
22   The technical interpretive issue related to the scope of paras xxi and xxii of s 51 of the *Constitution*. Briefly, the issue was that if the Commonwealth Parliament could make laws about parental rights as an exercise of the 'marriage' power under para xxi, could it also confer jurisdiction on the courts to enforce these rights as an exercise of its legislative authority for marriage? The argument against this interpretation rested on the assumption that Parliament had such authority to confer the necessary powers on the courts under para xxii and that operated to limit the scope of para xxi so that it did not include such powers. The High Court majority held that no such limitation to the marriage power could apply. In reaching this conclusion, the majority appeared to confirm the principle of constitutional interpretation that the heads of power under s 51 are to be interpreted separately and disjunctively. See *Russell v Russell; Farrelly v Farrelly* (1976) 134 CLR 495 (Stephen, Mason and Jacobs JJ); Dickey, above n 13, 24–5.

The High Court specifically had to determine whether the definition of matrimonial cause in the FLA was valid to the extent that it permitted custody, child-maintenance and spousal-maintenance proceedings to be initiated by anyone at all; and whether the definition of a child of the marriage, including an ex-nuptial child of either husband or wife from an earlier marriage who was ordinarily a member of the household, was within the legislative power of the Commonwealth. Furthermore, the Court had to determine whether it was permissible for the Commonwealth law to include in its definition of matrimonial cause proceedings between spouses with regard to property where there were no associated proceedings for principal matrimonial relief (such as dissolution or nullity of marriage), and whether such proceedings could be commenced at any time during the marriage and with respect to any property regardless of the circumstances.

With respect to the custody and maintenance provisions, the Court found that, in not placing any limitations on the parties to the proceedings, the provisions under challenge exceeded the marriage power. It was only by invoking s 15A of the *Acts Interpretation Acts 1901* (Cth) that the Court found that the provisions related to custody and maintenance were valid under the marriage power provided that the proceedings were between the parties of the marriage and that the children were the biological or adopted children of the marriage.

With regard to the property provisions of the FLA, the Court found that these provisions were not valid under the marriage power. Instead they were valid pursuant to the divorce and matrimonial causes power provided that the proceedings were in relation to proceedings for principal relief such as the dissolution of marriage.

While these conclusions appear consistent with principles of constitutional interpretation, we can also see how the Court's conclusions confirm the understanding of family as private and nuclear. One concern that was raised in *Russell v Russell* was that the property provisions would allow married parties to use the provisions at any time to resolve property disputes between them. In an ongoing marriage, a dispute of this kind was construed to be commercial in nature and not a matrimonial cause. In determining the issues this way, we can see the Court subscribing to the public/private distinction by invalidating the law under the marriage power because that would allow parties to resolve disputes that appear to have a public character (a commercial venture), and only validating the law under the divorce power to allow for the resolution of disputes that are seemingly private (at the time of marriage breakdown). Viewed in this way, we can see how the Court, in making decisions about the validity of laws made with respect to the marriage and divorce powers, understands the marriage relationship in terms of the nuclear family model. The custody and maintenance provisions had a similar fate because of the Court's implicit subscription to the heterosexual nuclear family, which resulted in the conclusion that proceedings for custody and maintenance could only be brought between spouses and in relation to their biological or adopted children and not in relation to any ex-nuptial children of either party.

In response to this decision, the Commonwealth Parliament amended the FLA to reflect the High Court's reasoning.[23] However, in 1983, and in reaction to High Court cases that appeared to widen the scope of the Commonwealth powers in the *Constitution*, the Commonwealth Parliament amended the FLA again with the enactment of the *Family Law*

---

23   *Family Law Amendment Act 1976* (Cth).

Amendment Act 1983 (Cth). This allowed a wider category of people to be parties to proceedings in child-related matters; broadened the category of children covered by the FLA; and permitted property proceedings to commence at any time as long as they related to the marital relationship.[24]

2.4.2   Children and the marriage power

After the 1983 amendments, the provisions of the FLA relating to ex-nuptial children were challenged again in the High Court.[25] In upholding these challenges the High Court found that the marriage power could not cover an ex-nuptial child of the husband or wife or a child of other parents, even though the child was living with the husband and wife as a member of their family. The emphasis of the High Court was on the fact that these children were not the children of their marriage. A law governing such children would be too remote from the institution of marriage and therefore outside the scope of the marriage power.

The main consequence of these cases was to declare that the scope of legislative power did not extend to making laws for children born outside a valid marriage, even when these children were living in the common household of the husband and wife and their biological children. In reaching these sorts of conclusions, judges may apply conventions of constitutional interpretation, but, in our view, underlying these decisions are choices that are informed by the traditional nuclear family. These decisions affect the lives of real people. By the mid-1980s, the Court's approach did not appear to stay in step with social realities. The Court, in striking down 'family' laws aimed at governing all of the children of a married couple, including their ex-nuptial children, was creating problems for blended families. The effect was that custody and maintenance proceedings relating to the biological children of a married couple could be brought within the federal family law jurisdiction; whereas proceedings for ex-nuptial children (stepchildren, foster children or other children living in the common household of husband and wife) could only be brought in a State or Territory court.

This problem was eventually resolved with the States' referral of family law powers to the Commonwealth (1986–90).[26] As a result the Commonwealth Parliament now has virtually unlimited legislative power with respect to children. State child-welfare legislation and adoption laws remain the only two exceptions. The result of the High Court's insistence that the marriage power requires that laws for children can only be made for the children of the marriage or children formally adopted by a married couple is an illustration of how the legal discourse manages to make the marriage between husband and wife the norm for creating a family. Children living in the same household, who are for all practical purposes members of the family, are deemed not to be children of the marriage unless they are the

---

24   For a more detailed coverage of the aims of the 1983 amendments, see Explanatory Memorandum, Family Law Amendment Bill 1983 (Cth) 4985–6.

25   *In the Marriage of Cormick; Salmon, Respondent* (1984) 156 CLR 170; *R v Cook; Ex parte C* (1985) 156 CLR 249; *Re F; Ex parte F* (1986) 161 CLR 376.

26   See *Commonwealth Powers (Family Law – Children) Act 1986* (NSW); *Commonwealth Powers (Family Law – Children) Act 1986* (Vic); *Commonwealth Powers (Family Law – Children) Act 1990* (Qld); *Commonwealth Powers (Family Law) Act 1986* (SA); *Commonwealth Powers (Family Law) Act 1987* (Tas). Western Australia did not refer its powers and it has continued to refer its family law matters to the Family Court of Western Australia pursuant to the *Family Court Act 1997* (WA).

biological or legally adopted children of both spouses. Legal analyses of the High Court's interpretation of the marriage power usually characterise the issue as one that is about the interpretation of constitutional provisions and the division of legislative powers between the Commonwealth and State parliaments. This is a relevant consideration, but what is also relevant for us as legal analysts is to ask whether these were the only outcomes available to the Court.

It is not difficult to argue that the High Court in these cases had options and could have interpreted the marriage power differently. The rules of interpretation available to the judges do not present themselves in any order of preference. The issue, for example, of whether the custody and maintenance of ex-nuptial children could be provided for in a law enacted as an exercise of the marriage power could be examined by considering the question of what a marriage is. As this is the term used in the *Constitution*, the question is not answerable by looking at the legislation defining marriage. However, the High Court never fully considered the meaning of 'marriage' in the *Constitution* in these cases; it only did this inadvertently.[27] When the High Court has found that the regulation of the rights of ex-nuptial children is too remote from the marriage, it assumes the marriage to be the legal union between two particular people of different sexes.

However, this is the very issue that requires interpretation by a court assigned the responsibility of interpreting the *Constitution* and it is plausible to expect that the judges would have at least considered the purpose of enacting these child-related provisions in the FLA in the first place.[28] The fact that the judges did not ask this question does not invalidate the choices they made. But raising the issue does illuminate the fact that matters of interpretation always require choices to be made. Furthermore, these choices have real consequences. The final interpretation does not make the law objective or value-neutral, but the conventions of legal reasoning that do not allow for the articulation of the idea that judges are always making choices help maintain the fiction of a pre-constituted law that judges find and apply.

Thus, the function of legal reasoning is also to delegitimise the questioning of what the judges are doing. In a federal system they have responsibilities to interpret the *Constitution*, which in the context of these cases requires maintaining the integrity of the division of legislative authority between the Commonwealth and the States. Moreover, there is no logical possibility of claiming that the judges are 'wrong' in their interpretations, for they are the ones who decide the meaning of the constitutional terms. It is also part of the legal lexicon that judges do so objectively and not by reference to their personal preferences. The High Court's interpretations are final and constitute the law at the given moment.

But inevitably these decisions have consequences for individuals, their families and the broader society. The idea that legal reasoning is an objective task, however, makes these consequences irrelevant in the process of legal interpretation whether of the *Constitution*

---

27   See the summary of the opinions of justices of the High Court to the question 'what is a marriage?' discussed in *Attorney-General for the Commonwealth v 'Kevin & Jennifer'* (2003) 30 Fam LR 1, 23–4 [91]–[100].

28   The conventions and rules of interpretation of constitutions and ordinary legislation are supposed to be different. However, the point here is that judges have to frame the issues and in order to interpret the marriage power they could have plausibly asked: what was the FLA trying to do? Was it designed to regulate an uncontroversial aspect of being married – that is, to nurture children?

or of ordinary legislation.[29] These ideas come together to normalise the idea that marriage has a definite meaning, yet this is not specifically articulated in the High Court judgments.

2.4.3   The marriage and divorce powers and proceedings involving third parties

Subsequent cases involving third parties in disputes over the custody of children further support these claims. For instance, in the case of *Dowal v Murray* the High Court had to consider the validity of s 61(4) of the FLA (now repealed) concerning the effect of a custody order after the death of the spouse who had been granted custody of a child.[30] The section provided that, upon the death of a spouse who had been granted the custody of a child under the Act, the other spouse was entitled to the custody of the child only by an order of the court. The section also provided that, upon a non-custodial spouse applying for an order for custody of a child after the death of the custodial spouse, any person having the care and control of the child was entitled to be a party to the custody proceedings. In upholding the validity of the provision, the High Court appeared to broaden the scope of the marriage power in allowing third parties to a marriage to be parties to proceedings for custody of a child.[31]

This seems apparent considering that in *Russell v Russell* the High Court had held that custody proceedings should be between the parties to the marriage.[32] Notably, however, the validity of the provision in *Dowal* did not depend on the rights of the third parties who had care and control of the child at the time the application was made, but on the rights of the surviving spouse that the Court found arose from the marriage relationship, such as their right to the custody of a child against a third party. As a result of cases like these, provisions for proceedings for custody of a child involving third parties would be valid pursuant to the marriage power, provided at least one of the parties to the marriage was also a party to the proceedings.[33]

These cases found that the provisions involving third parties were valid as the connection to the marriage power was that the child was a child of the marriage. As Gibbs J found in the case of *R v Lambert; Ex parte Plummer*,[34] for a law to be a law with respect to marriage there must be a 'close' connection (now referred to as 'sufficient' connection) between the law and marriage: 'The crucial question … is whether the legislation creates, defines or declares rights or duties that arise out of, or have a close connection with, the marriage relationship'.[35] However, in his view a law is not a law with respect to marriage simply because it has some operation with respect to a child or a party to a marriage. It is within a judge's discretion

---

29   The concept of legal reasoning as a jurisprudential concept functions to contain the judicial task as one of using prescribed rules of interpretation and confining the judges to apply the law. For an introduction, see Julie Dickson, 'Interpretation and Coherence in Legal Reasoning' in Edward N Zalta (ed), *The Stanford Encyclopedia of Philosophy* (Summer 2014 Edition) <http://plato.stanford .edu/archives/sum2014/entries/legal-reas-interpret/>.

30   (1978) 143 CLR 410.

31   *Dowal v Murray* (1978) 143 CLR 410.

32   *Russell v Russell; Farrelly v Farrelly* (1976) 134 CLR 495, 496.

33   Similar reasoning applied in *Vitzdamm-Jones v Vitzdamm-Jones; St. Claire v Nicholson* (1981) 148 CLR 383. See also Fiona Burns, 'Commonwealth Marriage Power and Third Parties in Custodial Proceedings: *Vitzdamm-Jones v Vitzdamm-Jones; St. Claire v Nicholson*' (1983) 10 *Sydney Law Review* 193; *Fountain v Alexander* (1982) 150 CLR 615; *V v V* (1985) 156 CLR 228.

34   (1980) 146 CLR 447.

35   *R v Lambert; Ex parte Plummer* (1980) 146 CLR 447, 456.

to determine whether a law has a 'close' connection to marriage or not. As Gibbs J put it himself, '[t]he question whether a law is one with respect to marriage is one of degree'.[36] Subsequent cases involving third parties show that the High Court continues to privilege the institution of marriage.

The scope of the marriage and divorce powers with regard to third parties arose in *Re Gould*,[37] where the wife sought to restrain the husband from dealing with certain overseas companies under s 85 (now s 106B) of the FLA and to prevent him from defeating her claim in property proceedings under the FLA. The husband (and third-party company) challenged the constitutional validity of these provisions and argued that the marriage power does not authorise the making of laws that enable orders to affect the property rights of third parties. The Full Family Court held that each grant of power under the *Constitution* must be read as capable of flexible application to changing circumstances, and the language of the marriage and divorce powers did not suggest that the power is limited in the sense claimed by the husband and the third-party company.

A similar conclusion was reached in the case of *Hunt v Hunt*.[38] In that case the validity of ss 90AE(2) and 90AF(2) that had been introduced by the enactment of the *Family Law Amendment Act 2003* (Cth) and provided for orders and injunctions binding third parties was upheld by the Family Court.[39] These provisions have gone further than any other third-party provisions in the FLA in empowering a court with family law jurisdiction to make property orders or injunctions that are directed to, or alter the rights, liabilities or property interests of, a third party in relation to a marriage. In upholding their validity, the Court found they fell within the marriage, divorce and incidental powers of the Commonwealth.

There are many ways of understanding the outcomes of these two cases. From a constitutional law perspective, these cases confirm well-established principles of constitutional interpretation. From an economic perspective, they can be seen as family law encroaching on commercial law. From a social-welfare perspective, they could have the effect of increasing the property pool in order to minimise the welfare dependency of the more vulnerable party to the marriage. So understood, these provisions may to some extent be bridging the public and private divide. However, from the perspective taken in this chapter, we can see how the outcomes of these cases continue to privilege the institution of marriage in so far as the validity of the provisions depended on their involving the interests of a party to a marriage in proceedings brought under the FLA.

2.5   Intrinsic meaning of 'marriage' in the *Constitution*

In the discussion below, we address three issues that arise in relation to the term 'marriage' in s 51(xxi) of the *Constitution* – namely, whether or not it empowers the Commonwealth Parliament to *only* make laws with respect to marriage as a monogamous, heterosexual,

---

36   Ibid.
37   (1993) FLC 92-434.
38   (2006) 36 Fam LR 64.
39   See Tom Altobelli, Editorial, 'Constitutional Challenge to Part VIIIAA' (2006) 20 *Australian Journal of Family Law* 114.

formal institution. The monogamous aspect of the legal definition of marriage has implications for polygamous marriages and directly affects the status of traditional Aboriginal marriages;[40] while the heterosexual aspect has implications for same-sex marriages,[41] and the formal aspect has implications for de facto relationships.[42]

2.5.1 Traditional Aboriginal marriages

The Australian Law Reform Commission ('ALRC') in writing its report, *Recognition of Aboriginal Customary Laws*, extensively engaged Aboriginal people through public hearings, research and discussion papers that were translated and distributed among Aboriginal communities, and ensured that Aboriginal women were engaged in the process.[43] The scope of the report was wide in its examination of the conditions and principles for the coexistence of state and traditional Aboriginal laws, but the central issue for the present discussion is whether the Commonwealth Parliament has power to make laws with respect to polygamous marriages such as traditional Aboriginal marriages or whether it can only make laws with respect to monogamous marriage.[44] The failure of Australian law to recognise traditional Aboriginal marriages except in limited circumstances has given rise to many legal and social problems for Aboriginal peoples in areas such as adoption, social security, compensation for accidents, and distribution of property after death. The report explored three different ways of recognising traditional marriages under Australian law to address these problems: recognition of traditional marriage as a de facto relationship, recognition of traditional marriage as marriage for all purposes, and recognition of traditional marriage for particular purposes, also described as 'functional recognition'.[45] Ultimately, the ALRC found that the preferred option was functional recognition of Aboriginal customary law and thereby the functional recognition of traditional marriages under Australian law.[46]

The functional recognition of Aboriginal law rests on examining each area of law that gives rise to legal or social problems for Aboriginal peoples in traditional marriages. A federal law could then provide for the recognition of traditional marriages for each of the purposes that were considered desirable.[47] The benefit of this approach is that it would

---

40   Australian Law Reform Commission ('ALRC'), *Recognition of Aboriginal Customary Laws*, Report No 31 (1986) ch 13.

41   *Commonwealth v Australian Capital Territory* (2013) 250 CLR 441. See also Mary Anne Neilsen, *High Court Decides the ACT's Same-Sex Marriage Law is Invalid* (12 December 2013) Parliament of Australia <http://www.aph.gov.au/About_Parliament/Parliamentary_Departments/ Parliamentary_Library/FlagPost/2013/December/High_Court_decides_the_ACTs_same-sex_ marriage_law_is_invalid>.

42   For arguments for and against giving Federal Parliament this power, see Mary Anne Neilsen, *Family Law Amendment (De Facto Financial Matters and Other Measures) Bill 2008*, No 9 of 2008, 25 August 2008, Bills Digest <https://www.aph.gov.au/binaries/library/pubs/bd/2008-09/09bd009.pdf>.

43   ALRC, above n 40, [9]–[20].

44   The main and more fundamental issue in this report was whether the Australian state legal systems could accommodate the recognition or existence of another legal system. Whether the Aboriginal peoples want such a recognition is an issue that points to the manner in which official discourse of recognition gets formulated. See also Michaela Ash, 'Preventing Harm or Fortifying the Borders? Political Discourse on Polygamy and Islam in Australia' (2013) 9(2) *Critical Race and Whiteness Studies* <http://www.acrawsa.org.au/files/ejournalfiles/209Ash201329.pdf>.

45   ALRC, above n 40, [241].

46   Ibid [270].

47   The principles to be used in deciding on recognition are set out in para 270 of the report.

leave Aboriginal communities with more freedom and flexibility to develop rules to adapt to new situations. It would avoid the introduction of externally imposed rigidity that would be inevitable if the Aboriginal marriage rules had to be written down. This approach would also avoid conflict between Aboriginal marriage law and Australian law. At the same time, it respects aspects of Aboriginal ways of life and customary law.

This reasoning is invoking the discourse of legal pluralism, where the idea that more than one law can exist at the same time surfaces repeatedly. That is, the mainstream legal system through its institution – the ALRC – is trying to be inclusive and move beyond the idea that only one legal system can exist within the nation-state. In this respect the ALRC appears to be contributing to the extensive literature on legal pluralism, where the progressive stance depicts pluralism as the norm rather than the exception.[48] However, the very fact that the state legal system has the choice as to whether to 'recognise' another system is indicative of the hierarchical position of systems of rules. Thus, ultimately the ALRC is legitimising the laws of the state irrespective of the actual recommendations in its report.

One of the reasons given by the ALRC for not recognising Aboriginal marriages as marriages for all purposes is that it could mean that many Aboriginal people would be guilty of the crime of bigamy.[49] It is worthwhile to pause here and consider why the ALRC did not instead suggest that the definition of marriage in the MA should change. The obvious answer is that the limited brief of the ALRC was to examine whether Aboriginal marriages could be recognised by the law of the state. It was not within the scope of the ALRC inquiry to ask whether the definition of marriage in the Commonwealth law could be different or modified to include Aboriginal customary marriages. In other words the category of marriage in the MA was not under review or consideration.

Admittedly, categories are necessary for any discussion to proceed, and of necessity categories are exclusionary. However, it is important to point out that the function of using some categories extends beyond the immediate task. Considering that the report is one of the most cited reports of the ALRC, its contribution to normalising the definition of marriage as a monogamous union can only be imagined. This is not a comment on the intentions of the ALRC but an illustration of how our assumptions about what is normal or natural find expression in different sites.

Thus the approach of the ALRC, albeit well intended, entrenched the idea of marriage as monogamous. It conceptualised its task as exploring how best another kind of marriage, the traditional Aboriginal marriage, could fit within the pre-existing legal system. This may have been inevitable considering the ALRC is a state institution and is operating within a legal system where marriage is defined as a monogamous institution. However, the presupposition of

---

48   The concept of legal pluralism is understood differently by authors in various disciplines and it is not an exaggeration to say that in legal scholarship the subject remains a fringe topic. See generally Martha Mundy (ed), *Law and Anthropology* (Routledge, 2002); Michael Freeman and David Napier (eds), *Law and Anthropology: Current Legal Issues Volume 12* (Oxford University Press, 2009); Antony Allot and Gordon R Woodman (eds), *People's Law and State Law: the Bellagio Papers* (Foris Publications, 1985); Marc Galanter, 'Justice in Many Rooms: Courts, Private Ordering, and Indigenous Law' (1981) 19 *The Journal of Legal Pluralism and Unofficial Law* 1; John Griffiths, 'What is Legal Pluralism' (1986) 24 *Journal of Legal Pluralism and Unofficial Law* 1; Sally Engle Merry, 'Legal pluralism' (1988) 22(5) *Law and Society Review* 869; Brian Z Tamanaha, 'A Non-Essentialist Version of Legal Pluralism' (2000) 27(2) *Journal of Law and Society* 296.

49   ALRC, above n 40, [317].

marriage as a monogamous union, and treating it as unchangeable in the process of 'recognising' another familial arrangement, should be seen as an exercise of power rather than a mere description of a natural state of affairs. The same argument can be made with respect to the High Court's response to attempts to recognise same-sex marriage.

2.5.2   Same-sex marriages

It is customary for family law texts to briefly discuss the issue of the legislative definition of marriage extending to same-sex marriage and to give an opinion on whether this could be possible or not. The matter is treated as an issue of constitutional interpretation that can be decided either by relying on the original intention of the framers of the *Constitution* or on the conception of the *Constitution* as a text that requires interpretation in its contemporary context. We wish to focus instead on the contingent choices always open to the courts. In this context, it is also important to identify how the High Court has appeared to be progressive while ultimately denying the status of marriage to same-sex unions.

The High Court has at times suggested that the legislature could legislate on the issue. Thus in *Re Wakim; Ex parte McNally* McHugh J in the High Court considered the possibility of the Commonwealth Parliament legislating with respect to sex-same marriages.[50] However, the issue was not tested directly in the High Court until the case of *Commonwealth v Australian Capital Territory*.[51] In this case the High Court was asked to decide whether the Australian Capital Territory could enact the *Marriage Equality (Same Sex) Act 2013* (ACT) ('ACT Act'), or whether, as the Commonwealth Parliament claimed, the law was inconsistent with the MA and therefore of no effect. In response, the Australian Capital Territory argued that the ACT Act was intended to fill a gap in the marriage law that was silent on the issue of same-sex marriage.

Unanimously, the High Court held that the ACT Act could not operate concurrently with the MA. In reaching its decision the High Court considered the scope of the marriage power. It found that, when used in s 51(xxi), 'marriage' is a term that can include marriages between people of the same sex.[52] Effectively, this means that the Commonwealth Parliament has the power to legislate with respect to same-sex marriage. The Court further found that the Commonwealth has only exercised this power in enacting the MA which, in its current form, is only intended to provide for marriages that can be solemnised between a man and a woman, and no other form of marriage. Therefore, the provisions of the ACT Act are not capable of operating concurrently with the Commonwealth law because the MA was intended to 'cover the field' and be 'a comprehensive and exhaustive statement of the law with respect to the creation and recognition of the legal status of marriage'.[53]

Thus, the fact that the MA does not 'allow' a same-sex union to be designated as a marriage means that the ACT Act cannot provide for these marriages either. The question of

---

50   *Re Wakim; Ex parte McNally* (1999) 198 CLR 511, 553–4; this was the observation made by McHugh J in arguing that the interpretation of constitutional terms must change with time.

51   (2013) 250 CLR 441.

52   The High Court said that it must decide whether s 51(xxi) permits the Commonwealth Parliament to make a law with respect to same-sex marriage (ibid 454 [9]); whether 'marriage' in placitum xxi refers to the status as understood at the time of Federation; and answered 'no' as it is a topic of juristic classification (ibid 455 [14]).

53   Ibid 467 [57]; if the MA had defined marriage as also including same-sex unions, then the ACT Act would not have operated.

concurrent operation depends upon the proper construction of the relevant laws and 'on its true construction, the *Marriage Act* is to be read as providing that the only form of marriage permitted shall be a marriage formed or recognised in accordance with that Act'.[54] The only form of marriage permitted under the MA is the marriage between a man and a woman. It is significant that the High Court uses the word 'only' even though it is not present in the MA definition of marriage.

The High Court's reasoning follows the principle of constitutional interpretation that does not depend on original intent but on finding the 'topic of juristic classification'.[55] This approach is not tied to any particular historical model, but is based on the understanding that marriage is a social institution that changes over time, evident for example in the fact that a marriage may no longer be a union for life. The High Court also reassessed the 19th century cases that formerly were treated as authority for the proposition that marriage is a union between a man and woman (for example, *Hyde v Hyde*).[56] It found that these cases were not primarily concerned with defining marriage; their scope was more limited and these cases did not then, and do not now, define the scope of the marriage power. Moreover, the Court found that more recent case law and legislation have changed various aspects of the definition of marriage that had applied in these cases; for example, polygamous marriages formed in overseas jurisdictions are now recognised under Australian law.[57] It concluded that, in the context of s 51(xxi) of the *Constitution*, 'marriage' is a term that includes a marriage between people of the same sex.

This is the first time that the High Court has interpreted the meaning of 'marriage' in s 51(xxi) in this way. This seems like a truly progressive stand, and some commentators immediately said so after the judgment was delivered.[58] However, it remains the case that, despite the High Court finding that the marriage power could be used to legislate with respect to same-sex marriage, the Court also found that, until the Commonwealth Parliament makes a law to this effect, marriage will continue to be defined as a union between husband and wife. Marriage equality will continue to be denied to people in same-sex unions.

The list of reasons the High Court gave to support its decision can help us identify the choices that it made; but this is not to say that it is doing something that it is not authorised to do.[59] On the contrary, this is one way of illustrating that the High Court is remaining within the bounds of formalism.[60] Formalism has many definitions, but we use it here to

---

54   Ibid 467 [56].

55   Ibid 455 [14].

56   (1866) LR 1 PD 130.

57   Most recently affirmed in *Ghazel & Ghazel and Anor* [2016] FamCAFC 31.

58   Trieste Corby and Chris Travers, *High Court of Australia Recognises Constitutional Power to Legislate with Respect to Same-Sex Marriage* (12 December 2013) Human Rights Law Centre <http://hrlc.org .au/high-court-of-australia-recognises-constitutional-power-to-legislate-with-respect-to-same-sex-marriage/>.

59   For constitutional analysis, see Margaret Brock and Dan Meagher, 'The Legal Recognition of Same-Sex Unions in Australia: A Constitutional Analysis' (2011) 22(4) *Public Law Review* 266. See also Patrick Parkinson and Nicholas Aroney, 'The Territory of Marriage: Constitutional Law, Marriage Law and Family Policy in the ACT Same Sex Marriage Case' (2014) 28 *Australian Journal of Family Law* 160.

60   For an introduction to the different forms of legal reasoning, see Andrei Marmor (ed), *Law and Interpretation: Essays in Legal Philosophy* (Clarendon Press, 1995); Linda Meyer (ed), *Rules and Reasoning: Essays in Honour of Fred Schauer* (Hart Publishing, 1999).

mean that the judges are expected to interpret the language of the rule rather than concern themselves with the effect of such an interpretation. Thus, the High Court reached its decision by using legal reasoning methods, by applying precedents, and determining the scope of the marriage power and intent of the legislation by reference to principles of interpretation. What the High Court failed to mention was that all of the same-sex marriages that had been formed under the ACT Act were now void as a result of its decision. In that way its decision was an act of discrimination on the basis of sexuality.

But even according to mainstream legal analyses, the High Court could have approached its task of interpretation differently. For instance, it could have legitimately applied other rules of interpretation to find that in enacting the MA the Commonwealth had exercised its power to make laws *only* with respect to marriage between people of the opposite sex but not with respect to same-sex marriage, which would be within the scope of the marriage power. This way it could have reached very different conclusions: that the MA did not cover the field, which would have allowed the ACT Act to fill the 'gap' left by the Commonwealth Parliament in not legislating with respect to same sex-marriages. Importantly, it would still be using the rules of interpretation permissible as an exercise of formal legal reasoning, but in a way which could have meant the difference between a decision that promotes discrimination and one that does not. Among various objections to this line of questioning is that the High Court is not completely free to do what it wants – it is obliged to maintain the integrity of a federal system and division of powers between the Commonwealth and the States and Territories. However, this argument depends on the acceptance of the objectivity of legal reasoning and obscures the choices that are made by judges.

The issue here is not that the Court acted intentionally to disadvantage people belonging to a minority group. Indeed, the High Court decision may be a good illustration of Queer theory and gay and lesbian claims that the existence of discrimination on the grounds of sexuality fails to even register as discrimination in mainstream reasoning.[61] The point is to illuminate, as critical theory has done, whether in fact neutral or objective interpretations of law are possible.[62] If we accept they are not, then how can the adoption of one perspective, and not another, be justified? The short and conventional answer is that the decision-maker is responsible for choosing one interpretation and not another. The difference in our argument is that decision-makers should not be able to hide behind the claim that they are engaging in legal reasoning and treat it as objective truth.

2.5.3 De facto relationships

The question of whether the marriage power extends to informal marriage-like relationships has not been tested before the High Court. Over time State laws have been introduced to regulate aspects of these relationships and inevitably there have been differences in their approaches, especially with respect to same-sex relationships. The States' referral of powers over the subject to the Commonwealth in 2008 enabled the Commonwealth Parliament

---

61   Carl F Stychin, *Law's Desire: Sexuality and the Limits of Justice* (Routledge, 1995).
62   For a general overview, see Ian Ward, *An Introduction to Critical Legal Theory* (Cavendish Publishing, 2nd ed, 2004); Margaret Davies, *Asking the Law Question* (Thomson Reuters, 3rd ed, 2008) where it is illustrated throughout how the construction of legal knowledge takes place in various legal theories.

to enact the *Family Law Amendment (De Facto Financial Matters And Other Measures) Act 2008* (Cth). The States (except Western Australia; South Australia referred its powers in 2010) have referred their powers to the Commonwealth with respect to de facto heterosexual and de facto same-sex couples. The 2008 amendments inserted a new Part VIIIAB. As a consequence the FLA now applies to de facto couples, both heterosexual and same-sex, in relation to property settlements (including superannuation splitting, third-party provisions, financial agreements and maintenance) and children.[63] Generally, the provisions of the FLA dealing with disputes arising in marriages and de facto relationships are mirror images of each other.[64] This is one example of how the law privileges the institution of marriage as a formal union and how other relationships are measured against this standard. Unlike the issue of monogamy and same-sex relations, in this context it is the mere formality of entering into the legally approved relationship of marriage that is attributed significance.[65]

The use of the legislative device of referring State powers to the Commonwealth illustrates the discursive significance of keeping de facto relations separate from marriage. The standard explanation for this development is that the *Constitution* divides legislative powers in such a manner that the Commonwealth Parliament cannot legislate for de facto relations and only the States and Territories are vested with the residual power to do so. The alternative question that is not posed is whether the Commonwealth Parliament could cover such relationships under a broadened definition of marriage. If such a question were asked, at the very least it would bring into focus how the contemporary definition of marriage is not immutable. It can be redefined and the fact that it is not so re-conceptualised demonstrates the discursive power of the category of 'marriage' used by the legal system. There are other possible ways to explain why the Commonwealth Parliament did not redefine marriage in the MA to include de facto relationships, but this discussion is only pointing out that there are other ways of interpreting what a marriage is.

2.6   Institutional structures: courts, their jurisdiction and the rise of ADR

In the following discussion, we examine the creation of a specialist family court under the FLA and the subsequent developments that seem to be rolling back the distinctiveness of the 'Family Court'. The creation of a specialist court goes far in legitimising family law as a distinct area of law. Moreover, a specialist institution has been created in most common law jurisdictions and the issue in every instance is whether the primacy given to procedural

---

63   This is in so far as they are relevant to the resolution of financial matters between the parties, while the class of children is confined to those born in married and de facto relationships (and can include born through artificial means and through surrogacy arrangements).

64   Discussed in greater detail in subsequent chapters; however, for an application relating to a de facto relationship, the initial jurisdictional issue is that the court must find that a de facto relationship actually existed. See Carl Boyd, 'Family Law: Challenging De Facto Relationships: Jurisdictional Issues' (2014) 52(4) *Law Society Journal* 40.

65   As we will see when we come to examine the hurdles of establishing a de facto relationship that occur when the relationship has broken down. A married couple does not experience the same hurdles, as their relationship is formalised by the marriage ceremony. See also Anne Barlow et al, *Cohabitation, Marriage and the Law* (Hart Publishing, 2005).

justice in common law systems is worth preserving. The FLA created the specialist court known as the Family Court of Australia ('FCA').[66] Originally the courts that were to exercise jurisdiction under the FLA were the FCA and, to a limited extent, the courts of summary jurisdiction and the State Supreme Courts.[67] In addition, now the Federal Circuit Court of Australia ('FCC', formerly the Federal Magistrates Court of Australia) exercises jurisdiction in all but a few areas of the FLA.[68] This development creates further issues about the continued relevance of a specialist Family Court.

2.6.1 Family Court of Australia

Part IV of the FLA deals with the creation and structure of the FCA. The creation of the FCA is made possible by s 21. It consists of a Chief Judge, a Deputy Chief Judge and other judges (maximum 54; currently 41). It is a superior court of record (s 21(2)) and is accordingly equivalent in status to the Federal Court of Australia and the Supreme Courts of the States and Territories. However, unlike the Supreme Courts, the statute defines its jurisdiction. The FLA provides for the Chief Executive Officer to assist the Chief Judge in the management of the administrative affairs of the Court and also defines their powers.[69] Moreover, the FLA provides for other officers of the Family Court of Australia, including registrars, family consultants (formerly court counsellors and mediators) and marshals.[70]

The FLA applies exclusively in matters that fall under the court's jurisdiction, in a matrimonial cause, or a de facto cause, or a proceeding under Part VII (s 8(1)).[71] The connection between the courts and the applicants is established by reference to the concepts of citizenship, domicile or ordinary presence. Thus, proceedings for divorce require that at least one party is an Australian citizen; or a person domiciled in Australia; or a person ordinarily resident in Australia for one year prior to proceedings.[72] Proceedings for all other matrimonial causes may be instituted if at least one party is an Australian citizen; or a person ordinarily resident in Australia or present in Australia at the relevant date.[73] Proceedings for a de facto financial cause may be instituted if either party or at least one party is an Australian citizen; or ordinarily resident; or present in Australia at the relevant date.[74] With respect to proceedings

---

66   Part IV of the FLA deals with the structure and personnel of the FCA.
67   Part V of the FLA deals with jurisdiction of courts. Originally the FLA had continued the jurisdiction of State Supreme Courts as a transition measure while the Commonwealth set up the FCA. This jurisdiction was to continue until revoked by a proclamation. The FLA also provided for the possibility that States could set up their own Family Courts. Western Australia is the only State that created its own Family Court, known as the Family Court of Western Australia.
68   With few exceptions – international child abduction; international relocation; special medical procedures; contravention of parenting orders of the FCA; serious allegation of child sexual or physical abuse; serious controlling family violence; complex jurisdiction questions; likely lengthy hearing; adoption; and validity of marriage or divorce. The FCA hears divorce applications in exceptional cases only.
69   See FLA pt IVA divs 1, 1A, 2.
70   See FLA pt IVA div 3.
71   Since 1987, proceedings relating to children do not require a reference to matrimonial cause.
72   s 39(3).
73   s 39(4). For proceedings under para (f) of the definition of 'matrimonial cause' in s 4(1), the requirements of citizenship, ordinary residence or presence are not necessary, but a few other conditions apply.
74   s 39A(2).

related to children, s 69B explains that if one can bring an action under this Part of the FLA, then he or she cannot institute proceedings elsewhere except with respect to child support. Section 69C(2) sets out who may institute these proceedings: either or both parents; the child; a grandparent; or any other person concerned with the care, welfare or development of the child.[75]

Primarily, the FCA is to administer the FLA, but in practice a number of courts are authorised to do so. The FCA and the FCC administer the FLA[76] in all States (except Western Australia, as it has its own Family Court). In the Northern Territory, the Supreme Court administers the FLA (in addition to the FCA and FCC).[77] Courts of summary jurisdiction have limited jurisdiction under the FLA as they can deal with all matrimonial causes except proceedings for nullity of a marriage or for a declaration as to validity of marriage or its dissolution or annulment.[78] The original jurisdiction of the FCA is defined in s 31 and it has additional jurisdiction in associated matters,[79] and accrued jurisdiction.[80]

In the FCA, a single judge exercises original jurisdiction.[81] Under the FLA an appeal from a single judge of the FCA or from a decision of a State or Territory Supreme Court lies to a Full Court of three or more judges, with a majority from the Appeal Division.[82] In some instances an appeal to the High Court can be made, but this can only be done with special leave granted by the High Court.[83] Appeals from the FCC in family law matters lie to the Full Court of the Family Court.[84] In some cases (determined by the Chief Justice of the FCA), an appeal from the FCC lies to a single judge, but no appeal lies to the Full Court in these cases.[85] This is significant as now the majority of applications are initiated in the FCC and not in the FCA.[86]

In the following section, we discuss three main issues: whether a distinct area of jurisprudence can be created by the specialist family court; explanations for and responses to the hostility towards the FCA; and whether the distinctive philosophy underlying the FCA continues to exist despite the removal of mediation from the FCA and the recent creation of the FCC.

---

75   FLA s 69E details the level of connection with Australia of the parent, child or any other party to the proceedings.

76   s 39 (1), (1A), (2). The practices of the Family Court and Federal Court under the FLA are regulated by ss 33A–33C and 45A of the FLA, pt V of the *Federal Circuit Court Act 1999* (Cth) and respective Rules of Court and regulations. For details see Richard Chisholm, Suzanne Christie and Julie Kearney, *Annotated Family Law Legislation* (LexisNexis, 2014) 219ff.

77   ss 39(5), 40(3).

78   s 39(6); see s 39(7), which allows that such jurisdiction can be limited by proclamation; s 44A, which allows dissolution proceedings in 'prescribed' courts; and s 46, which limits property proceedings to $20 000 or if the parties consent to the jurisdiction, for property of greater value than that.

79   s 33.

80   The concept of accrued jurisdiction has been developed in various High Court decisions; for an FCA example, see *In the Marriage of Warby* (2002) FLC 93-091.

81   s 28(1), but can be exercised by the Full Court.

82   s 28(3); s 28(2) provides that appeals from courts of summary jurisdiction lie to a single judge or the Full Court of the Family Court.

83   s 95.

84   94AAA(1). Appeals from Family Law Magistrate of Western Australia also lie to the Family Court: s 94AAA(1A).

85   s 94AAA(3).

86   The AIFS reports that Family Law Court filings for the period 2004–05 to 2012–13 show that the case load distribution between the FCA and the FCC in 2012–13 was 14% and 86% respectively: Rae Kaspiew et al, *Family Law Court Filings 2004–05 to 2012–13* (AIFS, February 2015).

2.6.2   Why a specialist court?

The significance of a specialist family court can be understood at various levels – for example, in terms of the federal system of government, the effort to create a federal court system, and the implications of this for the jurisdiction of the existing court systems in the States and Territories; the need for specialised expertise of judges who would administer the newly created FLA; the procedural reforms that would make the FCA a more accessible institution; and the substantive content of the FLA, which includes the no-fault divorce philosophy.

The enactment of the FLA was a bold step by the federal government, in terms of both its substance and the institutions designed to implement it.[87] The creation of the FCA could be understood as an effort to make the philosophy of the legislation work in practice. The literature on the establishment and subsequent history of the FCA identifies the distinctiveness of the FLA, its philosophy, structure and need for expertise, as the main reasons for the creation of the specialist court.[88] However, the legislative history of the FLA shows that initially there was no proposal to create a specialist court. The original plan was that the State Supreme Courts would administer the FLA and it was only during the review of the Family Law Bill [No 2] 1974 (Cth) by the Senate Standing Committee on Constitutional and Legal Affairs that a specialist court was proposed.[89] This issue is also relevant for assessing the more recent changes to the FLA and its administration.

The FLA introduced a number of procedural innovations that could support the claim that the FCA was a specialist court.[90] As originally enacted, the FLA provided that the FCA would conduct its proceedings so as to avoid undue formality;[91] judges of the FCA would require special qualities,[92] but they would also be assisted by a number of non-judicial

---

87   In addition to the creation of the FCA, the FLA also provided for the creation of two other institutions: the Family Law Council and the Australian Institute of Family Studies. Both of these have continued to be influential bodies in regard to family law reform.

88   Kep Enderby, 'The Family Law Act: Background to the Legislation' (1975–76) 1 *UNSW Law Journal* 10; Helen Rhoades and Shurlee Swain, 'A Bold Experiment?: Reflections on the Early History of the Family Court' 22(1) *Australian Family Lawyer* 11; Shurlee Swain, *Born in Hope: The Early Years of the Family Court of Australia* (UNSW Press, 2012); Leonie Star, *Counsel of Perfection: The Family Court of Australia* (Oxford University Press, 1996); Alastair Nicholson and Margaret Harrison, 'Family Law and the Family Court of Australia: Experiences of the First 25 Years' (2000) 24(3) *Melbourne University Law Review* 756; Helen Rhoades, 'The Family Court of Australia: Examining Australia's First Therapeutic Jurisdiction' (2010) 20 *Journal of Judicial Administration* 67. See John Biggs, 'Stability of Marriage – A Family Court' (1961) 34 *Australian Law Journal* 343 for an argument for a specialist court even before the FLA was proposed.

89   See Commonwealth, *Parliamentary Debates*, Senate, 26 November 1974, 2745–51. See also H A Finlay 'Family Law, Family Courts and Federalism: An Opportunity for Reform' (1974) 9(4) *Melbourne University Law Review* 567; Star, above n 88, 89–90.

90   Whether the proposed specialist court could also be described as a therapeutic court is a matter of debate. For an introduction, see Michael King et al, *Non-Adversarial Justice* (Federation Press, 2009); David Wexler and Bruce Winick (eds), *Law in a Therapeutic Key: Developments in Therapeutic Jurisprudence* (Carolina Academic Press, 1996); Michael King, 'Problem-Solving Court Judging, Therapeutic Jurisprudence and Transformational Leadership' (2008) 17 *Journal of Judicial Administration* 155: Diana Bryant and John Faulks, 'The "Helping Court" Comes Full Circle: The Application and Use of Therapeutic Jurisprudence in the Family Court of Australia' (2007) 17 *Journal of Judicial Administration* 93.

91   s 97(3).

92   FLA s 22(2) mentions the preconditions for appointment, and in sub-cl (b) says a person shall not be appointed as a judge unless by reason of training, experience and personality they are a suitable person to deal with matters of family law.

personnel, for example registrars, judicial registrars and court counsellors.[93] In addition, the provision of mediation and other forms of ADR within the FCA structure was significant even though the predecessor legislation, the *Matrimonial Causes Act 1959* (Cth), had also incorporated the use of marriage counselling.[94]

But the possibility of creating a radically distinct court while the rest of the legal system continues to operate conventionally remains to be realised. The fact that the High Court is the highest court of appeal arguably has been more significant in determining the mode of existence of a specialist court within the larger legal system. Early in its history the procedural practices of the FCA were challenged in the High Court and in *Re Watson; ex parte Armstrong*[95] the High Court affirmed that the FCA should follow traditional procedural practices and avoid what was derogatorily described as a tendency to do 'palm tree justice'. We suggest that since the High Court continues to emphasise the jurisprudence of legal reasoning and apparently does so according to the principle of formal equality in not being concerned with the social or personal effects of a particular interpretation of the *Constitution*, the authoritative precedents in the area of family law are formed in terms of the mainstream legal traditions rather than in the alternative or specialist traditions of the FCA. A stronger way of saying this is that the fact that the High Court remains the apex court circumscribes the power of the FCA to be radical in its practices.[96] In that sense, the hostility towards the FCA evident in cases like *Re Watson* appears to have been misplaced.

This raises the next issue, which is the hostility directed at the FCA, but it is necessary to identify whether the perceived problems relate to the FCA as an institution, or are in part related to the substantive content of the FLA. Over the years the FCA has attracted an unusual amount of anger from certain sections of the community.[97] Sections of the profession were not very supportive of the FCA either.[98] Rhoades and Swain report, on the basis of an impressive study of the early history of the FCA, how the attitudes of consumers, mostly men, were negative towards the FCA. They go on to say that legal professionals often explained that these negative attitudes were owing to the appearance of the judges without robes and wigs and because the FCA was housed in ordinary buildings and furnished more casually than other courtrooms. This is a valuable insight into how the profession reacted to the introduction of the FLA. It is also the implicit reason for the changes introduced in the 1980s with regard to the functioning of the court. However, it is important to critique these assumptions, as otherwise they help construct the discourse of legal authority as dependent on its formality.

Eventually a number of changes were introduced to make the FCA look like any other court.[99] It has been pointed out that by the mid-1980s a majority of judges of the FCA wished

---

93   John Fogarty, 'Establishment of the Family Court of Australia and its Early Years: a Personal Perspective' (2001) 60 *Family Matters* 90.
94   Harvey, above n 12.
95   (1976) 136 CLR 248.
96   This is illustrated in an early decision of the High Court in *In re Watson; ex-parte Armstrong* (1976) 136 CLR 248. For a discussion of other similar responses by the High Court, see H A Finlay, 'Towards Non-Adversary Procedures in Family Law' (1983) 10 *Sydney Law Review* 61, 70ff.
97   See Rhoades and Swain, above n 88, 105.
98   Elizabeth Evatt, 'The Administration of Family Law' (1979) 38 *Journal of Public Administration* 1.
99   Among the changes introduced are that judges wear robes and the court arrangements are now more like conventional courtrooms. For a history of court attire, see Charles M Yablon, 'Judicial Drag: An Essay on Wigs, Robes and Legal Change' [1995] *Wisconsin Law Review* 1129.

to take up the wigs and gowns and the legislation was amended.[100] It is probably not surprising that the legal profession desires the formality and regalia of the law. For example, Thompson has famously analysed the reliance of law on creating a spectacle for maintaining its authority.[101] However, by accepting rather than questioning the claims that the informality of the FCA was the problem, we endorse the discourse of legal authority as dependent on the outward forms of its institutions and it becomes a self-fulfilling prophecy.[102]

The provisions for judges to conduct trials without undue formality and without being bound by the general rules of evidence similarly affects the legal profession's stake in maintaining their privilege as the experts and in control of the conduct of proceedings. Moreover, the FLA in providing for judges to be assisted by other 'helping' professions, including counsellors and mediators, appears to depart from the common law system where emphasis is on procedural justice as the main focus of court proceedings. Arguably this may be more of a concern for the practitioners than for the litigants. It is important therefore to temper the interpretations of practitioners with the possibility that there might be another explanation for the hostility towards the FCA.

In fact, whether people were (or are) hostile to the FCA has a lot to do with the subject matter of the law and the design of the FLA that gives wide jurisdiction and discretion to the Court to decide how to distribute property and decide arrangements for children after separation.[103] In particular, the perceived challenge to the authority of fathers is a recurring theme in the literature and it is accepted as one of the reasons for the hostility towards the FCA.[104] Therefore, the creation of the specialist court and the substantive content of the legislation are distinct but interrelated issues that can help explain the hostility towards the FCA.

It is also likely that the controversies related to the FCA may have arisen because its processes made it look like it was a radical departure from the conventions of litigation in the mainstream courts. No doubt the FCA did innovate with regard to procedure,[105] and to a large extent the legislative design in the FLA was novel. It authorised the court to divide property between spouses and the emphasis on ADR (or primary dispute resolution/family dispute resolution ('FDR') as it has come to be known) was a distinctive feature of the legislation.[106] The fact that under the legislation a judge could direct the parties to engage in mediation was a departure from the traditional understanding of the role of a court as a non-interventionist

---

100   Fogarty, above n 93, 97.

101   This idea is very convincingly developed by E P Thompson, *The Making of the English Working Class* (Victor Gollancz, 1965).

102   The idea gets repeated and acquires a self-evident truth status. See, eg, Melinda Brown, 'Keeping Your (Horse) Hair On' (1999) 73(2) *The Law Institute Journal* 12.

103   Nicholson and Harrison, above n 88. For an example of how the legislative content and the institution are conflated, see John Hirst, '"Kangaroo court": Family Law in Australia' (2005) 17 *Quarterly Essay* 85.

104   For an introduction, see Miranda Kay and Julia Tolmie, 'Fathers' Rights Groups in Australia and their Engagement with Issues in Family Law' (1998) 12 *Australian Journal of Family Law* 19.

105   Even where the FLA provided for the use of social sciences knowledge and social-welfare expertise, the courts had to develop the practices and often these practices differed in various courts. See Swain, above n 88; see also Finlay, above n 96, 70 for the argument that the structure of the Family Court was in the mould of an adversary court.

106   FLA s 10F defines 'family dispute resolution' as 'a process (other than a judicial process): (a) in which a family dispute resolution practitioner helps people affected, or likely to be affected, by separation or divorce to resolve some or all of their disputes with each other; and (b) in which the practitioner is independent of all of the parties involved in the process'.

and neutral arbiter of a dispute. This blurring of the distinction between the court and counselling was a function of the design of the legislation.

One of the main innovations of the legislation was that the facilities for ADR were made part of the court structure. The symbolic significance of this innovation became even more acute with the availability of these facilities in the FCA as a one-stop institution.[107] The FLA provided for counselling and mediation services to be carried out by court personnel, albeit non-judicial officers. In addition a judge could also refer the parties to counselling or mediation during a trial. The cumulative effect of all these changes was to create in-house expertise and a cooperative ethos among various branches of the FCA. It leads us to the next issue of whether, in view of the amendments to the FLA with the enactment of the *Family Law Amendment (Shared Parental Responsibility) Act 2006* (Cth) ('the 2006 amendments'), the FCA can still be described as a specialist court. One significant aspect of the FCA being a specialist court was that it integrated the provision of ADR and conventional litigation under the same roof, thus enhancing the synergies of the institutional design and the legislative emphasis on ADR.

The 2006 amendments to the FLA strengthened the legislative insistence on using ADR methods, but separated the counselling and mediation services and moved them outside the FCA. The focus in particular was on child-related disputes, with the introduction of FDR mechanisms that would be administered by newly established family relationship centres and resolved by the appointment of family dispute resolution practitioners.[108] Parkinson[109] explains that this was a compromise response to the recommendation of the *Every Picture Tells a Story* report for the establishment of a specialist tribunal.[110] The rhetoric behind the change was that by providing counselling and mediation in stand-alone facilities, cultural change would occur and parents would understand that disputes about children are not legal disputes.[111]

However, at the same time that these ADR functions were excised from the FCA, the FLA reiterated and strengthened the legislative insistence on using FDR methods. It bears asking how the two moves could be justified simultaneously.[112] On the issue of making a

---

107   The value of counselling services within the court is explained in Audrey Marshall, 'Social Workers and Psychologists as Family Court Counsellors within the Family Court of Australia' (1977) 30(1) *Australian Social Work* 9.

108   For background information on the creation of family relationship centres, see *Operational Framework for Family Relationship Centres*, Department of Social Services, Australian Government <https://www.dss.gov.au/sites/default/files/documents/frcs_operational_framework.pdf>.

109   Patrick Parkinson, 'Keeping in Contact: the Role of Family Relationship Centres in Australia' (2006) 18(2) *Child and Family Law Quarterly* 157.

110   These changes were part of the 2006 amendments to the FLA. The precursor to these amendments was the House of Representatives Standing Committee on Family and Community Affairs, House of Representatives, *Every Picture Tells a Story: Inquiry into Child Custody Arrangements in the Event of Family Separation* (2003). It is mentioned in this report that only about 6% of decisions in the FCA go right through to judicial decision. A judge is required to address the best interests, but little is known of the basis for decision-making in the majority (94%) of cases: 6 [1.23].

111   The Commonwealth government funds the family relationship centres and therefore the economic rationale of moving these services out of the FCA is not entirely plausible.

112   For an explanation of the changes, see Tom Altobelli, 'A Generational Change in Family Dispute Resolution in Australia' (2006) 17 *Australasian Dispute Resolution Journal* 140. It is also important to acknowledge that in response to an earlier report (Family Law Pathways Advisory Group, *Out of the Maze: Pathways to the Future for Families Experiencing Separation: Report of the Family Law Pathways Advisory Group* (2011)) the *Family Law Rules 2004* (Cth) sch 1 pts 1, 1(1) and 2 had already introduced pre-action procedures in child-related and financial disputes.

distinction between ADR and litigation, the procedures followed by the FCA also require some comment. Right from its inception the FLA had incorporated an emphasis on conducting court proceedings in a less formal manner.[113] The *Every Picture Tells a Story* report had recommended that an alternative specialist administrative tribunal should be created to resolve child-related disputes in a genuinely non-adversarial manner. But the dual emphasis on the non-adversarial resolution of disputes through a tribunal and the parties finding their own solutions reveal a tension between the desire to delegalise the system and to keep some role for the legal regulation of child-related disputes.[114] We will return to these issues in the final section of the chapter, but now briefly address a related issue involving the creation of the FCC that has assumed responsibility for the majority of applications under the FLA.[115]

Originally the Commonwealth Parliament introduced the Federal Magistrates Bill 1999 (Cth) for the creation of the Federal Magistrates Court as a lower court in the federal court system. In the second reading speech, the Attorney-General said:

> The federal magistrates will be selected for their expertise in federal matters, including family law, and will deal with a range of matters of a less complex nature that are currently dealt with by the Federal and Family Courts. The Federal Magistrates Service is intended to provide a quicker, cheaper option for litigants and to ease the workload of both the Federal Court and the Family Court.[116]

This court was renamed the Federal Circuit Court in 2013.[117]

The significant issue here is that since the 2006 amendments to the FLA and their emphasis on pre-action procedures, the relevant *Family Law Rules 2004* (Cth) govern the proceedings in the FCA only and not in the FCC. Even though the FCC has its own set of rules,[118] and the general trend in the Australian legal system is now geared towards dispute resolution without litigation, it does seem anomalous that the specialist FCA has a set of rules to put its philosophy into action but the generalist FCC that now deals with most applications does not follow

---

113   For a concise history of legislative developments, see Margaret Harrison, *Finding A Better Way: A Bold Departure from the Traditional Common Law Approach to the Conduct of Legal Proceedings* (Family Court of Australia, 2007) 9ff. The FCA has made many innovations in its procedures, including the introduction of the less adversarial trial program ('LAT') and the Magellan Case Management Program, and formulating the Family Violence Best Practice Principles.

114   For an argument against the merger, see John Fogarty, 'Why Should the Federal Magistrates Court be Abolished?' (2009) 23 *Australian Journal of Family Law* 79. The compromise legislative solution in the 2006 amendments was to make pre-trial processes compulsory in child-related matters as detailed in the amended pt VII of the FLA.

115   For a chronology of events leading up to the institution of these courts, see 'Rudd Government to Reform Federal Courts' (Press Release, 5 May 2009) <http://parlinfo.aph.gov.au/parlInfo/search/display/display.w3p;query=Id%3A%22media%2Fpressrel%2F7WGT6%22>.

116   Commonwealth, *Parliamentary Debates*, House of Representatives, 24 June 1999, 7365 (Daryl Robert Williams, Attorney-General).

117   See the *Federal Circuit Court of Australia Legislation Amendment Act 2012* (Cth).

118   *Federal Court Rules 2011* (Cth) and the *Civil Dispute Resolution Act 2011* (Cth) say that as far as possible people should take steps to resolve disputes before certain civil proceedings are instituted. The nature of these activities is deliberately left vague. See *Civil Dispute Resolution Act 2011*, Attorney-General's Department, Australian Government <http://www.ag.gov.au/legalsystem/alternatedisputeresolution/pages/civildisputeresolutionact2011.aspx>.

the same rules.[119] Whether it can be argued that the FCA remains a specialist court or that such a court is even required becomes the relevant question. This leads us to the last issue in this chapter, which is to consider the implications of our family law system that emphasises alternative, primary or family dispute resolution as the preferred method of resolving disputes.

2.6.3   ADR to PDR to FDR

Alternative dispute resolution ('ADR') is the generic term used to describe methods of resolving a dispute outside the courtroom.[120] There are various models of ADR that include arbitration (where a third party who is not a judge decides a dispute according to the law) and mediation (where parties resolve the dispute among themselves with the help of a mediator).[121] The Australian legal system has come to rely heavily on ADR, with litigants in many areas of law being legally required to try ADR before they can have their case determined by a judge.[122] There are various analyses of the reasons for the enthusiastic turn to ADR in the legal system, and reducing costs and court workloads in a litigious society feature prominently.[123] In the literature it is almost considered inevitable that ADR is an integral part of the legal landscape and no longer a matter of debate.[124]

ADR is often presented to consumers as cheaper, more time efficient and providing better access to justice in contrast to litigation, but even if these claims are true the issue for us as legal thinkers is how conducive it is to achieving a fair family law. As an alternative to litigation, the focus is usually on the procedural benefits of ADR, not on whether ADR could or should produce substantive justice that seems to be beyond the reach of formal legal processes. When viewed in this way the rise of ADR may be better understood in terms of neoliberal concerns to promote economic efficiency by reducing the financial costs of litigation, and self-sufficiency in making the parties responsible for the outcomes of their disputes.

In the context of our argument, we illustrate how the FLA through its insistence on ADR promotes autonomy and privacy and thus functions to support the family as a private institution. In turn, the current emphasis on ADR reproduces a range of social hierarchies that already exist in society. The substantive contents of the FLA and its procedural preferences come together and function to legitimise gender hierarchies that exist in the nuclear family form. We also acknowledge that class, race and sexual hierarchies, among others, could also be replicated in this focus on ADR. A brief account of the legislative provisions of the FLA follows.

---

119   Although the imperative for pre-action procedures is part of the provisions of the FLA and to that extent governs applications filed in the FCC. See also <http://www.federalcircuitcourt.gov.au/wps/wcm/connect/fccweb/rules-and-legislation/rules/>, and *Thompson v Berg* [2014] FamCAFC 73 for a discussion of how the rules in the FCC are not the same as those in the FCA: [31]–[59].

120   A popular description of some of the processes is available in Roger Fisher, William Ury and Bruce Patton, *Getting to Yes: Negotiating Agreement Without Giving In* (Penguin, 1991).

121   For a history of the movement, see Carrie Menkel-Meadow, 'What Will We Do When Adjudication Ends? A Brief Intellectual History of ADR' (1997) 44 *UCLA Law Review* 161.

122   David Spencer and Samantha Hardy, *Dispute Resolution in Australia: Cases, Commentary and Materials* (Law Book Co, 3rd ed, 2014).

123   See, eg, Laurence Boulle, 'Minding the Gaps: Reflecting on the Story of Australian Mediation' (2000) 3(1) *ADR Bulletin* 1.

124   Also supported legislatively at the Federal Court level with the enactment of the *Civil Dispute Resolution Act 2011* (Cth).

In Australian family law, there has been a gradual transition towards ADR over time. The *Matrimonial Causes Act 1959* (Cth) provided for the possibility of reconciliation through counselling.[125] The trend has continued as successive amendments to the FLA have expanded the scope from voluntary to compulsory schemes and from reconciliation to dispute settlement.

In the FLA, the original description of these methods as conciliation and counselling was supplemented by mediation available in the FCA[126] and the introduction of the new terminology of primary dispute resolution ('PDR'), which has been subsequently replaced by the concept of family dispute resolution ('FDR') in child disputes.[127] Notably, there has been increased attention in the FLA to formally enforcing the resolution of disputes without litigation.[128] The major changes introduced in the 2006 amendments are briefly explained before assessing the implications of these changes.

The FLA now provides non-court-based services such as 'family counselling' (s 10B) by 'a family counsellor' (s 10C); 'family dispute resolution' (s 10F) by 'a family dispute resolution practitioner' (s 10G); 'arbitration' (s 10L) by 'an arbitrator' (s 10 M); and 'family consultants' (s 11B) to provide a variety of services to clients and the court (11A). More significantly, the FLA now provides for pre-action processes for financial and child-related disputes. In property and financial cases, the *Family Law Rules 2004* (Cth) ('*Family Law Rules*') stipulate mandatory pre-action processes only in the FCA.[129] Pre-action requirements in parenting cases (in all courts) are included in the FLA.[130] Parties to parenting cases are also subject to specifications in the *Family Law Rules*.[131] Few exceptions to comply with the *Family Law Rules* are included.[132]

In financial cases, the *Family Law Rules* stipulate that each prospective party to a case in the FCA is required to make a genuine effort to resolve the dispute before starting a case by (1) participating in dispute resolution such as negotiation, conciliation, arbitration and counselling; (2) exchanging a notice of intention to claim and exploring options for settlement by correspondence; and (3) complying as far as possible with the duty of disclosure.[133]

---

125   Harvey, above n 12.

126   Alistair Nicholson, 'Mediation in the Family Court' (1991) 65(2) *Law Institute Journal* 61.

127   For the concept of PDR, see Attorney-General's Department, *The Delivery of Primary Dispute Resolution Services in Family Law* (August 1997) and *The Delivery of Primary Dispute Resolution Services in Family Law: Next Steps* (1998). After the 2006 amendments, the terminology used is 'family dispute resolution', defined in FLA s 10F, above n 106.

128   For a discussion of aspects of successive changes to the FLA, see John Wade, 'Family Mediation: A Premature Monopoly in Australia?' (1997) 11 *Australian Journal of Family Law* 286.

129   *Family Law Rules 2004* (Cth) sch 1, pt I.

130   s 60I (7)–(12).

131   sch 1, pt II.

132   *Family Law Rules 2004* (Cth) r 1.05 states that compliance is necessary for all cases in the FCA unless the case is an application for divorce, child support or bankruptcy; or the case is an application that is in relation to a case commenced in the previous 12 months. Compliance is not necessary if there are allegations of child abuse, family violence or fraud; the application is urgent; compliance would be unfair to the applicant; the dispute is genuinely intractable; or there is another good reason for non-compliance. See FLA s 60I(9)(b)–(c), (e).

133   These rules apply to the FCA but not the FCC; *Civil Dispute Resolution Act 2011* (Cth) governs actions in the FCC and requires parties to take genuine steps to resolve a civil dispute before court proceedings are commenced.

Furthermore, the FLA also provides for the possibility of conciliation after filing a court application.[134]

The FLA emphasises FDR in child-related disputes and parenting cases in any court that can exercise jurisdiction under Part VII ('Children'). Exceptions are made,[135] but if these do not apply, the parties in parenting cases must attend FDR and make a genuine effort to resolve their dispute before filing an application in court.[136] If FDR fails, an FDR certificate must be filed in court when proceedings are initiated as evidence that the parties have attempted dispute resolution.[137] Before commencing the process of dispute resolution, a family dispute resolution practitioner must have regard to any history of family violence between the parties; the likely safety of the parties; the equality of bargaining power between the parties; the risk that a child might suffer abuse; the emotional and physical health of the parties; and any other matter the FDR practitioner considers relevant.[138] These practitioners are also given specific responsibilities in conducting the dispute resolution process.[139]

The court personnel have similarly specific responsibilities. For example, family consultants, along with their other duties, are expected to help the parties to resolve disputes,[140] and legal practitioners[141] have obligations to inform the applicants about the range of non-court-based family services available to assist in resolving their dispute; so too principal executive officers of courts and family counsellors, family dispute resolution practitioners and arbitrators have responsibilities to similarly inform applicants.[142]

---

134   s 79(9); *Family Law Rules 2004* (Cth) rr 12.03, 12.07.
135   Exceptions to filing a certificate – FLA s 60I(9) includes instances when application is made by consent of all parties, or the court believes that there has been abuse/family violence or there is a risk of abuse/family violence to the child by a party.
136   FLA s 60I(3) says that the dispute resolution provisions of the *Family Law Rules 2004* (Cth) also apply to an application to a court other than the FCA with suitable modifications if necessary.
137   There are four kinds of certificates in FLA s 60I(8) – that the person did not attend FDR because of the other party's failure to attend (s 60I(8)(a)) or because the practitioner considers it would not have been appropriate (s 60I(8)(aa)); that the person attended FDR and all attendees made a genuine effort to resolve the issues in dispute (s 60I(8)(b)); or that the person attended FDR but that person, or the other party, did not make a genuine effort to resolve the issue (s 60I(8)(c)); or that the person began attending mediation with the mediator and the other party, but that the mediator considered it not appropriate to continue the FDR (s 60I(8)(d)).
138   *Family Law (Family Dispute Resolution Practitioners) Regulations 2008* (Cth) reg 25(2).
139   reg 29. Note reg 29(d)(i)–(ii): a family dispute resolution practitioner must not provide legal advice to any of the parties unless the family dispute resolution practitioner is also a legal practitioner, or the advice is about procedural matters.
140   FLA s 11A. In addition they are expected to assist and advise people involved in the proceedings; assist and advise the court and give evidence; report to the court under ss 55A and 62G; and advise the court about appropriate programs and services to which the court can refer the parties.
141   FLA s 12E. They also have the obligation to inform applicants about the court's processes and services as well as reconciliation and marriage counselling services where clients are married (unless the practitioner thinks there is no reasonable possibility of reconciliation); and the objects, principles and other applicable law under Part VII proceedings.
142   FLA ss 12F, 12G.

2.6.4 Evaluation of the rise of ADR in family law

It is well accepted that litigation is not user-friendly,[143] and it is assumed that ADR has obvious advantages.[144] Rather than engage with the extensive literature in this area, we wish to ask how the shift to ADR may be assessed, as there is no agreed standard of measurement available. The following discussion focuses on three interrelated functions of the emphasis on ADR: it promotes the family as a private institution; it is paternalistic; and it entrenches gender hierarchies by maintaining the sexual division of labour. This focus could help in turn to challenge the easy acceptance of the claim that ADR is simply a dispute resolution mechanism.

The distinctive feature of the FLA in its financial provisions is that it aims to address the financial disparities, if not outright dependence, created through the non-financial work of caring for children (see Chapter 5). In fact, one of the main rationales for the existence of the FLA is that general property law and principles of equity fail to acknowledge the value of non-financial work. It thus enables the court to adjust property rights of former partners to achieve just and equitable outcomes. For the same law to turn around and say to the parties that they must cooperate with each other and reach an amicable agreement about property (and children) without going to court negates the reason for its own existence. Moreover, where children are involved, the expectation is that their parents will act less emotionally and more rationally. And all this is said to be in the interests of their children. These expectations in fact regulate the conduct of parents to reach an agreement rather than litigate.

Simultaneously, the law does not provide parents with any formal rights; instead, they have responsibilities towards their children, and this idea extends to the financial issues. In ADR, conflicts based on legitimate grievances are transformed into mere disagreements. Where there is disparity in power, this can result in weaker parties settling for less than their fair share.[145] The effect is to privatise disputes and undermine legal entitlements. Bottomley argues that the privatisation of disputes cloaks ongoing state regulation of families in the name of the best interests of the child.[146] Women, in particular, are coerced to focus on the best interests of the child and not consider their own interests. Inevitably, their bargaining

---

143   Stephen Grant, 'Alternate Dispute Resolution in Family Law: What's Not to Like?' (2008) 27 *Canadian Family Law Quarterly* 235. Commonly, the list of disadvantages includes the following: excessively formal and inflexible court procedures, incapable of tailored solutions; rules of evidence and other procedural formalities preventing the truth coming out; the acrimony of cross-examination; an intimidating and impersonal environment; expensive to hire lawyers and barristers; no surety of the outcome; a solution imposed from above rather than the parties contributing; the winner takes all; the possibility of losing and associated costs; and delays in the final resolution. See Richard Delgado et al, 'Fairness and Formality: Minimizing the Risk of Prejudice in Alternative Dispute Resolution' [1985] *Wisconsin Law Review* 1359.

144   The advantages of ADR over litigation include efficiency regarding time and money, the fact that ADR promotes a more cooperative, 'problem solving' approach to the resolution of disputes, and that these processes may be less intimidating and hence improve access because of their informality: Delgado et al, above n 143.

145   Hilary Astor and Christine Chinkin, *Dispute Resolution in Australia* (LexisNexis, 2nd ed, 2002) 342–61.

146   Anne Bottomley, 'What is Happening to Family Law? A Feminist Critique of Conciliation' in Julia Brophy and Carol Smart (eds), *Women-in-Law: Explorations in Law, Family, and Sexuality* (Routledge, 1985) 162.

power is affected. Furthermore, consideration of individual rights and of justice between the parties is subverted by notions of treatment and therapy in ADR.[147] This translates legal issues into relational issues where parties are expected to change their way of thinking or behaviour rather than claim legal entitlements or rights.[148] In the process the focus on emotional circumstances arising at the breakdown of the relationship distracts attention from the fact that there is a legal dispute remaining to be resolved. Goodman argues that the FLA thus conflates relationship breakdown with the resolution of disputes arising as a consequence of the breakdown.[149]

Privatisation thus is not to be confused with non-regulation. The insistence on private settlement regulates family relations through various professional experts such as counsellors, mediators, social workers and lawyers, to name a few.[150] There is ample literature that explains how, by appropriating therapeutic processes and practices, the insistence on ADR brings individuals under intensified state control and scrutiny of both legal and non-legal professionals.[151] This phenomenon has also been described as the triumph of the therapeutic.[152] The rhetoric of family autonomy creates possibilities for greater surveillance by various professionals (such as mediators, counsellors and social workers). Freeman even questions whether the expertise of these professionals is mere opinion.[153]

Moreover, the differences in opinion of these experts (for example, psychologists and social workers) on what may be best for a child are not analysed in a systematic manner in legal scholarship. This is despite how family law endorses these disciplinary orthodoxies by authorising these professionals to engage in court proceedings by facilitating out-of-court settlements (for example, the role of family consultants). The law thus becomes an avenue for the experts' opinions on what is a normal way of behaving to be incorporated into legal solutions. Moreover, in the process the fact that these professionals may have different understandings of the legal provisions is obscured.[154]

---

147   Ibid 162–77.
148   Ellen Goodman, 'Dispute Resolution in Family Law: Is "Conciliatory Procedure" the Answer?' (1986) 1 *Australian Journal of Family Law* 28.
149   Ibid 34.
150   Peter Goodrich, 'Social Science and the Displacement of Law' (1998) 32 *Law and Society Review* 473. For a discussion of the role of lawyers in mediation, see Bobette Wolski, 'On Mediation, Legal Representatives and Advocates' (2015) 38(1) *UNSW Law Journal* 5.
151   Bottomley, above n 146; Michael Freeman, 'Questioning the Delegalization Movement in Family Law: Do We Really Want a Family Court?' in John Eekelaar and Sanford Katz (eds), *The Resolution of Family Conflict: Comparative Legal Perspectives* (Butterworths, 1984) 7; Ann Milne, 'Mediation or Therapy – Which is it?' in James Hansen and Sarah Childs Grebe (eds), *Divorce and Family Mediation* (Aspen Systems Corp, 1985) 1, 2–7; A L Milne, 'Mediation and Domestic Abuse' in J Folberg, A L Milne and P Salem (eds), *Divorce and Family Mediation: Models, Techniques and Applications* (The Guilford Press, 2004) 283; J Dworkin, L Jacob and E Scott, 'The Boundaries Between Mediation and Therapy: Ethical Dilemmas' (1991) 9 *Mediation Quarterly* 107.
152   Freeman, above n 151.
153   Ibid 14. Freeman says that the courts generally accept the recommendations of experts, to the extent that if they do not they feel obliged to explain why.
154   Different professionals interpret legal provisions differently as illustrated in John Wade, 'Forever Bargaining in the Shadow of Law: Who Sells Solid Shadows? (Who Advises What, How and When)' (1998) 12 *Australian Journal of Family Law* 256. See also Christine Piper, *The Responsible Parent: A Study in Divorce Mediation* (Harvester, 1995).

This emphasis on ADR thereby functions as therapy underpinned by paternalism. The fact that ADR in the family law context shares its origins with the concept of the juvenile justice system is symbolic in so far as erring children and erring family partners are both perceived as requiring 'help' from the law.[155] That is, rather than the law being there to uphold the rights of people, it has adopted the role of assisting them to resolve their disputes. It is commonplace to explain this shift as necessary because of the identified drawbacks of using litigation to enforce legal rights.[156] However, it remains a relevant question to ask when a dispute is a legal dispute.[157] In other words, we can go to the law to solve any dispute but only if we have a right or entitlement that can be legally enforced.

The paternalism of family law manifests in the law by recommending the use of a 'better' or more appropriate dispute resolution method, but also making it a mandatory requirement for the parties to engage in ADR. This insistence takes away the autonomy of the participants.[158] It is, however, supported by the claim that the separating partners will still need to continue to have a 'working' relationship for the sake of their children. The implication is that both of them must learn to cooperate and not put their interests above those of their children. The latter is another aspect of paternalism, but it also has a significant influence in entrenching ideas about the private family and normalising the sexual division of labour.

For instance, in a 'typical' (allow us to make the claim) family law case when the parties have separated, the disputes between them may include financial matters and/or child-related arrangements. However, the law assumes that the two issues can be separated and furthermore, with respect to the child-related matters, that there is no place for parents to assert any rights. The strength of the idea that the deciding principle is 'in the best interests of the child' (discussed in Chapter 8) makes it culturally unacceptable for either parent to claim that they have any rights to enforce. It follows easily that out-of-court settlement is the rational thing to do. In the process, the relationship between child-related issues and financial matters is obscured in the name of the best interests of the child.

Furthermore, the emphasis on cooperation is the FLA's method of reinforcing gendered parenting arrangements.[159] It does this by allowing the parties to privately agree on how to

---

155   Freeman, above n 151, 12; Bottomley, above n 146, 162–77. Note that, because youth and crime intersect in juvenile justice, programs can range from welfare to punitive responses, and can incorporate restorative justice elements: ALRC, *Seen and Heard: Priority for Children in the Legal Process*, Report No 84 (1997) ch 18.

156   The literature in this area is too vast to be reviewed here. As an introduction to the issues, see Richard Abel, *The Politics of Informal Justice* (Academic Press, 1982) vols 1–2. For arguments in support, see L Fuller, 'Mediation: Its Form and Functions' (1971) 44 *Southern California Law Review* 305. For arguments against, see Owen M Fiss, 'Against Settlement' (1984) 93 *Yale Law Journal* 1073; Delgado et al, above n 143; Trina Grillo, 'The Mediation Alternative: Process Dangers for Women' (1991) 100 *Yale Law Journal* 1545; Jana B Singer, 'The Privatization of Family Law' [1992] *Wisconsin Law Review* 1443.

157   Different answers are available in scholarship of various disciplines. For an example of an anthropological take, see Sally Engle Merry and Susan S Silbey, 'What Do Plaintiffs Want? Reexamining the Concept of Dispute' (1984) 9 *The Justice System Journal* 151.

158   See Helen Rhoades, 'Mandatory Mediation of Family Disputes: Reflections from Australia' (2010) 32(2) *Journal of Social Welfare and Family Law* 183.

159   See Grillo, above n 156, 1572–81 for a discussion of how social norms do not allow women to express anger and how that translates into mediation settings.

allocate the costs of child care at the end of a relationship with the promise that virtually no scrutiny will follow. It can do this because underpinning ADR is the notion of gender neutrality, which assumes that both parties are equally able to negotiate an agreement. This is an apt illustration of how legislative gender neutrality facilitates the entrenchment of existing societal gender hierarchies. The substantive provisions of the FLA underpin these hierarchies further. The legislative scheme of the FLA does not assign identifiable rights to the applicants; instead it gives discretion to the courts whether in financial or in child-related matters. This creates a situation where the parties go into mediation without the legal tools to bargain in favour of their rights.[160]

Confidentiality and the private nature of these agreement-making processes make it difficult to ascertain the basis on which agreements are reached. The effect of seeking guidance from the FLA is to treat financial and child-related matters as separate issues. The FLA provides little space for articulating how agreements about financial matters and children may be linked and acknowledging the financially weaker position of primary carers because of their responsibilities for children.

The disparity of power between the two partners is ignored by this combination of the design of the FLA and the emphasis on ADR. This imbalance manifests itself in many ways and violence is one of its extreme forms. In response it is generally claimed that the FLA has progressively made it more explicit that ADR is not suitable for relationships where violence is present, especially in the resolution of child-related disputes; we will detail these provisions in Chapter 4. It is the argument here that by making an exception for relations involving violence, the FLA seeks to gain legitimacy while not being able to address the causes or effects of violence.[161] The legislative emphasis on private agreements exacerbates power asymmetries between disputants, especially if violence is undetected.[162]

However, for now it is important to pay heed to Esteal's claim that law impacts on women in many ways; the metaphor of an iceberg captures well the idea that some biases are visible, but the majority are not.[163] With respect to the effects or even the existence of domestic violence, the metaphor seems apt. It is undeniable that the FLA uses an expansive definition of violence, allows exceptions to using FDR for violent relationships, and relies on various professionals to manage cases involving violence. It is nevertheless necessary to acknowledge that in practice what ultimately qualifies as violence and how to detect it are extremely contentious issues.[164] Moreover, the responsibility for screening violence falls on the mediation programs and not on the lawyers.[165]

---

160   Robert H Mnookin and Lewis Kornhauser, 'Bargaining in the Shadow of the Law: The Case of Divorce' (1979) 88 *Yale Law Journal* 950.

161   See Rosemary Hunter, 'Adversarial Mythologies: Policy Assumptions and Research Evidence in Family Law' (2003) 30(1) *Journal of Law and Society* 156, 172ff for a discussion of how the presence of violence affects participants in private negotiations.

162   Astor and Chinkin, above n 145, 342–61.

163   Patricia Easteal (ed), *Women and the Law in Australia* (LexisNexis, 2010).

164   Rachael M Field and Mieke Brandon, 'A Conversation about the Introduction of Compulsory Family Dispute Resolution in Australia: Some Positive and Negative Issues for Women' (2007) 18 *Australasian Dispute Resolution Journal* 27; Deborah Kirkwood and Mandy McKenzie, 'Family Dispute Resolution and Family Violence in the New Family Law System' (2008) 19 *Australasian Dispute Resolution Journal* 170.

165   Rhoades, above n 158, 191.

Cumulatively, these issues raise the question of whether the celebration of dispute resolution alternatives to litigation in family law needs to be reviewed.

Freeman claims that there is no easy choice for disadvantaged groups between legal formalism that is characterised by the application of universal rules and informalism that seeks to tailor solutions for individual cases because both can result in injustice. He goes on to argue that it is necessary for legal scholarship on ADR to acknowledge that delegalisation does not achieve justice, equity or autonomy, but can result in interventionism, indirect controls and pervasive reliance on professional expertise in the name of the private family, all of which continue to be upheld as in the best interests of children.[166]

In a survey of the legal scholarship on ADR in the 1990s, another author[167] noted the reluctance to critique ADR in legal scholarship. In Australian family law scholarship, there are empirical studies of the processes of ADR but there is no sustained discussion of whether the problematic functions of ADR identified above have been addressed. The overall message of the empirical evidence is that to a large extent the disputants are satisfied and therefore the system is working.[168] Yet, as Hunter has observed, the research suggests that some cases that ought to be adjudicated are prevented from being able to do so because of the overzealous support for ADR.[169]

The reticence of legal scholars to question the inevitability of ADR in family law is another illustration of how the discourse of law takes shape in various ways. Family law simultaneously allows more autonomy to the parties in a relationship, yet manages to enhance intervention by insisting on mandatory dispute resolution without adjudication. In light of the discussion in this chapter, we ask readers to consider whether these developments are fair and just.

---

166   Freeman, above n 151, 19.
167   Eric K Yamamoto, 'ADR: Where Have The Critics Gone?' (1995–96) 36 *Santa Clara Law Review* 1055.
168   Rae Kaspiew et al, *Evaluation of the 2006 Family Law Reforms* (AIFS, December 2009) 105–10.
169   Hunter, above n 161, 175.

MARRIAGE AND MARRIAGE-LIKE RELATIONSHIPS

3.1   Introduction

The focus of this chapter is on the legal requirements for entering into a valid marriage, establishing a de facto relationship, and the legal recognition of other non-marriage types of relationship. The discussion continues to build on the argument made in the first two chapters: that family law relies on, and thereby constructs its understanding of the family based on, the nuclear family model.

The chapter begins by providing a short history of the rise of the modern nuclear family. This coverage links changes in understanding of the concept of family to the wider changes that transformed Europe from a feudal to a modern society. Economic, political and religious forces helped shape the family, but as we will see, there are competing views on whether these have had desirable effects on the family and its members. The history of the nuclear family will provide a foundation for understanding the regulation of the family in law and the present tensions that exist in the legal regulation of different family structures. This discussion connects to Chapter 1, where marriage and its suitability as the benchmark for governing all other personal relations was discussed. An overview of the debate on the (non) recognition of same-sex marriage in Australian law will tie the range of theories on the family together, illuminating the continuing stronghold of the nuclear conception of the family in law.

This chapter also draws on sociological theories of family to assist in understanding the changing responses of the law to other familial relations, such as de facto, polygamous, same-sex and domestic relationships. But the shift in understanding is far from complete. The hierarchy in relationships that law has created among married, de facto, registered relationships and domestic relationships will assist in developing our analysis of family law as continuing to privilege the particular social structure of the nuclear family based on the marriage model. In this regard, these developments can be seen not so much as the law merely reflecting the understanding of family life in the literature (for example, the literature canvassed in this chapter contains a mix of reactions to heterosexual marriage and its virtues and vices), but can be better understood as the law engaged in making ideological choices about which relationships should be given greater protection in law than others.

This literature will help explicate the legal provisions in the *Marriage Act 1961* (Cth) ('MA') and case law on the formation and nullity of marriage. As will become evident, the nuclear family construct informs even more progressive developments in the law – for example, the law recognising the validity of marriage entered into by a transsexual person. To further advance this claim, we will also examine the provisions of the *Family Law Act 1975* (Cth) ('FLA'), various State and Territory legislation and case law on de facto and domestic relationships. In view of this analysis, we argue that the law continues to privilege the traditional family construct despite the law's apparent decentralisation of marriage through the legal recognition of alternative family structures.

3.2   The marriage relationship

The concepts of family and marriage are often used interchangeably. The preliminary point that will help contextualise the following discussion is that the term 'marriage' is usually treated as synonymous with the term 'family'. The interchangeability of these terms goes a long way to normalising the dominant view that a proper family comes into existence as a consequence of marriage. Thus, the history of the rise of the nuclear family serves as a history of marriage also, and as the nuclear family grew in significance so too did marriage become significant in law. We provide an outline of this history below, starting with Stone, who provides an account of the historical developments that assisted in the formation of the nuclear family. His focus is on the external forces involved in the nuclear family formation. Other historians, like Poster, focus on the emotional or psychological aspects of the modern or bourgeois family, while yet others, like Harris, focus on the material effects of changing family morality on women and children. The juxtaposing of these accounts will reveal the complex processes involved in shaping family life. In considering their historical analyses side by side, we will be able to glean a history of the family that is subject to much contestation.[1] The debates over the concept of family and whether it is a beneficial or oppressive institution for its members have also been the subject of sociological research of the family, but, as we discuss below, the prevalent view continues to endorse the egalitarian family in this field as well. However, in our view, critical perspectives of the family cannot be ignored. Since family law continues to endorse the marriage relationship as the model for family life, critical perspectives on the family raise pertinent questions about the law in its regulation of marriage and other non-married forms of relationships. It follows that the law's endorsement of marriage needs to be questioned.

3.2.1   History of the nuclear family

Stone provides an influential historical analysis of the rise of the nuclear family.[2] Very briefly, Stone's argument is that between 1500 and 1700 the family in England changed or evolved in two ways. First, the importance of the nuclear core increased and that of extended kin declined; and, second, the importance of affective bonds increased while the economic functions of the family declined. Three interrelated causes led to these changes: a decline of kinship as the organising principle of society, the rise of the modern state, and the success of Protestantism. For some time the pre-existing patriarchal aspects of relationships were strengthened, but Stone finds that by the late 17th century and 18th century a more egalitarian and companionate type of family structure, bound by ties of affection, eventually prevailed. In his argument, Stone echoes Parsons' theory of the nuclear family, where the marriage union forms the basis of the family and in turn is the basis of a stable and functional society. Stone also finds that the patriarchal control stage of the family eventually yielded to an egalitarian stage where marriage became a true partnership between two equals. This helps to explain why the companionate marriage based on mutual love and respect eventually came to be extolled for providing emotional support to its members, especially children, whose care and support would become the central concerns of the family.

---

1   For an early review of the historical debates, see generally Barbara Harris, 'Recent work on the History of the Family: A Review Article' (1976) 3(3/4) *Feminist Studies* 159.

2   For the following account, see Lawrence Stone, 'The Rise of the Nuclear Family in Early Modern England: The Patriarchal Stage' in Charles Rosenberg (ed), *The Family in History* (University of Pennsylvania Press, 1975) 13, 13–4, 21–36, 54–7.

However, since the 1970s critiques of the family have challenged whether this transformation has in fact really happened. Poster, for example, challenges the idea that the nuclear family is the inevitable culmination of historical changes that resulted in the egalitarian companionate marriage union.[3] He argues that if we focus on the psychological dimensions of family relations and realise that the nuclear family (what he terms the 'bourgeois family') is not an inevitable product of history, we can ask how better outcomes for individuals and especially children may be constructed. Critical histories of the family thus ask whether the praise for the emotional solace the modern nuclear family provides is in fact justifiable. Poster explains the particular emotional structure within this family with the help of Freudian psychology. The emotional pattern of the bourgeois family is one where authority is confined to the parents, deep parental love is felt for children and, rather than physical punishment, sanctions are expressed in the form of withdrawal of love. The childhood dependency this creates forms the basis for learning to love one's superiors in adult life.[4]

Poster argues that the emotional enclosure of the family and the dependent child it creates is a product of psychosocial dynamics that are not natural or inevitable. This becomes evident when the experiences of children in other family structures that have existed in history are compared, such as in aristocratic, peasant or working-class families where the care and control of children were diffused among a range of adult figures and produced very different childhood experiences for these children. Moreover, as history has shown, the bourgeois family was never simply a progressive and morally beneficial nest of love, domesticity and individualism, because within it new forms of oppression of women and children could be expressed. As Harris argues in her overview of the history of family, although there is historical evidence to support the rise of a culture of domesticity and maternal love within western societies from the 18th century onwards, it did not supersede but coexisted with repressive, rigid and violent practices towards children by parents and educators. Her analysis also brings into question the social effects of the conjugal unit on women, and whether these effects were truly egalitarian in creating social roles where they were conceived of as the superior guardians of morality on the one hand, only to find themselves the non-financial party in the marriage relationship on the other.[5]

Critical histories of the family help explicate the contradictions that can exist in family life (in our examples, egalitarian marriage versus oppressive marriage). They also bring into question whether the history of the family is truly a history of progress, signalling that the patriarchal marriage has given way to the egalitarian marriage. Comparisons between different historical accounts of the family illuminate the significance of the theoretical perspectives used to explain the subject of family or marriage. This would be relevant to imagining what an ideal family could be – that is, non-hierarchical and augmenting individual development for everyone in the family – or whether it needs to be something else. To the extent

---

3   Mark Poster, *Critical Theory of the Family* (Pluto Press, 1978) ch 7.
4   This echoes the arguments of Foucault about how in modern society we create self-regulating individuals who do not have to be disciplined by external forces including the law. For an illustration of how these ideas explain the hold of body image for women, see Sandra Bartky, 'Foucault, Femininity and the Modernization of Patriarchal Power' in Lee Quinby and Irene Diamond (eds), *Feminism and Foucault: Paths of Resistance* (Northeastern University Press, 1988) 61.
5   Harris, above n 1, 159–70.

that law endorses the nuclear family, critical reflections on the family would be particularly relevant for assessing the historical development of family law as well.

Nonetheless, despite these critiques of the family the idea of the egalitarian family has prevailed. This has been particularly evident in the sociological literature relating to the changing nature of families in contemporary societies. This literature has been influential in explaining changes in family relations in terms of individualisation of relationships. For instance, Beck and Beck-Gernsheim have emphasised the idea that in pre-industrial societies there was an emphasis on communities held together through need while in contemporary times it is the individuals who create their own relationships based on, among other things, their interests and experiences.[6] In a slightly different vein, Giddens describes modern relationships as characterised by reflexive individualisation. He explains that modern intimacy is different from that in earlier times because intimate relationships can now last only as long as the partners decide to be together in a relationship. Changing ideas of love, intimacy and gender relations of the partners inform such decisions, and consequently the sense of obligation that each party has to the other and the commitment they have to their relationship are more negotiable in contemporary society.[7]

It may be possible to understand these changes as reflecting the understanding that marriage is becoming increasingly irrelevant in today's society. Indeed, contemporary family law is credited with being pluralistic and accommodating of many different kinds of relationships; it recognises de facto relations, including same-sex relations and different forms of domestic relationships. Law's inclusion of plural forms of family relations could also be understood as acceptance of the changing nature of close and personal relationships. In particular, the argument that law allows individuals to define their own relationships while they are together, and also when they separate, is meant to capture the individualistic conceptions of what is an acceptable relationship.

Yet, in the following discussion, we argue that family law continues to endorse the idea of romantic love and coupledom in ways that support the dependency model of marriage. The emphasis on these aspects of personal relationships detracts – indeed separates the relationship – from the implications that emotional dependency can have for the financial relationship between the parties. The point is that in treating marriage or de facto relations independently of the financial aspects of these relationships creates the idea that marriage/ coupledom is about emotional fulfilment only. When law regulates these relations based on the notion of individual autonomy, it conveys the understanding that individual choice is the defining feature of these relationships. However, by obscuring the wider financial implications of these relationships, the law creates a false impression that these relationships are truly egalitarian. This is particularly problematic as the marriage model continues to set the benchmark for the regulation of these relationships.

---

6   Ulrich Beck and Elisabeth Beck-Gernsheim, *Individualization: Institutionalized Individualism and its Social and Political Consequences* (Sage Publications, 2002).

7   Anthony Giddens, *The Transformation of Intimacy* (Polity Press, 1992). There is extensive literature addressing these theories, but this is not our main topic. We will not engage with these debates, but for an accessible critique see Julia Brannen and Ann Nielsen, 'Individualisation, Choice and Structure: A Discussion of Current Trends in Sociological Analysis' (2005) 53(3) *The Sociological Review* 412.

3.2.2 Legal regulation of family through marriage

Similar to the family, the history of family law is invariably depicted as a history of progress that is marked by shifts in the law away from supporting the patriarchal model of marriage to championing equality in marriage. This is most evident in the history of changes to laws relating to women, especially the recognition of the rights of married women evident in the *Married Women's Property Act 1882* (UK), which was duly adopted in the Australian colonies.[8] The legislation was significant in overcoming some of the disabilities inherent in the common law doctrine of coverture. It ensured that married women had separate legal personalities from their husbands by guaranteeing the right to hold property and enter into contracts in their own names. The enactment of Married Women's Property Acts was part of a broader movement seeking the same legal and political rights for women as were enjoyed by men. To the extent that women now have equal rights in areas such as voting, education and employment, it is a commonly held view that women have greatly benefitted from legal and political reforms in the past.[9]

However, feminists are critical of these developments. In family law, feminists have criticised the extension of equal rights to women because this approach uses the male standard of progressive individualism to measure progress. This approach measures equality according to the extent women have the same rights as men. In turn this approach fails to register the inequality that continues to exist in familial relations. Social historians argue that in focusing on the domestic roles of women the experiences of women become visible. This focus exposes the limits in the law in protecting the rights of women despite the extension of formal legal equality that has been granted to them.[10]

This critique alerts us to the significance of analysing the relationship between law and society, as Minow explains.[11] She argues that women have historically used their social roles as wives and mothers in seeking legal rights and protection.[12] This has had a paradoxical effect whereby women, in seeking law reform to advance their equality, have also managed to reinforce their family obligations and domestic roles, which are the source of their inequality. In our view this approach, in reinforcing women's roles as wives and mothers, also has the effect of reinforcing the economic dependency of women. Returning to the ideology of the sexual division of labour, women as the bearers of children are

---

8   The trend had begun in the United States in 1839 when individual States enacted Married Women's Property Acts. The 1882 UK legislation was initially received in the Australian colonies as imperial law and was subsequently enacted in the Australian colonies. See *Married Women's Property Act 1883* (NSW), *Married Women's Property Act 1890* (Qld), *Married Women's Property Act 1893* (SA), *Married Women's Property Act 1893* (Tas), *Married Women's Property Act 1884* (Vic), *Married Women's Property Act 1892* (WA).

9   Martha Albertson Fineman, *The Illusion of Equality: The Rhetoric and Reality of Divorce Reform* (University of Chicago Press, 1991).

10   For a critique of the opposition between domesticity and self-interest as explaining the behaviours of women and men, see Joan Williams, 'Domesticity as the Dangerous Supplement of Liberalism' (1991) 2(3) *Journal of Women's History* 69.

11   Martha Minow, '"Forming Underneath Everything that Grows": Toward a History of Family Law' [1985] *Wisconsin Law Review* 819, 830–9.

12   See also Eli Zaretski, 'Family in the Origins of the Welfare State' in Barrie Thorne and Marilyn Yalom (eds), *Rethinking the Family: Some Feminist Questions* (Longman, 1982) 188, 211–7.

assigned the role of primary carers of children as well. Differences in men's and women's reproductive capacities are difficult to equalise within the paradigm of formal equality. Arguably, children could be reared by either parent, or by both, or by other adults in any social configuration, but in the present time any of these arrangements would need to accommodate the consequences of the financial burden of caring for children. However, this is not what happens when the work of caring for children (or other family members) is carried out within a marriage. The work is naturalised and the discourse of love and affection that parents have for their children makes it difficult to formulate questions about the economic costs of such arrangements. Notably, traditional accounts of family that focus on its role in the procreation of children emphasise the love between husband and wife and their children, but they do not generally ask how the economic dependency created by the care for children during a marriage should be accommodated in law.

We will return to this topic in Chapter 5, but for now it is relevant to ask whether marriage is truly egalitarian if the economic dependency created by the sexual division of labour is not adequately accommodated in the family. Moreover, if the title of 'marriage' is legally extended to other affective relationships, do the same implications of economic dependency apply? Another way of formulating the same question is to ask: what purpose does marriage serve? The answers to that question will inform the role of law in the regulation of marriage. Is the legal regulation of marriage designed merely to confer special status on the married couple through the performance of certain rituals, does it confer certain duties and obligations on the parties, or does it involve a combination of these factors? If so, would the obligations of marriage also include the regulation of the economic consequences of the relationship?

In answering these questions, it is important to maintain a distinction between the social or cultural significance of relationships of love and affection and the need to represent that meaning in legal regulation. Thus, when we consider that marriage is an institution, this should alert us to the fact that we enter institutions not on our terms but on the terms of the institution.[13] It is evidently the case that legal regulation is to some extent responsible for maintaining a particular form of marriage. This multidimensionality is captured in O'Donovan's comment that marriage has both contractual and institutional aspects, but it is also a law unto itself.[14] It is this law of marriage that we turn to next. We will examine how far the legal notions of marriage have incorporated the wider societal understandings of marriage and other couple relationships. In so doing we will illuminate the tensions that exist between the dependency and autonomy models of family and that underpin the maintenance of the nuclear family in law.

The institution of marriage continues to be supported by the legal requirements of specific rituals or ceremonies. Yet there is a simultaneous loosening of regulation that makes marriage more akin to a contract. This is also evident in the legal recognition of de facto relationships. How can these legal developments be understood? Below we outline these developments. Schroter and Smart provide two very different accounts of these

---

13   Katherine O'Donovan, *Family Law Matters* (Pluto Press, 1993) 44.
14   Ibid.

developments and will enable us to demonstrate that any appraisal of the legal regulation of personal relationships requires a prior explicit articulation of why any legal regulation is required in the first place.

3.2.3   The ritual of marriage

Throughout history, marriage has been an act that requires specific rituals that in turn have status implications.[15] The connection between the two is encapsulated in the ancient concept of rites of passage, which are rituals that accompany major changes in the lives of people and can include initiations into adulthood, marriage and funerals. Three types of ritual that typically accompany the passage from one status to another are the rituals of separation, transition and incorporation. Of these, marriage is the most important transition from one social status to another, for marriage is as a rule a social act, not just the union of two individuals. There are always other groups interested in the marriage, as illustrated in the Roman *manus* marriage.

In entering this ancient marriage, solemn rituals were used to mark the passage of the woman from one social or legal state (the *potestas* of her *paterfamilias*) to another (the *potestas* of her husband's family). This example makes the contrast with the contemporary marriage evident, but also highlights that even though the status of being married no longer has the same legal meaning (of transferring ownership of a woman from one family to another), to the extent that modern marriage continues to be accompanied by rituals (whether in law or religion) it too is an indicator of status. However, given the change in the times, whether marriage as a status relationship retains any significance today remains to be seen.

Sir Henry Maine in his thesis, *Ancient Law*, argues that the transition from early to modern legal systems is characterised by a change from status to contract as the organising principle for relationships.[16] Maine's argument is that the waning of ritual in modern law is not just a change in taste or a change from formalism to a desire to give effect to the will of the parties. Rather, it is evidence of an underlying lessening of importance of status relationships in favour of consensual relations. This argument has implications for issues like whether law should continue to regulate marriage; and, moreover, whether law should regulate de facto relationships on the same basis as marriage (status relation) or as a consensual (contract) relation.[17]

The history of the legal regulation of marriage in England illustrates how, over time, marriage came to be less regulated by the Church and how, gradually, legal restrictions on marriage were relaxed.[18] Marriage laws since the 1800s have changed from prohibiting an extensive list

---

15   Peter Meijes Tiersma, 'Rites of Passage: Legal Ritual in Roman Law and Anthropological Analogues' (1989) 9 *Journal of Legal History* 3.

16   Sir Henry Sumner Maine, *Ancient Law: Its Connection with the Early History of Society, and Its Relation to Modern Ideas* (John Murray, 1861).

17   In both cases, the issue identified in Chapter 1 remains relevant – what is the purpose of such regulation?

18   Lawrence Stone, *The Road to Divorce: England 1530–1987* (Oxford University Press, 1990).

of possible marriages[19] to the contemporary law of marriage where only few marriages are prohibited.[20] Unlike earlier laws of marriage, the consent of two parties is now considered enough to constitute a valid marriage and the consent (or control) of parents is largely irrelevant. In addition, the law recognises non-married relationships such as de facto relations, which include same-sex relationships. Although in Australia the right to marry does not extend to same-sex couples, the trend in a number of overseas jurisdictions has been to permit same-sex marriage.[21] There are also very few constraints on the legal capacities or rights of each party to, for example, enter into marriage, own property, have custody or guardianship of children; or make contracts and wills and/or provide maintenance during marriage.[22]

Moreover, in Australian law today the family law provisions that apply to marriage also apply to legally recognised de facto relationships.[23] This raises a pertinent issue for us about why the law continues to regulate the formation of marriage as a specific relationship while also distinguishing between the concepts of marriage and de facto relations when they are now subject to the same family law legislation. One explanation is that the law is caught within the tension that exists between the view of marriage as losing its centrality

---

19   As Barbara Leigh Smith Bodichon noted in *A Brief Summary, in Plain Language, of the Most Important Laws Concerning Women; Together with a Few Observations Thereon* (John Chapman London, 1854):

> These marriages are prohibited: – A widower with his deceased wife's sister; a widow with the brother of her deceased husband; a widower with his deceased wife's sister's daughter, for she is by affinity in the same degree as a niece to her uncle by consanguinity; a widower with a daughter of his deceased wife by a former husband; and a widower with his deceased wife's mother's sister. Consanguinity or affinity, where the children are illegitimate, is equally an impediment (p 4).

Bodichon also listed the disabilities experienced by women on marriage:

> A man and wife are one person in law; the wife loses all her rights as a single woman, and her existence is entirely absorbed in that of her husband. He is civilly responsible for her acts; she lives under his protection or cover, and her condition is called coverture.
>   A woman's body belongs to her husband; she is in his custody, and he can enforce his right by a writ of habeas corpus.
>   What was her personal property before marriage, such as money in hand, money at the bank, jewels, household goods, clothes, &c, becomes absolutely her husband's, and he may assign or dispose of them at his pleasure whether he and his wife live together or not (p 6).

20   For instance, MA s 23B(2) prohibits marriage of a person and an ancestor or descendant and between a brother and sister (whole blood or half-blood) and s 23B(3) further provides that such prohibited relationships will include relationships created through adoption.

21   For a list of countries that allow same-sex marriages, see Australian Marriage Equality, *Marriage Equality Around the World* (2015) <http://www.australianmarriageequality.org/overseas-same-sex-marriages/>.

22   See Jill Cowley, 'Does Anyone Understand the Effect of "The Marriage Ceremony"? The Nature and Consequences of Marriage in Australia' (2007) 11 *Southern Cross University Law Review* 125.

23   With the enactment of *Family Law Amendment (De Facto Financial Matters and Other Measures) Act 2008* (Cth): (1) a new Part VIIIAB was inserted, and many of its provisions mirror the provisions in Part VIII (Property, Spousal Maintenance and Maintenance Agreements) of the Act; (2) Part VIIIB (Superannuation Splitting) has been amended to extend it to de facto couples; and (3) a new s 90TA was inserted which, by using a schedule, replicates Part VIIIAA (Orders and Injunctions Binding Third Parties) and amends it for de facto couples without setting out in full a new Part VIIIAA for de facto couples. For a fuller discussion of these provisions, see Justice Garry Watts, *De Facto Property Under the Family Law Act* (19 December 2008).

(evidenced by relationships formed simply on the consent of the parties and supported by laws that recognise cohabiting non-married couples) and the view that marriage continues to be of central importance in society (based on the understanding that marriage is a status relationship necessary for the emotional and financial support of children).

Schroter argues that the informalisation of marriage is happening simultaneously in marriage law and social practice.[24] He traces the history of marriage and its legal regulation to explain that the increasing reluctance of individuals to organise their relationships through marriage is reflected in the official laws of marriage that make entering into a marriage and divorce much easier than in earlier times. This indicates that marriage has lost its centrality as family has lost many of its former functions, and this has resulted in the individualisation of marriage as it is more about two individuals and their rights than about the unit composed of a husband and wife and their children.

In contrast, Smart in analysing the same issue presents a very different perspective.[25] She argues that, notwithstanding the changing social mores on sex and divorce (as identified by Schroter), marriage continues to be central to the family. This is because marriage is more than a legal contract that confers rights and duties and it is also more than a traditional social ritual that carries extra-legal expectations and obligations. By this she means that marriage is an ideological enclosure, which confers identity and meaning about what is an appropriate intimate relationship and how relations are to be organised within that relationship. Marriage is then the relationship against which every other relationship is measured. In this way marriage prioritises coupledom and heterosexuality.

It also continues to be the most socially accepted context for sexual relations, in part exemplified by the stigma attached to adultery, but mainly because marriage is considered to be the privileged context for the procreation of children. Even though the law no longer distinguishes between children born within marriage or otherwise, it remains the case that marriage – and not any family – is socially presented as the securest and most suitable institution for the raising of children. However, and unlike Schroter, Smart finds that the centrality of marriage to the family continues to be the site of oppression for women (which she implicitly links to the sexual division of labour). In Smart's view, social pressures and economic constraints mean that the desire to be a mother often leads women to contemplate marriage when they otherwise might not. Motherhood accentuates the dilemma for many women who do not wish to be dependent on men, but who cannot work and pay for child care alone. Smart explains that motherhood coincides with the material manifestation of women's inferior economic position and the social condemnation of the woman who, in refusing to marry, is refusing to provide the most secure environment for her child.

Smart further explains that the feminist critique of marriage as the idealised context for heterosexual coupledom and legitimate childbirth is not a critique of love and affection, nor is it an endorsement of individualism. Rather, in view of the identified drawbacks of marriage as an institution that is the mainstay of the oppressive family, it is necessary that we do not extend the definition of marriage to cover all relationships on the same basis. Smart therefore argues in favour of abandoning the status of marriage altogether and providing for

---

24   Michael Schroter, 'Marriage' (1987) 4 *Theory, Culture and Society* 317.
25   Carol Smart, *The Ties That Bind* (Routledge & Kegan Paul, 1984) 143–6.

the legal recognition of a much wider range of relationships based on a system of rights, duties or obligations that is not dependent on coupledom or marriage.

Therefore, the question arises again as to what is or should be the objectives of such legal recognition and regulation of rights and obligations. The suggestion[26] that law regulate 'family practices' rather than the family does not help. The fundamental issue remains that when individuals share their lives the resultant effects will continue to be unevenly felt between them as long as broader gendered cultural norms stay the same. Same-sex relationships may be able to avoid the gendered trappings of heterosexual relations. However, the legal recognition of same-sex relationships on the same basis as heterosexual relationships can function to normalise the patterns of heterosexual partnerships, and also be inadequate to accommodate the way same-sex relationships are organised. Furthermore, extending these norms to regulate non-married relations requires a prior articulation of what is the basis of regulation; that is, are these laws simply acknowledging the decentralised position of marriage or are they serving to maintain the privileged status of marriage?

Keeping these ideas in mind, we turn now to analyse the provisions of the MA. This will be followed by a comparison with the legal regulation of de facto and other non-married forms of relationships in Australian law. This comparison will help elucidate the issues further as we consider how the law juggles changing perceptions of the family with privileging the marriage institution.

3.2.4   The law of marriage

The law of marriage in Australia is contained in the MA. It sets out the formal requirements of marriage and the capacities of the parties needed to enter into a valid marriage.[27] The MA does not use the terminology of 'formalities of marriage' or the 'capacities for marriage' required by the parties to establish a valid marriage, but the provisions of the MA can be conveniently divided into these two categories and the provisions of each will be outlined in turn.

3.2.4.1   The formal requirements of marriage

Part IV of the MA prescribes the rules for the solemnisation of marriages. There are four subcategories of what may be loosely described as Australian marriages: (1) marriage performed in Australia by an authorised celebrant; (2) marriage of defence force personnel overseas; (3) marriage in Australia by consular officers of prescribed countries; and (4) marriage performed overseas but recognised in Australia. The first two categories relate to marriages where one person is Australian, but in the latter two that may not be the case.

The formalities required for creating a valid marriage when celebrated in Australia[28] and for solemnisation of marriages of defence force members overseas are detailed separately.[29]

---

26   Alison Diduck, *Law's Families* (Cambridge University Press, 2003) 36.

27   This terminology is used in private international law and invokes the general rule that, to create a valid marriage, formalities conform to the law of the place of celebration (*lex loci celebrationis*), and the capacity or essential validity is determined by the law of the place of domicile (*lex domicili*) of the parties.

28   MA pt IV.

29   MA pt V div 3. Part V of the MA was amended in 2002, removing the ability of Australian embassy and consular officers to perform marriages for Australian citizens overseas.

Authorised ministers of religion and civil celebrants can perform a marriage in Australia.[30] Part IV, div 1, sub-div A and C respectively detail how the ministers of religion and civil celebrants are to be registered.[31] The steps involved in the creation of a marriage require the parties to give notice to a registered celebrant. The celebrant uses a religious or civil form of ceremony and issues a certificate of marriage. The effects of non-compliance with these rules are specified in the MA.

The MA provides that in Australia religious and other celebrants can perform a marriage, and they must meet certain criteria to be registered celebrants.[32] Entering into marriage requires a notice of intention to marry. It is necessary that this notice be given to the celebrant who will solemnise the marriage at least one month, and up to six months, before the intended date of the marriage.[33] Evidence of age and marital status must be provided to the marriage celebrant pursuant to s 42, which requires that a marriage shall not be solemnised unless the parties produce their birth certificates or equivalent and the parties must make declarations in the prescribed form concerning their status and belief that they are free to marry.[34] Similarly, if a party has previously been married there must be evidence of the divorce or death of the former spouse, but there is no requirement that at the date of notice the person must be divorced.[35] Section 45(1) provides that a marriage performed by a minister of any religion may follow 'any form and ceremony recognised as sufficient for the purpose' by that religion.[36]

The MA prohibits a celebrant from solemnising a marriage where he or she has reason to believe there is a legal impediment present.[37] Significantly, an authorised celebrant is to give the parties a document outlining the obligations and consequences of marriage and indicating the availability of marriage education and counselling.[38] The celebrant, parties to the marriage and two witnesses must sign the marriage certificates after the ceremony.[39]

Notably, the prescribed list of required formalities in the MA is followed by what reads almost like a disclaimer that non-compliance in most instances does not prevent a marriage from coming into existence.[40] The main point deserving comment here is that the formalities required for entering into a marriage function to privilege the relationship of marriage. Moreover, non-compliance with most of the formalities sends ambiguous messages and bears a comparison with what is required in the case of creating a de facto relationship

---

30   This is an early innovation of Australian law. See Dally Messenger III, *Murphy's Law and the Pursuit of Happiness: A History of the Civil Celebrant Movement* (Spectrum Publications, 2012).

31   ss 25–38 and 39A–39M respectively deal with these matters.

32   ss 25–39; Part IV Division 2 prescribes the formalities of solemnisation and provides for the issue of marriage certificates.

33   MA s 42 and Form 13 of the *Marriage Regulations 1963* (Cth).

34   s 42(1)(b)–(c).

35   s 42(10). This was held in *In the Marriage of Warren* (1988) 12 Fam LR 245 (Kay J).

36   MA ss 45(2) and 46 provide that marriages performed by other celebrants must include a prescribed form of words. However, s 48 provides that not all non-compliances with formalities make a marriage void.

37   s 42(8).

38   s 42(5A).

39   s 50(1)–(2).

40   Sections 48(2)–(3), read in conjunction with s 23B(1)(c), make non-compliance with most formalities not relevant in creating a valid marriage. Section 45(4)(a) specifies that if the form of marriage is in dispute, then a certificate of marriage does not operate as conclusive proof of the marriage. For further discussion, see the analysis of s 23B(1)c below.

(discussed below). The status of marriage as an institution is further bolstered by the general rule of presumption of validity of a marriage. There are two aspects of this rule: the first relates to the ceremony of marriage and the second relates to the nature of the relationship between the parties.

With respect to the first aspect, if the two parties have gone through a ceremony of marriage it is presumed to be a valid marriage unless substantial contrary evidence is provided. This rule has its genesis in earlier times when documentation of marriages and divorces was less comprehensive, but is interpreted slightly differently now. For example, in the case of *In the Marriage of Kirby and Watson*, Watson J in the Family Court reviewed earlier cases that discuss the rule of presumption of validity and concluded that '[w]here status is involved it may avail little to erect artificial rules as to presumptions and onus of proof'.[41] The task before the Family Court was to infer as a matter of fact that the husband's first wife was dead at the time of his second marriage, but it declined to do so owing to the paucity of evidence available.

With respect to the second aspect, the presumption of validity of a marriage is based upon the social reputation of a couple living together as man and wife. If the man and woman cohabit as a husband and wife and have a public reputation to that effect, it is accepted as a common law marriage even if there is no evidence of a valid ceremony. The same general trend is present in the rules of private international law when, in making a choice of law, it is preferable to choose a rule that would enable recognition of a marriage.[42] Under the FLA a marriage certificate is considered to be sufficient proof of a marriage unless it is disproved.

One exception to the general rule of the presumption of validity of marriage in Australia arises in the case of consular marriages.[43] It is generally accepted that consular offices are deemed to be territories of their states. A general rule of private international law is that a marriage between people domiciled outside Australia must comply with the formalities prescribed by the local law, and the parties must possess the capacity to marry according to the law of their domicile. This rule was replaced by the amendments to the MA in 1985, primarily to give effect to the *Hague Convention on Celebration and Recognition of the Validity of Marriages* (*'Hague Convention on the Validity of Marriages'*), which Australia had signed in 1980 and which aims to facilitate easier recognition of marriages.[44] However, the amended MA also provided that where neither party is an Australian citizen but the marriage is solemnised in Australia by a foreign diplomatic officer, some rules of Australian domestic

---

41   (1977) 3 Fam LR 11, 318, 11, 322.

42   However, some rules of recognition in the MA go against this long-standing trend, discussed below.

43   Performed by consular officers pursuant to *Marriage Act 1961* (Cth) pt IV div 3. In some cases if neither party is an Australian citizen they can get married in a consular office by a foreign diplomatic or consular officer.

44   This amendment was made pursuant to Australia signing in 1980 the *Hague Convention on Celebration and Recognition of the Validity of Marriages*, opened for signature 14 March 1978, [1991] ATS 16, 16 ILM 18 (entered into force 14 May 1991). This convention replaced the earlier rules of recognition regarding formal and essential validity and was designed to facilitate recognition of marriages only by reference to the law of place of celebration. For a discussion of the various aspects of this convention and their presence in the MA, see G E Fisher, 'The Australian Adoption of the Hague Convention on Celebration and Recognition of the Validity of Marriages' (1986) 2(2) *Queensland Institute of Technology Law Journal* 17.

law with regard to capacity to marry (age, not married, not within prohibited degrees) must be complied with. This is worth noting, as the effect is that Australian marriage law is overriding a general principle of private international law (even though permitted by the *Hague Convention on the Validity of Marriages*), and doing so with respect to marriages where the two parties are not Australian citizens. It is difficult to see what public policy purpose is served by this rule, except to emphasise that the power of the Australian state is being exercised to define what is (and is not) a valid marriage.

The same is illustrated in the rules that determine the recognition in Australia of marriages celebrated abroad.[45] We acknowledge that rules of private international law have always permitted states to override their obligations arising from the principle of comity of nations and to refuse to recognise foreign marriages in some circumstances, including when such recognition would be against its public policy.[46] Nevertheless, the following examples illustrate an effort by the Commonwealth Parliament to determine the validity of a marriage by maintaining its right to define marriage. For example, the Australian law will not recognise a polygamous marriage, even if it is valid in the country in which it was entered into;[47] and if one of the parties to the marriage is an Australian domiciliary, then both parties must be of marriageable age according to Australian law.[48] Section 88E of the MA preserves the common law rules of recognition if they would enable recognition of a foreign marriage that would not otherwise be recognised under ss 88C and 88D, but even then it provides that if at the time of marriage either party was not of marriageable age such a marriage will not be recognised in Australia.[49] Moreover, the MA specifically prescribes that unions solemnised in a foreign country between a man and a man, or a woman and a woman, must not be recognised as a marriage in Australia.[50] These rules assume greater significance when juxtaposed with the legal recognition of de facto relations as discussed below.

3.2.4.2 The capacities required to establish a valid marriage

We now turn to consider the capacities required by the parties to establish a valid marriage. These are sometimes referred to as the rules for the essential validity of marriage. Notably, the MA does not specify the conditions for creating a valid marriage and instead specifies when a marriage will be void. The distinction between void and voidable marriages is no longer a part of the marriage law in Australia. Section 51 of the FLA supplements the MA in providing that an application for a decree of nullity of marriage under the MA shall be based

---

45   A cursory survey of cases shows that these issues arise mostly in relation to the application and interpretation of migration law. For a discussion of the family law cases, see Sirko Harder, 'Recent Judicial Aberrations in Australian Private International Law' (2012) 19 *Australian International Law Journal* 161, and especially 174–9 for the analysis of *Nygh v Kasey* [2010] FamCA 145.

46   The *Hague Convention on the Validity of Marriages* also provides for such exceptions in articles 11 and 14.

47   FLA s 6, however, allows a party to such a marriage to apply for principal or ancillary relief; see also MA s 88E(4), which saves any other Commonwealth law that deems a union a marriage. See also *Ghazel & Ghazel* [2016] FamCAFC 31, which involved a husband and wife who were married in Iran, where the husband could marry up to three wives. The parties' application for a declaration of validity of their marriage under the MA was refused by the primary judge, but was allowed on appeal to the Full Family Court.

48   MA s 88D(2)(b).

49   s 88E(2).

50   s 88EA.

on the grounds that the marriage is void. A decree of nullity renders a marriage void. This means that a marriage between the parties has never existed. This is very different from a divorce decree, which acknowledges that there once was a valid marriage between the parties and it has now come to an end. Even though the availability of divorce has reduced the significance that was once placed on nullity of marriage, it is still the case that having the capacity to enter into a valid marriage is essential in determining whether a marriage comes into existence or not.

The grounds for nullity of a marriage are detailed in s 23 of the MA.[51] In the following discussion we will refer to s 23B(1) only. Sections 23(1) and 23B(1) are the same, but it is the latter subsection that applies to a marriage that takes place after the commencement of s 13 of the *Marriage Amendment Act 1985* (Cth). This amendment was introduced to give effect to Australia's international obligations as a consequence of signing the *Hague Convention on the Validity of Marriages*. Rules of private international law are inapplicable to marriages covered in s 23B. Section 23B(1), in several paragraphs, details the conditions when a marriage is void. In summary, these include:

1. if either party is lawfully married to another person

2. if the parties are within a prohibited relationship

3. if the marriage is not valid by reason of s 48

4. if the consent of either party is not real consent because:

    (a) it was obtained by duress or fraud

    (b) one party is mistaken as to the identity of the other party or the nature of the ceremony performed

    (c) one party lacked the mental capacity to understand the nature and effect of the marriage ceremony

5. if either party is not of marriageable age.

As a preliminary issue, it is necessary to point out that the validity of marriage is always determined according to the law as it was at the time of the ceremony and not the law at the time of the court proceedings. For example, once the FLA commenced operation, all applications for 'matrimonial causes' including an application for a declaration that a marriage is void must be instituted under this Act.[52] However, the validity of the marriage is to be determined by the substantive law at the time of marriage.[53]

In keeping with the social significance of marriage, it is also evident that legal rules lean towards the recognition of marriages as far as possible. For example, in an application by a wife challenging the will of her deceased husband, a dispute arose relating to the validity of their marriage.[54] Evidence was adduced that showed that her husband was married to another woman prior to his marriage to the applicant and there was no evidence that the earlier marriage had ended. Thus, the issue before the Family Court was whether at the time

---

51   See also Fisher, above n 44.
52   ss 39, 4(1) (definition of 'matrimonial cause').
53   *In the Marriage of Schmidt* (1976) 1 Fam LR 11 355 (Ellis J).
54   *Fox v Public Trustee* (1983) 9 Fam LR 275 (Needham J). The same emphasis is evident in the rules of recognition of marriages entered into in another country.

of the marriage the husband had the capacity to marry the applicant. The Court held that on the balance of probabilities the presumption of validity applied. In other words, the Court was satisfied the marriage was valid based on the evidence that a valid marriage ceremony between the parties had taken place. The Court also focused on the circumstances of the marriage, such as its length, to establish proof.

3.4.2.3 Specific requirements for a valid marriage

The following discussion follows the sequence of issues listed in s 23B(1) of the MA that can apply to void a marriage, but it is useful to keep in mind that there are three broad requirements for creating a valid marriage: having the capacity to marry, giving consent to marry, and satisfying certain formal requirements of marriage.

SECTION 23B(1)(A) – IF EITHER PARTY IS LAWFULLY MARRIED TO ANOTHER PERSON

This is also described as the requirement for the marriage to be a monogamous union; that is, a person can only be lawfully married to one person at any given time.[55] The history of this requirement can be traced back to the Christian conception of marriage and, conventionally, *Hyde v Hyde* is quoted as the common law authority for this rule.[56] However, the use of these cases as authorities for the view of marriage as a monogamous union has recently been shaken by what the High Court said in *Commonwealth v Australian Capital Territory*.[57] In a detailed analysis of the common law authorities used to define marriage as a monogamous union, the High Court declared that what was said in *Hyde* only reflected the state of the common law at the time of that judgment; since that time both case law and statute have qualified the statements made in *Hyde*; it gave the example of s 6 of the FLA, which permits recognition of certain polygamous marriages for the purposes of proceeding under that Act.

Nevertheless, it remains the case that polygamous marriage unions cannot be entered into in Australian law, as was evident in the discussion of Aboriginal customary marriages in Chapter 2. However, the topic provides an occasion for the creation of a discourse about whether the practice of polygamy is morally reprehensible[58] and whether the law should continue to prohibit it. This is also an example of how Australian law, while insisting that marriage is a monogamous union, also allows recognition of more than one relationship in the context of de facto relations, as we will discuss below.

SECTION 23B(1)(B) – IF THE PARTIES ARE WITHIN PROHIBITED RELATIONSHIPS

Historically, laws of marriage have changed from prohibiting relatively long lists of relationships[59] to relatively few prohibitions. Section 23B(2) provides that a person cannot marry an ancestor or descendant, or a brother or sister (whether full- or half-blood).[60] Any relationship

---

55   Further supported by MA s 94 prohibiting a married person from marrying and a person from marrying another person who is married, and imposing criminal penalties in such cases.
56   (1866) LR 1 P & D 130.
57   (2013) 250 CLR 441, 461 [30]–[32]. See the discussion in Chapter 2.
58   See, eg, Mark Durie, 'The Rising Sex Traffic in Forced Islamic Marriage' (2014) 58(3) *Quadrant* 7.
59   See Bodichon, above n 19, 4, 6–8.
60   MA s 23B(6) defines the terms 'adopted' and 'ancestor'.

specified in this subsection includes relations created through adoption. Furthermore, for the purposes of prohibited relationships the MA assumes an adopted child to be a natural child of both sets of parents and the prohibitions apply even if the adoption is cancelled or ceases to be effective for any reason.[61] This is a significant effort by marriage law to maintain its hold on which relationships can be defined as marriage. Adoption law on the whole is premised upon the legal fiction of a child being a natural child of the adoptive parents. The incapacity of the law to deal with the idea of more than one set of parents for a child is given expression in this fiction. However, the risk of breaching the taboo of incest in some situations no doubt is a stronger motive for the law maintaining the 'natural' relationship of the child with its biological parents and adoptive parents at the same time. In the process, the artificial and constructed nature of such rules becomes apparent but is rarely commented upon in the legal literature. Similar prohibitions are included in laws dealing with de facto relationships as discussed below.

SECTION 23B(1)(C) – IF THE MARRIAGE IS NOT VALID BY REASON OF S 48

The inclusion of this subsection creates a certain degree of difficulty in separating the capacity and formalities distinctions for creating a valid marriage. We discuss it here as it is presented next in order in s 23B of the MA. Section 48 is contained in div 2 of the MA, which specifies the requirements for marriages solemnised in Australia by marriage celebrants. Section 48(1) provides the general rule that marriages not solemnised in accordance with this division are invalid. However, sub-s (2) enumerates specific instances where non-compliance with the rules does not make the marriage invalid. These subsections are a good illustration of the opposing pulls of the law to provide the conditions for creating a valid marriage and the reluctance to invalidate marriages for non-compliance with certain rules.[62] Reading s 48 as a whole, it seems as though a marriage will be invalid pursuant to it only if the ceremony does not comply with the s 48(3) requirement that *both* parties knew that the celebrant was not authorised to perform the marriage.[63]

SECTION 23B(1)(D) – IF THE CONSENT OF EITHER PARTY IS NOT REAL CONSENT

Consent of the parties to a marriage is also a requirement and lack of consent can result in a void marriage if:

1. it was obtained by duress or fraud
2. one party is mistaken as to the identity of the other party or the nature of the ceremony
3. one party lacked the mental capacity to understand the nature and effect of marriage.

---

61   s 48(3)–(5).

62   See *Oltman v Harper (No 2)* [2009] FamCA 1360 where the marriage was declared valid even though the religious celebrant was not a registered celebrant but the wife did not know this fact; and *Wold v Kleppir* [2009] FamCA 178 where the marriage was declared valid even though no notice was given pursuant to the MA and no marriage certificate was issued.

63   Anthony Dickey, *Family Law* (Thomson Reuters, 6th ed, 2014) 150.

The requirement for consent in marriage most obviously links the creation of a marriage and the creation of a contract. The major difference, of course, is that in a marriage the law provides certain minimum conditions that cannot be altered by the parties and it also specifies the consequences of being married. The lack of consent can be owing to fraud or duress, as explained in the following decisions. The courts have used the concepts of fraud and duress as developed in the law of contracts, often adapting these principles to the specific context of family law.

Lack of consent – duress

In *In the Marriage of S*, the applicant was a 17-year-old girl of Egyptian descent who had entered into a marriage, arranged by her parents, with an Egyptian man.[64] She had applied for a decree of nullity alleging lack of consent owing to duress. In the Family Court, Watson SJ accepted the evidence of the applicant, her parents and the priest. In granting the decree of nullity, he held that duress not only arises where there are threats of violence, imprisonment or physical constraint, but also when there was no consenting will. The applicant in this case was not physically threatened or in danger, but was caught in a psychological prison of family loyalty, parental concern and a culture of familial obedience. The case is notable in the judge's attempt to resolve the issues in a culturally sensitive way while at the same time emphasising the central tenets of Australian family law as contained in s 43 of the FLA to preserve and protect the institution of marriage, to protect the family, and to protect any children. It is also notable that, in broadening the scope of the legal meaning of the notion of duress to establish lack of consent in this case, the judge tailored an understanding of duress to suit the marriage relationship as distinct from a contractual relationship.

Lack of consent – fraud

In *In the Marriage of Deniz* the applicant was a woman of Lebanese descent who had married a man from Turkey.[65] After the marriage ceremony he told her that his reasons for marrying her were to gain a resident visa so that he could stay in Australia. The applicant was of the firm view that a divorce in her community would be a serious thing for a woman. Justice Frederico in the Family Court accepted that the consent of the applicant was induced by trick as the man had no intention to respect the obligations of marriage, and granted a decree of nullity. However, in *In the marriage of Al Soukmani* Kay J disagreed with the decision in *Deniz* and held that the marriage between the parties in this case was valid.[66] The marriage had been entered into under similar circumstances as *Deniz* (for the husband to gain Australian residency). The applicant wife claimed the marriage was void owing to fraud, but the Court held that as they had undergone a valid marriage ceremony the marriage was valid. The Court found that the parties' subjective intentions were irrelevant, and only the circumstances applying at the time of the ceremony were relevant in determining

---

64   *In the Marriage of S* (1980) 5 Fam LR 831. See also *In the Marriage of Teves III and Campomayor* (1994) 18 Fam LR 844, where the wife alleged duress in the form of physical violence and sexual assault. Justice Lindenmayer in the Family Court held that it is duress at the time of marriage that is relevant.

65   (1977) 31 FLR 114.

66   *In the Marriage of Al Soukmani and El Soukmani* (1989) 96 FLR 388. See also *In the Marriage of Osman and Mourrali* [1990] FLC 92-111 and *Hosking v Hosking* [1995] FLC 92-579.

whether the marriage was valid or not. The absence of a finding of fraud at the time of the marriage ceremony meant that the marriage was valid, and the Court found that the correct course of action was for the wife to apply for the dissolution of marriage (now referred to as a divorce order). Although the two cases came to different conclusions, we can see a common desire in both decisions to protect the institution of marriage whether in upholding what the judge described as the obligations of marriage in *Deniz* or the presumption of validity of marriage in *Al Soukmani*.[67]

One party is mistaken as to the identity of the other party or the nature of the ceremony performed

A similar inclination to uphold the institution of marriage by ensuring that the parties have entered into a valid marriage is evident in *In the Marriage of Najjarin and Houlayce*.[68] In that case the parties agreed to marry in front of an Islamic celebrant and a certificate of marriage was issued. Subsequently the respondent ceased his visits and contact with the applicant. The applicant argued that none of the ceremonies required under Islamic law took place at any time. Justice Nygh in the Family Court held that the marriage was invalid either because the applicant was mistaken as to the nature of ceremony and/or the essentials of the ceremony required according to Islamic law that are permitted by s 45(1) of the MA were not performed.

These decisions bring to the surface the idea that the consent required for the creation of a valid marriage may be interpreted differently from that in the formation of a contract. But the parallel requirement for consent in both demonstrates their similarities, as do the following requirements.

Lack of consent where one party lacked the mental capacity to understand the nature and effect of the marriage ceremony

In the case of *Oliver (decd) v Oliver* the issue before the Court was whether the deceased had the capacity to understand the nature and effect of the marriage he had entered into with the respondent at the time of the ceremony; if he did not, then the marriage was void.[69] The applicant was the granddaughter of the deceased and the dispute related to whether the marriage of the deceased to his carer was valid. At the time of marriage, the deceased and his carer were respectively 78 and 49 years of age. The marriage took place in April 2011 and Mr Oliver died in September 2013. The applicant claimed that the marriage should be declared void because at the time of the marriage Mr Oliver was mentally incapable of understanding the nature and effect of the marriage ceremony as provided for in s 23B(1)(d)(iii) of the MA. Justice Foster in the Family Court held that it is 'significant that the legislation not only requires a capacity to understand "the effect" but also refers to "*the* marriage" rather than "*a* marriage". … Taken together those matters require more than a general understanding of what marriage involves' (emphasis in the original).[70] Moreover, in view of

---

67   See also *Aird v Hamilton-Reid* [2007] FamCA 4, where the decision in *Al Soukmani* was again affirmed.
68   (1991) 14 Fam LR 889. See also *Rabab v Rashad* [2009] FamCA 69.
69   [2014] FamCA 57.
70   Ibid 255.

the evidence the Court was satisfied that the deceased had significant mental and cognitive incapacity before and at the time of the marriage ceremony. In these circumstances, the onus was on the respondent to adduce evidence that the deceased had the necessary capacity to understand the nature and effect of the marriage ceremony at the time of the ceremony, but failed to meet this requirement.

SECTION 23B(1)(E) – IF EITHER PARTY IS NOT OF MARRIAGEABLE AGE

The law requires that a party to a marriage must be of marriageable age, which at present is 18 years for both males and females. However, there are provisions for a court to make an order authorising a person to marry below that age in limited circumstances.[71] The person making such an application must be at least 16 years of age and they must seek permission to marry a particular person rather than seek general permission to marry. The MA further provides that, for the marriage of a minor, consent by certain prescribed people is required and, if not given, may be substituted by consent of other authorised people.[72] The MA also makes it an offence for someone to go through a ceremony of marriage with a person not of marriageable age.[73] There are defences available if the person believed on reasonable grounds that the other person was of marriageable age, or had been married before, or the consent of the relevant person who can consent to the marriage of a person not yet of marriageable age had been obtained or dispensed with legally.[74] The crossover between the age of consent laws and the MA is a significant issue in determining the role of law in regulating the sexuality of young people. It is significant in law's efforts to decide issues of sexual identity as well as sexual autonomy. For example, in *Family Violence – A National Legal Response*, the Australian Law Reform Commission notes how the age of consent to sexual activity differs in the laws of various States as well as the Commonwealth, and in some jurisdictions consent is not available as a defence.[75] The existence of such differences is in part an illustration of the competing legal impulses to protect children and recognise the autonomy of young people. The corresponding efforts of family law can be discerned in the law not imposing an age limit for recognising de facto relationships.[76]

3.2.5   The same-sex marriage debate

Whether the law can and should regulate same-sex marriage has been a recurring debate in family law across the industrialised world. There is halting progress in the direction of legally recognising same-sex relationships and, although same-sex marriages are recognised in a number of jurisdictions, the issue of marriage equality remains a contentious one, as is evident in Australia. This is a vast topic and we cannot cover all aspects of the debate. Three distinct but related issues discussed below are: does the marriage label matter? Are there any

---

71   MA ss 11–12.
72   ss 13–15.
73   s 95(1).
74   s 95(3)–(4).
75   Australian Law Reform Commission, *Family Violence – A National Legal Response*, Report No 114 (2010) ch 25.
76   See Patrick Parkinson, 'Taking Multiculturalism Seriously: Marriage Law and the Rights of Minorities' (1994) 16(4) *Sydney Law Review* 473, 490–6 for an argument that raising the marriageable age to 18 years for both men and women has implications for cultural sensitivity to minority communities.

plausible jurisprudential reasons for restricting the marriage label to a heterosexual union? If, as argued by feminists, heterosexual marriage is a patriarchal and oppressive institution, is it worth emulating as a standard for same-sex relationships?

In Australia the FLA now recognises de facto heterosexual and same-sex relationships. Moreover, the legal effects of marriage and de facto breakdown are the same under the FLA. Nevertheless, the Commonwealth government, at present, is not keen to legislate in favour of permitting same-sex couples to enter into 'marriages' recognised by Australian law.[77] Recently Ireland voted in favour of marriage equality for same-sex and heterosexual relations.[78] A recent decision of the Supreme Court of the United States has also upheld marriage equality for same-sex couples in ruling that State bans on same-sex marriage were unconstitutional.[79] These developments have increased pressure on the government to enact a law enabling same-sex marriages to be solemnised,[80] but it continues to resist these calls for marriage equality.

If we accept the general argument in this chapter that marriage is the most privileged social institution, then it follows that the label given to same-sex unions matters. The name matters because it provides the formal, public recognition of the relationship and this would matter to the individuals in the relationship.[81] The label 'marriage' signifies the acceptance that same-sex marriage has the same legitimacy and value as heterosexual marriage. This would guarantee marriage equality and thereby validate the individual choices that have been made in forming these relationships. However, some jurisdictions have fallen short of labelling these unions as 'marriages' and instead have permitted same-sex couples to enter into what have been labelled as 'civil unions'.[82] This labelling is problematic on a number of levels. A label like 'civil union' continues to privilege heterosexual marriage as the normative institution. It conveys the message that same-sex unions are different and inferior and therefore do not deserve the same status in law as can be conferred on heterosexual relationships. The symbolism of the label therefore perpetuates privilege of one and the disadvantage of other forms of intimate relationships.

This leads to the question of whether there are legitimate reasons for according same-sex relationships a lesser status than marriage. The main argument against same-sex marriage derives from the religious belief that the marriage union can only be between a man and a woman. The moral and philosophical arguments that favour the retention of the heterosexual aspect of marriage as its defining feature underline natural law theory. This is evident

---

77   The constitutional limits on the federal parliament with regard to legislating for marriage are discussed in Chapter 2.

78   Thirty-fourth *Amendment of the Constitution (Marriage Equality) Act 2015*.

79   *Obergefell v. Hodges*, 576 US __ (2015).

80   Attempts to introduce national legislation legalising same-sex marriage have so far failed to pass through Parliament. The current Turnbull government is opposed to legalising same-sex marriage, but is in favour of holding a plebiscite on the issue in 2017. At the time of writing, no draft legislation on the plebiscite has been put before Parliament.

81   Nancy F Cott, *Public Vows: A History of Marriage and the Nation* (Harvard University Press, 2000).

82   See *Freedom of Marriage World Map: Same Sex Marriage and Civil Unions*, Hiddush <http://marriage.hiddush.org/about/same-sex-marriage-and-civil-unions>, which provides a list of countries where same-sex marriage is permitted and a corresponding list of countries where civil unions are permitted. In some Australian jurisdictions, civil partnerships can be registered: *Civil Partnerships Act 2008* (ACT); *Civil Partnerships Act 2011* (Qld).

in the writings of Finnis,[83] among others. Natural law theory depends upon the idea that there are certain 'intrinsic goods' that we can identify and appreciate through our practical reasoning and that for a law to be valid it must be made in pursuit of such goods. Natural law theorists like Finnis identify marriage as one of these 'goods'. According to Finnis, there are two main reasons why marriage should be valued: first, for the procreation and bringing up of children; and, second, for the mutual support of spouses that arises because they are sexually complementary to one another.

In response to these claims, Zanghellini has brought into question whether these aspects are what make marriage valuable.[84] He mentions existing evidence that challenges whether nuclear families actually serve to nurture and promote the wellbeing of children in a special manner. Moreover, there are no definitive answers available in psychology or sociology about the best social arrangements for rearing children. Thus, the assumption that the nuclear family is the most appropriate institution for bringing up children cannot be a plausible conclusion through practical reasoning. The fact that Finnis makes the claim that children's wellbeing is best served in a heterosexual marriage is based on assumptions about the value of the complementary sex roles of the husband and wife to their children. Zanghellini claims this is highly problematic as it assumes coherency in the classification of 'man' and 'woman' in a way that presents this dichotomy as representing the entire spectrum of human sexual experiences, including individual psychological sexual identities. The subjectivities of sex/gender outsiders are erased by such a classification, and the false hypothesis of this classification enables the construction of discourses about intersexual people as an evolutionary aberration, a transgender person as having a non-integrated personality, and a woman as complementary to a man but the former always being conceptualised as the more inferior being.[85]

Critical analyses of marriage like these add to the feminist critiques of marriage discussed in Chapter 1 and question the value of marriage by illuminating its oppressive aspects – not only in perpetuating the unequal gendered relations based on the sexual division of labour, but also in upholding inequalities based on sex/gender identities. In view of these oppressive aspects of marriage, it then becomes pertinent to consider whether there are any valid reasons for recognising same-sex marriage in law.

The strongest argument in favour of same-sex marriage is based on the egalitarian model of marriage, which relies on liberal notions of formal equality and individual freedom of choice; in the same-sex marriage debate, these translate to the claim that two people, regardless of their sex, should be allowed to celebrate their love for one another in marriage. The argument in essence recognises that while the heterosexual marriage continues to be privileged it is a matter of principle that same-sex unions should be entitled to the same label. But is legal recognition desirable in view of the oppressive aspects of marriage? Within the

---

83   John Finnis, 'Law, Morality, and "Sexual Orientation"' (1994) 69(5) *Notre Dame Law Review* 1049. See also John Finnis, 'The Good of Marriage and the Morality of Sexual Relations: Some Philosophical and Historical Perspectives' (1997) 42 *American Journal of Jurisprudence* 97.

84   Aleardo Zanghellini, 'Marriage and Civil Unions: Legal and Moral Questions' (2007) 35(2) *Federal Law Review* 263, 283–96.

85   Ibid, where Zanghellini provides a detailed analysis of the arguments of Finnis and other natural law theorists.

lesbian and gay scholarship, there are proponents of both views: that marriage is a desirable label on the one hand, and that it is not the way to achieve equality or non-discrimination on the other.[86] In the context of the argument advanced in this book that law continues to privilege the nuclear family (and marriage as the quintessential expression of the family), we suggest that an argument for classifying same-sex unions as marriages reinforces the normative dominance of marriage. Polikoff has argued (following Martha Fineman) that the central issue in family law is not one about legal recognition of the relationship between two adults, but instead about legal recognition of enforced dependencies, primarily created by the rearing of children.[87] The power of naming a union is no doubt important, but demands for marriage equality need to simultaneously focus on the function of marriage in creating social hierarchies, and the role of law in supporting these hierarchies, which is most evident in how attention is deflected from the real costs of rearing children by the representation of marriage as a consensual, egalitarian union between equals. The marriage equality debate identifies well the norm-setting function of giving different names to different unions. It is equally important to identify how the marriage institution and the law intertwine to entrench social inequalities by disassociating the affective aspects from the economic aspects of relationships.

3.2.6   Marriage between a man and a woman

This brings us to the issue that is a matter of contemporary debate: whether same-sex relationships are or can be defined as marriage under the MA. It is evident that a marriage between two people of the same sex is not mentioned in the list of factors that can make a marriage void. Historically, the requirement for a marriage to be a heterosexual union was not included in the MA, but was treated as an essential part of the definition of marriage in the common law. However, the *Marriage Amendment Act 2004* (Cth) introduced the new definition of marriage in s 5 that now states that '"marriage" means the union of a man and a woman to the exclusion of all others, voluntarily entered into for life'. Despite this amendment to the definition of marriage, this requirement is not mentioned as a ground of nullity in s 23.[88] In Parliament, then Attorney-General Phillip Ruddock explained the need for the Bill to amend the definition of marriage 'because there is significant community concern about the possible erosion of the institution of marriage'.[89] He provided no evidence in support of this concern and only insisted that some other countries permit same-sex marriages but Australia will not.[90]

Conventionally, the courts have often referred to the requirement for marriage to be a heterosexual union as self-evident. However, since the decision in the *Commonwealth v Australian Capital Territory*, discussed in Chapter 2, the High Court has unanimously held

---

86   For an introduction to these debates, see William B Rubenstein et al, *Cases and Materials on Sexual Orientation and the Law* (West Academic Publishing, 5th ed, 2014).

87   Nancy Polikoff, 'Why Lesbians and Gay Men Should Read Martha Fineman' (2000) 8 *American University Journal of Gender, Social Policy & the Law* 167.

88   However, FLA s 88B now prevents recognition in Australia of a same-sex marriage formed in a foreign country.

89   Commonwealth, *Parliamentary Debates*, House of Representatives, 27 May 2004, 29 356 (Philip Ruddock, Attorney-General).

90   For a critique of this amendment as discriminatory and a retrograde step, see Alastair Nicholson, 'The Legal Regulation of Marriage' (2005) 29(2) *Melbourne University Law Review* 556.

that the Commonwealth Parliament has the power to make a law recognising same-sex marriage.[91] An extreme consequence of insisting that marriage can only be between a man and a woman is evident in cases where courts have had to address the issue of the legal significance of surgical gender reassignment procedures. The case of *Attorney-General for the Commonwealth v 'Kevin & Jennifer'* (*'Kevin and Jennifer'*) illustrates the issues that arise in such cases.[92] In that case, the applicants had initially applied to the Family Court for a declaration that their marriage, which had been solemnised in 1999, was valid pursuant to s 113 of the FLA. The declaration was made at first instance by Chisholm J.[93] The Commonwealth Attorney-General appealed the decision to the Full Family Court. The contentious issue was that Kevin was a post-operative transsexual male and the question was whether he was allowed to marry a woman. It was accepted by all parties that the legal position in other contexts is that a post-operative person is treated according to their reassigned gender. The respondents, Kevin and Jennifer, did not claim that same-sex marriage is or should be permitted but only that Kevin should be recognised as a man for the purpose of Australian marriage law.

The Attorney-General disagreed and argued that the trial judge had made a number of errors, which included his rejection of the idea that it is for the Parliament to decide whether a post-operative transsexual person may marry as a person of the sex other than their biological sex at birth. The Full Family Court did not accept these arguments and held that it was open to the trial judge to come to the conclusions he did; that the word 'man' has its ordinary meaning in the MA; and that it follows that since Kevin meets the definition of a man, the marriage was valid. In reaching this conclusion, the Full Court relied on the medical evidence, the fact that Kevin has been socially accepted as a man, the relevant international legal developments that are consistent with its decision in finding the marriage was valid, the criminal and social service laws that recognise the post-operative sex of a transsexual person, and that many State laws provide new birth certificates in these cases.

The two judgments in *Kevin and Jennifer* are considered sensitive and liberal decisions, but it cannot escape our notice that in the reasoning processes the legitimacy of marriage as a heterosexual union is being promoted. Although the argument was not advanced in this case, the judges could have questioned the need for determining the effect of gender reassignment for the purposes of marriage law. If in other areas of law such surgery is accepted as reassigning gender, why is it that marriage law is being treated as different or a special case? Alternatively, it is worth pondering whether the judges could have used the then existing provisions relating to the validity of marriage (as noted above, the definition of marriage in s 5 was inserted in 2004) to conclude that nothing in the legislation would make the marriage void even if Kevin was treated as a female, which was his biological sex at the time of birth.

This is not idle speculation, but an illustration of how the discourse of family law comes into existence by judges imposing restrictions on themselves. The judges did not expand their brief, but remained within the conventions of legal reasoning that the role of a court is strictly to decide on the issues presented to it. The same judges did mention the anomalous situation of whether a pre-operative transsexual person could marry according to his or her

---

91 *Commonwealth v Australian Capital Territory* (2013) 250 CLR 441.
92 (2003) 30 Fam LR 1.
93 *Re Kevin: Validity of Marriage of Transsexual* (2001) 28 Fam LR 158.

gender, but found it was not for them to decide this issue. In making this claim, the judges are repeating the mainstream view of legal reasoning that judges simply 'apply' the law. Nevertheless, it is also undeniable that such a view obscures how in common law systems judges participate in developing legal doctrine.[94] For this reason, the conventional view of the judicial role needs to be exposed for legitimising judicial authority while enabling judges to actively engage in the formation of legal discourse.

The other significant issue is that judges are 'constrained' by the arguments put before them. In the case of *Kevin and Jennifer*, counsel on behalf of Kevin was very well versed in the medical and sociopolitical discourses of transsexualism.[95] This case was exceptional in that people living with transsexualism were advised and represented by people living with transsexualism. They were able to explain the significance of maintaining a critical attitude to medical literature that continues to use psychiatry or psychology to treat transsexualism as an illness or disorder by ascribing a person's birth sex as their normal sex and the procedures they undergo as changing their sex or having 'a sex change'. They were able to present the argument convincingly to the trial judge, who was also open to the ideas and willing to develop the legal principles.[96] This happy coincidence does not always happen as is exemplified in cases involving children seeking treatment for gender identity disorder.[97]

These decisions illustrate how the courts do not see themselves as able to challenge or even question the legal classification of all humans into the binary categories of male and female. In *Kevin and Jennifer* the Court made it clear that this is supposed to be the task of the legislature. We use the word 'supposed' because it is a limitation the courts seem to endorse rather than question, and more so in family law than in other areas of law. It is this role of the judges in translating social discourse into legal discourse that necessitates a closer analysis of how legal discourse is formed in the courts. This is amply evident in the legal regulation of de facto relations, as detailed below.

3.3   Family relationships outside marriage

In this section, we illustrate how hierarchies of relationships are created and maintained in family law through the legal recognition of de facto relations and other non-married types of relationships. We will substantiate our argument by comparing the legal requirements for the formation of de facto and marriage relationships. As a preliminary point, it is worthwhile to dwell upon the meaning of the phrase 'de facto relationship' and to appreciate that the formal term is 'de facto marriage' which means a marriage in fact rather than in law. The close parity between the two terms 'de facto' and 'marriage' is never far from the surface, yet the law insists on maintaining this conceptual distinction. In the following discussion, we briefly

---

94   See the discussion in Chapter 2 of *Commonwealth v Australian Capital Territory* (2013) 250 CLR 441. The High Court decision in *Mabo v Queensland [No 2]* (1992) 175 CLR 1 is a more notable example.

95   See Rachael Wallbank, 'Re Kevin in Perspective' (2004) 9(2) *Deakin Law Review* 461 for a detailed account of the expertise of the counsel in the subject matter of intersex identities and its importance in how the argument was presented to the courts.

96   Appeal against the decision was refused by the Full Family Court and it accepted the reasons of the trial judge; see above n 92.

97   See, eg, *Re Alex: Hormonal Treatment for Gender Identity Dysphoria* [2004] FamCA 297; *Re: Alex* [2009] FamCA 1292.

canvas the various sociological explanations for the rise of the phenomenon of de facto relations and examine to what extent the law reflects these assumptions. This is followed by an analysis of the legal developments in recognising different forms of relationships, which will then be compared to the legal approach to marriage. In conclusion, we argue that the continued distinction between marriage and all other relationships is one of the chief mechanisms of maintaining the primacy of the nuclear family. As will become apparent, the law 'regulates' conjugal, monogamous heterosexual and same-sex relationships on the same set of assumptions, but elevates marriage over others.

3.3.1   Sociological theories of family without marriage

It is undeniable that in contemporary societies the need to be married in order to conform to social or cultural expectations is almost non-existent as compared to even 50 years ago.[98] In the literature this is often described as an expression of modernity where the earlier social, cultural or religious constraints are no longer the determinants of how people form conjugal relationships of affection. Smart observes that personal relationships of various kinds now fit under the concept of families.[99] Yet it is also the case that these relationships are organised in similar ways to marriage and are described as such by those people. This has been explained as an effect of the hold of marriage on our imaginations. O'Donovan describes marriage as having a sacred and magical status.[100] Diduck discusses how many individuals in de facto relationships speak about 'settling down' in marriage.[101] Fineman explains in a similar vein that, despite the fact that the married family is statistically a minority family unit, it remains central to our thinking about the family.[102]

At the same time, in the sociological literature there are various explanations for the rise of cohabitation in non-married relationships, but not everyone considers that this development has been a progressive step.[103] While the positive aspect of non-married cohabitation is captured by theories explaining that these relations are manifestations of increasing individualisation and more democratic or equal relationships,[104] others depict the same relationships as creating less stability and demonstrating less commitment than marriage.[105] It is not possible to state categorically why people enter into de facto relations instead of getting married, but among the possible reasons is that it is an ideological choice for some, while for others it is a pragmatic choice. That is, cohabitation without marriage may be seen as a

---

98   Admittedly, there are exceptions to this statement and in particular the religious and cultural traditions of various ethnic communities continue to expect marriage as the norm.

99   Carol Smart, *Personal Life: New Directions in Sociological Thinking* (Polity Press, 2007) 27.

100   O'Donovan, above n 13.

101   Diduck, above n 26, 33.

102   Martha A Fineman, 'Why Marriage?' (2001) 9 *Virginia Journal of Social Policy and the Law* 239, 246. Compare the discussion of Bittman and Pixley in Chapter 1. We would qualify this comment by saying that the nuclear family is central to thinking about the family in law.

103   Michael D A Freeman and Christina M Lyon, *Cohabitation Without Marriage: An Essay in Law and Social Policy* (Gower, 1983).

104   Ulrich Beck and Elisabeth Beck-Gernsheim, *The Normal Chaos of Love* (Polity Press, 1995); Anthony Giddens, *The Transformation of Intimacy: Sexuality, Love, and Eroticism in Modern Societies* (Stanford University Press, 1992).

105   Zygmunt Bauman, *Liquid Love: On the Frailty of Human Bonds* (Polity Press, 2003); Ruth Deech, 'The Case Against Legal Recognition of Cohabitation' (1980) 29 *International and Comparative Law Quarterly* 480.

rejection of the institution of marriage as a gendered and hierarchical set up. Or, with the increasing social and cultural acceptance of de facto relations it may not appear so much to be a rejection of marriage, but a prelude to it or at most an alternative but not necessarily different from marriage.[106] It is, however, suggested by some researchers that de facto relationships are more fragile than marriages.[107]

It is necessary in examining the legal responses to de facto relationships to consider why the law regulates these relationships and what the aims of legal regulation are. It is evident from the provisions of the FLA that the main features of legal regulation relate to child-related disputes, as the FLA now makes it irrelevant whether the parents are married or not. The FLA provisions regarding property and maintenance disputes that apply with respect to marriages also apply to de facto relationships. Equating de facto relationships and marriage in law in these ways suggests that de facto relationships have finally been accepted as functional families.[108] These legal developments also reflect the empirical evidence that challenges the idea that couples in de facto relationships are less committed than married couples.[109]

The question therefore is: why should de facto relationships be distinguished from marriage in law? We examine next the process of formation of de facto relations in the eyes of the law. The obvious issue that arises in this context stems from the fact that, by definition, de facto relationships are not formal relationships and they come into existence without specific rituals. In the following analysis, we illustrate how this informality gives rise to much closer scrutiny of de facto relations in comparison to marriage. Moreover, the benchmark of whether a de facto relationship exists is provided by what is generally considered to be the social (and not necessarily legal) norms of marriage. In the process, the legal privileging of marriage proceeds effortlessly.

3.3.2 Law of de facto relationships

There are many precursors to the contemporary legal regime regulating de facto relationships under the FLA. The extent of legislative recognition of de facto relations illustrates how family or personal relationships are not only the concern of marriage and divorce laws. Even before the various States introduced legislative measures recognising de facto relationships, there were many laws at both Commonwealth and State levels which 'recognised' these relationships for specific purposes. These laws extend to diverse areas like social welfare, domestic violence, intestacy and worker's compensation, to name a few.[110] More specific

---

106   For a collection of essays on the topic, see Alison Diduck (ed), *Marriage and Cohabitation: Regulation Intimacy, Affection and Care* (Ashgate, 2008).

107   See, eg, Ruth Weston and Lixia Qu, 'Trends in Family Transitions, Forms and Functioning: Essential Issues for Policy Development and Legislation' in Alan Hayes and Daryl Higgins (eds), *Families, Policy and the Law: Selected Essays on Contemporary Issues for Australia* (AIFS, 2014) 76.

108   Jenni Milbank, 'The Role of "Functional Family" in Same Sex Family Recognition Trends' (2008) 20(2) *Child and Family Law Quarterly* 155.

109   Lynn Jamieson et al, 'Cohabitation and Commitment: Partnership Plans of Young Men and Women' (2002) 50(3) *The Sociological Review* 356. See also Deborah Chambers, *A Sociology of Family Life* (Polity Press, 2013) ch 2.

110   For example, *Social Security Act 1947* (Cth), *Workers' Compensation Act 1926* (NSW), *Crimes (Domestic Violence) Amendment Act 1982* (NSW), *Family Provision Act 1982* (NSW), and *Family Relationships Act 1975* (SA) all provided for the existence of a de facto relationship relevant to their own purposes.

legislation aimed at resolving disputes over property arising at the end of a de facto relationship came into existence at the State and Territory levels in a non-coordinated manner, with each legislature providing slightly different rules for the resolution of these disputes.[111] These provisions were subsequently extended to heterosexual and same-sex de facto relationships. Some States and Territories now have legislation that provides for the registration of de facto relationships.[112]

The statutory definitions of de facto relationships have morphed over time and have gradually come to include same-sex relationships within their scope. For instance, initially legal recognition was extended to marriage-like relationships as is illustrated in the *De Facto Relationships Act 1984* (NSW). Section 3 originally provided the definition of a de facto spouse as a man (or woman) living with a woman (or man) on a bona fide domestic basis although not married to her (or him). When this legislation was amended in 1999 and renamed the *Property Relationships Act 1984* (NSW), the definition of a de facto relationship was also altered and now states in s 4(1) that 'a de facto relationship is a relationship between two adult persons: (a) who live together as a couple, and (b) who are not married to one another or related by family'.[113]

The Commonwealth Parliament's responses to the recognition of de facto relations have varied in different areas.[114] In the context of the present chapter, we will primarily examine how the FLA regulates de facto relationships. Section 51 of the *Constitution* does not mention de facto or family relations more generally, and as a result the accepted position is that the Commonwealth Parliament does not have the necessary legislative authority to make laws with respect to them. The States over time have referred their powers in this area to the Commonwealth,[115] and so Parliament was able to amend the FLA and provide for the regulation of children[116] and the financial aspects of de facto relationships.[117]

---

111   See, eg, *Property Relationships Act 1984* (NSW) ('PRA') (formerly *De Facto Relationships Act 1984* (NSW)); *Relationships Act 2008* (Vic); *Property Law Act 1974* (Qld); *Relationships Act 2003* (Tas); *Domestic Relationships Act 1994* (ACT); *De Facto Relationships Act 1991* (NT); *De Facto Relationships Act 1996* (SA); *Family Court Act 1997* (WA) as amended by *Family Court Amendment Act 2002* (WA).

112   *Relationships Register Act 2010* (NSW); *Relationships Act 2008* (Vic); *Relationships Act 2011* (Qld); *Relationships Act 2003* (Tas); *Domestic Relationships Act 1994* (ACT).

113   See New South Wales Law Reform Commission ('NSWLRC'), *Relationships*, Report No 113 (2006) Recommendation 5 at 39: 'The definition of "de facto relationship" in s 4(1) of the PRA should be amended to dispense with any suggestion that the parties to the relationship must cohabit'.

114   This has included recognition of same-sex de facto relationships. As part of this reform process the Australian government amended 84 pieces of legislation in the areas of taxation, social security, employment, Medicare, veterans' affairs, superannuation, workers' compensation and family law.

115   Except Western Australia, which is not a participating State, but under the *Family Court Act 1997* (WA) de facto couples are covered on the same basis as married couples; Western Australia referred powers over superannuation to the Commonwealth in *Commonwealth Powers (De Facto Relationships) Act 2005* (WA): South Australia referred its powers in 2010.

116   Referral of powers over children by the States to the Commonwealth was effected by the enactment of State laws. For example, Victoria enacted the *Commonwealth Powers (Family Law-Children) Act 1986* (Vic); this and similar laws of other States resulted in the federal parliament enacting the *Family Law (Amendment) Act 1987* (Cth).

117   *Family Law Amendment (De Facto Financial Matters and other Measures) Act 2008* (Cth) which came into effect on 1 March 2009 and for South Australia on 1 July 2010.

3.3.2.1   The FLA and de facto relationships

One of the obvious differences between marriage and de facto relationships is that in the case of the latter there is no document – like a certificate of marriage – proving that the relationship exists. This has resulted in a situation where the court has the authority to make a declaration about the existence of a de facto relationship where relief is sought under the FLA.[118]

In order to come within the jurisdiction of the court under Part VIIIAB of the FLA, a de facto couple must satisfy three threshold requirements: the geographical requirement that requires the parties of the relationship, or one of them, to be ordinarily resident in a participating jurisdiction (that is, one that has referred its powers to the Commonwealth) when the proceedings commenced;[119] the definitional requirement that requires the parties to have been in a de facto relationship within the definition in s 4AA of the FLA; and the requirements as set out s 90SB that the parties' relationship meets certain criteria.

Section 90SB sets out four bases that a court can rely on to make a relevant order: the de facto relationship is of at least two years' duration; or there is a child of the de facto relationship; or that the party to the de facto relationship applying for a property order made substantial contributions and not making an order or declaration would result in serious injustice to the applicant; or that the relationship is or was registered under a prescribed law of a State or Territory. The last basis allows parties to agree to be covered by the FLA even if none of the other bases for establishing jurisdiction is met.

However, just because a couple have a child together does not necessarily mean they are in a de facto relationship. It is important to bear in mind that the three threshold requirements are interrelated and the question of whether a de facto relationship exists also depends on FLA s 4AA. It states that '(1) A person is in a de facto relationship with another person if: (a) the persons are not legally married to each other; and (b) the persons are not related by family … ;[120] and (c) having regard to all the circumstances of their relationship, they have a relationship as a couple living together on a genuine domestic basis'. Subsection

---

118   'Declaration about existence of de facto relationships' under the FLA s 90RD: '(1) If: (a) an application is made for an order under section 90SE, 90SG or 90SM, or a declaration under section 90SL; and (b) a claim is made, in support of the application, that a de facto relationship existed between the applicant and another person; the court may, for the purposes of those proceedings (the primary proceedings), declare that a de facto relationship existed, or never existed, between those 2 persons. (2) A declaration under subsection (1) of the existence of a de facto relationship may also declare any or all of the following: (a) the period, or periods, of the de facto relationship for the purposes of paragraph 90SB(a); (b) whether there is a child of the de facto relationship; (c) whether one of the parties to the de facto relationship made substantial contributions of a kind mentioned in paragraph 90SM(4)(a), (b) or (c); (d) when the de facto relationship ended; (e) where each of the parties to the de facto relationship was ordinarily resident during the de facto relationship'.

119   ss 90RG, 90SD, 90SK, 90UA.

120   FLA s 4AA(6)(a)–(c) defines when two people are 'related by family': if one is the child of the other; if one is another descendant of the other; or if they have a parent in common. In each case the relation through adoption is included. Incest continues to be a criminal offence: *Crimes Act 1900* (NSW) s 78A. Similar prohibitions are mentioned in other enactments; for example, the *Relationships Act 2003* (Tas) includes a requirement that the two parties should not be related.

(2) provides guidance on how to determine whether the parties have a 'relationship as a couple'. Those circumstances may include any or all of the following:[121]

    (a) the duration of the relationship;

    (b) the nature and extent of their common residence;

    (c) whether a sexual relationship exists;

    (d) the degree of financial dependence or interdependence, and any arrangements for financial support, between them;

    (e) the ownership, use and acquisition of their property;

    (f) the degree of mutual commitment to a shared life;

    (g) whether the relationship is or was registered under a prescribed law of a State or Territory as a prescribed kind of relationship;

    (h) the care and support of children;

    (i) the reputation and public aspects of the relationship.

Moreover, no particular finding in relation to any circumstance is to be regarded as necessary in deciding whether the people have a de facto relationship. The court has the discretion to decide which factors to take into account and how much weight to attach to any particular factor. De facto relations can exist between two people of different sexes or of the same sex, or even if one of the people is legally married to someone else or in another de facto relationship.[122] If the FLA applies to a de facto relationship and financial matters therein, then State and Territory laws are excluded.[123]

In the following discussion, it must be kept in mind that the differences in legal treatment of marriage and de facto relationships are significant both at the legislative design level and at the level of judicial interpretation. The legislative provisions regulating the two kinds of relationships bear comparison, as now the financial provisions applicable to both kinds of relationships are the mirror images of each other in the FLA. This is a significant change from the previous State and Territory regulation of de facto relationships where the courts were often reluctant to treat them as the same as marriages.[124] The financial issues arising from these legislative regimes are discussed in subsequent chapters, but for now the point we want to stress is that the determination of whether or not a de facto relationship exists is primarily made in the context of assuming

---

121   Compare with the list of factors in the PDR s 4(2): 'In determining whether two persons are in a de facto relationship, all the circumstances of the relationship are to be taken into account, including such of the following matters as may be relevant in a particular case: (a) the duration of the relationship, (b) the nature and extent of common residence, (c) whether or not a sexual relationship exists, (d) the degree of financial dependence or interdependence, and any arrangements for financial support, between the parties, (e) the ownership, use and acquisition of property, (f) the degree of mutual commitment to a shared life, (g) the care and support of children, (h) the performance of household duties, (i) the reputation and public aspects of the relationship'.

122   FLA s 4AA(3)–(5).

123   s 90RC, but see exceptions in s 90RC(3)–(5).

124   Dorothy Kovacs, *De Facto Property Proceedings in Australia* (Butterworths, 1998).

jurisdiction for a financial dispute.[125] In that sense the two issues are interconnected. Thus, whether a court comes to the conclusion that a de facto relationship exists (whether under the State legislation or now under the FLA) would, in our view, be influenced by whether the court thinks that a property division is justified or not. Yet the legislation does not articulate this connection and the courts treat the two as not connected by separating the issues of whether a de facto relationship exists and the making of property orders. This is very different from how marriage is treated, where the legality of the relationship has been previously established by a valid marriage ceremony.

The legislative definition of a de facto relationship in the FLA requires two interrelated steps. In determining whether a relationship falls within the definition of a de facto relationship, a court may rely on a list of factors in establishing that the parties are not married and are living together as a couple on a genuine domestic basis. The privileging of coupledom is in this way written into the definition, but what constitutes living together on a genuine domestic basis is indicated by the enumeration of the list of factors. It is interesting to trace the origin of this list as it has over the years assumed a central importance in subsequent cases, but more importantly in the legislation as well.

It is generally accepted that the case of *D v McA* decided by Powell J in the Supreme Court of New South Wales is the source of the list of factors that are used to determine whether a de facto relationship of the relevant kind exists.[126] The Court in this case found that it was permissible and legitimate to take guidance from the decisions made in relation to similar statutory provisions in interpreting the definition of a de facto relationship in the NSW Act. The Court further enumerated a list of factors that now appears in almost identical form in s 4AA(2) of the FLA. In creating the list, it appears that the Court made general reference to a number of cases concerned with proving separation between married parties for the purposes of establishing the dissolution of marriage under the FLA and establishing welfare eligibility under the *Social Security Act 1947* (Cth).

In drawing up its list, the Court referred to *Pavey's* case,[127] which in turn had relied on *Todd's* case.[128] Both of these cases, decided in the Family Court, were concerned with (for the purpose of deciding whether to make an order for the dissolution of marriage) whether there had been an irretrievable breakdown of marriage while the respective parties continued to reside under the same roof. In *Todd* Watson J opined that '[m]arriage involves many elements, some or all of which may be present in a particular marriage – elements such as dwelling under the same roof, sexual intercourse, mutual society and protection, recognition of the existence of the marriage by both spouses in public and private relationships'.[129] The Full Family Court in *Pavey* (a case also involving an application for dissolution of marriage) added to this list 'the nurture and support of the children of the marriage'.[130] Evidently, this list

---

125   The other reason for finding the existence of a de facto relationship is to determine parentage in specific cases of medically assisted pregnancy. The existence of a de facto relationship for the purposes of FLA pt VIIIAB is covered by a slightly different definition. Section 60EA includes a registered relationship as conclusive proof of the existence of a de facto relationship for the purposes of s 60H, which relates to the parentage of children born as a result of artificial conception procedures.

126   (1986) 11 Fam LR 214.

127   *In the Marriage of Pavey* (1976) 10 ALR 259.

128   *In the Marriage of Todd (No 2)* (1976) 9 ALR 401.

129   Ibid 403.

130   *In the Marriage of Pavey* (1976) 10 ALR 259, 263 (Evatt CJ, Demack and Watson JJ).

has appeared in subsequent judgments and has been incorporated in legislation, but what is not often acknowledged is how the so-called elements of marriage are now used to measure the existence of a de facto relationship, whether it is a heterosexual or same-sex relationship.

Moreover, in *D v McA* Powell J's list of factors to determine a de facto relationship is not supported by more definite evidence, either by more detailed discussion of the case law or the social science literature. Nevertheless, his list has assumed a status of authoritative knowledge over time. It was used in subsequent decisions, then in the New South Wales de facto legislation and subsequently in the FLA. This history is important to assess the often-repeated claim that the concept of de facto relations has evolved over time and is no longer directly compared to marriage. We argue instead that the language of the statute has changed, but not much else. While it is true that the legislative definitions no longer refer to the requirement of 'a man and a woman living together as a husband and wife on a bona fide domestic basis', the FLA is still invoking the requirement of coupledom albeit with a different formulation of 'a relationship as a couple living together on a genuine domestic basis'.

The interpretation of what constitutes a couple is the task of the courts, and in *Baker v Landon* Riethmuller FM commented that the definitions in various pieces of legislation have different meanings due both to the different language used and the different purposes of the legislation.[131] The Court found that, for that reason, the definition of the term 'de facto relations' in other statutes can provide only limited guidance. The issue in this case was whether the applicant was in a de facto relationship with the respondent at the time of the conception of the child, as that would attribute parentage under s 60H of the FLA (see Chapter 8). The striking feature of the decision is that the discretion remains with the Court in deciding what weight to attribute to different factors. The Court quoted *Davies v Sparkes* in support of the idea that the term 'de facto' does not become any clearer by analysing the use of language.[132] Thus, the term 'living together' cannot be read in isolation and be understood as requiring that de facto couples always live together.

Moreover, in the course of the decision in *Baker v Landon*, the Court managed to reiterate the distinction between marriage and de facto relations by explaining that the definitions of de facto relations in the New South Wales and Commonwealth laws are different. It did so by quoting with approval *Evans v Marmont*, where it was found:

> There are some similarities between the provisions of the *Family Law Act* and those of the *De Facto Relationships Act*. There are also differences. Those differences are substantial, conspicuous, and deliberate … The second [difference] relates to the essential legal nature of marriage, which is referred to in the *Family Law Act* (s 43) as an institution, and which is given by that Act its common law meaning as being the union of a man and woman to the exclusion of all others voluntarily entered into for life.[133]

This is an apt illustration of how the judicial construction of the discourse of the special nature of marriage is accomplished by mere repetition of earlier statements. The quote from *Evans v Marmont* stating the differences between de facto relationships and marriage was

---

131   (2010) 43 Fam LR 675.

132   (1989) 13 Fam LR 575, 577 citing *Davies v Sparkes* (1989) 13 Fam LR 575.

133   *Evans v Marmont* (1997) 42 NSWLR 70, 78, cited in *Baker v Landon* (2010) 43 Fam LR 675, 681.

made with respect to the NSW law relating to de facto relationships and at a time when the FLA only related to marriages. When repeated in *Baker v Landon* the statement operates in the context of the FLA that now regulates de facto relationships and marriages with identical even though separately stated rules. Moreover, there is no effort to engage with the extensive discussion in the literature about whether de facto relations and marriages demonstrate essential differences. Even in legal scholarship, for example Chisholm et al, it has been argued that the tendencies of some courts to make a distinction between de facto and marriage relationships is mistaken partly because the *De Facto Relationships Act 1984* (NSW) had itself elected to treat the two kinds of relationships as similar for some purposes and different for other purposes.[134] In areas where the legislation had modelled itself on the relevant FLA provisions, it should not be the task of the court to give a different and less generous interpretation to the NSW rules. In particular, Chisholm et al criticise the idea that the two kinds of relationships are different because when parties are entering into marriage they do so consciously. They quote from the decision in *Wilcock v Sain*, where it was found that parties who have deliberately refused to enter into marriage, but are deemed for all purposes to have gone through the ceremony of marriage, completely defeat their common intentions.[135] The authors criticise the idea that the intentions of parties entering into marriage or de facto relations are necessarily different, and also point out how this attitude results in an unnecessarily narrow interpretation of the *De Facto Relationships Act*.

The issue, therefore, is this: if de facto relationships are marriage-like (as per *D v McA*) but not quite like marriage (as per *Baker v Landon*), how then should a court interpret the property provisions of the FLA when they apply to de facto relationships? This raises the question of whether judicial views and methods of reasoning have changed since the FLA was amended to include a Part VIIIAB regulating de facto financial matters. Before these issues can be examined, it is essential to consider how the courts have determined whether or not a de facto relationship exists. Rather than discuss every factor mentioned in the list in s 4AA(2), in the following analysis an effort is made to draw comparisons in judicial pronouncements between different kinds of de facto relationships. A brief outline of the facts is included, as most decisions turn on the judicial interpretation of facts.

Moby v Schulter was one of the earliest cases decided under the amended FLA.[136] The parties had lived together and separately on various occasions between 2002 and 2009. Justice Mushin determined that the Court would have jurisdiction in accordance with s 90RD(2) if the total duration of the relationship was two years. In deciding whether a de facto relationship existed under the definition in the FLA, Mushin J held that, for the purposes of the definition, 'a couple' is constituted by two people, whether of the same or opposite sexes. In addition, the second element of the definition of a de facto relationship is the concept of 'living together'. The Court was of the view that if a couple does not live together at any time, they cannot be seen as being in a de facto relationship. However, it also found that the concept of 'living together' does not require any particular proportion of time that the couple must live together.[137]

---

134   Richard Chisholm, Owen Jessep and Stephen O'Ryan, 'De Facto Property Decisions in NSW: Emerging Patterns and Policies' (1991) 5(3) *Australian Journal of Family Law* 241, 256.
135   Ibid 258, citing *Wilcock v Sain* [1986] DFC 95-040.
136   [2010] FamCA 748.
137   Ibid [140].

The Court then discussed the factors in s 4AA(2) and whether they were present in this relationship. It found that, in engaging in this task, drawing parallels between marriage and a de facto relationship was not appropriate, inter alia because a marriage certificate is conclusive proof of a marriage but no such proof is available for a de facto relationship (with the exception of it being registered under relevant legislation). This was not the only difference it found. There are other differences, as that a marriage can only be between a man and a woman but a de facto relationship can exist between two people of the same sex, and more than one such relationship can exist at the same time. It also found that there is no requirement for *consortium vitae* to exist between two partners in a de facto relationship, although it is one of the relevant circumstances in determining the existence of such a relationship. The legislation envisages de facto relationships as diverse, as is indicated by the list of relevant circumstances in determining its existence, and no single circumstance is essential.[138]

Jonah v White concerned a relationship that lasted from 1996 to 2009; during this time the respondent was married to another woman.[139] The trial judge declined to find that a relevant de facto relationship existed and the appeal against that order was unsuccessful as well. The accepted facts were that the appellant had commenced working for the respondent's business in 1992 and shortly after that they entered into a relationship. The respondent had a wife and children and the existence of the relationship between the applicant and respondent was kept a secret. They never shared any accommodation, but the respondent visited the applicant at her place first in Brisbane and since 2006 in Sydney, and they retained financial independence of one another. The respondent commenced paying a monthly amount to the applicant in 1999 and she stopped remunerative work from that time.

On appeal, the Full Court accepted that the time spent together can vary, but went on to say that it had to determine not merely whether the parties were 'living together' at the relevant time but whether they were 'a couple living together on a genuine domestic basis'.[140] The appellant's argument that they were living together not only in each other's physical presence but also by their emotional communion was rejected by the Court as not falling within the definition of living together. Instead the Court endorsed the trial judge's view that at the core of a de facto relationship is the manifestation of 'coupledom', which involves the merger of two lives. Even though the two parties came together and spent time together when they could, the following factors indicate two separate lives: each of the parties kept and maintained a household distinct from the other; the respondent continued the maintenance of his family, including the support of children; there was no evidence of any relationship between the applicant and the respondent's children; the relationship between the applicant and the respondent had no social reputation and they spent time with each

---

138   Ibid [163]–[164]. A particularly disturbing aspect of this decision is Mushin J's discussion of the serious violence perpetrated against the applicant by the respondent. With respect to those events he found 'that the respondent perpetrated very serious family violence against the applicant which had a profoundly negative effect on her, physically, emotionally and psychologically. The applicant was very seriously adversely affected by the respondent's actions. However, my experience in this jurisdiction persuades me that events of that kind, no matter how serious, do not inevitably bring the relationship to an end': [180]–[181].

139   (2012) 48 Fam LR 562 (May, Strickland and Ainslie-Wallace JJ).

140   Ibid [43].

other rather than with others; they rarely mixed with each other's friends; and even though the respondent supported the applicant financially they had no other joint financial dealings.

However, considering the legal provision that a de facto relationship can coexist with a marriage or other de facto relationships, this raises questions about how a de facto relationship could fulfil the requirement of 'living together on a genuine domestic basis' when it is coexisting with another relationship.[141]

Moreover, the flat rejection by the Court of the emotional involvement as relevant in deciding whether a de facto relationship existed demonstrates how the 'truth' of what constitutes a de facto relationship is constructed in judicial discourse. The relevant factors that had been set out to make up a helpful list in earlier cases have assumed the status of essential factors, and any factor not mentioned there is now considered irrelevant. This judicial response also brings into sharp focus the sociological and legal discourses about the changing nature of contemporary relationships. This is what we mean by the myth of the decline of nuclear family, and the law, by continuing to privilege the nuclear family, preferably in the form of marriage, extends this regulation to marriage-like relationships as well. In the process, it manages to privilege marriage as the standard against which every other relationship must be measured and this becomes starkly evident in its responses to same-sex de facto relationships.

In *Regan v Walsh* the parties had known each other since 2005 and for varying periods had shared a residence.[142] The applicant claimed a de facto relationship while the respondent denied it and explained it as a 'situation of friends with benefits'. Judge Coker in the FCC found that the financial dependence of the applicant was not proof that there was a genuine domestic relationship between the parties, but that he had manipulated the respondent to meet his expenses and provide a home for him to live in.

The Court went on to acknowledge that the meaning of the expression 'a genuine domestic basis' is difficult to state with any precision and the task is not that different for same-sex relationships. In this instance, although the shared residence existed for a significant period of time it is the nature of the common residence that is relevant, but it is to be assessed in the light of other circumstances. The Court found this was a case where the applicant used the respondent's stronger financial position to his own benefit rather than a situation where the applicant was dependent on the good grace and support of the respondent.[143] Moreover, there was no evidence of mutual commitment to a shared life, as they had no future plans, nor any property in joint names and the respondent had made a will without mentioning the applicant.

This decision bears comparison with *Cadman v Hallett*, where the issue related to when a de facto relationship had come to an end.[144] The facts were that Mr Cadman at the time of the hearing was 70 years of age, suffered from dementia and was represented by his case guardian, who was also his sister. Mr Hallett was 48 years of age and he had initiated the proceedings for a declaration that a de facto relationship existed between him and Mr Cadman. There was no dispute that the parties met in 1991 and were in a de facto

---

141   Dorothy Kovacs, 'A Federal law of De Facto Property Rights: The Dream and the Reality' (2009) 23(2) *Australian Journal of Family Law* 104.

142   [2014] FCCA 2535.

143   Ibid [71].

144   (2014) 52 Fam LR 149 (Strickland, Ainslie-Wallace and Aldridge JJ).

relationship until 2000. In January 2000 Mr Hallett travelled to the United States and over the following 10 years he travelled back and forth and at times Mr Cadman had visited him in the United States. When Mr Hallett was in Australia he stayed with Mr Cadman, who continued to support him financially. While in the United States Mr Hallett had apparently tried to arrange a sham marriage so that he could remain there.

In the appeal to the Full Family Court it was argued that Mr Hallett had returned to Australia at the end of 2009 because he could not get a green card and not because he returned to live with the appellant on a genuine domestic basis. There were relationship difficulties and the appellant changed his will in July 2010, withdrawing the earlier specified benefits from Mr Hallett. The appellant contended that Mr Hallett, in trying to arrange the marriage, had formed an intention to end the relationship with Mr Cadman. The Court found that '[e]ven if the intention was formed there is no evidence it had been communicated to Mr Cadman'.[145]

These two decisions bear comparison in so far as in both cases one partner was supporting the other financially and arguably the support was one-sided. Yet in the case of *Regan v Walsh*, the Court was highly critical of what it considered to be the manipulative misuse of the generosity of one partner.[146] In contrast, in the case of *Cadman v Hallett* the Court came to the conclusion that the fact that the partner had tried to arrange a marriage with another person was not necessarily indicative of any change in the continuation of the de facto relationship. These decisions illustrate well how the value preferences of judges find expression in the interpretation of the laws. It is a matter of speculation how far the facts that the appellant in the case of *Cadman* was suffering from dementia and that he was probably not likely to be able to enjoy his wealth influenced the final decision. In contrast, in the case of *Regan* the Court was very favourably inclined towards the respondent and viewed the applicant as trying to gain advantage from a generous man. These comments should bring into focus that there is no certain way of knowing when a de facto relationship will be found to exist. This is also evident in *Regan*, where the Court recounts how the respondent's original legal team strongly advised him to accept that a de facto relationship existed, but to also argue that the nature of the relationship would require no financial adjustments. Instead the respondent changed his legal advisers and eventually the Court agreed with him that no de facto relationship was established.

More tellingly, in both cases the marriage model was used implicitly in determining whether a de facto relationship did exist or not. In *Regan* the applicant failed because he was unable to prove there was sufficient interdependency in the relationship to fulfil the requirements in s 4AA(2), while in *Cadman*, where a longstanding de facto relationship had been established, the Court echoed the requirements for a divorce order that the respondent communicate his intention to end the relationship (see Chapter 5).

Keaton v Aldridge involved a dispute about parenting rights, but the issue turned on whether the applicant was a parent of the child.[147] The determination of whether she was a parent depended on whether the parties were in a de facto relationship at the time the child was conceived. Ms Aldridge was the biological mother of the child, who was conceived

---

145   Ibid 157. The main emphasis in the Full Court's reasoning when it rejected the appellant's arguments was that the trial judge was exercising discretion, and there was no error in this exercise of discretion.

146   [2014] FCCA 2535, [46]–[47].

147   [2009] FMCAfam 92.

through artificial insemination procedures. Ms Keaton had been involved in attending the fertility clinic with the mother and was present at the hospital at the time of the birth. However, disagreements about parenting styles resulted in the mother leaving the applicant's home in November 2006. The mother progressively reduced the time the applicant could spend with the child. At the time of the application the child was three years old and the applicant argued that she should be deemed to be a parent by reference to s 60H as she and the mother of the child were living in a de facto relationship at the time of conception of the child (see Chapter 8).

Chief Federal Magistrate Pascoe found inter alia that the applicant and the mother were in a relationship but not in a de facto relationship at the relevant time. He explained that ultimately the task is to decide whether the parties at the relevant date (when the child was conceived) had 'a relationship as a couple living together on a genuine domestic basis'.

Although Pascoe CFM accepted that 'living together' does not necessarily require a common residence, as it is a broader concept than just a common residence, he was nevertheless of the view that a common residence is a good starting point in this endeavour. But even when the couple was sharing a residence they did not consider themselves to be living jointly. Among other things, the Court commented on the fact that the parties did not cook for each other, did not share other household chores, there was no intermingling of finances and their sexual relationship had ceased early on in the relationship. However, they did attend counselling with regard to that aspect of the relationship and in attending the fertility clinic they represented themselves as a couple. In all the circumstances of this case and '[w]ithout the "solemnities and formalities" by which some hetero-sexual couples declare that relationship in marriage, same-sex relationships are fluid in the sense that it is difficult for them to discern what, if any, circumstances will carry them across an invisible threshold to be a relationship recognised by law'.[148]

The Court went on to say that determining whether the parties in this case crossed that threshold was related to their commitment to raising a child together. That they participated in the fertility program as a couple, that they had a social reputation as a couple, and at least some witnesses thought they were having a child together, were not enough to prove mutual commitment to a shared life together. Instead the Court was of the view that evidence suggested that one of the main reasons for having the child was for the respondent to have the experience of motherhood and not because they wanted to raise the child together. It was up to the respondent to decide what role the applicant would play.[149]

It is salutary to read Pascoe CFM's decision to see how the meaning of 'a couple' and 'a mutual commitment to a life together' invokes comparisons with what is socially expected of heterosexual couples. The facts that the two people did not share living expenses, nor did they shop or cook together, and one even offered to pay rent for staying in the home of the other partner, are treated as significant indicators of lack of commitment to a life together. In the process this judicial discourse functions to normalise ideas of domesticity. Moreover, the hierarchy of relationships becomes established in that if the relationship in question were a marriage, all these factors would be irrelevant in determining the status of the parties as

---

148   Ibid [112].
149   The Federal Magistrate's Court ordered that Ms Keaton have sole parental responsibility for the child and that she also spend time with Ms Aldridge. Ms Keaton's appeal to the Full Family Court was dismissed: *Aldridge v Keaton* (2009) 42 Fam LR 369.

married or not. If it was a de facto heterosexual relationship in the context of social-welfare law, an assumption of economic dependency is made readily without examining the actual arrangements (see Chapter 10). In the case of a same-sex de facto relationship, the absence of economic dependency is more readily taken as evidence that a de facto relationship has not been established. The fact that both parties were involved in the decision to have a child through a fertility program was interpreted as the respondent's desire for the experience of motherhood rather than the desire that they wanted to raise the child together. The same circumstances within a marriage or in a heterosexual relationship are not likely to be as easily interpreted as one partner only wanting a motherhood experience. They would be interpreted as a couple deciding to have a child together. Thus, same-sex relationships are scrutinised for their sameness to heterosexual relationships, but they are also judged on a different scale.

In an earlier response to the proposed changes to the NSW de facto legislation,[150] the Gay and Lesbian Rights Lobby had suggested that there should be a broader category of domestic relationship recognised in the *Property (Relationships) Act* – one that was not limited to cohabiting couples. Among the recommendations in its report *Relationships*,[151] the New South Wales Law Reform Commission recommended that the requirement of cohabitation should be removed because it should be possible to recognise many social reasons why two people may not have a public reputation of a couple. The Commission also recommended that registration of a relationship should be considered conclusive proof of the existence of a de facto relationship even in relation to the Commonwealth law.[152]

Furthermore, the kind of information that is made available and scrutinised by the courts in determining the existence of a de facto relationship lays bare the regulation of sexuality in non-married relationships. It also challenges the assumption that not entering into a marriage can be construed as an expression of an intention not to be regulated by state laws. The level of scrutiny and the value judgments made by the courts are inevitable. For instance, in *Baker v Landon* (discussed above) the Court referred to *Davies v Sparkes* in support of the proposition that the language used in a statute does not determine the content of a de facto relationship.[153] A technical analysis of the Latin term 'de facto', or even an analysis of the statute word by word, would yield little meaning. However, the striking feature of the *Davies* decision was how the judicial discretion exercised in assessing the factual situation was blatantly infused with the making of subjective value judgments. In *Davies*, the Court was assessing a relationship of approximately 16 years between the plaintiff, who was 68 years of age, and the defendant, who was 71 years old. In its assessment of the defendant, the Court described him as a very simple person in his behaviour and deportment, and as primitive in other respects. Among its various observations, the Court noted with disapproval that the parties 'sometimes had intercourse in his motor car, which shows a lack of dignity. A sexual relationship was a continuing aspect of their relationship over this long period … '.[154] There are many other examples of a similar function performed by the courts in ascertaining the existence of a relevant kind of de facto relationship. So too in *Jonah v*

---

150   NSWLRC, *Review of the Property (Relationships) Act 1984* (NSW), Discussion Paper 44 (2002).
151   NSWLRC, above n 113.
152   Ibid 85.
153   Above n 132.
154   *Davies v Sparkes* (1989) 13 Fam LR 575, 578.

White the Court expressed scepticism about the existence of a de facto relationship, in part because the man's children from a subsisting marriage were not in contact with the woman with whom he was in a long-term relationship.[155]

In a slightly different context, Roseneil argues that law privileges heterosexual marriage when coupledom is understood in terms of how married couples are supposed to act. The author goes on to argue that law can and should think about relationships that can be formed on bases other than conjugal ones.[156] We suggest that this becomes an option only after it is acknowledged openly that family law – whether understood as relating to marriages or marriage-like relationships – is primarily interested in reallocating the costs of interdependence in relationships between the parties. It would appear that when there is no acceptable reason to reallocate these costs, such as in cases like *Regan*, *Keaton* and *Davies*, because the parties have not acted in sufficiently marriage-like ways, then there is no finding of a de facto relationship. And, as we will see in the chapters on financial relations, family law seems most interested in reallocating the cost of child care between the parties of a relationship, but, by keeping it a private cost as far as possible, undermines the fairness of these decisions.

Among other things, the cases discussed above bring into question whether seeking the existence of a de facto relationship and a property order are two separate issues. Considering that judges are willing to acknowledge that different enactments using the concept of de facto relationship have different aims, our argument that if a court decides that it is not a proper case for property redistribution it will determine that a de facto relationship is not established seems plausible. This claim is not conclusive; indeed, it is in direct competition with the claim to objectivity of judicial reasoning in determining the existence of a de facto relationship. That judicial subjectivity is an inevitable part of the nature of the judicial task is obscured by repeatedly conflating the exercise of discretion and the ascertainment of a fact in determining a 'question of fact'. This was done, for example, in *Jonah v White* and repeated with approval in *Ricci v Jones*.[157]

3.3.3   Registered relationships, domestic relationships and other close personal and caring relationships

The possibility of registering non-married relationships in various jurisdictions already exists, but may also contribute to the dilemma of further entrenching a hierarchy of relationships with marriage at the pinnacle, followed by registered relationships, de facto relationships, domestic relationships and other close, personal and caring relationships.

In some States and Territories, it is possible to register a de facto relationship. At present the following Acts provide for the registration of relationships between couples irrespective of their sex: the *Relationships Register Act 2010* (NSW); the *Relationships Act 2008* (Vic); the *Relationships Act 2003* (Tas); the *Civil Partnerships Act 2008* (ACT); and the *Civil*

---

155   (2012) 48 Fam LR 562, [25].
156   Sasha Roseneil, 'Why We Should Care About Friends: An Argument for Queering the Care Imaginary in Social Policy' (2004) 3 *Social Policy and Society* 409.
157   [2011] FamCAFC 222 [60].

Partnerships Act 2011 (Qld). The literature contains arguments for and against registration,[158] but we wish to ask the prior question: what is the distinguishing feature between a marriage and de facto relationship (whether registered or not) that means the latter merits a separate title? Unless this question is addressed, 'marriage' will continue to be the standard relationship against which all other relationships are measured. Yet the legal consequences of being in one or the other kind of relationship are becoming more similar rather than different. Moreover, the similarities of outcome assume that all relationships entail economic dependence and that unless the law steps in the vulnerable partner will be subjected to injustice.

Similarly, the inclusion of personal or caring relationships within various enactments dealing with de facto relationships brings into sharp focus the unstated but primary rationale for these laws as financial compensation to the person who may have made non-financial contributions to a relationship.[159] The problem, of course, is that care work under this model is sought to be compensated by an extremely flawed model of legal regulation, as we will argue in later chapters. If the issue is to compensate someone for his or her caregiving role, the rationale for including that category under de facto relationships legislation is confused at the very least, as it is a very different type of relationship from an affective relationship. It is also beyond the scope of the relationships that family law usually addresses. However, this is not an effort to expand the scope of family law. Rather, it is legitimising poor compensation for care work and in the process legitimising the idea that dependencies in human relationships can only ever be addressed imperfectly.

It is necessary to formulate a question at this point about whether the difficulties of regulating various kinds of personal relationships could be better managed by the law regulating all relationships as contracts negotiated by the parties. The earlier objections in the literature to treating marriage as a contract may not be as relevant now, as many more marriage-like relationships are recognised by law.[160] Thus, any two people (and not only a man and a woman, or two men, or two women) may enter a contract, set their own terms and specify how, if the relationship ends, the issues of property division will be decided. An interesting example in this regard is the French model of *pacte civil de solidarité* ('PACS'), which allows the parties to contract on the terms they decide to include in their agreement. It is described

---

158   See NSWLRC, above n 113, ch 4.
159   The *Property (Relationships) Act 1984* (NSW) s 5 provides for domestic relationships that include de facto and close personal relationships. The latter exist 'between two adult persons, whether or not related by family, who are living together, one or each of whom provides the other with domestic support and personal care' (s 5(1)(b)) and where the care is provided without fee or reward (s 5(2)(a)).

Apart from providing for the registration of domestic relationships that exist between individuals in a couple, the *Relationships Act 2008* (Vic) s 5 provides for registrable caring relationships, which are defined in a similar manner to close personal relationships in New South Wales, except that the parties need not be living together to qualify.

The *Relationships Act 2003* (TAS) ss 4, 5 and 6 respectively provide for significant relationships that relate to couples; caring relationships, which have similar requirements to close personal relationships in New South Wales; and personal relationships, which include both significant and personal relationships.

The *Domestic Partners Property Act 1996* (SA) s 3 provides for close personal relationships, which appear to simultaneously relate to de facto relationships and close personal relationships.

160   Carole Pateman, *The Sexual Contract* (Polity Press, 1988); O'Donovan, above n 13, 59.

as a means of recognising people's autonomy to determine the shape of their relationships.[161] This approach could be a potential response to the legal privileging of marriage and could commence a process of addressing the prevalent disjuncture in the discourse that our relationships are changing despite the law's ongoing endorsement of marriage.[162]

Moreover, the concept that the decline of the nuclear family is a myth becomes relevant once again when it is acknowledged that the FLA attaches similar consequences to various relationships of marriage, heterosexual de facto and same-sex de facto relationships.[163] It retains the separate categories of relationships and thus uses its power to name as the device to privilege marriage as the standard relationship whereby other relationships are measured. The possible response that the law now regulates different kinds of relationships without any preference is not convincing. This argument fails to recognise how the law attributes certain consequences to the status of being married, and then extends the same status consequences to marriage-like relationships. Notably, one major status consequence of marriage – the incapacity to marry another – does not apply to de facto relationships. In fact, no such restriction applies to forming multiple de facto relationships – a married person is only prohibited from marrying another, but is free to enter into a simultaneous de facto relationship.

3.4   Conclusion

It is evident that by creating a hierarchy of relationships the law manages to privilege heterosexual marriage as the standard relationship that every other relation must emulate. As O'Donovan argues, legal marriage thrives as an institution and those excluded pay homage in their desire for admission.[164] We argue that, rather than maintain a hierarchy of relationships, it is more desirable that legal regulation of affective relationships follows a prior articulation of the aims of such regulation. If it is acknowledged that the legal and religious meanings of marriage are not the same, it becomes possible to articulate the purposes or aims of a law of marriage. Rather than endorsing coupledom and domesticity, such a law would be able to provide for the documentation of a relationship for the purposes of providing remedies for clearly articulated goals. Thus, whether a person is married or cohabiting and whether it is a heterosexual or same-sex relationship would be irrelevant if the aim was to provide a fairer distribution of the costs and gains of a relationship. Alternatively, the discussion above can be a catalyst for a fundamental rethinking about the aims of family law and whether a marriage or marriage-like relationship needs to be the foundation of such a law. Thus, the real benefit of a discourse about relationships becomes evident, allowing us

---

161   For an introduction, see Carl F Stychin, *Governing Sexuality: The Changing Politics of Citizenship and Law Reform* (Hart Publishing, 2003) ch 3; Claude Martin and Irene Thery, 'The PaCS and Marriage and Cohabitation in France' in Alison Diduck (ed), *Marriage and Cohabitation: Regulation Intimacy, Affection and Care* (Ashgate, 2008), 431. Compare the discussion of agreement-making in Australian family law in Chapter 7.

162   In fact Diduck addresses this literature and questions whether it is true that these are the current trends: Alison Diduck, 'Introduction' in Alison Diduck (ed), *Marriage and Cohabitation: Regulation Intimacy, Affection and Care* (Ashgate, 2008), xiv.

163   Discussed in detail in Chapter 1.

164   O'Donovan, above n 13, 56.

to systematically examine whether and why these institutions require legal recognition in the first place. The next step would be to consider the objective of such regulation. In our view, it would be to uphold our collective responsibility to value caregiving functions in a realistic manner rather than allowing the façade of marriage or de facto relationship nomenclature to divert attention from this central issue in family law.

DIVORCE AND VIOLENCE IN FAMILY LAW

4.1   Introduction

This chapter is focused first on the law of divorce, and second on the family violence provisions in the *Family Law Act 1975* (Cth) ('FLA'). The discussion aims to illuminate how the tensions that exist in the law continue to uphold the nuclear family construct and perpetuate inequalities in society.

In the 20th century there was a significant shift in western family law jurisdictions from fault-based divorce to no-fault divorce. This chapter links the history of these legal developments to the effects of market liberalism and the notion of personal autonomy that underpins it. However, as will become apparent, the liberal transition in divorce law has not been complete. In the Australian context the specific provisions of the FLA challenge this understanding and illustrate the continuing influence of the Christian conception of marriage and its need for legal protection. The scope of the jurisdiction of the courts to bring about reconciliation between the parties using alternative measures, such as marriage counselling, provides a good example of the investment the law continues to have in maintaining the institution of marriage. A sociological analysis of the no-fault basis of divorce will explicate the unresolved tension between the individualism of liberal ideas and the interdependencies of family relations that maintain marriage as a status relationship.

The tension between the private and public is also relevant here. Whether we accept that familial relationships are autonomous or dependent, the understanding of the family as a private institution continues to prevail in law. As long as that distinction exists in law, the issue of when and in what circumstances it is appropriate for the law to regulate the family continues to arise.

However, the effect of the public and private distinction is somewhat paradoxical, as we see in relation to the FLA provisions that continue to perpetuate the private nuclear family through the regulation of divorce. Golder observes, in a historical study of the introduction of divorce laws in New South Wales, how the public and private spheres converged in divorce proceedings when the courts discussed issues of women's sexuality, women's domestic labour and men's financial responsibility for women and children.[1] The same could almost be said about divorce discourse in contemporary times, for although the legislative grounds of divorce have radically changed, it is evident that the state continues to maintain a stake in marriage through the regulation of divorce. As we see in this chapter, this is most evident in contested applications for divorce that give the court scope to scrutinise marriage breakdown in determining whether a divorce order should be made.

The individualism of liberal ideas that shape no-fault divorce comes into sharp question with the acknowledgement of violence in intimate relations. The availability of divorce in family law is supposed to be separate from issues of fault that could arise, for example, in violent relationships. Indeed, the autonomy of agency inherent in the no-fault divorce provisions elides the issue of family violence completely. It is not a ground for divorce, nor is its presence necessarily an indicator of relationship breakdown. The implicit message

---

1   For a history of early developments in New South Wales, see Hilary Golder, *Divorce in 19th Century New South Wales* (UNSW Press, 1985) 5. Golder critiques the analysis of women in Australia in Patricia Grimshaw, 'Women and the Family in Australian History' in Elizabeth Windschuttle (ed), *Women, Class and History: Feminist Perspectives on Australia 1788–1987* (Fontane/Collins, 1980) 46.

of no-fault divorce is that all individuals, even targets of violence, are equally free to file for divorce. However, in examining divorce law and family violence provisions side by side in this chapter, our aim is to contribute to existing critiques of no-fault divorce by illuminating how the notion of individual autonomy that underpins it can be difficult to reconcile with the presence of violence in familial relationships. Our purpose in raising this issue in this chapter is not to support the resurrection of fault-based divorce, but to examine whether the provisions in the FLA are actually equipped to respond to violence or whether they in fact can be implicated in perpetuating a cycle of violence against women and children that can exist within families.

This is a serious charge considering the extensive amendments to the FLA made in recent times to strengthen its responses to family violence, especially in the context of parenting disputes. We will provide an overview of these provisions.[2] However, in our analysis we continue to remain mindful of the competing assumptions about the family made in the law – assumptions that are based on freedom and autonomy on the one hand and dependency on the other. Once it is accepted that the FLA normalises dependencies in ongoing relationships and then switches to a discourse of autonomy when relationships break down, it becomes relevant to ask whether family law is itself implicated in maintaining the relative powerlessness of women and children in family relations despite its recognition of and attempts to address violence in families and uphold individual autonomy more generally.

In the context of this chapter, we explore these issues initially through the property and parenting provisions in the FLA and how they in fact can be seen to undermine the autonomy of targets of family violence – usually women. With respect to the property provisions, it is argued that a woman's autonomy is undermined as long she does not have property in her own name and any entitlement to property under the FLA remains subject to the discretion of the court.

Similar claims can be made with respect to parenting disputes. The history of reform of the FLA shows the ideological contestations in this terrain, most starkly illustrated in the amendments to the FLA in 2006 (which introduced the presumption of shared parental responsibility in tandem with compulsory family dispute resolution ('FDR'))[3] and 2011 (which introduced additional family violence protection measures).[4] Evidently, the emphasis of the FLA on promoting FDR and shared parental responsibility while also protecting against family violence proves that they are ongoing concerns for the Commonwealth Parliament. But in our view these concerns are also contradictory and further compound the tensions that exist in the law. This will become clearer in our discussion of the limitations of the violence provisions, particularly evident in the difficulties experienced in detecting and screening violence that undermine the effectiveness of these provisions.

---

2   Note that the family violence provisions are canvassed here. The child abuse provisions will be canvassed in the later chapters on children. The procedural frameworks for resolving disputes involving family violence and/or child abuse, such as the less adversarial trial, the Magellan Case Management Program, and the Family Violence Best Practice Principles, are introduced in this chapter and discussed in more detail later in this chapter. See also Chapter 8.

3   *Family Law Amendment (Shared Parental Responsibility) Act 2006* (Cth) ('2006 amendments') came into effect on 1 July 2006.

4   *Family Law Legislation Amendment (Family Violence and Other Measures) Act 2011* (Cth) ('2011 amendments') came into effect on 7 June 2012.

4.2   History and philosophy of divorce

If our main argument that family law supports the nuclear family model that is based on marriage is plausible, then the existence of divorce requires explanation. The fact that divorce was not readily available but is now available even unilaterally supports the opposite claim – that the law is actually weakening the ties of marriage. We use historical analyses of how the law of divorce has changed to examine whether the availability of 'easy' divorce is indicative of the changing nature of personal relations, including marriage. The idea that contemporary relationships are an expression of individuality rather than conforming to societal, including religious, expectations is aptly captured by Giddens, as discussed below.

However, the history of divorce begins earlier and is inextricably bound to the history of marriage, as Stone explains in his book *Road to Divorce*.[5] He reminds us that the affective, procreative and companionship aspects of marriage, while always present, were, well into the 17th century, of only secondary importance. Marriage as an institution helped create an economic partnership where both spouses performed specialised functions. It also functioned to create alliances between families and kin groups that spanned social, economic and political ties. Moreover, 'marriage acted as the most important vehicle for the transfer of property, far more important than purchase and sale'.[6] Thus, the history of how the concept of divorce was formulated goes beyond the interpersonal issues and incorporates religious and other social influences.

In the religious doctrine of Roman Catholicism, marriage was and in fact continues to be a sacrament that is not dissoluble. Within this religious view the only way to end a marriage was if it was declared *void ab initio* – not a marriage at all. The rules of nullity of marriage were developed in the ecclesiastical law and were extended to certain situations where a marriage was voidable. The technical terms used were divorce *a vinculo matrimonii* and divorce *mensa et thoro*. The effect of the former term was to void a marriage, while the effect of the latter was that the parties were treated as separated but not free to marry again, as technically the marriage continued to subsist.[7]

Family law historian Phillips explains that with the rise of Protestantism this early Catholic view on divorce and remarriage was challenged.[8] However, the Protestant support for divorce should not be seen as a manifestation of the permissiveness associated with modern conceptions of marriage. Instead he argues that the 16th century divorce doctrines, laws and the associated literature focused on the importance of marriage as the consequence of divorce. Marriage was considered to be the institution that maintained the moral and social order through the family. Single men and women could avoid the temptation to sin if allowed to marry. This was also the reason for Protestant support for remarriage after divorce. Moreover, the Protestant view acknowledged the unworkability of celibacy as a practice for most people and therefore wanted to allow remarriage to prevent 'sinful' activities.

---

5   Lawrence Stone, *Road to Divorce: England 1530–1987* (Oxford University Press, 1990).
6   Ibid 6.
7   Archana Parashar, 'Do Changing Conceptions of Gender Justice Have a Place in Indian Women's Lives? A Study of Some Aspects of Christian Personal Laws' in Michael R Anderson and Sumit Guha (eds), *Changing Concepts of Rights and Justice in South Asia* (Oxford University Press, 1998) 114.
8   The following account draws on Roderick Phillips, *Putting Asunder: A History of Divorce in Western Society* (Cambridge University Press, 1988) 92–4, 513–5, 562–7, 571–2.

The significant point is that permitting divorce was a sign not of weakening of the institution of marriage but of an overriding concern to preserve the integrity of individual marriages. There were many steps in the lead up to divorce that were aimed at the reconciliation of the marriage. However, if none of these steps succeeded, the next step was to make it possible for the parties to enter into another marriage. Therefore, Phillips argues that early divorce reform by the 19th and 20th centuries was a dialogue between two kinds of conservatives: those who wished to protect the family by allowing a restricted form of divorce and those who wished to protect the family by not allowing divorce at all. There were various contradictions in divorce doctrine and law, including the effort to allow divorce while also preserving the institution of marriage. The effects were that marriage became subject to tighter regulation and, although divorce was available, it was very expensive and controlled by rigorous procedures that did not acknowledge mutual consent or incompatibility as a ground for divorce. Notably, most of the grounds on which divorce was available were for behaviour associated with the working class, but the cost of obtaining a divorce put it out of their reach. Thus, divorce was allowed in a way that the legislators hoped would make it a rare occurrence and leave marriage fundamentally unaffected.

Over time the grounds of divorce changed and eventually the rules combined a range of fault and no-fault grounds for divorce. Phillips explains that the period from the 1960s constitutes a third generation of divorce legislation, following the Protestant laws of the 16th century (the first generation) and the wider legalisation and liberalisation of divorce in the latter half of the 19th century (the second). Although the no-fault ground was present in many earlier laws, in the 1960s it came to be the focus of legislation. The distinctiveness of this change lay in the fact that the individual spouses no longer had the responsibility to establish that they were innocent or needed relief. Instead all that was required was the establishment of the fact that the marriage had ended, and this could be achieved by reference to specific objective criteria. The remarkable change in this law was that the responsibility of deciding what constituted a particular marriage and when it had broken down now lay with the individual spouses. The law would only concern itself with the fact of breakdown, usually indicated by non-cohabitation, and was no longer concerned with the reasons why cohabitation had ceased.[9]

Phillips argues that the emphasis on no-fault divorce has displaced the long-held view that the Church or state must closely regulate divorce. In the process the no-fault divorce laws have shifted the responsibility of defining the criteria for a satisfactory marriage directly to the spouses themselves. He suggests that among the causes of this shift in the legislative attitude to marriage and divorce was the influence of sociological theory that espoused the understanding that divorce was no longer explicable according to individual actions, but according to social, economic and other environmental factors.[10]

---

9   For a history of legislative developments in regard to divorce in Australia, see generally Henry Finlay, *To Have But Not to Hold: A History of Attitudes to Marriage and Divorce in Australia 1858–1975* (Federation Press, 2005); see also Elizabeth Evatt, 'Foreword' in *To Have But Not to Hold: A History of Attitudes to Marriage and Divorce in Australia 1858–1975* (Federation Press, 2005) for a brief discussion of how demands for equality for women were articulated and accepted over time.

10   Whether this constitutes an example of the increasing delegalisation of personal relations remains to be determined and we will return to this issue below.

Glendon similarly argues that the changes in legal attitudes to divorce are a result of wider social developments rather than an indicator of the weakening of the institution of marriage.[11] She explains that, just as individuals have gained the freedom to decide whom to marry, so too they have gained the right to decide when to end a marriage. Glendon locates the trend in family laws towards individualism and egalitarianism in the broader social and economic developments that have undermined the 19th century assumption that family and marriage are essential determinants of an individual's security. She argues that family law has always been about the regulation of property rights and that now includes the regulation of 'new forms of property'. That is, in contemporary societies one gains status or standing in society not just from inherited wealth but also from one's capacity to earn or generate an income.

However, in her view the law's retreat from regulating closely who might marry whom, the respective rights and duties of married spouses, and how such unions may be termi-nated is not necessarily an indication of a shift towards individualism in family life. Instead she argues that poor families tend to be governed by public and administrative law and middle-class families are regulated through other aspects of family law like spousal sup-port, marital property, and inheritance and tax laws. She goes on to say that this change is not a reflection of families losing functions, but, instead, of sharing them with distant bureaucratic entities rather than with neighbours, patrons or parish. In this sense family dependencies continue to exist, but in complex relationships with different administrative and legal institutions.

These are important observations, particularly as they bring into question the common assertion in the literature that the introduction of no-fault divorce law was a response to the social changes that had already happened. For instance, Freidman argues that in the United States the introduction of no-fault divorce was more the law catching up to already exist-ing practices and social attitudes.[12] Similarly, the parliamentary debates in the case of the Family Law Bill 1974 [No 2] (Cth) ('Family Law Bill') show an often-repeated comment that the proposed law would help make the dissolution of a marriage a more civil procedure. For example, Whitlam, during the parliamentary debates on the Family Law Bill, claimed:

> The vast majority of persons whose marriages have failed turn to divorce only as a last resort. What this Bill will do is enable them to have the marriage dissolved without having to be put to the additional distress of making formal, undignified charges against the other party that that party's cruelty or adultery or wilful desertion was the cause of the breakdown, and because of it that party deserves to be divorced.[13]

Eekelaar, in a different vein from Glendon, cautions that social reality and legal reality are not the same and even though they influence each other there is much to be gained by see-ing law as having its own 'reality'.[14] This legal reality is no doubt constituted and affected

---

11   The following account is based on Mary Ann Glendon, *The Transformation of Family Law: State, Law and Family in the United States and Western Europe* (University of Chicago Press, 1989) 292–7.

12   Lawrence Friedman, 'Rights of Passage: Divorce Law in Historical Perspective' (1984) 63(4) *Oregon Law Review* 649.

13   Commonwealth, *Parliamentary Debates*, House of Representatives, 28 November 1974, 1 (Gough Whitlam, Prime Minister).

14   John Eekelaar, *Regulating Divorce* (Clarendon Press, 1991) 15–22.

by other social forces, but it is important to critique the assumptions underlying it and the directions implicit in it. This makes it possible to at least aim to change or modify these assumptions and directions for the benefit of everyone in society. We argue that this is an important issue for any discussion of no-fault divorce as endorsed in the family law provisions. The danger in accepting the idea that no-fault divorce provides for already existing social practices is that it relies on a model of individual autonomy, which is not the reality for marriages where spousal dependency continues to exist. And it follows that, in subscribing to an autonomy model, divorce is treated as independent of the related unequal consequences of marriage and its breakdown arising from the sexual division of labour.

Once it is accepted that dependency exists in familial relationships, then it is apparent that family sociologists who subscribe to an autonomy model only tell a partial story about the changing nature of intimate relationships. For instance, Giddens explains that we are part of a social world undergoing profound transformations where, among other things, women no longer comply with male sexual dominance. Both men and women have to deal with the implications of these transformations in the nature of family, marriage and sexuality. However, he argues that men have always behaved in a manner that has allowed them to pursue their passions whether overtly or otherwise, but what has changed is that women are now in a position to pursue their own desires as well. Thus, intimate relationships are being restructured in a fundamental sense. The resultant 'pure relationship' is a relationship entered into for its own sake and lasts only so long as it delivers satisfaction to each individual. Marriage, for many in society, is veering towards a pure relationship in this sense. Giddens, however, cautions that this is part of the generic restructuring of intimacy happening in many aspects of our lives and not only in heterosexual marriages.[15]

Giddens's account depends on two interrelated assumptions that are associated with the nature of social reality and family law, and deserve further attention. The first is that both men and women engage in such pure relationships to the same extent and the second that various institutions, including family law, do actually facilitate this reflexive intimacy. We argue that existing gender hierarchies in contemporary societies make it difficult for women to engage in such pure relationships as suggested, and also that the institution of family law only selectively facilitates this reflexive intimacy. This is obvious if the entire FLA, not just the no-fault divorce provisions, is taken into account. The later chapters will substantiate this claim with respect to the financial relations provisions and the provisions related to children and child support. But for now it is important to identify how a tension exists in the law between the concept of marriage based on interdependence and marriage as a union between equals. This tension is illustrated well by the debates between those who want to reintroduce the concept of fault-based divorce and those who wish to resist such change.

It is sometimes argued that marriage is like a business partnership. It is an institution of trust that enables two people to have the confidence to make long-term investments in their relationship. The idea of fault is central to the notion of marriage as a commitment, binding each party to their marital obligations. In this way a fault-based divorce law protects those who fulfil their obligations.[16] In contrast there are arguments against reintroducing

---

15   See especially Anthony Giddens, *The Transformation of Intimacy* (Polity Press, 1992) 8, 58.
16   Robert Rowthorn, 'Marriage and Trust – Some Lessons From Economics' (1999) 23(5) *Cambridge Journal of Economics* 661.

fault as the basis of divorce. It is argued that there is no evidence that no-fault divorce leads to an increase in the rate of marriage breakdown; nor does it lead to unjust property or alimony decisions; nor it is necessary to apportion blame as meeting the parties' psychological needs is no longer required once a marriage breaks down.[17]

However, both sides of the debate seem to assume that fault and no-fault regimes can produce fair outcomes notwithstanding the inequalities that may have existed during a marriage, whether owing to unequal sharing of property and financial resources, unequal parenting arrangements, or violence. It also appears to be an assumption made during the parliamentary debates on the Family Law Bill where most of the discussion focused on the grounds of divorce and not, for example, on how the property provisions would apply to resolve the financial consequences of marriage breakdown.[18] Once that connection is made, then the arguments in favour of fault or no-fault divorce are not necessarily opposed to one another. Indeed, in the next section we see how the law of no-fault divorce is not interested so much in remediating the effects of marriage, but functions to support the institution of marriage through its regulation of divorce. This may be an inevitable consequence of the design of the FLA that provides for separate orders to be sought whether, for example, it is a divorce, property or parenting order. But with respect to the making of these orders it is important to ask which conception of marriage informs them. Both the dependency model and the autonomy model of marriage have inherent failings. Historically, the dependency model has supported patriarchal relations between the parties, with men placed at the head of households and women and children subordinate to them. The autonomy model may appear to be a progressive development in familial relations in upholding the principle of equality with respect to marriage partners; however, it may assume that equality exists and so obscure the reality of dependency in relationships. Currently in Australia, the no-fault divorce regime is based on the autonomy model but, as we shall see in later sections, the autonomy of the more vulnerable party to a marriage is yet to be fully realised within the area of family law.

4.3   Legal requirements of divorce in the FLA

According to the Australian Bureau of Statistics, in 2014 there were 46 498 divorces granted in Australia and of these 19 281 divorces were granted from joint applications, compared with 15 127 from female applicants and 12 090 from male applicants.[19] Legislative provisions regulating divorce are contained exclusively in Part VI of the FLA (ss 48–59). The following discussion focuses on the overall pattern of these provisions that simultaneously support the continuation of a marriage while they allow one party to end the marriage for any reason whatsoever. A discussion of the single ground for divorce will form the context for analysing the emphasis in the legislation on reconciliation. When first enacted, the FLA used the term

---

17   See, eg, Ira Ellman, 'The Misguided Movement to Revive Fault Divorce' (1997) 11(2) *International Journal of Law, Policy and the Family* 216.

18   See details in Finlay, above n 9, ch 7.

19   Australian Bureau of Statistics, *Marriages and Divorces, Australia* (2015) <http://www.abs.gov.au/ausstats/abs@.nsf/mf/3310.0>.

'dissolution' rather than divorce, supposedly in an effort to make the process non-adversarial. The *Family Law Amendment Act 2004* (Cth) introduced the change in terminology, from 'decree of dissolution of marriage' to 'divorce order' (s 48).

4.3.1   Irretrievable breakdown of marriage

Section 48(1) and (2) of the FLA provides that irretrievable breakdown of marriage is the only ground for an application for divorce and it is established by the fact of 12 months' separation.[20] If this fact of separation is proved, the court must grant a divorce order. There are very few exceptions (loosely so described) to this rule. For example, s 48(3) states that 'a divorce order shall not be made if the court thinks there is a reasonable likelihood of cohabitation being resumed'. The court can also withhold granting a divorce if it is not satisfied that suitable arrangements have been made for the child(ren) (s 55A(1)(b)(i)).

Immediately after the enactment of the FLA there was a dramatic increase in the number of applications for dissolution of marriage made to the court, some of which were defended applications. The main issue in defended applications involved statutory interpretation relating to the provisions in s 48(1) and (2) and whether they constitute two requirements or one. That is, does it have to be proved that the marriage has broken down irretrievably and that the parties have separated for a minimum period of 12 months? Dickey claims that this is a misconceived question as the fact of irretrievable breakdown is proved only by 12 months' separation.[21] What constitutes separation is answered in part by s 49. It provides that '[t]he parties to a marriage may be held to have separated notwithstanding that the cohabitation was brought to an end by the action or conduct of only one of the parties' (s 49(1)). Furthermore, '[t]he parties to a marriage may be held to have separated and to have lived separately and apart notwithstanding that they have continued to reside in the same residence or that either party has performed some household services to the other' (s 49(2)).

The courts have identified the three elements of separation as the intention to separate, action putting that intention into effect, and communication of the intention to the other spouse.[22]

In the Marriage of Todd (No 2) has come to be accepted as providing the authoritative interpretation of what constitutes separation under s 48.[23] It is a good illustration of the contributions judges make to legal discourse formation as in this case both parties sought the

---

20   FLA s 48: 'Divorce (1) An application under this Act for a divorce order in relation to a marriage shall be based on the ground that the marriage has broken down irretrievably. (2) Subject to subsection (3), in a proceeding instituted by such an application, the ground shall be held to have been established, and the divorce order shall be made, if, and only if, the court is satisfied that the parties separated and thereafter lived separately and apart for a continuous period of not less than 12 months immediately preceding the date of the filing of the application for the divorce order. (3) A divorce order shall not be made if the court is satisfied that there is a reasonable likelihood of cohabitation being resumed'.

21   Anthony Dickey, *Family Law* (Thomson Reuters, 6th ed, 2014) 190. In *In the Marriage of Bozinovic* (1989) 99 FLR 155, Kay J held that 12 months should be calculated to include an extra day for filing the application. See also *Campbell v Cade* [2012] FMCAfam 508, [32] where Scarlett FM held that the parties should have lived separately and apart for 12 months immediately preceding the filing of the application and not at the time of the hearing.

22   Dickey above n 21, 192.

23   (1976) 9 ALR 401 (Watson J).

order for dissolution of marriage and were in agreement that separation and thus irretrievable breakdown had occurred. A notable aspect of this case is how the Court, in determining whether to make the order, referred to earlier decisions under the *Matrimonial Causes Act 1959* (Cth) ('MCA') and indicated that they continued to be good authorities despite the introduction of the FLA and the shift to no-fault divorce the new Act represented.

As a preliminary issue the Court observed that separation can occur even if cohabitation is brought to an end by one party, and it may occur even if the parties continue to reside under the same roof and perform some household services to the other, but the Court will decline to grant a decree if it finds that there is a likelihood of resumption of cohabitation. The Court found that in establishing separation three concepts require consideration: separation, living separately and apart, and resumption of cohabitation. It found that separation requires more than physical separation: it involves the destruction of the marital relationship (*consortium vitae*) and occurs when one or both spouses form the intention to end the relationship or not resume the relationship, and act on that intention or act as if the relationship has ended.

The form or content of a marital relationship will vary for each couple, but there are a few elements all or some of which would be present in any individual marriage: dwelling under the same roof, sexual relations, mutual support, and public and private recognition of the relationship. Whether a separation has occurred is a question of fact that would require a consideration of the particular relationship before and after the claimed separation. For example, in *In the Marriage of Pavey*,[24] the Full Court endorsed the view expressed in *Todd's* case[25] and emphasised that the task of the court is to understand what constituted the particular marriage under consideration rather than applying a definition of what a marriage relationship ought to include. Therefore, a list of relevant factors of what constitutes marriage was useful but not to be applied mechanically, as will be discussed further below.

The second concept – living separately and apart – is established unless it can be shown that the parties have substantially resumed cohabitation after the initial separation. A mere intention to resume cohabitation is insufficient and it must be a bilateral intention, as was held in *Todd's* case. So too with respect to resumption of cohabitation; only if there is a reasonable likelihood that cohabitation will resume will the order not be made. If a party asserts that there is a reasonable possibility of parties reconciling, the person making this assertion must support it with relevant facts.[26] In other cases, it has been held that physical separation is neither a necessary nor a sufficient condition; for example, in *In the Marriage of Falk* it was found that separation means a departure from a state of things rather than from a particular physical place.[27] Mere intention to separate is not enough to constitute separation and has to be accompanied by some action.[28]

Whether the intention to separate must be clearly communicated to the other spouse has been a topic of discussion since the inception of the FLA. The requirement that intention should be communicated whether by actions or words finds its origin in the earlier cases under the MCA dealing with desertion as a ground for divorce. In view of the fact that divorce

---

24   (1976) 10 ALR 259 (Evatt CJ, Demack and Watson JJ).
25   *In the Marriage of Todd* (No 2) (1976) 9 ALR 401.
26   *In the Marriage of Bates and Sawyer* (1977) 29 FLR 221 (Evatt CJ, Marshall SJ and McGovern J).
27   (1977) 15 ALR 189 (Evatt CJ, Fogarty and Bulley JJ).
28   *In the Marriage of Batty* (1986) 83 FLR 153 (Wilczek J).

was not easily available, courts developed the concept of constructive desertion for situations where the relationship or *consortium vitae* had finished but the spouses continued to live in the same house. It was supposedly a safeguard against collusion that the courts insisted that the intention to end the relationship should have been communicated. After the enactment of the FLA, with the availability of no-fault divorce and the legislative provision for separation under the same roof, it is arguable that the earlier interpretation of the law was no longer necessary. However, the Family Court has grappled with this notion and commentators have expressed conflicting opinions on the issue as well.[29]

The relevance of communication of intention has arisen again more recently – for example, in a case where separation was occasioned by one spouse moving into a care facility.[30] The earlier insistence on communication of intention to constitute separation and the more recent revival of this notion are, however, informed by very different considerations. In the earlier cases, it is easy to discern an effort by the courts to ensure that the law not be misused in a way that avoids compliance with the requirement of the 12-month separation period. It could be justified as particularly necessary in cases where separation under the same roof was claimed. The insistence on communication may also be aimed at capturing how at the time of physical separation the intention to end the marriage may or may not have been formed. For example, in *In the Marriage of Tye* the husband moved to Singapore and told his wife that he would ask her to join him later.[31] He subsequently informed the wife of his intention to end the marriage, but claimed that he had formed the intention before his departure from Australia. The Court allowed him to calculate the 12-month period from the earlier date. It is plausible that the Court found that nothing was to be gained by delaying the dissolution of this marriage, but in other cases the courts have insisted on the 12-month period commencing from when the intention is made known to the other spouse whether expressly or by their actions.[32]

The rationale for these decisions could be that the end of marriage is an objective fact and one spouse should not be able to claim that the marriage has ended if they have not made their intentions clear to the other spouse. However, in more recent cases the fact of separation has been asserted to invoke the jurisdiction of the court to make a property order.[33] We argue that, rather than rely on the need to communicate the intention to separate, such cases require a finding about separation on other grounds. For example, in the *Jennings* case the couple lived together in a marriage from 1975 to 1994 when the husband was hospitalised for severe dementia.[34] The wife continued to visit him regularly but the Public Trustee, who had been appointed as the guardian of the husband, initiated proceedings for a property order under the FLA. The Court held that there was no separation as the intention

---

29   See, eg, P E Nygh, *Guide to the Family Law Act* (Butterworths, 4th ed, 1986) 611; Lisa Young et al, *Family Law in Australia* (LexisNexis, 8th ed, 2013) 312ff.

30   *Jennings v Jennings* [1997] FLC 92-773, discussed below.

31   *In the Marriage of Tye* (1976) 9 ALR 529 (Emery J).

32   *In the Marriage of Whiteoak* [1980] FLC 90-837 (Evatt CJ, Bulley and Nygh JJ); *In the Marriage of Batty* (1986) 83 FLR 153; *In the Marriage of Falk* (1977) 15 ALR 189.

33   See the decision in *Wilson & Wilson* [2010] FMCAfam 435 (Lapthorn FM) for an example of the application for divorce being rejected because the Court accepted one version of events over another. The applicant husband claimed separation from July 2008, but the respondent wife claimed it was from January 2009.

34   *Jennings v Jennings* [1997] FLC 92-773 (Dessau J).

of either spouse to separate had not been established. The outcome was that the Court refused the application for divorce and made a scathing criticism of the administrator, who had simply 'reached the decision' that the marriage had ended. The misguided action of the Public Trustee overlooked how physical separation, by itself, has never been a sufficient condition for establishing the end of a marriage.

When the Court in *Price v Underwood* discussed *Jennings*, it was dealing with a different set of circumstances and it acknowledged the increasing frequency of cases being brought by case guardians of older people or those suffering from dementia or other debilitating conditions.[35] One of the main issues was whether the case guardian could bring an application for divorce, and it was held that the rules permit the institution of such an application. However, the case guardian had to convince the Court that the person on whose behalf the application was brought had formed the requisite intention to end the marriage and had lived separately and apart for 12 months from the other spouse. The requirement of showing the requisite intention was supported by the earlier authorities of *Todd, Pavey* and *Falk* but, as argued above, the function of the legal requirement for communicating intention was very different in those cases.

4.3.2   Separation under the same roof

Pavey is the authoritative statement of what constitutes separation under the same roof (s 49(2)). This legislative rule was an acknowledgement of the difficulties faced by a financially dependent wife and children, who may not have financial means to find alternative accommodation. In the parliamentary debates on this provision the rationale given for 'separation under the same roof' was that it would assist those who did not have the necessary resources to set up two households during separation. Senator Murphy opposed an amendment to the clause (cl 27) that parties to a marriage shall not be found to have separated if they continued to live under the same roof. He argued that, if accepted, this proposal would create difficulties for people who could not afford to live elsewhere. It would be a class-based amendment, affecting poor people, who would simply not have the finances to set up another home.[36]

The Full Court in *Pavey* was cautious that the provision should not be misused to circumvent the requirement for 12 months' separation and held that in cases alleging separation under the same roof the kind of evidence required would go:

> beyond inexact proofs, indefinite testimony and indirect inferences. The party or parties alleging separation must satisfy the court about this by explaining why the parties continued to live under the one roof, and by showing that there has been a change in their relationship, gradual or sudden, constituting a separation.[37]

It also endorsed the view expressed in *Todd's* case that a claim of separation under the same roof may require comparing the elements of that particular marriage before and after separation.

---

35   *Price v Underwood (Divorce Appeal)* (2009) 41 Fam LR 614, [135]–[145] (Boland and Ryan JJ).
36   Commonwealth, *Parliamentary Debates*, Senate, 27 November 1974, 2863 (Lionel Murphy, Attorney-General).
37   *In the Marriage of Pavey* (1976) 10 ALR 259, 265.

An interesting aspect of the case was how it acknowledged that very often in these cases the evidence turns on facts related to cooking, washing and housework, but that as men increasingly turn their hands to such activities their significance as indicators of the state of the marriage relationship will lessen.[38] This expectation that the gender roles of men and women are changing, and thus becoming equal, is introduced casually, but has the potential to be the device through which common sense ideas of what constitutes a standard marital relationship are included in the law. As we saw in Chapter 3, when same-sex couples do not conform to similar patterns, courts find it difficult to conclude that a relevant de facto relationship existed.

The *Pavey* decision is also authority for the proposition that the fact that the parties have stayed under the same roof for the sake of the children may challenge an application for divorce, as this would indicate that the marriage was still intact. Thus, the Court added to the list of factors found in the *Todd's* case 'the nurture and support of the children' as a constituent element of a marital relationship.[39] By itself, this factor seems uncontroversial, but it is also an example of how the discourse of the nuclear family finds its way into the legal lexicon. This is illustrated by the respondent counsel's argument that s 49(2) required only examining what remained of the marriage; the fact that the parties stayed under the same roof and that one spouse continued to perform household services is irrelevant. The Full Court disagreed and found that s 49(2) is aimed at the situation where the parties have physically separated, as well as the situation where parties continue to reside under the same roof and perform household services.

As a result of the *Pavey* decision, the courts are able to examine the minutiae of a marriage in any contested separation. It is also necessary to remember that the *Pavey* decision is to a large extent endorsing the *Todd* decision, though in the latter case the Court stated the general interpretation of ss 48 and 49 also. In *Pavey's* case, the dispute was over whether the parties had legally separated, as they continued to reside under the same roof. The husband, though not averse to the application, disagreed with the wife, particularly as they continued to prepare and eat meals together during the period of separation. Notably, in determining whether the parties had legally separated, the Court considered the evidence that the husband had forced entry into the wife's bedroom and had intercourse with her despite her efforts to secure her room with a lock and chain. However, these facts were only commented upon as evidence of the parties' sleeping arrangements in separate rooms in the Court's efforts to determine whether or not to make the order for dissolution.

Here we can see how the courts can pick and choose which aspects of the facts to rely on in determining whether a marriage has irretrievably broken down, but also that the Court's treatment

---

38   Ibid. The Court also uncritically accepted the trial judge's assessment of the relationship that the husband and wife 'gave as much as they got' in the later years of their unhappy marriage; this is a questionable assumption considering the obvious physical and financial inequalities between them, as discussed below.

39   Ibid 263. This idea was endorsed in the case of *Falk*, where the Full Court expounded a distinction between parties remaining together for the sake of children or remaining in the matrimonial home for the sake of children. In this case the wife explained that she stayed in the matrimonial home because it was less disruptive for the children and also that she had been advised to stay for reasons to do with the property distribution application. At trial, Lindenmayer J had, however, refused to grant the divorce on this and two further grounds. It was the Full Court that agreed that separation of the relevant kind was established. See also Young et al, above n 29, 321.

of these particular facts suggests that it accepted that sexual violence in marriage is a normal occurrence. Moreover, in its rigorous assessment of the facts, it seems that the Court is more concerned about protecting the institution of marriage by ensuring the parties have met the statutory requirements of separation than ensuring that the wife is protected from violence. This may reflect the state of the law in 1976 when rape in marriage was not considered to be a crime. It is notable in this respect that the Court gave most weight to the fact that the wife had obtained a maintenance order against the husband, which proved that he was in breach of a fundamental legal duty owed to the wife. Ultimately, it was this fact that established that the marriage had irretrievably broken down, as an important aspect of the marital relationship (that of providing mutual support and protection) was now being enforced by court order.

The point we wish to emphasise is that the judicial discourse of what constitutes a marital relationship appears to be constructed on a common sense view of marriage, but nevertheless as a result of choices made by judges about the relative significance of some and not other issues. It is plausible to imagine that the initial interpretations of ss 48 and 49 could have been in conformity with the broader philosophy of the FLA: that if one person decides that the marriage is no longer existing, there is not much the other spouse can do except delay the process of divorce. Instead the courts have opened up the possibility of examining the details of particular marriages inter alia in the name of asking how manifest separation must be to the world at large. The differing conclusions simply illustrate the inevitability of different judges using different interpretations of what constitutes separation. Thus, in *In the Marriage of Fenech* it was held that:

> To the outside observer, matters go on much as usual, and only within the family itself – between the husband and wife – is there any acknowledgment of the breach. To comply with the Act there must be some overt separation, some evidence that there are two households, not one; it is not established in this case.[40]

Yet in *In the Marriage of McLeod* the spouses continued to present as a couple socially and the wife was not interested in a divorce.[41] The Court held that separation under the same roof was established as they lived separate lives at home. The judge was convinced that the marriage had broken down irretrievably as, among other things, the husband had a long-standing relationship with another woman and planned to marry her once the proceedings were finalised.

Similarly, there is virtually no judicial comment on the desirability of having the 12-month separation period before a divorce may be granted. There are arguments for and against this period, but the remarkable point is that everyone seems to accept that a separation period is required.[42] In the parliamentary debates on the Family Law Bill, the focus was on the length of the period of separation rather than on whether any period should be stipulated. Senator Murphy supported the 12-month period because in his opinion a longer

---

40   *In the Marriage of Fenech* (1976) 9 ALR 527, 527–8 (Evatt CJ).

41   (1976) 10 ALR 190 (Wood J). For a recent contrary example, see *Campbell v Cade* [2012] FMCAfam 508.

42   See Commonwealth, *Parliamentary Debates*, Senate, 27 November 1974, 2845ff for the debates on the separation period, where arguments were advanced in favour of 12 months to two and even three years' separation.

period would just encourage the parties to perjure themselves. He also argued that overseas literature suggested that a longer period of separation does not enhance the possibility of reconciliation.[43]

This non-discussion exemplifies how the need to protect the stability of marriage as a social institution remains entrenched in family law. But it raises the question of why family law entrusts the parties to determine the nature of their marriage while it is intact, and then imposes a 12-month separation period before a divorce order can be granted. The argument that this period of separation is an objective criterion of irretrievable breakdown is plausible, but does not explain why the decision of one of the spouses to end the marriage is not enough.[44] The FLA permits divorce on the basis of a unilateral decision made by one of the spouses, but requires them both to wait 12 months before a divorce order is made. Whether making the parties wait for 12 months adds anything to the stability of their marriage or marriage more broadly is a question not often discussed as it is somehow considered as destabilising for the institution of marriage.[45] At the same time, however, the FLA allows for the possibility of ending a de facto relationship without a specified period of separation, as we detail below. The same imperative to support the institution of marriage is evident in a number of other legislative provisions, which we turn to next.

4.3.3 Legislative efforts to protect the marriage institution

It is intriguing to find a number of provisions in the FLA that appear to support the institution of marriage while permitting one party to end a marriage for any or no reason at all. We enumerate these examples in order to ask whether it is paternalistic for the state law to 'tell' adults that they must consider reconciliation. They also serve as further illustration of our argument that the FLA continues to support the nuclear family. Section 43 is an apt example as it contains the general statement that the courts shall have regard to a number of matters that support the institution of marriage.[46] The 1974 parliamentary debates on the Family Law

---

43   Ibid 2846–7.
44   See *In the Marriage of Spanos* (1980) 6 Fam LR 345 (Evatt CJ, Fogarty and Maxwell JJ), where the Full Court accepted that, despite the husband having frequent sexual intercourse with the wife and repeatedly telling her that he loved her, wanted the marriage to continue, and intended to return home and live with her, objectively the separation had taken place. Thus, the unilateral intention of one spouse, even when contrary to their assertions, was taken as sufficient to establish the fact of separation, but the Court had to be satisfied and not the other spouse. The decision-making thus remains with the Court rather than the spouses.
45   For an argument about its cost effectiveness, see Richard Ingleby, 'Regulating the Termination of Marital Status: Is It Worth the Effort?' (1990) 17(4) *Melbourne University Law Review* 671.
46   FLA s 43(1): 'The Family Court shall, in the exercise of its jurisdiction under this Act, and any other court exercising jurisdiction under this Act shall, in the exercise of that jurisdiction, have regard to: (a) the need to preserve and protect the institution of marriage as the union of a man and a woman to the exclusion of all others voluntarily entered into for life; (b) the need to give the widest possible protection and assistance to the family as the natural and fundamental group unit of society, particularly while it is responsible for the care and education of dependent children; (c) the need to protect the rights of children and to promote their welfare; (ca) the need to ensure safety from family violence; and (d) the means available for assisting parties to a marriage to consider reconciliation or the improvement of their relationship to each other and to their children'. See also Frank Bates, 'Principle and the Family Law Act: The Uses and Abuses of Section 43' (1981) 55 *Australian Law Journal* 181; Frank Bates, '" … Which Comforts While it Mocks … ": Some Paradoxes in Modern Family Law' (2000) 4(2) *Newcastle Law Review* 17, 27–9.

Bill show that the proposed definition of marriage as the union of a man and a woman was defeated, but in cl 21A (now s 43(1)(a) of the FLA) the definition was modified to include at the end of the clause 'the need to preserve and protect the institution of marriage' the words 'as the union of a man and a woman to the exclusion of all others voluntarily entered into for life'.[47] It has thus served as a means of promoting one vision of the marriage and family.

It has been accepted by some judges that this provision is mandatory in that it provides that the courts 'shall' have regard to it and they cannot override or ignore express provisions of the FLA.[48] But it is also evident that the mere presence of this provision does not give any substantive rights to the spouses and it is more akin to a mission statement that is open to interpretation by different judges. Accordingly, it provided an occasion for one judge to state that s 43 is 'directive' and requires the court to have regard to the need to recognise marriage as a heterosexual union and the need to give the widest possible support to the family as the fundamental unit of society. Although it does not define 'family', it is clear that the family is the nuclear family comprised of man, woman and children.[49] Another Court, however, came to the conclusion that this section can only be regarded as propaganda that is contradicted by the substantial provisions of the Act.[50] Thus, the presence of this section provides the opportunity for judges to articulate their preferred philosophy regarding marriage and family.[51]

Another example of the law supporting the institution of marriage is evident in cases of marriages of less than two years. Section 44(1B) requires that, before filing an application for divorce in these cases, the applicant must file a certificate that the parties have considered reconciliation with the help of a specified counsellor or organisation. Presumably the rationale of this provision is that if the parties have entered into a marriage they should not be in a haste to end it. However, s 44(1C), which was introduced in 1983, enables the court to waive this requirement in special circumstances. In *In the Marriage of Kelada* the parties had considered counselling but not presented a certificate.[52] The Court, however, insisted that the effect of the 1983 amendments was that 'the court may find "special circumstances" if the parties have not considered a reconciliation; but cannot do so if the parties have considered a reconciliation, but the appropriate certificate has not been filed'.[53] The Court further explained this outcome as indicating that the Parliament must have intended that the only exception to the rule was when consideration of reconciliation was impossible. In addition,

---

47   Commonwealth, *Parliamentary Debates*, Senate, 21 November 1974, 2643 and 26 November 1974, 2783.

48   See *In the Marriage of Warne* [1977] FLC 90-241, 76 301. See also *In the Marriage of Opperman* (1978) 20 ALR 685, 694, where a majority of the Full Court (Watson CJ and Murray J) found that if this section is to have any meaning, then the children, including step-children, should be able to look to the family unit for nurture and protection. See also *In the Marriage of Giammona* (1985) 10 Fam LR 17 and *In the Marriage of Grimshaw* (1981) 8 Fam LR 346.

49   *Oldfield and Anor & Oldfield and Anor* [2012] FMCAfam 22, 32, [111], [113] (Coker FM).

50   *Seidler v Schallhofer* (1982) 8 Fam LR 598, 614 (Hope, Reynolds and Hutley JJA), although the dispute in this case related to a financial agreement entered into by the parties that depended on whether, after a specified period of time, they would either marry or the relationship would end. The comment was made by Hutley JJA while he explained how the nature of marriage has changed to the extent that non-marital relationships are no longer considered immoral.

51   See also Richard Chisholm, Susanne Christie and Julie Kearney, *Annotated Family Law Legislation* (LexisNexis, 2nd ed, 2014) 235 for the comment that after the enactment of the *Family Law Amendment Act 1987* (Cth) the family in s 43 would include a wider group of people.

52   *In the Marriage of Kelada* (1984) 9 Fam LR 576 (Asche J).

53   Ibid 578.

the emphasis on alternative dispute resolution ('ADR') in the FLA means that, under relevant regulations, the people approaching the legal system (whether a legal practitioner or the courts) must be given information about the 'services available to help with a reconciliation between the parties to a marriage'.[54]

The emphasis on reconciliation in the FLA is further evident in s 50. Section 50(1) provides that the separated spouses may try reconciliation and may resume cohabitation for up to three months, and if they do not reconcile the period of cohabitation will not interrupt the computation of 12 months' separation required under s 48(2). However, only one such effort is permissible and it should not exceed a period of three months. Section 50(2) states that '[f]or the purposes of subsection (1), a period of cohabitation shall be deemed to have continued during any interruption of the cohabitation that, in the opinion of the court, was not substantial'.

The rationale for this provision is to enable the parties to try reconciliation without prolonging the process of divorce in case they are not successful.[55] In *Clarke* the decree nisi for dissolution of marriage was rescinded by application of the husband and wife. The spouses subsequently resumed cohabitation from 20 December 1985 to 25 January 1986, and then separated again. The husband applied for divorce on 26 February 1986, but the trial judge refused to accept that a period of 12 months could include time before December 1985. The Full Court overturned this decision based on reasoning that s 50(1) is designed to encourage reconciliation and it would be against the policy of the Act to deny the parties the benefit of this section. In comparison, the Court in *In the Marriage of Keyssner* refused to make the order on the basis that the parties had resumed cohabitation more than once in the 12-month period.[56] Even though they had resumed cohabitation for less than three months, the fact that they had separated and resumed cohabitation several times meant that they did not satisfy the requirement in s 50(1) that resumption of cohabitation must be for one period only.

These two cases make it obvious that the deeper issue is not whether the parties are undecided but whether the courts accept that they have finally separated. Whether s 50 upholds the autonomy of the parties is less than certain, as illustrated by different decisions of the courts. Considering that in *Keyssner* both spouses were in agreement that they had separated, what is the rationale of the Court not allowing them to divorce? The lawyers' answer, of course, is that this is what the legislation requires, but that does not address the spirit or the policy of the Act. If we accept that it is to preserve the institution of marriage, does it make sense to put legal obstacles in the way of married couples who no longer want to stay together?

Other circumstances that could result in a divorce order not taking effect are contained in s 55A(1). The section provides that a divorce order will not take effect unless the court declares either that there are no children under the age of 18 years; or, where there are children under the age of 18 years, that proper arrangements have been made for them. However, the section also provides that there can be circumstances by reason of which the divorce

---

54   FLA s 12C; *Family Law Regulations 1984* (Cth) reg 8A.
55   *In the Marriage of Clarke* (1986) 11 Fam LR 364 (Fogarty, Lindenmayer and Nygh JJ). The section is relevant for calculating the period of separation before an application for divorce can be filed with evidence of 12 months' separation.
56   (1976) 11 ALR 542 (Demack J). The parties initially separated for 11 months, resumed cohabitation for 14 days, separated again for 17 days, resumed for 10 days, separated for four months, and resumed for eight days before finally separating.

order should take effect even though the court is not satisfied that arrangements for the children have been made.[57] Considering that the courts have very wide discretionary powers with regard to children, it is questionable whether this provision is required. The discourse of a normal family as one based on the stability of marriage thus comes into existence continuously, subtly and at many sites. None of these issues is relevant in the courts dealing with the end of de facto relationships. In this respect these provisions hold up marriage at a higher standard than de facto relations, as we discuss below. Before we turn to these issues, however, a brief mention of the procedural issues with regard to divorce is necessary.

4.3.4   Filing an application for divorce

Section 39 of the FLA grants jurisdiction in matrimonial causes to the Family Court and the Supreme Court of a State or Territory,[58] while s 39(1A) grants jurisdiction to the Federal Circuit Court ('FCC').[59] In effect, since the Family Court's introduction of *Practice Direction No 6 of 2003*, all divorce applications are to be instituted in the FCC.[60] The applicant must have the relevant connection to the jurisdiction, which is established by the fact of being a citizen/domicile/ordinarily resident for 12 months prior (s 39(3)). The application can be made by one party or by a joint application and in the latter case it is possible for the court to determine the case in the absence of the parties.[61] In a joint application, the role of the court is more akin to being administrative in nature and raises the issue of whether divorce by mutual consent should be made available in the FLA.

The earlier terms of decree nisi and decree absolute are no longer used in the FLA. A divorce order takes effect automatically one month after the court's order or from the court making an order under s 55A. The court has the power to shorten or extend this period, but once the time has passed there is no appeal against this order. Parties can apply jointly to have the order rescinded within one month – that is, before the order becomes final (s 57). In very limited circumstances, the court can rescind a divorce order before it has taken effect if there is a miscarriage of justice (s 58). One effect of a divorce order is that a property- and/or maintenance-related application can only be made within 12 months of such an order or with the leave of the court.[62] If a divorce order has taken effect, a person is free to marry again (s 59). However, as we explain below, none of these formalities applies in cases of a de facto

---

57   *In the Marriage of Opperman* (1978) 20 ALR 685.

58   In effect, only the Supreme Court of the Northern Territory retains such jurisdiction now.

59   When read in conjunction with s 31 and the definition clause s 4(1); s 39(2) read with s 44A and reg 10A of *Family Law Regulations 1984* (Cth) enables divorce proceedings in the 'proclaimed' courts of summary jurisdiction in Australian Capital Territory and Western Australia.

60   Family Court of Australia, *Practice Direction No 6 of 2003 – Divorce Applications to be Filed in Federal Magistrates Court* (13 November 2003). See also Family Court of Australia, *Protocol for the Division of Work between the Family Court and the Federal Circuit Court* (12 April 2013) <http://www.familycourt.gov.au/wps/wcm/connect/fcoaweb/about/corporate-information/protocol-for-division-of-work-fcoa-fcc>.

61   Provided it is satisfied that adequate arrangements have been made for the children: FLA s 98A(2A). See also *Federal Circuit Court Rules 2001* (Cth) r 25.14. It corresponds to *Family Law Rules 2004* (Cth) r 3.10.

62   FLA s 44(3). The general rule is that an application out of time can be made only with the leave of the court, but this limitation is not applicable to divorces obtained overseas. See *Anderson v McIntosh* (2013) 283 FLR 361 (Bryant CJ, May and Thackray JJ).

relationship breakdown. This is significant because maintaining these procedural distinctions further legitimises the idea that marriage is a relationship that needs the support and protection of the law and that a de facto relationship does not require the same level of protection. This seems particularly problematic for de facto parties who, in the absence of formal proof that their relationship existed, must resort to making an application to the court for a determination of the existence of their relationship at a time when their relationship has ended and when relations between them are likely to be the most acrimonious. Inevitably, this gives the court wide discretion in determining whether or not a de facto relationship existed and thereby it becomes actively engaged in constituting what is (and what is not) a de facto relationship.

4.4 Ending a de facto relationship

The informality of entering or exiting a de facto relationship comes to a rather abrupt halt when the courts have to decide an application for a property and/or maintenance order, or a parenting order relating to children born through artificial means (see Chapter 3). In this section, we are most interested in cases where the applicant is seeking property and/or maintenance orders. Unlike marriage, in an application relating to a de facto relationship, the issue before the court is not whether the relationship has broken down but more about when the relationship broke down. The date when the relationship ended is relevant in computing the duration of the relationship, which determines whether a relevant de facto relationship existed pursuant to s 90SB of the FLA. The finding that a de facto relationship existed is relevant for the court to assume jurisdiction in property and/or maintenance proceedings. Applications for these proceedings should be brought within two years of the relationship ending.[63]

In the case of *Smyth v Pappas* the Court held that determining whether a de facto relationship (and not any relationship) existed and when it ended necessitates an examination of the parties' statements and actions over the life of the relationship as well as after it ended.[64] The Court remarked on the very little guidance available in the law and other decisions, and said that mere 'indications' that a relationship has ended once the parties are no longer living together will not be sufficient to show that a relationship has broken down. Among other things, the ending of a de facto relationship must have permanence about it rather than a temporary suspension. In this instance, the issues turned on whether a de facto relationship was in existence on 1 March 2009, because only then would the Court have jurisdiction to determine the issues between the parties.[65] The Court, in assessing the evidence and

---

63   FLA s 44(5). The court can grant leave to a party to apply out of time 'if the court is satisfied that: (a) hardship would be caused to the party or a child if leave were not granted; or (b) in the case of an application for an order for the maintenance of the party – the party's circumstances were, at the end of the standard application period, such that he or she would have been unable to support himself or herself without an income tested pension, allowance or benefit' (s 44(6)). This provision mirrors s 44(4), which relates to married couples.

64   [2011] FamCA 434 (Cronin J).

65   Ultimately, the Court found that the parties' de facto relationship began in 1999 and finally ended in 2009. Between 1999 and December 2005 and then from July 2006 to December 2009, the relationship was in existence. During the 12 months between December 2007 and December 2008, the relationship was suspended, but not ended in any permanent sense: ibid [118].

credibility of both parties, examined inter alia the other relationships of each party in the relevant timeframe, which in the judgment were referred to as 'a fling',[66] 'seeing other people'[67] or 'a sexual relationship'.[68] It observed that the legislation itself acknowledges the possibility of a de facto relationship coexisting with other relationships or even a marriage. Yet the decision demonstrates that the level of scrutiny of the parties' sexual activity is intense and the Court has of necessity to make subjective assessments of the significance of such activity.

In the course of its discussion the Court mentioned the earlier decision of *Hibberson v George*.[69] In that decision Mahoney JA had made a distinction between a marriage and a de facto relationship and said that marriage has its basis in law, which means that it continues to be valid even when all the things for which it was created have ceased. However, a de facto relationship has its existence in fact, and when one party keeps away from the other in the sense that they determine not to 'live together', that brings the relationship to an end. Notably, in *Hibberson* it was found that since there was no overt act by the defendant to indicate to the plaintiff that she was staying away only temporarily and intended to return, the Court found that the relationship had ceased.[70]

This judicial stance can be compared with other decisions regarding separation under the one roof and other de facto cases as well. Such a comparison helps to illustrate how the particular court gets to define what constitutes a relationship in the relevant sense and inject subjective assessments into the substance of law. It is also relevant to remember that the finding of the existence or non-existence of a de facto relationship has a bearing on whether the court has jurisdiction to determine the financial disputes between the parties.

In *Dahl v Hamblin*, it was found that there could be an aggregation of periods even if in between the relationship had broken down.[71] Significantly, the breakdown here was of 10 years' duration. The fact that during the period of breakdown a party had engaged in sexual activity outside the relevant relationship, or entered into a relationship with another person outside this relationship, would not be a bar to consolidating the periods of the relationship before and after the breakdown. It is obvious that unless this view had been taken the Court would not have had jurisdiction in this case. Yet it is stretching the imagination to say that the 'same' relationship was resumed after all the intervening time and events. Furthermore, this decision can be used to justify similar interpretations in subsequent cases and thus functions to form the legal discourse about the nature of de facto relationships.

Again in *Cadman v Hallett* the issue was when the relationship between the parties had ended.[72] The Full Court agreed with the trial judge that for the relationship to end one party at least should form such an intention and the intention should be communicated to

---

66   *Smyth v Pappas* [2011] FamCA 434, [26].
67   Ibid [46], [50].
68   Ibid [20], [46].
69   [1989] DFC 95-064, cited in ibid [10].
70   This decision also amounts to saying that separation may occur by a unilateral act of one partner and express communication of intention is not necessary. However, this has not been followed in later cases.
71   (2011) 254 FLR 49 (Finn, Coleman and Austin JJ).
72   (2014) 52 Fam LR 149 (Strickland, Ainslie-Wallace and Aldridge JJ). Mr Cadman was 70 years of age and Mr Hallett 46 years. It was not in dispute that they had been in a de facto relationship from 1991 until 2000. After that Mr Hallett travelled frequently to the United States for studies and other activities, but kept coming back to Mr Cadman's house. Mr Cadman, through his case guardian, asserted that the relationship ended in January 2000, but Mr Hallett argued that it ended in October 2010.

the other party. Such an intention on the part of Mr Cadman was formed when he changed his will, but it still had to be communicated to the other partner. Many factors were considered and among them was the fact that Mr Hallett had tried to organise a sham marriage in the United States to enable him to get a visa to remain in that country. The Full Court did not consider this a significant issue and concluded that the de facto relationship was in existence. Therefore, the Court could determine the property distribution issues. Thus, court pronouncements on the existence of a de facto relationship illustrate how ideas about marriage and de facto relationships are constructed in judicial discourse. The agency of judges in resolving disputes and formulating discourses about the nature of relationships will be further examined in the following section.

In conclusion, we can now assess the claim that contemporary family law has receded from regulating the content of personal relations, whether in the form of a marriage or a de facto relationship. This claim is made by reference to the no-fault divorce regime with respect to marriage and the absence of any formal requirements to bring a de facto relationship to an end in the FLA. The discussion above makes it amply clear that once we look beyond the rhetoric of autonomy informing no-fault divorce and the establishment of de facto relations, the intense regulation of personal relations comes into view. Judicial scrutiny of marriage breakdown may be justified on the broader basis of protecting the institution of marriage, while scrutiny of de facto relations may be explained as necessary to ascertain the status of the parties for the court to assume jurisdiction in order to resolve the disputes between them. But in both contexts this scrutiny means that the conduct of the parties continues to be monitored. Thus, instead of the law retracting, it is apparent that the law is heavily invested in family regulation. This is most evident with regard to the family violence provisions discussed below.

4.5   Violence in family law

In this part, we discuss the rationales for the regulatory regimes for family violence; explain briefly the remedies available to the targets of violence; and extend the analysis to other parts of the FLA to examine how the provisions on FDR, the relevance of conduct in financial matters and the emphasis on shared parental responsibility create the structural realities for women experiencing violence in personal relationships. The discourse of family violence is constructed in all these sites in ways which we claim perpetuate the vulnerabilities of women by not acknowledging the existence of gender hierarchies in contemporary society. The remedies available to the targets of family violence, when linked to the other provisions of the FLA, make it evident that the law functions to disempower women by putting structural hurdles in the way of the exercise of their autonomy.

Although violence is an unfortunate feature of many ongoing relationships, it becomes especially visible at the breakdown of a relationship. Empirical evidence shows that violence is a significant contributing factor to relationship breakdown,[73] and can increase and

---

73   See, eg, Elspeth McInnes, 'Single Mothers, Social Policy and Gendered Violence' (2003) 13 *Women Against Violence: An Australian Feminist Journal* 18, 18 where she refers to a 1999 Australian Bureau of Statistics study in which it was found that 62% of women nominated violence as the reason their relationship ended. See also Ilene Wolcott and Judy Hughes, 'Towards Understanding the Reasons for Divorce' (Working Paper No 20, AIFS, 1999), which found that abusive behaviour and personality traits were the second most common reasons for marriage breakdown.

become fatal after separation.[74] The following discussion should not be read as a denial of the efforts made to combat family violence in law and policy, but more as a critique of the design of the FLA in this regard. The provisions of the FLA are especially significant at the time of relationship breakdown, when issues of a financial nature and child-related arrangements require judicial resolution. It is these very factors that bring into view the gendered nature of family violence and its specific cultural connotations.

Family violence is a ubiquitous topic in family law, but it is relevant to consider why the existence of violence in personal relationships is accepted as almost inevitable.[75] Family violence has gained a great deal of attention in recent times and extensive research on the topic exists. That said, there also exist debates about the definitions, causes and remedies for violence.[76] In the context of this book, it is pertinent for us to connect the existence of family violence to the argument that the law continues to support the nuclear family. That means acknowledging the social reality that we live in a gender-hierarchical society and violence in families is to a large extent a manifestation of the extreme disparities of power that can exist between men and women. These disparities are directly linked to the caring roles performed by women.[77] But it must also be acknowledged that gendered violence has very different meanings for differently situated women, as the experiences of Aboriginal and Torres Strait Islander women demonstrate.[78]

Gendered inequalities are not only economic – they are also culturally embedded in various levels of society. In this context, it is salutary to remember that 'the moral texture of a violent act is contingent on its context',[79] and the abusiveness of a blow is dependent on the larger patterns of dominance. For example, Petersen del Mar explains that the slave's blow to a master or a child's blow to an adult carries different significance because of the wider context in which their actions occur. It does not mean that women are never violent

---

74   Janet Phillips and Penny Vandenbroek, 'Domestic, Family and Sexual Violence in Australia: an Overview of the Issues' (Research Paper Series 2014–15, Parliamentary Library, Parliament of Australia, 2014) 8, citing Christine Coumarelos and Jaqui Allen, 'Predicting Violence Against Women: The 1996 Women's Safety Survey' (1998) 42 *Crime and Justice Bulletin* 1; Jacquelyn C Campbell et al, 'Risk Factors for Femicide in Abusive Relationships: Results From a Multisite Case Control Study' (2003) 93(7) *American Journal of Public Health* 1089; Tina Hotton, 'Spousal Violence After Marital Separation' (2001) 21(7) *Juristat* 1.

75   See, eg, the National Council to Reduce Violence against Women and their Children, *Time for Action: The National Council's Plan for Australia to Reduce Violence against Women and their Children, 2009–2021* (2009) 153. For a review of the report, see Australian Domestic and Family Violence Clearinghouse (2009) *Newsletter* 37, 1, 8–10.

76   For an introduction to the wide range of issues, see Belinda Fehlberg et al (eds), *Australian Family Law: The Contemporary Context* (Oxford University Press, 2nd ed, 2015) ch 5. For the wider policy issues, see also Suellen Murray and Anastasia Powell, *Domestic Violence: Australian Public Policy* (Australian Scholarly Publishing, 2011).

77   It is notable that the evidence shows that women are most vulnerable to violence during pregnancy and following separation: Phillips and Vandenbroek, above n 74, 8.

78   Ibid 9–10. See also 8–12, where the report discusses the particular circumstances of younger women, women living in remote and rural areas, women with disabilities, and women from culturally and linguistically diverse backgrounds who may be experiencing violence.

79   For the following argument see, eg, David Peterson del Mar, *What Trouble I Have Seen: A History of Violence Against Wives* (Harvard University Press, 1996) 1–8.

or that men who are subjected to violence do not suffer.[80] Nor is it a denial of the existence of violence in same-sex relationships or elder abuse perpetrated by carers or other family members.[81] However, if we are to avoid the trap of treating the actions of everyone in society as the same and thereby subscribe to the principle of formal equality as the only legitimate way of understanding violence, it needs to be acknowledged that male violence against women is a societal problem of a different order.[82]

More specifically, the repeated claims that family is the cornerstone of our society and the unarticulated assumptions about the desirability of the nuclear family exist side by side with the prevalence of violence against women and children. This is in part because the heterosexual marriage continues to be a patriarchal arrangement, with the family based on a nuclear model of man, woman and child. The fundamental issue for us is that such a family obscures the cost of child rearing. In a slightly different context, Dolan argues that marital conflict is rooted in the models of marriage inherited from early modern England.[83] She describes these models of marriage as hierarchy, as fusion and as contract between a man and a woman. However, her claim is that the hierarchy of the marriage relationship has never been resolved. Indeed, it is often explained away as a natural consequence of gender differences. She explains that we may no longer maintain gender differences so strictly, but this does not mean that the patriarchal marriage has transformed into an equal and companionate union. A critique of the family in the 20th century (and now the 21st century) requires an acknowledgement of the incomplete project of meeting the demands of women for equality within family relationships. In Dolan's terms, it requires an open acknowledgement that the family continues to depend on possessive individualism on the one hand, and on familial selflessness on the other. Dolan describes this notion of marriage as an economy of scarcity, as this conception can only accommodate one 'individual'.[84]

---

80   This is an issue that men's rights group 'One in Three' pursues, but in stressing the experience of violence by men, they significantly downplay the violence experienced by women at the hands of men: Male Family Violence Prevention Association, *No To Violence: Response to the One in Three Organisation's Comments About Male Victims* <http://ntv.org.au/wp-content/uploads/141125-senate-dv-inquiry-NTV-1in3campaign-response.pdf>.

81   See Catherine Donovan et al, *Comparing Domestic Abuse in Same Sex and Heterosexual Relationships* (2006) <http://www.equation.org.uk/wp-content/uploads/2012/12/Comparing-Domestic-Abuse-in-Same-Sex-and-Heterosexual-relationships.pdf>; Marianne James, 'Abuse and Neglect of Older People' [1994] 37 *Family Matters*.

82   See Russell P Dobash and Rebecca E Dobash, 'Women's Violence to Men in Intimate Relationships: Working on a Puzzle' (2004) 44(3) *British Journal of Criminology* 324 for a careful analysis of a number of empirical studies claiming that men and women are equally violent in personal relationships. The authors find that women are more often the targets of violence. See also Michael Johnson, 'Conflict and Control: Gender Symmetry and Asymmetry in Domestic Violence' (2006) 12(11) *Violence Against Women* 1003, where it is argued that it is important to distinguish between four major types of intimate partner violence because they have different causes, patterns of development and consequences, and need different kinds of intervention. See also Michael Johnson, *A Typology of Domestic Violence: Intimate Terrorism, Violent Resistance, and Situational Couple Violence* (Northeastern University Press, 2008).

83   Frances E Dolan, *Marriage and Violence: The Early Modern Legacy* (University of Pennsylvania Press, 2008).

84   Ibid 6, where the author is agreeing with the analyses of C B McPherson and Wendy Brown. See ibid 1–25 for the complete argument.

She adopts the concept of familial selflessness as used by Brown,[85] and claims that this concept can be extended to expose how women's contributions as caregivers are legitimised and normalised in such conceptions of the family. It is the presence of children and the need to care for them that creates the 'need' for selflessness. Even though both parents may contribute to the rearing of children (and even to domestic household chores), they do so in different ways. Women's roles create economic dependence, but for most women it is normalised by various arguments that prioritise their roles as carers. We rely on this analysis to stress that the care functions and economic dependence of women need to be at the forefront of any discussion of family violence. It is also the reason that violence against children cannot be treated as though it occurs independently of the violence against women/mothers. This is not an argument that the economic dependence of women is the only explanation for the occurrence of family violence, but it is most directly relevant in the context of the FLA.

It is also necessary to acknowledge that experiences of gendered violence are not uniform and that, in particular, the complex intersections of race and gender mean that it has very different meanings for differently situated women, such as Aboriginal and Torres Strait Islander women. In this context, for instance, it is argued that there can be no justice without healing.[86] However, the FLA, in keeping with its gender (and race) neutral language, makes no specific provisions for the particular needs of Indigenous women who experience family violence.[87] At a more fundamental level, their experiences of colonisation mean that it is very difficult for Aboriginal and Torres Strait Islander women to trust state institutions such as the police or the law in general because they historically symbolise colonial domination and continue to be instrumental in maintaining colonial power and control.[88] Critical analyses that identify law as an institution that makes it possible for the colonial domination of Aboriginal and Torres Strait Islander peoples are not part of the mainstream legal scholarship or ways of conceptualising law.[89] And, even if they were, this would raise issues about how the law could respond. Presumably women would be central in directing any reform agenda. However, as Nancarrow has shown, Indigenous and non-Indigenous women have very different responses about how to address violence within relationships;[90] this could

---

85   Wendy Brown, *States of Injury: Power and Freedom in Late Modernity* (Princeton University Press, 1995) especially ch 6.

86   Dorinda Cox et al, 'No Justice Without Healing: Australian Aboriginal People And Family Violence' (2009) 30 *Australian Feminist Law Journal* 151. See also Victoria Hovane, *White Privilege and the Fiction of Colour Blindness: Implication for Best Practice Standards for Aboriginal Victims of Family Violence* (Australian Domestic and Family Violence Clearinghouse, *Newsletter* 8, 2007) 11.

87   For an analysis of NSW domestic violence laws and experiences of Indigenous women, see Belinda Russon, *The Law of Equality and Justice: Evaluating Domestic Violence Outcomes for Aboriginal Women in New South Wales* (PhD Thesis, University of New South Wales, 2014).

88   Melissa Lucashenko, 'Violence Against Indigenous Women: Public and Private Dimensions' in Sandy Cook and Judith Bessant (eds), *Women's Encounters with Violence: Australian Experiences* (Sage Publications, 1997) 147.

89   See, eg, Irene Watson, 'First Nations Stories, Grandmother's Law: Too Many Stories to Tell' in Heather Douglas et al (eds), *Australian Feminist Judgments: Righting and Rewriting Law* (Hart Publishing, 2015) 46 for the argument that it is not possible to write a feminist judgment from an Indigenous perspective so long as the state legal system continues its dominance. See also Joan Kimm, *A Fatal Conjunction: Two Laws Two Cultures* (Federation Press, 2004).

90   Heather Nancarrow, 'In Search of Justice for Domestic and Family Violence: Indigenous and Non-Indigenous Australian Women's Perspectives' (2006) 10(1) *Theoretical Criminology* 87.

mean that the existing colonial hierarchy would merely take on a new form. It is important to acknowledge how far-reaching these issues are, and that the way they are constructed is central to understanding them. However, keeping within the much narrower theme of how the FLA addresses violence, it is disappointing but not surprising that the legislation does not acknowledge and make provision for violence as it is experienced differently according to gender and race.[91]

While the occurrence of family violence is a widely acknowledged fact in contemporary times, its causes and possible remedies are debated. The extensive literature in this area spans disciplines and, not surprisingly, the responses to the phenomenon reflect particular disciplinary concerns. Thus, psychologists are likely to address issues related to behaviour and the need for therapy,[92] while sociologists focus more on wider social causes and the need for broader social changes.[93] It is only to be expected that law's focus will be on prevention or making remedies available to the targets of violence. While this compartmentalisation of disciplinary concerns is understandable, it needs to be challenged. Among other things, this could mean that legal responses of necessity have to take into account wider issues of social, economic or psychological causes. This in turn requires a conception of law as an integrated part of the network of other societal institutions that could lead to acknowledging and addressing existing gender hierarchies. Yet ours is a legal system that is dominated by a positivist understanding of law. The jurisprudential implications of conceptualising law independently of other institutions are starkly evident in the legal responses to the phenomenon of family violence. It is a function of such an understanding of law that the legal responses to family violence are primarily about providing remedies to the victims and do not extend to examining how law is implicated in maintaining a hierarchical society.

Legal categories inevitably function to normalise a state of affairs. For instance, asking what is distinctive about family violence and why it needs a specific category of its own rather than being treated as any other violence can make visible the continued valence of the public/private sphere ideology.[94] The use of the concept of family violence within the legal discourse itself legitimises the distinction. This is not an intentional manipulation of legal categories but is nonetheless a function of utilising analytical categories of public and private. Unless this use of analytical categories becomes the central focus of critique, law will keep facilitating the classification of violence among intimates as somehow of a special kind and thus requiring special treatment. In the process, the prevailing gender hierarchies and power imbalances that contribute to the occurrence of violence in intimate relations are rendered invisible in law. More importantly, it absolves legal analysts from

---

91   The contributions the courts make to address the particular issues that arise for Aboriginal and Torres Strait Islander children will be addressed in later chapters.

92   See, eg, Jacquelyn W White, Mary P Koss and Alan E Kazdin (eds), *Violence Against Women and Children, Volume 1: Mapping the Terrain* (American Psychological Association, 2011).

93   See Sylvia Walby, Jude Towers and Brian Francis, 'Mainstreaming Domestic and Gender-Based Violence into Sociology and the Criminology of Violence' (2014) 62 *The Sociological Review* 187 for the argument that social theory does not adequately address three gendered concepts of domestic violence, gender-based violence, and violence against women.

94   There are arguments about the inappropriateness or inability of criminal law to capture the specific harms of intimate violence, but for reasons of space we will not engage in these debates. Our argument is not with the inadequacies of civil remedies but with the conceptualising of domestic violence as a special kind of violence.

linking different responses of the law to various aspects of family relations, making it possible for the analysis of family violence to be treated as a stand-alone issue. The debates over whether providing an adequate response to the presence of family violence requires a civil, a criminal or a human rights law approach remain within such a paradigm. Each of these approaches conceptualises the 'wrong' in a specific way and provides remedies accordingly.[95]

Owing to constraints of space, we can only raise these issues, without further developing the theoretical critique of legal categorisation, but we aim to illustrate some of these issues with respect to the FLA. Therefore, we confine our discussion below to the design of the FLA. As a preliminary issue it is important to note the jurisdictional complexities of the federal and State laws regulating different aspects of family violence.[96] A brief explanation of the State and Commonwealth legal remedies available to targets of violence is followed by a discussion of three aspects of the FLA: its overall emphasis on ADR, the wide discretion of the courts in determining the relevance of conduct in financial and child-related issues, and the move towards emphasising shared care of children after separation. We argue that these aspects of the FLA function cumulatively and individually to exacerbate the vulnerabilities of those experiencing violence in personal relationships.

4.5.1   Remedies for family violence in State, Territory and Commonwealth laws

Theoretically, anyone experiencing family violence could seek a range of remedies – file a complaint for assault in criminal law, seek an injunction against the perpetrator in equity, claim compensation in civil law, or seek a family violence order under statute. In practice, specific domestic/family violence orders are used most often, but we begin with a brief explanation of the remedies in criminal and civil law. One of the consequences of Australia being a federation is that legislative authority for specific matters is divided among the parliaments of the States (and Territories with self-government) on the one hand, and the Commonwealth on the other. Criminal laws relating to family violence and child abuse that constitute criminal offences continue to be governed by State laws and thus these laws are different in each State and Territory. However, not all incidents of family violence constitute criminal offences. For that reason, each jurisdiction has enacted civil remedies – notably,

---

95   For an overview of criminal law remedies and other non-specific remedies, in addition to
      FLA remedies, see Renata Alexander, *Domestic Violence in Australia* (Federation Press, 3rd ed,
      2002). For a review of research on the criminal and civil law responses to domestic violence
      in the United States, see Carol E Jordan, 'Intimate Partner Violence and the Justice System: An
      Examination of the Interface' (2004) 19(12) *Journal of Interpersonal Violence* 1412. For Australia,
      see especially Australian Law Reform Commission, *Family Violence – A National Legal Response*,
      Report No 114 (2010) ch 8; Heather Douglas, 'The Criminal Law's Response to Domestic Violence:
      What's Going On?' (2008) 30(3) *Sydney Law Review* 439. For an argument that strangulation should
      be included as a harm in civil remedies for domestic violence, see Heather Douglas and Robin
      Fitzgerald, 'Strangulation, Domestic Violence and the Legal Response' (2014) 36(2) *Sydney Law
      Review* 231.
96   For a brief account, see Hilary Astor and Rosalind Croucher, 'Fractured Families, Fragmented
      Responsibilities: Responding to Family Violence in a Federal System' (2010) 33(3) *UNSW Law
      Journal* 854.

apprehended violence orders – especially in response to family violence.[97] However, the way these laws interrelate can be quite complex. For instance, federal laws such as the FLA can override State laws, so that a parenting order under the FLA may override an apprehended domestic violence order.[98] Thus, anyone trying to escape family violence faces the complexities of navigating the legal system where State or federal and criminal or civil laws may be relevant in the same case situation.[99] It should, however, be remembered that in practice the State/Territory laws are used more than the federal FLA. This is in part owing to the general view that FLA injunctions are not very useful or effective.[100]

The States and Territories have followed slightly different legislative paths in enacting laws. For example, some have amended the existing Justices Acts or summary procedure laws that cover everyone – not only family members (South Australia, Tasmania and the Australian Capital Territory). Others have enacted specific domestic violence laws (New South Wales, Victoria, Queensland). Others have initially modified Justices Acts, but then enacted specific domestic violence legislation (Western Australia and the Northern Territory). The key relevant legislation is as follows: *Domestic Violence and Protection Orders Act 2008* (ACT); *Crimes (Domestic and Personal Violence) Act 2007* (NSW); *Property (Relationships) Act 1984* (NSW) ss 53–55; *Domestic and Family Violence Act 2007* (NT); *Domestic and Family Violence Protection Act 2012* (Qld); *Intervention Orders (Prevention of Abuse) Act 2009* (SA); *Family Violence Act 2014* (Tas); *Family Violence Protection Act 2008* (Vic); and *Restraining Orders Act 1997* (WA).

Some of the common features of the State/Territory laws are that a person or a police officer can apply for an order; a person can seek an order from a court of summary jurisdiction to restrain another person from committing an act of violence; the person against whom such order is made does not have to be present or even know about the order; orders can exclude the assailant from a premises as well as their own residence; and orders can be directed at restraining expected violence or harassment. In most legislation it is possible to seek or make separate orders for the protection of children, but in the discussion below we will primarily refer to adult applicants. We briefly discuss the provisions in the New South Wales legislation to illustrate the main issues.

In New South Wales the two pieces of legislation that are utilised in applications related to family violence are the *Crimes (Domestic and Personal Violence) Act 2007* (NSW) ('CDPVA')

---

97   See above n 95. Casting family violence remedies as civil remedies has its own problems. It could be taken to signify that the really serious violence is regulated by criminal law while civil law is sufficient to deal with the less serious violence that takes place in family contexts. See for an example of this argument Jocelyn Scutt, *Women and The Law* (Law Book Co, 1990) 451; also discussed in ALRC, above n 95, ch 8.

98   FLA ss 68P, 68Q.

99   These issues are analysed comprehensively in ALRC, above n 95 and New South Wales Law Reform Commission, *Family Violence – A National Legal Response*, Report No 128 (2010).

100   There are various explanations for this, including that the police are more used to enforcing State legislation; the Family Court and the police do not communicate very well; and both police and parties have to be aware of injunction powers to enforce them effectively. See also Geoff Monahan and Lisa Young, *Family Law in Australia* (LexisNexis, 7th ed, 2009); and a collection of articles in the special issue of the (2010) 33(3) *UNSW Law Journal*. See also for an overview of the enforcement provisions of all relevant legislation Annabel Taylor et al, *Domestic and Family Violence Protection Orders in Australia: An Investigation of Information Sharing and Enforcement: State of Knowledge Paper* (Australian National Research Organisation for Women's Safety, 2015).

and the *Property (Relationships) Act 1984* (NSW) ss 53–55. When first enacted, the CDPVA dealt with violence in domestic relationships but now it extends to any kind of personal violence. Thus, it provides for two kinds of orders: apprehended domestic violence orders ('ADVO') and apprehended personal violence orders. Moreover, the definition of 'domestic relationship' is very wide and includes people in domestic but other than sexual relationships (s 5).

The court has wide discretion to make an ADVO if on the balance of probabilities it is satisfied that a person fears or has reasonable grounds to fear the commission of an act of personal violence, intimidating conduct or stalking by the other person. In specified circumstances the court does not even need the balance of probability test to make the order (s 16(2)). The application can be made by the person in need of protection or the police (s 48), but in certain circumstances the police must apply for an ADVO (s 49).

The court may make provisional, interim or final orders. It has the power to impose restrictions and prohibitions on the behaviour of the defendant that it considers necessary and desirable to ensure the safety and protection of the person needing such protection (s 35). These prohibitions and conditions are in addition to the mandatory provisions of every ADVO that prohibit behaviour that is assaulting, molesting, harassing, threatening or otherwise interfering with the protected person, intimidating conduct, or stalking the protected person or another person who is in a domestic relationship with the protected person (s 36). The police have the power of arrest and the final ADVO can carry with it the warrant of arrest (s 88). A breach of the ADVO is a criminal offence (s 14).[101]

4.5.2   Remedies for family violence under the FLA

The FLA defines family violence in s 4AB(1) as 'violent, threatening or other behaviour by a person that coerces or controls a member of the person's family (the family member), or causes the family member to be fearful'. Examples of family violence are included in s 4AB(2). It is mentioned separately that a child is exposed to family violence if the child sees or hears family violence or otherwise experiences the effects of family violence (s 4AB(3)). A non-exhaustive list of examples of situations that constitute a child being exposed to family violence is included in s 4AB(4). There are extensive obligations of the parties and other personnel as well as the courts to report and respond to allegations of family violence.[102]

The specific remedies for family violence under the FLA are injunctions for married people (s 114), for those in de facto relations (s 90SS) and for children (s 68B). In the following discussion, we use s 114 as the illustration but roughly the same observations can be made with respect to s 90SS (with some concessions as identified below). The first point to make is that an injunction is a discretionary remedy that the court decides to grant or withhold.[103] Moreover, the court can decide to 'make such order or grant such injunction as it considers

---

101   In New South Wales, it is also possible for an applicant to use the *Property (Relationships) Act 1984* (NSW) pt V provisions to obtain an order for personal protection, restraining the other person from entering the place where the applicant lives or works or an order related to the occupancy of the premises where the partners reside.

102   For example, s 60CF(1), which places the onus on the parties to report violence to the court; ss 60J(1)–(2), 67ZBB(3) and many other sections.

103   *Fedele v Fedele* [2008] FamCA 836.

proper' in the matter before it. A preliminary requirement is that proceedings under s 114(1) must involve circumstances arising out of the marital relationship.

Section 114(1) has two parts: the first gives a general power to courts (in certain circumstances) exercising jurisdiction under the FLA to make such order or grant such injunction as it considers proper. The second part contains a non-exhaustive list of six purposes for which an injunction may be granted.[104] Under s 114(2), an injunction may be granted for the purpose of relieving a party to a marriage from any obligation to perform marital services or render conjugal rights.

A person wishing to restrain marital violence can proceed not only under s 114 but also under any relevant State or Territory law that has been prescribed (s 114AB(1)).[105] However, if a person takes action under any prescribed State/Territory law, they cannot subsequently start proceedings under s 114 or s 68B (s 114AB(2)). The relative ease of using the State/Territory laws has in part to do with the enforcement mechanisms. As explained above, the police can arrest a person who breaches a court order, but the injunctions under the FLA have to be enforced. Earlier, the Family Court was given discretion to attach a power of arrest to an injunction order. However, s 114AA now provides for an automatic power of arrest on the breach of an injunction in certain circumstances.[106] Moreover, a police officer can arrest without a warrant in certain circumstances.[107] Nevertheless, these FLA remedies are still not utilised widely.

An injunction for personal protection of a party to marriage (s 114(1)(a)) includes non-molestation-type orders to be issued for the protection of one party to a marriage. It can only be issued against the other party to a marriage and not against a third party.[108] It cannot be issued for the personal protection of, for example, adults in a de facto relationship, flatmates or siblings, as s 114(1) requires the application to be a matrimonial cause.[109] The terms of the

---

104   For the personal protection of a party to the marriage; the restraint of a party to the marriage from entering or remaining in the matrimonial home or from a specified area; restraint of a party to the marriage from entering the place of work of the other party to the marriage; the protection of the marital relationship; for the purposes relating to the property of a party to the marriage; and for the purposes relating to the use or occupancy of the matrimonial home.

105   *Family Law Regulations 1984* (Cth) reg 19. For s114AB of the FLA, the following are prescribed laws: (1) the *Crimes (Domestic and Personal Violence) Act 2007* (NSW); (2) the *Family Violence Protection Act 2008* (Vic); (3) the *Domestic and Family Violence Protection Act 2012* (Qld) and the *Peace and Good Behaviour Act 1982* (Qld); (4) the *Restraining Orders Act 1997* (WA) pts 1–6; (5) the *Intervention Orders (Prevention of Abuse) Act 2009* (SA); (6) the *Family Violence Act 2004* (Tas) and the *Justices Act 1959* (Tas) pt XA; (7) the *Domestic Violence and Protection Orders Act 2008* (ACT); (8) the *Domestic and Family Violence Act 2007* (NT); and (9) the *Domestic Violence Act 1995* (NT).

106   An injunction under the FLA allows the automatic power of arrest to the police only when it states that it is for the personal protection of a party or child.

107   s 114 AA(1) allows this in circumstances where the action causes or threatens to cause bodily harm to the person for whose protection the injunction is granted or that person is harassed, molested or stalked.

108   For example, in *Oates v Crest* [2008] FamCAFC 29 (Boland J) an appeal was upheld against an order obtained by the husband preventing the wife from coming within 100 metres of a house in which his new partner was living. It was found that the order could not be made because it was not for the personal protection of the husband.

109   Renata Alexander, 'Family Violence' in Springvale Legal Centre (ed), *Lawyers Practice Manual Victoria* (Thomson Reuters, 2015) 208–1059, [2.8.313].

order can use broad concepts, but an effort should be made not to be vague or use words that are too broad.[110]

The other main ground for granting an injunction in family violence-related applications is an exclusive occupation order. It has been accepted from the beginning that an order for exclusive occupation of the matrimonial home cannot be made lightly and should not be made on the basis of the balance of convenience.[111] In *Davis* the Court enumerated a non-exhaustive list of factors that may be taken into account and, among other things, held that an injunction to allow one party the exclusive use of the house may take into account the 'conduct of one party which may justify the other party in leaving the home or in asking for the expulsion from the home of the first party'.[112] Moreover, it was held in *In the Marriage of O'Dea* that an order for exclusive occupation should be made only if it is not practicable or reasonable for the parties to remain living in the same house.[113] However, there is still a strident opinion that such orders are used inappropriately and to gain a collateral purpose rather than to deal with domestic violence.[114]

It is perhaps not surprising that there is not a lot of case law on the use of injunctions under the FLA as a family violence remedy. However, in the FLA (and to a lesser extent in State and Territory laws) the important question is whether, in excluding the other party from the home, the court should pursue the principle of 'welfare' of the applicant or 'justice' to the ousted party. The implied question here is: what if, as can happen, the applicant is 'at fault' also? The wider issue for family law is whether it is to be used as a law pursuing values of welfare or justice.[115] Moreover, as we discuss below, a real problem is that very often violence is not raised and, even if it is, it is not easily proven in family law proceedings.

4.5.3   The FLA and family violence

This leads us to the issue of whether negative behaviour should be equated with fault. There seem to be no principled arguments about whether conduct should be relevant and, if so, what kind of conduct would be relevant in FLA matters such as those that relate to granting injunctions for sole occupancy of the home (above); or for that matter in determining property, spousal maintenance or child-related disputes. All of them have a bearing on how the discourse of family violence as a special kind of violence is constructed. In the next two sections, we discuss the implications of the FLA's emphasis on ADR and how the courts and/ or the legislature deal with the presence of violence in property and child cases.

---

110   *In the Marriage of English* [1986] FLC 91-729 (Fogarty, Murray and Ross-Jones JJ), where it was said that using the concept 'annoy' would make the order too vague and difficult to enforce.

111   *In the Marriage of Davis* [1976] FLC 90-062 (Evatt CJ, Pawley and Ellis JJ); endorsed by the Full Court in *Fedele v Fedele* [2008] FamCA 836. See also *In the Marriage of Dean* [1977] FLC 90-213; *In the Marriage of Jolly* [1978] FLC 90-458; *In the Marriage of Aly* [1978] FLC 90-519; *In the Marriage of Healey* [1979] FLC 90-706.

112   *In the Marriage of Davis* [1976] FLC 90-062, 75 309.

113   (1980) 6 Fam LR 675 (Murray J).

114   See for an example of this kind of writing in the context of State domestic violence orders Augusto Zimmermann, *'Without Restraint': the Abuse of Domestic Violence Orders* (14 March 2015) *News Weekly*, 9 <http://newsweekly.com.au/article.php?id=56865>.

115   Asked in the context of English family law but equally relevant to Australia. See Andrew Bainham, 'Men and Women Behaving Badly' (2001) 21(2) *Oxford Journal of Legal Studies* 219, 224ff.

4.5.3.1   Emphasis on FDR and family violence provisions

As we saw in Chapter 2, the FLA incorporates an institutional design that provides for the invocation of the jurisdiction of the courts only after ADR of various kinds has been explored. Thus, the overall message of the legislation is that (depending on the kind of dispute) the preferred method of resolving family disputes is through mediation, arbitration and counselling, if needed. Given this emphasis on alternative dispute settlement, the question for present purposes is how someone subjected to violence can negotiate with the perpetrator. The formal answer that the FLA makes exceptions for relationships involving violence (particularly in parenting disputes) is only part of the story. This approach does not address how unreported violence affects the targets; that effective screening is difficult; that it relies on professionals (mediators or counsellors) to identify the presence of violence, but they may not be equipped to do so; and that the wider structural impediments steer in the direction of private settlement.

The trauma of family violence is debilitating on many fronts. In a study about the difficulties of navigating the family law system, one participant observed that it was very difficult to go through the repeated mediation sessions with a person who had 'pushed me around for fifteen years, was now sitting across the table and glaring at me and I had to articulate what I wanted'.[116] The same report points out that the system seems unable to comprehend the traumatic effect of abuse that in turn affects the ability of the targets of violence to participate in negotiations and mediation. So too the ALRC report, *Family Violence*, acknowledges the difficulties faced by targets of violence when there are no formal reports or other kinds of tangible evidence indicating the existence of violence.[117] When violence is not formally reported or detected, the targets of violence end up in very challenging situations. Krieger argues that mandated mediation forces the target of violence to collaborate with the perpetrator and should itself be recognised as a form of structural abuse.[118] The legislative exclusion from mediation for cases involving violence is dependent on the reliable identification of such violence, which, as Astor argues, is a very difficult task.[119]

The point we wish to emphasise is the difficulty of identifying family violence in the present cultural context, where it is silenced and made invisible. We acknowledge that efforts at better screening are constantly being made. One such initiative is the development of the DOORS framework.[120] Although there are ongoing government efforts to address the social policy issues, as illustrated in the establishment of the National Council to Reduce

---

116   Lesley Lang, 'No Way to Live: Women's Experiences of Negotiating the Family Law System in the Context of Domestic Violence' (Research Paper, The Benevolent Society, 2010) 12.

117   ALRC, above n 95, 831–3.

118   Sarah Krieger, 'The Dangers of Mediation in Domestic Violence Cases' (2002) 8(2) *Cardozo Women's Law Journal* 235.

119   Hilary Astor, 'Violence and Family Mediation: Policy' (1994) 8 *Australian Journal of Family Law* 3. See also Hilary Astor, 'The Weight of Silence: Talking About Violence in Family Mediation' in Margaret Thornton (ed), *Public and Private: Feminist Legal Debates* (Oxford University Press, 1995) 174.

120   Jennifer McIntosh, *The Family Law DOORS: A New Whole-of-Family Approach to Risk Screening* (AIFS, Child Family Community Australia, 2013). This initiative is supported by the Attorney-General's Department, Commonwealth Government.

Violence against Women and their Children,[121] it is also unfortunately true that resources to deal with the effects of violence are in dwindling supply.[122]

The powerlessness of the targets of violence is exacerbated by the legislative design that relies on formal reporting of violence or on the ability of the professionals (mediators at the first instance) to identify the occurrence of violence.[123] The legislative response to the social reality that a lot of violence is not reported in any formal manner includes broadening the definition of violence; making specific exemptions (especially in child-related disputes) for an applicant exposed to violence from attending family dispute resolution ('FDR'); and imposing responsibilities on family dispute practitioners and lawyers to screen cases where violence is present (see Chapter 2). Thus, the FLA can legitimately claim that it responds to the presence of violence by excluding such relationships from mandatory FDR. Despite this, it is widely reported that the majority of people who attend family relationship centres ('FRCs') have experienced violence in their former relationships.[124]

This requires us to address the design issues in the legislation differently. For example, the Explanatory Memorandum to the 2011 Bill that introduced a wide definition of family violence states that 'the definition is intended to cover a wide range of behaviour including assault, sexual assault or other sexually abusive behaviour, stalking, emotional and psychological abuse, and economic abuse. The definition encompasses patterns of family violence and single violent events.'[125] However, if for cultural and structural reasons such violence is not reported or substantiated by targets, the broad definition cannot assist them. It would require additional resources to detect the violence, but as the legislation stands it does not provide the mechanisms for this.[126]

It is true that in their contact with FRCs or equivalent organisations the parties have to be screened and assessed for the presence of violence. But it is also accepted that more effort is required to develop mechanisms that can better screen for domestic violence.[127] While the

---

121   See the National Council to Reduce Violence against Women and their Children, above n 75 for the council's 12-year plan.

122   For a discussion of some of the effects of such practices in New South Wales, see, eg, Wendy Bacon, 'Updated: The Gutting and Gagging of Feminist Women's Refuges', *New Matilda* (online), 25 July 2014 <https://newmatilda.com/2014/07/25/updated-gutting-and-gagging-feminist-womens-refuges>.

123   Research shows that domestic violence is an under-reported phenomenon: see Enrique Gracia, 'Unreported Cases of Domestic Violence against Women: Towards an Epidemiology of Social Silence, Tolerance, and Inhibition' (2004) 58 *Journal of Epidemiology and Community Health* 536. See also Debbie Kirkwood and Mandy McKenzie, 'Family Dispute Resolution and Family Violence in the New Family Law System' (2008) 19(3) *Australasian Dispute Resolution Journal* 170.

124   See, eg, Rae Kaspiew et al, *Evaluation of the 2006 Family Law Reforms* (AIFS, 2009) Table 4.15.

125   See, eg, the Explanatory Memorandum at point 16: Explanatory Memorandum, Family Law Legislation Amendment (Family Violence and Other Measures) Bill 2011.

126   It is of course true that there is a lot of institutional recognition of the inappropriateness of mediation in violent relations. See Susan Gribben, 'Violence and Family Mediation: Practice' (1994) 8 *Australian Journal of Family Law* 22; Alastair Nicholson, 'Mediation in the Family Court' (1991) 65(5) *Law Institute Journal* 61; Family Law Council of Australia, *Report on Family Mediation* (1992); *Family Violence Plan* (3 May 2016) Federal Circuit Court of Australia <http://www.federalcircuitcourt.gov.au/wps/wcm/connect/fccweb/family-law-matters/family-violence/family-violence-plan/family+violence-plan>.

127   Jane Murphy and Robert Rubinson, 'Domestic Violence and Mediation: Responding to the Challenges of Crafting Effective Screens' (2005) 39(1) *Family Law Quarterly* 53.

FLA specifically mentions that FDR is not suitable in cases involving violence, it has virtually nothing to say about screening. The task of screening is made more difficult in the absence of agreement about who should be assessed and why; what behaviour actually constitutes family violence and how it should be assessed; whether screening and assessment of violence are different tasks; who should perform these tasks; and what kind of training they need.[128]

Similarly, the skills of various professionals asked to screen for violence are questioned in the literature. Thus, Rhoades illustrates how the mediators (family dispute resolution practitioners or 'FDRPs' under the FLA) and lawyers adopt, or are perceived to adopt, differing approaches in identifying safety risks.[129] In this study, Rhoades inter alia identifies the concerns of mediators that lawyers are not well equipped to detect violence. But whether the mediators are well trained for this task is also a matter of some debate. The system of training and accreditation for mediators is developing, but the philosophies that inform this training need much more public debate.[130] Moreover, questions remain about whether there is any way of judging what the mediators are doing in practice. It is the very nature of mediation that makes empirical evidence of such practices difficult to collect. Both of these issues illustrate how family law manages to privatise disputes as we simply have no way of knowing how legally enforced FDR operates. Thus, the skills of those asked to screen for the presence of violence is an important issue, but the privatisation of violence by the legal system ought to be a more serious concern.

A further complication results from the structure of the legal system, which makes legal aid inaccessible for a lot of separating couples. This presents a structural hurdle to parties who cannot afford legal representation and is an outcome of policy decisions in different locales that come together to compel a vulnerable parent to 'settle' with a spouse irrespective of the merits of the agreement. This is also the experience of some FRCs, which report that the FDRPs are well aware of their role in facilitating the parties entering into an agreement that is not coerced. However, since there is an absence of avenues of legal representation for their clients, they do not suggest litigation as a realistic option. Thus, the possibility that a vulnerable parent would enter into an agreement that is not

---

128   Elly Robinson and Lawrie Moloney, 'Family Violence: Towards a Holistic Approach to Screening and Risk Assessment in Family Support Services' (2010) 17 *Australian Family Relationships Clearinghouse* <https://aifs.gov.au/cfca/sites/default/files/publication-documents/b017.pdf>. See also Alexandria Zylstra, 'Mediation and Domestic Violence: A Practical Screening Method for Mediators and Mediation Program Administrators' [2001] (2) *Journal of Dispute Resolution* 253 for a similar assessment for screening methods in the US legal system.

129   Helen Rhoades, 'Mandatory Mediation of Family Disputes: Reflections from Australia' (2010) 32(2) *Journal of Social Welfare and Family Law* 183.

130   See Rachael Field, 'Using the Feminist Critique of Mediation to Explore "the Good, the Bad and the Ugly": Implications for Women of the Introduction of Mandatory Family Dispute Resolution in Australia' (2006) 20(5) *Australian Journal of Family Law* 45. Over the years, we have seen the mediation profession go from being largely unregulated to being much more regulatied. The FLA now requires FDRPs to be accredited (s 10A). See the requirements for accreditation at *Becoming a Family Dispute Resolution Practitioner*, Attorney-General's Department, Australian Government <https://www.ag.gov.au/FamiliesAndMarriage/Families/FamilyDisputeResolution/Pages/Becomingafamilydisputeresolutionpractitioner.aspx>.

freely negotiated becomes real.[131] The federal government has made well-intentioned efforts to make legal assistance available at the initial stages of the process in the FRCs.[132] In the context of our argument, this approach demonstrates an acknowledgement of the importance of upholding legal entitlements, while simultaneously demonstrating a reluctance to enforce those legal entitlements by emphasising that FDR is the preferred method of dispute resolution.

In addition to these structural hurdles are the well-documented effects of power imbalances owing to the effects of existing gender hierarchies in society. The assurance given in the legislation that FDR is not appropriate where violence exists[133] does not capture the debilitating effects of violence that is not even reported and in all probability cannot be 'proved'.[134] In a different context – of restorative justice being offered to the victims of crime – it has been argued that the incompatibility of the interests of victim and perpetrator needs to be acknowledged.[135] This insight applies equally to dispute settlement through mediation where violence is present but has not been formally reported. Moreover, if the different sets of empirical evidence are put together and respectively show that a greater majority of separated partners acknowledge the existence of family or partner violence *and* that most disputes in family law get settled out of court, it is worth asking how many of these settled cases involve the silencing of the targets of violence.[136]

---

131   Ringwood Family Relationship Centre, Submission to Victoria Legal Aid, *Family Law Legal Aid Services Review* (2015).

132   See the initiative by the federal government to make such legal services available at FRCs: R McClelland, 'Building Better Partnerships Between Family Relationship Centres and Legal Assistance Services' (Media Release, 4 December 2009). See also Lawrie Moloney et al, *Evaluation of the Family Relationship Centre Legal Assistance Partnerships Program, Final Report* (AIFS, 2011). More generally, Commonwealth funding priorities for family law services are with respect to (1) matters involving allegations of family violence; (2) matters where the safety or welfare of children is at risk; (3) matters involving complex issues about the living arrangements, relationships and financial support of children; and (4) assisting people with property settlement matters if they are experiencing financial disadvantage or are at risk of homelessness. For legal aid commissions, the representation of children in family law proceedings and family dispute resolution processes should also be a focus. Legal aid commissions determine the financial eligibility of applicants, which is usually (though not always) dependent on an income and assets test. Council of Australian Governments, *National Partnership Agreement on Legal Assistance* (1 July 2015), sch B 1, 3–4 <https://www.ag.gov.au/LegalSystem/Legalaidprogrammes/Documents/NationalPatnershipAgreementOnLegalServices.pdf>.

133   s 60I(9)(b)(iii)–(iv).

134   Anne Bottomley, 'What is Happening to Family Law? A Feminist Critique of Conciliation' in Julia Brophy and Carol Smart (eds), *Women-in-Law: Explorations in Law, Family, and Sexuality* (Routledge, 1985) 162; Pauline Bryan, 'Killing Us Softly: Divorce Mediation and the Politics of Power' (1992) 40(2) *Buffalo Law Review* 441; Field, above n 130; Andree G Gagnon, 'Ending Mandatory Divorce Mediation for Battered Women' (1992) 15 *Harvard Women's Law Review* 272. For an argument that women's concerns in mediation can be adequately addressed, see Claire Downey, 'Family Law Mediation: Compromising Justice for Women?' (2000) 8 *Women Against Violence: An Australian Feminist Journal* 45.

135   See Julie Stubbs, 'Relations of Domination and Subordination: Challenges for Restorative Justice in Responding to Domestic Violence' (2010) 33(3) *UNSW Law Journal* 970.

136   John De Maio et al, *Survey of Recently Separated Parents: A Study of Parents Who Separated Prior to the Implementation of the Family Law Amendment (Family Violence and Other Measures) Act 2011* (2012) Attorney-General's Department <https://www.ag.gov.au> (widely known as the 'SRSP 2012 Report'). In a slightly different context, it is argued that the victims of violence have both survival needs and justice needs. See Judith Herman, 'Justice from the Victim's Perspective' (2005) 11(5) *Violence Against Women* 571.

The extremely debilitating effects of insisting on mediation without the certainty of detecting violence lead to a recognition, in the words of one commentator, that:

> It is time to recognize that the entrapment of women in personal life is not primarily 'domestic,' in that it is rooted in sexual politics, nor mainly about 'violence.' CC [Conflict and Control] involves the violation of rights that are so basic to the conduct of our everyday lives, so critical to our capacity to imagine ourselves as autonomous and free, that it is difficult to conceive of personhood or citizenship apart from them.[137]

If the FLA were not so insistent on prioritising FDR, one possible option could be to suggest, as others have done, that the choice of having mediation should be left to the person experiencing violence; she, with appropriate support, could decide whether mediation would actually give her better control over her future.[138] The broader design of the FLA in the provisions relating to financial matters and child-related matters similarly significantly affects the possibility of a dependent spouse or partner leaving a violent relationship, as we discuss next.

4.5.3.2 Judicial and legislative approaches to property and children at the end of a violent relationship

As discussed above, a distinctive feature of the FLA is the introduction of no-fault divorce,[139] but the FLA also has provisions for a court to make orders with respect to the property of the parties. Even though under the earlier MCA, the court was authorised to settle any property on the wife (s 86), in the overall scheme of that legislation this was understood as providing for the maintenance of the spouse (and children) at the end of a marriage. It was the FLA that introduced the idea that the property of the parties could be distributed between them partly based on their respective contributions to the property. While this was a major innovation of the FLA, the court has the ultimate discretion to determine whether to make a property order if sought by one of the parties. The effect of an order can be to transfer the property held by one party to the other party (see Chapter 5).

Although these provisions appear progressive in acknowledging each party's contributions, particularly of a non-financial nature, to the property, one consequence of these provisions is that a woman in a long-term marriage or relationship and without property in her own name can find that she must rely on the benevolence of the court to decide whether she should get a share of the family property. This uncertainty about her entitlements (if any) can only exacerbate the vulnerability of a woman trying to leave a violent relationship. When combined with the legislative emphasis on ADR, it creates a situation where the woman entering into mediation and negotiations does not have a clear bargaining

---

137   Evan Stark, 'Commentary on Johnson's "Conflict and Control: Gender Symmetry and Asymmetry in Domestic Violence"' (2006) 12(11) *Violence Against Women* 1019, 1024.

138   Nancy Ver Steegh, 'Yes, No, and Maybe: Informed Decision Making About Divorce Mediation in the Presence of Domestic Violence' (2003) 9 *William and Mary Journal of Women and the Law* 145. See Katrina Markwick, 'Appropriate Dispute Resolution in Cases of Family Violence and the Collaborative Practice Model' (2015) 5(1) *Family Law Review* 4 for a critique of mediation and for supporting a collaborative law approach.

139   Lawrie Moloney, 'Lionel Murphy and the Dignified Divorce: Of Dreams and Data' in Alan Hayes and Daryl Higgins (eds), *Families, Policy and the Law: Selected Essays on Contemporary Issues for Australia* (AIFS, 2014) 245.

chip as the law lacks the requisite certainty or predictability.[140] Neave argues that a necessary condition for privileging private settlement is that it should recognise that the earning capacity of women is affected by their responsibilities for child rearing.[141] We would add that a fundamental issue is that the woman in a partnership of marriage or marriage-like relationship with no property of her own has no property entitlement as a matter of right. It can thus be little consolation that in some cases the courts, in assessing what distribution of property to give to the woman, are willing to take the presence of violence into account, as explained below.

The courts have grappled with the question of whether conduct of the party who perpetrates violence should be taken into account in assessing contributions to the property. The early cases under the FLA adopted the position that evidence of conduct is irrelevant but financial consequences of conduct could be considered.[142] In an early article Behrens analyses the response of the Family Court to the effects of violence in determining property distribution.[143] She explains that the legislation itself requires that courts should take violence into account because it is relevant to assessing the contributions to the property (negative contributions) and the needs that are created in part by the ongoing violence, and s 75(2)(o) permits any other fact or circumstance to be taken into account if the justice of the case requires it. Moreover, the reluctance of the law to intervene in the details of a marriage is a misplaced argument, as violence is neither a 'lifestyle' choice nor a legitimate way of behaving. Rather, it is a gendered harm and, when left unacknowledged in property distribution decisions, results in the law's maintenance of the status quo in the name of non-intervention.

The Full Court in *Kennon v Kennon* ultimately declined to accept the idea that a negative contribution is made by the violent spouse in these cases.[144] But the Court made it explicit that violent conduct would be a relevant consideration in property distribution, irrespective of whether such conduct had economic consequences or not.[145] We argue that it is a no-win situation when women subjected to violence in their personal relations either have to get some 'compensation' through a property distribution order or have to bear the consequences of financial as well as physical and psychological violence without any recognition.

140   Kathy Mack, 'Alternative Dispute Resolution and Access to Justice for Women' (1995) 17(1) *Adelaide Law Review* 123.

141   Marcia Neave, 'Private Ordering in Family Law – Will Women Benefit?' in Margaret Thornton (ed), *Public and Private: Feminist Legal Debates* (Oxford University Press, 1995) 144, 164.

142   *In the Marriage of Soblusky* (1976) 28 FLR 81; *In the Marriage of Barkley* [1977] FLC 90-216: *In the Marriage of Hack* [1980] FLC 90-886; *In the Marriage of Sheedy* [1979] FLC 90-719; *In the Marriage of Fisher* (1990) 99 FLR 357, the claims of violence were considered not relevant as it was the nature of the contributions rather than their causes that were relevant.

143   Juliet Behrens, 'Domestic Violence and Property Adjustment: A Critique of "No Fault" Discourse' (1993) 7(1) *Australian Journal of Family Law* 9. See also Regina Graycar, 'The Relevance of Violence in Family Law Decision-Making' (1995) 9(1) *Australian Journal of Family Law* 58.

144   (1997) 139 FLR 118 (Fogarty, Baker and Lindenmayer JJ). Discussed in greater detail in Chapter 5.

145   In response Nygh argues that: '[b]y specifically linking the existence of increased contribution to conduct, the Full Court has opened the door to a punitive approach which is not the function of the Family Law Act, and which is not helpful in the long run to the cause of women either': Peter Nygh, 'Family Violence and Matrimonial Property Settlement' (1999) 13(1) *Australian Journal of Family Law* 1. See also Sarah Middleton, 'Matrimonial Property Reform: Legislating for the "Financial Consequences" of Domestic Violence' (2005) 19(1) *Australian Journal of Family Law* 9 for an argument against the *Kennon* approach.

There are arguments for and against such recognition,[146] but they can be assessed only in the wider context of the FLA, which does not give women any defined rights to property. Whatever adjustment is made in the property distribution order, it cannot compensate for the FLA creating a situation where the woman does not have a right to property.

The same discomfort is evident in Altobelli FM's comments that more thought has to be given to the very rationale of *Kennon*-type adjustments to explore whether better, fairer and more transparent methods can be found to deal with issues of conduct in financial matters.[147] The enormity of the inadequacy of the FLA is evident in *Coad & Coad*, where it was found that:

> the injuries inflicted to the wife by the husband made the discharge of her care of the child more onerous than it would otherwise have been. I accept that the wife was seriously disabled in the months after the attempted murder but, very significantly, that she has sustained residual and life long disabilities which cause her pain and interfere with her capacity to work and, presumably, make it more difficult for her to care for the child.[148]

Although the fact that he almost killed her was factored into the assessment of the relevant contributions of the parties to the family property, this approach seems vastly inadequate when the outcome is considered whereby the respective contributions of the parties were divided 40% for the husband and 60% for the wife.

There are various ways in which women could find empowerment in walking out of a difficult and violent situation, but surely securing financial independence must be an important factor. The FLA, however, seems more concerned about 'saving' marriages than declaring that violence in any form is antithetical to family relations. If the FLA were serious about condemning violence in all of its forms, then it would hold the perpetrator responsible for such conduct and make him compensate the target of his violence accordingly. Hypothetically, it could be imagined that the FLA would declare all violence unacceptable and would attach serious penalties to anyone engaging in such conduct. It is worth asking why this kind of discourse is not part of family law debates. There are two issues here: one is to make use of the existing provisions, but the other, and according to us the more significant issue, is to challenge the status quo that accepts that the existence of violence against women is private and inevitable.

Regrettably, this was not the path the legislative developments followed when, as the result of the enactment of the 2006 amendments, the widely available evidence that women are the main victims of violence was turned on its head, and the post-separation nexus between children and their parents was elevated in the form of a rebuttable presumption of shared parental responsibility in the FLA.[149] Briefly, the 2006 amendments were made in response to the report *Every Picture Tells a Story*.[150] The legislation

---

146   See Nell Alves-Perini et al, 'Finding Fault in Marital Property Law: A Little Bit of History Repeating' (2006) 34(3) *Federal Law Review* 377.
147   *Kozovski v Kozovski* [2009] FMCAfam 1014, [77].
148   [2011] FamCA 622, [179] (Bennett J).
149   See ss 60CC, 61DA.
150   House of Representatives Standing Committee on Family and Community Affairs, House of Representatives, *Every Picture Tells a Story: Inquiry into Child Custody Arrangements in the Event of Family Separation* (2003).

emphasises that the involvement of both parents in the child's life is in the child's best interests (s 60CC(2)(a)). The rebuttable legislative presumption that equal shared parental responsibility is in the best interests of the child (s 61DA) serves as the normative standard of the legislation.

The involvement of both parents in their child's life is evidently not a concern of the FLA in an ongoing marriage or relationship, presumably on the basis that how parents bring up their children is a private matter that the law should not interfere with except in extreme circumstances (see Chapter 11). This is not only an example of inconsistency in the responses of the law, but is also an illustration of how the nuclear family form is privileged without the law having to say anything specific about it. The repeated idea in the FLA discourse on the best interests of children – that both parents are necessary for a normal childhood – continues to invoke the nuclear family as the normal family in a strangely uncontested manner.[151] It is only when shared parental responsibility and violence are in conflict that concern that the two-parent family may not be in the best interests of the child has been raised. This is evident in the legislative history of the FLA after the 2006 amendments.

The effects of the 2006 amendments were, among other things, to make it difficult for a parent to claim domestic violence. For example, it was possible for a court to make a costs order against a parent found to have 'knowingly' made false statements (s 117AB). The so-called 'friendly parent' provision, which required the court to consider the extent to which a parent has enabled the child to have an ongoing relationship with the other parent (s 60CC(4)(b)), was also introduced. Not surprisingly, the 2006 amendments led to many reviews, and on the whole the conclusions were that women experiencing domestic violence were being silenced, which eventually resulted in some modifications being made.[152] The 2011 amendments to the FLA that came into force in 2012 made it clear that in cases involving violence the safety of children was to be given priority.[153] The friendly parent provision was repealed and so was s 117AB. The 2011 amendments articulate more strongly than ever before the law's concern to protect children from violence (s 60CC(2A)). But whether these amendments can have positive practical effects is in part affected by the procedural practices of the courts, discussed next.

---

151   Linda Gordon, *Heroes of Their Own Lives: The Politics and History of Family Violence* (University of Illinois Press, 1988) 82–3, especially ch 4, where she traces the construction of discourse about normal families in the context of debates relating to child protection in Boston in the United States. She explains how the concern with protecting children from cruelty was in fact a reflection of deeper concerns over the rise of individualism, the corresponding erosion of domesticity, and inadequate parental authority, and thus of an overarching desire to protect the traditional family.

152   For an empirical assessment of the 2011 amendments, see Rae Kaspiew, Sarah Tayton and Monica Campo, Submission to the Royal Commission into Family Violence, *Issues Paper*, 29 May 2015; Richard Colin Chisholm, *Family Courts Violence Review: A Report* (Attorney-General's Department, 2009) also made recommendations that led to the 2011 amendments.

153   Adiva Sifris and Anna Parker, 'Family Violence and Family Law: Where to Now?' (2014) 4 *Family Law Review* 3. For a critical assessment of various empirical studies of the effects of the 2006 amendments, see Karen Wilcox, *Intersection of Family Law and Family and Domestic Violence* (Australian Domestic and Family Violence Clearinghouse, 2012); Karen Wilcox, *Family Law and Family Violence: Research to Practice* (Australian Domestic and Family Violence Clearinghouse, 2012).

4.5.3.3   Violence and the family courts

The Family Court of Australia faces a formidable task in dealing with disputes involving allegations of family violence and child abuse that cannot be resolved without litigation. The combination of legislative provisions and practice guidelines for the court creates a working environment where the system takes allegations of violence and abuse very seriously. For example, it has introduced a number of procedural innovations, such as the 'less adversarial trial'[154] and the Magellan case management program.[155] Cases involving allegations of serious physical or sexual abuse of children are designated as Magellan cases, and the court overseeing the coordination of such cases is meant to deal with such issues as expeditiously as possible. In other cases of allegations of violence, the court is supposed to take prompt action (s 67ZBB).[156] Moreover, the Family Court and the FCC have developed best practice principles in cases where family violence or abuse is alleged.[157] Yet there is consistent criticism of the courts from both the targets and the perpetrators of violence.[158] Whether it is an issue of institutional design or a deeper systemic issue, it is clear that violence needs more robust scrutiny. While it is commonly accepted that family violence requires more than a legal response, it is also the case that the legal response needs to change. Therefore, it is for the legal thinkers to shift the discourse from only an instrumental view of the law in the direction of a 'no tolerance to violence' stance.

Thus, the question of how anything can change needs to be answered at a deeper level than simply legislative reform or procedural change. It is customary in the literature on law reform to argue that women's and children's voices should be heard by the legal system. However, as Graycar claims, the issues are not only about silencing targets, but also about how their experiences are 'processed' by legal mechanisms, including court personnel.[159] Feminist-led reforms have failed to create situations where women no longer experience violence. Although there are many reasons for this, the fact that women are not the dominant constructors of the discourses of law (including family law and domestic violence discourses) may be a contributing factor. So too, Hunter identifies the specific ways in which members of the legal profession, including judges and magistrates, have been unable to take the enormity of the violence experienced by women into account – including social, cultural and common sense understandings of violence.[160]

---

154   For a review, see Margaret Harrison, *Finding a Better Way: A Bold Departure from the Traditional Common Law Approach to the Conduct of Legal Proceedings* (Family Court of Australia, 2007).

155   Daryl J Higgins, *Co-operation and Coordination: An Evaluation of the Family Court of Australia's Magellan Case-Management Model* (AIFS, 2007) 190.

156   *Family Law Rules 2004* (Cth) r 2.04e. The interconnection that exists between the violence against the partner and its effects on the child becomes evident in these programs. See also *Chapa v Chapa* [2013] FLC 93-538, in which it was found that it is not essential for the court to make specific reference to this section.

157   *Best Practice Principles for Use in Parenting Disputes When Family Violence or Abuse is Alleged* (Family Court of Australia and Federal Magistrates Court of Australia, 3rd ed, 2012) ('Family Violence Best Practice Principles').

158   John Faulks, 'Condemn The Fault and Not The Actor? Family Violence: How the Family Court of Australia Can Deal with the Fault and the Perpetrators' (2010) 33(3) *UNSW Law Journal* 818.

159   Regina Graycar, 'Telling Tales: Legal Stories about Violence Against Women' (1997) 7 *Australian Feminist Law Journal* 79.

160   Rosemary Hunter, 'Narratives of Domestic Violence' (2006) 28(4) *Sydney Law Review* 733.

One of the remedies suggested by Hunter is appropriate legal education at both undergraduate and postgraduate levels. We would like to broaden her suggestion and argue in favour of genuine engagement with the formation of legal knowledge and of acknowledging the inevitable roles of all legal thinkers, whether scholars, judges or legislators, in the construction of law. The constructed nature of legal knowledge is accepted in critical scholarship, but somehow does not find a central place in legal education. The disconnect between critical legal theory and how law is conceptualised in most curricula is time and again manifested in the criticism that the judiciary does not engage with feminist critiques of domestic violence. It is also necessary to take seriously the claims of Aboriginal and Torres Strait Islander scholars that academics, to become true allies, must acknowledge their privileged position and work towards creating knowledges that challenge rather than endorse colonial power structures.[161] We argue that such a rethinking of how various knowledges are constructed about family violence is the main task facing us as family law writers. Unless legal analysts make the connections between the social realities of gender (for example, the care work of women) and race hierarchies (for example, the ongoing colonial project) and their perpetuation by law, we will remain incredulous that so much effort is made to address family or domestic violence and yet not much is achieved.

---

161   Leanne R Simpson, 'Anticolonial Strategies for the Recovery and Maintenance of Indigenous Knowledge' (2004) 28 (3&4) *The American Indian Quarterly* 373, 381.

FINANCIAL RELATIONS

5.1   Introduction

This chapter begins by providing a background to the current property regime in the *Family Law Act 1975* (Cth) ('FLA') and includes an overview of the current statutory provisions and key case law. The interaction between the legislation and the cases will provide an illustration of how family law remains a mechanism for privileging the nuclear family structure and maintaining the gender hierarchy created by the sexual division of labour. This is achieved by the unequal distribution of the costs of relationship breakdown between men and women, while the cost to the state is minimised. This analysis will demonstrate the need for everyone engaged in the law to understand how the family property relations form part of wider financial relations in society. In particular we argue that in family law the issue of financial inequality stems from the FLA's inability to address the issue of attributing an adequate economic value to non-financial work – that is, care work. Our argument is directed at the limitations of the substantive provisions of the legislation as well as those of the judicial interpretations of these provisions, illuminating how both legislators and judges have been unable to adequately address the prevalent social reality of the sexual division of labour.

The most significant legal reform in the family laws of western states has been the granting of a share of property to the financially dependent spouse, usually the wife. A share of property rather than ongoing maintenance is supposed to facilitate a clean break for individuals when their relationships break down. These principles were extended to the regulation of de facto relations, most notably with the introduction of the *Family Law Amendment (De Facto Financial Matters and Other Measures) Act 2008* (Cth).

The changes to the law appear progressive in the way they break with the past by allowing women to claim a share in the family property. This change can be understood as the law upholding the norm that marriages (and other affective unions) are partnerships where the two partners may predominantly perform either financial or caring work. It is a joint undertaking and the law acknowledges that each of them may be entitled to a share of the accumulated property or wealth. Yet the disjuncture between the law's discourse on marriage as a partnership and the unequal gendered financial consequences of marriage breakdown requires explanation. We will demonstrate how the concepts of nuclear family, family as a private institution, and the claims of family law as merely providing a neutral dispute resolution mechanism come together to produce this gendered outcome.

Over time, courts have determined ways of approaching a property distribution between the parties. We provide an overview of these cases and the steps involved in determining a just and equitable property distribution under the FLA. This includes discussion of recent developments such as the inclusion of superannuation within the property pool, and the extension of the FLA jurisdiction to cases of bankruptcy. It also includes a discussion of the way violence is treated in the case law. The potential effects of the recent High Court decision in *Stanford v Stanford* ('*Stanford*') are also examined.[1]

Discussion of the incorporation of superannuation and some bankruptcy issues in property proceedings under the FLA also assists to establish that financial relations within the family context have connections to wider financial arrangements in society and legal actors need to understand these interconnections. Therefore, a study of family law must include an

---

1   (2012) 247 CLR 108.

analysis of how financial dependence is created or maintained through market relations, industrial laws and financial institutions. This analysis will be taken up again in Chapter 10, where
some of the interrelationships between family law and social welfare are discussed. In view of
these legal developments, and the overarching principle in property proceedings – to reach a
'just and equitable' settlement between the parties – the chapter will consider the norm-setting
functions of the law.

5.2   Altering property interests in family law

5.2.1   Philosophical issues

A brief history of matrimonial property law is necessary to contextualise the contemporary
debates about the role of family law in creating a fair society.[2] The common law doctrine of
coverture meant that married women could not own property, and at marriage their property
vested in their husband. Rich families could subvert this legal arrangement through the device
of family trusts. Eventually the Married Women's Property Acts were enacted to meet changing
circumstances in law and society.[3] In part, the need for change was felt because of the legislative enactment of divorce. Once women could be divorced more easily, it became necessary
to also provide for them financially. This was broadly the rationale for spousal maintenance.
Initially, the distinction between spousal and child maintenance was not clear. The subsequent history of spousal maintenance (discussed in Chapter 6) shows that child maintenance
was a contentious issue. Furthermore, the spousal maintenance amounts awarded by courts
were very often unrealistically low. In addition, the enforcement of maintenance orders was
notoriously difficult. Courts, in response to this unsatisfactory state of affairs, began settling
property in the name of the wife as part of the maintenance order.

More recently, the legislative response has been to provide no-fault divorce provisions, as well as provisions for the division of property between the spouses.[4] In part, this
response was informed by the need for the 'clean break' principle to operate effectively.
That is, in keeping with the concept of no-fault divorce, if the parties were expected to finish a non-functioning marriage and start again, it could hardly be feasible that spousal maintenance to a former spouse would continue as well.[5] The combination of no-fault divorce
and the 'clean break' principle in turn invoked the conception of marriage as a voluntary
partnership of two equal individuals, justifying the idea of sharing the gains and burdens of

---

2   The definition of 'matrimonial property' differs in various contexts. We use the term to include
       property subject to the jurisdiction of the FLA in marriages as well as de facto relations.
3   The first to be enacted in England was the *Married Women's Property Act 1870* (UK), but it was
       not until the enactment of the *Married Women's Property Act 1882* (UK) that a system of separate
       property within marital relationships was created.
4   There is extensive scholarship about the possible reasons for this change and the absence of
       feminists in the reform process. See, eg, in the context of the United States Martha Minow and
       Deborah Rhode, 'Reforming the Questions, Questioning the Reforms: Feminist Perspectives
       on Divorce Reform' in Stephen D Sugarman and Herma Hill Kay (eds), *Divorce Reform at the
       Crossroads* (Yale University Press, 1990) 191. In the legislative developments in Australia, it
       is striking that the possibility of dividing the property was not discussed in any detail in the
       Parliament: see Commonwealth, *Parliamentary Debates*, Senate, 26 November 1974, 2744–95.
5   It was also widely acknowledged that recovering child-support payments from fathers was difficult.
       See William J Goode, *World Changes in Divorce Patterns* (Yale University Press, 1993).

a marriage at its end. Division of property between the spouses thus became the preferred device for dealing with financial aspects of marriage breakdown, and family law provisions supporting these arrangements made their appearance in the 1970s in most western industrialised countries.[6]

Correspondingly, the concept of spousal maintenance became less attractive even though it was not abandoned altogether. Instead, it became the secondary consideration in ensuring financial support for a divorced and economically weaker spouse – usually the wife. For example, under the FLA, if a property allocation application under s 79 and a maintenance application under s 72 are made together, the court will determine the matter of property allocation before deciding whether the maintenance application needs to be addressed. This very brief historical sketch of property division in family law, however, needs to be juxtaposed with the contemporary social, economic and philosophical explanations of family law taking it upon itself to override principles of private property by distributing property according to various other principles.

As an initial point, it should be acknowledged that, in the context of family law, most of the issues relating to property ownership and division arise because affective relationships are organised in our societies as partnerships based on mutual support between the two spouses or partners in the context of labour that is divided on a gendered basis.[7] As explained in Chapter 1, the concept of sexual division of labour encompasses different kinds of work done by women both within the family and in the paid workforce. Even though the model of breadwinner husband and stay-at-home wife is no longer the norm, because many women with children now participate in paid work,[8] it is still true that most women with children are the economically weaker partners in marriages or de facto relationships owing to the effects of sexual division of labour.[9] It is this social reality that is obscured by the conception of marriages/relationships as voluntary partnerships between two equal and autonomous individuals. Moreover, women, as the weaker economic partners, can no longer rely on the continuation of the partnership and the availability of the financial benefits of having invested in the relationship.[10] In these circumstances, the tension between the equality and autonomy of the two partners is inevitable.[11] Whether the response of family law can adequately compensate for the effects of the prevailing sexual division of labour is one of the recurring questions addressed below.

6   Mary Ann Glendon, *State, Law and Family: Family Law in Transition in the United States and Western Europe* (North Holland Publishing Co, 1977).

7   Catherine Ross, 'The Division of Labour at Home' (1987) 65(3) *Social Forces* 816.

8   Matthew Gray and Jennifer Baxter, *The Longitudinal Study of Australian Children: Annual Statistical Report 2010* (Growing Up in Australia, 2011), ch 4 <http://www.growingupinaustralia.gov.au/pubs/asr/2010/asr2010d.html#top>.

9   The evidence of gendered hierarchies in contemporary societies is overwhelming. We disagree with the argument that women simply choose to be economically dependent, and instead examine how such hierarchies are legitimised. For patterns of paid work participation by mothers, see Jennifer Baxter, *The Longitudinal Study of Australian Children: Annual Statistical Report 2014* (Growing Up in Australia, 2015), ch 3 <http://www.growingupinaustralia.gov.au/pubs/asr/2014/asr2014c.html>. See also Janeen Baxter, 'The Joys and Justice of Housework' (2000) 34(4) *Sociology* 609.

10   Jacqueline Scott and Shirley Dex, 'Paid and Unpaid Work: Can Policy Improve Gender Inequalities?' in Joanna Miles and Rebecca Probert (eds), *Sharing Lives, Dividing Assets* (Hart Publishing, 2009) 41.

11   Carolyn Vogler, 'Managing Money in Intimate Relationships: Similarities and Differences Between Cohabiting and Married Couples' in Joanna Miles and Rebecca Probert (eds), *Sharing Lives, Dividing Assets* (Hart Publishing, 2009), 61.

To set the background context for the following discussion, it is useful to consider the possible property regimes for married or couple relationships. The Australian Law Reform Commission ('ALRC') in its report on matrimonial property listed the most common property ownership regimes in the family laws of western industrialised societies.[12] The very necessity of devising specific property ownership regimes for family members is indicative of how emotions and finances are not separate or watertight aspects of our lives. Nevertheless, the cultural meanings attached to the companionate aspects of marriage, or other similar relationships, have the effect of diverting attention from the financial aspects of entering into such relationships. The relevant question for lawyers, therefore, is how law can regulate such financial aspects of a relationship in a fair and just manner.

One model is based on maintaining the spouses' property as separate property. The spouses continue to hold property in their individual capacity and the fact of marriage or separation does not have any effect on their property rights. The Married Women's Property Acts that were adopted in jurisdictions such as the United States, England and Australia created this ownership regime. However, in most common law jurisdictions this model has been modified, so that when marriage breaks down the separate property of the spouses can be adjusted by judicial discretion. The spouses continue to own property separately during the marriage, but at separation the law gives authority to the court to adjust the property rights of the two spouses. In contrast, in most civil law jurisdictions the law operates in such a manner that marriage results in a community of property ownership. Any property acquired during a marriage is treated as owned jointly by both spouses. A slightly different regime operates in the deferred community property ownership. The spouses own property separately during the marriage, but at the end of the marriage the property is treated as community property owned by both parties.

In discussing these models, the ALRC report recommended that 'the law must be both fair and practical. It should strike an acceptable balance between flexibility and predictability, and encourage spouses to settle their property disputes with a minimum of cost and distress'.[13] It also explained that 'the major question' for them was not 'whether the law of property allocation on divorce should be formally based on judicial discretion or on legislatively prescribed entitlements'.[14] Their brief was to consider 'whether the post-separation circumstances of the spouses and their children should be taken into account in the allocation of property, or whether these circumstances are primarily matters for the law of spousal and child maintenance and social security'.[15] Keeping in view the fact that there is no ideal matrimonial property law, the ALRC report supported the adoption of criteria where matrimonial property law would be assessed on whether it provided a clear statement of law, equal status between the parties, universal application, and conciliation and harmony with other laws.

---

12   Australian Law Reform Commission ('ALRC'), *Matrimonial Property*, Report No 39 (1987) 13–4 [27]. For the background to this report and the process of law reform, see Regina Graycar, 'Feminism and Law Reform: Matrimonial Property Law and Models of Equality' in Sophie Watson (ed), *Playing the State: Australian Feminist Interventions* (Verso, 1990) 153, 162ff.
13   ALRC, above n 12, 16 [31].
14   Ibid 119 [270].
15   Ibid.

5.2.2   Rationales for altering property interests in family law

Above is a commendable general statement about workable laws, but it does not attend to the central issue of why family law needs to affect the property rights of spouses when there exists a separate and specific property law system. Moreover, these developments in family law are taking place in the wider context of liberal capitalist societies that are organised around the notions of private property as a fundamental right. Therefore, principles that permit such over-riding of private property rights need to be articulated, examined and justified.

Thus, the question of what would be an ideal matrimonial property law is the central one that must be addressed before it can be decided whether the law is fair or just. Yet the reticence in articulating what are, or should be, the ideals of matrimonial property laws keeps surfacing. For instance, in a widely used study of the property awards under the FLA,[16] a list of possible principles or rationales for property distribution included that marriage is a partnership of equals; an individual has an exclusive right to his or her own personal resources; parents, according to their respective financial resources, are responsible for the support of their children who have not attained the age of 18 years; and, if following the equitable distribution of resources upon marriage breakdown an individual's resources are insufficient for his or her support, or for the support of his or her children, then the state must bear the responsibility for dependencies created through marriage. However, these rationales are based on the existing provisions of the FLA and do not address the central question of what an ideal matrimonial law should be designed to achieve. We will focus on the Australian contemporary context, but similar issues have arisen in other legal systems.

For example, Krauskopf explains that in the North American context the no-fault divorce reformers made two assumptions.[17] The first was that at the end of a marriage both home-makers and children would be in an adequate economic position. This was so because the homemakers would either remarry or start to earn a living, those continuing to care for children would have child support available, and a share of property awarded to the homemaker would cover their other needs. The second major assumption was that a 'clean break' was in everyone's interest, so no economic ties would continue between the parties after the dissolution of marriage. Ample empirical evidence now exists to demonstrate the inaccuracy of both these assumptions.[18] Yet there is a curious lack of public discourse on the desirable rationales for property distribution at the end of a marriage or similar relationship. Fehlberg et al note that major property reform has not been considered in Australia since the 1980s.[19]

We agree with Krauskopf that it is necessary to articulate the ultimate goals of property distribution in family law before we can assess the fairness of property settlements.[20]

---

16   Peter McDonald et al, 'Directions for Law Reform and Social Policy' in Peter McDonald (ed), *Settling Up: Property and Income Distribution on Divorce in Australia* (AIFS, 1986) 308.

17   Joan M Krauskopf, 'Theories of Property Division/Spousal Support: Searching for Solutions to the Mystery' (1989) 23(2) *Family Law Quarterly* 253.

18   Empirical evidence in the Australian context is well documented; see, eg, David de Vaus et al, 'The Economic Consequences of Divorce in Australia' (2014) 28(1) *International Journal of Law, Policy and the Family* 26. See also other references in n 27 below.

19   Belinda Fehlberg et al, *Australian Family Law: The Contemporary Context* (Oxford University Press, 2nd ed, 2015) 408.

20   Krauskopf, above n 17.

The fundamental issue is whether the goal of property distribution is to share the loss and gain in earning capacity owing to marriage, or is it the need of one partner, and the capacity to pay of the other, that justifies redistribution? Furthermore, this initial issue cannot be settled in isolation and must be considered in the wider context of the conception of marriage/relationship used in the legislation. As we saw earlier, the FLA incorporates no-fault divorce and thus treats marriage as a voluntary union that any party can exit at any time. It thus conceptualises both spouses as equally competent individuals who are able to decide how to live their private lives. The idea that each individual is autonomous, however, leaves out issues of gender, especially in cases where there are children or where property disputes arise later.

It is the presence of children and the need to look after them that creates dependencies – usually of women and children – on men who are usually the primary financial actors.[21] It is necessary to note at this point that our argument is not about what the role of men and women should be in providing care to children. Rather, we ask the narrower question: how does the FLA deal with the contemporary social reality that most caregiving is performed by women and the resultant financial dependencies make women financially weaker than men? This central issue does not hold the attention of many commentators on the provisions of the FLA. For example, Saunders gives an elegant exposition of what may constitute fairness in family law property proceedings.[22] He explains the different emphases of the philosophical arguments in terms of egalitarian, meritocratic or classical liberal traditions. Yet in elaborating his argument he relies on the example of a childless couple. He also mentions that the gender of each partner is not relevant as the principles under consideration apply equally to men and women.[23] These theoretical assumptions are problematic if not outright flawed when the need to care for children is factored in.

Turning to the FLA provisions, it is possible to say that in this regard the FLA is progressive as it acknowledges that individual needs are to be balanced with the interests of children and societal interests in ensuring that financial dependencies are managed efficiently.[24] This is where the FLA provisions regarding property distribution become relevant.[25] At a glance, Part VIII of the FLA expresses values of gender equity and marriage as a partnership of equals doing different kinds of work; it acknowledges the sexual division of labour in the

---

21   For a discussion of related issues, see Martha Fineman, *The Autonomy Myth: A Theory of Dependency* (The New Press, 2004).

22   Peter Saunders, 'What is a Fair Divorce Settlement' (1999) 53 *Family Matters* 48.

23   Ibid 50.

24   It is often argued in the literature that family law is retreating from regulating the relationships of the spouses/partners and instead now regulates the parent–child relationship. We disagree in so far as property distribution is regulating conduct of the spouses, even if retrospectively. See, eg, Mavis Maclean and John Eekelaar, *The Parental Obligation* (Hart Publishing, 1998).

25   See FLA pts VIII, VIIIAB. Property distribution is authorised under s 79 for marriage and s 90SM for de facto relations. The latter is a mirror image of s 79 and, for reasons of space and ease of reading, we will only refer to s 79. Also, it is useful to remember that while the power to alter property rights is directed primarily at parties of marriages, it extends to parties to void marriages (s 71), but no corresponding provision is available for a de facto relationship.

    Although property distribution under the FLA is designed to take into account spousal maintenance and to a lesser extent child-support responsibilities, they are treated as separate issues under the FLA, the *Child Support (Assessment) Act 1989* (Cth) and the *Child Support (Registration and Collection) Act 1988* (Cth). The following discussion reflects these artificial boundaries, although we are conscious that the issues are interrelated.

nuclear family and, in keeping with the overall emphasis of the FLA on alternative dispute resolution, prefers private settlement. Accordingly, s 79(1) authorises the court to redistribute the property of the spouses and make any order it considers appropriate, and s 79(2) specifies that 'the court shall not make an order under this section unless it is satisfied that, in all the circumstances, it is just and equitable to make the order'. In view of these provisions, the continued financial disadvantage of women with children needs to be explained. In our view, it seems that, despite the apparent progressive approach of the FLA provisions that can override general rules of property ownership, we need to take seriously how the application of these provisions may in fact have a bearing on producing disadvantageous outcomes.

The possibility of sharing the property, rather than only providing an entitlement to maintenance, would seem to be a revolutionary advance in the rights of women, as they are the non-financial or weaker financial partners in most unions. It was possible for the court to settle property in the name of the non-owner spouse, even under the former *Matrimonial Causes Act 1959* (Cth). A distinctive feature of the FLA, however, is that it looks beyond the formal title to property and links the property order to contributions, thus suggesting that there is an entitlement or even a right to property because a person has contributed to its accumulation.[26]

However, empirical evidence from the commencement of this, and similar legislation in other jurisdictions, has revealed surprising outcomes for women. That is, women with children under family laws that have incorporated no-fault divorce and property distribution have suffered economic hardship.[27] What is more surprising is that, after separation, disadvantages for women with children continue to persist even today.[28] While it is a truism that the gender disparities in our society are caused by complex structural factors, in the context of this book it is the narrower issue of the role of family law that concerns us. In particular, it is relevant to inquire whether the shape of family law also structures choices made by the individual partners. We suggest that the FLA does operate in such a structural manner.

---

26   There is very little discussion in the literature about the need to enact these property provisions, considering that various kinds of trust instruments exist in law that could be developed by courts to override strictly legal title. For a brief discussion of whether such doctrines were adequate and whether they continue to be relevant under the FLA, see Patrick Parkinson, 'Quantifying the Homemaker Contribution in Family Property Law' (2003) 31(1) *Federal Law Review* 1, 20–1. See also Marcia Neave, 'Three Approaches to Family Law Disputes – Intention/Belief, Unjust Enrichment and Unconscionability' in Timothy G Youdan (ed), *Equity, Fiduciaries and Trusts* (Law Book Co, 1989) 262. However, we question whether the provisions in the FLA create a legal right to property for the spouse who has no property in their own name when it is up to the court to determine whether it is just and equitable to make a property order in their favour (see discussion below and in Chapter 6).

27   The path-breaking study in this regard is Lenore J Weitzman, *The Divorce Revolution* (The Free Press, 1985). Her findings were replicated in Australia: see generally Peter McDonald (ed), *Settling Up: Property and Income Distribution on Divorce in Australia* (AIFS, 1986). For suggestions of reform, see especially McDonald et al, above n 16. Although there exists extensive literature critiquing aspects of Weitzman's methodology, there is consensus that women with children do suffer economic disparities after divorce or relationship breakup. See also Kathleen Funder, Margaret Harrison and Ruth Weston, *Settling Down: Pathways of Parents after Divorce* (AIFS, 1993).

28   See, eg, Bruce Smyth and Ruth Weston, 'Financial Living Standards after Divorce: A Recent Snapshot' (Research Paper No 23, AIFS, 2000) 1. Almost three decades after the enactment of the FLA, the outcomes seem to continue to be disadvantageous to women with children: see de Vaus et al, above n 18. See also Grania Sheehan, 'Financial Aspects of the Divorce Transition in Australia: Recent Empirical Findings' (2002) 16(1) *International Journal of Law, Policy and the Family* 95; Grania Sheehan and Jody Hughes, 'The Division of Matrimonial Property in Australia' (2000) 55 *Family Matters* 28.

Therefore, the fundamental issue for all family law thinkers must be to imagine how the outcomes of divorce or relationship breakup could be equitable, or at least comparable, for the two partners. Put another way, the issue requiring analysis is the design of the FLA. Thus, the scope provided in s 79(2) to the court to make a property alteration order only if it is just and equitable to do so requires a prior articulation of what may constitute justice and equity between divorcing or separating parties. This issue is in turn dependent upon a clear understanding of why property redistribution is required. The two obvious justifications are that it is to recognise contributions made by both parties to the accumulation and preservation of property, or, alternatively, it is required to provide for the 'welfare' needs of the relatively financially weaker party. The distinction between these two justifications is that the former invokes a sense of entitlement, while the latter invokes a sense of being helped or given a gift. However, in both cases unequal access to property or financial wellbeing is firmly connected to the costs of rearing children. The question that remains unasked specifically is: who should bear this cost and in what proportion?

5.3   Design of the FLA financial provisions

Very briefly, the design of the FLA financial provisions enables the court to alter the property interests of the two parties and, in deciding what order to make, it can take into account respectively the contributions and needs of both of them. The paragraphs in s 79(4) seem to combine the two rationales of entitlement and need.[29] Its first three paragraphs are generally understood to be referring to the respective contributions of the parties and the remaining four paragraphs are taken as referring to the future needs of the parties. Thus, in s 79(4) (a)–(c), direct and indirect financial contributions to property, non-financial contributions to property and contributions to the welfare of the family are to be taken into account. On the strength of these contributions, the court is supposed to reach a notional distribution of property that can then be modified by reference to the matters in s 79(4)(d)–(g), which embody spousal maintenance principles. Very broadly, these matters can be described as addressing the future needs of the parties, but they are more commonly described as the retrospective and prospective elements of the property order.[30]

It is the recognition that non-financial and caregiving work is relevant in property proceedings that is the FLA's most distinctive feature. Yet it is a partial or halting recognition, as evidenced in the rules and court decisions about property division. The judicial authority to alter individual interests in property is a radical departure from the approach to property

---

29   Section 79(4) provides a list of seven factors that must be taken into account: '(a) the direct and indirect financial contributions of the parties; (b) the non-financial contributions of the parties; (c) contributions to the welfare of the family, including contributions as homemaker or parent; (d) the effect of any order on the parties' income earning capacity; (e) the list of considerations in s 75(2) of the FLA; (f) any other order made under the FLA affecting a party or child of the marriage; and (g) any child support payable, or likely to be paid in the future'. The rationales of property distribution are discussed extensively in the literature. See, eg, Anthony Dickey, 'The Moral Justification for Alteration of Property Interests under the Family Law Act' (1988) 11(1) *UNSW Law Journal* 158.

30   Rebecca Bailey, 'Principles of Property Distribution on Divorce – Compensation, Need or Community' (1980) 54 *Australian Law Journal* 190.

acquisition and entitlement found in property law more generally.[31] A central tenet of capitalist liberal societies is that property has economic or money value and those who can pay for it, own it.[32] However, the FLA does not explicitly articulate and justify the departure from this tenet and this could be a reason why there is so much dissatisfaction with the FLA among both men and women. As this is a very extensive topic, we can only discuss the conceptual difficulties in translating non-financial work into a financial value as a share in the matrimonial property. This will provide the framework for analysing the approach to financial relations in the FLA and the case law.

5.4   Attributing financial value to non-financial work: feminist economics versus neoclassical economics

The following is a broad-brush account of the incapacity of economic discourse to deal with non-economic work. Our aim is not to critique economic theories per se, but to identify the disconnect that exists between economics and family law discourses. Mainstream economics, also sometimes described as neoclassical economics, provides the definitions of work, and distinguishes between production and social reproduction. Production and work relate to market transactions and, by definition, activities undertaken for non-market activities do not merit the classification of work and do not attract a financial or monetary value. Thus, the goal of family law to treat a marriage/marriage-like relationship as a partnership where different, but presumably equally valuable, paid and unpaid work is done by two people comes up against a definitional hurdle of defining both kinds of activities as 'work' in economic terms.[33]

Scholars in feminist economics challenge such definitions, and have persistently made the argument for using the concepts of caring labour and care economy in identifying and measuring the work done within families and households.[34] This includes not only work related to child rearing and the sustenance of adult workers, but also extends to the care of those unable to work, including the sick, severely disabled and elderly members of society. This kind of care work is undertaken within families, and also in the community sector; yet, mainstream

---

31   The main exception to the sanctity of property rights is present in principles of equity but, other than that, liberal free-market societies are premised upon the security of property rights. For an introduction, see Janice Gray et al, *Property Law in New South Wales* (LexisNexis, 3rd ed, 2012).

32   For an introduction to theories of private property, see Jeremy Waldron, *The Right to Private Property* (Clarendon Press, 1988); Margaret Jane Radin, 'Property and Personhood' (1982) 34(5) *Stanford Law Review* 957. The nexus between private property and capitalism is a major topic of analysis. For an introduction, see Paul H Rubin and Tilman Klumpp, 'Property Rights and Capitalism' in Dennis C Mueller (ed), *The Oxford Handbook of Capitalism* (Oxford University Press, 2012) 204.

33   Luisella Goldschmidt-Vermont, *Unpaid Work in the Household: A Review of Economic Methods* (International Labour Office, 1989); Susan Himmelweit, 'The Discovery of "Unpaid Work": The Social Consequences of the Expansion of "Work"' (1995) 1(2) *Feminist Economics* 1.

34   For an introduction to the issues, see Diana Strassmann, 'Feminist Economics' in Janice Petersen and Margaret Lewis (eds), *The Elgar Companion to Feminist Economics* (Edward Elgar, 1999) 360.

economics seems to be able to ignore these insights.[35] This is an example of how dominant discourse formation takes place within disciplinary knowledge, but is anything but objective.

The difficulty of capturing care work within the definition of work is further exacerbated by the lack of agreement about how to attach financial value to such work.[36] Whether it should be valued on a uniform basis as wages for housework, or whether specific activities should be attributed a market value as if they were purchased in the market, are different ways of approaching the issue, but each has its shortcomings. The 'wages for housework' model has come up against the issue of who would be responsible to pay for it, and there has been disagreement over whether it would be a private or public cost. Payment at market rates for domestic work has also encountered problems, especially because care work is generally undervalued even in the marketplace. For example, being a professional attracts much higher wages than being a worker in hospitality or in the childcare industry. This is sometimes described as the feminisation of work,[37] and if this model is used to give value to domestic work, such work will always be classified as a low-paid activity.

This very brief overview of the economic issues in attributing financial value to non-financial work allows us to reflect on the virtual absence and lack of significant discussion of this kind of knowledge in the law. However, if the judicial discourse on domestic work does not grapple with these conceptual difficulties, it is not a particular failure of the judges. Rather, it demonstrates the function of the idea of legal reasoning that locates the meaning of any legal rule within the legal doctrine. Even when judges make efforts to incorporate such knowledge in their reasoning, they are invariably faced with the obstacle posed by the understanding that legal reasoning has a specific and technical meaning.[38] Thus, the judges are not obliged to inform themselves of the social sciences' knowledge about the gendered aspects of domestic work, nor are they expected to use other (than law) disciplinary knowledges to inform their views about what would constitute a fair recognition of the respective contributions made by parties engaging in paid and unpaid work. Moreover, when making their decisions about a fair distribution of property, the guidance provided to the judges in the legislative formula in the FLA is problematic on a number of counts, which will be discussed in the following sections. Before that, a brief enumeration of procedural issues is provided.

---

35   Dianne Elson, 'Micro, Meso and Macro: Gender and Economic Analysis in the Context of Policy Reform' in Isabella Bakker (ed), *The Strategic Silence: Gender and Economic Policy* (Zed Press, 1994) 33; Nancy Folbre, 'Measuring Care: Gender, Empowerment, and the Care Economy' (2006) 7(2) *Journal of Human Development* 183. Increasingly in this literature, a distinction is made between domestic and care work. See, eg, Silvia Federici, *Revolution at Point Zero: Housework, Reproduction, and Feminist Struggle* (PM Press, 2012); Encarnacion Gutierrez-Rodriguez, 'Domestic Work–Affective Labour: On Feminization and the Coloniality of Labor' (2014) 46 *Women's Studies International Forum* 45.

36   Susan Himmelweit, 'Domestic Labour' in Janice Petersen and Margaret Lewis (eds), *The Elgar Companion to Feminist Economics* (Edward Elgar, 1999) 126.

37   Leslie Hossfeld, 'Feminization of Labor' in Jodi O'Brien (ed), *Encyclopedia of Gender and Society* (Sage Publications, 2009) 318. For an international dimension of the issue of low economic value attributed to care work, see Majella Kilkey, Helma Lutz and Ewa Palenga-Möllenbeck, 'Introduction: Domestic and Care Work at the Intersection of Welfare, Gender and Migration Regimes: Some European Experiences' (2010) 9(3) *Social Policy and Society* 379.

38   There is a significant amount of scholarship on the issue of how the courts may not be able to take adequate note of social science knowledge. For an introduction to some of the issues, see Alan Hayes, 'Social Science and Family Law: From Fallacies and Fads to the Facts of the Matter' in Alan Hayes and Daryl Higgins (eds), *Families, Policy and the Law: Selected Essays on Contemporary Issues for Australia* (AIFS, 2014) 283.

5.5   Family property proceedings

Parts VIII and VIIIAB of the FLA provide the legislative scheme regarding financial relations for married and de facto couples respectively.[39]

5.5.1   Procedural issues

In keeping with the FLA's emphasis on alternative dispute resolution, there are provisions in the *Family Law Rules 2004* (Cth) ('*Family Law Rules*') for pre-action processes.[40] There are also provisions in the FLA for the court to order conciliation even after filing a court application.[41] Thus, with very few exceptions, the parties must try to settle the matter without litigation, but if this fails and the dispute reaches the court, it is still possible for the court to direct them to try to negotiate a settlement.[42]

Although both the Family Court of Australia ('FCA') and the Federal Circuit Court ('FCC') have jurisdiction in a property dispute application (ss 39, 39(1A) and 39B), the protocol for the division of work between them means that all applications must be filed in the FCC, except if any of the specified criteria apply.[43] An application for a property order must be made within 12 months from the time the divorce order becomes absolute (s 44(3)), or two years after the end of a de facto relationship (s 44 (5)).[44] Property proceedings must be filed

---

39   For the legislative provisions governing de facto relations, see Rachel Carson, 'Property and Financial Matters Upon the Breakdown of De Facto Relationships' (Child Family Community Australia Paper No 24, 2014).

40   Such rules are mandatory for child-related disputes, but less so for financial disputes. However, non-compliance can be taken into account by the court: *Family Law Rules* rr 1.10, 11.03, 19.10. Part 1 in sch 1 of the *Family Law Rules* provides that each party is required to make a genuine effort to resolve the dispute before starting a case by participating in dispute resolution such as negotiation, conciliation, arbitration and counselling. The *Civil Dispute Resolution Act 2011* (Cth) governs applications in the FCC and under it the parties are required to take genuine steps to resolve a civil dispute before court proceedings commence.

41   s 79(9); *Family Law Rules* rr 12.03, 12.07. See also the less adversarial trial process introduced by the FCA to expedite resolution of litigated cases. Special procedures apply for cases involving allegations of violence. The Family Violence Best Practice Principles were first announced in March 2009 and now govern both the FCA and the FCC: see *Federal Circuit Court of Australia Legislation Amendment Act 2012* (Cth).

42   For an early discussion of the advantages of arbitration in this context and an exploration of reasons why it could become a more commonly used dispute resolution method, see John Wade, 'Arbitration of Matrimonial Disputes' (1999) 11(2) *Bond Law Review* 395.

43   Family Court of Australia, *Protocol for the Division of Work between the Family Court and the Federal Circuit Court* (12 April 2013) <http://www.familycourt.gov.au/wps/wcm/connect/fcoaweb/reports-and-publications/publications/administrative/protocol-for-division-of-work-fcoa-fcc>. The criteria are international child abduction; international relocation; disputes as to whether a case should be heard in Australia; special medical procedures (of the type such as gender reassignment and sterilisation); contravention and related applications in parenting cases relating to orders that have been made in FCA proceedings, that have reached the final stage of hearing or judicial determination and that have been made within 12 months prior to filing; serious allegations of sexual abuse of a child warranting transfer to the Magellan list or similar list where applicable and serious allegations of physical abuse of a child or serious controlling family violence warrant the attention of a superior court; complex questions of jurisdiction or law; or, if the matter proceeds to a final hearing, it is likely it would take in excess of four days of hearing time. The FCA exercises exclusive jurisdiction in matters of adoption and the validity of marriages and divorces.

44   Sections 44(4)/(6) enable the court to extend the time limit if not doing so would cause hardship to a party or a child.

before one of the parties to a marriage dies (s 79(8))/s 90SM(8)). If there is a dispute about the ownership of property, s 78 empowers the court to make a declaration. The court can refuse to make such a declaration if it is intended to prejudice a third party. Property orders are a final determination of financial relations, but the possibility to vary such orders does exist in limited circumstances.[45] The court has very wide discretion in deciding what kinds of property orders to make and, subject to a few exceptions, has this authority with respect to all of the property of either spouse.

5.5.2   Property proceedings: an overview

In the following discussion, we focus on the specific issues where the legislative design and conventions of legal reasoning come together to produce gendered outcomes. These issues are: parties in a marriage or relationship can opt out of the application of the FLA; the financial provisions operate in the context of the wider emphasis of the FLA on private settlement; the FLA does not articulate a specific right to property for the non-financial partner; and the judiciary has wide discretion to decide how to allocate property between the two parties.

As a preliminary point for the following discussion, it should be noted that it is now possible to contract out of the jurisdiction of the FLA altogether (s 71A). This was not always the case and, when initially enacted, the rules of the FLA were applicable to all financial disputes arising in the context of a matrimonial cause (as defined in s 4(1)). In other words, the law assumed jurisdiction over a matrimonial dispute if one spouse came to it, and it was not open to the parties to foreclose this possibility. Admittedly, it was always possible for the parties to avoid Family Court proceedings by settling their property issues privately, and the possibility of entering into maintenance agreements (ss 86, 87) or consent orders (s 79) always existed. However, some level of judicial oversight was involved. The significant difference between the earlier and the current rules is that now the law is making a normative statement that it is permissible for the parties to quarantine their property or opt out of the jurisdiction of the FLA.[46] These developments are concerning, especially as the FLA stands out in its (albeit implicit) acknowledgement that domestic work is work and is to be accorded an economic value.

It is also significant that the FLA does not create any legal rights that the financially weaker party, usually the woman as the primary caregiver, can assert to claim a share in the property. For a start, its language is fiercely gender-neutral, and it only grants both parties a right to ask the court to make a property distribution order. A related issue in this regard is that the legislative emphasis on settling property matters without litigation, but also without

---

45   Sections 79A/90SN provide that variations can be requested by mutual consent on the application of one party where there has been a miscarriage of justice by reason of fraud, duress, suppression of evidence (including failure to disclose relevant information), the giving of false evidence or any other circumstance; circumstances have made it impracticable for the order to be carried out; a person has defaulted and justice and equity require the order to be set aside or modified; circumstances related to the care and welfare of a child require setting aside or modification; or a proceeds of crime order has been made.

46   Although in limited circumstances the court can set aside a binding financial agreement. See Chapter 7 for further details.

articulating clear rights to a share of property or maintenance, creates a false sense of the law being progressive. Thus, the statistical detail that a majority of disputes are settled privately, without litigation, means that there is no way of knowing whether the property settlements are influenced by the legislative provisions. This is privatisation of family on a large scale, and achieved with the help of a law that was meant to make the end of a marriage (and now de facto relationship) relatively more equitable. Empirical studies that try to measure people's satisfaction with the property outcomes are no doubt useful, but they do not address the normative issue that what may be fair and what may be acceptable to people are two very different matters.[47]

The specific legislative rules that a court may take into account in making a property order are included in s 79.[48] The distinctive feature of this section is that in all aspects it relies on the discretion of judges. The following discussion focuses on some of these issues: that the judge has the discretion to decide whether to make a property order; what form that order should take; what relative weight is to be attributed to different kinds of contributions (including financial and non-financial contributions); and what relative weight should be given to the contributions and needs components of the property order. Before discussing these issues, it is useful to consider the procedures involved in a property application under s 79.

Section 79(1) begins with the words '[i]n property settlement proceedings, the court may make such order as it considers appropriate', and explains that the court may alter the interests in property of either or both parties to the marriage and, in the case of vested bankruptcy property, the interests of the trustee of bankruptcy.[49] This broad judicial discretion is further elaborated in s 79(2): '[t]he court shall not make an order under this section unless it is satisfied that, in all the circumstances, it is just and equitable to make the order'. Some commentators have interpreted this subsection as the overriding clause; that is, the court must consider when making an order that it is just and equitable to do so. Only if the court is satisfied of this primary consideration can it then determine what order to make.[50]

Two issues arise with respect to this interpretation. The first relates to the technical nature of statutory interpretation, and the second to the confidence that law can be interpreted without taking into account social realities. Going to the first point about technical

---

47   See, eg, Lixia Qu et al, *Post-separation Parenting, Property and Relationship Dynamics after Five Years* (AIFS, 2014).

48   Section 90SM is the corresponding provision for de facto relationships; they are mirror images of each other, but for easier reading we will only refer to s 79 from here on. There is extensive literature discussing whether it is advisable to equate the financial provisions for married and de facto couples. For an introduction, see Dorothy Kovacs, 'The Federal law of De Facto Property Rights: The Dream and the Reality' (2009) 23(2) *Australian Journal of Family Law* 104; Jenni Milbank, 'De Facto Relationships, Same-sex and Surrogate Parents: Exploring the Scope and Effects of the 2008 Federal Relationship Reforms' (2009) 23(3) *Australian Journal of Family Law* 160.

49   Section 79(1)(b) states: 'in the case of proceedings with respect to the vested bankruptcy property in relation to a bankrupt party to the marriage – altering the interests of the bankruptcy trustee in the vested bankruptcy property; including: ... (c) an order for a settlement of property in substitution for any interest in the property; and (d) an order requiring: (i) either or both of the parties to the marriage; or (ii) the relevant bankruptcy trustee (if any); to make, for the benefit of either or both of the parties to the marriage or a child of the marriage, such settlement or transfer of property as the court determines'.

50   Patrick Parkinson, *Australian Family Law in Context* (Thomson Reuters, 5th ed, 2012) 564; Anthony Dickey, *Family Law* (Thomson Reuters, 6th ed, 2014) 589; Fehlberg et al, above n 19, 515–7.

rules of interpretation, in following the interpretation that s 79(2) is mandatory and governs the issue of the power of the court, it could as easily be said, within the conventions of statutory interpretation, that it is illogical to read s 79(1) as giving wide power to the court, only to take it away. It would be more logical for the legislation to begin by stating that there is a limited power to alter property interests, to be exercised only if to do so is just and equitable. Once it is ascertained that the court can exercise this power, the next provision would be that the extent of the court's power is to make 'such order as it considers appropriate'. We raise this issue as a strictly technical issue of statutory interpretation, but, in pointing it out, wish to bring into focus the artificiality of such rules. The existence of statutory rules of interpretation diverts attention from the obvious fact that there is always the possibility of more than one interpretation of a rule. The explicit faith in the possibility of reaching a correct interpretation lends legitimacy to the existing legal system.

That is, it is a particular claim of legal reasoning that judges 'apply' the law rather than make it. Judicial interpretation of law is a principled activity as the judges are bound by rules of interpretation, and thus can be relied upon to find out the meaning of any rule.[51] It is assumed that the meaning of any rule of law is ascertainable, and rules of interpretation provide the method of reaching that meaning. Although extensive critiques of this view exist, most of them do not find their way into mainstream legal thinking or teaching. Legal education and training rely heavily on statutory interpretation as a core skill and teach that, if applied correctly, such rules obviate the danger of judges' personal value systems conditioning their legal thinking and interpretation of the laws.[52] This is done without any acknowledgement that scholarship in post-structuralism has challenged comprehensively this view of knowledge.[53] In the process, the discourse of law is constructed on the basis of a technique of interpretation that completely ignores the alternative and plausible view that all knowledge is partial and not objective. It follows that legal professionals confidently use the rules of interpretation, but in the process manage to underplay their reliance on the method to gain the truth,[54] and act as if it is possible to ascertain the meaning of any legal rule independently of its context.

Thus, in the context of s 79(2) of the FLA, commentators confidently assert that the message of this rule is that the courts should refrain from making a property order and modifying the property interests of the parties unless justice and equity require it. The main issue we have with this interpretation is that it ignores how the sexual division of labour continues to operate in our society, and that, unless family law modifies the prevalent rules of property ownership, the financially dependent spouse (usually the wife) will come off second best at the end of a marriage/relationship.[55] That is, the social reality continues to be that raising

---

51   For an introduction to this literature, see Neil MacCormick, *Rhetoric and the Rule of Law: A Theory of Legal Reasoning* (Oxford University Press, 2005). For an example of how legal education uses the concept, see John H Farrar, *Legal Reasoning* (Thomson Reuters, 2010) referred to in Malcolm Voyce, 'Family Farming and Property Settlements under the "Family Law Act 1975" and the Category of "Special Contributions"' (2015) 34(2) *University of Queensland Law Journal* 341.

52   For example, textbooks teaching such skills are part of most legal curricula. See as an example Catriona Cook et al, *Laying Down the Law* (LexisNexis, 9th ed, 2015).

53   See Michael Kirby, 'Statutory Interpretation: The Meaning of Meaning' (2011) 35(1) *Melbourne University Law Review* 113.

54   For a critique of the claim that correct method allows one to reach the truth of any matter, see Hans-Georg Gadamer, *Truth and Method* (Sheed and Ward, 1975).

55   Although a remedy in equity was always available, it was impractical, expensive and thus not much used.

children requires money and effort, and usually one spouse (mostly the husband) generates an income and the other spouse (mostly the wife) primarily focuses on child-rearing activities. This appears to be the most plausible reason why the legislature included s 79 in the FLA, especially considering that it allows the court to take into account the parties' contributions to the welfare of the family when making property orders. If, in the process of legal interpretation, this understanding of the FLA, taking upon itself to address the sexual division of labour, is rendered irrelevant, we can only wonder why s 79 was required in the first place.

In other words, in the gendered hierarchy that exists in our contemporary society, justice and equity would almost always require that the property interests of the parties are adjusted to acknowledge the financial consequences of the immense amount of care work involved in bringing up children. When rules of statutory interpretation permit legal commentators and judges to deny this social and cultural reality, the question has to be asked whether this is how law helps maintain such hierarchies. It bears pointing out that the individual commentators or judges are not entirely to blame as they are 'permitted' by the conventions of legal reasoning to come up with such interpretations. Moreover, as Thornton says, '[l]egal method is accepted as neutral and authoritative, not only by the relevant legal hermeneutic community but by the wider community as well'.[56] This critique is primarily directed at the view of knowledge that supports the idea that the correct method allows us to access the singular truth. This trust in judges' abilities to find the true meaning of legal rules is further complicated by the provisions in the FLA that stop short of having clearly articulated goals, as illustrated below.

5.5.3   The steps in making a property order

Since the enactment of the FLA, the courts have developed practices with regard to a property application.[57] Until relatively recently the received wisdom was that the court mostly followed a four-step process.[58] However, since the High Court decision in *Stanford*, debate about whether it is a three- or four-step process has arisen. We will address that, but first explain the long-standing practice of the Family Court.

The four steps in a property application are:[59]

1. to identify and value the net property of the parties (usually as at the date of trial)

2. to consider the contributions of the parties within paragraphs (a)–(c) of s 79(4)

3. to consider paragraphs (d)–(g) of s 79(4) and the s 75(2) factors, and

4. to consider whether the proposed distribution is 'just and equitable'.

56   Margaret Thornton, 'The Judicial Gendering of Citizenship: A Look at Property Interests During Marriage' (1997) 24(4) *Journal of Law and Society* 486, 488.

57   The identification of steps in making the property order was considered necessary to explain how the court reached a particular conclusion about the allocation of property. The courts were not prescriptive in their formulations. See, eg, *In the Marriage of Ferraro* (1992) 16 Fam LR 1; *In the Marriage of McLay* (1996) 131 FLR 31; *In the Marriage of Clauson* (1995) 18 Fam LR 693.

58   Many of the cases follow the four-step process and are listed or discussed in *In the Marriage of Hickey* (2003) Fam LR 355, 370 [39].

59   Reiterated in *In the Marriage of Omacini* (2005) 33 Fam LR 134, 147 [46], where the court also referred to *In the Marriage of Ferraro* (1992) 16 Fam LR 1.

Step one: identify and value the property

Once a property adjustment application reaches the court, the first task is for the court to ascertain the total pool of property available for distribution.[60] The definition of 'property' in s 4(1) is broad and does not make a distinction between matrimonial and other property. It provides that property means property to which both or either party in a marriage/de facto relationship are 'entitled, whether in possession or reversion'. At this initial stage, the relevant property includes a very wide range of different kinds of assets and includes 'business' assets.[61] It does not matter how, or when, the property was acquired. These matters become relevant later on in deciding how to divide the property. It is usual for the extent and value of the property of the parties to be ascertained as at the date of the hearing. The extensive reach of the FLA to include all types of property has now been extended to superannuation, in certain conditions (s 90MC).[62]

Courts have accepted a very wide variety of interests as property, including the family home, savings and investments, as well as gifts, inheritances, lottery wins, compensation claims and money awards in other litigation, and notional property as add-backs.[63] Significantly, the courts have looked at the substance of the interest in property rather than its description only.[64] For example, property subject to a discretionary trust is treated as property of the parties if one of the parties had the power to vest the property in either of them since the High Court decision in *Kennon v Spry*.[65] Whenever the person has a present entitlement it is treated as property, and for this reason any potential, future or contingent interests are not property. Correspondingly, a mere personal right – for example, the right to occupy the matrimonial home – is not treated as property.[66] As part of the process of determining the property interests of the two parties, the courts take into account any debts or liabilities and may also determine the claims of creditors if required.[67]

Courts have explained the distinction between three sources of wealth: property, financial resources and income. It was pointed out early in *In the Marriage of Duff* that only property could be the subject of an order of a court.[68] Despite the fact that the courts have interpreted very widely what may constitute property, if any source of wealth is defined as

---

60   Subject to the proviso that since the High Court decision in *Stanford* the first step might be to ask whether the division of property is just and equitable.

61   For examples of the kinds of assets included, see Jacqueline Campbell and Grant Riethmuller, 'Property' in Renata Alexander et al, *Australian Master Family Law Guide* (CCH, 7th ed, 2015) 338.

62   The effect of the *Family Law Legislation Amendment (Superannuation) Act 2001* (Cth) was to treat superannuation as property with respect to matrimonial causes (s 4(1)(ca)) in the FLA. These superannuation provisions were extended to de facto financial causes (s 4(1)(a)) in 2009 (except in Western Australia; 2010 in South Australia).

63   Since the decision of the High Court in *Stanford*, the Family Court has been hesitant to treat notional property as property; see, eg, *Bevan v Bevan* (2013) 279 FLR 1; *Panagakos and Panagakos* [2013] FamCA 463 for refusal to take existing debts into account in ascertaining property.

64   See *Sand v Sand* (2012) 48 Fam LR 458, 465 for a discussion of earlier cases dealing with the issue of what constitutes property.

65   (2008) 238 CLR 366. See also *Pittman v Pittman* (2010) 43 Fam LR 121, in which the husband's interest was treated as property where, under a trust, he was entitled to a share of the capital and income.

66   *Mullane v Mullane* (1983) 158 CLR 436.

67   *In the Marriage of Bailey* (1989) 98 FLR 1.

68   (1977) 29 FLR 46 (Watson SJ, Murray and Wood JJ). In this case the Full Court held that shares in a company were property in the relevant sense.

a financial resource it will be taken into account at the later stage of making an adjustment of property interests (when considering s 75(2) factors).[69] Financial resources cannot be split (like property interests), but can be taken into account in adjusting the parties' interests in the property that can be split.[70] Initially superannuation was treated as a financial resource when making a property order.

The court requires the parties to make full and frank disclosures of their assets. Under the *Family Law Rules* each party has the obligation to disclose all its property and assets.[71] The court may look negatively upon a party who does not disclose all of his or her financial circumstances.[72] In case of disagreement about the value of property, it is the responsibility of the court to determine what value to give to the property.[73]

Step two: ascertain each party's contributions

The very broad discretion in s 79(1) of the FLA is to be exercised by reference to matters mentioned in s 79(4). This subsection directs the court that 'in considering what order (if any) should be made under this section in property settlement proceedings, the court shall take into account' paragraphs (a)–(g). It is generally accepted that s 79(4) is divided into two broad limbs: the first limb (s 79 (4)(a)–(c)) is commonly described as the 'contribution' factors, and the second limb (s 79(4)(d)–(g)) is referred to as the 'future needs' factors or the s 75(2) factors (taken into account in step three of the process of decision-making).

In step two of the property allocation process, the court takes into account the 'contribution' factors mentioned in paragraphs (a), (b) and (c) respectively. Paragraph (a) requires the court to assess the financial contribution made by each party, directly or indirectly, to the acquisition, conservation or improvement of any property of the parties. The cumulative scope of paragraph (a) is very wide as it includes financial contribution (to the accumulation, conservation or improvement), made directly or indirectly, and whether by the parties or on their behalf. Over time, courts have included initial contributions in long and short marriages (but have given them different significance) and post-separation contributions (gifts and inheritances, windfalls, damages awards), and have taken note of reduction of assets owing to one party's conduct.[74]

---

69   See *In the Marriage of Kelly (No 2)* (1981) 7 Fam LR 762: that financial interests cannot be split like property, but can be taken into account in distribution of property interests that can be split.

70   The FLA does not contain a definition of 'financial resource', but courts have elaborated the meaning: see *In the Marriage of Crapp* (1979) 35 FLR 153; *In the Marriage of Gould* (1996) 128 FLR 401.

71   r 13.04: full and frank disclosure; *Federal Circuit Court Rules 2001* (Cth) r 24.03.

72   There is a long list of decisions where the court has taken an adverse view of non-disclosure. See, eg, *In the Marriage of Weir* (1992) 110 FLR 403; *Jacks v Parker* (2011) 248 FLR 9.

73   See *Phillips v Phillips* [2002] FLC 93-104, 88 982 for a discussion of authorities on valuation of property. See *Kapoor and Kapoor* [2010] FamCAFC 113 for consideration of some issues arising in the valuation of superannuation. The *Family Law Rules* also provide for restricting expert evidence to issues that are in dispute; where possible, single experts are used; and adversarial experts are allowed only with the permission of the court: *Family Law Rules* div 15.5.3.

74   One of the contentious issues in this regard is to ascertain the reasons why the legislation includes contributions made before or after the marriage. See Parkinson, above n 26; Patrick Parkinson, 'Judicial Discretion, the Homemaker Contribution and Assets Acquired after Separation' (2001) 15(2) *Australian Journal of Family Law* 155.

Paragraph (b) refers to contribution, other than financial contribution to the acquisition, conservation or improvement of any property of the parties. It was added later,[75] presumably to make it clearer that the aim of property distribution is to acknowledge that accumulation of property is made possible by the financial as well as the non-financial contributions of the parties to the relationship. The distinctive effort of the FLA to attribute a financial value to non-financial contributions is partly present in paragraph (b), which mirrors paragraph (a), but also refers to other than financial contributions, whether made directly or indirectly. However, these contributions must be to the acquisition, conservation or improvement of the property, or are otherwise related to the property.

Paragraph (c) refers to contributions that relate to the performance of non-financial care work in the family.[76] It authorises the court to take into account contributions made to the welfare of the family (that is, to the parties of the marriage and any children of the marriage), including any contributions made in the capacity of homemaker or parent. The separation of non-financial contributions into paragraphs (b) and (c) is partly a legislative effort to clarify that such work is relevant both in the accumulation of property and in the care of family members.[77] These are two different kinds of contributions. In response to a suggestion that only contributions made when the family was constituted by marriage are relevant, and not those made during pre-marital cohabitation, the Court in *In the Marriage of Gill* explained that the insertion of paragraph (c) was 'to affirm the existing jurisprudence of the Family Court on housewifely contributions and not to destroy it'.[78] The same instinct to expand the definition of family, however, was not extended to include other relatives or members of the household.[79]

It has been the accepted practice of the courts to make a notional division of property on the basis of the respective contributions by the two parties. However, the most contentious issue for the courts is how to assess and balance different kinds of contributions, as the FLA provides no guidance in this regard.[80] A brief look at some of the decisions will illustrate the difficulties faced by the judges which are created by the paucity of relevant interdisciplinary knowledge available and utilised by them. It also helps explain the resultant inevitability of common sense views about the relative values of financial and care work finding expression in the judicial assessments.

As discussed above, there is a paucity of knowledge, even in disciplines other than law, as to the method of attributing financial value to domestic and care work. This is true even in the discipline of economics, but the FLA expects judges to be able to give a financial value to non-financial contributions by exercising their discretion. Thus, if the outcomes are less than satisfactory, the judges are not necessarily to blame. Such less-satisfactory outcomes may be more an illustration of the fact that family matters cannot be treated as stand-alone issues. The FLA vacillates between trying to recognise the prevailing social realities and creating a gender-neutral set of rules. But the real issue is that it does not even formulate the necessary

---

75   *Family Law Amendment Act 1983* (Cth).
76   Inserted also by the *Family Law Amendment Act 1983* (Cth).
77   *In the Marriage of Shaw* (1989) 95 FLR 183. Unlike paras (a) and (b), this provision does not extend to contributions made on behalf of a party by some other person: see *AB v ZB* (2002) 30 Fam LR 591.
78   (1984) 9 Fam LR 969, 977 (Nygh J).
79   *In the Marriage of Mehmet* (1986) 11 Fam LR 322.
80   Frank Bates, 'Discretion, Contributions and Needs' [2005] *International Family Law* 218.

rules in sufficient detail. Its preferred method of giving discretion to the judges to decide what relative weight to give to different kinds of contributions only transfers the responsibility to another set of functionaries. The judges (just like any other decision-makers) do not have available to them the specific tools, or special training, to be able to attribute financial value to non-financial work. Instead, they resort to the technicalities of legal reasoning to attempt this task with, not surprisingly, unsatisfactory results.[81]

The main issue relates to conventions of legal interpretation that require that the unfettered discretion given to the judges in the legislation cannot be subsequently fettered by judicial interpretation. The High Court in *In the Marriage of Mallet*[82] had to decide, among other issues, whether the respective contributions of both the parties should be given an equal value. It is a significant decision as the High Court was, for the first time, addressing specific provisions of the FLA, and its views continue to inform the interpretation of the lower courts. Briefly, the dispute related to property allocation at the end of a marriage of 29 years. The value of the assets jointly owned was ($240 000); $261 000 was solely owned by the husband; $5700 was solely owned by the wife; and each owned 26% of shares in a family company valued at $86 996 each. At first instance, Bell J ordered that the wife should receive one-half of the jointly owned property; the value of her shares; and 20% of property solely owned by husband. The wife appealed to the Full Family Court, which held that, since all assets were acquired in a similar way, 'a just and equitable result would be to adopt the 50 per cent figure overall'.[83] The husband appealed to the High Court, and it restored the judgment of Bell J. In separate judgments it was emphasised that there is no legal presumption that in long marriages equality should be regarded as the starting point of making a property distribution based on the contributions of the parties.

The High Court had to respond to the developing trend in a number of earlier decisions that tended to treat the contributions of both parties as equal, especially in marriages of long standing. This was referred to as the proposition that 'equality is equity', and in marriages of long duration it was one way of attributing financial value to non-financial work. All five judges of the High Court wrote separate judgments, but we will refer to two of them that demonstrate how the High Court was primarily concerned with the conventions of legal interpretation rather than with developing a position on what may constitute equitable outcomes for the two parties of the marriage based on their financial or non-financial contributions.

Chief Justice Gibbs said that court decisions 'cannot put fetters on the discretionary power which the Parliament has left largely unfettered'.[84] Parliament had not provided expressly, or by implication, that the contribution of the homemaker or parent should be equated with the financial contribution of the other party. It had also not provided that there should be an equal division of property at divorce, or that equality of distribution should be the starting point in the exercise of the court's discretion. Justice Mason reviewed the earlier decisions that had applied a presumption of equality in evaluating the parties' contributions, and said that the language of s 79(4) imposes a duty on the court to evaluate the respective contributions of husband and wife. In undertaking this task, the court may decide that the respective

81   Parkinson, above n 26.
82   (1984) 156 CLR 605.
83   Ibid 613 quoted by Gibbs CJ.
84   Ibid 609.

contributions of husband and wife are of equal weight, but it can only reach this conclusion if the materials before the court show that the efforts of the wife, in her role, were equal to those of the husband, in his role.

He then went on to explain that such a conclusion of equality of contributions would be more readily reached in regard to property consisting of the matrimonial home, superannuation or other pension funds, but more difficult in cases where extensive business assets had been accumulated by one party owing to his or her ability and energy, and to which the other party had made no financial contribution.[85] According to him, the flaw in the Full Court's decision was its reliance on the proposition, developed in other Family Court decisions, about equality of contributions that had elevated it to a legal presumption. This step had allowed the court to arbitrarily give equal value to the direct financial contribution of one and to the indirect contribution of the other as a homemaker and parent. It thus had not undertaken the task of evaluating the relative worth of these different contributions.

Both of these judgments focus on legislative design that grants discretion to the court in a specific matter, and conventions of legal interpretation that do not permit the courts to restrict the scope of such discretion. The High Court in *Mallet* identified the main problem, which was that the Family Court, in earlier decisions, had tended to assume, rather than calculate, an equality of contributions to the property. What was not discussed in detail was how the courts may calculate the financial value of non-financial work. Economics does not provide any workable formula, and the lawyers fumble with concepts like discretion and the limited role of the judiciary in applying the law. The comment in Mason J's decision that a conclusion of equality of contributions would be more readily reached for property in the form of the matrimonial home, rather than for extensive business assets, is the central issue that needs explanation. This reasoning typifies the common sense attitude that non-financial caregiving work will only result in a share (perhaps even a greater share) of the matrimonial home, but there is no justification for valuing this kind of work as on par with business activities.

This is, however, not a representation of marriage as a partnership where two individuals do different kinds of work and should be treated as equal partners. Care work is undervalued in both domestic and market spheres and if judges hold the same views (even though the rhetoric is different) it should not come as a surprise. Initially there was some resistance to equating the consequences of marriage and de facto relationships,[86] but since the FLA has assumed jurisdiction over the latter, judges are now more inclined to attribute economic value to non-financial work in a similar manner.[87]

What is more difficult to accept is the judicial insistence that they function within the boundaries of the law and cases where a lesser value is allocated to domestic work than

---

85   Ibid 625.

86   There are repeated references to de facto relations not being the same as marriage in earlier de facto cases. See, eg, *Dwyer v Kaljo* (1992) 15 Fam LR 645. See also Judith Housego, 'De Facto Relationships Property Claims – Some Certainty, At Least For Now' (1997) 11(3) *Australian Journal of Family Law* 239.

87   For a discussion of how far judges' attitudes are the same as those likely to use the law, see Nareeda Lewers, Helen Rhoades and Shurlee Swain, 'Judicial and Couple Approaches to Contributions and Property: The Dominance and Difficulties of a Reciprocity Model' (2007) 21(2) *Australian Journal of Family Law* 121.

market work can be explained by reference to an objective assessment of facts.[88] The judicial responses since *Mallet* have to be understood as the triumph of legal reasoning that privileges procedure over substance.[89] In the vast number of cases decided by courts pursuant to s 79, there is thus an understandable reluctance to create rules (much less binding rules), even as general guides, because of the discretion granted in the legislation.

A series of decisions dealing with the allocation of large assets and introducing the notion of special skills (usually of the husband) exemplifies how entrenched this attitude is, but, even when judges find reasons to reject the special skills argument, attributing equal value to both kinds of work is not the inevitable outcome. This analysis not only exposes the values these decisions reflect, but also demonstrates the flawed formulation of s 79 of the FLA.

In the Marriage of Ferraro is a well-known decision where the concept of 'special skills' in accumulating substantial assets was discussed.[90] In a marriage that had lasted about 27 years, the trial judge valued the total property at $10.26 million. Most of these assets were created through the business conducted by the husband. The wife had devoted herself virtually entirely to the care of the home and children, but she was a company director. At first instance, Treyvaud J divided the property, 70% to the husband and 30% to the wife. He found that the husband had acquired, improved and conserved the parties' property almost without assistance from the wife, their marriage was one of traditionally divided roles, and the wife's contribution was limited in quantum and value. In rejecting the wife's claim of equality of contribution, the trial judge commented that doing otherwise would be:

> akin to treating the contributions of the creator of Sissinghurst Gardens, whose breadth of vision and imagination, talent, drive and endeavours led to the creation of most beautiful gardens in England, with that of the gardener who assisted with the tilling of the soil and the weeding of the beds.[91]

The wife appealed and inter alia argued that the trial judge had erred in assessing her contributions. The Full Family Court identified the two main issues: how are the quality of the parties' respective roles to be assessed; and how are those disparate roles to be compared in making a s 79 order?[92] It acknowledged the difficulty of assessing the 'quality' of very different kinds of contributions in the normal range of activities of a breadwinner and a homemaker, as that would lead to undervaluing the role of the homemaker. The Court analysed the practice of courts,[93] repeating the comments of Wilson J in *Mallet*,[94] that the contributions of

---

88   For a review of a number of such decisions, see Belinda Fehlberg, '"With All My Worldly Goods I Thee Endow?": The Partnership Theme in Australian Matrimonial Property Law' (2005) 19(2) *International Journal of Law, Policy and Family* 176; Juliet Behrens, 'De Facto Relationship? Some Early Case Law under the Family Law Act' (2010) 24(3) *Australian Journal of Family Law* 350.

89   For a then contemporary argument favoring equal sharing of family assets, see Elizabeth O'Keefe, 'Property Rights in Marriage and Property Distribution on Divorce: Room for Maneuver' (1983) 18(2) *Australian Journal of Social Issues* 136.

90   (1992) 16 Fam LR 1 (Fogarty, Murray and Baker JJ).

91   Ibid 28. For a trenchant critique of this comment, see Lisa Young, 'Sissinghurst, Sackville-West and "Special Skill"' (1997) 11(3) *Australian Journal of Family Law* 268.

92   *In the Marriage of Ferraro* (1992) 16 Fam LR 1 35–6, where it was also acknowledged that undervaluing of the homemaker's contributions could be levelled out by taking account of future needs in s 75(2). This issue is discussed in greater detail below.

93   Ibid 37–49.

94   Ibid 36.

the homemaker should be recognised in a substantial and not a token manner. It, however, continued the practice of the court to not require a detailed assessment of the respective roles of the homemaker and breadwinner in the 'normal range' of such roles.

Furthermore, the Court went on to say that the 1983 legislative amendments to s 79, as well as social changes, have given a greater emphasis to the equality and partnership aspects of marriage. Nevertheless, the Court felt bound by the *Mallet* decision, which had rejected emphatically the presumption of equality of contribution. It further said that, in cases of considerable wealth, there was no reason in principle or logic why the special skills or acumen of the breadwinner should be treated differently from the high level of skill of a professional or tradesperson such as a surgeon, lawyer or electrician. The difference is in the resultant accumulation of wealth. However, having said all that, the Court modified the order of the trial judge from a 30% to a 37.5% share to the wife.

We mention these details in the *Ferraro* decision for a number of reasons. First, they demonstrate the function of legal reasoning that can prioritise the technical aspects of the rule of interpretation that, when granted by the legislature, discretion cannot be fettered by judicial interpretation. The courts thus feel compelled to exercise discretion in every case as if each case is dealing with issues that are unique to it. Second, the diversity of assessments of relative contributions is undertaken without any tools of calculation or comparison. Thus, in *Ferraro*, the Full Court assessed the 'correct' share of the wife as 37.5% as opposed to the trial judge's 30% assessment, but it is not possible to discern why the assessment was increased by 7.5%. It is a subjective valuation, and it cannot be anything else given the legislative design and the insistence that courts must not fetter the discretion granted to them. Third, whether the courts have abandoned the 'special skills' aspect of assessing the worth of contributions by the financially more active partner, usually the husband, is a question that will keep arising precisely because the discretion allowed to the judges is not to be curtailed.[95]

More recently, the decision of the Full Family Court in *Fields v Smith*[96] addressed the issue of how to weigh the respective contributions of an entrepreneur husband and a wife who was engaged in raising the children and also participating in the running of the business as a director and shareholder. At first instance, Murphy J awarded the wife a share of 40% and the husband 60% of the total assets at the end of a 29-year marriage.[97] On appeal, the Full Family Court readjusted this distribution of property to 50% each. It declined to accept the implied assumption in the husband's claim that he should be attributed a larger share because of his business acumen and special skills.[98] In particular, the Court endorsed the views in the earlier Full Family Court decisions of *Hoffman v Hoffman* and *Kane v Kane*,[99] that nothing in the words of s 79 endorses the view that there is a special category of

---

95   Soon after *Ferraro* the Full Court commented that the concept of 'special skills' ought to be reconsidered in a suitable case: see *In the Marriage of Figgins* (2002) 173 FLR 273 (Nicholson CJ, Ellis and Buckley JJ). See also Lisa Young, 'Rich Women and Divorce: Looking for a "Common Sense" Approach' (2004) 22(1) *Australian-Canadian Studies: An Interdisciplinary Social Science Review* 95. Whether legislative reform is required is briefly discussed in Frank Bates, '"Exceptional Contributions" by a Spouse in Australian Family Law – A Road Mistaken' [2003] *International Family Law* 176.

96   (2015) 53 Fam LR 1 (Bryant CJ, May and Ainslie-Wallace JJ).

97   Ibid 29 [109]. More pertinently, he constructed a table of cases dealing with special skills and large assets. Even though he denied that he was relying on this table as a guide, on appeal the Full Family Court accepted that the trial judge had in fact relied on this table and thus fettered his discretion.

98   Ibid 13 [42]–[43], 34 [130].

99   Respectively (2014) 51 Fam LR 568; (2013) 50 Fam LR 498.

property that is more valuable than other kinds. The Court went on to say that its obligation was to weigh the respective contributions of both parties, and to give appropriate weight to their contributions.

What was not explained was how their respective contributions were finally weighed. The trial judge had done this by finding in the previous decisions general guidelines that involved large pools of assets, but also specifically denying that he endorsed the 'special skills' argument. Since the Full Court disagreed with his method, and redistributed the property on the strength of its assessment, the crucial question is: what method did it use? If all that has happened is that this particular set of judges considered the respective contributions of the parties as equal, what stops another set of judges from coming to a different conclusion? We say this despite decisions like *Fields v Smith*, which involve large asset pools where equal distribution of property, on the strength of respective contributions, has been ordered. The point is that, ultimately, everything seems to hinge on the subjective judgment of the particular judges. We argue that the reliance in the FLA on judicial discretion as the central device used to achieve just and equitable outcomes is a major flaw in the legislative design.[100] Whether introducing more definite rules of distribution of property can rectify this is discussed below.

The difficulties in attaching financial value to contributions are made more evident in cases involving family violence and where the asset pool is modest. In this regard, the halting efforts of the Family Court to take into account domestic violence when assessing respective contributions are a poor substitute for the law proclaiming unequivocally that any kind of violence is unacceptable in personal relations. Attributing a financial value to unacceptable violence cannot be a form of justice in the absence of adequate criminal sanction of this behaviour. Moreover, as was explained above, the courts face conceptual difficulties in attributing financial value to non-financial conduct. Given this fact, how a court can fairly 'compensate' for the presence of violence remains a puzzle. The matter is doubly confused as the FLA's emphasis on no-fault divorce is extended to all other aspects of the Act as well. Thus, the initial resistance to acknowledging the relevance of violence in property applications was based on the claim that since the FLA is premised on no-fault divorce, fault should not become relevant in an indirect manner.[101] One device used by the court to acknowledge the consequences of violence was to claim that violent conduct is not per se relevant, but if it has an effect on the ability of the target of violence to contribute to property accumulation, welfare of the family and so on, it would be taken into account.

For instance, in *In the Marriage of Sheedy*[102] the Court was asked to rule on the admissibility of allegations made in a paragraph of the wife's affidavit concerning the respondent's behaviour towards her. Justice Nygh found that, as a result of decisions like *In the Marriage of Soblusky*[103] or *In the Marriage of Ferguson*,[104] the conduct of parties in an application

---

100   But see John Dewar, 'Reducing Discretion in Family Law' (1997) 11(3) *Australian Journal of Family Law* 309.

101   For example, in *In the Marriage of Fisher* (1990) 99 FLR 357, 360 (Nygh J) it was said that the primary subjects of investigation were the contributions and needs of the parties rather than the causes of the breakdown.

102   [1979] FLC 90-719 (Nygh J).

103   (1976) 28 FLR 81.

104   (1978) 34 FLR 342.

under s 74 or 79 is only relevant if it has financial consequences, such as financial misbehaviour resulting in the waste or suspension of family assets,[105] or physical misconduct resulting in the applicant's illness or disability.[106]

The Full Family Court in *Kennon v Kennon*[107] reviewed the earlier cases and held that when there is violent conduct by one party against the other which has made the target's contributions significantly more arduous than they ought to have been, it is a fact that can be taken into account. Moreover, the Court said it preferred this approach to the concept of negative contributions.[108] At first instance, Coleman J had acknowledged and assessed the contributions of the wife pursuant to s 79 at $200 000, but admitted that there was no pretence that such a figure represented a scientifically precise assessment. More significantly, the trial judge, in assessing the wife's s 79(4)(c) contributions, assumed that they were offset by the very lavish lifestyle of the parties. The Full Court majority disagreed, and increased this sum to $400 000 on the basis that the wife performed her role as she was expected to in an affluent family, and her contributions under paragraph (c) were substantial.[109] Significantly, it did not overrule the trial judge's assessment that the wife's capacity to contribute had not been lessened by the violence. The Full Court did, however, make a number of general statements about the relevance of violence in assessing the contributions of the target of violence. What is most surprising is that this decision is often quoted as endorsing the idea that violent conduct can affect the property order.[110] Yet, on the facts in this case, the decision rested on a consideration of s 75(2) factors to 'compensate' for the violence. It is on the basis of this assessment that the Full Court majority differed from the trial judge, and increased the sum of $200 000 awarded by the trial judge for these factors to $300 000. It is virtually impossible to explain why this sum, and not another, is a more appropriate quantification of the needs of the wife.[111]

---

105   For example, in *In the Marriage of Cordell* (1977) 30 FLR 308.
106   For example, in *Barkley v Barkley* (1976) 25 FLR 405. See also Richard Chisholm and Owen Jessup, 'Fault and Financial Adjustment under the Family Law Act' (1981) 4(2) *UNSW Law Journal* 43; Juliet Behrens, 'Domestic Violence and Property Adjustment: A Critique of "No Fault" Discourse' (1993) 7(1) *Australian Journal of Family Law* 9; Regina Graycar, 'The Relevance of Violence in Family Law Decision-Making' (1995) 9(1) *Australian Journal of Family Law* 58. See a response by Peter Nygh, 'Family Violence and Matrimonial Property Settlement' (1999) 13(1) *Australian Journal of Family Law* 1.
107   (1997) 139 FLR 118 (Fogarty, Baker and Lindenmayer JJ). In this case the parties had cohabited for about five years and the total assets were valued at approximately $8.7 million. They did not have children, but the husband had children from earlier marriages who visited them regularly. The application by the wife for a property order, and for common law damages for the violence she was subjected to and its consequences, was heard by the Family Court (under the then existing cross-vesting legislation). The trial judge, Coleman J, awarded $400 000 in total ($200 000 under s 79 and $200 000 under s 75(2)) and $43 000 in response to her claim of $50 000 for damages.
108   Ibid 140 (Fogarty and Lindenmayer JJ).
109   Ibid 154 (Fogarty and Lindenmayer JJ; Baker J dissenting on the final amount). After taking s 75(2) factors into account, the Full Court majority replaced the trial judge's total order of $400 000 with an order of $700 000.
110   See, eg, Sarah Middleton, 'Family Court Property Proceedings: Rethinking the Approach to the "Financial Consequences" of Domestic Violence' (2002) 25(3) *UNSW Law Journal* 704.
111   For another view, see Patricia Easteal, Catherine Warden and Lisa Young, 'The Kennon "factor": Issues of Indeterminacy and Floodgates' (2014) 28(1) *Australian Journal of Family Law* 1.

Similar observations could apply to the Family Court's efforts to give financial value to domestic or care work in cases involving more modest asset pools.[112] It is generally accepted that in such cases the Family Court has more readily accepted the equality of contribution by the two parties. Moreover, in cases where children are young and being cared for by one parent, usually the mother, the courts have been willing to readjust the notional distribution in view of the s 75(2) factors.[113] It is through this readjustment to provide for future needs that the conventional wisdom that the Family Court is a court biased towards women comes into being.[114]

Thus, the issue of how to give financial value to non-financial work remains uncertain, as judicial precedent is open to revision at any time. While courts draw a fine distinction between restricting discretion and providing guidelines for subsequent cases, either way it is difficult to discern the rationale for any particular case. Would it be a better option to enact a legislative rule that equality of contribution would be a starting point for making a property allocation order?[115] The suggestion to introduce equality of contributions as a legislative starting point was made, but rejected mainly on the basis that families require individualised solutions that cannot be reached through the application of general rules.[116]

No matter how definite the legislative rules are, it remains the case that they need to be interpreted. It may help if the legislation contained more definite guidelines, but as legislation is always open to interpretation, ultimately it is the conventions of legal reasoning that need to be reviewed; this is true for all areas of law, not only for family law.[117] This also becomes evident in the courts' consideration of the s 75(2) factors, or what are sometimes referred to as the 'future needs' aspect of s 79(4) as part of step three in property allocation decisions.

---

112   See, eg, *In the Marriage of Best* (1993) 116 FLR 343 (Fogarty, Lindenmayer and McGovern JJ), where modest assets were divided by the trial judge, Gee J, in the ratio of 70:30 for the wife and husband. On appeal by the wife, the Full Family Court awarded the wife all the assets, in part because the husband had substantial and continuing capacity to generate an income as a senior partner in a Sydney law firm. At the same time the wife had significant responsibilities for herself and the four children of the marriage.

113   See, eg, a survey of 261 cases where the Family Court gave a judgment between October 1983 and May 1984; frequently equal division of assets was adjusted by a further 10% in favour of the parent responsible for housing children – usually the woman: ALRC, 'A Study of Family Court Property Cases in Australia' (Research Paper No 1, 1985) 167.

114   For a brief review of some of these arguments, see Peter Nygh, 'Sexual Discrimination and the Family Court' (1985) 8(1) *UNSW Law Journal* 62.

115   Patrick Parkinson, 'The Yardstick of Equality: Assessing Contributions in Australia and England' (2005) 19(2) *International Journal of Law, Policy and the Family* 163.

116   There was a tentative move towards introducing a presumption of equality of contributions in the FLA, but it was not enacted. See Commonwealth Joint Select Committee on Certain Aspects of the Family Law Act, Parliament of Australia, *The Family Law Act 1975: Aspects of its Operation and Interpretation* (1992); Attorney-General's Department, Commonwealth, *Property and Family Law: Options for Change*, Discussion Paper (1999). See, for a discussion about this proposal, Angela Lynch, Zoe Rathus and Rachael Field, 'The Future of Family Law Property Settlement in Australia: A 50:50 Split or a Community of Property Regime? Some Issues for Women' (1999) 15 *Queensland University of Technology Law Journal* 77.

117   Feminists have long argued for making the method of legal reasoning responsive to gender. See, eg, Mary Jane Mossman, 'Feminism and Legal Method: The Difference it Makes' (1986) 3 *Australian Journal of Law and Society* 30.

Step three: future needs/maintenance or something else?

Over time, the Family Court has developed the practice that a notional distribution of property is made on the basis of contributions and, if required, it may be adjusted by reference to factors in s 79(4)(d)–(g) of the FLA. Very broadly, such readjustment is described as the 'future needs' component, and at times it is also designated as the maintenance component of the property order. The two broad categories of the relevant provisions in s 79(4) are the s 75(2) factors referred to in s 79(4)(e), and those included in s 79(4)(d), (f) and (g). In the latter category, the court must consider the effect of the orders on the earning capacity of either party to a marriage (s 79(4)(d)); any other order made under the FLA affecting a party to the marriage or a child of the marriage (s 79(4)(f)); and any child support under the *Child Support (Assessment) Act 1989* (Cth) that a party to the marriage is to provide or has provided for a child of the marriage (s 79(4)(g)). The focus in this section is on the s 75(2) factors in s 79(4)(e). We will have occasion to analyse these factors in the following chapter and, therefore, mention them only briefly here.

In making a property order, s 79(4)(e) requires the court to take into account matters referred to in s 75(2) so far as they are relevant. As a preliminary issue, it is necessary to distinguish between the relevance of the s 75(2) factors in a property order and in spousal maintenance proceedings.[118] It is possible that the applications for property allocation and spousal maintenance are considered at the same time. However, it is accepted practice in the courts that, in such instances, the property application is finalised before the maintenance application is considered.[119] Therefore, the court's treatment of s 75(2) factors as part of the property order does not have to comply with the requirement to satisfy 'need' in s 72.[120] Moreover, an order for property under s 79 might obviate the need of one party to be maintained by the other.[121]

A primary purpose of including s 75(2) factors in the property order is to give effect to the s 81 imperative that as far as possible the court should try to finalise the financial relations between the parties. One way of doing this is to anticipate the future needs and provide for them. The FLA thus anticipates that spousal maintenance will be required only if the property distribution is unable to provide for the needs of the financially weaker party. However, a number of issues arise from the legislative design which make the judicial task extremely onerous. The FLA does not specify the relative weight to be given to the contributions and maintenance/need/future components of the property order. The extent of discretion granted to the court under s 75(2) is extremely wide. Thus, in determining whether to modify the entitlement to the property on the basis of contributions (arrived at in step two of the process), it is up to the individual judge to attribute any weight to the factors mentioned in s 75(2). Judges acknowledge that the criteria are expressed very broadly, but also that they refer to the future and are prospective in nature.[122] Thus, another element of subjective assessment is added to the exercise.

---

118   *In the Marriage of Collins* (1990) 100 FLR 340. The court is authorised to award spousal
         maintenance under s 74 and in doing so it must take into account the matters referred to in s 75(2);
         the entitlement to spousal maintenance is determined in s 72.
119   *In the Marriage of Clauson* (1995) 18 Fam LR 693.
120   *In the Marriage of Williams* (1984) 9 Fam LR 789.
121   *In the Marriage of Clauson* (1995) 18 Fam LR 693.
122   *In the Marriage of Waters and Jurek* (1995) 126 FLR 311.

Moreover, the relationship between the two rationales for a property order – entitlement on the basis of contributions and requirement because of need – is not articulated. Distribution of property on the basis of need sits uneasily in the FLA, which seems to treat the two members of a marriage (and now also of a de facto relationship) as equal partners. It is an undeniable fact that many women would require support at the end of a marriage or relationship, especially if they are the primary carers of children. What is not so evident is why that should be the sole responsibility of the former husband or partner. What is the state's role or the role of the economic market in this context? In raising this issue we are pointing out the ready assumption made in the FLA that seems to emphasise the individual autonomy of both spouses and expects them to exit an unsatisfactory marriage at will, assuming they will both fare equally well in society. At the same time, it cannot ignore the financial dependencies that intimate relations can create. One obvious rationale for adjusting property between the parties is to acknowledge how one spouse/partner has benefitted from the unpaid labour of the other spouse in exercising his or her capacity to earn a wage, but it is only one factor among the 14 included in s 75(2).

Illuminating these issues exemplifies how the law enforces the idea of family as a private unit, and that the cost of marriage or de facto relationship breakdown is best borne by the individuals involved. This assumption sits uneasily with the reality of the dependencies created through the sexual division of labour, and it also absolves the state from establishing a safety net that sufficiently provides for the financially vulnerable party. The fact that family law facilitates women taking on the care roles and consequent financial vulnerabilities is one of the most important facts that needs to be the central focus of any analysis of the FLA. This has become even more evident in light of the High Court decision in *Stanford*, as discussed in the next section.

Once the court has given consideration to all of the potentially relevant matters in the step-three process, it must decide how to make the property order, both in terms of the proportion of shares and in actually making an order to that effect. This is where the so-called fourth step becomes relevant.

Step four: proposed orders to be 'just and equitable'

The Family Court, over time, had established the practice of making a property order in four steps, with the fourth step requiring the court to stand back and consider the entire case as a whole before making an order.[123] The fourth step refers to the Court's obligation to take into account s 79(2), namely, '[t]he court shall not make an order under this section unless it is satisfied that, in all the circumstances, it is just and equitable to make the order'.[124] However, the High Court decision in *Stanford*[125] has led to suggestions that the first issue to

---

123   See, eg, *In the Marriage of Hickey* (2003) Fam LR 355; *Russell v Russell* [1999] FLC 92-877.
124   For other aspects of what may be just and equitable, see also *In the Marriage of Schokker and Edwards; Re Leith Sinclair & Co* (1986) 11 Fam LR 551; *Doherty v Doherty* [2006] FamCA 199.
125   For ease of reading, we will refer to it as the High Court judgment and not the main judgment by French CJ, Hayne, Kiefel and Bell JJ, or separate but concurring judgment by Heydon J. However, we note that Heydon J's judgment was confined to examining whether a property order in this case satisfied s 79(8)(b) of the FLA in view of the fact that the wife had died while the proceedings were being determined. Thus, the issue turned on whether under s 79(2) it would have been just and equitable to have made an order with respect to property if the wife had not died. While the rest of the Court was concerned with this issue also, the main judgment has broader implications for the relationship between ss 79(2) and 79(4), which is the focus of our discussion.

require determination in a property claim is whether equity and justice require a property order to be made.[126] We argue that the main significance of this judgment lies in how it constructs the discourse of property ownership.

In considering the relationship between ss 79(2) and 79(4), the High Court in *Stanford* said '[t]he requirements of the two sub-sections are not to be conflated. In every case in which a property settlement order under s 79 is sought, it is necessary to satisfy the Court that, in all the circumstances, it is just and equitable to make the order'.[127] Although it was specifically acknowledged that the power granted by s 79 is not to be exercised by using fixed rules, the High Court did articulate three fundamental propositions:

1. Existing property interests are identified by reference to ordinary common law and equity principles, and it is in the context of these existing interests that the court must be satisfied that it is just and equitable to make a property settlement order.

2. The very wide discretion under s 79 must be exercised in a principled fashion, without assuming that the parties' rights and interests in property should be different from those that exist. It is also relevant that a community of property ownership arising from marriage has no place in common law. Therefore, questions of ownership of property between husband and wife must be decided by reference to the same rules as govern property rights of any two persons.

3. Whether a property distribution order is 'just and equitable' is not to be decided by assuming that one or other party has a right to have the property of the parties divided between them by reference to s 79(4) factors. If the court concludes what is a 'just and equitable' property order only by reference to matters in s 79(4) without a separate consideration of s 79(2), this would act to conflate the two provisions and ignore the principles laid down by the FLA.[128]

It is not clear why the High Court chose these three propositions and whether these were the only propositions available to it. But in doing so it has departed from what has been the accepted approach of the courts in the exercise of judicial discretion in property cases. Considering that it is the High Court laying down these fundamental propositions, every other court will now be bound by them.[129]

---

126   See, eg, Patrick Parkinson, 'Family Property Law and the Three Fundamental Propositions in *Stanford v Stanford*' (2013) 23(2) *Australian Family Lawyer* 4; Martin Bartfeld, *Stanford v Stanford Lots of Questions – Very Few Answers* (Leo Cussen Centre for Law, 2013).

127   247 CLR 108, 120 [35].

128   Ibid 121 [40].

129   Later cases have interpreted *Stanford* in ways that work around the implications of the case. For example, in *Bevan v Bevan* (2014) 51 Fam LR 363, also known as *Bevan 2*, the Full Court (Bryant CJ, Finn and Thackray JJ) said that the judges in *Stanford* were describing the classical judicial discretion where no single consideration or any combination of considerations necessarily determines the result. It also said that the High Court had neither approved nor disapproved of the four-step process. In the later case of *Chapman v Chapman* (2014) 51 Fam LR 176 (Bryant CJ, Strickland and Murphy JJ), it was held by different judges that, when the court is deciding whether it would be just and equitable to make an order under s 79(2), it is not a requirement to take into account s 79(4) factors. Justices Strickland and Murphy also said that if *Bevan v Bevan* (2013) 279 FLR 1 ('*Bevan 1*') decided that taking s 79(4) factors into account was mandatory, then they disagreed with that interpretation. The *Chapman* decision was approved of in *Scott v Danton* [2014] FamCAFC 203; *Fitzgerald-Stevens and Leslighter* [2015] FCWA 25, [182] where Walters J said that 'the "just and equitable requirement" – to use the words appearing in the heading to s 79(2) – is neither "a threshold issue" nor some sort of "factor" to be considered wholly within one or more of the steps or stages referred to. Instead, it pervades and informs the entire process'.

The High Court emphasised that, during a marriage, the explicit or implicit assumptions made by the parties about their property interests are matters for the parties to determine. It is only if the marriage comes to an end, and they are no longer living together, that it would be 'just and equitable' to make a property order, as there will be no common use of property for the two parties. In that case, the Court would then rely on the factors of s 79(4) to decide what may be a proper order. Thus, the bare fact of involuntary separation (as was the case in *Stanford*) does not establish that it is just and equitable to make a property order. However, it went on to say that even when the separation is involuntary there might be circumstances when it would be permissible to make a property order. However, that was not shown to be the case in this instance.[130]

The exact scope of the High Court decision continues to be interpreted in subsequent decisions that grapple with the respective implications of ss 79(2) and 79(4) for a court asked to make a property order.[131] The basic facts in *Stanford* were that the wife was living in a residential care facility. Before that she was living in the matrimonial home. It was found that physical separation did not establish that the marriage had ended. In determining whether to make an order in this case, the Court emphasised that the just and equitable requirement is independent of the contribution considerations. The Court gave examples of the sorts of things that could be considered in working out what is just and equitable. But in the factors they used to determine whether it is just and equitable we can see certain discourses getting preference over others: marriage as a private contract, which in this instance focused on an inquiry into the intention of the parties and what they planned to do with the property; who owned the property and, in this instance, why the husband who owned the property should have to sell it; and marriage as creating dependencies – in this instance, if the husband was not meeting her needs, then a property order would have to be made.

This case was decided the way it was because it was an involuntary separation and the wife's needs were being met, but it is open for other courts to apply this reasoning in other cases. The Court said that the just and equitable requirement will usually be met when the marriage has broken down, despite the intentions of the parties during the marriage, because there will no longer be common use of the property. This is an example of how family law maintains the idea of family as a private sphere institution. The Court made it clear that it would only have intruded in this case if the needs of the wife were not being met (under s 79(8)). It did not examine at what level the needs were required to be met, and from the facts it seems the Court thought it was enough that her subsistence requirements were being met – it was not expected that she would require more.[132]

Moreover, the Court drew distinctions between the kinds of factors that can be taken into account in working out what is just and equitable. Notably, it mentioned legal factors, including the common law, equity and the FLA itself, but not moral factors. In effect (though the Court did not say this), in validating the legal factors and not moral ones, the Court

---

130   The High Court, in rejecting the argument of the husband that the FLA allows no jurisdiction to divide property in intact marriages, emphasised the significance of reasons and circumstances that would make it 'just and equitable' for a court to override the private arrangements of the two parties about the common use of property.

131   See above n 129.

132   See Chapter 6, where the maintenance cases on the standard of living provide a notable comparison.

affirmed the husband's legal ownership of the property (the wife made no financial contribution to the property), and in effect refused to give any weight to the wife's contributions to the property as the wife in a long marriage. Thus, the Court reconstructed the discourse that in an intact marriage the parties 'choose' how to organise their affairs and, as long as the wife's basic needs are being met, the Court would not interfere in their financial relations. The final message is – who owns the property owns the property.

Its emphasis that the 'just and equitable' requirement in s 79(2) has to be read independently of s 79(4) supports the option of interpreting s 79 in the abstract, oblivious to the wider social context in which the FLA is operating, and the disputants are living. At its most fundamental level, the issue can be identified by posing the question: when is it not 'just and equitable' for someone to be denied a share of the property? In general, responses to this question would point to the ownership of property by reference to legal title, which would justify the reticence of the court to disturb those normal rules of ownership. Decisions like *Stanford* seem to reiterate that property belongs to those who paid for it and the existence of the FLA has done very little to disturb this idea. A person, usually a woman, who has not paid for the property can thus, legitimately, be described as 'not the owner'. If she is not the owner of property, denying a property distribution application would not be unjust and, in fact, it would be unjust to take away a part of the property from the 'real' owner. Thus the idea that marriage/relationship is a partnership gets overlooked. This is the function of the FLA that uses a property ownership model based on separate property and does not articulate a specific right to share the property for the non-financial spouse. This becomes further evident once the particular facts in *Stanford* are explained in detail.

In this case the parties married in 1971 and both had children from prior marriages. For 37 years they lived in the matrimonial home that the husband owned and brought into the marriage. The wife suffered a stroke in 2008 and was eventually moved to a residential care facility. The husband put about $40000 in an account to provide for the care of the wife. In 2009 a daughter of the wife, as her case guardian, applied to the Family Court for a property order including that the house be sold and proceeds divided equally between the husband and wife. At first instance, the Magistrate's Court divided the property. The husband appealed against this order, but the wife died before the Full Court made its orders. Subsequently, the Full Court made the orders that the sum representing 42.5% of the assets should be paid to the legal representatives of the wife when the husband dies. The husband appealed against this decision to the High Court on two main grounds: that the courts did not have the power to make the orders; and if they did have the power it should not have been exercised.

The High Court decided that the power to make the orders existed but it was not just and equitable to make the orders. It is easy to see how it is not just or fair that a man who has lived all his life in his home should at the very late stage in his life be asked to sell his home so that the wife's children from a prior marriage might inherit 'her' estate. The High Court decided by a circuitous argument that the decision to make the property order turns on whether the wife's needs in an intact marriage are being met adequately. The separation was for medical reasons, it was not voluntary, and the fact that a case guardian represented the wife, as she could not represent herself, did not support the conclusion that the marriage had ended. It was also the case that the husband was continuing to meet the needs of the wife, and therefore this was a case where it was not just and equitable to make a property distribution order.

Thus far there seems little to disagree with, but, as becomes evident in the decision of Heydon J, there were disputes between the husband and the daughters of the wife about her care arrangements.[133] The daughters wished to keep her in a facility that required a $300000 bond, but the husband did not agree to that. Subsequently, the wife was placed in a high-care facility that did not require the payment of a bond. Nonetheless, the suggestion that the needs of the wife were being met adequately was readily accepted by the High Court. Ultimately, the decision turned on the particular facts of this case, but since it is the High Court's decision, the statement of legal principles is now the law for all other courts to follow.

Thus, the real significance of the High Court's judgment is that it decided what is just and equitable by reference to 'need' only and did not discuss contributions by the wife. At the end of a long life and marriage, the wife in this instance had no property or assets to show for it. The particular facts of this case were that the wife had died during the proceedings and no longer had a need, but the facts also lead to the conclusion that she had no property either. It is unavoidable that after *Stanford* the message of the High Court to non-financial spouses in an ageing population is that they should not expect to have a right to a share of the property to provide for their care at a level to which they are entitled – except if they seek a divorce order, and even then there is no guarantee that they will obtain an order in their favour. Marriage may be a partnership of equals, but property still belongs to the one who paid for it under the FLA. Is this a just and equitable outcome? According to the High Court it seems that it is. It remains possible that, according to general principles of law and equity, one may get a share of the 'matrimonial' property, but this was possible even before the FLA was enacted.

The outcome in *Stanford* demonstrates how abstract legal reasoning functions to distance the decision-maker from the result. Thus, the judges did not explicitly say that justice or fairness to the husband requires that he can stay in his house as he is old, has always stayed in this house and his wife is already dead. Moreover, making a property distribution order will only enable the wife's daughters from a previous marriage to get a share of the property. This was implicit in their reasoning. But the Court managed to give credence to these outcomes by laying down a general proposition that the Court must first determine whether it is just and equitable to make a property order according to general principles of law; only if it is just and equitable to make the order will it then consider the s 79(4) factors to decide what order to make. This is legal reasoning at its abstract best. It can, and does, avoid addressing the reason why provisions to make property orders based on the contributions of the parties were inserted in the FLA in the first place. It requires no acknowledgement of the need to redress the consequences of sexual division of labour that is an everyday part of our lives – including the lives of judges. It is for the same reason that the High Court can say that it is not possible to chart the metes and bounds of what constitutes just and equitable, but then go on to articulate three 'fundamental propositions' that could shape what this is.[134]

---

133   247 CLR 108, 126 [56].
134   Ibid 121 [41].

It is also the case that the possibility of creating a particular kind of jurisprudence by creating specialist courts, like the Family Court, falters when the apex court is embedded in the mainstream methods of legal interpretation. The possibility of creating an island of family law jurisprudence, while all other law continues to be formalist in orientation, is thus limited. This is also evident in the FLA's interactions with other areas of property law.

5.6   The reach of the FLA in other property law regimes

This limitation is illustrated in the interaction of the FLA with three other areas of property law: the legal regulation of superannuation, bankruptcy laws and the lending practices of financial institutions. This discussion substantiates our claim that family law cannot be considered a stand-alone area of law. In all three instances 'the problem' is that the FLA does not give the woman or non-financial partner a right to property as a co-contributor. The response has been to use the FLA to try to manage the situation by making forays into other areas of law and at times affecting the property interests of third parties, as is the case in superannuation or bankruptcy matters. In non-FLA-related cases, other rules of financial institutions treat women as full legal subjects, who are held responsible for the debts of their partners even if the relationship had ended some time ago. While the FLA epitomises the efforts of the legislature and the courts to acknowledge (however imperfectly) the sexual division of labour within affective relations, the other areas of law operate virtually oblivious to this social reality. The FLA on its own will not be able to modify the deeply entrenched ideas about entitlement to property and the significance of cultural ideas about care work or domestic work.

5.6.1   New forms of property: superannuation

Prior to the 2002 amendments to the FLA that introduced Part VIIIB,[135] courts could take superannuation entitlements into account only as a financial resource rather than as property (s 75(2)(g) and (f)). Owing to the higher and more regular income received by men from paid employment, they have greater super entitlements.[136] In the third step of making a property order, a court could adjust the allocation of property in favour of the spouse who did not have access to superannuation. Alternatively, a court would postpone making a property order and wait for superannuation entitlements to vest in the member (s 79(5)).

---

135   *Family Law Legislation Amendment (Superannuation) Act (2001)* (Cth) came into effect on 28 December 2002. Mirror provisions with respect to de facto relationships came into effect in 2009 (except in Western Australia; South Australia in 2010). For an explanation of these changes, see Federal Magistrate Judy Ryan, 'Superannuation on Marriage Breakdown: A Work in Progress' [2004] *Federal Judicial Scholarship* 6. For a discussion of the principles underlying this amendment, see John Dewar, 'Property and Superannuation Reform in Australia' (1999) *International Family Law* 118.

136   Margaret Harrison, 'Australia's Family Law Act: The First Twenty Five Years' (2002) 16(1) *International Journal of Law, Policy and the Family* 1, 14–5.

However, this latter option could come into conflict with the imperative of s 81, which is to finalise the property relations. As Harrison explains, a court could not divide superannuation as it was not vested property, and therefore could not bind trustees to enforce its orders, as they were third parties. Since 2002, courts have been given specific powers with regard to superannuation and their orders can bind the trustees of superannuation funds, who are third parties. The separating parties can agree to split or divide superannuation, or the court can make orders to this effect.[137] Such court orders, or private agreements, can bind the trustees of superannuation funds.[138] Whether these changes have modified the court property orders under s 75(2) is not clear.

It was held in *Coghlan v Coghlan* ('*Coghlan*') that a superannuation interest is not property but another species of asset altogether that can be dealt with under s 79.[139] However, in order to the make a determination about superannuation, the court needs to determine the value of the interest (s 90MT(2)). However, as explained above, courts have struggled with attributing a financial value to non-financial work, and the same issue has arisen about assessing contributions of the non-financial spouse to superannuation funds.[140]

In keeping with the overall design of the financial provisions in the FLA, the legislation does not articulate a clear right to a share of the superannuation by the financially weaker spouse or partner. Specifically, the discretion granted to judges continues to be the defining feature of the legislation. This is in addition to the options available to the parties to come to a private agreement about sharing the superannuation entitlements, or to enter into a superannuation financial agreement under the FLA that would oust the jurisdiction of the courts under the FLA with regard to the superannuation funds of either party.

It is not surprising, then, that the difficulties experienced by the courts in determining an appropriate property order extend to making orders with regard to superannuation funds as well. There is, as yet, no discernible pattern in the judgments about quantifying contributions to superannuation funds, and how to factor in the lack of direct financial contributions to super by the financially weaker spouse. So too, it is not clear what significance should attach to the relative weight of the contributions and prospective needs components of the property order relating to superannuation.[141]

There are many decisions of the courts before and since the amendments in 2002, but as an illustration of the issues that come up with regard to assessing contributions to

---

137   *Coghlan v Coghlan* (2005) 193 FLR 9.
138   The other major change is that the parties or the court can impose a payment flag on a superannuation fund. Such a payment flag operates as an injunction to the trustees that they cannot deal with the funds without such flag being lifted (s 90ML). Courts also continue to create an offset of superannuation against other assets. The main difference from earlier practices of the court in acknowledging superannuation as a financial resource is that now it is treated as property that enlarges the 'pool' available for making a property order. For details, see Jacqueline Campbell, 'Superannuation' in Renata Alexander et al, *Australian Master Family Law Guide* (CCH, 7th ed, 2015) 645.
139   (2005) 193 FLR 9, 18 [43] (Bryant CJ, Finn, Coleman, Warnick and O'Ryan JJ).
140   For pre-reform analysis, see Jenni Milbank, 'Hey Girls, Have We Got a Super Deal For You: Reform of Superannuation and Matrimonial Property' (1993) 7(2) *Australian Journal of Family Law* 104.
141   In the period prior to the 2002 amendments, one approach often used was to apply the formula stated in *In the Marriage of West and Green* (1991) 114 FLR 74, but it also attracted disagreements. In the post-2002 amendments period, this formula is used more as a basis of calculating the split of superannuation interest for the non-contributing spouse. See *PJM v STM* [2005] FLC 93-242.

superannuation, and what weight to assign to those contributions, *Coghlan* is instructive. In this case, the wife appealed against the orders of the trial judge, claiming that he had erred in not including superannuation as part of property subject to the s 79 application. Both husband and wife had separate superannuation entitlements and were employed, although the husband later stopped working. The Full Family Court did not accept this argument, and said there is nothing in the FLA that compels the Court to treat superannuation as property in a s 79 order, but the Court retains the discretion to do so. In this case the Court preferred to treat superannuation entitlements separately from the rest of property. Moreover, it explained that where such interests are considered they would be subject to the factors in s 79(4), and thus 'not only will any contributions, both direct and indirect, by either party to such superannuation interests be more likely to be given proper recognition, but the real nature of the superannuation interests in question can also be taken into account, both in consideration of the s 75(2) matters and in the final assessment of whether the ultimate order is just and equitable'.[142]

It explained that the meaning of 'the real nature of superannuation entitlements' refers to the fact that, even though it may be calculated as a significant sum at present, the real value of such entitlement in the future may be a periodic sum or a lump sum of unknown amount.

There were no children in this case and the marriage (of 11 years) had been relatively short. The Court did not have occasion to elaborate on the possibility of assessing non-financial contributions to superannuation entitlements, but it is evident that, in cases involving a primary caretaker, such non-financial contributions to superannuation of the other spouse would be a significant issue. Yet there is no definite trend evident in how the courts assess such indirect and non-financial contributions.[143]

Most of the commentary in this area deals with the technical rules in the FLA,[144] and the constitutional authority of the Federal Parliament to affect the property rights of third parties. We would like to depart from this emphasis and ask: what is the significance of this change for improving the financial independence of the spouse in the carer role, namely the wife in most cases? The changes in the FLA's response to superannuation are welcome, but do not go far enough. It bears repeating that, even if the superannuation interest is treated as property and divided between both spouses, the disparity between the two will continue if the primary carer continues to have an interrupted or part-time attachment to the workforce.

The extensive literature on women's lesser access to superannuation points out how women in later years of their lives will be poorer than their male counterparts for this reason.[145] This demonstrates the limitations of relying on the FLA for the post-divorce wellbeing of the person who incurred economic disadvantage owing to their primary caretaking

---

142   (2005) 193 FLR 9, 24 [67] (Bryant CJ, Finn and Coleman JJ); but see *Paul v Paul* [2012] FLC 93-505 (May, Thackray and Crisford JJ), where the Full Court said that the approach suggested in *Coghlan* has merit, but does not exclude other ways of dealing with the issue.

143   Grania Sheehan, April Chrzanowski and John Dewar, 'Superannuation and Divorce in Australia: An Evaluation of Post-Reform Practice and Settlement Outcomes' (2008) 22(2) *International Journal of Law Policy and the Family* 206.

144   See, eg, Campbell, above n 138.

145   See David de Vaus et al, 'The Consequences of Divorce for Financial Living Standards in Later Life' (Research Paper No 38, AIFS, 2007).

responsibilities. Family law is one among a range of factors which have a bearing on how the costs of child care are distributed in our society. It cannot alter the lack of access to regular wage work for the primary carers. Nor can it have any influence on the shape of conditions of work, part-time work, or other aspects of labour laws that determine a person's financial wellbeing. Family law nevertheless holds out a promise that cannot be fulfilled – that it operates to achieve equitable outcomes for the spouses at the end of a marriage or relationship. But even within its sphere of influence, family law has not developed adequately to address the economic disparities created in familial relationships.

5.6.2   Third-party interests: bankruptcy

Changes to the FLA with regard to bankruptcy are another instance of the FLA extending its reach into other areas of law. Very briefly, the law of bankruptcy vests the property of a bankrupt in the bankruptcy trustee.[146] One consequence of this legal principle was that a spouse could not claim a share of property under s 79 if the other spouse had been declared a bankrupt.[147] Amendments in 2005 have made far-reaching changes to the authority of the courts dealing with property applications under the FLA.[148] The amendments, however, fall short of securing the interests of the non-bankrupt spouse before the interests of other creditors. The deciding authority remains with the court in the exercise of its wide discretionary power – a recurring pattern in the provisions for property proceedings under the FLA.

More specifically, the courts administering the FLA have gained the authority to affect certain property rights of third parties – that is, people other than the spouses or relevant de facto partners. As mentioned above, the FLA was amended in 2005 by the *Bankruptcy and Family Law Legislation Amendment Act 2005* (Cth).[149] One consequence of these changes is that the simultaneous operations of the FLA and the *Bankruptcy Act 1966* (Cth) are streamlined to some extent, but without specifying whether the non-bankrupt spouse has a prior claim to other non-secured creditors to the property in the name of the bankrupt spouse/partner. Thus, the court dealing with a family property dispute can make property orders with regard to property vested in the bankruptcy trustee, and so affect the property rights of third parties. Accordingly, the trustee can join the FLA proceedings (ss 90AE and 90AF).[150]

As noted, under the general principles of bankruptcy law, once a person becomes a bankrupt their property vests in the trustee of bankruptcy. It is for the trustee to decide how to deal with the claims of the non-secured creditors. Prior to the 2005 amendments, the claims of the non-bankrupt spouse were not given any special status.[151] The official

---

146   *Bankruptcy Act 1966* (Cth) ('*Bankruptcy Act*').

147   There is extensive case law but see, eg, *Deputy Commissioner of Taxation v Swain* (1988) 81 ALR 12.

148   *Bankruptcy and Family Law Legislation Amendment Act 2005* (Cth). See also Dorothy Kovacs, 'The New Face of Bankruptcy in 2005: The Bankrupt Spouse, the Trustee in Bankruptcy and the Family Court' (2005) 19 *Australian Journal of Family Law* 60 (Development and Events) for a detailed academic review.

149   The *Bankruptcy Act 1966* (Cth) was also amended in relevant areas.

150   See, eg, *Commissioner of Taxation v Worsnop* (2009) 40 Fam LR 552.

151   Patrick Parkinson, 'Property Rights and Third Party Creditors – The Scope and Limitations of Equitable Doctrines' (1997) 11(1) *Australian Journal of Family Law* 100, where he argues that not all the risks should be sheeted home to the wife.

explanation for these amendments was that they would provide new procedures and protections to the non-bankrupt spouse and also alert the court to the interests of the creditors of the bankrupt spouse.[152] It was made clear by the Family Court in *Lemnos*[153] that the 2005 legislative amendments removed the priority given to the unsecured creditors of the bankrupt spouse over the non-bankrupt spouse's claim for s 79 relief, but it did not accept that the legislation established an effective priority in favour of the non-bankrupt spouse.

These amendments to the FLA are a step in the right direction, but again do not go far enough. The most that has happened is that the non-bankrupt partner can now make an effort to claim a share of the property – unlike earlier times when the rules of the law of bankruptcy took precedence.[154] Whether a spouse will succeed in claiming a share of the property remains dependent on the discretion of the court. The main issue that seems to be unaddressed by the FLA rules in this regard is that the spouse/partner is treated as one of the many creditors. It could even be described as a denial of the FLA's own effort, however halting, to link property distribution to the contributions made by the two partners. Thus, even in this new regime the non-financial partner remains vulnerable to the commercial decisions of the other partner.

It is not an uncommon scenario for the equity in the matrimonial home to be used as a guarantee to secure loans for business or commercial activities. If and when such activities fail, the financial institutions step in to claim the matrimonial home to recoup their money. The non-financial spouse/partner is extremely vulnerable under the FLA, but also under other laws. In the literature this phenomenon is described as 'sexually transmitted debt'.[155] We refer to it here to bring into focus the rather limited, or non-existent, influence of the principles of the FLA on other areas of law that deal with the consequences of economic dependencies created within affective relations. It also reinforces the point that family law is not an island on its own that can deliver justice to both spouses in a gendered society.

5.6.3   Women as guarantors of debts of their partners

A recurring issue before the courts is where the applicants challenge the consequences of relationship debt. Very often third-party guarantors are women who support the borrowings of their male partners, usually for the purposes of small business enterprises. As detailed

152   Commonwealth, *Parliamentary Debates*, House of Representatives, 17 February 2005, 30–2 (Philip Maxwell Ruddock, Attorney-General). Section 35 of the *Bankruptcy Act* also provides that if there are pending property settlement or spouse maintenance proceedings the Family Court has jurisdiction in relation to any matter connected with a bankruptcy.

153   *Lemnos v Lemnos* [2007] FamCA 1058, [60] (Coleman J).

154   For example, on appeal in *Trustee of the Property of G Lemnos v Lemnos* (2009) 223 FLR 53 (Coleman, Thackray and Ryan JJ) the Full Court held that the court has to address s 75(2)(ha) factors and consider the effect of any orders on the creditors of the bankrupt. See also *Lasic v Lasic* [2007] FamCA 837. See also Grant T Riethmuller, 'Family Law and Bankruptcy: An Alternative Conceptualisation' (2014) 28(3) *Australian Journal of Family Law* 290.

155   R D Wilson, 'Sexually Transmitted Debt: Family Law and Bankruptcy' (2002) 22(3) *Australian Bar Review* 225; Kristie Dunn, '"Yakking Giants": Equality Discourse in the High Court' (2000) 24(2) *Melbourne University Law Review* 427; Janine Pascoe, 'Guarantees – They're Just Not Fair' (2005) 19(1) *Commercial Law Quarterly* 9.

in the NSW Law Reform Commission study,[156] these guarantors have often mortgaged the family home as part of the guarantee. In a high number of instances they have not received legal advice and have signed the 'all moneys' clause as part of the guarantee. It is recognised in the literature, and in decided cases, that the terms of the loans determined by financial institutions are onerous for vulnerable, emotionally involved partners.[157] In fact Baron argues that the concept of emotionally transmitted debt, rather than sexually transmitted debt, captures the core issue; that is, most women accept liability for the business loans taken out by their partners because of their emotional involvement with their partners.[158] Women are still expected to act altruistically and conform to other gender-stereotype legacies. She claims these include 'the prevalence of dependency and/or control inherent in many relationships; and the fact that many women lack business education, experience and information'.[159] Various suggestions for modifying the laws dealing with financial institutions' responsibilities include proposals designed to compel them to make full disclosure to the guarantor of the codes of conduct and similar provisions available in the law. But they only address the issues of misinformation or inadequate information. They do not deal with the fundamental issue of power imbalance which is gender-related.[160] While there is wide recognition of the vulnerabilities of guarantors, it is also the case that the law allows the financial institutions to enforce the sureties given by the partners. When seen in conjunction with the approach of the FLA, which does not give women a right to share property, we can see how the law constructs dependencies in various arenas.

5.7   Conclusion: transforming aspirations

In conclusion, we wish to emphasise that the above analysis of s 79, both as a legislative rule and how it is interpreted judicially, is not meant as an exercise in legalese. Simply reforming the rules without acknowledging the underlying reason why family law needs to deal with property rights will not change much. Thus the efforts, even if not carried through, to introduce a rule of equal distribution of property as the starting point in a s 79 order may be well intentioned, but they stop short of naming the problem of economic dependency created in affective relationships.[161] In most cases, the links between caring functions and the financial dependency of the caregivers are evident, but there also exist situations where cultural norms make it permissible for women to 'choose' to be economically dependent. The FLA, by holding out a promise that it can ensure a just and equitable outcome at the end of a relationship, facilitates the continuation of dependencies. It is this coming together of social, cultural and legal mores that requires more sustained analysis.

---

156   NSW Law Reform Commission, 'Darling, Please Sign This Form: A Report on the Practice of Third Party Guarantees in New South Wales' Research Report No 11 (2003).

157   Ibid ch 3.

158   Paula Baron, 'The Free Exercise of Her Will: Women and Emotionally Transmitted Debt' (1995) 13(1) *Law in Context* 23.

159   Ibid 25.

160   Renata Gross, *Looking for Love in the Legal Discourse of Marriage* (Australian National University Press, 2014) ch 3.

161   See references in above n 95 about the merits of legislative introduction of a presumption of equality of contributions.

A discussion of the arguments for and against a legislative presumption of equality of contributions is a necessary first step in the process of imagining a fairer family law system. However, it is also necessary to be alert to feminist critiques that have consistently examined the 'persistence of an understanding of equality as merely formal equality – the notion that the way to achieve gender equality is to treat women and men in exactly the same way'.[162] We argue that it is time to recast the debate, and that it is more useful to develop better ways of identifying the base causes of dependency, and then address those causes. For example, if it could be acknowledged that the responsibility for bringing up children is the main issue that needs to be addressed, then debates about public versus private responsibilities become relevant. Whether areas such as social-welfare law, tax law and employment law have a legitimate role to play in creating a fairer society becomes an inevitable part of family law debates.

Our main conclusion from the preceding discussion is that family law treats family disputes about property as private disagreements between two individuals, but ultimately creates discontent for both. It legitimises the financial dependencies of mothers, initially by holding out a promise of sharing the property, but then changes its emphasis to the desirability of autonomy in the maintenance discourse, and in social-welfare discourse, as will be illustrated in the following chapters. This is a function of the legal compartmentalisation of issues and of treating each distinct area of law as an autonomous subject, unaffected by other institutions or laws. One way to change this way of understanding law is to focus on the power of law to name realities and struggle with those contestations. As Fineman argues:

> The problem with many feminist analyses is that they have failed to realise the degree to which the possibility for the transformation of the family is dependent on corresponding radical and massive transformations of the workplace and accompanying ideological shifts that validate assumption of responsibility by the state in an unstigmatised manner.[163]

It is therefore necessary that we understand law reform in an expansive sense so that the specific rules are formulated by making the right assumptions, the interconnections of family law and other institutions are addressed, and the conventions of legal reasoning are included in the reform agendas. For example, while it is true that 'changes to laws can only ever constitute a small part of any profound social change',[164] the law should at least make the right assumptions. As long as the FLA does not give vested property rights to the wife, and continues to use gender-neutral language, the difficulties of attributing adequate financial value to care work as identified in this chapter will continue to surface. Policy-makers within family law cannot eliminate dependency, but they can manage it in an efficient and

---

162   Regina Graycar and Jenny Morgan, 'Examining Understandings of Equality: One Step Forward, Two Steps Back?' (2004) 20 *Australian Feminist Law Journal* 23. See also Margaret Davies and Kathy Mack, 'Legal Feminism – Now and Then?' (2004) 20(1) *Australian Feminist Law Journal* 1 and other articles in this issue.

163   Fineman, above n 21, 7.

164   Regina Graycar and Jenny Morgan, 'Law Reform: What's in it for Women' (2005) 23(2) *Windsor Year Book of Access to Justice* 393, 395. See also John Wade, 'Matrimonial Property Reform in Australia: An Overview' (1988) 12(1) *Family Law Quarterly* 41, 68 for an early acknowledgement that reform of family law on its own will not be enough to achieve fair outcomes for both spouses.

fair manner.[165] For this to happen, the study of family law has to be combined with the study of other laws and disciplines so that the institutions that continue to view the worker as an unencumbered individual,[166] with no caretaking responsibilities, can be changed. This requires a wider conception of family law than is presently used. Thus, a conception of a fair family law may require that policy-makers address the causes and consequences of the diminished earning capacity of caregivers, rather than only devising property ownership regimes, which on their own cannot adequately address these consequences and causes.[167] But even more importantly, the conventions of legal reasoning have to change in such a manner that law is interpreted in a contextual and embedded sense rather than as abstract rules. We will elaborate on this statement in the following chapter, where we discuss the legislative provisions for spousal maintenance and the judicial interpretation of these provisions.

---

165   Fineman, above n 21, 11.
166   Judy Fudge and Rosemary Owens (eds), *Precarious Work, Women, and the New Economy: The Challenge to Legal Norms* (Hart Publishing, 2006).
167   Discussed in the following chapter. See also Eva Cox, 'Beyond Community of Property – A Plea for Equity' (1983) 18(2) *Australian Journal of Social Issues* 142.

SPOUSAL MAINTENANCE

6.1   Introduction

This chapter begins by examining the concept of alimony, which will provide the historical and theoretical background of maintenance understood as a right, but which is limited in scope in the current provisions of the *Family Law Act 1975* (Cth) ('FLA'). Drawing on our analysis of property distribution in the previous chapter, this chapter will further develop the analysis of family law as maintaining the unequal effects of economic dependence in heterosexual relations in marriage, whether de jure or de facto.

The property division provisions of family law are not very relevant in poorer families, where no or very little property is available for distribution. However, the effect of the philosophy of the clean break principle in family law functions to delegitimise ongoing maintenance in these families as well. The economic dependence generated in an ongoing relationship becomes the individual problem of the financially weaker spouse. Moreover, at the breakdown of a marriage the legal discourse changes from marriage as a partnership with different but complementary roles, to one that is more about individual autonomy and self-sufficiency. While property provisions appear to acknowledge the need to compensate the caregiver, in cases where not much property is available, the expectation is that at the end of the marriage both parties should be able to fend for themselves. This analysis will illustrate the significance of family law moving between these different conceptions of relationships: as a partnership between two interdependent parties on the one hand, and as a contract between two equal partners on the other.

We will develop our argument by analysing the specific provisions of the FLA in the context of the widespread social reality that most women are neither generating incomes to the same extent as men nor generally the owners of substantial property in their own right. An analysis of the legislative provisions and case law on maintenance will lend support to our argument that there is an urgent need to revisit the maintenance discourse in family law.

6.2   History of the concept of alimony and maintenance

In any discussion of spousal maintenance the issue is, to put it starkly: why are women dependent financially, and why is it the responsibility of their former husbands to provide for them? This can be answered only if the historical development of ideas about marriage, divorce and financial work are considered together.

As we discussed earlier, Christian marriage was considered a sacrament that could not be dissolved by human agency. Therefore, the early religious and legal institutions, with few exceptions, did not have to provide for maintenance outside marriage. The necessity of spousal maintenance is intertwined with the possibility of marriage being dissolved. Its increased relevance as a legal concept coincided with the rise of the availability of divorce, evident in the enactment of the *Matrimonial Causes Act 1857* (UK), which was duly adopted in Australia.[1] The concept of maintenance relies on the model of marriage in which the husband is the primary wage earner and the wife is the primary homemaker or care provider. In that regard, the law as it developed with respect to maintenance reflected the prevailing ideology of the nuclear family as the ideal family,[2] and acknowledged the common law duty of the husband to maintain the wife, who did not have the legal capacity to own property.

Although married women have had the capacity to own property since the Married Women's Property Acts, the provision of maintenance at a fundamental level is a response of policy-makers to the social reality of the financial dependence of the wife. For if no spousal maintenance could be provided by the husband, the wider society, through poor laws, and later through social-welfare schemes, would have to step in to support the divorced wife and children. It was a logical response to marriage as a lifelong enterprise, so that if it had to be dissolved because of one person's fault, the wife could make a claim to maintenance, provided the husband could pay.[3] In earlier laws, even though spousal maintenance or alimony was available to the wife, very often conduct, whether or not she was the 'innocent' or not at fault spouse,[4] was taken into account in various other ways.

The legislative developments in the Australian colonies followed the broad contours of the *Matrimonial Causes Act 1857* (UK) and were eventually replaced by the federal *Matrimonial Causes Act 1959* (Cth) ('MCA').[5] Under this law spousal or child maintenance was available as an ancillary form of relief. State laws continued to be relevant if maintenance was required in circumstances other than in conjunction with an application for matrimonial relief under the MCA. The FLA, which replaced the MCA in 1975, was more sweeping in its application and covered most maintenance claims, with de facto partners and ex-nuptial children being notable exceptions. This changed partially after the States (except Western Australia, and subsequently Queensland in 1990) referred their powers over

---

1   Earlier the ecclesiastical courts could allow judicial separation and women in those circumstances also needed financial support. See Chester G Vernier and John B Hurlbut, 'The Historical Background of Alimony Law and its Present Statutory Structure' (1939) 6(2) *Law And Contemporary Problems* 197; John Eekelaar and Mavis Maclean, *Maintenance After Divorce* (Clarendon Press, 1986). See also John Witte Jr, *From Sacrament to Contract: Marriage, Religion, and Law in the Western Tradition* (Westminster John Knox Press, 2nd ed, 2012) for the historical correspondences between religious and legal regulation of marriage.

2   The term 'prevailing ideology' captures the well-documented fact that women have always contributed to household incomes by economic and non-economic activities. It is the cult of domesticity, mainly in bourgeois marriages, that overshadowed the economic contributions of women in working-class families. See Leonore Davidoff et al, *The Family Story: Blood, Contract and Intimacy 1830–1960* (Longman, 1998). We suggest that the ideology continues to thrive in contemporary social assumptions, as illustrated in the previous chapter on property proceedings under the FLA.

3   For a social history of this law, see Gail L Savage, 'The Operation of the 1857 Divorce Act, 1860–1910: A Research Note' (1983) 16(4) *Journal of Social History* 103; Marilyn J Coleman and Lawrence H Ganong, 'Alimony and Child Support' in Lawrence H Ganong (ed), *The Social History of the American Family: An Encyclopedia* (Sage Publications, 2014) 53.

4   David I Kertzer and Marzio Barbagli, *The History of the European Family: Family Life in the Long Nineteenth Century: 1789–1913* (Yale University Press, 2002) 119. The authors also explain how the maintenance laws allowed a de facto form of judicial separation for poorer Victorian women who could not afford to petition for divorce.

5   For this and the following discussion, see Anthony Dickey, *Family Law* (Thomson Reuters, 6th ed, 2014) 372–3.

ex-nuptial children to the Commonwealth so that the FLA could provide for the maintenance of all children.[6] In 2009 the Commonwealth relied on the referral of powers to it by the States (except Western Australia, and subsequently South Australia in 2010) over de facto relationships to extend its coverage to financial aspects, including maintenance claims in de facto relationships.[7]

Moreover, it is now usual for the claim to be made that, despite the legal definition continuing to insist that marriage is a union for life, the availability of no-fault divorce has changed the nature of marriage.[8] Attitudes to marriage as a lifelong commitment have morphed into affective unions lasting only as long as they satisfy the needs of the two adult partners (see Chapter 3). Other societal changes, particularly in the employment patterns of men and women, have supported this rise in individualism. It is an empirical fact that many women with children now participate in paid work, and therefore the question arises: why should the law make provision for spousal maintenance at the end of a relationship?[9]

The literature in this regard contains arguments that broadly pose a choice between two conceptions of spousal maintenance. On the one hand, it is seen as a useful legal acknowledgement of, and a means of redressing, the consequences of the dependency of women on men during marriage or similar relationships.[10] On the other hand, it is portrayed as contravening the principle of equality and perpetuating the problem of dependency by providing a disincentive to be financially independent.[11] An assessment of the relative merit of these claims is necessary, but it can only be undertaken adequately in the context of wider societal patterns.

An adequate discussion of the issue of spousal maintenance requires a prior acknowledgement of the cultural mores that legitimise women being the primary carers in families.[12] There is nothing in law that demands the allocation of caring tasks to women. The financial dependence of women, which is a result of the culturally accepted sexual division of labour within ongoing relationships, is justified on many grounds, including that it is a matter of choice for free individuals, that it is a private matter between the spouses/partners, or that the equality discourse is not appropriate in the context of affective relations as it valorises commodification and undermines care and love in the family. All of these responses are accepted views in society and we do not wish to engage in an exercise of validating one view over another, but it is important to address the consequences of these views.

---

6   This change took place with the *Family Law Amendment Act 1987* (Cth).
7   This change took place with the *Family Law Amendment (De Facto Financial Matters and Other Measures) Act 2008* (Cth).
8   See *Marriage Act 1961* (Cth) s 5(1) for the definition of 'marriage'.
9   Technically, spousal maintenance can be awarded in an ongoing marriage but only at the end of a relevant de facto relationship: see definitions of 'matrimonial cause' and 'de facto financial cause' in s 4(1) of the FLA.
10   For an illustrative example, see Belinda Fehlberg, 'Spousal Maintenance in Australia' (2004) 18(1) *International Journal of Law, Policy and the Family* 1.
11   See, eg, Ruth Deech, 'The Principle of Maintenance' (1977) 7 *Family Law Review*; Baroness Ruth Deech, 'What's a Woman Worth' (2009) 39 *Family Law* 1140.
12   Judith McMullen, 'Alimony: What Social Science and Popular Culture Tell Us About Women, Guilt, and Spousal Support After Divorce' (2011) 19(1) *Duke Journal of Gender, Law and Policy* 41 discusses the social science research findings about why women may not negotiate hard enough to obtain property or spousal support at the end of a relationship. We aim to connect these insights to the assumptions made in the legislative design of the FLA and the process of judicial reasoning.

The disagreements about the legitimacy of the concept of maintenance usually do not confront the fundamental issue that in a liberal market economy the financial wellbeing of individuals is primarily determined by their capacity to generate an adequate income. The trend of mothers participating in greater numbers in wage employment is celebrated, but obscures the difficulties faced by them in juggling paid work and caregiving roles.[13] Impairment of the capacity to be financially independent is inevitable for the primary caregivers because of the way work is organised to suit an ideal worker who does not have such responsibilities. Women, as the primary caregivers, are thus disproportionately disadvantaged.[14] Given this empirical reality, the question may be posed: why do women keep making these choices?[15] In economic terms this is not 'rational' behaviour, and in liberal terms it is not an option to explain this phenomenon as the result of differences between men and women. That is, liberals cannot explain such 'choices' as a result of women being less rational beings.[16] So the liberal legal system, being premised on the basis of formal equality and universal rules, ignores the significance of gender differences.

However, it is through the application of gender-neutral laws that structural inequalities become entrenched. Thus, labour laws that structure work conditions, or tax laws or social-welfare laws, among others, that structure decisions about workforce participation, are fiercely gender-neutral and not designed to name the social reality that women are the primary carers in our society.[17] This is despite the fact that feminist critiques of the effects of gender-neutral laws include the maintenance of gender hierarchies in society.[18] Furthermore, the choice is not only between gender-neutral and gender-specific laws. The fundamental issue is how law manages to construct a discourse that legitimises outcomes that are less than fair.[19] This is an extensive topic that we can only flag here, and in keeping with the theme of the book we ask the more specific question of what role the FLA plays in this regard. The maintenance provisions in the FLA use gender-neutral language (as the MCA had done), but their very presence in the legislation could also be viewed as an effort

---

13   In Australia 66% of mothers with children below 15 years of age were employed in 2011, compared to 42% of mothers in 1981. Over the same period, employment rates for mothers with children less than five years of age were 30–56%: see Jennifer Baxter, 'Child Care Participation and Maternal Employment Trends in Australia' (Research Report No 26, AIFS, 2013).

14   For example, Baxter notes that there is an upward trend of mothers in wage work. For families with children aged less than 18 years old, the proportion of mothers who were employed increased from 55% in 1991, to 56% in 1996, 59% in 2001, 63% in 2006 and 65% in 2011. However, over the period 1991–2011, there was no increase in the percentage of families with two full-time employed parents. The most significant change in family employment patterns was that the number of families with one parent employed full time and the other parent employed part time increased. In most families women undertook the part-time work. Jennifer Baxter, *Parents Working Out Work* (AIFS, 2013) <https://aifs.gov.au/publications/parents-working-out-work>.

15   Janeen Baxter, 'The Joys and Justice of Housework' (2000) 34(4) *Sociology* 609.

16   Neil Gilbert, *A Mother's Work: How Feminism, the Market, and Policy Shape Family Life* (Yale University Press, 2008).

17   See, eg, Joan Williams, *Unbending Gender: Why Family and Work Conflict and What To Do About It* (Oxford University Press, 2000).

18   For a comprehensive analysis of various feminist arguments about the nature of legal knowledge, see Katharine T Bartlett, 'Feminist Legal Methods' (1990) 103(4) *Harvard Law Review* 829.

19   Judith Baer, 'Feminist Theory and the Law' in Robert E Goodin (ed), *The Oxford Handbook of Political Science* (Oxford University Press, 2013) <http://www.oxfordhandbooks.com/view/10.1093/oxfordhb/9780199604456.001.0001/oxfordhb-9780199604456-e-016> 305. See also Judith A Baer, *Our Lives Before the Law: Constructing a Feminist Jurisprudence* (Princeton University Press, 1999).

of the law to address the gendered consequences of relationship breakdown. An analysis of the connections between legislative assumptions and modes of legal reasoning yields a complex picture.

The following discussion analyses the consequences of the financial provisions in the FLA, which make property and maintenance interdependent issues. We focus on three issues. The first is that the provision of maintenance under the FLA is circumscribed by the wider legislative context of the financial provisions that are mainly concerned with property division and upholding the 'clean break' principle. Second, the broader context of the legislation informs the practices of the courts that grant maintenance sparingly within the legislative model. This is made possible by the legislative model that grants wide discretion to the judges while also making s 75(2) factors relevant both in a property order and in granting periodic maintenance, and together they function to delegitimise claims for spousal maintenance. Third, the separation of spousal and child maintenance functions to confine maintenance as an economic issue rather than linking it to the far-reaching difficulties involved in combining paid work with child-rearing responsibilities. This is evident in how maintenance is usually ordered for a limited time, whether to allow the caregiver to retrain or to allow the children to grow up, with the expectation that she will be able to gain financial independence in the future.

In brief, we argue that the FLA maintains the salience of the nuclear family and the family as a private institution at different stages of the life of a relationship through the discourses of dependency and autonomy. It supports the formation of marriage and marriage-like relationships and the dependencies created by the sexual division of labour by not concerning itself with how the relationship is structured, but also by holding out a promise that the partners would be treated fairly by the law at the end of the relationship. However, it adopts the discourse of independence at the end of the same relationship, which cannot fully account for the effects that dependency has had for the financially weaker partner.

These issues lead us to question whether the concept of maintenance should be abolished altogether. We begin with a brief discussion of whether there is an argument for abolishing spousal maintenance and relate it to an examination of the possible rationales for providing spousal maintenance in the FLA.

6.3   Should all maintenance be abolished?

In a seminal and still relevant article, O'Donovan addresses the responses of the public, law reformers, popular writers and scholars in the debate regarding the continuing need for spousal maintenance at the end of a marriage.[20] The central point she makes is that most arguments about abolishing spousal maintenance invoke an ideal (egalitarian) society, which does not exist. More than three decades after O'Donovan wrote this article we are still far from such an ideal society, and therefore we need to take seriously the connections she is drawing between the economic, cultural and legal structures that support the status quo.

---

20   Katherine O'Donovan, 'Should All Spousal Maintenance be Abolished?' (1982) 45 *Modern Law Review* 424. In this article she is responding to two Law Commission reports, from England and Scotland respectively: Law Commission, *Family Law: The Financial Consequences of Divorce* (Law Com No 112, 1981); Scottish Law Commission, *Family Law: Report on Alimony and Financial Provision* (Scot Law Com No 67, 1981).

O'Donovan, in addressing the arguments of those who say that ongoing spousal main-tenance is a problem and should be abolished, identifies how the woman requiring ongo-ing maintenance is often portrayed as the problem because she expects to be maintained for life even after the marriage has ended. It is therefore not surprising that many feminists have been reticent in supporting spousal maintenance as it carries with it the stereotype of a victim woman who lacks the agency to take control of her life. Rejecting the idea or expecta-tion of ongoing support would in contrast endorse the conception of women as equal and capable individuals, which in turn would support the idea that at the end of a dead marriage ongoing maintenance should be abolished.

However, O'Donovan argues that this requires an ideal society to already exist, and one that meets the following conditions: equality of partners during marriage, including financial equality; equal participation by both partners in wage-earning activities; wages geared to people as individuals and not as heads of families; treatment of people as individuals and not as dependants by state agencies, such as social security and tax departments; and provi-sion for children by both parents, including financial support, child care, love, attention and stimulation.[21] This is far from the case in our society, where the ideology of equality has not been followed by material equality.

O'Donovan finds that questions of material equality arise within and outside the home. Thus, within the home family law does not intervene in an ongoing marriage despite the empirical evidence that the patterns of consumption are gendered, with no social or legal compulsion for equal sharing of wages, material goods or property ownership.[22] Outside the home, women find that opportunities for material equality are largely non-existent, and to an extent this is manifest in the lesser earnings of women compared to men as a group. This is largely the consequence of the continuing persistence of the family wage that is manifest in a dual labour market where women on average have lower wages and/or are engaged in part-time work so that they can also juggle childcare responsibilities and waged labour. It is a situation that is also largely supported by the failure of government departments to reform social security and taxation law to address the financial effects of the nuclear family on women, and the burden of child care falling primarily on mothers.

These conditions of work deploy the notion of a breadwinner wage earner and a depen-dent spouse with children. The concept of a breadwinner may not be a legal concept, but work conditions and industrial laws are structured in such a manner that the primary care-giver becomes dependent on the main wage earner in the process of raising children. The tax laws and social-welfare laws also assume the family to be the relevant unit in allocating many resources, such as tax breaks or social-welfare measures. So, too, the fact that mothers carry the main burden of child care may be a cliché, but we continue to speak of child care and the need for spousal maintenance primarily in non-financial terms. As a consequence, the time and effort spent in caring for children and other members of family are ignored or inadequately acknowledged.

However, O'Donovan explains that the discourses of dependence during marriage and after marriage are very different. The continued dependence of women as primary

21   O'Donovan, above n 20, 428.
22   As illustrated in the context of Australian family law in the discussion of property ownership and division in Chapter 5.

caregivers on their husbands is not only a personal or individual choice, but also one that is buttressed by legal provisions in family laws, taxation laws and social-welfare laws, to name a few of them. Thus, maintenance during the marriage is supported by the very legal system that at the end of such a relationship expects the woman to be financially independent. If we accept that dependence is undesirable, why do we not wish to abolish it in an ongoing marriage? If the material conditions existed that made the need for ongoing maintenance obsolete after marriage breakdown, it would be logical to expect that they would make dependence in an ongoing marriage also unnecessary.

In such an ideal society, each spouse would be an economically independent and self-sufficient individual with the safety net of social welfare available if needed. As a consequence, spousal maintenance would not be required and the stereotypically dependent woman wanting to be supported for the rest of her life would no longer exist. But this raises a pertinent question about the nature of marriage. If dependency between marriage partners were abolished altogether, would we still need marriage?[23] To answer this question it is essential to distinguish between religious and cultural understandings of marriage and to consider what the legal institution of marriage should entail.[24]

We agree with Diduck and Orton that the goal ought to be to abolish the systemic social and economic disadvantage of women associated with their roles as primary carers within marriage.[25] If true equity in employment and pay as well as affordable, good quality child care and fair valuation of domestic work existed, either partner could adopt any role. In such conditions, if maintenance were required at the end of a relationship it would not only be women asking for it, and it would be available as a right, based on the person's entitlements, instead of being an act of benevolence, made reluctantly available to dependent women. However, this connection between dependence during a marriage and at the end of it is not articulated often enough in the legal literature on spousal maintenance.

These analyses also illustrate how the concepts of choice,[26] and of public and private spheres, legitimise the idea that if two parties decide to create dependencies in an ongoing marriage, that is their private choice and not the concern of law or wider society. Moreover, a logical consequence of this private choice is that at the end of the marriage, or similar relationship, the law assumes that both individuals can and should move on with their lives. The law does not completely ignore the social realities of the hierarchies and dependencies

---

23   We would add any family organised as the two parents and child unit, whether in a marriage or a de facto relationship.

24   O'Donovan goes on to make the argument that child maintenance is a different issue, and that from the perspective of children it is necessary to provide for their needs, and this can be done through the institution of parenthood. We will return to this issue in later chapters on child-related matters. See O'Donovan above n 20, 432–3.

25   Alison Diduck and Helena Orton, 'Equality and Support for Spouses' (1994) 57(5) *Modern Law Review* 681. See also Mary E O'Connell, 'Alimony After No-fault: A Practice in Search of a Theory' (1988) 23 *New England Law Review* 437; June Carbone, 'Economics, Feminism and the Reinvention of Alimony: A Reply to Ira Ellman' (1990) 43(5) *Vanderbilt Law Review* 1463.

26   In the different context of surrogacy, the concept of choice is discussed by Charlotte Kr--løkke, Karen A Foss and Jennifer Sandoval, 'The Commodification of Motherhood: Surrogacy as a Matter of Choice' in Sara Hayden and Lynn O'Brien Hallstein (eds), *Contemplating Maternity In An Era of Choice: Explorations into Discourses of Reproduction* (Lexington Books, 2010) 95.

created during an ongoing relationship,[27] and provides for maintenance in limited circumstances. Whether this is an entitlement, or simply the possibility for the court to exercise its discretion, is partly answered by analysing the relevant provisions of the FLA as discussed in the following section. However, the broader philosophical and moral justifications underlying such legal rules also need to be articulated. We use the examples of the rationales for maintenance in the FLA and its use of gender-neutral provisions to argue that this particular shape of the maintenance provisions is not inevitable, and could be different.

As we discussed in the preceding chapter, the rationale for providing for property division in the FLA is neither articulated nor evident from court decisions. The same can be said with regard to spousal maintenance – for example, whether it is treated as an entitlement or is meant to provide for the needs or welfare of one spouse. Although the FLA is silent on the issue, it is useful to articulate the possible rationales for awarding maintenance before analysing the FLA provisions. The Family Law Council, in its discussion paper on spousal maintenance, describes different rationales as 'Rehabilitative Maintenance'; 'Custodial Maintenance'; 'Compensation for Past Contributions'; 'Lifestyle Maintenance'; 'Punitive Damages'; and 'Reduction of Welfare Expenditure'.[28] While this classification allows for a clear articulation of the possible rationales behind spousal maintenance, the categories are in fact overlapping and the existing provisions in the FLA depict a combination of these rationales. This is inevitable because the FLA does not explicitly justify the basis of the authority of the courts to override general rules of property ownership whether with regard to the division of property or maintenance provisions. In the former, the implied rationales simultaneously invoke the entitlement and need bases, but, under the maintenance provisions, the need of one party is to be balanced against the capacity of the other to pay.[29]

It is also an example of how the law assumes gender equality in the no-fault divorce regime and extends it to the provisions relating to maintenance. The MCA that was the immediate precursor of the FLA also contained maintenance provisions that gave wide discretion to the court to make such orders as it thought proper for maintenance of a party or children of the marriage.[30] However, in making an order, s 84(2) directed the court to have regard to the means, earning capacity and conduct of the parties to the marriage and all other relevant circumstances. It was not necessary for the applicant, mostly the wife, to show that she was in need before she was entitled to maintenance. Nor was her right to maintenance affected because she had the capacity to work and earn an income.[31] The conduct

---

27   See Jennifer Baxter, 'Employment Characteristics and Transitions of Mothers in the Longitudinal Study of Australian Children' (Occasional Paper Number 50, Department of Social Services, 2013) for an analysis of how mothers with young children negotiate the paid labour market. It analyses data from the first four waves of Growing Up in Australia: the Longitudinal Study of Australian Children. See Matthew Gray and Jennifer Baxter, *The Longitudinal Study of Australian Children: Annual Statistical Report 2010* (2011) Growing Up in Australia, <http://www.growingupinaustralia.gov.au/pubs/asr/2010/asr2010d.html#top>.

28   Family Law Council, *Spousal Maintenance* Discussion Paper (1989) [6.3].

29   Attorney-General's Department, Commonwealth, *Property and Family Law – Options for Change*, Discussion Paper (1999) included a proposal to separate the s 75(2) spousal maintenance factors from the provisions governing property division, but the entire proposal was abandoned. For the response of the Family Law Council, see Family Law Council, *Submission on the Discussion Paper Property and Family Law – Options for Change* (1999).

30   *Matrimonial Causes Act 1959* (Cth) s 84(1).

31   Ian J Hardingham and Marcia Neave, *Australian Family Property Law* (Law Book Co, 1984) 494.

of the parties, while not relevant in determining the entitlement to maintenance, could be taken into account in assessing the amount.[32] Hardingham and Neave claim that s 72 of the FLA imposes a reciprocal and identical duty of maintenance on both spouses, and that this is consistent with the increasing equality of men and women. It also makes marital misconduct irrelevant to the issue of liability of the other spouse to pay.[33] We agree that the main focus of s 72 in the FLA is on a reciprocal duty, but are less confident about the assertion regarding the increasing equality of men and women.[34]

A preliminary note about the terms used in the FLA is that it only uses the term 'maintenance' and does not use the terms 'spousal maintenance' and 'periodic maintenance ', but in this discussion we will use these terms for ease of discussion. This is in part necessary to distinguish between the maintenance/future needs/s 75(2) component of the property order under s 79 and maintenance payable under ss 72 and 74, which may be ordered as a periodic payment or lump sum payment that represents the capitalisation of periodic payments (s 80).[35]

6.4 Interdependence of property distribution and spousal maintenance provisions

6.4.1 The legislative context

The FLA contains the provisions for spousal maintenance in Part VIII.[36] The procedural rules for making an application for maintenance include provisions specifying that a matrimonial cause (s 4(1)(c), (f) and (caa)) or de facto financial cause (s 4(1)) is to be instituted in courts with jurisdiction under the FLA (ss 8(1) and 39A(5)). In practice most applications for spousal maintenance are made in conjunction with a property application under s 79. The main difference between a maintenance order and a property order is that the former does not need to be made in relation to existing property. For instance, in cases where there is no property but there is a capacity to generate an income, a maintenance order can be made for the spouse in need. It is possible to institute maintenance proceedings during a marriage,[37] but

---

32   Paul Toose, Ray Watson and David Benjafield, *Australian Divorce Law and Practice* (Law Book Co, 1968) 420ff.

33   Hardingham and Neave, above n 31, 495.

34   For an argument that the FLA provisions do not depict a clear policy rationale, see Belinda Fehlberg, 'Spousal Maintenance in Australia' (2004) 18(1) *International Journal of Law, Policy and the Family* 1.

35   See, eg, *In the Marriage of Vautin* (1998) 23 Fam LR 627.

36   Titled 'Property, Spousal Maintenance and Maintenance Agreements'. Part VIIIAB provides similar provisions for de facto relationships: see particularly div 1 subdiv B ('Maintenance'). The corresponding sections for maintenance in regard to a marriage and relevant de facto relationships are: right to maintenance (s 72/s 90SF(1)); power to order maintenance (s 74/s 90SE); matters to be taken into consideration (s 75/s 90SF); particular factors (s 75(2)/s 90SF(3)); urgent maintenance (s 77/ s 90SG); specification in orders (s 77A/s 90SH); cessation of orders (s 82/s 90SJ); modification of orders (s 83/s 90SI); and an extension of time to make an application for maintenance (s 44(4)(b)/s 44(6)(b)).

37   *In the Marriage of Eliades* (1980) 6 Fam LR 916. It is possible to make an application for maintenance even if the parties' marriage is void (s 71).

not during a de facto relationship.[38] Time limits apply for applications at the end of a marriage or de facto relationship. Generally, a maintenance application must be made within 12 months of the decree of divorce (s 44(3)), but the court can grant an extension of time.[39] In the case of a de facto relationship, an application must be made within two years of the end of the relationship (s 44(5)).[40] The court has wide discretion under s 74 to make any order that it considers proper and, pursuant to s 72(1), it must decide what is proper by reference to the s 75(2) factors. It can order periodic payments and lump sum payments,[41] as well as urgent or interim maintenance.[42]

Maintenance proceedings cannot be instituted after the death of one or both of the parties, or if a binding financial agreement covering maintenance bars such an application (s 90G/s 90UC), or during an existing de facto relationship.[43] Unlike a property order, a maintenance order can be modified relatively easily – that is, when the circumstances of a party change (s 83/s 90SI). For example, a court can discharge the order if there is any just cause for doing so (s 83(1)(c)/s 90SI(1)(c)); it can suspend the operation of the order wholly or in part and either until a further order or until a fixed time or the happening of some future event (s 83(1)(d)/s 90SI(1)(d); and when either party dies the order ceases to have any effect (s 82(1)–(3)/s 90SJ(1)). An order for periodic maintenance ceases, with few exceptions, upon the recipient getting married (s 82(4)/s 90SJ(2)). The underlying assumption seems to be that

---

38   s 90SE(1) and the court must be satisfied that the parties satisfy the geographical requirement in s 90SD and one of the factors in s 90SB.
39   See, eg, *In the Marriage of Atwill* (1981) 7 Fam LR 573 (Ngyh J), where an extension of time was granted in a case where a decree nisi was made absolute in 1960 and a deed was entered into by the parties for the maintenance of the wife on the same date. Under the FLA the parties can consent to the institution of proceedings out of time (s 44(3)(b)). In granting leave to institute out of time proceedings, the court must consider conditions mentioned in s 44(4), which include: '(a) hardship would be caused to the party or a child if leave were not granted; or (b) in the case of an application for an order for the maintenance of the party—the party's circumstances were, at the end of the standard application period, such that he or she would have been unable to support himself or herself without an income tested pension, allowance or benefit'.
40   A court can grant an extension of time (s 44(6)) for the same reasons as stated in s 44(3). However, the parties in a de facto relationship cannot consent to the making of an application out of time.
41   The court may make a permanent order, an order pending the disposal of proceedings, or an order for a fixed term or for a life or during joint lives, or until a further order. In *In the Marriage of Clauson* (1995) 18 Fam LR 693 (Barblett DCJ, Fogarty and Mushin JJ), the Full Court explained that periodic maintenance in the form of a lump sum would not be granted readily if the husband was not likely to default. This was because the court can modify a maintenance order relatively easily. See s 83/s 90SI for variation of maintenance orders and ending an order. For a discussion of the principles used in making lump sum payments, see *Budding v Budding* [2009] FamCAFC 165 (Ryan J).
       An application for variation under s 83 still requires fulfilling the conditions in s 72(1), so it requires evidence that the applicant has the relevant need, and the matters listed in s 83(2) are in the alternative. It is possible for an order for lump sum maintenance to be made as a variation of an existing order for periodic payments. Note that only the provisions for married couples are cited here, but equivalent provisions apply to de facto couples.
42   ss 77, 90SG; ss 80(1), 90SS(1). See *In the Marriage of Ashton* (1982) 8 Fam LR 675 and *Sadlier v Sadlier* [2015] FamCAFC 130 for a discussion of the differences between urgent and interim maintenance. *In the Marriage of Vautin* (1998) 23 Fam LR 627 discusses the suitability of a lump sum payment in certain circumstances. However, the reluctance of the courts to do this is made clear in other cases. See, eg, *Budding v Budding* [2009] FamCAFC 165.
43   s 90SF(1) and definition of de facto financial cause (s 4(1)).

the recipient of maintenance can expect to be dependent on the new spouse. However, the discharge of the maintenance order is not automatic when the party remarries.[44]

The legislative design for spousal maintenance in the FLA is discernable from ss 72–75. Section 72 provides the threshold requirements that each party to a marriage is obliged to maintain their spouse according to their respective ability to pay and the need for maintenance.[45] Conventionally, these are described as the two limbs of the rule in s 72(1), but it is also made clear in paragraphs (a)–(c) that the need of one party is due to their responsibility for looking after a child of the marriage who is under 18 years of age; or because of their incapacity for gainful employment on account of age or physical or mental incapacity; or for any 'other adequate reason'. In making an order, the court must consider these issues by having regard to the matters referred to in s 75(2).[46] In addition, the court must pay due regard to the imperative of the clean break principle, as discussed next.

6.4.2 Clean break philosophy and maintenance

The conception of marriage as a voluntary union of two autonomous individuals informs the no-fault divorce regime, but the notion of autonomy seems somewhat inconsistent with the provisions for maintenance. As discussed above, a distinctive feature of the FLA is provision for no-fault divorce and, consistent with that, the clean break philosophy in s 81.[47] The obvious issue is how the provisions for ongoing maintenance fit this philosophy.

Finalising the financial relationship between the parties pursuant to s 81 is conditional on it being practicable. There could be many situations where it is not practicable to finalise the financial relationships between separating parties. The most obvious is where there is insufficient property available to be divided to provide for the maintenance needs of one of the parties. As we saw earlier, a property order can only deal with the presently vested property of either party. However, one spouse may be generating regular or ongoing income and in such circumstances the needs of the other party could be met by making a maintenance order.[48]

---

44 Sections 82(4) and 90SJ(2) provide that '[a]n order with respect to the maintenance of a party to a marriage ceases to have effect upon the re-marriage of the party unless in special circumstances a court having jurisdiction under this Act otherwise orders'. Thus, it is possible for the court to order that maintenance continues despite remarriage of the recipient. Note that a maintenance order can be modified if the circumstances of the party in receipt of maintenance change, 'including the person entering into a stable and continuing de facto relationship' (s 83(2)(a)(i)/s 90SI(3)(a)(i)).

45 See s 90SF(1) for parallel provision relating to de facto relationships, but for ease of reading in the following discussion, we will mention only ss 72, 74 and 75.

46 Section 72(2) provides that the court may order the transfer of vested property of the bankruptcy trustee to fulfil the liability of a bankrupt spouse to maintain the other party.

47 Section 81 states that: '[i]n proceedings under this Part, other than proceedings under s 78 or proceedings with respect to maintenance payable during the subsistence of a marriage, the court shall, as far as practicable, make such orders as will finally determine the financial relationships between the parties to the marriage and avoid further proceedings between them'. For de facto relations the corresponding provision is s 90ST. Belinda Fehlberg et al, *Australian Family Law: The Contemporary Context* (Oxford University Press, 2nd ed, 2015) 606 observe that the clean break principle does not apply to maintenance proceedings in the same way as to property proceedings. However, we wish to emphasise the normative effect of the principle.

48 See, eg, *In the Marriage of Best* (1993) 116 FLR 343. See *In the Marriage of Mitchell* (1995) 120 FLR 292 (Nicholson CJ, Fogarty and Jordan JJ) for an acknowledgement of the existence of the feminisation of poverty owing to the long-term effects of financial dependence of women within marriages or similar relationships.

Section 81 could be viewed as trying to balance the competing needs of freeing the parties to start their lives again and fulfilling the obligations created while the marriage or relationship was ongoing.[49] Thus, in *In the Marriage of Bevan* the Full Family Court articulated the relationship between the responsibilities of the court under s 81 and s 74 as the former giving way to the latter.[50] That is, s 81 does not require the court to finalise the financial relations in absolute terms, but only if it is practicable. Thus, in a maintenance application, once the threshold test of s 72 is met, the court must make an order under s 74 that it considers proper.

However, the very presence of s 81 in the FLA conceives the parties as equally able to walk out of a marriage or relationship and start their lives again. When this is combined with the overall emphasis of the courts, and of the legislation, on making an order for property division rather than for periodic maintenance, it further demonstrates a propensity in family law to uphold the formal equality model of relationships between two adults. Thus, when a property division application and a periodic maintenance application are made simultaneously, the practice of the courts is to determine the property application before considering the application for periodic maintenance.[51] This ensures that, as far as practicable, the financial relations can be finalised by factoring the future needs of the financially weaker spouse into the property order. At times the periodic maintenance is ordered as a lump sum payment and can also function to finalise the financial relations.[52]

Despite the efforts of the courts to be sensitive to the particulars of each case, it is inevitable that the normative effect of s 81 is to legitimise the conception of men and women as equally able to begin again after relationship breakdown. The gender hierarchies of our contemporary society are thus written out of existence at a conceptual level in these provisions. A possible counter-argument, that the very availability of periodic maintenance in the FLA is designed to acknowledge the consequences of men and women undertaking different kinds of work within an ongoing or finished relationship, does not deal adequately with the force of the normative power of the law. Thus, the clean break principle conveys the main message of the legislation. Combined with the availability of property distribution, s 81 functions to subtly delegitimise a decision to award periodic maintenance. The same normative message – that maintenance is less than desirable – is reinforced by s 72, which says an award of maintenance is contingent on one party having the need and the other having the capacity to pay. Since the FLA does not articulate the rationale for maintenance as either need or entitlement, it also avoids the difficult question of why one party should continue to be responsible for the maintenance of the other after their relationship has ended.

There are many plausible answers to this question. For example, it can be assumed that the superior capacity of one party to generate an income came from the other party

---

49   Pamela Symes, 'Indissolubility and the Clean Break' (1985) 48(1) *Modern Law Review* 44.
50   (1993) 120 FLR 283 (Nicholson, CJ, Lindenmayer and McGovern JJ); see also *DJM v JLM* (1998) 23 Fam LR 396.
51   ss 75(2)(n)–(naa), 90SF(3)(n)–(p).
52   *Brown v Brown* (2007) 37 Fam LR 59 (Kay, Warnick and Boland JJ), where the Full Family Court calculated the lump sum payment on the basis of the capitalisation of the wife's needs for a period of 25 years. The husband had not paid periodic maintenance regularly and had the capacity to pay the lump sum amount.

supporting them by adopting the primary role of a caregiver. Thus, their need for support is the result of their adoption of a primarily non-financial role. It could also be seen as the entitlement of the non-financial partner as they have contributed through non-financial care work to the superior income-generating capacity of the other partner – usually the man. Maintenance can be rationalised as compensation for the lost opportunities of the caregiver.[53] However, none of these rationales seems to be evident in the FLA provisions, as the need of one is linked to the capacity of the other to pay. If, for a moment, we could abandon the gender-neutral language and name the social reality that it is mostly women who are the financially weaker partners, and this is because they are the primary carers of children, it becomes evident that the FLA is not acknowledging this social reality. By adopting gender-neutral language, the FLA manages to avoid naming the issue of maintenance as one related to the costs of child rearing, which is performed mainly by women.

Moreover, it functions to deflect attention from the fact that the issue is a broader structural issue than the living arrangements 'chosen' by the two partners. Instead, the FLA provides a practical solution, one that tries to provide for maintenance in the context of property division and thus finalise the financial relationship in that way. As an additional safeguard, it allows the possibility that in certain circumstances a maintenance application can be made as a stand-alone application. However, a maintenance award is not an inevitable outcome of an application for maintenance because the legislation fails to acknowledge that the primary carer has or should have a right or an entitlement to be provided for. This is made amply clear in the substantive rules in ss 72, 74 and 75(2), discussed next.

6.4.3 General principles in assessing a maintenance claim: need and capacity to pay

The decision-making process in a maintenance application generally follows the steps as explained in *Saxena v Saxena*.[54] The court first needs to determine whether the applicant was unable to support herself adequately without an order of maintenance. Next it ascertains the reasonable weekly needs of the applicant, followed by the assessment of the capacity of the respondent to meet an order if one were to be made, and finally decides the order having regard to s 75(2) of the FLA.

The threshold finding under s 72(1) corresponds to the existence of the need of the applicant and the capacity to pay by the respondent. The first limb of this rule requires that the applicant is 'unable to support herself or himself adequately'. As in other parts of the FLA, the discretion rests with the court to decide what would constitute the relevant inability to support oneself. For instance, in an early case it was explained as referring to whether the wife could generate funds from her own resources or earning capacity to fulfil her own needs and would exclude help from others.[55] However, in *In the Marriage of Bevan*, the husband opposed the wife's claim for maintenance, partly on the basis that the wife could use the capital sum available to her to support herself. In this case, the assets available to the wife were very meagre. The Full Court said that 'we do not think that the law requires that

---

53 See the literature in above n 25.
54 [2006] FLC 93-268, 80 551 (Coleman J).
55 *In the Marriage of Murkin* (1980) 5 Fam LR 782, 784 (Nygh J).

a wife should deplete an already comparatively meagre capital sum' to enable a husband to avoid paying for her maintenance.[56]

Similarly, the issue of what may constitute adequate support is answered in the particular context of the two parties.[57] Adequate support is determined by what may be considered a reasonable standard of living and is usually decided by reference to the fact that the parties are no longer a husband and wife and the resources that supported one household are now to be divided between two.[58] However, courts have been reticent in requiring a parity of standard of living even in cases where the means of the other spouse permit it. Thus, it is repeated often in the cases that there is no fettering principle that an order that can support the pre-separation standard of living should be awarded.[59]

This outcome is an obvious illustration of the rule of statutory interpretation that discretion granted by legislation cannot be fettered by judicial decision-making. It is evidently not an attempt by the courts to achieve gender equality in balancing need and capacity to pay. Indeed, it is demonstrative of a reluctance to interpret s 72 in a way that would place the man and the woman on par at the end of a relationship even when the financial circumstances could allow it. In this respect, these sorts of cases appear to illuminate a need for judges to foster a better understanding of the gendered inequities that familial relationships can engender. But it is also evident that judges' interpretation of the law falls within the bounds of legal reasoning. In that respect it is important to identify how the legislative provisions are able to be interpreted by judges in ways that entrench their value judgments about the different entitlements that men and women deserve. Thus, what requires change are the conventions of legal reasoning, to prioritise fairness in outcomes more than the technicalities in the relationship between legislative and judicial authority. Principled guidance in the legislation could assist in this regard to temper the value judgments of judges that are concealed by the claims that their decision-making is value-free.

The second requirement of the threshold test in s 72(1) is that the respondent has the capacity to pay. This capacity is assessed more broadly than the income of the person and may include capital or the capacity to borrow against capital assets.[60] For example, in *Sampey v Sampey*[61] the Court awarded interim maintenance to the wife despite the husband claiming very limited income. The wife argued that the two proprietary companies were his alter ego, but the Court decided it was not able to make such a finding. It did, however,

---

56   *In the Marriage of Bevan* (1993) 120 FLR 283, 288. Compare *Hall v Hall* [2016] HCA 23, where a majority of the High Court (French CJ, Gageler, Keane and Nettle JJ) accepted that the wife was not entitled to maintenance from the husband because she could access a financial resource in the form of her brothers' obligation to support her, as had been the wish of their deceased father. The Court made this finding notwithstanding that she had not sought financial support from her brothers and that on the evidence the brothers' obligation to support her was a moral, though not a legal, obligation.

57   *Brown v Brown* (2007) 37 Fam LR 59.

58   *Nutting and Nutting* [1978] FLC 90-410.

59   *In the Marriage of Bevan* (1993) 120 FLR 283, 290. See also *Brown v Brown* (2007) 37 Fam LR 59, 90 [161] for the statement that 'an applicant is not entitled to live at a level of considerable luxury or comfort merely because the other party is very wealthy'. Similarly in *In the Marriage of Aroney* (1979) 5 Fam LR 535, 545, Nygh J opined that the ex-wife of a rich businessman cannot expect the same standard of living as during the marriage. Instead it would be more appropriate to expect a standard comparable to what a high official after retirement might expect.

60   *Maroney v Maroney* [2009] FamCAFC 45.

61   [2015] FamCA 89 (Stevenson J).

find that the husband had access to funds from these entities from which he met part of his fixed and discretionary expenditure. Thus, it was held that he had the capacity to pay maintenance to the former spouse.

The discretion granted to the court in determining need and capacity is further reiterated in s 74, where the court 'may make such order as it considers proper for the provision of maintenance in accordance with this Part'. It is this latter phrase, 'in accordance with this Part', which makes s 72(1) relevant in that the court must only have regard to the matters mentioned in s 75(2) (discussed below).[62]

6.4.4   Section 75(2) factors and judicial interpretation

It is expected that the court must take into account each of the factors in s 75(2) if they are relevant to the particular facts. It is for the court to decide, in exercise of its discretion, the weight to be placed on each of the relevant factors. It is accepted practice that the court should first determine which factors in s 75(2) should be taken into account. After all the factors have been determined, the next step is to assess the weight that should be assigned to each of them and determine the amount that should be adjusted.[63] We reproduce below the exact language of s 75(2)[64] to emphasise the very broad reach of these factors and the absence of legislative guidance as to their relative significance:

> Section 75(2): The matters to be so taken into account are:
>
> (a) the age and state of health of each of the parties; and
>
> (b) the income, property and financial resources of each of the parties and the physical and mental capacity of each of them for appropriate gainful employment; and
>
> (c) whether either party has the care or control of a child of the marriage who has not attained the age of 18 years; and
>
> (d) commitments of each of the parties that are necessary to enable the party to support:
>
> > (i) himself or herself; and
> >
> > (ii) a child or another person that the party has a duty to maintain; and
>
> (e) the responsibilities of either party to support any other person; and
>
> (f) subject to subsection (3), the eligibility of either party for a pension, allowance or benefit under:
>
> > (i) any law of the Commonwealth, of a State or Territory or of another country; or
> >
> > (ii) any superannuation fund or scheme, whether the fund or scheme was established, or operates, within or outside Australia;

---

62   Dickey, above n 5, 387. See also *In the Marriage of Plut* (1987) 11 Fam LR 687. The three matters mentioned in s 72(1) as the reasons for the inability to maintain oneself will also be discussed with s 75(2) factors.

63   See, eg, *In the Marriage of Beck (No 2)* (1983) 48 ALR 470, 474.

64   The corresponding provisions for de facto relationships are included in s 90SF(3)(a)–(r) but we will not discuss them; there is no corresponding provision in s 75(2) for s 90SF(3)(p) and (t).

and the rate of any such pension, allowance or benefit being paid to either party; and

(g) where the parties have separated or divorced, a standard of living that in all the circumstances is reasonable; and

(h) the extent to which the payment of maintenance to the party whose maintenance is under consideration would increase the earning capacity of that party by enabling that party to undertake a course of education or training or to establish himself or herself in a business or otherwise to obtain an adequate income; and

(ha) the effect of any proposed order on the ability of a creditor of a party to recover the creditor's debt, so far as that effect is relevant; and

(j) the extent to which the party whose maintenance is under consideration has contributed to the income, earning capacity, property and financial resources of the other party; and

(k) the duration of the marriage and the extent to which it has affected the earning capacity of the party whose maintenance is under consideration; and

(l) the need to protect a party who wishes to continue that party's role as a parent; and

(m) if either party is cohabiting with another person – the financial circumstances relating to the cohabitation; and

(n) the terms of any order made or proposed to be made under section 79 in relation to:

(i) the property of the parties; or

(ii) vested bankruptcy property in relation to a bankrupt party; and

(naa) the terms of any order or declaration made, or proposed to be made, under Part VIIIAB in relation to:

(i) a party to the marriage; or

(ii) a person who is a party to a de facto relationship with a party to the marriage; or

(iii) the property of a person covered by subparagraph (i) and of a person covered by subparagraph (ii), or of either of them; or

(iv) vested bankruptcy property in relation to a person covered by subparagraph (i) or (ii);

(na) any child support under the *Child Support (Assessment) Act 1989* that a party to the marriage has provided, is to provide, or might be liable to provide in the future, for a child of the marriage; and

(o) any fact or circumstance which, in the opinion of the court, the justice of the case requires to be taken into account; and

(p) the terms of any financial agreement that is binding on the parties to the marriage; and

(q) the terms of any Part VIIIAB financial agreement that is binding on a party to the marriage.

As explained in the previous chapter, s 75(2) factors are relevant in determining property orders.[65] The same factors are relevant in making a maintenance order, but this time the court has to first determine the need and capacity to pay of the two parties respectively. However, in most reported cases s 75(2) factors are assessed in the context of making a property order, as (periodic) maintenance is granted comparatively less frequently.[66] Courts have construed these provisions broadly for the purpose of property proceedings.[67]

In the following discussion we explore, though not exhaustively, how the courts have interpreted some of these factors.[68] Our aim is to relate this analysis to the theme of the book that legal discourse about the sexual division of labour is constructed differently during the continuation of a marriage or de facto relationship and after it ends. A comparison of the interpretation of rules regarding the division of property and those regarding maintenance illustrates the two different judicial conceptions of marriage: as a partnership and as a contract. This analysis further demonstrates how legal discourse is constructed as a result of complex interactions between the legislative assumptions and ideas about the nature of the judicial task.

A preliminary point about s 75(2) that ought to be noted is that the factors included in more than one paragraph come into operation in most cases.[69] For instance, paragraph (a) directs attention to the age and state of health of each of the parties, and in that respect the paragraph (k) factor (the duration of the marriage and the extent to which it has affected the earning capacity of the party whose maintenance is under consideration) may also become relevant. Moreover, the courts have tried to accommodate the practical aspects of the effect of age on the earning capacity of the parties, among other things, by taking into account the available social sciences knowledge.[70] The following paragraph (b) is obviously relevant also insofar as it directs the court to consider 'the income, property and financial resources

---

65   s 79(4)(e) – in s 79 applications, the matters in s 75(2) must be taken into account 'so far as they are relevant'. A party's entitlement to an order under s 79 is assessed before the question of entitlement for spousal maintenance under s 72 is considered. This is most likely owing to the possibility that a s 79 settlement may remove the need for one party to be maintained by the other party.

66   See Grant Reithmuller and Robin Smith, 'Spousal Maintenance: Is It Time to Roast the Old Chestnut?' (Paper presented at the 13th National Family Law Conference, Adelaide, 7 April 2008), where the authors report that an analysis of the judgments of the Family Court found that the database of more than 10 000 judgments listed 115 judgments on maintenance; quoted in Fehlberg et al, above n 47, 605.

67   In *In the Marriage of Browne and Green* (1999) 25 Fam LR 482 (Lindenmayer, Finn and Holden JJ), the Full Court rejected the husband's argument that s 75(2)(k) was relevant only in maintenance proceedings and not in property proceedings. It reiterated that the accepted practice in dealing with s 75(2) factors was to consider paragraphs (g), (h) and (k) as referring to proceedings for property settlement.

68   For a discussion of the difficulties of relying on s 75(2) in the contexts of making an order for division of property, or awarding maintenance, or child support, see *In the Marriage of Mee and Ferguson* (1986) 10 Fam LR 971, 975 (Asche ACJ, Fogarty and Cook JJ).

69   See Richard Chisholm, Suzanne Christie and Julie Kearney, *Annotated Family Law Legislation* (LexisNexis, 3rd ed, 2015) 623.

70   For example, in *In the Marriage of Mitchell* (1995) 120 FLR 292 the Full Court noted the literature on the effects of 'feminisation of poverty' and how the Canadian courts have dealt with this issue in *Moge v Moge* (1992) 43 RFL (3d) 345. In *In the Marriage of Atwill* (1981) 7 Fam LR 573, Nygh J commented on the lack of evidence about the wife's employability, but then said the Court could take judicial notice of the fact that 60 years of age was the retirement age for women and the wife was 57 years old.

of each of the parties and the physical and mental capacity of each of them for appropriate gainful employment'. This paragraph can be read in conjunction with paragraph (a), as the consideration of health as well as physical and mental capacity of the parties is more often relevant in marriages of long duration.[71] All of these factors also have a bearing on the earning capacity of the parties.

The Full Family Court in *DJM v JLM* analysed the meaning of 'earning capacity' in some detail.[72] It explained that, with respect to assessing the earning capacity of the respondent, cases need to be determined according to their circumstances; that is, child-support cases need to be considered in a different light from spousal support and property cases. The child-support provisions emphasise and prioritise the obligations of the parents to support their children (see Chapter 10). The level of support is to be ascertained by reference to the parents' capacity to provide financial support. The Court went on to explain that property adjustment orders and spousal maintenance are governed by different tests – that is, according to what is 'appropriate' and 'proper' respectively. For a property adjustment, the judge determines this by weighing the competing factors, while a maintenance application requires the judge to have regard to the reasonable ability of the liable spouse to provide for the needs of the other spouse. Therefore, there can be different answers to the issue of the earning capacity of the person. In child-support cases, a parent would not be able to easily avoid child-support obligations simply by reducing his or her income, but the same may not apply with respect to spousal maintenance.[73]

This is a clear judicial articulation of the lesser importance of spousal maintenance as an obligation or entitlement. We suggest that this is due to the unarticulated assumption that at the end of a marriage the spouses, unlike children, are expected to look after themselves. Moreover, both of them are equally expected to do so, despite the fact that during the marriage, or a similar relationship, it was accepted socially, culturally and legally that the woman would be financially dependent. In *DJM v JLM* both the trial judge and the appeal court accepted unreservedly that the wife did not have the capacity to earn because of her responsibilities for the children, and that her prospects of employment had been affected by the fact that she had never worked in Australia. Despite all this, the outcome of the appeal was that the amount of spousal maintenance payable by the husband was reduced from the $500 awarded by the trial judge to $150 per week.

In this case the wife was an American school teacher, initially reluctant to stay on in Australia, but who continued in the marriage from 1980 to 1994. During this time the parties had five children and at trial four of them lived with the wife and one with the husband.

---

71   *Hand v Bodilly* [2013] FamCAFC 98 (Faulks DCJ, Ryan and and Watts JJ), where the Full Court rejected the appeal of the husband against the order of the single judge. In this case, the marriage lasted 15 years and the wife was suffering from a serious health condition related to multiple sclerosis.

72   (1998) 23 Fam LR 396 (Baker, Kay and Morgan JJ).

73   Since then, the legislative trend in child-support legislation in this regard has moved in the same direction of minimising the relevance of assessing earning capacity of the parent and restricting the instances where this may be a relevant issue. See the recommendations with respect to determining 'capacity to earn' for the purposes of the *Child Support (Assessment) Act 1989* (Cth) made by the Ministerial Taskforce on Child Support, *In the Best Interests of Children – Reforming the Child Support Scheme* (2005) 203–5 <http://www.dss.gov.au/our-responsibilities/families-and-children/publications-articles>.

Throughout the marriage the wife did not work for wages and the husband earned approximately $200000 per annum, but just before the Family Court heard the property application he had changed his job and reduced his income to approximately $80000 per annum. They had a modest asset pool of less than $500000. At trial, the judge made an order dividing the property in the ratio of 80% and 20% respectively for the wife and husband. It was accepted that the wife would use most of the capital to buy a house for her and the four children.

In addition, the husband paid child support and the wife was awarded $500 per week maintenance by the trial judge. On appeal, the Full Court retained the first two assessments of property division and child support, but reduced the spousal maintenance to $150 per week. It justified this by attributing different significance to the husband's earning capacity for the purposes of child support and spousal maintenance. In assessing his capacity to earn, which was relevant to calculating his child-support liability, the Court relied on his capacity to earn $200000 per annum rather than what he was earning at present. In contrast, when considering his capacity to pay spousal maintenance, the Court used his present income of $80000 per annum as the relevant figure. In part, the reasoning adopted was that it is not appropriate to expect the husband to work in a different job from the one he had chosen so that he can pay maintenance to his former wife. Thus, in calculating the husband's capacity to pay, the Court accepted that, after taking care of his expenses, only $150 remained available to be paid for spousal maintenance. As a result, in a case where the wife had claimed more than $900 per week for spousal maintenance, she ended up with $150 per week. The Full Court explained this outcome as partly due to the fact that the case was conducted around the issue of the husband's capacity more than the wife's needs. Presumably the Court was sympathetic to the wife's claim for a larger amount of maintenance but felt constrained, as her claim was not argued on the basis of her needs.

In giving these details, we reiterate that it is not entirely a criticism of the judges that this outcome was reached. It is mainly to illustrate how the process of legal reasoning allows an outcome where child maintenance is considered more important than spousal maintenance. The judges are able to emphasise different aspects in the existing legislation to yield different interpretations of the concept of 'capacity to earn'. They can further support their interpretations of this concept based on the conception of judicial task as one of applying the law. For instance, it is indisputable that the court has to operate within the constraints of the legislation that makes the capacity of the liable spouse to pay a relevant issue in deciding a maintenance application. Evidently, it is the system of the law in which judges decide cases that allows them to make the decisions they make, and where their value systems are rendered invisible by their application of the law.

On the basis of 'capacity to earn' it was open to the Court to find that the husband's capacity was much more than his present income and to assess spousal maintenance according to how it had assessed child support. Thus, the explanation given by the Full Court, that the capacity to generate income must be assessed differently in cases of child and spousal maintenance, is not an entirely convincing argument. Moreover, it is also not plausible to assert that this is the only interpretation available to the judges. Interpretation by its very nature permits more than one meaning. The judges perform their task within the constraints of accepted norms of legal reasoning, including that they apply the law rather than make it. Yet in doing so, they constantly have to make choices and it is no surprise that such choices are informed by the prevailing ideas about responsibilities of the two partners: on the one hand, to be self-sufficient after the marriage has ended; and, on the other, to fulfil their parental responsibilities to their children.

Thus, the finding that a person cannot be forced to work long hours or in certain jobs so that the other spouse can obtain maintenance is not an inevitable conclusion. It is a partial story that manages to convey the meaning that the obligation to one's spouse is less compelling than that to one's children. What may be the basis of such a view is a matter of speculation, but it evidently invokes the idea of two spouses as equally expected to look after themselves at the end of a relationship. This enables the Full Court to simultaneously endorse the dependency of the wife owing to her role as the primary caregiver when the relationship was intact, while also managing to reduce the award of maintenance after the relationship came to an end. The fact that she will be responsible for looking after the children in the immediate future is somehow not translated into an entitlement to maintenance in her own right. Moreover, it seems to be at cross-purposes with statements often made in these cases that the capacity to generate an income is the most valuable asset a party can take out of a marriage.[74]

Evidently, the Full Court is contributing to the construction of the legal discourse about the distinctiveness of spousal maintenance and child support. In a different vein, Young and Wikeley argue convincingly that a review of recent case law reveals that the concept of earning capacity has greater significance in courts determining the applicant's capacity to support herself and not so much in calculating the ability of the respondent to pay.[75] They explain that the payees have the obligation to establish need for maintenance, which would depend upon their income or their capacity to generate an income. It follows that the applicants have a heavy onus and must explain why they cannot support themselves. These examples illustrate how the concept of 'earning capacity' is constructed in different ways in judicial discourse. Moreover, it is a function of the legislative design of the FLA, where wide discretion is granted to the judges, that facilitates different interpretations of the concept of earning capacity.

The judicial trend that has made the earning capacity of the applicant (wife) a relatively more relevant factor in determining the entitlement or the quantum of maintenance payable helps convert into legal discourse the prevailing social idea that after a marriage has ended, as far as possible, the wife should support herself financially. That is a perfectly reasonable idea except that it does not seem to be the expectation in an ongoing marriage, either socially or legally. Put differently, while the marriage or similar relationship lasts, the law considers it to be a private matter for the two parties to decide for themselves. After the marriage ends, if they cannot agree on their respective entitlements, the court has to step in but, in doing so, it assumes a model of equal partnership that goes against the very rationale for the property provisions in the FLA. That is, if we accept that the FLA property provisions are an acknowledgement of the social reality that men and women are differently situated financially owing to the sexual division of labour, then it could and it may be necessary for judges

---

74   *In the Marriage of Best* (1993) 116 FLR 343; *In the Marriage of Clauson* (1995) 18 Fam LR 693.
75   Lisa Young and Nick Wikeley, '"Earning Capacity" and Maintenance in Anglo-Australian Family Law: Different Paths, Same Destination?' (2015) 27 *Child and Family Law Quarterly* 129, 141–2 citing (at footnote 105) *Carse v Carse* [2012] FMCAfam 1202, [62]–[64]; *Lester v Lester (No 2)* [2012] FMCAfam 388, [201]–[212]; *Beklar v Beklar* [2013] FamCA 327, [225]; *Marsden v Baker* [2013] FamCA 320, [308]; *Harper v Harper* [2013] FamCA 202, [35]–[45].

to override normal rules of property ownership to reach a just outcome for the primary carer. In contrast, the same FLA in its maintenance provisions has been enacted and interpreted as if the social reality has changed. Thus, decisions about maintenance are linked to the effects on the applicant's earning capacity arising from the applicant's child-related responsibilities, but granting maintenance is also construed as a relatively short-term solution to these effects. As a result, the conception of the husband and wife as autonomous individuals, allowed to walk out of a relationship anytime, goes a long way in rendering spousal maintenance almost anachronistic. Yet if the same parties had continued in the relationship the law would have averted its gaze from the financial dependency existing within it. This is an apt illustration of how the law endorses the ideology of family as a private institution.

Legislative support for this approach is evident in s 72(1)(a) and a number of other factors in s 75(2) that link maintenance decisions to the consequences of the applicant's child-related responsibilities. For example, if the party has the care and control of a child of the marriage who is under 18 years of age, it is a relevant factor in s 72(1)(a) and s 75(2)(c). In addition, s 75(2)(d), (l) and (na) all direct the court to consider the effects of child-related responsibilities. Additionally, if the person has commitments for maintaining another child or person, s 75(2)(d) is also relevant,[76] as well as if someone wishes to continue his or her role as a parent (s 75(2)(l)). Similarly, s 75(2)(na) requires the court to take into account the person's liability for child support.[77] However, the courts are often faced with the argument by the father/husband that, since child support is being paid, the wife may not be able to argue need on the grounds that she has a 'duty to maintain the children' as well. Moreover, in *Stein v Stein* the Court said that s 75(2)(d) ('the commitments of each of the parties that are necessary to enable the party to support') is more significant in determining the capacity of the payer than in determining the need of the recipient.[78]

When the court is considering the effects of a person having the care and control of a child less than 18 years of age, whether it should assess only economic issues, or the wider social and moral issues as well, has been debated in some cases.[79] This is somewhat surprising because the legislation itself acknowledges the social and moral aspects of caring for children in s 75(2)(l), which could be described as protecting the parental role. As a result, the courts generally would support a parent who could participate in paid work, but chose instead to be a full-time parent.[80]

However, this is in the context of the same parent being expected to be in paid work once the child has attained 18 years of age (s 72(1)(a)). Thus, the mixed messages of the provisions in the FLA, including s 75(2), are that if one wishes to be a full-time parent, that would be a legitimate decision and one supported by the law, but once the marriage or relationship has ended, the primary carer would be expected to retrain (s 75(2)(h)) and participate in paid work

---

76 *Stein v Stein* [2000] FamCA 102 (Kay, Holden and Dessau JJ). This refers to the party's duty to maintain another person or child.

77 This addition was made corresponding to the enactment of the *Child Support (Assessment) Act 1989* (Cth). For an example of the court balancing child-support liabilities with making an order for spousal maintenance, see *Kitman v Kitman* [2007] FamCA 822, [36] (Bryant CJ, Kay and May JJ).

78 [2000] FamCA 102, [1]. But see *Drysdale v Drysdale* [2011] FamCAFC 85 (Coleman J), where the Court was dealing with an application for interim maintenance. It indicated that in a final order a clearer separation of the wife's and children's needs might be required.

79 *In the Marriage of Collins* (1990) 100 FLR 340; *Farmer v Bramley* [2000] FLC 93-060.

80 *In the Marriage of Nixon* [1992] FLC 92-308.

as far as possible.[81] However, all the difficulties of combining paid work and childcare responsibilities do not end magically when the last child turns 18. The effects of these constraints would most likely continue to be felt by the primary carer, who is usually the mother. For the law to expect that she can now retrain or resume full-time or other wage work is to deny the long-term consequences of being a primary carer. Combined with the interpretation of s 75(2) factors, that there is no imperative that the court should make orders that create a parity of living standards for both parties, it contributes to the discourse of two autonomous individuals equally able to make choices about engaging in the workforce. The cost of being the primary carer is thus shifted onto individual mothers. This is the issue underlying various analyses of the rationales for maintenance, and the scholarship on maintenance as compensation for foregone opportunities adverts to these costs.[82] However, no amount of 'compensation' can replace the outcomes that result from exercising one's capacity to earn an income.

At the same time, expecting former husbands or partners to keep paying maintenance in all circumstances has its own set of difficulties, as illustrated in the following case. In *Hilare v Hilare* the parties commenced cohabitation and later married.[83] The arrangement lasted for about seven years, at which time the wife informed the husband that the marriage was over and she left with the two children. After separation both parents were involved in caring for the children. She made an application for property distribution and maintenance. There were very few assets to be divided and the husband earned a substantial income even when working part-time. The wife was studying and had established a new relationship, but her only source of income was the maintenance paid by the husband. The Court acknowledged that some in the community might struggle with the concept that the husband should pay maintenance to a former wife who is in a committed relationship with another man. However, the Court held that the legislation does not disqualify a person from receiving maintenance in such circumstances. The Court placed substantial significance on the fact that the maintenance award was for approximately two years and would enable the wife to finish her studies and earn an income.[84] What was not articulated was the rationale for expecting the former husband to pay maintenance to a wife who had decided to leave the marriage and the husband. It is not a sufficient explanation that the FLA makes conduct irrelevant in most cases.

A similar difficulty is evident in *Hand v Bodilly*.[85] This is an interesting case that brings into focus the difficulties presented by the legislation in not articulating the rationales for

---

81   *Hilare v Hilare* [2010] FamCA 108.
82   See, eg, Mavis Maclean and Lenore J Weitzman, 'Introduction' in Lenore J Weitzman and Mavis Maclean (eds), *Economic Consequences of Divorce: The International Perspective* (Clarendon Press, 1992) 3; Hilaire Barnett, 'Financial Provision: A Compensatory Approach?' (1983)13 *Family Law* 124.
83   [2010] FamCA 108, [166] (Brown J).
84   Compare this with the mixed reactions towards the applicant wife who left the husband for another man in *In the Marriage of Issom* (1976) 7 Fam LR 305.
85   [2013] FamCAFC 98. In this case, at the time of the marriage the wife had multiple sclerosis. In 1998, after 15 years of marriage the parties separated and later divorced. They entered into a financial agreement and divided the assets in a manner that gave the wife 32% of the assets. In addition the husband agreed to pay periodic maintenance of $500 a week, which was not indexed. In 2007 the wife's condition deteriorated and she could no longer engage in part-time work. She also required structural modifications to the house and tried to negotiate an increase in the maintenance amount. The husband had remarried and had two children. He also had substantial assets and an annual salary package of $1.7 million. At trial the husband was ordered to pay periodic spousal maintenance of $3323 per week (backdated weekly payment for nine months), a lump sum of $120000, and the wife's costs of $331188. On appeal the Full Court upheld this order.

spousal maintenance in terms other than need and capacity to pay. In this case, the marriage ended a long time ago and the parties had already agreed to divide their assets, which included the husband paying ongoing maintenance. Subsequently he re-partnered, and the needs of the former wife changed. In December 2009 the wife initiated proceedings seeking an increase in the maintenance amount. He had the capacity to pay but if he did not, or was not expected to meet these needs, she would of necessity require social-welfare assistance. In the context of the discourse of private responsibility, it may be understandable that the legal system discourages this outcome, but what was not clear was why the wife's changing needs should continue to be the responsibility of the former husband. There was no suggestion that her new needs were the result of the former marriage. Moreover, if the parties had agreed only upon a property division, and not on periodic maintenance, it is likely that there would be no expectation that the husband should now meet the changed needs of the wife.[86]

These outcomes bring into sharp focus the design of the legislation to contain the cost of marriage or relationship breakdown as a private cost as far as possible. The same emphasis is reiterated more explicitly in ss 75(3) and 75(2)(f). The availability of a pension entitlement is directly related to the ability of a person to support himself or herself. It could be relevant at the threshold test stage under s 72(1), but it is generally accepted that if a person needs a pension, then he or she lacks the capacity to be able to adequately support himself or herself.[87] Section 75(2)(f) becomes relevant when the court has to decide the quantum of maintenance, and since the 1987 amendments it is clear that the amount payable by the respondent is not to be reduced by taking into account any social-welfare entitlement of the applicant.[88]

Another example of the legislation trying to contain the cost of relationship breakdown by making it a private cost is s 44(4)(b). It provides that the court may grant leave to apply outside the limitation period if the applicant can show that he or she would have been unable to maintain himself or herself without an income-tested pension, allowance or benefit. In a similar vein, s 77A provides that if the court orders maintenance, and that requires the payment of a lump sum or the transfer or settlement of property, and one of the purposes of such payment, transfer or settlement is to make provision for the maintenance of a party to the marriage, the order must specifically be expressed as one to which s 77A applies. Moreover, it must specify the portion of the payment, or the value of the portion of property, which is maintenance. This is meant to ensure that the recipient's entitlement to any pension or social security payment is calculated by taking into account any maintenance payments.[89]

Efforts to contain the cost of relationship breakdown between the parties are further facilitated by the absence of an explicit articulation of the rationales for spousal maintenance in the FLA. The threshold tests in s 72(1) related to need and capacity to pay are not interpreted as necessarily arising because of the relationship. The resultant arbitrariness of the decisions,

---

86   A maintenance order can be varied in many circumstances under s 83/s 90SI, but a property order may be varied in comparatively more limited circumstances under s 79A/s 90SN.

87   *In the Marriage of Kajewski* [1978] FLC 90-472.

88   The *Family Law Amendment Act 1987* (Cth) introduced a new s 75(3), which provides that: '[i]n exercising its jurisdiction under section 74, a court shall disregard any entitlement of the party whose maintenance is under consideration to an income tested pension, allowance or benefit'.

89   See also ss 66R and 87A.

at least from some perspectives, does nothing to enhance confidence in the capacity of the FLA to deliver justice or fair results. Judicial discretion granted in the legislation has the benefit of enabling courts to make nuanced adjustments for each case, but it cannot replace the need for clear articulation of the rationales for granting maintenance. Various cases have relied on s 75(2)(o), which directs the court in making an order to consider 'any fact or circumstance which, in the opinion of the court, the justice of the case requires to be taken into account' to try to ameliorate the need of one spouse, but it is not always or entirely clear why the other spouse should bear the responsibility. Nor is a maintenance order the most suitable means of dealing with all cases. It is used because no other identifiable remedy may be available in a situation that nevertheless demands some response from the legal system.

For example, in *In the Marriage of Steinmetz*[90] the husband refused to grant the Jewish wife the religious divorce, Gett. She could not marry again without it. The trial judge doubled the amount of lump sum maintenance to provide for the needs of the wife. On appeal the Full Court agreed that the trial judge was entitled to take this fact into account under paragraph (o). The husband was denying the wife the opportunity to marry again and thus the benefit of financial support that remarriage might bring. Thus, the Court was trying to help the wife in a difficult situation, but in the process it also legitimised the idea that dependence on the next husband is acceptable and something that the applicant should expect. The construction of this notion of a dependent woman happens unintentionally and in the guise of helping the wife.

The issue has arisen as to whether paragraph (o) allows any factors to be taken into account or whether, in keeping with the financial nature of the rest of the factors in s 75(2), this paragraph confines the court to taking into account only financial factors. In the early case of *In the Marriage of Issom*, it was said that three interpretations are possible.[91] The first two are that, in keeping with other paragraphs, this paragraph should allow consideration of only economic factors, or that it should be interpreted to give effect to the ordinary meaning of the words 'any facts or circumstances', which would include conduct of the parties. The third interpretation would acknowledge that conduct of the parties is not ordinarily relevant, but there may be exceptional cases where the conduct of one of the parties is so outrageous or gross that to make an order would be to offend the most basic views on maintenance. The Court finally decided that, despite the philosophy and approach of the FLA in endorsing the no-fault principle, paragraph (o) enabled it to take account of the conduct of the wife as a factor.

As mentioned above, s 75(2) factors are also relevant in the court making a property order under s 79. We discuss some of the salient issues of this area next.

6.4.5   The relevance of s 75(2) in a property order and maintenance order

Since s 75(2) factors are relevant in a s 79 application for a property order, as well as in a s 72 application for a maintenance order, the practice has developed that the property application is considered before an application for maintenance under ss 72 and 74, as such an

---

90   [1980] FLC 90-801 (Hogan J); *In the Marriage of Steinmetz* [1981] FLC 91-079 (Evatt CJ, Ellis and Emery JJ).

91   (1976) 7 Fam LR 305, 313 (Fogarty J).

order may remove the need for maintenance.[92] Courts are able to differentiate the meaning to attach to s 75(2) factors in a property division order from that used for a spousal maintenance order.[93] Rationales for making a s 75(2) adjustment are discussed in *In the Marriage of Waters and Jurek*.[94] It was also held in *In the Marriage of Clauson* that, in making a property order and considering s 75(2), the exercise is not an exercise of the maintenance power, and it is not a backdoor maintenance order.[95] However, the discussion below relies on cases discussing s 75(2) factors either in property distribution or maintenance applications.[96]

A few general propositions that may be discerned from the decided cases are discussed next, but we do not aim to give an exhaustive account. For example, one of the recurring themes is whether the consideration of s 75(2) factors is meant to equalise the economic position of the two parties. In *In the Marriage of Dickson* the Full Court addressed this issue and said that, even though there was no general principle, in making a s 79 order a court should try to equalise the standard of living of both parties and a consideration of s 75(2) factors may yield such a result.[97] In this case, the marriage ended after 26 years and the Court said it was reasonable to expect that the two parties would continue to have a similar standard of living. As we saw above, similar observations could be made in spousal maintenance matters. However, if the order was for ongoing maintenance it is an open question whether a similar approach would be taken as readily.[98] We say this because the ongoing nature of a maintenance order means that there will be an ongoing financial relationship, which creates an ideological tension with the legislative efforts to bring the financial relationship to an end; a property order does not create the same sort of tension.

Another difference in considering s 75(2) factors in property and maintenance applications is that, in the former applications, the court does not have to be constrained by the threshold factors of s 72(1). Thus in *Waters and Jurek*,[99] both husband and wife earned substantial incomes: the husband earned $170000 per annum and the wife $70000 per annum. After considering their shares on the basis of contributions, the Court made a $50000 adjustment for the wife by reference to the s 75(2) factors. The Court explained that this would equalise the income of both for one year. Two observations worth noting are that the Court did not articulate why such an equalisation was necessary, and, if it was desirable, why it was only for one year. Second, this outcome would not have been possible in a maintenance application as the wife would not be able to show need and meet the threshold condition in s 72(1). While this demonstrates the different functions of s 75(2) factors in making property and maintenance orders, it does not explain the underlying rationales of each order.

---

92   *In the Marriage of Clauson* (1995) 18 Fam LR 693. There are many cross-references within s 75(2) factors and s 79; for example, see ss 75(2)(n), 79(4)(e) and (f).
93   *In the Marriage of Collins* (1990) 100 FLR 340.
94   (1995) 126 FLR 311, 333–4 (Fogarty, Baker and Hase JJ), discussed below.
95   (1995) 18 Fam LR 693, 706. See also Adiva Sifris, 'Lump Sum Spousal Maintenance: Crossing the Rubicon' (2000) 14(1) *Australian Family Law Journal* 1.
96   This is necessitated partly by the fact that very few maintenance-only judgments are reported. See Young and Wikeley, above n 75, 138–9.
97   (1999) 24 Fam LR 460, 473 (Lindenmayer, Kay and Warnick JJ).
98   For example, in *Carmel-Fevia v Fevia (No 3)* [2012] FamCA 631 the asset pool of the parties was worth almost $435 million. Justice Cronin made a property order in favour of the wife in the amount of $19.5 million, and declined to accept the wife's application for spousal maintenance.
99   (1995) 126 FLR 311.

In *Clauson* the Full Court, when discussing how to compute the s 75(2) component of a property order, noted the practice of courts in allocating a percentage value in the range of 10–20% for s 75(2) factors. A deviation from these parameters could be made when there were legitimate justifications. In this case the Full Court modified the trial judge's assessment of s 75(2) factors from 15% to 25%.[100]

It was also said that it is important to give a monetary value to the percentages that will determine the true effect of the order.[101] The other significant observation the Court made was that even though the wife was qualified and had the capacity to generate an income, her responsibilities for four children of relatively young ages were relevant under various factors in s 75(2). The husband had made substantial initial financial contributions, but also had a higher earning capacity. Evidently, the Court was very mindful of the wife's responsibilities for the four young children and was doing the best it could in giving a generous value to the s 75(2) factors in making the property order. However, the outcome also illustrates how the law functions to entrench economic disparity between the spouse who earns money and the spouse who looks after the children.

Evidently, family law, as a combination of the legislation and cases, is supportive of the woman who is dependent because of her child-rearing responsibilities, but can do very little to address the long-term consequences of such dependence. Once the children of this marriage have grown up, the wife must start fending for herself. Presumably, by the time the youngest child, now three years old, attains majority, the $300 000 paid to the wife as part of her property settlement would have long disappeared. The argument is not that she should be awarded maintenance, but to point out how primary responsibility for child care inevitably causes economic dependency and the mere transfer of a share of property to the primary carer is an immensely inadequate response. The courts are given very wide discretion to accommodate the specifics of each case, but that cannot create an income-generating capacity for the carer. This is why we think that the justification of maintenance as compensation for lost opportunity or as a rehabilitative measure is inadequate and misplaced. The fundamental issue is to recognise how the financial well-being of any person is dependent on their capacity to generate an income. Thus, the wide discretion given to the courts to make appropriate maintenance orders does not suffice, as we explain next.

The very wide discretion of the courts is illustrated in the outcome in *In the Marriage of Best*, where, on appeal, the Full Court assessed the s 75(2) factors as requiring the wife to

---

100   (1995) 18 Fam LR 693, 711. Briefly, the facts were that the parties cohabited for approximately 10 years. There were four children, between the ages of three and eight years. They were living with the wife and she applied for property orders and spousal maintenance. With respect to the property orders, the wife on appeal was awarded 50% of the $1.4 million asset pool. The Full Court also held that, in view of the dimension of the property order, it was not legitimate to make an order for spousal maintenance whether in the form of a lump sum or periodic payment. After taking into account the accommodation and day-to-day living costs for the wife and children, she was left with approximately $300 000. The Court said that the possession of such a sum would normally prevent the wife from demonstrating that she was unable to support herself adequately.

101   This suggestion is usually followed by the courts, but not always. For example, in *Marsh v Marsh* (2014) 51 Fam LR 540, [174] Le Poer Trench J observed that, even though nothing in s 79 requires it, courts have developed the general practice of converting a percentage sum into dollar terms when making a property order.

have 100% of the available assets.[102] The Full Court said that the award of 70% of the assets to the wife by the trial judge was an illusory order as there were virtually no assets available. Moreover, the wife had no relevant skills to generate an income, and had responsibilities for four children, while the husband had a high present income and continuing capacity to generate very high income. The Full Court also observed that, in a case like this, a lump sum payment could be ordered, even if it would be paid by periodic sums. However, the wife had not pursued this line of argument.[103]

Similarly in *In the Marriage of Mitchell*,[104] at the end of a marriage of 27 years the trial judge, Moore J, ordered 90% of assets to the wife and the order included s 75(2) adjustment of 40%. It also dismissed the spousal maintenance application of the wife. The asset pool was approximately $300000 without taking into account the superannuation of the husband. The husband was a barrister with a high income, which fluctuated, but was around $100000 per annum, while the wife was a registered nurse at the time of marriage, but had not worked as a nurse since the birth of the second child in 1972. She had resumed part-time paid work in 1990 and for a while earned about $200 per week, but she no longer held these positions.[105]

On appeal, the Full Court retained the property order giving her 90% of the assets, which amounted to $281907. It disagreed with the trial judge on the matter of spousal maintenance. The trial judge had said that the wife had not made enough effort to find more paid work and in view of the property order she could not establish need under s 72(1). The Full Court agreed that the threshold test in this section requires the applicant to be unable to support himself or herself adequately, but said that the determination of what constitutes 'adequate standard' must be more than at the subsistence standard. It also said that there is advantage in the courts taking judicial notice of social science research that establishes the economic disadvantages of marriage and divorce for mothers who drop out of the workforce to take on full-time childcare responsibilities. Yet it also found that such research evidence could not be used as a substitute for evidence in a particular case.[106]

---

102   (1993) 116 FLR 343 (Fogarty, Lindenmayer and McGovern JJ). In this case the wife had supported the husband to acquire professional training as a lawyer, worked as a nurse for the first couple of years but then gave up paid work to look after the children. At the end of a marriage of approximately 16 years, the trial judge, Gee J, assessed her contributions as 45% and adjusted that for s 75(2) factors by 25%. As a result, the wife was entitled to 70% of the assets. In addition, a departure order for child maintenance was challenged; this had reduced child maintenance from approximately $860 to $500 per week, while spousal maintenance of $400 was also ordered. On appeal, one of the main issues was whether the husband's partnership interest in the law firm was 'property'. The Full Court answered that it was. See also *Gollings v Scott* [2007] FLC 93-319 (Finn, Kay and Boland JJ), where the Full Family Court said the trial court was in error as the effect of its order was that it gave the wife more than 100% of the pool of available assets.

103   (1993) 116 FLR 343, 369.

104   (1995) 120 FLR 292.

105   The husband claimed that his monthly personal expenses were $16460 and the wife claimed expenses of $933 per week and an order that she should be allowed to retain the matrimonial home, worth $525000 less liabilities of $100000. This sum included some expenses for the two adult sons living with her.

106   Thus, the legal emphasis on evidence in the individual case allows the courts to disregard persistent empirical evidence of the gendered differences in earning capacities of men and women. These differences are exacerbated by women taking on primary childcare responsibilities: see Jessica Irvine, 'Australia's Top 10 Jobs with the Biggest Gender Pay Gap Revealed', *Sydney Morning Herald* (online), 19 June 2016 <http://www.smh.com.au/comment/australias-top-10-jobs-with-the-biggest-gender-pay-gap-revealed-20160608-gpezg8>.

In disagreeing with the trial judge's finding that the wife had not established an inability to support herself adequately, the Full Court observed that, in view of 'her age, her legitimate needs, the standard of living enjoyed by the parties during the course of the marriage, and the husband's professional skills and prospects of high future earnings for the foreseeable future', any future earnings that the wife might be able to generate would be unable to meet her needs.[107] The Full Court made an interim maintenance order of $150 per week and remitted the case for the assessment of spousal maintenance.

However, the Full Court also observed that at trial no consideration was given to a limited maintenance order that would have enabled the wife to retrain. In the Court's view, such an approach would have been very useful in this case. In making this statement, the Court supported the dominant discourse in maintenance cases that, even at the end of a long marriage, the wife is expected to start making efforts to be financially independent. There is no entitlement to maintenance as the property order has made as much adjustment as possible within the constraints of the legislation.[108] However, even with regard to property division there is some debate whether the wife would be entitled to a share if the available property were in the form of a windfall, as detailed next.

The Full Court in *Farmer v Bramley* had to decide whether a Lotto win of $5 million by the husband should be divided between the husband and the former wife.[109] At separation the parties had no assets, but at the time of trial the husband had won Lotto and both had re-partnered with other people. It was reiterated by all judges that there was no requirement that the contributions of either party are directly related to specific property. However, there was disagreement about the relevance of s 75(2) in making a property order that could lessen the disparity of financial circumstances of the two parties. Justice Guest in this case was of the view that any readjustment of property allocation under s 75(2) must be related to the incidences of marriage of the parties. The husband's financial position arose solely due to the Lotto win and had no connection to how the parties had lived before separation.[110] At the same time it has been held in other cases that s 75(2)(b) could be interpreted as requiring that the two parties be situated in a similar economic position after separation, especially if one person has substantially more superannuation.[111]

Duration of marriage is relevant and generally, in short marriages, the courts are reluctant to give much significance to s 75(2), as illustrated in *GBT v BJT*.[112] The parties had cohabited before marriage and the marriage lasted for 19 months. There were no children of the marriage. The Full Court assessed the contributions of the wife as 7.5% and s 75(2) factors as 2.5% of the total assets. The Court said the trial judge, Strickland J, erred in addressing the disparities in the parties' incomes and earning capacity, and gave insufficient regard to the fact that the wife had made very few contributions during the short marriage. Moreover,

---

107   (1995) 120 FLR 292, 312.
108   See also *Goddard v Patterson* [2011] FamCAFC 14 (Bryant CJ, Coleman and Strickland JJ), where the Full Court refused to accept the wife's argument that, even though she could not establish a 'need', she needed ongoing maintenance until the two children finished school and only then would she be able to undertake full-time paid work. The reason for this decision, according to the Court, was that these were not the relevant considerations under s 72.
109   [2000] FLC 93-060 (Finn, Kay and Guest JJ).
110   Ibid 87 981.
111   *GBT v BJT* [2005] FamCA 683 (Kay, Holden and Warnick JJ).
112   Ibid. See also *In the Marriage of Browne and Green* (1999) 25 Fam LR 482.

the Court added that the contributions were as the homemaker, but, even then, the husband paid for a good deal of domestic help. We argue that it is comments like these that function to devalue the role of the wife and domestic work. For it is eminently plausible to suggest that the Court could have achieved the same outcome by saying that she did not suffer any substantial loss of her earning capacity while she was married.

However, the Full Family Court has observed that trying to discern the philosophy underlying the values or philosophy of s 79 is an irrelevant exercise. More specifically, the intention of the legislation and compensation for economic disadvantages arising from the marriage, by themselves, are not the relevant criteria in deciding to make a property or maintenance order. The concept of loss of income during marriage and compensation for loss of living standard, on their own, should not influence the outcome of a property settlement.[113] This illustrates how the legislative design of granting wide discretion to the court can also work to entrench societal norms, but without having to name them as such. But it is evidently the case that if the concepts of intention or compensation are not the guiding criteria of the legislation, it is up to the individual judge to decide why any property distribution ought to be made. The legislation purports to contain the judicial discretion by providing a set of factors that must be considered. However, that assumes these factors can have a universal meaning. We challenge whether this can be possible. Instead we ask: how does a judge give weight to, or interpret these factors, if not by reference to broader values in determining whether to 'compensate' the less well-off spouse or partner depending on how she fulfilled her role as wife and mother? The broad discretionary approach also demonstrates how the judges can avoid having to engage with other discourses.[114]

Another issue arising in these cases is whether violent conduct is relevant in resolving the financial disputes between the parties. For instance, the Full Court in *Kennon v Kennon*,[115] among other things, observed that spousal maintenance is essentially concerned with issues of need and capacity, and conduct is not relevant in that regard.[116] It reviewed the legislative change from fault to no-fault divorce law in the FLA and also reviewed the earlier decisions discussing the relevance of violent conduct under the property provisions. Significantly, it

---

113   In *CCD v AGMD* [2006] FLC 93-300, 81 072 Warnick J quotes with approval similar statements from *In the Marriage of Beck (No 2)* (1983) 48 ALR 470 (Evatt CJ, Emery and Haese JJ). This was a marriage of a short duration (five years). The husband had substantial assets and the wife had given up modestly paid wage work at the time of marriage. The trial judge (Gibson J) awarded her 15% of the total assets, but the Full Court allowed the husband's appeal against that outcome. The trial judge had said that intention, contribution, reliance, compensation and need were recognised justifications for making property distribution orders.

114   The existence of extensive literature and debates among scholars about the possible rationales for maintenance are thus rendered irrelevant. For an example of such debates, see Mavis Maclean and James Johnston, 'Alimony or Compensation?: What Can We Learn from the Language of Economists?' (1990) 20 *Family Law* 148; Rebecca Bailey-Harris, 'The Role of Maintenance and Property Orders in Redressing Inequality: Re-opening the Debate' (1998) 12(1) *Australian Journal of Family Law* 3.

115   (1997) 139 FLR 118 (Fogarty, Baker and Lindenmayer JJ). The marriage lasted five years and involved violence by the husband towards the wife. The husband had assets worth about $8 million and earning capacity of $1 million per annum. The wife's earnings were approximately $36 000 per annum. The trial judge awarded her $200 000 as contributions under s 79 and a further adjustment of $200 000 for s 75(2) factors. In addition, $43 000 was awarded as damages in torts for specific assaults.

116   Ibid 137, where the Court agreed with the decision in *In the Marriage of Soblusky* (1976) 28 FLR 81.

held that a court can take conduct into account, in this case domestic violence, as a relevant factor in s 79 because it may have made the contributions of the recipient of violence more difficult to make. Thus, the emphasis of the Court was on the rationale for taking conduct into account, not because violence is reprehensible, but because it makes contributions to property of the target more onerous.[117]

Moreover, in the particular facts of this case the Full Court was very scathing of the trial judge, Coleman J, acknowledging that the s 75(2) factors required a substantial adjustment in favour of the wife, but then awarding only $200 000 as an adjustment for those factors. This amount represented about 2% of the total assets. The Court held that the trial judge had severely undervalued the significance of the s 75(2) factors, but in turn, when modifying this adjustment, the Full Court changed the sum to $300 000. The final adjustment for the s 75(2) factors thus amounted to 3% of the total assets. Thus, the judgment functions simultaneously as a site for constructing the law as responsive to the needs of the target of violence; it is not obliged to create a parity in outcome for the two parties.

The case of *Stanford v Stanford*[118] is one concerning a long marriage and involuntary separation (also see Chapter 5). The wife was living in a care facility, and her daughter from a previous marriage approached the court as her case guardian for a property order to pay for the wife to be moved to a better quality nursing home. This would require the matrimonial property to be sold. The husband was in his eighties and wished to remain in the home where he had resided for the last 45 years. The trial judge made a property order, but the husband appealed. The Full Court (Bryant CJ, May and Moncrieff JJ) allowed the appeal and in stating that a rehearing may be necessary, observed:

> the wife did not have a need for a property settlement as such and that her reasonable needs could be met in other ways particularly by maintenance. In considering what was just and equitable under s 79 and s 75(2) the Magistrate was required to consider the effect of these orders on the husband and the fact that this was an intact marriage.[119]

The subsequent judicial history of this case is that the High Court allowed the appeal by the husband with respect to orders made by the Full Court that 42.5% of the marital property be paid to the wife's legal representatives after his death. In allowing the appeal the High Court also made a few observations that function to undermine the idea of entitlement of the wife on the basis of contributions.

The main judgment of the High Court applied a technical interpretation of s 79(2) and found that the provision authorises a property division only if the court is convinced that it is just and equitable to do so.[120] The interpretation of this imperative by the High Court makes for disturbing reading. It is the highest court in the legal system in Australia and it is virtually

---

117   For a more detailed discussion of the *Kennon* judgment, see Chapter 5, and for later cases using the *Kennon* judgment, see Chapter 4.

118   (2012) 247 CLR 108.

119   (2011) 46 Fam LR 240 [112]. Before the Full Court made its orders, the wife died. Both parties agreed that if the Court had jurisdiction it should make appropriate orders rather than send the case for rehearing. It was held in *Stanford v Stanford* (2012) 47 Fam LR 105, [52]–[53] that, at the end of a long marriage and on the basis of the wife's contributions, the moral obligations ought to be discharged by a property settlement. The husband appealed to the High Court, which overruled the Full Court decision in *Stanford v Stanford* (2012) 247 CLR 108.

120   *Stanford v Stanford* (2012) 247 CLR 108 (French CJ, Hayne, Heydon, Kiefel and Bell JJ).

endorsing the interpretive possibility that a woman at the end of a long marriage may not be entitled to a share of property. It also demonstrates how the specialist expertise of the family court in these cases is assigned a relatively subordinate position in the wider legal system, as appeals from the Full Family Court must be decided by the High Court, which operates according to the mainstream conventions of legal reasoning.

Before 2002, superannuation was treated as a financial resource and was one of the significant factors in s 75(2) for making a property division order (see Chapter 5). Since the 2002 amendments to the FLA, superannuation may be split or flagged in making a property order if required by the circumstances of the case. Many issues about splitting super, and the relevance of s 75(2) factors in dividing super funds when making a property order, remain.[121] Where superannuation is not 'splittable', it may still be treated as a financial resource.[122] Similarly, since the amendments related to bankruptcy, it remains the case that the court can decide how to balance the interests of the non-bankrupt spouse and the trustee. It was observed in *Pippos v Pippos* that the Court had to consider the just and equitable outcome between the trustee and the non-bankrupt spouse and 'the provisions of section 75(2)(ha) and (n) [have] the effect that she will indeed be in part sharing responsibility for payment of some of the debt due to the husband's creditors'.[123]

In conclusion, the above discussion illustrates the precariousness of any claims for maintenance despite the apparent attempts of judges to reach reasonable outcomes. The issues in these cases arise not only from the judges' understanding of the facts and application of the law, but also from their method of interpretation of the law in a context where the legislation refuses to spell out the bases for an entitlement to a share of property. The same problematic outcomes are inevitable in the law that separates spousal and child maintenance. This is further illustrated in Chapter 10 on child maintenance or support, where it will be evident that child support has been provided greater security than spousal maintenance. However, the rationale for this appears tenuous when the caregiving role of the primary carer is taken into account.

6.5   Separation of spousal and child maintenance

The discussion above illustrates graphically how applications for spousal maintenance are conceptualised as secondary to applications for property division and, for the most part, are kept separate from claims for child maintenance or support. This separation manages to deflect attention from the background social context of the legislation where women with children have childcare responsibilities that make it difficult for them to participate in the

---

121   *Clives v Clives* [2008] FLC 93-385 (Warnick, Boland and Cronin JJ), where the Full Court approved the trial judge's decision regarding s 75(2) factors to make a 15% adjustment in the wife's favour with regard to non-superannuation funds. For dividing the superannuation funds, s 75(2) factors were again taken into account and the Full Court noted that the husband was older than the wife and she would be able to work longer. This was balanced against the husband's present capacity to earn a higher income.

122   *Lesbirel v Lesbirel* [2006] FLC 93-301.

123   [2008] FamCA 542 [65] (Burr J).

paid work sector on the same basis as men.[124] Yet the rules for maintenance in the FLA are gender-neutral and create the false impression that the law is there to 'help' anyone who undertakes primary childcare responsibilities. We argue that the conceptual separation of child and spousal maintenance functions to construct maintenance as a private issue to be resolved between the parties, and while there is some attempt to acknowledge that the need for maintenance mostly arises from caring for children, this is not articulated in a principled way in the FLA. Indeed, this recognition is competing with other concerns to ensure that formerly dependent spouses establish financial autonomy at the end of a relationship. In view of these competing concerns, the law ultimately fails to acknowledge the far-reaching effects that child rearing has on the financial autonomy of the person providing the care. As the discussion above and in the previous chapter has amply demonstrated, any amount of allocation of available property or maintenance does not and cannot make up adequately for the costs of assuming primary childcare responsibilities.

The fundamental cause of economic disparities between parents (whether married or in de facto relations involving men and women or same-sex partners) is linked to the need to look after young children in a society that does not adequately acknowledge these costs.[125] It is a fact that there are no other groups in society, other than mothers, who are given the option of choosing to be financially dependent. This happens in the wider context of a capitalist–materialist society where the need for economic self-sufficiency requires everyone to earn a living. To borrow an idea made famous by Glendon, this is the new property that determines our place in current society.[126] Women who have children are unable to participate in wage work as easily as men who have children. Thus even when most women with children engage in paid work, they consistently earn less than men; the concept of the gender gap captures this difference.[127]

This is a result of many factors coming together and it is a more extensive issue than one about the shape of family law.[128] There is nothing in family law to compel a mother or father to become financially dependent. Supposedly, this is a private choice that law does not concern itself with. Family law in this way maintains the discourse of family as a private

---

124   The technical aspects of the interrelationship between spousal maintenance and child support are discussed in *Kitman v Kitman* [2007] FamCA 822.

125   Iain Campbell, Gillian Whitehouse and Janeen Baxter, 'Australia: Casual Employment, Part-time Employment and the Resilience of the Male-breadwinner Model' in Leah Vosko, Martha MacDonald and Iain Campbell (eds), *Gender and the Contours of Precarious Employment* (Routledge, 2009) 60.

126   Mary Ann Glendon, *The New Family and The New Property* (Butterworths, 1981).

127   Beth Gaze, 'Gender Equality: Do Women Enjoy Human Rights in Australia?' (2015) 128 *Precedent* 21, 23 states that 'the gender pay gap is currently increasing. Having reached a low point of 14.9 per cent in 2004, it is now over 18 per cent and is continuing to increase'. For more recent statistics, see the Workforce Gender Equality Agency <https://www.wgea.gov.au/learn/fact-sheets-and-research-reports>; the *2015 Pay Equity Report Card*, Workforce Gender Equality Agency <https://www.wgea.gov.au/sites/default/files/2015_pay_equity_report_card.pdf>; see also Tanya Livermore, Joan Rodgers and Peter Siminski, 'The Effect of Motherhood on Wages and Wage Growth: Evidence for Australia' (2011) 87 *The Economic Record* 80.

128   For example, a comparative study of OECD countries conducted by AIFS shows that the social security system, labour market, family models and the family law system of any country influence the effects of divorce for women. The most important indicators of women's post-divorce economic wellbeing were their engagement in paid work and re-partnering. Spousal maintenance, social-welfare benefits and availability of child care were relevant but not as significant; David de Vaus et al, *The Economic Consequences of Divorce in Six OECD Countries* (Research Report No 31, AIFS, 2015).

institution, but also promises fair results if the relationship breaks down.[129] The normative function of the property and maintenance remedies of FLA is to create a (false) sense of security that if the marriage or relationship ends the primarily non-financial partner will be provided for. This false promise is amply illustrated in the empirical evidence of the consequences of marriage or relationship breakdown. The empirical evidence of Australian Institute of Family Studies (AIFS) studies shows that women with children suffer the most economic hardships when long marriages end.[130]

However, it is important to emphasise that these outcomes may not solely reflect patriarchal views of judges and the remedy may not simply lie in 'educating' judges in gender matters. It should be seen as a broader social issue requiring better understanding of the economic dynamics of relationships when they are intact and when they break down. This could assist in cases where there is a significant disparity in the property and financial resources between the parties. However, we should also bear in mind that in most cases of separation there is not a lot of wealth available for distribution. The resources that supported one household are often not enough to support two households. The courts very often divide the basic assets in the proportion of two-thirds to the wife and one-third to the husband, and very often the husband ends up with the non-basic assets.[131] Very often in practice the woman is the one providing for the housing needs of the children and needs this allocation of assets to provide a dwelling place rather than to generate an income. It has also been established that the single mother with ongoing caregiving responsibilities will face all the hurdles of engaging in paid work.[132] However, despite the seemingly generous property allocation in family law and the ample evidence of mothers entering paid work in ever-increasing numbers, it remains the case that property division outcomes continue to produce disadvantageous results for women with children.[133] This is an illustration of the limited capacity of family law to achieve economic parity for men and women.

Thus, it is evident that the remedies provided in the FLA for property division and maintenance fall short of the implied promise of fairness, but even within the limitations of these remedies there are many assumptions that refuse to acknowledge either the long-term effects of being the primary caregiver that most of the time it is the mother who has this role. This is most starkly illustrated in the separation of child support from spousal maintenance

---

129   The theoretical underpinnings of law thus maintaining dependencies is discussed in Martha Fineman, 'Masking Dependency: The Political Role of Family Rhetoric' (1995) 81(8) *Virginia Law Review* 2181.

130   There are many AIFS studies; for a review see Grania Sheehan, 'Financial Aspects of the Divorce Transition in Australia: Recent Empirical Findings' (2002) 16(1) *International Journal of Law, Policy and Family* 95. See also Grania Sheehan and Jody Hughes, *Division of Matrimonial Property in Australia* (Research Paper No 25, AIFS, 2001). Ruth Weston and Bruce Smyth, 'Financial Living Standards after Divorce' (2000) 55 *Family Matters* 10 report that 59% of women with children were still living in poverty six years after separation.

131   Sheehan and Hughes, above n 130.

132   See, eg, Matthew Gray et al, *Determinants of Australian Mothers' Employment: An Analysis of Lone and Couple Mothers* (Research Paper No 26, AIFS, 2002), who explore the possible reasons for the facts that lone-parent families have a higher rate of unemployment than couple families and the majority of lone-parent families are headed by women.

133   de Vaus et al, above n 128 found that in the United Kingdom, Germany and Australia, even though women's earnings started to recover, after six years of divorce women still earned substantially less than they would have done if they had remained married.

under the FLA and the creation of a separate regime for child support.[134] Two normative outcomes are achieved simultaneously in this process. First, the moral imperative of providing for the children (unlike providing for the former spouse or partner) is not politically controversial[135] and the difficulties associated with enforcing maintenance orders are avoided by making child support an administrative task of the relevant agency. Second, child support is more easily justified as a moral and legal responsibility of both parents, thus denying the existing social reality that most mothers are economically weaker than fathers and, even after the relationship breakdown, they continue to be the primary carers. The effects are that the concept of spousal maintenance and entitlement of the spouse to maintenance are subtly delegitimised. The link between the Child Support Acts and the concept of equal shared parental responsibility further entrenches the idea that fathers, as typically the non-resident parents, pay child support. A corollary to this responsibility to pay child support is that they are also entitled to a right of contact with the child. But it is not asserted as a right per se, but conceptualised as in the best interests of the child (see Chapter 10).[136]

The financial remedies of the FLA are inadequate because they do not identify the base cause of the problem – the source of wellbeing is not access to property but access to income.[137] This problem itself stems from a failure in family law to acknowledge the real cost of childcare responsibilities. Ultimately, these issues bring into focus the inadequacy of conceptualising family law as a stand-alone area of law.[138] The gender-neutral language of the FLA makes a mockery of the idea that family law recognises social realities and provides for them. The language of the FLA in this regard endorses formal equality between men and women, and denies the prevalent social reality that child care is predominantly a gendered activity and carries with it a heavy price. It does, however, make it possible for judges to accommodate the specifics of any relationship. Faith in the judiciary to make an appropriate order is premised on the assumption that judges can more readily recognise social realities and 'compensate' for the existing gender hierarchies. The issue, however, is: why should the judges be expected to do so? What are the tools available to them? As discussed in the previous chapter, there are no guides available to attribute financial value to non-financial work. Judges thus exercise discretion with very real constraints on their ability to reach a fair outcome. An additional and, in our view, more problematic issue is that what is a 'fair' outcome is left unarticulated by the legislation.

---

134   *The Child Support (Registration and Collection) Act 1988* (Cth) and the *Child Support (Assessment) Act 1989* (Cth).

135   For example, the claim that the child-support scheme has been conducive to gaining greater public support for the idea that parents bear these obligations is reiterated in the Ministerial Task Force on Child Support, *In the Best Interests of the Children – Reforming the Child Support Scheme* (Commonwealth of Australia, Attorney General's Department, 2005) 2.

136   Belinda Fehlberg, Christine Millward and Monica Campo, 'Post-Separation Parenting Arrangements, Child Support and Property Settlement: Exploring the Connections' (2010) 24(2) *Australian Journal of Family Law* 214.

137   See, eg, Robert Paul Wolff, *Understanding Rawls* (Princeton University Press, 1977) 197, where he claims that in capitalist societies what is important is 'how much your job pays, not how big your portfolio is or how much land you have inherited'.

138   The presence of extensive debates about the impact of government policies on how families, and particularly mothers, navigate wage work is not represented adequately in family law rules or their interpretations. See, eg, Alan Hayes and Jennifer Baxter, 'Work and Family Approaches in Australia' in Jackie Griffiths (ed) *Family Futures* (Tudor Rose, 2014) 187.

While it is true that the award of periodic maintenance is rather uncommon in family law cases,[139] the significance of these particular legislative measures lies beyond that fact, in so far as these rules legitimise a normative expectation that at the end of a relationship the cost of the breakdown would be met by the parties rather than by the wider society. Thus, the equation of the need of one partner and the capacity to pay of the other not only privatises the costs of sexual division of labour and the breakdown of the relationship, but it also goes against its own earlier assumption of formal equality. Ultimately, the consequences of providing periodic maintenance are that those asked to pay are usually men, who feel aggrieved, and those receiving maintenance are usually women, who do not attain a parity of living standard with their former partners. The discontent on all sides is a product of the family law judges being expected to achieve outcomes that are influenced by a complex array of factors not created solely by the individual choices of the two people in a relationship. The absence of any aspiration on the part of the FLA to create a parity of outcomes is most starkly illustrated in the provisions for entering into financial agreements that oust the jurisdiction of the FLA, as discussed in the next chapter.

---

139   Juliet Behrens and Bruce Smyth, *Spousal Support in Australia: A Study of Incidence and Attitudes* (Working Paper No 16, AIFS, 1999).

PRIVATE ORDERING OF FINANCIAL RELATIONS

7.1   Introduction

The 2000 amendments to the *Family Law Act 1975* (Cth) ('FLA') introduced the concept of financial agreements. The main significance of this change is that a financial agreement can be binding on the parties, allowing them to opt out of the jurisdiction of the FLA.[1] This chapter juxtaposes the trend in the FLA of providing private ordering arrangements through mechanisms such as financial agreements and the social reality of dependencies created through family care arrangements that usually arise from caring for children.[2] We analyse how notions of individual autonomy and private ordering are endorsed in a law that was apparently meant to provide for the dependencies created by these caregiving roles (see Chapter 5). The rationale behind the new provisions is to promote individual autonomy and free choice, which are principles based in the ideology of capitalism, and aligned to the liberal understanding of family as a contract. We argue that, with the possibility of creating binding financial agreements, the potential normative message of the FLA to promote just and equitable property distributions at the end of a marriage or de facto relationship is wiped clean.

However, the argument that the introduction of binding financial agreements is merely reflecting either the individual autonomy or privacy of the parties does not provide a full explanation for this change to the law. This is because there are provisions in the FLA that override private agreement-making in specific circumstances. This is exhibited most strongly in instances when the social-welfare system is called upon to make up for any shortfall in the ability of financially weaker parties to provide for themselves after marriage or relationship breakdown. Provisions for financial agreements exist parallel to those that apply in cases of spousal maintenance (discussed in Chapter 6) and child support (discussed in Chapter 10). These provisions allow courts to scrutinise maintenance arrangements made between parties if and when social-welfare payments are claimed. Thus, the ideology of autonomy operates to protect the financial interests of the parties, but only so long as the finances are sufficient for the parties to bear the costs of relationship breakdown. The analysis below will thus demonstrate how the tension between autonomy and dependency also exists in the context of agreement-making, and how the nuclear family in this context is relied upon in the FLA as a means of containing the costs of family dependencies to the state.

The chapter includes an overview of the statutory provisions regulating the creation of financial agreements and the provisions that authorise the court to scrutinise these agreements and that serve to protect more vulnerable family members (and the public purse). Similarly, the discussion of the jurisdiction of the courts to vary orders and set aside agreements will reveal the investment the law continues to have in the family. An analysis of the courts' interpretations of these provisions will provide an interesting contrast between the approaches of the legislature and the judiciary to the role of the FLA in achieving fair outcomes for both partners at the end of a relationship. Essentially, the difference between them is one of interpretation of what is fair: for the legislature it is largely upholding the private

---

1   The *Family Law Amendment Act 2000* (Cth), which commenced on 27 December 2000, inserted a new pt VIIIA ('Financial Agreements') into the FLA.

2   Similar observations can be made with respect to the move to compulsory family dispute resolution in children's matters, discussed in Chapter 8.

agreement, while for some members of the judiciary it is protecting the institution of the family based on the traditional marriage model. We contend that in an unequal gendered society the former scenario could favour the stronger financial party, while the latter may favour the interests of the more financially vulnerable party. The discussion will also link to Chapter 6 on spousal maintenance and Chapter 10 on child support and social welfare to demonstrate the contrary pulls of private versus public ideologies present in family law.

7.2   Financial agreements in the FLA: the dilemmas of treating personal relationships like contracts

It is important to understand the context of the changes to the FLA in 2000 that have made it possible for parties to enter into binding financial agreements before, during or after a marriage.[3] The provisions for financial agreements were extended to de facto relationships from 1 March 2009.[4] Unlike all other (earlier) methods of entering into private agreements, the parties entering into binding financial agreements are able to oust the jurisdiction of the courts in making a determination over the nominated property covered by an agreement. The significance of this possibility of quarantining all or some property from court interference goes beyond the enhancement of the parties' freedom of choice. We argue that this change represents an increase in the privatisation of family relations with the additional (albeit unstated) aims of protecting the financial interests of the parties, on the one hand, and of saving the public purse, on the other. It thus helps transform the cost of dependency within personal relationships into a private rather than a social cost.

Let us begin by repeating the reasons why the FLA (or the earlier matrimonial causes law) exists. The conventional understanding of family law as a dispute resolution mechanism is based on the understanding that the family is a private institution and the role of law is to regulate the boundary-marking aspects of it – for example, how to enter into a marriage (or de facto relationship) or how to dissolve it. In addition to these functions, the law can assist in making decisions about how children will be cared for and property distributed when a relationship breaks down. Associated with these functions is the distinctive feature of the FLA: providing for the possibility for primary caregivers to claim a share of the property because of the non-financial contributions they made to the accumulation of property and to the welfare of the family during the relationship. We saw in Chapter 5 that in pursuance of this idea the courts are given wide discretion to readjust the property entitlements of

---

3   *Family Law Act 1975* (Cth) ss 90B–90D (for married couples); cf ss 90UA–90UD (for de facto couples).

4   The *Family Law Amendment (De Facto Financial and Other Measures) Act 2008* (Cth) ('2008 amendments') was passed by Federal Parliament on 11 November 2008 and received royal assent on 21 November 2008. The provisions relating to the regulation of the financial affairs of de facto couples commenced on 1 March 2009. The Act extends the property and maintenance provisions of the FLA to de facto couples in referring States upon relationship breakdown. The new pt VIIIAB effectively replicates for de facto couples the provisions in the existing pt VIII ('Property, Spousal Maintenance and Maintenance Agreements') and pt VIIIA ('Financial Agreements') for married couples.

the two parties. This authority to reallocate property rights is not easily available under any other laws or principles of equity, and is a distinctive feature of the FLA. Thus, it is entirely plausible to argue that the main message of the property provisions is to acknowledge the prevailing social realities that caregiving functions continue to be gendered and result in financial disadvantage for the primary carer. In this way the FLA recognises that parties may have engaged in financial and non-financial activities to different degrees. In providing for the recognition of non-financial contributions to the property and the family, the FLA provides the possibility for the more financially vulnerable partner to get a share of property at the end of a relationship. This approach is based on an understanding of the relationship as a partnership of equals, who are engaged in different activities during an intact relationship. However, our contention is that all of these potential safeguards are negated at a normative level by the possibility of entering into a binding financial agreement.

We argue that this change represents enhanced privatisation of the family through the discourse of contract law; however, contract is an inappropriate regulatory model for personal relations that are based on dependency arising from the care of children. When originally enacted, the FLA had jurisdiction over all property, but it came with the proviso that private agreements were also possible. However, the complete quarantining of property from the jurisdiction of the FLA is now available by the parties entering a binding financial agreement. This represents the entrenchment of the idea of family relations as contractual. This is a problematic development for a number of reasons, including that: (1) financial agreements do not provide greater equity and certainty, but give priority to procedure over the substance of the agreements; (2) autonomy of the parties is not taken to its logical conclusion and instead the protection of the law is provided by lawyers and not the courts; (3) there is an inconsistent attitude to the autonomy of the parties in the FLA and financial agreement provisions; and (4) the contract model treats the two individuals as autonomous adults, but is ill-suited for family relationships based on gendered relations of dependency, especially where children are involved. These issues are elaborated upon in the following discussion.

7.2.1 Financial agreements: procedure prioritised over substance

As originally enacted, the FLA assumed jurisdiction over all of the property of both spouses for the purpose of ascertaining the pool of property, irrespective of how that property was acquired. Simultaneously, the FLA has favoured private settlement of disputes, but also maintained, at least in principle, a role for judicial scrutiny of these private agreements. This changed in 2000 with the introduction of provisions in the FLA for the making of binding financial agreements.[5] For the first time, it became possible to oust the application of the FLA property provisions and thus court scrutiny of property settlements between the parties. The explanations for amending the FLA implicitly use

---

5   The idea was canvassed and supported earlier in the Australian Law Reform Commission, *Matrimonial Property*, Report No 39 (1987) and in the Commonwealth Joint Select Committee on Certain Aspects of the Family Law Act, Parliament of Australia, *The Family Law Act 1975: Aspects of its Operation and Interpretation* (1992). However, in both cases there was a recognition that the court should be able to oversee that the agreement was fair or just.

the changes in society, and, in particular, changes in social attitudes towards marriage since the introduction of the legislation in 1975, as the main justifications for modifying the legislation.

The Commonwealth government's reasons for introducing binding financial agreements are evident in the second reading speech of the then Attorney-General, Daryl Williams. His stated reasons for the change include that:

> it will provide greater equity and certainty in matters relating to the party's finances by allowing couples to make binding financial agreements. … This will offer couples improved choice and greater control in arranging their financial affairs. It will also allow couples to avoid costly court proceedings.[6]

The aim of giving greater certainty in financial settlements between the parties is impliedly referring to the distinctive feature of the FLA property provisions that invests judges with wide discretion in making property orders.

However, if the issue is 'uncertainty' of outcomes, how to approach the resolution of this problem should at the very least require an open discussion of potential options to remedy the situation, instead of making private agreement the only option (see Chapter 5). Moreover, the idea that private financial agreements provide greater equity in financial matters assumes that everyone stands to benefit from them equally. However, we contend that the interests of the more financially secure parties will benefit most. This is because binding financial agreements are contrary to the very rationale of the FLA, which enables readjustment of property entitlements at the end of a relationship, and deny the existing social reality that necessitated the FLA in the first place – that is, to address the consequences of gendered roles within families. This disjuncture between social and legal realities brings into sharp focus why contracts have not been the preferred model of regulating personal relations.

There are further problems in how financial agreements are conceptualised in the FLA. For instance, the idea that the goal of the amendments is to keep people out of court prioritises procedural efficiency at the cost of substantive fairness. Admittedly, the same emphasis is present in the FLA's insistence on family dispute resolution as the preferred method of dispute settlement (see Chapters 2, 4 and 8).

7.2.2   Autonomy of the parties versus legal protection provided by their lawyers

The FLA also does not consistently apply the assumption that two autonomous adults can look after their own affairs. This is illustrated by the FLA providing for an ongoing role of the law to oversee the division of the parties' property. Similarly, with regard to financial agreements the 'protection' offered by the law continues to be relevant. However, legal protection

---

6   Commonwealth, *Parliamentary Debates*, House of Representatives, 30 August 2000, 19729. See also Williams's response to the debate on the following day: Commonwealth, *Parliamentary Debates*, House of Representatives, 31 August 2000, 19 807.

is now provided by the parties' respective lawyers rather than by the courts. The trouble with this is that lawyers are not equipped to provide the authoritative interpretations of the law that the courts provide. Furthermore, the lawyers operate in a legislative context that does not set out clear rights of the parties, but gives wide discretion to the courts and so does not produce binding precedents that lawyers can in turn use as a guide.

For instance, it is possible to interpret the introduction of financial agreements (and how they allow parties to quarantine some or all property from the jurisdiction of the courts) in a strictly technical manner as adhering to the principle of formal equality by enabling the parties to decide how to divide their property. It is not such a radical idea since the law already allows the partners in commercial transactions to decide the terms of their agreements and the same autonomy is now being extended to intimate relationships. The implication of such a stand is that family law has no role to play when two capable adults agree to organise their financial relations in a particular manner.[7] They are already relatively free of legal oversight while their personal relationship is ongoing, and the same idea is being extended to their relationship when it comes to an end.

However, this is not the complete picture as the FLA has not made the role of law and legal professionals irrelevant in providing freedom of choice to the parties. Instead, it has replaced judicial oversight with assigning responsibility to legal advisers to assist their clients when planning to enter into a financial agreement.[8] Thus the legislation makes it clear that legal rights are at stake and in entering into a private agreement both parties should have legal advice.[9] This emphasis on the role of lawyers, however, has its own set of problems as it is questionable whether the legal advisers can perform the original role of the courts to ensure some semblance of a fair agreement.

This is especially so in the context of the legislative design of the FLA, which does not specifically articulate the legal rights of the parties. It also brings into view the tension between a conception of family law as a guarantor of rights or of fairness on the one hand, and a conception of family law as merely a dispute resolution mechanism on the other hand. The implicit assurance is that, since the parties' lawyers will give advice to each party respectively, both of them can be sure of entering into a fair settlement. The FLA thus gives a (false) assurance that the involvement of lawyers will safeguard the rights of both parties. The task of the lawyer is made more difficult by the design of the FLA, which emphasises

---

7   For an argument that distinctions between commercial and family agreements cannot be maintained, see Mary Keyes and Kylie Burns, 'Contract and the Family: Whither Intention?' (2002) 26(3) *Melbourne University Law Review* 577.

8   The criteria for a binding financial agreement pursuant to s 90G(1) of the FLA include: '(a) the agreement is signed by all parties; and (b) before signing the agreement, each spouse's party was provided with independent legal advice from a legal practitioner about the effect of the agreement on the rights of that party and about the advantages and disadvantages, at the time that the advice was provided, to that party of making the agreement; and (c) either before or after signing the agreement, each spouse party was provided with a signed statement by the legal practitioner stating that the advice referred to in paragraph (b) was provided to that party (whether or not the statement is annexed to the agreement); and (ca) a copy of the statement referred to in paragraph (c) that was provided to a spouse party is given to the other spouse party or to a legal practitioner for the other spouse party ...'.

9   But note that paragraph (1) in s 90G(1) is subject to paragraph (1A), which provides that a financial agreement can still be binding on the parties in certain circumstances, including when one or more of the paragraphs in s 90G(1)(b)–(ca) are not satisfied in relation to the agreement.

the exercise of the court's discretion in deciding how to distribute the property of separating parties. Therefore, it does not lend itself to interpretations that identify the property rights of the parties with any certainty, as the courts' discretionary judgments do not yield precedents in the conventional sense. The legal advisers cannot do more than note the trend in the judgments on property matters. But as we saw in the previous two chapters, the number of variables are simply too many and legal advisers have no more insight into likely outcomes than any other legal actor.

7.2.3 Inconsistency between the FLA's approach to provisions for financial agreements and other FLA provisions

There are a number of inconsistencies in the FLA's approach to the issues of autonomy and free choice of the parties. In its regulation of relationships, family law adopts a gender-neutral stance: that the two partners are equally able to decide which roles they will choose in an ongoing relationship. It follows from this logic that the economic dependency that arises from being the primary carer is construed as a consequence of these individual choices rather than being a structural reality. However, assumptions about the autonomy of both partners are not taken to their logical conclusion as the FLA also includes property adjustment provisions. In these provisions the FLA selectively acknowledges that primary caretakers (though its gender-neutral language obscures the fact that they are mostly mothers) are likely to be financially weaker partners who require legal protection to ensure a fair outcome at the end of a relationship. As we saw in the previous two chapters, many aspects of the property distribution provisions fall short of creating a just outcome for the financially dependent or weaker spouse/partner, but it is also undeniable that the mere presence of these provisions has wider functions. They set up the normative expectation that justice and fairness might require that the two partners should share the available property or wealth at the end of a relationship. It is this normative message that is being overridden by the possibility of the parties entering into a financial agreement and contracting out of the jurisdiction of the FLA.

Furthermore, the notion of individual autonomy is inadequate in fully explaining various other provisions of the FLA, and the financial agreement provisions, for that matter. These provisions adopt an inconsistent stand with regard to the social reality of gender hierarchies and the dependencies created owing to the performance of caregiving work by according selective recognition to this work and its effects on the financial standing of the parent who performs it. Two illustrations of these inconsistencies are evident when (1) individual autonomy to enter a financial agreement is overridden when it clashes with social-welfare policies and laws and (2) the autonomy to enter into financial agreements is not extended to the parties in other areas of family law.

For instance, the same FLA that allows parties to enter into a financial agreement also allows the law to override the private agreement if at the time the agreement was made the applicant would otherwise have had to rely on social-welfare payments for survival. Thus the FLA provisions for spousal maintenance (discussed in Chapter 6) and child support (discussed in Chapter 10), which allow courts to scrutinise maintenance arrangements when social-welfare payments are being claimed, are also made relevant with respect to financial agreements, as discussed later in this chapter.

So too, in other provisions of the FLA the invocation of the legal fiction of two autonomous contracting parties is not taken to its logical conclusion. For example, the same two parties who are free to enter into a financial agreement are not free to set the terms of their marriage or de facto relationship. It is accepted without question that people do not have absolute freedom to choose the terms of their relationship.[10] Thus the two parties are restricted by law in choosing various other aspects of their relationship:[11] the duration of their relationship, the nature of the relationship (polygamous, same-sex), or even the terms of how they will perform their respective roles in an ongoing relationship. Most of these 'conditions' would be unenforceable either as contracts or under the FLA. For instance, it is uncontroversial that the principle of freedom of contract is subject to the wider concerns of public policy, as well as to prevent unconscionable conduct and guard against fraud, duress and so on.[12] Similarly, and by analogy, the law not allowing contracts for marriage relationships of short duration is understandable.[13]

Extending this line of argument, it could be asked whether the FLA, in allowing people to contract out of their financial obligations at the end of a (gendered) relationship, is also problematic and unconscionable, and therefore against public policy.[14] However, this question is rendered irrelevant by deploying the discourse of two autonomous individuals, free to decide how to organise their personal lives.[15] In this picture, socially existing gender hierarchies are obliterated as law uses formal equality as its standard. The surprising thing is that this is being done in a piece of legislation that can also function to address the consequences of gendered roles within families.

The question therefore is whether contracts constitute the appropriate model for organising personal relationships. In posing this question, our aim is not to endorse the concept of complete freedom of contract as the organising principle of personal relations, but to articulate the problems with this idea. The discourse of autonomy deployed in contracts invokes ideas that two adult parties should be able to organise their lives as they wish; and any interference with this autonomy is paternalistic as it denies them freedom in their transactions, and is unwarranted interference with their choices. If accepted in family law, this reasoning

---

10   Nor is there complete freedom to choose the terms of your private agreement, as is famously discussed in Robert N Mnookin and Lewis Kornhauser, 'Bargaining in the Shadow of the Law: The Case of Divorce' (1979) 88 *Yale Law Journal* 950.

11   See a critique of marriage as contract in Carol Smart, *The Ties that Bind* (Routledge & Kegan Paul, 1984) 143. For an economist's perspective, see Helmut Rainer, 'Should We Write Prenuptial Contracts?' (2007) 51(2) *European Economic Review* 337. For a feminist argument in favor of marriage as a contract, see Lenore Weitzman, *The Marriage Contract* (Free Press, 1993).

12   John Gooley, Peter Radan and Ilija Vickovich, *Principles of Australian Contract Law* (LexisNexis, 3rd ed, 2014). See also F H Buckley (ed), *The Fall and Rise of Freedom of Contract* (Duke University Press, 1999) for a review of the resurgence of ideas about freedom of contract.

13   See also an argument as to why marriage as a covenant may be a desirable regulatory model: Elizabeth S Scott, 'Marital Commitment and the Legal Regulation of Divorce' in Antony W Dnes and Robert Rowthorn (eds), *The Law and Economics of Marriage and Divorce* (Cambridge University Press, 2002) 35.

14   See the discussion below of *Black v Black* (2008) 38 Fam LR 503.

15   A related issue here is whether individuals are free to decide when and how to have children as reproductive technologies become more sophisticated. Legal regulation of surrogacy and other forms of assisted reproduction throw up many drawbacks of contracts as the model. See, eg, Janet L Dolgin, *Defining the Family: Law, Technology, and Reproduction in an Uneasy Age* (New York University Press, 1997).

could justify the structuring of personal relationships as contracts between two autonomous individuals.[16] It follows that there is nothing specific that family law does (other than provide a neutral dispute resolution mechanism) and therefore it can be replaced with the law of contracts. The obvious objection to this line of reasoning is that at the end of a marriage/relationship children have to be provided for, as they are vulnerable and dependent on adults for their wellbeing. Could contracts replace family law if the issues of the rights of parties to a marriage or de facto relationship are separated from the issue of the rights of children, as the FLA already does? This line of questioning could justify family law being reconceptualised as parenting law,[17] but we resist this suggestion, as explained below.

7.2.4 The concept of individual autonomy does not suit the dependency model of family relationships

The debates about regulating marriage as akin to a contract have a long history,[18] but for this approach to produce fair results certain conditions must be met. In brief, we argue that contract as the model for organising personal relationships may work only if there are two adults involved. It simply does not work fairly if children are also involved in the particular family set up. Treating an intimate relationship like a contract assumes formal equality between the parties, but this is a flawed understanding.[19] Underpinning the abstract notion of two equal contracting parties is the discourse of self-interest and individualism that denies the social realities and consequences of dependencies that exist in affective human relationships,[20] especially when children are present.[21] It is for this reason that we contend that a contractual model favours the stronger financial partners in relationships, and in an unequal gendered society they would be less likely to be mothers with dependent children.

Furthermore, the discourse of family relations as the private concern of the parties contributes to the creation and legitimising of ideas that conceptualise public and private spheres as independent of each other. As Smart has argued, it is not possible to separate the parents from their relationship with each other or from their relationship with their children.[22]

---

16 The trend towards contractualisation of family is evident across nations. See, eg, Frederik Swennen, 'Private Ordering in Family Law: A Global Perspective' in Frederik Swennen (ed), *Contractualisation of Family Law – Global Perspectives* (Springer, 2015) 1.

17 For the argument that parenthood and the relationship of the partners are separable considerations, see Gillian Douglas, 'Marriage, Cohabitation and Parenthood – From Contract to Status' in Stanford N Katz, John Eekelaar and Mavis Maclean (eds), *Cross Currents: Family Law and Policy in the United States and England* (Oxford University Press, 2005) 211.

18 For a discussion of possibilities related to contracts, see Antony W Dnes and Robert Rowthorn (eds), *The Law and Economics of Marriage and Divorce* (Cambridge University Press, 2002).

19 Martha Fineman, 'Responsibility, Family, and the Limits of Equality: An American Perspective' in Jo Bridgeman, Craig Lind and Heather Keating (eds), *Taking Responsibility: Law and the Changing Family* (Ashgate, 2011) 37.

20 Alison Diduck, 'Autonomy and Vulnerability in Family Law: the Missing Link' in Julie Wallbank and Jonathan Herring (eds), *Vulnerabilities, Care and Family Law* (Routledge, 2013) 95.

21 Martha L A Fineman, 'Masking Dependency: the Political Role of Family Rhetoric' (1995) 81(8) *Virginia Law Review* 2181.

22 Carol Smart, 'The New Parenthood: Fathers and Mothers After Divorce' in Carol Smart and Elizabeth Silva (eds), *The New Family* (Sage Publications, 1999) 100.

In this respect, we also recall Poole's analysis, as outlined in Chapter 1, that a particular kind of public sphere inhabited by individualistic, contracting parties can be imagined only because of the existence of a private sphere. In this private sphere, emotional sustenance, altruism, generosity and care structure our relationships. It is also the case that women are more associated with these attributes, and thus notions of femininity and masculinity are constructed as though they are a true depiction of the essential natures of men and women. The separation between public and private spheres seems inevitable, and the allocation of specific roles to men and women follows. However, if the so-called organising values of the public sphere were to regulate the private sphere, society would simply not survive, as it would not be able to replicate itself. For example, personal relations organised as contracts would make it irrational for women to become financially vulnerable in 'choosing' to be the primary carers. It would not make economic or rational sense to either invest in relations with the other partner or invest in children. Thus, the 'rationality' of the public sphere constructed by contractual relations can only exist if there is a different kind of sphere of life – a private sphere – which operates to fulfil the emotional and physical needs of individuals and society more generally.

Pateman makes a similar point in her celebrated book, *The Sexual Contract*.[23] She explains that western conceptions of public and political authority, as based on a contract of autonomous individuals, become possible only because these individual (male) contracting agents have the sexual contract available to them in the private sphere. It is the sexual contract between men and women in their personal relationships that ensures that the services of women as nurturers are available to men, so that they can function as autonomous individuals in the public sphere. This insight is of direct relevance to the present discussion of the FLA. On the one hand, the law invokes the construct of private contracting agents exercising free choice in entering a financial agreement. On the other hand, the law acknowledges that if personal relationships end the economically vulnerable partners (mostly women) may require legal intervention to achieve a fair or just outcome – if not also to protect the public purse.[24]

It is, of course, the case that emotional and financial dependencies are intertwined,[25] and yet the law takes no responsibility for the emotional or psychological aspects of personal relationship breakdowns.[26] Family law is designed to address the financial aspects of relationship breakdown, as it would seem that no other area of law is able to address these issues. However, by allowing the parties to 'contract out' of the application of the property adjustment provisions of the FLA, the very law that was apparently meant to deal with the consequences of caring for children, in both material and non-material terms, seems to deny its own reason for existence.

23   Carole Pateman, *The Sexual Contract* (Polity Press, 1988).

24   See also Julie Wallbank, '(En)Gendering the Fusion of Rights and Responsibilities in the Law of Contact' in Julie Wallbank, Shazia Choudhry and Jonathan Herrings (eds), *Rights, Gender and Family Law* (Routledge, 2010) 93.

25   Jo Bridgeman, 'Relational Vulnerability, Care and Dependency' in Julie Wallbank and Jonathan Herring, *Vulnerabilities, Care and Family Law* (Routledge, 2013) 199.

26   See also Jennifer Nedelsky, *Law's Relations: A Relational Theory of Self, Autonomy and Law* (Oxford University Press, 2011) for an argument that individuals are not self-contained or bounded units, but take shape in relational terms. We suggest that this insight is particularly significant as a counter-position to when the law 'allows' two individuals to act as contracting agents in personal relations.

Thus the FLA, in providing for financial agreements, makes the issue of fairness in the distribution of property a private affair, not the legitimate business of anyone other than the parties. In the process, it hides the cost of ongoing financial dependence behind the ideology of autonomy, but only so long as the parties bear the costs of relationship breakdown. The constructs of individual autonomy and public/private come together in the discourse of family law in this regard. This in turn illustrates the wider function of family law to rely on the nuclear family as a mechanism for containing the cost of family dependencies to the state.

The raising of these issues illuminates an insight of post-structuralism that the meaning of law is always in the process of construction. It is therefore necessary for legal thinkers to engage with the processes of law at various sites. In the context of financial agreements, it is particularly significant to understand the different approaches of the legislature and the judiciary in promoting individual autonomy on the one hand, while also extending the 'protection' of the law to the more financially vulnerable parties on the other, and how the private and nuclear family is re-created in this process. The tension between the objectives of the legislature to promote choice and autonomy, and the judiciary to protect the interests of more vulnerable parties, will be evident in the discussion of the cases below. Before that, it is important to overview the relevant legislative provisions.

7.3   Financial agreements

7.3.1   The legislative provisions

The *Family Law Amendment Act 2000* (Cth) inserted a new Part VIIIA into the FLA (Part VIIIAB came into effect on 1 March 2009 for de facto relationships). Part VIIIB of the FLA also provides for the making of financial agreements that split or can otherwise affect superannuation entitlements.[27] These provisions allow for the making of binding financial agreements that oust the jurisdiction of the court in relation to property and maintenance.[28] They replaced FLA s 87 maintenance agreements, which allowed for a similar result but only when the court approved the agreement. They also replace FLA s 86 agreements, which allowed for private agreements to be registered with the court without the scrutiny of the court, but which did not oust the jurisdiction of the court under s 79 of the FLA (subject to the time requirement in s 44).

'Financial agreement' in s 4(1) relates to marriages and is defined to mean 'an agreement that is a financial agreement under section 90B, 90C or 90D, but does not include an ante-nuptial or post-nuptial settlement to which section 85A applies'. 'Part VIIIAB financial agreement' relates to de facto relationships and is defined to mean 'an agreement: (a) made under section 90UB, 90UC or 90UD; or (b) covered by section 90UE'.

The term 'financial matters' in s 4(1) is defined to mean:

> (a) in relation to the parties to a marriage – matters with respect to:
>
> > (i)   the maintenance of one of the parties; or

---

27   A financial agreement that deals with superannuation is effective under pt VIIIB and not pt VIIIA even though superannuation is treated as property by s 90MC.

28   It has been held by the court that it is possible to have a financial agreement that is binding under pt VIIIA and pt VIIIAB: see *Piper v Mueller* [2015] FLC 93-686.

(ii) the property of those parties or of either of them; or

(iii) the maintenance of children of the marriage; or

(b) in relation to the parties to a de facto relationship—any or all of the following matters:

(i)   the maintenance of one of the parties;

(ii) the distribution of the property of the parties or of either of them;

(iii) the distribution of any other financial resources of the parties or of either of them.

7.3.2   Who may enter into financial agreements?

Financial agreements can be entered into by couples who are intending to marry (s 90B); are married but not separated (s 90C); are married and separated but not divorced (s 90C); or are divorced (s 90D). Third parties can now be a party to an agreement as a result of the *Family Law Amendment (De Facto Financial Matters and Other Measures) Act 2008* (Cth) ('2008 amendments'), which commenced on 1 March 2009. Similar provisions (ss 90UB–90UD) are available to de facto couples who meet the s 90UA requirements to enter into financial agreements (s 90UE agreements also apply).[29] Financial agreements made in relation to a marriage may deal with four broad categories of matters, including how all or any property or financial resources of the parties is to be 'dealt with';[30] spousal maintenance during marriage and/or after divorce;[31] matters 'incidental or ancillary to' the above matters;[32] and 'other matters' (that is, child maintenance).[33]

The language of each subsection reflects whether the financial agreement is made before or during the marriage or after divorce. For example, financial agreements before marriage and during marriage may include any of the enumerated matters in s 90B(2) or s 90C(2) respectively. In an agreement made before marriage, these are how, in the event of the breakdown of marriage, all or any of the property or financial resources of either or both parties at the time when the agreement is made, or at a later time and before divorce, are to be dealt with (s 90B(2)(a)); in an agreement made during marriage, it can deal with how the property or financial resources at the time when the agreement is made, or at a later time during the marriage, are to be dealt with (s 90C(2)(a)). Thus, the property or financial resources that can be dealt with must be acquired before or during the subsistence of the marriage. A financial agreement after divorce is made under s 90D and the slight variation of language reflects this. This agreement can be made only after divorce is finalised (s 90D(1)). It can deal with property or financial resources the parties had or acquired during the former marriage (s 90D(2)(a)). The first two kinds of financial agreements can also deal with maintenance of either of the spouses during the marriage, after divorce or both during the marriage and after divorce (s 90B(2)(b) and s 90C(2)(b)), but financial agreements made after divorce can deal with maintenance of either of spouse parties after divorce (s 90D(2)(b)).

---

29   We will not refer repeatedly to these provisions in order to avoid complexity of the text, but the corresponding provisions for de facto couples to enter into financial agreements are present in pt VIIAB, div 4.

30   ss 90B(2)(a), 90C(2)(a), 90D(2)(a).

31   ss 90B(2)(b), 90C(2)(b), 90D(2)(b), but subject to the requirements in s 90E.

32   ss 90B(3)(a), 90C(3)(a), 90D(3)(a).

33   ss 90B(3)(b), 90C(3)(b), 90D(3)(b) but subject to the requirements in s 90E. Compare the corresponding provisions for de facto relationships: ss 90UB(3), 90UC(3), 90UD(3), 90UH.

There are additional requirements for a separation declaration for certain provisions of financial agreements to take effect, and these are included in s 90DA. In financial agreements dealing with the property or financial resources of one or both parties at the end or break-down of marriage, the provisions concerning how the property or financial resources of one or both parties are to be dealt with upon marriage breakdown will have no effect unless the parties are divorced, one has died or a separation declaration is made (s 90DA(1)). This provision came into force in April 2005 and is designed to prevent the transfer of property between parties who have not separated. A separation declaration is a written declaration, signed by at least one of the parties, that states that there has been an effective break-down of their matrimonial relationship, and that there is no likelihood of cohabitation being resumed (s 90DA(2)–(5)). A financial agreement can be binding on the parties after divorce or death of the parties/party and therefore a separation declaration is not required in these circumstances (s 90DA(1A)).

7.3.3   Binding financial agreements: developments in legislation and cases

As a preliminary point, it must be emphasised that for a financial agreement to be a bind-ing agreement it must meet both formal and substantive requirements. Formal requirements include that it must be in writing and it must specify the relevant provision of the FLA under which it is made.[34] Only one financial agreement can exist at any time; if a prior financial agreement already exists, the new agreement must specifically terminate it. Substantive requirements of a financial agreement include that it must relate to how either or both par-ties' property and financial resources are to be dealt with following the marriage breakdown (not necessarily divorce); or the maintenance of either of them, whether during marriage or after divorce; or it may deal with both of these matters. Such an agreement effectively ousts the jurisdiction of the courts under the FLA (s 71A). An agreement that does not meet these formal requirements can still operate as a contractual agreement,[35] but it is not 'bind-ing' on the parties as required under the FLA and therefore does not oust the jurisdiction of the court under the FLA. Moreover, the court can order maintenance despite the existence of a financial agreement if the applicant is unable to support himself or herself without an income-tested pension, allowance or benefit (s 90F(1A)).

Section 90G(1) explains when a financial agreement becomes a binding financial agree-ment. It provides that, subject to sub-s (1A), a financial agreement is binding on the parties to the agreement if and only if the following four formal requirements are met: the agree-ment must be signed by all parties; each party must obtain independent legal advice before signing; each party is provided with a signed statement by the legal practitioner that the required advice was provided; and a copy of the statement signed by the legal practitioner is to be given to the other party or their legal practitioner.

Section 90G(1) has been the source of an ongoing tussle between the legislature and the judiciary in defining the scope of the legislative provision. Discussion has centred on the

---

34   s 90B(1)(a)–(b).

35   See *ASIC v Rich* [2003] FLC 93-171 for the proposition that the agreement has effect according to the ordinary law of contract.

nature of the legislative requirement that both parties must receive legal advice if they are to enter into a financial agreement that is binding. We discuss the salient cases in some detail and the subsequent legislative amendments, as they represent a good illustration of how legal discourse is formulated at various sites. Moreover, these different sites do not always produce a consistent or harmonious discourse. This discussion therefore serves as a practical example of our argument throughout the book that the construction of meaning of law is always an ongoing process. Furthermore, the developments in the cases and legislation illustrate how the content and meaning of law are products of contestation, which is essential in understanding how law can change and develop, and is not merely discovered. We also discuss these developments as an example of the courts' view of their role as one of providing legal protection to the individuals who come before them. This is evident in how the courts are reluctant to endorse the legislative intention of taking away the very limited 'protection' given by the FLA to the non-financial contributions of the primary carers of children.

In this way, our analysis illuminates the multiple sites where legal meaning is formed. It further serves to demonstrate the importance of engaging in contestation over meaning, and challenges the easy confidence that mainstream legal analyses have in understanding that law is unambiguous, waiting to be discovered and available by engaging in the correct method of interpretation. Equally, it serves as a corrective to the tendency to analyse law as somewhat peripheral to how people organise their lives. For example, Auchmuty argues that marriage is no longer relevant to how most women organise their lives and thus it proves that Smart was right when she had argued in the 1980s that feminists ought to 'decentre' law and use non-legal strategies to change the position of women.[36] According to this view, it is not the changes in law but in social conditions that have made marriage not as relevant. We would like to counter-argue, as we have been claiming throughout the book, that the power of law lies precisely in its reach in regulating all affective relationships. There is no option to ignore the normative and practical reaches of law in defining what constitutes 'normal' relationships, and it is incumbent on all of us to be alert to how the law constructs notions of what is an acceptable or unacceptable relationship.

The case of *Black v Black* set in train a course of events and we therefore begin with its analysis.[37] In this case, the parties were married for the relatively short period of 18 months. In the course of their marriage, they signed an agreement that the husband would sell his house and the wife would put monies she was about to receive from a personal injuries claim into a joint pool. With this total pool of money, they would buy a house together. They also entered into a financial agreement that in the event of marriage breakdown they would sell the house and divide the money in the proportion of 50:50.

They bought a house, but the money the wife received from her personal injury claim was less than was expected by the husband. They subsequently separated and the husband initiated proceedings asking the court to set aside the financial agreement, as it did not comply with s 90G. The husband sought an order that the assets of the parties be divided 80:20, reflecting his greater contribution. The trial judge, Benjamin J, held that there was a binding financial agreement. Specifically he said that, although the legislative intent was that

---

36   See Rosemary Auchmuty, 'Law and the Power of Feminism: How Marriage Lost its Power to Oppress Women' (2012) 20(2) *Feminist Legal Studies* 71; Carol Smart, *Feminism and the Power of Law* (Routledge, 1989).

37   (2008) 38 Fam LR 503 (Faulks DCJ, Kay and Penny JJ).

the parties should have legal advice, it would be defeating the purpose of the legislation if the courts insisted that the parties and their legal advisers should 'cross all of the "t's" and dot all of the "i's" to enter into and give effect to financial agreements'.[38] He further said that the FLA did not create a regime of strict compliance. But he also said that, in case he was wrong, he would have found 2:1 division in favour of the husband, thus indicating that the binding financial agreement was not fair or equitable.

The husband appealed to the Full Court and argued that the financial agreement was not binding because it did not comply with the requirements of the relevant provisions of the FLA. This assertion was based on the fact that after the parties executed the agreement it was amended, but the husband's solicitor did not re-certify the agreement after the amendment was made. The wife argued that the trial judge had correctly interpreted the legislation using a purposive approach. The Full Court allowed the appeal and in its reasoning referred to the history of legislative changes regarding property and financial matters. The Court said that the *Matrimonial Causes Act 1959* (Cth) and the FLA gave parties of a marriage 'rights of application in respect of property and maintenance. The parties could not by agreement outside the confines of that legislation contract themselves out of the right to institute such proceedings'.[39] This restriction reflected a long-held principle that agreements like these were against public policy. The compromise reached by the legislature (in the 2000 amendments of the FLA) 'was to permit the parties to oust the court's jurisdiction to make adjustive orders but only if certain stringent requirements were met'.[40]

Prior to the *Family Law Amendment Act 2003* (Cth) ('2003 amendments'),[41] s 90G(1)(b) expressly required that the agreement contain a statement from each party that, before they executed the agreement, they received independent legal advice from a legal practitioner in relation to the matters in clauses (i) to (iv), including 'the effect of the agreement on the rights of that party' and 'whether or not, at the time when the advice was provided, it was to the advantage, financially or otherwise, of that party to make the agreement'.[42] Furthermore,

---

38   Ibid quoted at 510 [37].
39   Ibid 511 [41].
40   Ibid 511 [42].
41   Before these amendments, s 90G provided: '(1) A financial agreement is binding on the parties to the agreement if, and only if: (a) the agreement is signed by both parties; and (b) the agreement contains, in relation to each party to the agreement, a statement to the effect that the party to whom the statement relates has been provided, before the agreement was signed by him or her, as certified in an annexure to the agreement, with independent legal advice from a legal practitioner as to the following matters: (i) the effect of the agreement on the rights of that party; (ii) whether or not, at the time when the advice was provided, it was to the advantage, financially or otherwise, of that party to make the agreement; (iii) whether or not, at that time, it was prudent for that party to make the agreement; (iv) whether or not, at that time and in the light or such circumstances as were, at that time, reasonably foreseeable, the provisions of the agreement were fair and reasonable; and (c) the annexure to the agreement contains a certificate signed by the person providing the independent legal advice stating that the advice was provided; and (d) the agreement has not been terminated and has not been set aside by a court; and (e) after the agreement is signed, the original agreement is given to one of the parties and a copy is given to the other. (2) A court may make such orders for the enforcement of a financial agreement that is binding on the parties to the agreement as it thinks necessary.'
42   This requirement was considered onerous for lawyers providing advice as they are not equipped to give financial advice. See also John Wade, 'The Perils of Prenuptial Financial Agreements: Effectiveness and Professional Negligence' (2012) 22(3) *Family Lawyer* 24. It is also important to remember that the FLA itself does not provide a clear statement and lawyers would be unable to give definite advice as to the parties' legal rights as well.

the section provided that the agreement must also annex a certificate executed by the legal practitioner stating that the matters referred to in (i) to (iv) were provided to that party.[43]

In *Black v Black*, the Full Court held that the statements in the financial agreement did not meet all the requirements set out in s 90G(1)(b) and particularly did not make any reference to advice whether the agreement was fair or prudent. Moreover, it found that care must be taken in interpreting any provision of the FLA that had the effect of removing the jurisdiction of the court and which in the process reversed a long-held principle that such agreements were contrary to public policy.[44] It held that strict compliance with the statutory requirements is necessary to oust the jurisdiction to make property adjustment orders under s 79.[45]

The legislative response of the Commonwealth Parliament to this decision was to amend the relevant provisions of the FLA in the *Federal Justice System Amendment (Efficiency Measures) Act (No 1) 2009* (Cth) ('2009 amendments'). These changes included the introduction of a new provision and the modification of s 90G(1)(b). The new s 90G(1A) now provides that the court has power to declare that the agreement is binding (1) provided it is signed by all the parties; and (2) even though one or more of the formal requirements in paragraphs (1)(b), (c) and (ca) are not met; and (3) a court is satisfied that it would be unjust and inequitable if the agreement were not binding; and (4) the court makes an order under subsection (1B) declaring that the agreement is binding on the parties; and (5) the agreement has not been terminated/set aside by a court.

The Explanatory Memorandum and the second reading speech for the Federal Justice System Amendment (Efficiency Measures) Bill (No 1) 2008 (Cth) made by the then Attorney-General, Robert McClelland, explicitly stated that the amendments were necessary to overcome the effect of the Full Court's decision in *Black v Black*. He added that:

> The bill amends the Family Law Act to ensure that people who have made an informed decision to enter into one of these agreements cannot later avoid or get out of the agreement on a mere technicality, resulting in court battles that the agreement was designed to prevent.[46]

In these changes it is evident that the legislature is seeking to change the legal discourse on agreement-making in the context of family law financial disputes from the 'long-held principle' that these agreements were against public policy to the understanding as contained in s 90G(1A)(c) 'that it would be unjust and inequitable if the agreement were not binding on the spouse parties to the agreement (disregarding any changes in circumstances from the time the agreement was made)'. However, the language of this provision, and of s 90G as a whole, is far from unambiguous, as the following discussion of the cases reveals. The effect is that the courts have maintained a role in resolving property disputes between the parties even when they have entered into a financial agreement.

Subsequently, courts have had to determine the nature of these amendments and, among the issues that have arisen, in *Wallace v Stelzer* the Full Family Court upheld the constitutionality of the retrospective effect of these amendments.[47]

---

43   Schedule 5 of the 2003 amendments deleted s 90G(1)(b)(ii)–(iii) and inserted '(ii) the advantages and disadvantages, at the time that the advice was provided, to the party of making the agreement'.
44   (2008) 38 Fam LR 503, 511 [40].
45   Ibid 512 [45].
46   Commonwealth, *Parliamentary Debates*, House of Representatives, 3 December 2008, 12297.
47   (2013) 51 Fam LR 115.

The construction of s 90G(1A) came before the Full Family Court for interpretation in the case of *Senior v Anderson*.[48] The relevant facts of this case were that the parties were married in 1989, separated in March 2006 and divorced in January 2009. In July 2009 they executed an agreement, which was titled 'Section 90C Financial Agreement'. The wife made an application to the Family Court in March 2010, seeking orders that the agreement was not a binding financial agreement. The contentious issues were that the agreement made an incorrect reference to s 90C, which makes provision for financial agreements during marriage. Second, the parties were incorrectly referred to as 'Patricia' and 'Chris' in both of their respective solicitors' certificates that specified that the requisite legal advice had been given.

At first instance, Young J determined that both errors could be rectified; that is, each of the references to s 90C should be changed to s 90D and the parties' names rectified in the solicitors' certificates. He explained that the recent amendments (in 2009) allowed the technical details to be rectified, the effect of which made the agreement a binding financial agreement pursuant to s 90G. The Full Court upheld the appeal (2:1) by the wife against the trial judge's orders that the agreement was a binding financial agreement and that the identified errors could be rectified.

The Full Court disagreed with the trial judge's interpretation of the 2009 amendments. All three judges of the Full Court agreed that the court has the power to rectify inaccuracies, but the power to rectify (that is, the references to s 90C in the agreement) derives from equity and not from the amendments to s 90G of the FLA. Justices Strickland and Murphy specifically said that the trial judge made an error in using extrinsic material related to the 2009 amendments in interpreting ss 4 and 90D. This was because the amendment did not affect those provisions, either directly or indirectly. However, their Honours found that the trial judge was wrong to rectify the errors in the solicitors' certificates pursuant to ss 90G(1A) and (1B). Justice May in dissent found that it would be unjust and inequitable pursuant to s 90G(1A)(c) for the agreement not to be binding on the basis of this technical fault.

Justice Strickland, in explaining the legislative framework, said that the FLA draws a distinction between financial agreements and binding financial agreements. Parties to a financial agreement would be bound (or not bound) by its terms (s 90KA); but it will not oust the jurisdiction of the court. Section 90G is irrelevant to the contractual rights of the parties. This section becomes relevant only when the issue is whether the parties are barred from making any claims under Part VIII of the FLA because the agreement is 'binding' within the meaning of s 90G. Thus there is a difference between the validity and enforceability of a financial agreement by reference to principles of contracts and equity on the one hand, and the statutory precondition for making a 'binding' financial agreement within the meaning of s 90G on the other. The remedy of rectification is available where the question is whether the contract or agreement exists.

Furthermore, the strict compliance test as stated in *Black v Black* is relevant only in deciding whether a financial agreement is binding under s 90G. It has no application to the question of whether there is a financial agreement. Although the trial judge erred in rectifying the references to s 90C in the agreement by reference to the amendments to the FLA, after *Black v Black* he had the authority to rectify that error even though his reasoning was incorrect. In contrast, the error of rectifying the solicitors' certificates was not open to the judge. Compliance with s 90G is mandatory as it is the foundation for ousting the court's

---

48   (2011) 45 Fam LR 540 (May, Strickland and Murphy JJ).

jurisdiction to make Part VIII orders. Moreover, Strickland J found that on the face of it the certificates must comply with the terms of the section. A court could not be satisfied about this if, as in this case, the certificates refer to advice that was provided to person A but there-after refers to advice being provided to person B.

It was also found that the amendments made in 2009 did not permit the court to 'cor-rect' non-compliance with any or all of the requirements of s 90G. The relationship between s 90G(1) and the amendments, including s 90G(1A), is such that the amendments permit the court to make a declaration under certain circumstances that the agreement is binding, even if one of the requirements in s 90G(1) is not met. One of the circumstances when the court may make such a declaration is that it is satisfied that it would be unjust or inequitable if the agree-ment were not binding (s 90(1A)(b)). However, the remedy is not rectification but a statutory remedy that the agreement becomes binding despite its deficiencies. For these reasons, the Court remitted the case for rehearing, as it had not heard sufficient argument to be able to decide whether it would be unjust and inequitable if the agreement were not binding.

In the course of his judgment, Strickland J commented also that the use of adjectives such as 'strict' or 'full' or 'complete' as qualifiers to the word 'compliance' are ways of rein-forcing the fact that it is only a 'financial agreement' as defined by the Act that is 'binding' can oust the jurisdiction of the court under Part VIII of the FLA. The legislation itself does not require or justify the use of such qualifiers. In the course of the judgment, it was also said that if a financial agreement is not valid under s 90G(1A) it might still be taken into account by the court at its discretion. However, such an agreement would not oust the jurisdiction of the court to make an order under Part VIII of the FLA.

Justice Strickland also referred to his decision in *Parker v Parker* that the court must look at the nature of non-compliance with respect to s 90G(1), and determine whether in the circumstances it would be unjust and inequitable if the agreement were not binding.[49] In *Parker* he had said that the 2009 amendments did not use the word 'technicalities' even though the expression is present in the second reading speech accompanying the Federal Justice System Amendment (Efficiency Measures) Bill (No 1) 2008 (Cth). He had come to the conclusion that each party must receive independent legal advice about entering into a financial agreement. In *Parker*, the wife had not been advised by her solicitor about the full implications of the amended clauses in the agreement and it could well be unjust and ineq-uitable if she were bound by that agreement. However, the Full Court allowed the husband's appeal and held that the agreement was a binding financial agreement.

The relevant issue for us is that one judge in *Parker* (Coleman J) disagreed with the trial judge's interpretation of s 90G(1A)(c) and said this section should be given a broader interpre-tation. As a consequence, the advice provided to the wife by her solicitor complied with the requirements of the provision. Another judge (May J) allowed the appeal, but held that the trial judge was entitled to conclude on the basis of evidence before him that the wife's solicitor had not given her the advice on the advantages and disadvantages of the amended agreement. The third Judge (Murphy J) found on this issue that it was open to the trial judge to come to the con-clusion that there was insufficient evidence that the wife's solicitor had given the relevant advice.

We dwell on the reasons in the three judgments in some detail because the Full Court decision in *Parker* has been referred to as authority for the proposition that a narrow

---

49   (2010) FamCA 664.

interpretation of the 2009 amendments would not promote its objectives.[50] This was certainly said by Coleman J, but not by the other two judges. This interpretation of *Parker*, however, has been the subject of further court decisions. For instance, in *Hoult v Hoult* all three judges of the Full Court discussed this decision, but they have not necessarily made its meaning any clearer.[51]

The facts in *Hoult* were that the parties had entered into a financial agreement in 2004, before getting married. There was evidence that the marriage would not have taken place unless the wife signed the agreement. The wife claimed that she did not receive the legal advice that the FLA requires. They separated in 2011 and the wife instituted proceedings under Part VIII. The husband opposed this and argued that there was a binding financial agreement between the parties. The trial judge (Murphy J) found that the financial agreement was not 'binding' in the relevant sense, but used s 90G(1A) to hold the parties to the agreement as otherwise it would be unjust and inequitable. One of the issues was whether the court could exercise unfettered discretion under s 90G(1A)(c). The trial judge had understood it to be unfettered discretion.

Justice Thackray noted that one significant legislative change is that it is now an express requirement for advice to be given to the parties by their respective lawyers.[52] However, in the present case that was not a contentious issue; one of the main issues was the extent of discretion available to the court under s 90G(1A)(c). Justice Thackray agreed with the trial judge that the discretion is wide and, if the legislature had wanted, it could have provided that absence of the requisite legal advice would be a bar to relief under this section. However, he next referred to the comment by the trial judge that the inherent 'fairness' of the agreement cannot be totally irrelevant to the exercise of discretion under s 90G(1A)(c). His Honour held that it was not necessary for him to form a concluded view on the view of the trial judge.[53] Significantly, he went on to state that:

> Although the Act now undoubtedly allows parties to enter into bad or grossly unfair bargains, it is perfectly consistent for the legislation to permit consideration of the fairness of the bargain (judged at the date of execution) in those cases where the safeguards in s 90G(1) have not been met.[54]

Justices Strickland and Ainslie-Wallace, however, disagreed with Justice Murphy's view that the court could assess the fairness or justice of the agreement. They quoted with

---

50   See, eg, Richard Chisholm, Julie Kearney and Suzanne Christie, *Annotated Family Law Legislation* (LexisNexis, 3rd ed, 2015) 869.
51   (2013) 50 Fam LR 260 (Thackray, Strickland and Ainslie-Wallace JJ).
52   Justice Thackray narrated the legislative history of these provisions and identified that the express requirement that each party have independent legal advice only became part of the legislation after the 2009 amendments. These amendments were given retrospective effect and all agreements would be validated under the new s 90G(1A) if applicable. Although this was not an issue in the present case, Thackray J was of the opinion that in earlier agreements it was expected that legal advice would have been given before the lawyers certifed them, though this was not a legal requirement. He further noted that '[t]his subtle change in the Act leaves all agreements open to challenge on the basis of absence of the prescribed legal advice, even though the lawyers have exchanged statements certifying the advice was given': 264 [23]. See also *Weldon v Asher* [2014] FLC 93-579, 79 120, where Thackray J reiterated the view that the 2009 amendments have imposed an additional requirement that legal advice must have been given.
53   *Parker v Parker* (2013) 50 Fam LR 260, 299 [197].
54   Ibid 300 [200].

approval Strickland J's view in the first instance in *Parker* that 's 90G(1A)(c) does not refer to whether the *terms* of the agreement are unjust and inequitable, but whether it would be unjust and inequitable if the agreement was not binding'.[55] Therefore, the content of the bargain has no relevance to the exercise of discretion in s 90G(1A)(c). The factors that might be relevant in deciding whether to set aside an agreement would include the nature of non-compliance and the circumstances surrounding the making and use of the agreement. The matter was remitted for rehearing by a different judge, and a definite interpretation of what 'unjust and inequitable' means in s 90G(1A)(c) is still not available.[56]

7.3.4   Restrictions in financial agreements: spousal maintenance and child maintenance

Spousal maintenance can be included in all financial agreements subject to the specific restrictions discussed below. There is no specific mention that child support can be included in financial agreements. If an agreement is made after the 2008 amendments, it can include child support as an instance of 'other matters' in ss 90B(3)(b), 90C(3)(b) and 90D(3)(b). Binding and limited child-support agreements can also made under the *Child Support (Assessment) Act 1989* (Cth) (s 81).[57]

Section 90E of the FLA states that if a financial agreement relates to the maintenance of a party to the agreement, or of a child or children, it must specify for whom maintenance provision is being made, and it must specify the amount provided or the value of the portion of property attributable to the maintenance of that party/child. In the absence of these specifics, the financial agreement would be void. In keeping with the goal of making the cost of relationship breakdown a private cost, it is provided in s 90F(1) that, in circumstances where sub-s (1A) applies, no provision of a financial agreement excludes or limits the power of a court to make an order in relation to the maintenance of a party to a marriage. Section 90F(1A) applies if the court is satisfied that at the time the agreement was entered into the party was not able to support himself or herself without an income-tested pension, allowance or benefit. The inability to support is assessed at the time the agreement takes effect, which may not be the same as when the agreement was made.

Non-compliance with s 90E can open the possibility for the other spouse to bring an application for maintenance under ss 74 and 72 of the FLA. Courts have generally adopted the course of action to sever the parts of the agreement that did not comply with s 90E requirements and declare the rest of the agreement to be binding.[58] However, in interpreting the parallel provision for de facto financial agreements (s 90UH) it was found by Altobelli FM that if the purpose of the provision is to protect the public revenue it is not open to

---

55   Ibid quoted at 318 [302] (emphasis added).

56   In response to the different judicial interpretations of s 90G and the confusion caused by past changes to the section, the Family Law Amendment (Financial Agreements and Other Measures) Bill 2015 (Cth) was introduced by the Commonwealth government in November 2015. If enacted, s 90G would be deleted and replaced by other provisions, the aim being to clarify when a financial agreement is binding. The Bill has subsequently lapsed in Parliament.

57   These provisions were introduced in the *Child Support Legislation Amendment (Reform of the Child Support Scheme – New Formula and Other Measures) Act 2006* (Cth).

58   See, eg, *Otero v Otero* [2010] FMCAfam 1022.

the parties to opt out of the application of the provision.[59] Similar views were expressed about the purpose of this provision being the protection of the public purse in *Boyd v Boyd*, where the father tried to argue that, since the financial agreement did not name the children or specify the amount of child maintenance he had to pay, it was non-compliant with s 90E(b).[60] Federal Magistrate Brown rejected this argument, among other things, on the ground that the identity of the children could be readily ascertained from other recitals.

7.3.5   Third parties and financial agreements

It is a generally accepted fact that financial agreements are usually entered into when one party has substantial assets. It follows that third parties may have an interest in the assets that form a part of the financial agreement. For instance, company creditors or the parents of one of the spouses may be such third parties. The 2003 amendments expanded the jurisdiction of the court to set aside financial agreements entered into for the purpose of defeating or defrauding a creditor of one of the parties, or with reckless disregard for the interests of a creditor of either party. This is a significant change from the legal position before the amendments and was a direct response to *ASIC v Rich*, discussed below.[61] The financial agreement provisions were further amended by the 2008 amendments so that it is now possible for third parties to enter financial agreements.

7.4   Alternatives to financial agreements

A financial agreement is not the only means available to the parties to make a 'private' agreement. The alternatives are to enter into a consent order pursuant to a s 79/90SM application; pre-nuptial or post-nuptial agreements; or a financial agreement that may not conform to the requirements of a binding financial agreement, and therefore not be in lieu of the right to make an application under Part VIII of the FLA. It is possible for an application under s 79 to be finalised through consent orders for property and/or spousal maintenance (s 79/90SM and s 72/90SF(3)). Parties can also enter into ante-nuptial and post-nuptial settlements to which s 85A applies (ss 4(1), 85A(3)).

There are certain advantages of making consent orders under s 79. They operate as court orders and finalise the financial relations of the parties. Courts scrutinise the content of the agreement to ensure that it 'complies' with the requirements of the FLA, but the scrutiny is less than when the court makes an order in a litigated case. Note that the High Court in *Harris v Caladine* found that, in making consent orders under s 79, the court must examine the propriety of the provisions relating to financial matters.[62] Whether the parties consenting to the provisions had legal advice would be a relevant factor in the court deciding whether the agreement was appropriate to be the basis of the consent order. Such legal advice is much less onerous in comparison to the requirements of independent legal advice for entering into a binding financial agreement. A consent order can be enforced relatively easily compared to a financial agreement.

---

59   *Corney v Hose* [2010] FMCAfam 1462.
60   [2012] FMCAfam 439.
61   [2003] FLC 93-171.
62   (1991) 172 CLR 84.

Ante-nuptial and post-nuptial settlements to which s 85A applies are another alternative to entering into a financial agreement. This section was introduced in the FLA in 1983 as a way for the Family Court to deal with the practice of much wealthier parties using discretionary family trusts to structure their property ownership and avoid the jurisdiction of the FLA at the end of a marriage. The court is authorised under s 85A(1) to make such an order as it considers just and equitable, and it can deal with either the whole or a part of the property that is the subject of an ante-nuptial or post-nuptial settlement. A financial agreement or another agreement that does not comply with the requirements of Part VIIIA or Part VIIIAB of the FLA can be taken into account by a court making a property readjustment order. The court may decide to follow the agreement or ignore it either fully or in part.[63]

7.5   Setting aside financial agreements

Financial agreements can end by the actions of the parties or by making an application to the court.

Section 90J of the FLA provides that the parties can end a financial agreement by making a termination declaration. Such a termination may be achieved if the parties include in another financial agreement a clause that terminates the previous financial agreement (s 90J(1)(a)). Similar to the conditions of entering into a binding financial agreement, a termination agreement is binding on the parties (subject to s 90J(2A)) if and only if the agreement is signed by all the parties to the agreement and each party received independent legal advice by a legal practitioner; such advice should deal with the legal rights of the parties, and the advantages and disadvantages of making the agreement. It should be provided before the signing of the agreement and a signed statement that the relevant legal advice was provided should be given to the other spouse or their legal representative (s 90J(2)). Where a financial agreement has been terminated, the court may make an order it considers just and equitable to preserve or adjust the rights of people who were parties to the financial agreement and any other interested people (s 90J(3)).

The other main avenue for ending a financial agreement is for the court to make a relevant order under s 90K. The relevant grounds are listed in s 90K(1). Before analysing the grounds on which the financial agreement may be set aside by the court, it is useful to mention that after the 2003 amendments such an application may be brought by a third party. As mentioned above, this legal amendment was made as a consequence of the decision in *ASIC v Rich*.[64] The husband was a founding director of the 'One.Tel' company. He resigned from the board of directors in May 2001, and the other members of the board resolved to

---

63   However, see *Patel v Patel* [2015] NSWDC 2, where Colefax SC DCJ held that the NSW District Court could hear a case involving a deed between the husband, the wife and the brother of the husband. The interesting issue here was that the wife had already initiated proceedings for spousal maintenance and property adjustment under the FLA. The judge held that the parties to a marriage could agree among themselves to provide remedies at common law with regard to their property adjustment rather than under the FLA. This is, however, a wider issue than the courts applying the FLA and in the process upholding, either partially or fully, a private agreement. The judge here seems to be saying that the courts, other than those authorised to apply the FLA, can enforce the rights under common law principles. If this line of reasoning is followed widely, it could presumably mean that the FLA would become even more irrelevant in regard to property matters for those who choose to make 'private' agreements.

64   See above n 61.

place the company into administration. Two days later the husband and wife entered into a financial agreement under s 90C of the FLA. The company was placed in liquidation in July 2001. The Australian Securities and Investments Commission ('ASIC') applied for orders under s 90K(1)(b) and 90KA for setting aside the financial agreement. The court held that, as such proceedings are a 'matrimonial cause', the Family Court had exclusive jurisdiction in relation to any proceedings to set aside the agreement. Since ASIC was not a party to the marriage, its application did not fit the description of a matrimonial cause. Moreover, since there were no proceedings when the parties entered into a financial agreement as a husband and wife, para (f) of the definition of matrimonial cause also did not give jurisdiction to deal with the application by ASIC. The FLA was amended in 2003 to insert a new provision in the definition of matrimonial cause in order to enable third party proceedings. So too, s 90K(1)(aa) was inserted to authorise the court to set aside an agreement entered into with the purpose of defrauding or defeating a creditor.

A court may, under s 90K(1), order that a financial agreement or a termination agreement be set aside if, and only if, the court is satisfied that the agreement was obtained by fraud; or entered into to defraud or defeat the creditors and with reckless disregard of the interests of creditors; or the agreement is void, voidable or unenforceable; or since the agreement was made circumstances have arisen that make it or part of it unenforceable; or since the making of the agreement there has been a material change in circumstances relating to the care, welfare and development of a child of the marriage, such that if the agreement is not set aside a child or carer of the child will suffer hardship; or a party to the agreement has engaged in unconscionable conduct. In *Parkes v Parkes* the Court set aside the financial agreement on grounds of duress, and also because there was a material change in circumstances, and if the court did not take that into account the wife would suffer undue hardship.[65]

The last two grounds in s 90K(1)(f) and (g) refer to situations where a payment flag is operating under Part VIIIB on a superannuation interest covered by the agreement and there is no reasonable likelihood that the operation of the flag will be terminated by a flag-lifting agreement under that Part; or the agreement covers at least one superannuation interest that is an unsplittable interest for the purposes of Part VIIIB.

This section reflects the same concerns as present in s 87(8), which allows the court to set aside a maintenance agreement. Such maintenance agreements can no longer be made, but those already made can still be enforced and the significant parallel with financial agreements is that a valid s 87 agreement finalised the parties' financial interests under the FLA. Similar authority is available to the court to set aside s 79 orders (s 79A). The court has discretion in deciding whether to set aside a financial agreement on these grounds. The court would be reluctant to set aside a financial agreement under this section if the party was trying to escape from a 'bad' bargain,[66] although in the case of *Logan v Logan* the Federal Magistrate said at the trial stage that a bad bargain might make the court suspicious as to whether the bargain was obtained by unconscionable conduct.[67]

Part VIIIB enables the parties to a financial agreement to deal with their superannuation interests in the agreement as if these were property, and the parties can deal with present

---

65   [2014] FCCA 102 (Phipps J).
66   *Sanger v Sanger* [2011] FLC 93-484.
67   [2012] FMCAfam 12.

and future superannuation interests. A superannuation agreement is not a separate form of financial agreement as it is a part of a financial agreement that deals with superannuation. Sections 90MD and 90MDA specify that the terms of a superannuation agreement are binding on the trustee of the superannuation fund.

7.6   Conclusion

The discussion in this chapter has illustrated the continuum in the trend in the FLA to impose private ordering arrangements in the resolution of family disputes, the law now enabling the parties to enter into binding financial agreements. Indeed, we may have entered into the next phase of this trend with the introduction of the Family Law Amendment (Financial Agreements and Other Measures) Bill 2015 (Cth). Although the Bill has lapsed, if passed in Parliament it would have introduced a new section setting out the objects of financial agreements. The Explanatory Memorandum explains:

> The new section would reinforce that parties to a marriage should be able to take responsibility for resolving their financial affairs, and that the intention and purpose of financial agreements is to provide certainty and finality to these parties about the resolution of their financial affairs.[68]

Even though the possibility of entering into private financial agreements has always existed in the FLA, the provision of binding financial agreements has assumed a normatively distinct status in their potential to oust the jurisdiction of the FLA over the financial affairs of the parties. This possibility of quarantining one's property from the oversight of the courts operating under the FLA sends a confusing signal to a person in a marriage or de facto relationship. Family law is promoting a person to be an autonomous bearer of the right to contract out of the limited legal protection that the FLA was geared to provide to primary carers. But it does not allow the same freedom in many other aspects of personal relations. Simultaneously, it promises fair outcomes owing to a person adopting the primary carer role and the consequent dependencies this creates. It thus acknowledges the social reality of gendered outcomes in parenting but, while it also permits the formation of binding financial agreements, it treats the two individuals as formal equal partners in a relationship. We argue that the selective use of the rhetoric of freedom of contract only denies the promise of fairness at the end of a relationship rather than creating autonomous agents able to safeguard their interests or wellbeing.

Even though the use of binding financial agreements is not widespread, it is the norm-setting function of the provisions that is significant. Treating both parents as equal in a formal sense combines ideas about privacy of the family and the autonomy of the individual to organise their lives as they wish. This is made to look plausible by the separation of the interests of parents from those of children. It is an illustration of our argument throughout the book that the concepts of public and private are used to underpin the maintenance of the nuclear family in legal discourse. Moreover, this confidence of the law in allowing complete

---

68   Explanatory Memorandum, Family Law Amendment (Financial Agreements and Other Measures) Bill 2015 (Cth) sch 1 para 69.

freedom to the two adult individuals parallels another legal development, where the responsibility for the maintenance of children is secured through the child-support system, which is non-discretionary and operates with the assumption that the maintenance of children is separable from spousal maintenance. Thus, the legal system functions to conceptualise children as vulnerable and needing the 'protection' of the law in a very different way to how it sees the financial needs of the primary carer parent. It is difficult to critique this separation, as the rhetoric of the best interests of the child is used to deflect any suggestion that mothers are mostly the primary carers and after separation their wellbeing and that of their children would of necessity be intermeshed. But irrespective of that, mothers who are predominantly the primary carers should, in their own right, be able to access fair outcomes once the relationship has ended. In its present form, the FLA invokes the notion of formal equality of two adults and combines it with the rhetoric of protecting the interests of the child to preclude a closer scrutiny of the fairness of the FLA. We analyse the FLA's response to the needs of the child to be cared for and protected in the following three chapters.

CHILDREN IN FAMILY LAW: CHILD-RELATED DISPUTES UNDER THE *FAMILY LAW ACT*

8.1   Introduction

This chapter provides an overview of the development of the concept of 'the child' in its historical and theoretical context. Central to the development of this concept is the understanding of the child as the most vulnerable member of society, in need of protection by the law. This understanding permeates family law provisions, whether in the context of resolving disputes over children when family relationships have broken down (discussed in this and the following chapter); or in the legal regulation of child protection, adoption and assisted reproductive technologies (discussed in Chapters 11 and 12). However, the influence of liberal notions of autonomy has also seen a parallel development in promoting the discourse of the rights of the child. In our discussion we will analyse the concept of 'the child' in terms of these competing discourses to explain the consequences of the law simultaneously adopting a paternal concern for the vulnerable child and recognising the child as a bearer of rights.

These discourses of the dependent or autonomous child come together in parenting disputes when courts are determining whether shared parental responsibility is in the best interests of the child. The discussion in this chapter includes an overview of changes in terminology in the *Family Law Act 1975* (Cth) ('FLA') that are indicative of changing ideology about the role of adults in the lives of children: the concept of parental responsibility imports the understanding that children have certain rights and their parents have certain responsibilities that need to be fulfilled. Notably, the legislation has been very prescriptive in setting out what these rights and responsibilities should be in making parenting orders, as is most evident in the *Family Law Amendment (Shared Parental Responsibility) Act 2006* (Cth) ('2006 amendments'), which commenced on 1 July 2006. These provisions, however, show that the legal conception of the rights of children, and the responsibilities of the adults involved in their care, continue to be informed by the nuclear family model. In emphasising the importance of both parents in the child's life, the law normalises the two-parent family as the ideal environment for rearing children. But it also functions to erase the reality of the sexual division of labour in ongoing relationships and replace it with the concept of parenting as a gender-neutral activity after the relationship ends.

In the context of these substantive norms, the procedural aspects of the FLA that prioritise agreements without litigation also assist in the privatisation of families. The FLA makes exceptions to family mediation in cases of family violence and child abuse; these exceptions carry cultural messages about the gender hierarchies of contemporary society and provide a very significant illustration of how law helps to construct the social environment. The *Family Law Legislation Amendment (Family Violence and Other Measures) Act 2011* (Cth) ('2011 amendments') that came into effect on 7 June 2012, and are aimed at protecting children from violence and abuse, in particular demonstrate the contrary pulls in balancing the protection of children from violence, and parents sharing parental responsibility and maintaining contact with their children. The discussion of these reforms goes to the heart of the underlining theme in this chapter relating to the values that should be pursued through family law.

An overview of the procedures involved in resolving disputes, including family dispute resolution ('FDR') as the primary dispute resolution mechanism and the role of the courts, including the introduction of the less adversarial trial ('LAT') process, will further explore the tensions that exist between autonomy and dependency of the various family members as child-related disputes are processed through the family law system. The substantive law in this part will include provisions in Part VII of the FLA and related case law. The developments in the law will be analysed within the broad framework of international law on the rights of the child, the influence of interest groups such as fathers' rights groups on the law, and domestic inquiries that have led to changes to the law. As in the other chapters, these sources will illuminate the choices that are made in regulating family life and how they could be different.

8.2   The conceptual terrain: childhood, welfare, or the rights of the child

This section begins by asking the question: what is a child? At an instinctive level the answer is evident, because being a child seems to be a natural stage of human development. But articulating this issue compels an acknowledgement that there is no single understanding of who may be defined as a child and, by implication, what constitutes childhood. Different disciplines, such as biology, psychology, sociology and philosophy, among others, are likely to yield different answers.[1] Even within a discipline, it is the context that determines a particular definition of the child. So too, within law there is no single definition of the child. It varies depending on the area of law and the purpose of legal regulation.[2] Some of the constructs of childhood include the views of the child as dependent, autonomous, incompetent, the undeveloped adult, the unruly child and/or the marginalised child.

We argue that it is important to understand that the concept of childhood is a construct and it is not necessarily the case that children are naturally vulnerable and need protection, but that societal practices and ways of talking about them also contribute to making them so.[3] Prefacing any legal analysis with this insight can help to identify the mechanisms used in the construction of childhood in legal discourse. This is an important task to undertake in family law because it plays a significant role in the creation and legitimisation of ideas of vulnerable children, in need of law's protection through concepts like the 'best interests of the child' principle.

---

1   For examples, see the essays in Julia Fionda (ed), *Legal Concepts of Childhood* (Hart Publishing, 2001); Gareth B Matthews, 'Getting Beyond the Deficit Conception of Childhood: Thinking Philosophically with Children' in Michael Hand and Carrie Winstanley (eds), *Philosophy in Schools* (Continuum, 2008) 27; Michael Freeman (ed), *Law and Childhood Studies: Current Legal Issues* (Oxford University Press, 2012) vol 14.

2   Julia Fionda, 'Legal Concepts of Childhood: An Introduction' in Julia Fionda (ed), *Legal Concepts of Childhood* (Hart Publishing, 2001) 3.

3   The distinction between biological and social childhood is discussed in Neil Postman, *The Disappearance of Childhood* (Vintage, 1994). For a contemporary theory based on neuroscience and philosophy that promotes the idea that children are not 'defective' adults but have special abilities, see Alison Gopnik, *The Philosophical Baby* (Farrar, Straus and Giroux, 2009).

8.2.1   Concept of childhood

Very briefly, Firestone, in her very well-known book, explains what she refers to as the myth of childhood.[4] Building on Ariès's ideas,[5] she draws parallels between the construction of children and women as vulnerable and thus in need of protection. The medieval view of children was that they were miniature adults and there was no special vocabulary to describe them. In this worldview children differed socially from adults only in their economic dependence. In aristocratic households, the child was just another member of the large patriarchal household, not even essential to family life. The child was usually wet-nursed by a stranger and thereafter, if a boy, sent to another home to be an apprentice, and as a result never developed a heavy dependence on his parents. They in turn did not 'need' their children. There were no special toys, games, clothes or classes designed just for children.

As Firestone further explains, the moralists and pedagogues of the 17th century were at the origins of both the concept of childhood and its institutionalisation, namely in the modern concept of schooling. They were the first espousers of the weakness and 'innocence' of childhood and put childhood on a pedestal just as femininity had been put on a pedestal. They preached the segregation of children from the adult world. 'Discipline' was the keynote to modern schooling, more than learning or education, and the function of the school became 'child rearing'. This segregation of the child from adults, among other things, indicated a growing disrespect for, and a systematic underestimation of, the abilities of the child. Schools as disciplining institutions became necessary to keep children under the jurisdiction of their parents for as long as possible. Segregation reinforces the oppression of children even today, and to an extent laws structure their physical and economic dependence.[6]

We acknowledge that this account of the construction of the concept of childhood is challenged in the literature,[7] but it also identifies a core issue for us. That is, the capabilities of a child are different from those of adults, but the importance attached to those capabilities is informed by moral or ethical values. For example, the idea that the child is an undeveloped adult in the process of developing into adulthood is a common motif. The idea of the vulnerability of the child is taken as a given in legal discourse, but it is worthwhile to focus on the mechanisms of how this ideology of childhood functions to construct children as vulnerable and in need of protection.[8] Family law has assumed an ever-greater role

---

4   Shulamith Firestone, *The Dialectic of Sex: The Case for Feminist Revolution* (Farrar, Straus and Giroux, 2003).

5   Philip Ariès, *Centuries of Childhood: A Social History of Family Life* (Robert Baldick trans, Vintage, 1962) [trans of *L'Enfant et La Vie Familliale Sous L'Ancien Regime* (first published 1960)]. For a discussion of challenges to Ariès's views, see David Kennedy, *The Well of Being: Childhood, Subjectivity, and Education* (SUNY Press, 2006).

6   For a contemporary argument that the child–adult relationship is one of hierarchy and the child of necessity suppresses feelings of anger, rage and unfairness that the ideology of benevolent childhood entrenches, see Joseph Zornado, *Inventing the Child: Culture, Ideology and the Story of Childhood* (Taylor and Francis, 2001).

7   Lloyd de Mause, 'The Evolution of Childhood' in Lloyd de Mause (ed), *The History of Childhood* (Souvenir Press, 1976) 1; Gareth B Matthews, *The Philosophy of Childhood* (Harvard University Press, 1994).

8   Allison James, Chris Jenks and Alan Prout, *Theorizing Childhood* (Polity Press, 1998).

as the guardian of children's welfare and rights.[9] In this role, the idea implicit in the law is that parents cannot always be trusted to safeguard the best interests of the child. A number of questions arise: is this assumption justified? Is it undermining the autonomy of the parents? Is the state better able to protect children through its institutions and laws?

8.2.2   Concept of the welfare of the child

Some of these issues become visible if the concept of welfare of the child or best interests of the child is analysed as a construct. Maidment explains how in the 18th century the concept of childhood was created; in the 19th century the welfare principle was developed; and the 20th century saw almost all aspects of a child's life the subject of some law, usually in pursuance of their welfare.[10] The issue, however, is whether these developments show an increasing emancipation of the child. Maidment demonstrates the connections between the greater possibility of divorce, increasing rights of mothers and the development of the concept of 'welfare of the child', converging as a guiding principle in law. In a nuanced analysis, she argues there is no doubt that the *Guardianship of Infants Act 1925* (Imp), the first legislation to incorporate the welfare of the child principle as the paramount consideration in child custody disputes, owes more to the fight of separated women for joint guardianship over their children than to any child protection philosophy. Claims of a mother to joint custody of her child (in contrast to the then legal position of the father as the natural guardian) were deflected by legislators introducing the welfare principle and subjecting the decision to the judicial oversight of the child's interests. Thus, the legal developments could be justified in the interests of the child rather than being seen as women/mothers gaining more rights.

Maidment argues, and it is a common view in the literature, that the 'welfare of the child' is an indeterminate standard for judicial interpretation of the needs of children. While the welfare principle is ostensibly child-centred, it has also been, and probably always will be, a code for decisions based on religious, moral, social and, perhaps now, social science-based beliefs about child rearing. Custody decisions have been made for and by adults, despite the apparent child-centred direction in the law. Not only is it the case that the adults bestow a right to protection and nurturance on children, but they also do it by using notions of what is best for the children from adult perspectives.

Significantly, she claims that the centrality of the child's welfare in divorce and custody decisions as understood nowadays continues the child protection tradition of the 19th century. The concern for the wellbeing of children of broken relationships can and does become the justification for the ever-increasing regulation of the family. Moreover, the humanitarian and philanthropic interventions on behalf of the state mask many other purposes. For instance, the identification and treatment of juvenile delinquency at the turn of the century

---

9   The *Matrimonial Causes Act 1857* (UK) gave the court wide authority to decide what orders to make with regard to the custody, maintenance and education of the children of the marriage in a case of judicial separation, nullity or divorce; the *Guardianship of Infants Act 1886* (Imp) enabled a court to make custody and access orders for an infant on a mother's application without the requirement, for example, of a divorce application. See Andrew Bainham and Stephen Cretney, *Children: The Modern Law* (Jordan Publishing, 1993) 12.

10   The following account is taken from Susan Maidment, *Child Custody and Divorce* (Croom Helm, 1984) 100–6, 149–68.

owed as much to child protection ideals as to the imposition of social order, and even to the worthwhile occupation of middle-class women.

8.2.3   Rights of the child

Since Maidment wrote her book, there have been phenomenal developments in the discourses on the rights of the child and the law's role in protecting them.[11] The rights discourse is most evident in the international *Convention on the Rights of the Child*.[12] However, we argue that, the discourse of the rights of the child notwithstanding, children continue to be denied a full legal subject position. In the context of family law, this needs to be understood in relation to the role law has assumed to protect the interests of children above the interests of their carers, who are assigned responsibilities towards their children but not any rights with respect to them.

Discourses about the rights of the child are grounded in many sources, but two issues need to be noted. Guggenheim explains that one source of the demand for the 'rights of the child' is informed by ideas of children's rights,[13] understood as protection against the exercise of state power. Another source of the demand for the rights of the child is in the context of the family, specifically in relation to parental rights. The progressives in the late 19th century in the United States were interested in creating a more humane society, and in part this required the state to take responsibility for children. Among other things, this manifested in policies on child labour and compulsory education. The creation of the juvenile court as a child-friendly court in criminal matters was also part of this initiative. However, the second movement for the rights of the child was related to the civil rights movement in the 1960s. It challenged the very things the progressives had achieved in the interests of children. Thus, among other things, the modern children's rights movement questioned the rationale of the juvenile court on the basis that it was paternalistic.

Guggenheim argues that the trend towards an increasing recognition of the rights of the child comes with a downside, resulting in courts and legislatures treating the legal disabilities attached to children as suspect. Thus, the legal protections available to the child are diminishing with questionable gains made under the rubric of rights. Legal developments with respect to the rights of the child are thus not an unequivocal advance of the interests of the child. There are unresolved tensions in protecting the rights of the child, with corresponding issues arising with respect to ascribing moral agency to children and whether or not they should be treated with full legal capacity and thus no differently from an adult legal subject.[14]

In the family law context, contemporary responses to the issue of children's rights or interests are based on less than clear principles. While it is well known that law is not always principled, the ready acceptance of the idea that the interests or rights of the child are being upheld by family law functions to deflect scrutiny of the combined role of legislation and

---

11   Extensive literature in this area exists and the specialty of Child Law is a recognised area of study. For an introduction, see essays in Andrew Bainham (ed), *Parents and Children* (Ashgate, 2008).

12   *Convention on the Rights of the Child*, opened for signature 20 November 1989, 1577 UNTS 3 (entered into force 2 September 1990).

13   Martin Guggenheim, *What's Wrong With Children's Rights* (Harvard University Press, 2005) 11. See also John Tobin, 'Justifying Children's Rights' (2013) 21(3) *The International Journal of Children's Rights* 395.

14   See below n 21.

judicial interpretation in translating certain social attitudes into legal discourse. One effect of such attitudes is that children are viewed as relatively independent beings whose interests need protecting, but the fact of their dependence on their carers is effaced. The very category of 'child', however, makes it evident that the child is not an independent human being. Carers are important to the child's survival, but family law functions to erase their significance. It also assumes the authority to be the final arbiter of how parents who have separated should care for their children.

This may not be a premeditated approach, but it is nevertheless the case that legal discourse makes it morally unacceptable to scrutinise the wider effects of the ideology of law protecting the vulnerable child. Therefore, the discourse of family law as the protector of the best interests of the child functions to make it impossible to question whether the outcomes may be disadvantageous to mothers as primary carers. While an ever-increasing number of women with children are participating in wage work, it is also well documented that to fulfil their carer responsibilities their attachment to the workforce is usually casual or part-time and therefore lower paid.[15] Similarly, time-share studies about how much time men and women spend on child-related activities only tell part of the story, as greater participation of men in childcare activities does not mean that women are doing lesser amounts of care work.[16]

Family law, by disassociating children and mothers (and, in some cases, fathers) as the caregivers, renders the cost of caring an irrelevant issue in decisions about children. Most notably, the concept of the best interests of the child simultaneously invokes the vulnerable child in need of law's protection, and parents who have responsibilities towards the child, but who cannot claim any recognition of their caring role. The law in this regard is supposed to be forward looking and only concerned with the best interests of children, not their parents. This dual emphasis leaves no space for considering that it may not be necessary to construct an opposition between the rights of children and their carers. While it is undeniable that the needs of children cannot be ignored, it is less than clear why the interests of primary carers can be considered irrelevant.[17] Nor is it evident why it is acceptable that the law is concerned with fair outcomes with respect to one and not the other. As discussed in Chapter 1, Okin explains that justice requires that if the need arises, everyone should be able to rely on rules that are fair and non-discriminatory. It is this issue that is rendered irrelevant by constructions of the vulnerable child in need of protection. The argument that the child needs protection is only part of the answer.

This issue also raises questions about private responsibility or collective and public responsibility for children. But since even asking the question is not considered appropriate,

---

15   Discussed in chapters 5 and 6. See also Alan Hayes et al, *Families Then and Now: 1980–2010* (AIFS, 2010).

16   Jennifer Baxter, Matthew Gray and Alan Hayes, *A Snapshot of How Australian Families Spend Their Time* (AIFS, 2007) <https://aifs.gov.au/publications/snapshot-how-australian-families-spend-their-time>; Anne Hollonds, 'Mothers Still do the Lion's Share of Housework' (Media Release, 9 May 2016) <https://aifs.gov.au/media-releases/mothers-still-do-lions-share-housework>.

17   See Martha Fineman, 'The Vulnerable Subject: Anchoring Equality in the Human Condition' (2008) 20(1) *Yale Journal of Law and Feminism* 1 for an argument that the vulnerability of all humans is an undeniable fact. The interdependencies this creates, particularly through carer and cared-for relationships, ought to be acknowledged in the law: Michael Fine and Caroline Glendinning, 'Dependence, Independence or Interdependence? Revisiting the Concepts of "Care" and "Dependency"' (2005) 25 *Ageing and Society* 601.

there is no space for exploring the possibilities of other models of allocating responsibility for children. It is also an illustration of how family law normalises the nuclear family of two parents and their children. Moreover, the process of law proclaiming itself the protector of the vulnerable child also means that, instead of the child being treated as a bearer of rights, he or she becomes subject to the paternalistic regulation of the law. The rights discourse thus functions not so much to provide rights protection to the child, but to privilege the law by enacting legislation and conferring jurisdiction on courts to make decisions for the child.

8.3   The child in law: legal capacity

Even though it is now accepted that ideas about childhood and the child are constructed by social scientists, it is also the case that most attention is focused on how the child is different from the adult and on integrating that difference into our concepts of order and organisation in adult society. The basic ontological question of 'what is a child?' does not even get asked or is answered in advance of theorising.[18] The child in law is someone less than capable of looking after himself or herself and it is generally accepted that the child's parents have this responsibility. The issue of capacity is the main legal idea that creates a distinction between legal subjects and those in need of legal protection. However, what constitutes sufficient capacity for legal subjecthood has many answers. Moreover, it is a morphing idea and illustrates well the fact that the concept of legal capacity is a construct rather than reflecting a natural state of affairs.

Different statutes use different ages as the age of majority that applies to determine legal capacity. For example, family law uses the age of 18 years in regard to capacity to marry and for the purposes of child support, but also provides exceptions and judicial discretion to modify this age. Similarly, the FLA has always acknowledged that the views and wishes of the child should be considered by a court in determining what is in the child's best interests, but the final decision is that of the court. Thus, the initial identification of the child as someone less than 18 years of age has gradually been modified by legislation and by judicial pronouncements. The celebrated 'Gillick competency'[19] test acknowledges that in certain matters it is the maturity of the child, rather than age, that should be relevant in determining whether he or she can make his or her own decisions.

At the international level the success of the *Convention on the Rights of the Child* is rightly celebrated.[20] Somewhat disturbingly, however, the increasing recognition of the rights

---

18   Chris Jenks, *Childhood* (Routledge, 1996) 2–4.

19   *Gillick v West Norfolk and Wisbech Area Health Authority* [1985] 3 All ER 402. The issue in this case was whether a minor could consent to contraceptive treatment or whether the parents had to give consent. The House of Lords decision elaborated the point that as minors gain competence they may be able to make important decisions. Any parental rights must be exercised to advance the welfare of the child and with the increasing maturity the child may be able to make decisions with a corresponding lessening of the parental decision-making authority. See also M D A Freeman, 'England: The Trumping of Parental Rights' (1986) 25(1) *Journal of Family Law* 91.

20   For an introduction, see Said Mahmoudi et al, *Child-Friendly Justice: A Quarter of a Century of the UN Convention on The Rights of the Child* (Brill Nijhoff, 2015). John Tobin, 'Understanding Children's Rights: A Vision Beyond Vulnerability' (2015) 84(2) *Nordic Journal of International Law* 155 argues that the *Convention on the Rights of the Child* uses the paradigm of vulnerability of children, but that this carries the risk of defining children by reference to their vulnerabilities. It is necessary that the concept of the child should be defined by reference to evolving capacities and his or her right to participation.

of the child runs parallel to the developments in law attaching full moral responsibility and the consequent criminal liability to the acts of ever-younger children.[21] Nor is it sufficiently acknowledged how claims to protect the rights of the child go hand in hand with courts retaining the power to decide whether to give effect to those rights, as illustrated well in the arena of family law. Moreover, the parents are subject to state scrutiny to make sure that they are discharging their responsibilities appropriately. Thus, in any dispute there are at least three perspectives that need to be accommodated – the child, the parents and the state.[22] In the following section, we explore the function of legal terminology in reinforcing the concept of the nuclear family as a unit with one set of parents and their children. This is achieved primarily through the introduction of the concept of shared parental responsibility as being in the best interests of the child.

8.4 The legislative terminology of the FLA

Historical legal developments with regard to parents and children begin with the common law position of the father as the natural guardian of children.[23] It is possible to describe the changes in law over time as moving from the rights of the father, to the rights of parents, to the position it is currently, where both parents have obligations to protect the welfare of their children. It is also now the case that, instead of talking about the rights of parents, we talk about the rights of the child. However, these are imperfect transitions, and the parents and children are not the only relevant actors. The state through its laws has always played a significant role in, for example, defining who is a parent for legal purposes, and what parental obligations and the rights of the child are. In the three-way relationship between the state, parents and children, many sites are created for the construction of legal discourse about 'normal' families.

---

21 For changes in criminal law, see Thomas Crofts, 'The Criminal Responsibility of Children' in Geoff Monahan and Lisa Young (eds), *Children and the Law in Australia* (LexisNexis, 2008) 167. See also Michael Freeman, 'The James Bulger Tragedy: Childish Innocence and the Construction of Guilt' in Anne McGillivray (ed), *Governing Childhood* (Dartmouth, 1997) 115. The exposé in *Australia's Shame* (reported by Caro Meldrum-Hanna and presented by Sarah Ferguson, ABC, *Four Corners*, 2016) of the Don Dale Youth Detention Centre, Darwin, Northern Territory, revealed the extreme vulnerability of Indigenous children in juvenile detention where children as young as 10 were being held, while others aged 13 had been put in long-term solitary confinement – treatment which has been rightly condemned as having violated their human rights.

22 There is extensive literature analysing these interconnections. For an introduction, see Michael Freeman (ed), *The State, the Law and the Family: Critical Perspectives: Critical Perspectives* (Tavistock, 1984). See also Alison Diduck and Felicity Kaganas, *Family Law, Gender and the State: Text, Cases and Materials* (Hart Publishing, 3rd ed, 2012). For an overview of the legal provisions, see Australian Law Reform Commission, *Seen and Heard: Priority for Children in the Legal Process*, Report No 84 (1997) ch 3.

23 This is the legal position only for legitimate children. Until relatively recently, the mother was the natural guardian of illegitimate children in the common law: Sir William Blackstone, *The American Students' Blackstone: Commentaries on the Laws of England in Four Books* (Banks and Brothers, 3rd ed, 1899) vol 1, 175.

8.4.1   Shared parental responsibility

Legislative terminology, in particular, functions to construct these discourses. The concepts and terms used by the FLA at the breakdown of the parental relationship have changed over time. When the FLA was first enacted, the concepts of guardianship and custody were used to denote different parental duties.[24] This terminology has since been replaced by the all-encompassing concept of parental responsibility that relates to all of the duties the parents have to their children. On the one hand, the change in terminology reflects how the understanding of 'rights' relating to children has changed. The earlier terminology, especially the concept of 'custody', suggested that parents own, or have some form of property rights with respect to, their children. The introduction of the concept of parental responsibility was intended to move away from this understanding and entrench a principle that stressed the responsibilities of both parents for their children.[25] On the other hand, this change in terminology coincided with a growing dissatisfaction with the outcomes in disputed cases where the custody of children was granted to one parent and 'non-custodial' parents (usually fathers) were being deprived of having a say in their children's lives.[26]

These ideas came together in the 2006 amendments to enshrine the rights of the child to know and be cared for by both parents and the right of contact on a regular basis with both their parents and other people significant to their care (FLA s 60B(2)(a) and (b)). The terminology changed again with the 2011 amendments, which replaced the language of contact with the broader language of providing for the rights of the child to know and be cared for by both their parents and the right to spend time on a regular basis with both their parents and other people significant to their care (FLA ss 60B(2)(a) and (b)). This change was in response to claims that the term 'contact' was too reminiscent of the language of the old regime, which had cast the non-custodial parent as the parent who had 'access' as opposed to the parent (usually the mother) who had custody (and who, in contrast to the 'contact parent', was referred to as the 'resident parent'). Thus, these 2011 amendments can be seen as a legislative attempt to promote the importance of both parents' involvement in the life of the child and avoid any differentiation in their roles in the child's life.

The philosophy behind the 2006 amendments may be discerned from the press release by the then Attorney-General explaining that the Family Law Amendment (Shared Parental Responsibility) Bill 2005:

> reflected the Government's determination to ensure the right of children to grow up with the love and support of both of their parents ... These initiatives represent a generational change in family law and aim to bring about a cultural shift in how family separation is managed: away from litigation and towards cooperative parenting ... The major changes in the Bill are to: insert a presumption, or starting point, of equal shared

---

24   See, eg, John Faulks, 'Children's Rights and Family Law' in Kathleen Funder (ed), *Citizen Child: Australian Law and Children's Rights* (AIFS, 1996).

25   See Anthony Dickey, *Family Law* (Law Book Co, 6th ed, 2014) 251–2 for a discussion of the 1995 and 2006 amendments to the FLA.

26   Henry Gordon Clarke, 'What is Parental Responsibility' (1996) 70(9) *Law Institute Journal* 30. For an overview of the 2006 amendments, see Anne-Marie Rice, 'Shared Parental Responsibility' in Renata Alexander et al (eds), *Australian Master Family Law Guide* (CCH, 7th ed, 2015) 85.

parental responsibility. This means that both parents have an equal role in making decisions about major long term issues involving their children.[27]

The emphasis on the concept of shared parental responsibility can be traced to the introduction in the late 1980s of the Child Support Scheme, which enforced the responsibility of the liable parent (usually fathers) to pay child support at a higher rate than the usual family court allocations.[28] It also made the collection of child support an administrative task that could be performed more effectively. As a result, fathers' rights groups lobbied for joint custody and were influential in the establishment of a major inquiry into family law by the Commonwealth government in 1991.[29] The report of this committee formed the basis for the introduction of the *Family Law Reform Act 1995* (Cth) ('1995 amendments'), which introduced the concept of shared parental responsibility. Although it is accepted that these 1995 amendments were a result of consultations with fathers' rights groups concerned about custody arrangements and women's groups concerned about the presence and effects of violence within families, this gave rise to a tension in the law between the aim of maintaining contact with both parents after separation and the aim of protecting family members – mostly women and children – from violence and abuse.[30] The same tension continued to be evident in the amendments to the FLA made in 2006, which explicitly entrenched the legislative aims of promoting shared care and protecting children from violence and abuse.[31] Whether the 2011 amendments have adequately addressed this issue by giving legislative priority to protecting children from violence and abuse, remains to be seen (see Chapter 4 and discussion below).

But if we accept that the introduction of the concept of shared parental responsibility in the FLA was appeasing the claims of fathers' rights groups for joint custody, was this a legitimate step for the legislature to take? Arguably, it could have been if the concept of shared parenting was actually reflecting the social reality or if the law, in pursuing the normative goal of having both parents involved in the lives of children, would benefit these children. However, both of these rationales have been contradicted by the statistical research and evidence of lived experiences. In contemporary society, women are still the primary caregivers in intact families as well as in separated families where parenting is not a contested matter. Moreover,

27   Philip Ruddock, 'Bill Marks "Cultural Shift" in Dealing with Family Breakdown' (News Release, No 232, 8 December 2005) <http://parlinfo.aph.gov.au/parlInfo/search/display/display .w3p;query=Source%3A%22ATTORNEY-GENERAL%22%20MajorSubject_Phrase%3A%22access%20 (family%20law)%22;rec=1>. The antecedents of these reforms are present in, eg, House of Representatives Standing Committee on Family and Community Affairs, House of Representatives, *Every Picture Tells A Story: Inquiry into Child Custody Arrangements in the Event of Family Separation* (2003); Standing Committee on Legal and Constitutional Affairs, *Exposure Draft of the Family Law Amendment (Shared Parental Responsibility) Bill 2005* (Parliament of Australia, 2005).

28   See, eg, Colin James, 'Media, Men and Violence in Australian Divorce' (2006) 31(1) *Alternative Law Journal* 6; Miranda Kaye and Julia Tolmie, 'Fathers' Rights Groups in Australia and their Engagement with Issues in Family Law' (1998) 12(1) *Australian Journal of Family Law* 19.

29   Joint Select Committee on Certain Aspects of the Operation and Interpretation of the Family Law Act, *The Family Law Act 1975: Aspects of its Operation and Interpretation* (Parliament of Australia, 1992).

30   Alistair Nicholson, 'Key Note Address: Court Management of Cases Involving Child Abuse Allegations' (Paper Presented at 7th Australasian Conference on Child Abuse and Neglect, Perth, 19 October 1999); Helen Rhoades, Reg Graycar and Margaret Harrison, *The Family Law Reform Act: The First Three Years* (University of Sydney and Family Court of Australia, 2000).

31   See Richard Chisholm, Suzanne Christie and Julie Kearney, *Annotated Family Law Legislation* (LexisNexis, 3rd ed, 2015) 320.

Fehlberg et al analyse the available empirical evidence about parenting arrangements in separated and intact families, compare it to the outcomes of court orders about time allocation, and relate it to the social science literature about shared care arrangements after separation. They argue convincingly that there is a lack of clear connection between shared care arrangements and better outcomes for children.[32] Thus, the legislative provisions and their application by the courts are combining to produce outcomes that are neither better for children nor reflective of the existing social patterns.

Rhoades further shows the disconnection between the prevailing social patterns of care work and the outcomes of the cases after the 2006 amendments.[33] She demonstrates with the help of pre-reform data how shared care was once a relatively rare phenomenon, but post-reform data indicates that almost half (46%) of the families have an arrangement in which the children spent five nights or more per fortnight with each parent.[34] This research suggests the 2006 amendments have been successful in producing more shared care outcomes. But such success has come at a cost to the psychological wellbeing of many children who are caught in the middle of their parents' conflict.[35]

If these provisions are seen as law pursuing a normative goal of both parents being involved in the lives of their children, another issue arises. In legal terms, the level and type of involvement of parents in a child's life is usually a private issue before relationship breakdown, but not after it.[36] Thus, in endorsing the concept of shared parental responsibility only after separation, the legislation functions to normalise ideas about the need for two parents in the lives of children, arguably in an effort to reconstruct the nuclear family on the premise that it provides the best environment for bringing up children. If this is the aim, then we can see how the law is informed by the structural functional view of the family advanced by Parson (see Chapter 1). However, the nuclear family constructed by the shared parenting provisions is very different from the model envisaged by Parsons. As we saw in Chapter 1, Parsons' ideas about the need for the nuclear family were to a large extent dependent upon the mother and father performing different roles in the socialisation of the child. According to Parsons' theory, for the child to develop into a well-adjusted adult required the father (who is instrumental-oriented) to navigate the external world, while the mother (who is expressive-oriented) was required to navigate relations between family members. Thus, in his

32　For a persuasive analysis, see Belinda Fehlberg et al, *Australian Family Law: The Contemporary Context* (Oxford University Press, 2nd ed, 2014) 176–90. The authors analyse John De Maio et al, *Survey of Recently Separated Parents* (AIFS, 2013) and Rae Kaspiew et al, *Evaluation of the 2006 Family Law Reforms* (AIFS, 2009) (particularly the discussion of the AIFS Longitudinal Study of Separated Families Wave 1). They also refer to Judy Cashmore et al, *Shared Care Parenting Arrangements since the 2006 Family Law Reforms: Report to the Australian Government Attorney-General's Department* (Social Policy Research Centre, UNSW, 2010); and Jennifer McIntosh et al, *Post-separation Parenting Arrangements: Patterns and Developmental Outcomes for Children: Report to the Australian Government Attorney-General's Department* (Family Transitions, 2010).

33　Helen Rhoades, 'The Dangers of Shared Care Legislation: Why Australia Needs (Yet More) Family Law Reform' (2008) 36(3) *Federal Law Review* 279.

34　Ibid 283, citing Jennifer McIntosh and Caroline Long, *Children Beyond Dispute: A Prospective Study of Outcomes from Child Focused and Child Inclusive Post-Separation Family Dispute Resolution* (Attorney-General's Department, 2006) 21.

35　Kaspiew et al, above n 32.

36　The concept of the 'best interests of the child' functions to divert attention from this, as the argument is put forth that the matter has to do with children and not with any presumed rights of parents.

theory a stay-at-home mother and a breadwinner father would achieve the task of producing well-adjusted adults for a smoothly functioning society.

The FLA in promoting shared parenting is eclectic in pursuing the idea that both parents are necessary for a child to grow up into a well-adjusted adult. We say this because it cannot contribute to the creation of families comprising a stay-at-home mother and a breadwinner father that will provide the necessary conditions for well-adjusted children while it also provides for a regime of divorce on demand and continues to enforce shared parenting after separation in high-conflict cases that end up in court (even after the 2011 amendments). At the same time, the amendments (both in 2006 and 2011) continue the past practice of not imposing any obligations on the 'contact parent' or 'non-resident parent' to maintain contact with the child.[37]

Our aim in raising these arguments is not to critique the processes of law reform, but to raise awareness of the fact that the law is not grounded in research or reality, and that the imposition of a model of the family that requires cooperation between parents will not create optimal conditions for children, if those conditions do not already exist. Legal critics carry the responsibility of illustrating how the legal provisions are constructed and how they may be able to pursue fairness for everyone rather than the child or one or the other parent.

8.4.2   The child and the parent in the FLA

Who is a child? The definition of 'child' in s 4(1) of the FLA is a person under the age of 18 years (for specified purposes). Common law terms of legitimate and illegitimate children are used in the *Marriage Act 1961* (Cth), but the FLA refers to nuptial or ex-nuptial children. The legal effects of distinctions between children because of their parents' marital status are now virtually irrelevant as laws for the equality of status of children have been adopted by all States and Territories, although various rules using the terms continue to exist.[38] The early history of the FLA demonstrates the restrictions on the Commonwealth Parliament enacting laws about children as an exercise of the 'marriage' power under the Constitution (see Chapter 2). The initial attempt of inserting a wide definition of the child in the FLA that would encompass more than the 'child of the marriage' was rejected by the High Court.[39] As a consequence, the FLA only covered children of a marriage,[40] but subsequently the States referred most of their powers over ex-nuptial children to the

---

37   For a brief discussion of these issues, see David Monaghan, 'Can a Contact Parent Contravene a Contact Order?' (1999) 73 *Australian Law Journal* 20.

38   For example, the *Marriage Act 1961* (Cth) ss 89–90 explain that children may be legitimated by the subsequent marriage of their parents or if a child is adopted by a husband and wife. See also s 55A(3) of the FLA.

39   *Russell v Russell; Farrelly v Farrelly* (1976) 134 CLR 495 (Barwick CJ, Gibbs, Stephen, Mason and Jacobs JJ).

40   The *Family Law Amendment Act 1976* (Cth) provided that the children must be the natural or adopted children of both spouses. The *Family Law Amendment Act 1983* (Cth) ('1983 amendments') widened the scope of the FLA regarding the children covered by it and included once again the children who were ordinarily members of the household of the husband and wife. These provisions were held invalid by the High Court in *Cormick v Salmon* (1984) 156 CLR 170; *R v Cook; Ex parte C* (1985) 156 CLR 249.

41   Between 1986 and 1990 all States except Western Australia referred their powers with respect to ex-nuptial children to the Commonwealth. The two exceptions are powers regarding adoption and child welfare. South Australia has not referred parentage testing to the Commonwealth.

Commonwealth.[41] As a result, the FLA now applies to all children, nuptial and ex-nuptial.[42] These legislative changes are readily explained as resolving the constitutional issues, but they are also recognition of the changing social attitudes about the conditions in which childbirth is acceptable. Nevertheless, the FLA still insists on identifying one set of parents, as explained below.

Who is a parent? The term 'parent' is not defined in s 4(1), and it only says that 'parent', when used in Part VII in relation to a child who has been adopted, means an adoptive parent of the child. It can be assumed that 'parent' means a biological parent, but there are certain provisions that provide for parentage of children born as a result of artificial conception procedures or under surrogacy arrangements (ss 60H and 60HB). There are specific presumptions (rebuttable) of parentage in the FLA (ss 69P–69U) and broadly they relate to the presumption of parentage arising from marriage, cohabitation, registration of birth, findings of courts and acknowledgements.[43] In addition, the court has powers under the FLA to declare the parentage of a child in certain proceedings (s 69VA).[44] Section 60H of FLA specifies the parents of a child born with the help of assisted reproductive procedures. It provides that children born as a result of artificial conception procedures to a woman who was married or in a de facto relationship are the children of the woman and her partner. The proviso is that the procedure was undertaken with the consent of both partners and the donor of genetic material.[45] This makes it clear that the person providing genetic material does not become a parent under the FLA.[46] Section 60HB affirms parentage orders made pursuant to prescribed State or Territory laws with respect to children born under surrogacy arrangements. In outlining these provisions, our point is to highlight how they allow for the construction of the norm that a child can only ever have two parents (whether biological or through artificial means). They thus function as a mechanism of reinforcing the naturalness of the nuclear family.

---

42   The FLA gives a non-exhaustive definition of 'child' in s 4(1), but for the purposes of Part VII the term includes an adopted child and a stillborn child; 'child of a marriage' is defined in s 60F(1) as including a child adopted since the marriage by the husband and wife or by either of them with the consent of the other; a child of the husband and wife born before the marriage; a child who is, under s 60H(1) or s 60HB, the child of the husband and wife. The wide ambit of the FLA is affirmed by s 69ZE(1).

43   Dickey explains that two are presumptions of paternity and the remaining are presumptions of paternity and maternity and are rebuttable except when the presumption is made by the court during the lifetime of a parent: Dickey, above n 25, 236. *The Child Support (Assessment) Act 1989* (Cth) has six presumptions.

44   The court is authorised to order that parentage testing orders be carried out if it is relevant for parenting proceedings and there is evidence that the parentage of the child is in doubt (s 69W).

45   What may constitute relevant consent is a matter of discussion in *Keaton v Aldridge* [2009] FMCAfam 92, where the two partners disagreed about whether the requisite consent was given by both partners. See discussion in Chapter 3. In *Maurice v Barry* (2010) 44 Fam LR 62, both partners asked the Court to declare the other intended parent as a parent and the Court granted that application.

46   s 60H(2)–(3) preserves any prescribed Commonwealth, State or Territory laws that recognise the woman and the man respectively as the mother or father of a child.

8.5   Parental responsibility

As the law accepts that children need protection, the obvious next issue is who should be responsible for the children. As previously noted, the FLA's answer is that the parents are primarily responsible for their children.[47] But in constructing the rules about parental obligations, the law articulates or assumes the bases of such obligations.

The concept of parental responsibility that replaced the earlier concepts of guardianship and custody was introduced in the 1995 amendments. In its present version in the FLA it means, in relation to a child, 'all the duties, powers, responsibilities and authority which, by law, parents have in relation to children' (s 61B).[48] Each parent has such responsibility towards their child of less than 18 years of age, irrespective of whether the parents' relationship is continuing or has ended (s 61C(1)–(2)). The scope of parental responsibility is not defined precisely in court decisions either.[49] It is possible to reallocate parental responsibilities by the parents entering into a parenting plan or by the court making a parenting order.

In the normal course, both parents are expected to discharge these responsibilities, but there are times when such obligations have to be enforced for the benefit of the child, and the state assumes that role. Law responds in three different contexts: in intact, separated and dysfunctional families. The idea that both parents ought to be involved in the lives of their children is the cornerstone of the nuclear family, and so, in intact families, family law virtually leaves it to the parents to decide how to bring up their children. The involvement of both parents is 'enforced' only after separation, but even then parents are expected to settle their arrangements privately. It is when the parents separate and are unable to agree about child-related matters that the law steps in through the courts to make such arrangements in the name of the best interests of the child.

The third scenario is when the state steps in to protect the child in a dysfunctional family. If the child is at risk and is not being looked after by either parent, the law authorises state agencies to step in, but they do so in the name of protection of the child (see Chapter 11). This also brings into focus the limited scope of the rights of the child arguments, as protection conveys ideas of paternalism rather than autonomy. There is a tension

---

47   For an interdisciplinary analysis of the concept of parent, see Andrew Bainham, Shelley Day Sclater and Martin Richards, *What is a Parent? A Socio-legal Analysis* (Hart Publishing, 1999). See also Jennifer McIntosh, 'The Care of Very Young Children After Parental Separation' (2014) 36(4) *In Psych*, explaining the differences of opinion among psychologists regarding the benefits of equal time care for very young children.

48   The phrase 'duties, powers, responsibilities and authority' that parents have in relation to their children is not given any content in this section. Section 65DAC provides that if an order for shared parental responsibility is made, then decisions about major long-term issues must be made jointly by those people; the order is taken to mean that the people must consult each other and make a genuine effort to come to a joint decision. The definition of 'major long term issues' in s 4(1) refers to 'the care, welfare, development of the child of a long-term nature'. Thus, there is no finite list prescribed in the FLA, but it can include issues about education, religious and cultural upbringing, health, the child's name and the child's living arrangements. Also see *B and B: Family Law Reform Act 1995* (1997) 21 Fam LR 676, discussed in Chapter 9.

49   *W v G (No 1)* [2005] FLC 93–247.

between the simultaneous acknowledgement of rights and the need for protection that permeates all aspects of the child–law relationship. We discuss these three issues below and start by examining how the FLA regulates the family in these different contexts.

8.5.1   Autonomy of parents in intact families

In an intact family, parents have considerable latitude regarding their children and their upbringing. The state, through family law, assumes that children are being cared for by the parents and gives more significance to the autonomy of the parents than to the rights of the child. There is virtually no effort made under family law to regulate parents or prescribe how they are to behave with regard to their children as long as there is no dispute before the court. It is assumed that both parents are acting responsibly (whatever that means) and that it is not appropriate for the law to intervene in people's private lives and tell the parents how to parent. In this way the concept of family as a private institution is reinforced through law.

In contemporary family literature, as we discussed in previous chapters, it is invariably acknowledged that there is no one form of family and we live in pluralist times where people define for themselves what kind of relationships they wish to form. In part, the changing nature of affective relationships is a result of the loosening of the social constraints of religion, morality and even legal regulation. The increasing individualisation described by sociologists seeks to explain how people enter and exit relationships in their quest for self-fulfilment. Very broadly, it means that in contemporary times we stay in relationships only so long as our needs are met, and exiting a relationship is now an easier legal and social option than in previous times.[50] But, as we have seen, this transition is far from complete and the reality is that families continue to be sites where emotional and financial dependencies exist. These two contradictory pulls are present in the marriage, divorce and financial provisions, but while the tendency in these provisions has been increasingly towards promoting the individualism and autonomy of the adult parties, the same approach has not been adopted with respect to parenthood. It remains the case that parents are held accountable and responsible for the wellbeing of their children irrespective of whether their relationship with the other parent has ended. This 'indissolubility of parenthood',[51] however, is different from what sociologists have to say about the needs or rights of children.

For example, Smart and Neale explain how individuals now invest more in their relations with children, supposedly because the parent–child relationship holds out a greater promise of permanence and satisfaction.[52] In comparison, the philosophical debates on the possible rationales for attaching the responsibility for children to their biological (or other) parents include moral obligations, notions of parental autonomy and balancing the interests

---

50   Carol Smart and Bren Neale, *Family Fragments* (Polity Press, 2007) ch 1 discuss the contemporary trends in sociology as present in the writings of Anthony Giddens, *The Transformation of Intimacy* (Polity Press, 1992); Ulrich Beck and Elisabeth Beck-Gernsheim, *The Normal Chaos of Love* (Polity Press, 1995); and David Morgan, *Family Connections* (Polity Press, 1996) to emphasise that the connection between parenting and care functions can explain the increased emphasis on the importance of children to both men and women, especially after separation.

51   This is because the sociological literature depicts the needs of parents as defining the ideas about continuing relationships while family law eschews this emphasis and claims to decide everything in pursuit of the best interests of the child. See Patrick Parkinson, *Family Law and the Indissolubility of Parenthood* (Cambridge University Press, 2011).

52   Smart and Neale, above n 50, 17.

of parents and children.[53] The FLA does not make explicit which rationale, if any, it uses to nominate parents as responsible for children. However, a general pattern where biological or genetic parenthood is the relevant connection used to link parental responsibility to the child is discernible. It is further supplemented by the idea that in some instances the relationship between partners determines parenthood.

Decisions about the day-to-day arrangements for children are the exclusive reserve of the parents. As long as the parents are in agreement about their respective roles, family law in particular has very little to say to them.[54] Family law literature is silent on how children are, or ought to be, cared for in intact families. This is in contrast to the extensive literature on what constitutes ideal situations for children in the allied disciplines of child development or child psychology. Thus, within family law the notions of parental autonomy and privacy of the family are given full expression in so far as the law has virtually nothing to say about children in intact families. However, there are notable exceptions to this approach, such as cases involving non-therapeutic medical treatment of children – for example, the sterilisation of a girl child with disabilities, and gender reassignment procedures. In these situations, the courts have assumed the role of the reliable guardian of children's rights.[55]

The technical ground on which the courts assume this responsibility is located in the 'welfare' power of the courts,[56] but another aspect of this matter relates to the powers of the state vis-à-vis those of the parents. The effect of the High Court decision in *Marion's* case is that, in cases involving certain serious medical procedures to be performed on children, the oversight of the court is necessary. There seems to be no evident reason for the lack of trust in the parents who continue to be responsible for all other aspects of the welfare of the child. In assuming that the parents' self-interest may clash with the best interests of the child or that the consequences of making a 'wrong' decision are very serious, the law, through the court, assumes the mantle of impartiality and objectivity that cannot be achieved by anyone else. Consequently, the capabilities of the experts in medical or other professions are also subjected to the oversight of the court. Since all this is done in the best interests of the child, there is not much space to ask: what special expertise do courts have that makes them the most capable to make these decisions?

The majority judgment of the High Court in *Marion's* case explicitly found that children with intellectual disabilities are extremely vulnerable owing to their disability and minority status, and that decisions affecting their welfare should be made by the court as that would

---

53   John Eekelaar, 'Are Parents Morally Obliged to Care for Their Children?' (1991) 11(3) *Oxford Journal of Legal Studies* 340.

54   Other areas of law would step in to regulate parental conduct in regard to, for example, corporal punishment or withholding necessary medical treatment.

55   *Secretary, Department of Health and Community Services v JWB and SMB* ('*Marion's* case') (1992) 175 CLR 218; *Re Alex: Hormonal Treatment for Gender Identity Dysphoria* [2004] FamCA 297; *Re: Alex* [2009] FamCA 1292. See also Felicity Bell, 'Children with Gender Dysphoria and the Jurisdiction of the Family Court' (2015) 38(2) *UNSW Law Journal* 426.

56   The welfare power of the courts in s 67ZC(1) gives courts similar powers to the traditional *parens patriae* powers of the Supreme Courts. The varied use of welfare power is illustrated in Dickey, above n 25, 301–2. It has been held by the High Court that the welfare jurisdiction of the Family Court in s 67ZC does not extend to children in immigration detention, primarily because the Family Court is restricted to making orders in relation to Part VII of the FLA: *Minister for Immigration and Multicultural and Indigenous Affairs v B* (2004) 219 CLR 365 (Gleeson CJ, McHugh, Gummow, Kirby, Hayne, Callinan and Heydon JJ).

reduce the likelihood of intentional or unintentional abuse of the rights of the child.[57] This decision is an example of the law simply declaring itself the expert or the most trustworthy decision-maker. The fact that the medical procedure would sterilise a girl with intellectual disabilities and would be an irreversible removal of a human right (to procreate) provided the basis for the Court's authority to decide whether the procedure was in the best interests of the child.[58] It needs to be pointed out that most probably the law would not countenance the abrogation of an acknowledged human right of any other section of the population.[59] The role of courts as experts who can decide what is in the best interests of the child when parents cannot agree becomes even more evident in Part VII proceedings.

Similar issues are illustrated in the Family Court decision in *Re Alex*.[60] This case was discussed in the later case of *Re Jamie*, where the parents raised the specific issue of whether hormonal treatment for managing gender identity disorder of the child[61] was a medical procedure of the kind that required court approval. The parents had obtained an order from the single judge authorising the stage one treatment as it was found to be in the child's best interests. However, the parents appealed and challenged the need for court approval for the treatment when the child, the parents and the medical doctors were in agreement about the need for such treatment. They argued that parents had the authority to permit medical treatment for their child identified as having gender identity disorder. This issue was particularly pertinent with respect to the stage two treatment as the trial judge had found that it was not possible to make an order authorising this treatment because it would commence after a long period of time and the court could not say what would be in the best interests of the child at that time.

The Full Court identified two issues to be determined: who has the authority to give consent to medical procedures when a child is *Gillick* competent; and who should determine whether a child is *Gillick* competent. The outcome in this case to a large extent turned on the treatment comprising two stages, one being reversible and the other not.

In this case it was accepted that stage one of the treatment was reversible and there was no controversy since the parents, the child and the medical experts all agreed that such treatment was needed. It was held that the child, if *Gillick* competent, could consent to such treatment without the involvement of the court. Stage two treatment, however, was irreversible and therefore the involvement of the court may be necessary in giving consent. With regard to this second question, there were some differences between the judgments of the three Full Court judges.

---

57   The High Court sent the case back to the Family Court to decide whether it was in Marion's best interests to undergo the proposed hysterectomy. The answer of the Family Court was yes: *In re Marion (No 2)* [1994] FLC 92-448 (Nicholson CJ).

58   Margaret Harrison, 'What's New in Family Law? Parental Authority and its Constraints: The Case of Marion' (1992) 32 *Family Matters* <https://aifs.gov.au/publications/family-matters/issue-32/whats-new-family-law>.

59   See also John Tobin and Elliot Luke, 'The Involuntary, Non-Therapeutic Sterilisation of Women and Girls with an Intellectual Disability – Can It Ever Be Justified?' (2013) 3(1) *Victoria University Law and Justice Journal* 27.

60   *Re Alex: Hormonal Treatment for Gender Identity Dysphoria* [2004] FamCA 297 (Nicholson CJ). See the discussion in Chapter 3 also.

61   *Re Jamie* [2013] FamCAFC 110 (Bryant CJ, Finn and Strickland JJ).

Chief Justice Bryant was of the view that the *Gillick* competent child could consent to stage two treatment, but also said that the Court would have to decide whether the child is *Gillick* competent. She explained that this decision was made reluctantly because the Court is bound by the High Court's decision in *Marion's* case. Justice Finn said that the Court must decide whether the child has the necessary competence to consent to irreversible medical treatment. Furthermore, if there was any doubt about such competence, then the Court would be required to decide whether to authorise the same. Justice Strickland said that whether the child is able to understand and give informed consent to stage two treatment is a threshold issue that the Court must decide.

In each instance, the judges were somewhat apologetic for putting the parents through the expense and stress of making another application to the Court, but they all came to the same general conclusion that the Court was the only reliable decision-maker with respect to the stage two treatment. This decision is lauded for clarifying the rights of children with gender identity dysphoria,[62] but there is no further explanation of why judges are the most competent decision-makers. The discussion of *Re Alex* in *Re Jamie* alludes to the issue of whether, in circumstances where no possible benefit could be gained by the parents in authorising the medical treatment, they could not make the decision. This case thus illustrates how the discourse of the best interests of the child is deployed to make the courts the final arbiters, but very often the courts reach the same conclusions that the parents and the medical experts were proposing. Notably, in the process 'the Court has positioned itself as part of the machinery of social regulation of non-normative gender identity'.[63]

8.5.2 Parents in separated families and equal shared parental responsibility

Part VII of the FLA governs issues related to children, primarily after separation. The discussion in this part focuses on the two distinct aspects of the 2006 amendments: the introduction of the legislative rebuttable presumption of shared parental responsibility and the compulsory requirement of FDR in child-related matters (see chapters 2 and 4). Cumulatively they illustrate how the law functions to legitimise the notion of family as a nuclear unit as well as a private institution. The norm-setting function of these legislative changes influences court decisions as well as private agreements. Despite the fact that most child-related disputes do not proceed to litigation, the effect of these legislative provisions is to set normative standards.[64] This is because the legislative provisions have a necessary influence on how people reach private agreements. The same can be said about the insistence of the FLA on FDR. Notwithstanding the fact that the legislative scheme and the courts allow many applicants

---

62   See also Michael Williams, John Chesterman and Phil Grano, '*Re Jamie (No 2)*: A Positive Development for Transgender Young People' (2014) 22(1) *Journal of Law and Medicine* 90.

63   Bell, above n 55.

64   Even when the cases reach the court, it is evident that a greater number of disputes relate to financial matters. Family Court of Australia, *Annual Report* (2014–2015) 53 explains that the issues sought on applications for final orders are 'parenting only' (30%); 'financial only' (55%); 'parenting and financial' (13%); and 'other' (2%).

to avoid engaging in FDR,[65] it is the normative force of private settlement as the preferred method of dispute resolution that functions to legitimise the notion of the private family.

8.5.2.1   Compulsory FDR in Part VII proceedings

Separating parents who cannot agree among themselves on arrangements for their children may seek legal assistance, but the legislation directs them to engage in private agreements as far as possible. The design of the FLA has always incorporated provisions that steer the parents towards private settlement of child-related disputes.[66] The development of this imperative culminated in the 2006 amendments to the FLA.[67] Two distinctive features of these amendments are the strengthened emphasis on private settlement, and the introduction of a set of responsibilities for advisers (legal, practitioners, family counsellors, family dispute resolution practitioners and family consultants) to inform disputing parent/s that the best interests of the child are the paramount consideration, and to encourage them to meet the child's best interests (ss 60D and 63DA). The insistence on FDR in the FLA Part VII proceedings serves to privatise family disputes more than any other set of provisions.[68] Moreover, combined with the legislative presumption in favour of shared parental responsibility, the normative function of these provisions is to normalise two parents as providing the most desirable parenting arrangement for all children. They in turn contribute to the lack of visibility of how most children are being brought up after the separation of their parents.

With regard to FDR, Part II of the FLA sets out the available non-court-based services.[69] The emphasis on pre-action procedures is now incorporated in Part VII, s 60I(2)–(6).[70] For a child-related matter to be heard by the court, it is necessary to provide a 'certificate' from a family dispute resolution practitioner ('FDRP') (s 60I(7)). Exceptions to this rule are included

---

65   Fehlberg et al, above n 32, 228–32. See also below n 69.

66   The *Matrimonial Causes Act 1959* (Cth) also contained provisions promoting reconciliation and private settlement, but they were not used widely. See Chapter 2 for further discussion.

67   The ideas and reports informing these changes include the House of Representatives Standing Committee on Family and Community Affairs, *Every Picture Tells a Story: Report on the Inquiry into Child Custody Arrangements in the Event of Family Separation* (Parliament of Australia, 2003); Department of the Prime Minister and Cabinet, *Framework Statement on Reforms to the Family Law System* (Commonwealth of Australia, 2004); Attorney-General's Department, *A New Approach to the Family Law System: Implementation of Reforms* (Australian Government, 2004); Department of Social Services, *A New Family Law System: Government Response to Every Picture Tells a Story* (Australian Government, 2005).

68   For a critique of the faith in mediation underlying these changes, see Rachel Field, 'Using the Feminist Critique of Mediation to Explore "the Good, the Bad and the Ugly" Implications for Women of the Introduction of Mandatory Family Dispute Resolution in Australia' (2006) 20(5) *Australian Journal of Family Law* 45.

69   Part III provisions relate to family consultants; pt IIIA provisions state the obligations of various personnel to inform the parties about non-court-based family services and court processes and services; pt IIIB elaborates the provisions regarding the court's powers in relation to both court and non-court based family services. See Chapter 2 for a detailed discussion; one of the key features of this reform was that simultaneously the government planned the setting up of family relationship centres as one-stop shops for the parties intending to separate. For a brief overview, see Sue Pidgeon, 'Australia's Family Relationship Centre: From Policy To Implementation – How Family Relationship Centres Became A Reality' (2013) 51(2) *Family Court Review* 224; Patrick Parkinson, 'The Idea of Family Relationship Centres in Australia' (2013) 51(2) *Family Court Review* 195.

70   Hilary Astor, 'Making a "Genuine Effort" in Family Dispute Resolution in Australia: What Does it Mean?' (2008) 22(2) *Australian Journal of Family Law* 102.

in s 60I(9) and broadly do not oblige the parties to produce a certificate if the orders are sought by consent; there are reasonable grounds for the court to believe that there has been or there is a risk of child abuse or family violence; the application relates to the contravention of a recently made parenting order and there is reason to believe that the person has serious disregard for their obligations under the order; the matter is urgent; or one of the parties is unable to participate effectively in FDR owing to specific reasons.[71]

The FDRP can issue one of five kinds of certificates (s 60I(8)). If the applicant parent has applied for an order, and has not attended FDR and obtained a certificate, or does not fall within the exceptions of s 60I(9), the court may order the parties to attend FDR (s 60I(10)). The court has the additional option of considering, at any stage in the proceedings, whether the parties should attend counselling or FDR (s 13C). A controversial aspect of the interaction between the general rule that FDR should be tried and the possibility of being exempted arises in cases involving family violence.[72] It is possible for the FDRP to grant a certificate saying that FDR is not appropriate owing to family violence, but it is nevertheless a matter of some discussion whether the existence of family violence is readily detectable.[73]

In giving advice on a parenting plan, advisers must also inform their clients, among other things, that if the child spending equal time with each parent is reasonably practicable and is in the best interests of the child, an arrangement of that kind is an option to consider (s 63DA(2)(a)). If not, the child spending substantial and significant time with each parent is another option to consider (s 63DA(2)(b)). They must also inform their clients of the matters that may be dealt with in a parenting plan in accordance with s 63C(2) (s 63DA(2)(d)); and that if there is a parenting order in force in relation to the child, the order may (because of s 64D) include a provision that the order is subject to a parenting plan entered into by the parents (s 63DA(2)(e)); and inform them of the various matters that are desirable in a parenting plan (s 63DA(2)(f)).

If the participation in the FDR process is successful and parents can reach an agreement, the FLA provides the option of entering into a parenting plan (s 63B).[74] Parenting plans are agreements in writing made between the parents of the child and entered into without any threat, duress or coercion (s 63C(1)). They are signed agreements but are not enforceable, although a parenting order may be subject to a subsequent parenting plan (s 64D). The parenting plans

---

71   There is a possible objection that FDR cannot be considered compulsory in view of the fact that many exemptions are granted. See, eg, the Family Court of WA, *Annual Review* (Family Court of Western Australia, 2011–2012) 16 that: '[d]uring 2011/12, 974 FDR Exemptions were lodged. With 803 of these lodged against a final orders application, about 53.4% of all final order parenting applications were commenced on the basis that a ground for exemption was established, hence FDR was not conducted prior to filing'.

72   Georgina Dimopoulos, 'Gateways, Gatekeepers or Guiding Hands? The Relationship Between Family Relationship Centres and Legal Practitioners in Case Management and the Court Process' (2010) 24(2) *Australian Journal of Family Law* 176.

73   s 60I(8). See also *Family Law (Family Dispute Resolution Practitioners) Regulations 2008* (Cth) reg 25(2); ALRC, *Family Violence—A National Legal Response*, Report No 114 (2010) ch 23.

74   The 1995 amendments introduced parenting plans, which could be registered with the court. They could then be enforced. The *Family Law Amendment Act 2003* (Cth) removed the possibility of registration and the plans are no longer enforceable. After the 2006 amendments they are encouraged by various means, but are not able to be registered (s 63DA(1) and (2)). However, a parenting order in certain circumstances can be modified by a parenting plan (s 64D(1)).

must be made between the two parents, but they can refer to non-parents (s 63C(2) and (2A)). They can deal with any of the matters mentioned in s 63C(2).[75] Before 2003, parenting plans could be registered and enforced by the court. This is no longer the case and has resulted in a decrease in the number of parenting plans, and an increase in the making of consent orders.

8.5.3   Parenting with the help of the court

If, however, no agreement is reached, the next step is to approach the court.[76] Disputes involving children, including disputes about where children should live and how much time they should spend with each parent (or other significant adults in their lives), are governed by various specific provisions in Part VII. The wide ambit of these provisions includes all children, parents, grandparents, and anyone concerned with the care, welfare and development of the child.[77] The 2006 amendments combine a set of procedural and substantive innovations (either introducing new ones or re-emphasising old ones) and are discussed below. The application for a parenting order must be made in compliance with the pre-action requirements. Usually, such an application will be made to the Federal Circuit Court (although other courts can exercise jurisdiction under ss 69H–69K) and the order can relate to a number of issues regarding the child (s 64B(2)).[78]

---

75   Section 63C(2) provides that: '[a] parenting plan may deal with one or more of the following: (a) the person or persons with whom a child is to live; (b) the time a child is to spend with another person or other persons (c) the allocation of parental responsibility for a child; (d) if 2 or more persons are to share parental responsibility for a child – the form of consultations those persons are to have with one another about decisions to be made in the exercise of that responsibility; (e) the communication a child is to have with another person or other persons; (f) maintenance of a child; (g) the process to be used for resolving disputes about the terms or operation of the plan; (h) the process to be used for changing the plan to take account of the changing needs or circumstances of the child or the parties to the plan; (i) any aspect of the care, welfare or development of the child or any other aspect of parental responsibility for a child. Note: paragraph (f) – if the *Child Support (Assessment) Act 1989* applies, provisions in a parenting plan dealing with the maintenance of a child (as distinct from child support under that Act) are unenforceable and of no effect unless the provisions in the plan are a child support agreement (see section 63CAA and subsection 63G(5) of this Act)'.

76   Moloney et al report that in 21% of cases no agreement was reached and a certificate was issued. In a further 31% of cases no agreement was reached but no certificate was issued either: see Lawrie Moloney et al, 'Evaluating the Work of Australia's Family Relationship Centres: Evidence from the First 5 Years' (2013) 51(2) *Family Law Quarterly* 234.

77   Section 65C provides that the following people may apply for a parenting order: a parent; a grandparent; a child; or any other person concerned with the care, welfare or development of a child. Section 69C specifies a list of who may institute proceedings in relation to a child. Section 69E specifies that the child or parent should be present in Australia when proceedings are commenced.

78   Section 64B(2) provides that: '[a] parenting order may deal with one or more of the following: (a) the person or persons with whom a child is to live; (b) the time a child is to spend with another person or other persons; (c) the allocation of parental responsibility for a child; (d) if 2 or more persons are to share parental responsibility for a child – the form of consultations those persons are to have with one another about decisions to be made in the exercise of that responsibility; (e) the communication a child is to have with another person or other persons; (f) maintenance of a child; (g) the steps to be taken before an application is made to a court for a variation of the order to take account of the changing needs or circumstances of: (i) a child to whom the order relates; or (ii) the parties to the proceedings in which the order is made; (h) the process to be used for resolving disputes about the terms or operation of the order; (i) any aspect of the care, welfare or development of the child or any other aspect of parental responsibility for a child'.

Section 69ZQ(1) further specifies general duties of the court in giving effect to the principles in s 69ZN (set out below) and, among other things, directs the court that it must decide which issues may be decided summarily and which require full investigation and hearing; decide the order in which issues would be decided, the timing of the steps in the proceedings, and whether the costs in taking these steps are justified; make use of appropriate technology; deal with as many aspects of the matter as it can on one occasion; where appropriate, deal with the matter without requiring the parties' physical attendance in court; and, if appropriate, encourage the parties to attend FDR or counselling.

Section 69ZR gives the court power to make determinations, findings of fact and orders at any stage of the proceedings that it considers will assist in the determination of the dispute between the parties; and this can be done by the judicial officer without having to disqualify himself or herself from a further hearing of the proceedings. Section 69ZX gives the court wide powers and duties in relation to evidence, particularly in relation to giving effect to the principles in s 69ZN and the application of s 69ZR.

8.5.3.1   Procedural innovations for the conduct of child-related proceedings

The Family Court of Australia ('FCA') in particular has been pro-active in developing procedures for the conduct of cases, especially those involving children. Two examples of such innovations are the less adversarial trial ('LAT') and the Magellan Case Management Program. Both these innovations have since been incorporated into the substantive provisions of the FLA. Further legislative innovations relate to the personnel that can help the court and include independent children's lawyers ('ICLs') and family consultants. Another distinctive feature of Part VII is that it includes a set of principles that the court must use in deciding child-related disputes.

THE LESS ADVERSARIAL TRIAL

The FLA has from its inception incorporated the idea that the FCA should conduct its proceedings without undue formality. However, the exact scope of how far the court can go in this regard has been the subject of controversy.[79] Nevertheless, in various cases dealing with the best interests of the child, the FCA has articulated general statements that in such cases the proceedings are not strictly adversarial proceedings.[80] Consistent with this philosophy, the FCA instituted the Children's Cases Program in the early 2000s as recognition of the fact that too many children's matters were unduly long and that the problem lay in the adversarial system of litigation more than in the legislation.

In designing the Children's Cases Program, the architects of the plan were influenced by the approaches of certain European courts that follow civil law practices.[81] They thus introduced certain practices where the judge could assume a more active role in deciding how the

---

[79] See, eg, *T v S* [2001] FLC 93-086 (Nicholson CJ, Ellis and Mullane JJ), where the Full Court said that, although proceedings regarding the best interests of the child are not adversarial in the usual sense, they are not inquisitorial either.

[80] See *Separate Representative v JHE and GAW* [1993] FLC 92-376 for a discussion of a number of earlier cases; *M v M* (1988) 166 CLR 69.

[81] See, for a comprehensive analysis of the program, Margaret Harrison, *Finding A Better Way: A Bold Departure from the Traditional Common Law Approach to the Conduct of Legal Proceedings* (Media Release, 27 April 2007).

trial was conducted, in defining the issues that needed to be determined, and whether a particular witness was necessary and how they could provide evidence.[82] Initially the Children's Cases Program was introduced as a pilot or trial program in the Sydney and Parramatta registries. It required the parties to agree that the judge could exercise greater control over the proceedings and would not be bound by the ordinary rules of evidence. Among other things the judge could determine what issues needed to be resolved, and direct what evidence was required and how it may be given. The judge could limit cross-examination, could interview children, and could act upon what the children said. The judge could direct the parties to try to settle their dispute rather than go to court.[83] It is significant that the then contemporary FCA *Annual Report* also contains the statement that the process is designed to take up less court time in reaching a determination as compared to the traditional (adversarial) trial.[84] The ready conflation of the aims for making the trial process less traumatic for the child and making the trial more efficient requires more analysis, as institutional economics and the interests of the child are not necessarily synonymous. These practices have now been translated into Part VII Division 12A of the FLA, which was introduced in the 2006 amendments. Among other things s 69ZN(4) articulates that the court is to actively direct, control and manage the proceedings.[85]

THE MAGELLAN CASE MANAGEMENT PROGRAM

The FCA, and now the Federal Circuit Court ('FCC'), deals with cases relating to children and very often they involve allegations of abuse – sexual and/or physical. In the late 1990s, the then Chief Justice of the Family Court, the Hon Alistair Nicholson, initiated a case management program to deal with such cases. A pilot program, known as the Magellan Case Management Program, was run in the Melbourne and Dandenong registries in 1998. It was designed to coordinate the work of the FCA with that of other statutory agencies involved in child protection. These include the police, child protection departments, forensic investigators, directors of public prosecutions and the criminal courts, as all of them could be involved in protecting children, prosecuting criminals and enforcing criminal laws. In initiating the program, the FCA sought to improve the resolution of disputes involving allegations of child abuse. One of the issues facing the FCA was that, when allegations of child abuse were raised in parenting cases, the court was not equipped to investigate the abuse or to determine the veracity of the respective claims of the parents. Yet it had the responsibility to resolve the dispute in line with the 'best interests of the child' principle. Since 2003 the program has been available in all FCA registries.[86] Only if there are insufficient resources available in the FCA can a case involving child abuse be filed in the FCC.

The FCA manages Magellan cases with the help of a Magellan Team[87] and a Magellan Steering Committee.[88] Very generally, Magellan procedures require that when the court

---

82   For details, see Family Court of Australia, *Annual Report* (2002–2003).
83   Family Court of Australia, *Annual Report* (2004–2005).
84   Ibid 3.
85   See also *Choudhary v McDonald* [2016] FamCA 304.
86   According to the Family Court of Australia, *Annual Report* (2014–2015) 68, 129 Magellan cases were commenced and 117 finalised.
87   Consisting of judges, registrars and mediators/family consultants who handle these cases from start to finish.
88   Constituted of representatives from the Family Court's Magellan Team, State/Territory legal aid commissions, child protection departments, and police services.

becomes aware of the allegations of abuse it should appoint an independent children's lawyer (ICL), consider whether any procedural or interim orders should be made to protect the child or any of the parties to the proceedings, enable expeditious collection of appropriate evidence about the abuse, and request that the officer of the relevant State/Territory child protection authority should intervene. Furthermore, the court requests that the Magellan Report relating to the allegations of abuse is prepared.[89]

PRINCIPLES AND PERSONNEL

The FLA contains specific principles for conducting child-related proceedings that the courts must follow.[90] In addition, as explained next, the court is able to obtain assistance from specific personnel, including ICLs and family consultants. The FLA also emphasises the importance of taking the child's views or wishes into consideration. One of the means by which the court can determine the views of the child is to ask for a report by the family consultant.

In child-related proceedings, the court is required to give effect to five articulated principles as set out in s 69ZN.

The principles for conducting child-related proceedings are that the court must consider the needs of the child and the impact of the proceedings on the child; it is required to actively direct, control and manage the conduct of the proceedings; it must conduct the proceedings in a way that safeguards the child from family violence, child abuse and neglect and the parties from family violence; it should conduct proceedings in a way that promotes cooperative and child-focused parenting as far as possible; and, to the extent it is possible, it should conduct proceedings without undue delay and with as little formality, legal technicality and form as possible. The judicial officers hearing matters in chambers are also governed by these provisions (s 69ZO) and the powers under Part VII Division 12A may be exercised by the court on its own initiative or on the request of one of the parties (s 69ZP).

VOICE OF CHILDREN

In keeping with the role of the court as the protector of the best interests of the child, the FLA provides for the court to take into account the views of the child.[91] Section 60CD specifically provides that when making a parenting order the court may take into account the views of the child. The court can inform itself of such views by ordering a report (s 62G(2)), by appointing an ICL, or by any other means it considers appropriate. However, it is made clear in s 60CE that neither the court, nor any other person, can compel a child to express a view. We discuss next the issue of how children are heard in the family law processes.[92]

---

89   *Magellan Manual* (Family Court of Australia, 2007). See also Daryl J Higgins, *Cooperation and Coordination: An Evaluation of the Family Court of Australia's Magellan Case-management Model* (AIFS, 2007).

90   These principles were first introduced in the 1995 amendments and included in the 2006 amendments with some variations.

91   There is extensive literature in this area; for an introduction to some of the issues, see the ALRC, above n 22, ch 17.

92   The discussion of less adversarial trials and the Magellan Case Management Program is also relevant in this context.

THE INDEPENDENT CHILDREN'S LAWYER

The FLA provides for the possibility that the court may appoint a separate lawyer as an independent children's lawyer (ICL).[93] The possibility of appointing a separate representative for the child existed in the *Matrimonial Causes Act 1959* (Cth) and has existed in the FLA since its enactment (originally in s 65). This person was formerly known as the child's representative, then as the child's separate representative, and now s 4(1) defines an ICL as 'a lawyer who represents the child's interests in proceedings under an appointment made under a court order under [sub-s] 68L(2)'. The court can appoint an ICL on its own initiative, or if an application is made by the child, or by an organisation pursuing the welfare of the child, or any other person (s 68L(3)).[94] The ICL is not the child's legal representative (s 68LA(4)). The role of the ICL is elaborated in s 68LA.

In *In the Matter of P v P; Legal Aid Commission of NSW* the Full Court accepted the statement of the role of the separate representative formulated by the Legal Aid Commission:[95]

> The separate representative ought:
>
> 1. Act in an independent and unfettered way in the best interests of the child.
>
> 2. Act impartially, but if thought appropriate, make submissions suggesting the adoption by the court of a particular course of action if he or she considers that the adoption of such a course is in the best interests of the child.
>
> 3. Inform the court by proper means of the children's wishes in relation to any matter in the proceedings. In this regard the separate representative is not bound to make submissions on the instructions of a child or otherwise but is bound to bring the child's expressed wishes to the attention of the court.
>
> 4. Arrange for the collation of expert evidence and otherwise ensure that all evidence relevant to the welfare of the child is before the court.
>
> 5. Test by cross examination where appropriate the evidence of the parties and their witnesses.
>
> 6. Ensure that the views and attitudes brought to bear on the issues before the court are drawn from the evidence and not from a personal view or opinion of the case.
>
> 7. Minimise the trauma to the child associated with the proceedings.
>
> 8. Facilitate an agreed resolution to the proceedings.
>
> These statements are of general application to all cases and we are in broad agreement with them.

---

93 According to the AIFS study, the role of the ICL was developed by the Family Court cases and later incorporated into the FLA: see Rachel Carson et al, 'The Role and Efficacy of Independent Children's Lawyers: Findings From the AIFS Independent Children's Lawyer Study' (2014) 94 *Family Matters* 58. The cases mentioned in this study are *In the Matter of P v P* (1995) 19 Fam LR 1; *In the Marriage of Bennett* (1991) 17 Fam LR 561; *DS v DS* (2003) 32 Fam LR 352; and *R v R: Children's Wishes* (2000) 25 Fam LR 712.

94 See also *Family Law Rules 2004* (Cth) r 8.04.

95 (1995) 19 Fam LR 1, 33 (Nicholson CJ, Fogarty and Finn JJ). See an earlier formulation in *In the Marriage of Lyons and Bosely* [1978] FLC 90-423. The guidelines were first laid down by the Full Court in *Re K* (1994) 17 Fam LR 537 (Nicholson CJ, Fogarty and Baker JJ).

The Court also said that the separate representative should be appointed early in the proceedings. Usually, it should be the role of counsel to call the expert evidence. The appointment of ICLs in their capacity as lawyers submitting evidence to the court on the child's best interests has caused some confusion about the nature of their role.[96] The Explanatory Memorandum for the 2006 amendments emphasises that the ICL should represent a child's interests rather than act on the instructions of the child.[97] Among other things it is expected that the ICL will ascertain the views of the child and put them before the court (s 68LA(5) and (6)). However, if the ICL believes that it is not in the best interests of the child to give effect to the views of the child, it can say that to the court. The ICL cannot compel the child to express his or her views, but how the ICL can assess the views of the child is also not settled, as has been illustrated in the empirical research conducted by the AIFS.

The AIFS conducted research into the approaches and practices of ICLs and identified two main views among them: those who took a cautious approach to having contact with the child, and those who took a more robust approach to having contact with the child.[98] The latter approach was less common, but in this category the ICLs utilised all three purposes of direct contact – familiarisation, explanation and consultation with the child in ascertaining his or her views. The ICLs in the former group explained their role more in terms of traditional advocates who collect information and manage litigation. They also felt that they did not have the necessary training to consult with the child and interpret his or her views. Interestingly, the expectations of most children that the ICL would listen to them, protect them, and understand their views and concerns were not met. Issues of family violence and child abuse dominated the caseload of ICLs, and it was found that parents were dissatisfied with their professional practices in this regard. Many parents felt that the ICLs were insensitive to child safety concerns and in some cases they seemed to assume that no or insignificant violence or abuse had occurred.

In response to the question of whether the involvement of an ICL improves the outcomes for children, different professionals gave different responses. Interestingly, the judicial officers were more positive about the usefulness of ICLs than any other professionals. The non-ICL lawyers were the least positive in their responses. Moreover, other professionals raised concerns about accreditation, training and ongoing professional development of ICLs. The coordination between ICLs and other professionals, most notably family consultants, was also perceived as less than satisfactory. These findings are a cause for concern, especially since ICLs are often described as a 'voice' for children and as facilitating children's participation in family law proceedings.[99]

---

96   See, eg, Family Law Council, *Pathways for Children: A Review of Children's Representation* (Commonwealth of Australia, 2004); Patrick Parkinson and Judy Cashmore, *The Voice of the Child in Family Law Disputes* (Oxford University Press, 2008).

97   Explanatory Memorandum, Family Law Amendment (Shared Parental Responsibility) Bill 2006 (Cth) 14 [55].

98   See ALRC, above n 22.

99   Felicity Jane Bell, *Independent Children's Lawyers in Family Law Disputes: 'All Care and No Responsibility'?* (PhD Thesis, University of Sydney, 2015).

FAMILY CONSULTANTS

In parenting cases the court can seek the assistance of family consultants at any time during the proceedings and the court can order a family report from the family consultant assigned to a case (s 62G).[100] Formerly the family consultants were known as the 'family and child counsellor' or as the 'welfare officer'. The Full Court, in discussing the weight to be given to a family report, made general observations in *In the Marriage of Hall* about how a family report is to be treated by a court.[101] Among other things, the Court found that a judge is not bound to accept a family report. Family reports assist the judge, but it is for the judge to decide whether they are consistent with the rest of the evidence. The counsellor's views will normally have weight, but it is only the judge who has the benefit of observing the witnesses in the court under examination or cross-examination. Therefore, if the court does not accept the report it should not be a cause for the counsellor to be disturbed. Similarly, the court may at times need to cross-examine the counsellor, just like any other expert. The court concluded that it is important as a matter of public policy that no party leaves the court feeling that he or she was denied an opportunity to test the evidence.[102]

The FLA now provides that reports of family consultants received under s 62G are admissible (s 62G(8)). Moreover, the rules of evidence have been relaxed under s 69ZT. Thus, hearsay evidence of children that may be included in a report may be admitted into evidence (s 69ZV). However, some rules of evidence apply; for example, if a person (such as a family consultant) is present in court, they can be compelled to give evidence (FLA s 69ZT(1); *Evidence Act 1995* (Cth) s 36).

The reports prepared by family consultants can be a major avenue for introducing social science research into family law.[103] This is a problematic state of affairs, as the judge remains the final arbiter of assessing the views expressed in such reports. The difficulty arises because the discipline-specific knowledge in any area is produced from specific perspectives. If judges trained in law are asked to assess these views, they can only do so as laypeople. However, their particular status in the legal system as the final interpreters of legal meaning creates the situation that judges also assess other disciplinary knowledge. It is not a particular failing of the judges but instead the institutional design of the family law system that the judges have the final say, and the views, opinions and even professional judgments of parents, children and various other professionals are subordinated to the 'judgment' of judges. More significantly, no space is available within the system to ask why, or on what bases, the judges are equipped to discharge this role.

---

100   Section 11A specifies the functions of family consultants, but not all courts with jurisdiction under the FLA may have them available; the court has very wide discretion in deciding whether to order a family report: see *Roe v Creswick* [2013] FLC 93-554, where the trial judge was found to have erred in exercising her discretion and not ordering the report.

101   (1979) 29 ALR 545 (Evatt CJ, Asche SJ and Hogan J).

102   Ibid 552–3.

103   See John Monahan and Laurens Walker, 'Twenty-five Years of Social Science in Law' (2011) 35(1) *Law and Human Behavior* 72; Kyle D Pruett, 'Social Science Research and Social Policy: Bridging the Gap' (2007) 45(1) *Family Court Review* 52; Zoe Rathus, 'The Role of Social Science in Australian Family Law: Collaborator, Usurper or Infiltrator?' (2014) 52(1) *Family Court Review* 69.

8.5.3.2   Substantive principles: concept of shared parental responsibility

Family law has over time used the concepts of the welfare of the child or best interests of the child as guides for the reallocation of parental responsibilities.[104] However, irrespective of the terminology, the overwhelming emphasis of the courts has been to maintain (as far as possible) the relationship between the child and both parents. Thus, courts have always been very reluctant to deny access to the non-resident parent, usually the father. This aspect of post-separation parenting has assumed much more prominence since the 2006 amendments to the FLA. The discussion below explores the implications of using the concept of shared parental responsibility; the legislative scheme that defines the task of the court in determining the best interests of the child by reference to primary and additional considerations and the overarching rebuttable presumption of shared parental responsibility; the link between the presumption and care time allocation; and, finally, some judicial interpretations of these provisions.

We argue that the emphases of the law function to normalise ideas about ideal parenting and parental responsibilities, but in the process also obscure the fact that it is the law's construction more than the law responding to existing realities.[105] The following discussion also illustrates stark differences in the way the legislative provisions address child-related disputes and financial disputes (discussed in chapters 5 and 6). In the former, the norm-setting function of the legislative changes and the significance of the FLA introducing legislative presumptions about parental responsibilities can be contrasted to the latter, where the emphasis is on the courts having unfettered discretion. Being prescriptive in one context and not in the other does not adequately account for the realities of the sexual division of labour and the care of children, predominantly by mothers.

CONCEPT OF SHARED PARENTAL RESPONSIBILITY

The historical developments in family law that saw the concepts of guardianship and custody (and allied notions of the 'non-custodial' or 'access' parent) morph into the notions of shared parental responsibility (and allied notions of the 'resident' and 'contact' parent), and morph again into the notion of 'parents the child spends time with', put into legal practice common sense ideas about what is good for the child. The overarching goal is the continued involvement of both parents. This is the standard interpretation of what is in the best interests of the child, even if that means achieving that goal with judicial oversight. However, the pursuit of this goal is done with varying emphases. On the one hand, after separation the law enforces the financial obligations of the non-resident parent most strictly. On the other, if a parent wants the non-resident parent to maintain contact with a child, the law is most reticent about enforcing contact if the non-resident parent does not want it. Moreover, the emphasis on shared parenting reflects neither social realities nor any specific knowledge from other disciplines. The imposition of financial responsibilities on biological parents is also not explicitly linked

---

104   See Chapter 9 for a detailed discussion of specific factors mentioned in s 60CC(3) that the court must take into account in determining the best interests of the child.

105   See Carol Smart, 'The Ethics of Justice Strikes Back: Changing Narratives of Fatherhood' in Alison Diduck and Katherine O'Donovan (eds), *Feminist Perspectives on Family Law* (Routledge-Cavendish, 2006) 123 for the argument that the concept of shared parental responsibility prioritises justice to fathers and downplays the ethics of care that is often more relevant for mothers.

to any philosophical views about parental obligations. Similarly, the idea that shared parental responsibility is good for children is not explicitly justified by reference to child-development theories or psychological schools of thought or any other disciplinary knowledge.[106]

In the following discussion, we outline the legislative design of Part VII before discussing the details of the specific provisions. Part VII begins with enumerating the underlying objects and principles, followed by the reiteration of the principle of the best interests of the child as the paramount consideration in the resolution of disputes over children. Next we explain that what constitutes 'best interests' must be determined with the help of primary and additional considerations. The two primary considerations relate to the child having a meaningful relationship with both parents and to being protected from violence (with greater weight given to the protection from violence consideration). After the enumeration of these principles, the FLA next defines parental responsibility and states that each parent has parental responsibility for their children irrespective of the status of their relationship. After separation, if the parents cannot agree, the court can reallocate parental responsibility in a parenting order, but must do so in the context of the rebuttable presumption that it is in the best interests of the child for the parents to continue to exercise shared parental responsibility. If the presumption is rebutted, the court must substitute it with an appropriate order. In making these orders, the court must decide whether the child should spend equal time with each parent and, if that is not in the child's best interests, to determine the proportion of time to be spent with each respective parent, again, if that is in the best interests of the child. We now elaborate on these specific aspects of the relevant provisions.

8.5.3.3   Best interests of the child are the paramount consideration

The objects of Part VII and principles underlying it are enumerated in s 60B.[107] Of note is that the rights of Aboriginal and Torres Strait Islander children to enjoy their culture, including the right to maintain, explore and develop an appreciation of their culture, is specifically articulated in the FLA (s 60B(2)(e) and (3)).

---

106   There is extensive literature in various disciplines and trenchant critique of the idea that both parents should be jointly responsible for the child after separation. For an example of such analysis, see Dawn Borque, 'Reconstructing the Patriarchal Nuclear Family: Recent Developments in Child Custody and Access in Canada' (1995) 10(1) *Canadian Journal of Law and Society* 1; Helen Rhoades, 'The Rise and Rise of Shared Parenting Laws' (2002) 19 *Canadian Journal of Family Law* 75.

107   Section 60B(1) provides: 'The objects of this Part are to ensure that the best interests of children are met by: (a) ensuring that children have the benefit of both of their parents having a meaningful involvement in their lives, to the maximum extent consistent with the best interests of the child; and (b) protecting children from physical or psychological harm from being subjected, or exposed to, abuse, neglect or family violence; and (c) ensuring that children receive adequate and proper parenting to help them achieve their full potential; and (d) ensuring that parents fulfill their duties, and meet their responsibilities, concerning the care, welfare and development of their children. (2) The principles underlying these objects are that (except when it is or would be contrary to a child's best interests): (a) children have a right to know and be cared for by both their parents, regardless of whether their parents are married, separated, have never married or have never lived together; and (b) children have a right to spend time on a regular basis with, and communicate on a regular basis with, both their parents and other people significant to their care, welfare and development (such as grandparents and other relatives); and (c) parents jointly share duties and responsibilities concerning the care, welfare and development of their children; and (d) parents should agree about the future parenting of their children; and (e) children have a right to enjoy their culture (including the right to enjoy that culture with other people who share that culture).'

In deciding whether to make a particular order, the best interests of the child are the paramount considerations (ss 60CA and 65AA). The court is given mandatory directions to consider specific matters, described as primary considerations and additional considerations, in deciding what may constitute the best interests of the child (s 60CC).[108] The Full Court in *Goode v Goode* stated that '[t]he child's best interests are ascertained by a consideration of the objects and principles in s 60B and the primary and additional considerations in s 60CC'.[109]

The courts have taken the view that they are all equally relevant considerations and there is no hierarchy intended in using these considerations to determine the best interests of the child.[110] However, it is also undeniable that courts have to decide what weight to attach to any considerations and have also taken the view that not every consideration needs to be discussed.[111] In view of this interpretation, the significance of making a nomenclature distinction between primary and additional considerations can only be described as serving a normative function.

A significant innovation of the 2006 amendments is that it changed the steps the court must take in determining what constitutes the best interests of the child. The courts must use the two new primary considerations in conjunction with additional considerations. These additional considerations replicate and build on the list of factors the courts were expected to take into account even prior to the 2006 amendments.[112] The primary considerations are enumerated in s 60CC(2) as '(a) the benefit to the child of having a meaningful relationship with both of the child's parents; and (b) the need to protect the child from physical or psychological harm from being subjected to, or exposed to, abuse, neglect or family violence'.[113] In the discussion below, we analyse aspects of the first primary consideration and how it incorporates the concept of shared parental responsibility. The second primary consideration is analysed in greater detail later in the section on abuse and violence. However, the separation of the issues is not easy or always possible. Therefore, some level of overlap and repetition is unavoidable.

The interrelationship between these two primary considerations[114] gave rise to considerable disquiet as empirical evidence mounted that children were being exposed to family

108   Section 60CC(1) directs the court (subject to sub-s (5)) to consider the matters set out in both sub-ss (2) and (3). Subsection (5) directs the court in making consent orders that it may, but is not required to, have regard to all or any of the matters set out in sub-s (2) or (3). See Chapter 9 for a detailed discussion of s 60CC(3) factors in determining the best interests of the child.

109   (2006) 36 Fam LR 422, 440 [9] (Bryant CJ, Finn and Boland JJ).

110   *Slater v Light* (2011) 45 Fam LR 41; see also *Aldridge v Keaton* (2009) 42 Fam LR 369.

111   *SCVG v KLD* (2014) 51 Fam LR 340 (Ainslie-Wallace, Ryan and Stevenson JJ); see also *Banks and Banks* [2015] FamCAFC 36 (Thackray, Murphy and Kent JJ), where it was said that, especially in interim proceedings, the court need not discuss each and every consideration. The Court also explained and distinguished what was said in *Goode v Goode* as not requiring undisputed facts to be discussed as well.

112   A list of relevant factors was introduced in s 64 of the 1983 amendments. This list was modified in the 1995 amendments and s 68F replaced the earlier provision.

113   This subsection includes a note stating that '[m]aking these considerations the primary ones is consistent with the objects of this Part set out in paragraphs 60B(1)(a) and (b)'. Subsection (2A) provides that '[i]n applying the considerations set out in subsection (2), the court is to give greater weight to the consideration set out in paragraph (2)(b)'.

114   For a history of these changes, see Richard Chisholm, 'Making it Work: The Family Law Amendment (Shared Parental Responsibility) Act 2006' (2007) 21(2) *Australian Journal of Family Law* 143.

violence.[115] As a result, the 2011 amendments were introduced and sub-s (2A) was added to s 60CC. It states that if there is any inconsistency in respect of the two primary considerations stipulated in s 60CC(2), then the right of the child to be protected from harm is to be given greater weight than the right of the child to have a meaningful relationship with each parent. Nevertheless, the 2011 amendments retained the presumption of equal shared parental responsibility as well as the legislative provisions for making orders for equal shared care in cases where shared parental responsibility is presumed to be in the child's best interests.[116]

8.5.3.4   Mandatory presumption of shared parental responsibility and care time allocation

In deciding what parental order to make the court is bound to consider whether it is in the best interests of the child for the parents to have 'equal shared parental responsibility' (s 61DA). The presumption of equal shared parental responsibility is rebuttable. Specifically, the presumption will not apply if there are reasonable grounds to believe the presence of abuse or violence (s 61DA(2)). Generally, it will not apply if the court is satisfied, on the basis of the evidence, that it is not in the best interests of the child (s 61DA(4)). It also applies in applications for interim orders unless the court thinks it is not appropriate in the circumstances (s 61DA(3)).

If the presumption of equal shared parental responsibility applies – that is, it is not rebutted – the court must consider making an order that the child should spend equal time with both parents, provided it is in the best interests of the child and is reasonably practicable (s 65DAA(1)).[117] However, even if the presumption of shared parental responsibility applies, the court in the exercise of its discretion may decide not to order equal time. If the court does not make an order for an equal time arrangement, it must then consider whether an order for the child to spend 'substantial and significant time' with each parent should be made, subject to an assessment of the best interests and reasonably practicable tests (s 65DAA(2)). 'Substantial and significant time' is defined to include days falling on weekends, weekdays and holidays, time that would enable each parent to share in the child's daily routine, and occasions and events that are special to both child and parent (s 65DDA(3)). The interrelationship between the presumption of equal shared parental responsibilities and time allocation for care has generated a lot of doubt and debate. *Goode v Goode* was the first judgment to spell out the precise relationship between sharing parental responsibility and sharing time with the child. In this case the Full Court felt

---

115   For a review of some of the relevant provisions of the 2006 changes to the FLA, see Richard Chisholm, *Family Courts Violence Review: A Report* (Attorney-General's Department, 2009).

116   The Explanatory Memorandum, Family Law Legislation Amendment (Family Violence and Other Measures) Bill 2011 (Cth) 2 provides: '[t]he Family Violence Bill retains the substance of the shared parenting laws introduced in the *Family Law Amendment (Shared Responsibility) Act 2006* (Cth) and continues to promote a child's right to a meaningful relationship with both parents where this is safe for the child'. For a comprehensive account of the considerations leading up to the amendments, see Mary Anne Nielsen, *Bills Digest Service*, No 126 of 2010–11, 25 May 2011.

117   In *MRR v GR* (2010) 42 Fam LR 531 (French CJ, Gummow, Hayne, Kiefel and Bell JJ) the High Court said that before an equal time order is made both tests should be fulfilled.

it necessary to spell out the steps involved in making a parenting order, and we reproduce them below:

> In summary, the amendments to Pt VII have the following effect:
>
> 1. Unless the Court makes an order changing the statutory conferral of joint parental responsibility, s 61C(1) provides that until a child turns 18, each of the child's parents has parental responsibility for the child. 'Parental responsibility' means all the duties, powers, and authority which by law parents have in relation to children and parental responsibility is not displaced except by order of the Court or the provisions of a parenting plan made between the parties.
>
> 2. The making of a parenting order triggers the application of a presumption that it is in the best interests of the child for each of the child's parents to have equal shared parental responsibility. That presumption must be applied unless there are reasonable grounds to believe that a parent or a person who lives with a parent has engaged in abuse of the child or family violence (s 61DA(1) and 61DA(2)).
>
> 3. If it is appropriate to apply the presumption, it is to be applied in relation to both final and interim orders unless, in the case of the making of an interim order, the Court considers it would not be appropriate in the circumstances to apply it (s 61DA(1) and 61DA(3)).
>
> 4. The presumption may be rebutted where the Court is satisfied that the application of a presumption of equal shared parental responsibility would conflict with the best interests of the child (s 61DA(4)).
>
> 5. When the presumption is applied, the first thing the Court must do is to consider making an order if it is consistent with the best interests of the child and reasonably practicable for the child to spend equal time with each of the parents. If equal time is not in the interests of the child or reasonably practicable the Court must go on to consider making an order if it is consistent with the best interests of the child and reasonably practicable for the child to spend substantial and significant time with each of the parents (s 65DAA(1) and (2)).
>
> 6. The Act provides guidance as to the meaning of 'substantial and significant time' (s 65DAA(3) and (4)) and as to the meaning of 'reasonable practicability' (s 65DAA(5)).
>
> 7. The concept of 'substantial and significant' time is defined in s 65DAA to mean:
>
>   (a) the time the child spends with the parent includes both:
>
>   (i) days that fall on weekends and holidays; and
>
>   (ii) days that do not fall on weekends and holidays; and
>
>   (b) the time the child spends with the parent allows the parent to be involved in:
>
>   (i) the child's daily routine; and
>
>   (ii) occasions and events that are of particular significance to the child; and
>
>   (c) the time the child spends with the parent allows the child to be involved in occasions and events that are of special significance to the parent.

8. Where neither concept of equal time nor substantial and significant time delivers an outcome that promotes the child's best interests, then the issue is at large and to be determined in accordance with the child's best interests.

9. The child's best interests are ascertained by a consideration of the objects and principles in s 60B and the primary and additional considerations in s 60CC.

10. When the presumption of equal shared parental responsibility is not applied, the Court is at large to consider what arrangements will best promote the child's best interests, including, if the Court considers it appropriate, an order that the child spend equal or substantial and significant time with each of the parents. These considerations would particularly be so if one or other of the parties was seeking an order for equal or substantial and significant time but, as the best interests of the child are the paramount consideration, the Court may consider making such orders whenever it would be in the best interests of the child to do so after affording procedural fairness to the parties.

11. The child's best interests remain the overriding consideration.[118]

8.5.3.5   Mandatory presumption and the distinction between the rebuttal and inapplicability of the presumption

At the level of judicial interpretation, it is particularly instructive to see how the courts have adopted the position (which they are entitled to do within the ordinary rules of statutory interpretation) that the presumption of shared parental responsibilities is mandatory unless it is rebutted. The emphasis in this interpretation is on the mandatory aspect rather than the rebuttable aspect of the presumption. It is a peculiarly legal way of reasoning that enables the courts to focus on requiring a rebuttal rather than inquiring whether the presumption is justifiable. Two examples of such interpretation are discussed next.

In *Dundas v Blake* the dispute between parents related to a child who was 15 months old at the time of separation and aged two years and 10 months at the time of hearing.[119] Initially, under interim orders both parents had shared parental responsibility and were involved in the care of the child, but eventually Sexton FM made an order for sole parental responsibility in favour of the mother. To a large extent the federal magistrate had relied on the report of the family consultant that the child was showing behaviour consistent with attachment insecurity and that in his view the child should live with one parent or the other. Her Honour had further said that the child should live with the mother, but with the proviso that if the mother continued to be depressed and engaged in excessive drinking the child would have to live with the father. The issue according to the consultant was whether the mother was a neglectful parent.

On appeal, the Full Court found that Sexton FM erred in ordering sole parental responsibility:

> Section 61DA is mandatory in its requirement that the presumption must be applied until a level of satisfaction upon the evidence is reached that it would not be in the

---

118   (2006) 36 Fam LR 422, 439–441 [65]. See also *SCVG v KLD* (2014) 51 Fam LR 340, 355 [73] for the proposition that *Goode* does not require that the court must begin its inquiry about what is in the best interests of the child by reference to s 61DA. Moreover, the Court said that s 60CC drives the application of s 65DAA(1) and (2).

119   [2013] FamCAFC 133 (Bryant CJ, May and Ainslie-Wallace JJ).

interests of the child for it to apply. In our view that level of satisfaction could not have been reached in this case.[120]

Primarily, the Full Court was of the view that the factors relating to the mother and father had been present throughout. By this the Court is presumably meaning that if these factors did not prevent a shared parental responsibility order with respect to the interim consent orders, and were not addressed in the trial by either party, they could not be evidence that the presumption had been rebutted. Moreover, the Full Court said that the evidence of the family consultant did not address the issue of rebutting the presumption. The Full Court went on to say that s 61DA is a significant provision and requires significant attention in the evidence. The mandatory requirement to apply the presumption requires that there should be explicit and cogent reasons why it should be rebutted.[121]

The function of this analysis becomes evident when it is seen that the Full Court modified the order of the trial judge and restored shared parental responsibility, but did not significantly alter the shared care time arrangements. The primary effect of the judgment thus seems to be to endorse shared parental responsibility as the norm.

In *Doherty v Doherty* the Full Court found that it was not correct for the trial judge to say that:

> the s 61DA presumption 'is capable of being rebutted' by findings of child abuse or family violence. The legislation makes plain the seriousness with which each must be treated by the court by rendering the presumption *inapplicable* if those relevant findings are made and, by contrast, rebuttable if relevant findings as to best interests are made. The distinction is underscored by each being the subject of different subsections of the Act (s 61DA(2) and (4) respectively).[122]

It was further explained by the Full Court that s 65DAC (requiring parties sharing parental responsibility to make joint decisions on long-term issues) also applies in situations other than when the presumption of shared parental responsibility applies. Moreover, parental responsibility for some long-term issues may be shared while others may not be shared, and such sharing may be equal sharing or other than equal sharing.

Further issues arise when shared parental responsibility is ordered and the court is then required to allocate the time the child will spend with each parent under s 65DAA. The issues that can arise in allocating time become particularly pronounced in cases where the parents are no longer residing in the same locality, as this can have an impact on the child maintaining a meaningful relationship with both parents. In *McCall v Clark* the Full Court explored three possible interpretations of the meaning of the phrase 'the benefit to the child of having a meaningful relationship with both of the child's parents' in s 60CC(2)(a).[123] The Court considered the present relationship approach, the presumption approach and the prospective

---

120   Ibid [57].
121   Ibid [61].
122   [2014] FamCAFC 20, [35] (Ainslie-Wallace, Murphy and Tree JJ). This was a case where the father unsuccessfully challenged the trial judge's orders under which parental responsibility for some matters was awarded to the mother and for other matters shared parental responsibility was retained.
123   (2009) 41 Fam LR 483, 509 [118] (Bryant CJ, Faulks DCJ and Boland J).

approach. It indicated a preference for the prospective approach; that is, the inquiry is about the benefit to the child, in the light of available evidence, of having a relationship with both parents. It rejected the presumptive approach, claiming that if the legislature had wished to elevate the benefit to a child of a meaningful relationship to a presumption it would have said so in clear and unambiguous terms.[124] The Court also preferred the prospective to the present approach in order to create the conditions for a meaningful relationship in the future as the child did not already have a meaningful relationship with his father. These judicial interpretations only serve to reinforce the underlying legislative design.[125]

NORM-CREATING FUNCTION OF THE LEGISLATION

A focus on the norm-creating function of legislative language and design can illustrate how the legitimisation of ideas works at various levels and creates normative expectations. Thus, the significance of these legal rules extends much beyond the decisions made by courts. For example, an important aspect of the provisions of shared parental responsibility and shared care time orders is the relevance of family violence in deciding whether the presumption is applicable or not. Collectively these provisions have attracted a lot of attention[126] and many subsequent changes have been made to the legislation, especially with regard to the relevance of family violence.

The decisions discussed above illustrate how the presumption of equal shared parental responsibility applies mandatorily except in the circumstances when it is rebutted or is inapplicable. At one level it could be said that the cumulative effect of the provisions of the FLA is that enough safeguards are available to protect the vulnerable as s 61DA(2) provides that the presumption of equal shared parental responsibility is not applicable if there is abuse or violence.[127] Moreover, it is to be read in the context of s 60CC(2), which specifies the two primary considerations relevant in determining the best interests of the child, including the imperative of protecting the child from harm of violence. However, there was sufficient disquiet about the tension arising between the two primary considerations and the consequences of exposing children to risks to their safety that change was prompted.[128]

---

124   Ibid 509–10 [119]–[120].

125   See Justice Grant Riethmuller, 'The 42 Easy Steps for Deciding Straightforward Parenting Cases Under Part VII of the Family Law Act 1975' (2015) 24(3) *Australian Family Lawyer* 39.

126   See above n 32 for various empirical studies related to the assessment of the 2006 amendments; Richard Chisholm and Jennifer McIntosh, 'Cautionary Notes on the Shared Care of Children in Conflicted Parental Separation' (2008) 14(1) *Journal of Family Studies* 37; Judy Cashmore, Patrick Parkinson and Judi Single, *Shared Care Parenting Arrangements Since the 2006 Family Law Reforms* (Social Policy Research Centre, 2010); Dale Bagshaw et al, *Family Violence and Family Law in Australia; The Experiences and Views of Children and Adults from Families who Separated Post-1995 and Post-2006* (Attorney-General's Department, 2010); see also above n 31 for the issues that led to the 2011 amendments.

127   s 61DA(2) provides: '[t]he presumption does not apply if there are reasonable grounds to believe that a parent of the child (or a person who lives with a parent of the child) has engaged in: (a) abuse of the child or another child who, at the time, was a member of the parent's family (or that other person's family); or (b) family violence'.

128   See, eg, Richard Chisholm, *Family Courts Violence Review* (Attorney General's Department, 2009); ALRC, above n 73 and NSW Law Reform Commission, *Family Violence – A National Legal Response*, Report No 128 (2010).

However, the normative effect of the presumption of shared parental responsibility pro-vision has been greater than the provisions aimed at protecting children from violence. That is, the legislative design uses two distinct matters in s 60CC – one related to the presumption that equal shared parental responsibility is applicable and the second that the child needs to be protected from abuse, neglect or violence.[129] This may be so even after the 2011 amendments, which direct the court to give greater weight to the need to protect the child (s 60CC(2A)). The main contentious issue that remains after the 2011 amendments is that the FLA continues to uphold the concept of equal shared parental responsibility as a rebuttable presumption and has not adopted a stronger position that the presumption does not apply in cases of violence or abuse at all.[130] This is not a claim of *mala fides* on the part of the leg-islature. Instead, the point of this critique is to demonstrate how the desire to maintain the primacy of the conception of the two-parent family is incompatible with protecting children from violence, and the legislation may still need to reconcile these issues.

Moreover, the normative and cumulative effect of these provisions is problematic as the legislative message against violence is enmeshed in the FLA's preference for private settle-ment of disputes. For example, even though the legislation contains safeguards against violence, detection of violence is imperfect.[131] One consequence of the non-detection of family violence is that the targets of violence engage in FDR processes with all the attendant drawbacks. But even if they are exempted from engaging in FDR, they still have to navigate the legislative regime that re-emphasises FDR at the level of court proceedings, and the leg-islation clubs together equal shared parental responsibility and protection from violence or abuse as primary considerations.

For instance, if the parties come to court without having a certificate from a FDRP because one of the exceptions in s 60I(9) applies, the court must consider whether an order should be made for the parties to attend FDR (s 60I(10)). In case the exception in s 60I(9)(b) applies – that is, there is violence or risk of violence and therefore the parties are not required to participate in FDR – the court cannot hear the application unless the applicant explains in writing that he or she received information about the services, including non-court options, available to them (s 60J(1)). If the applicant did not receive such information, the court must refer him or her to a family counsellor or FDRP to receive such information (s 60J(4)). It seems that only if s 60J(2) applies can the applicant avoid these provisions, and that depends on the court being satisfied on reasonable grounds that there is 'a risk of abuse of a child if there is a delay in applying for the order', or 'there is a risk of family violence by one of the parties to the proceedings'.

---

129   When initially enacted, these provisions were supplemented by the so-called 'friendly parent' provision and the possibility that a parent could be ordered to pay costs if his or her allegation of family violence was not proven (ss 60CC(3)(c) and 117AB). For a critique, see Tracey de Simone, 'The Friendly Parent Provisions in Australian Family Law: How Friendly Will You Need to Be?' (2008) 22(1) *Australian Journal of Family Law* 56.

130   The other salient changes in the 2011 amendments include a more expansive definition of family violence; inclusion of examples of family violence; a more expansive definition of child abuse; repeal of the friendly parent provision; and a costs provision regarding false statements.

131   This is notwithstanding the valiant efforts of the Family Court in this regard. For example, in the Family Court of Australia, *Annual Report* (2014–2015) 19, it is explained that a screening tool is being trialled and that 'there are comprehensive professional directions for family consultants regarding the assessment of violence risks. These outline a clear, stepwise, and prescriptive process that clinical staff must undertake when addressing family violence during assessments'.

We acknowledge that the FLA is exceptionally strong in its efforts to create the setting for courts to follow child-friendly practices as detailed above in the discussion of procedural matters. However, it is important to recognise the discursive strategies used by the legislation and by the judiciary that make it difficult to question the disassociation of the rights of the child and the interests of the parents. It is evident that the provisions regarding the presumption of equal shared parental responsibility and time allocation are completely entwined with each other. Rathus,[132] in a persuasive analysis of these provisions, points out two particularly noteworthy issues: that the idea of the presumption functions as though it reflects a truth rather than being a legal construction; and that the inevitable understanding in the community, as well as among judges, is that if the presumption applies an order for equal time will follow. The language of the provisions is sufficiently complex for the message that shared parental responsibility is the norm to prevail, despite there being exceptions and provisos in other related provisions.

The design of the FLA provisions for conducting child-related proceedings and the institutional responses of the court in cases of violence are in many respects path-breaking, but may not be sufficient to protect the child. This is partly because of a reluctance to admit that the child may not be an autonomous actor because of their closely connected relationships with both parents. Further complications arise in cases of alleged abuse. Courts dealing with family disputes simply do not have the mechanisms to assess the existence of abuse. It takes us to the unfortunate consequences of the divide between child protection being a State matter and parenting disputes falling within the ambit of the FLA.

8.6   Child abuse, child-welfare laws and the FLA

The FLA has long treated abuse of the child (understood as sexual abuse) as a serious matter,[133] and has progressively treated abuse, violence and neglect as belonging to a spectrum, rather than as separate issues.[134] The three main issues discussed below are the changes in the judicial and legislative emphases in regard to child abuse and family violence; the jurisdictional complexity produced by the intersection of State/Territory laws on child welfare and the FLA; and the inability of the courts in a family matter to determine whether sexual abuse has been established.

Initially, and for some time after the FLA was enacted, family violence was treated as an issue affecting the adult parties and not the children. Combined with the emphasis on no

---

132   Zoe Rathus, 'Social Science or "Lego-Science"? Presumptions, Politics, Parenting and the New Family Law' (2010) 10(2) *Queensland University of Technology Law and Justice Journal* 164.

133   The FLA introduced a definition of 'child abuse' in 1991 (s 60D(1)).

134   The expanded definition of abuse in relation to a child in s 4(1) is: '(a) an assault, including a sexual assault, of the child; or (b) a person (the *first person*) involving the child in a sexual activity with the first person or another person in which the child is used, directly or indirectly, as a sexual object by the first person or the other person, and where there is unequal power in the relationship between the child and the first person; or (c) causing the child to suffer serious psychological harm, including (but not limited to) when that harm is caused by the child being subjected to, or exposed to, family violence; or (d) serious neglect of the child'. Further elaboration of what constitutes family violence is provided in s 4AB(1), namely: 'family violence means violent, threatening or other behaviour by a person that coerces or controls a member of the person's family (the *family member*), or causes the family member to be fearful'.

fault as the guiding idea for dealing with matters related to separation, it resulted in courts being reticent to accept that violent conduct of a parent was relevant in deciding matters of child custody and access.[135] In later decisions, the Family Court adopted the view that family violence is a significant factor in deciding what living arrangements are in the best interests of the child, or enhance the child's welfare.[136]

The trend changed in the opposite direction with the introduction of the concept of parental responsibility in the 1995 amendments and the child's 'right of contact' with both parents in the 2006 amendments. The latter provisions helped create the situation where greater emphasis was placed on both parents being involved in the care of the child, even when the parents had separated. One consequence of this was that allegations of violence and abuse were to be scrutinised in the wider context of the FLA, where the involvement of both parents in the child's life was given priority. This was despite the 2006 amendments including two primary considerations in determining the best interests of the child: to maintain a meaningful relationship between the child and both parents; and to protect the child from abuse, neglect and family violence (s 60CC). The priority given to maintaining the two-parent family was evident in how the legislative attempts to protect children were themselves undermined by other legislative provisions that aimed to ensure that a parent facilitated contact with the other parent (the 'friendly parent' provision), and which could be used to penalise a parent who alleged violence or abuse but could not prove it (see also Chapter 4).

This latter provision was severely criticised for assuming that women make false allegations of violence and abuse and for effacing the difficulties faced by targets of violence to even report violence.[137] It was also contrary to the empirical evidence. For instance, a review of the international literature on child abuse allegations in the context of family disputes found that generally the proportion of cases involving allegations of child abuse was low, but it was relatively more in high-conflict cases.[138] Moreover, deliberately false allegations of abuse were found to be relatively low, fathers are more likely to make false allegations, and allegations made by mothers are more likely to be substantiated.[139] It was, therefore, disappointing that the legislation assumed that false allegations of abuse were the problem. This is an illustration of how gender stereotypes find expression in legislation, and why awareness of the mechanisms used in the construction of legal knowledge is necessary for all legal actors, starting with students of law. Eventually the 2011 amendments repealed these provisions, but the FLA has retained the two primary considerations in s 60CC, and although the court is to now give greater weight to protecting the child from violence and abuse under this section, this does not necessarily preclude a court from making an order maintaining contact between the child and a violent or abusive parent.

---

135   See, eg, *In the Marriage of Chandler* (1981) 6 Fam LR 736.
136   See, eg, see *In the Marriage of G* (1994) 18 Fam LR 255; *In the Marriage of Patsalou* [1995] FLC 92-580. See also Helen Rhoades, Charlotte Frew and Shurlee Swain, 'Recognition of Violence in the Australian Family Law System: A Long Journey' (2010) 24(3) *Australian Journal of Family Law* 296; Lisa Young, Sandeep Dhillon and Laura Groves, 'Child Sexual Abuse Allegations and s 60CC(2A): A New Era?' (2014) 28(3) *Australian Journal of Family Law* 233.
137   See, eg, Merrilyn McDonald, 'The Myth of Epidemic False Allegations of Sexual Abuse in Divorce Cases' (1998) 35(1) *Court Review* 12; Lawrie Moloney et al, *Allegations of Family Violence and Child Abuse in Family Law Children's Proceedings: A Pre-reform Exploratory Study*, Research Report No 15 (AIFS, 2007) ch 1.
138   Moloney et al, above n 137, ch 2.
139   Ibid.

State and Territory laws apply in matters of child protection and thus the FLA and State/ Territory laws coexist, but at times operate in a non-coordinated and fragmented manner. The FLA imposes a duty to report abuse on a diverse number of people. For example, parties to proceedings must inform the court of the existence of a family violence order relating to the child or a member of the child's family (s 60CF(1)), while a person not a party to the proceedings may inform the court of the existence of such an order (s 60CF(2)). A party to the proceedings must also inform the court that he or she is aware that the child, or another child who is a member of the child's family, is under the care of a person under child-welfare law (s 60CH(1)), or has been the subject of a notification, report, investigation or inquiry of a prescribed State or Territory agency (s 60CI(1)). A person who is not a party to the proceedings may also inform the court of these circumstances (ss 60CH(2) and s 60CI(2)). However, any failure to inform the court under ss 60CF, 60CI or 60CH does not affect the validity of any order made by the court.

If any court personnel (registrars), family counsellor, family dispute resolution practitioners or arbitrators suspect child abuse, they may notify a prescribed child-welfare authority of their suspicion and the basis for it (s 67ZA).[140] If an interested person (for example, a party to the proceedings or ICL) makes an allegation of child abuse (s 67Z) or family violence (s 67ZBA), he or she must file a notice with the court and arrange for it to be served on the person who is the alleged abuser (ss 67Z(2) and s 67ZBA(2) respectively).[141] The ALRC report, *Family Violence*, illustrates the problems of such an uncoordinated approach. Among other things the report mentions that:

> there is a division of jurisdiction in Australia between states and territories as administrators of the public domains of criminal and child protection laws, and the federal family courts as adjudicators of private law disputes. Inadequate communication, coordination or information sharing between courts and child protection agencies has been identified as a critical problem.[142]

It also reports that the authors of an Australian study argue that the competing discourses of child protection and family violence create difficult dilemmas for women.[143]

Similarly, the response of the courts to allegations of child abuse is problematic. The High Court in *M v M* continues to be the authority for the view that it is not the task of the Family Court to determine whether a parent has abused the child.[144] This view has been endorsed by later cases.[145] The Court held that it is the role of a criminal court to determine

---

140   In comparable circumstances judges, magistrates and lawyers (except ICLs) have no obligation to report to the child-welfare authority.

141   The notice must be in accordance with Form 4, *Family Law Rules 2004* (Cth) r 2.04E. The court has the obligation to take prompt action in relation to allegations of child abuse or family violence (s 67ZBB).

142   ALRC, above n 73 [19.34].

143   Ibid [19.36], quoting Heather Douglas and Tamara Walsh, 'Mothers, Domestic Violence and Child Protection' (2010) 16(5) *Violence Against Women* 489.

144   (1988) 166 CLR 69. For examples of assessment of risk, see *Napier v Hepburn* (2006) 36 Fam LR 395; *Potter v Potter* [2007] FLC 93-326.

145   See *Johnson v Page* [2007] FLC 93-344 for a summary of the main points. See also Richard Chisholm, 'Child Abuse Allegations in Family Law Cases: A Review of the Law' (2011) 25(1) *Australian Journal of Family Law* 1.

the criminal issues, and the Family Court's task is to ascertain whether there is an unaccept-able risk of harm to the child in a particular arrangement of access and custody. In coming to these conclusions, the Court found that the Family Court has the responsibility to balance the risk of harm with the desirability of the child maintaining contact with both parents. The Court also found that the focus of the Family Court should not be on proving abuse in the past, but rather on the future arrangements that do not expose the child to unaccept-able risk. The main task of the Family Court is to determine what is in the best interests of the child, and that matter cannot be subservient to the resolution of an allegation of sexual abuse on the balance of probabilities.[146]

It is understandable that the High Court requires the Family Court to focus on its primary task of pursuing the best interests of the child rather than acting as a criminal court. However, the ability of the court to judge what is unacceptable risk is assumed rather than established. While it is true that an unsubstantiated allegation is not the same as a false allegation,[147] the issue remains whether judges are the only reliable authorities who can determine the truth or future risk.[148] This is another illustration of how courts assume the mantle of infallibility with regard to children because, ultimately, what constitutes unacceptable risk is entirely dependent on the assessment of the particular judge. The fundamental issue remains that courts and the legislation are committed to the two-parent model as the basis of a normal childhood.

8.7   Conclusion

There is considerable academic commentary on the input of men's rights groups in bring-ing about the 1995 and 2006 amendments to FLA.[149] It is instructive to follow these analyses to understand how legislative formulations come into existence, but there is also a need to acknowledge that all legislation follows value preferences of some kind. Thus, the argument that the 2006 amendments pursue the agenda of men's groups is only the first step in asking why that is a problem. It needs to be linked with identifying whether the assumptions made in the FLA result in justice or fairness for everyone. Moreover, as Collier argues, the attention in the literature on the disproportionate influence of fathers' rights groups focuses on the deploy-ment of the analytical category of 'masculinity', but in the process effaces broader questions about the development of a political, economic and materialist analysis of gendered labour.[150] However, this inquiry is effectively silenced by the rhetoric that child-related decisions are decided by reference to what is in the best interests of the child and not by any other values.

What is not asked is whether it is, or should be, the aim of family law to be fair to every-one. In a liberal system it is a basic tenet that everyone is to be treated as an end in himself

---

146   There is extensive scholarship on this issue. For an introduction, see Alastair Nicholson, 'Child Sexual Abuse – Problems in Family Law' (1989) 4 *Australian Family Lawyer* 1.

147   McDonald, above n 137.

148   See also John Fogarty, 'Unacceptable Risk: A Return to Basics' (2006) 20(3) *Australian Journal of Family Law* 249 for a critique of the standard of balance of probabilities used by the High Court. However, we argue that the more problematic issue is that the High Court ultimately did not apply a standard of proof.

149   See references above n 32.

150   Richard Collier, 'Feminist Legal Studies and the Subject(s) of Men: Questions of Text, Terrain and Context in the Politics of Family Law and Gender' in Alison Diduck and Katherine O'Donovan (eds), *Feminist Perspectives on Family Law* (Routledge-Cavendish, 2006) 235.

or herself rather than as a means to someone else's ends. This basic premise is, however, not relevant when a child has to be protected and provided for, as notions of moral responsibility for children demand that.[151] But there is no plausible reason why, in protecting the interests of the child, the interests of parents, or the interests of one parent rather than the other, should be ignored. Therefore, we argue that it is not fair that women's work or contributions as primary carers are effaced in the introduction of the presumption of equal shared parental responsibility. As we saw in chapters 5 and 6, women become financially dependent because they undertake care work. That the law at the end of a relationship turns around and says that as a father and a mother both are to exercise equal shared parental responsibility denies the social and cultural realities of how care work is primarily performed by women.

It is evident that the FLA seeks to disassociate the 'best interests of the child' principle from its social and cultural context.[152] At the stage of child-related decision-making, to frame the issue as one which is about the best interests of the child deploys the idea that children can be treated as independent of their parents. That is, the law can determine what is in their best interests without having to also consider what is in the interests of the parents who are supposed to care for these children. A defining feature of liberal legal thinking is its use of the concept of the legal subject as an independent and autonomous being. Thus, the idea of the child's interests as independent of the parents' interests comes easily to legal thinkers.[153] The ambiguity of the child not being a full legal subject is handled by invoking ideas about the autonomy of the child.[154] However, in the process the law assumes the competing function as the guardian of the interests of the child.

In listing the above problems with various aspects of the law relating to children, we do acknowledge the valiant efforts made by the legislature and courts in making child-related proceedings sensitive to the needs of children. However, we also argue that the discursive device of separating the child from the parents is not working fairly. It is highly problematic for the law to assume that the child can find protection in a law that seeks to protect the child from his or her parents while simultaneously encouraging an ongoing relationship between the child and both parents. Moreover, the recurring emphasis of the legislation and cases on maintaining contact with both parents creates a disjuncture between the social and legal realities. It also functions to legitimise the idea of a proper childhood as requiring the involvement of two parents. Thus, the FLA pursues the ideal of the nuclear family in the name of the best interests of the child.

---

151   Harry Brighouse and Adam Swift, *The Ethics of Parent-Child Relationships* (Princeton University Press, 2014).

152   But similar ideas have been part of the family law discourse since the enactment of the FLA in 1975. Courts have also been unequivocal in saying that the 'best interests of the child' principle requires that no other consideration determines the issue. For example, in *In the Marriage of Smythe* (1983) 8 Fam LR 1029 (Evatt CJ, Asche SJ and Gee J) the Full Court held that, even when the welfare of the child is evenly balanced, it is not permissible to refer to notions of justice between the parties.

153   It is critiqued by feminist thinkers for denying the understanding of motherhood and pregnancy as a symbiotic rather than an antagonistic relationship. See, eg, Amy Mullin, *Reconceiving Pregnancy and Childcare: Ethics, Experience, and Reproductive Labor* (Cambridge University Press, 2005); Laura Purdy, 'Are Pregnant Women Fetal Containers?' (1990) 4(4) *Bioethics* 273.

154   Amy Mullin, 'Children, Autonomy and Care' (2007) 38(4) *Journal of Social Philosophy* 536; Amy Mullin, 'Children, Paternalism and the Development of Autonomy' (2014) 17(3) *Ethical Theory and Moral Practice* 413.

9

CHILDREN IN COURT PROCEEDINGS

9.1   Introduction

Despite a significant shift to family mediation in family law, not all child-related disputes are resolved through these processes. Indeed, family mediation may not be appropriate in all cases. Thus, family courts continue to maintain a role in determining child-related disputes. In this chapter the focus is on a selection of different factors that could affect the making of a parenting order which, pursuant to s 60CA of the *Family Law Act 1975* (Cth) ('FLA'), requires that 'a court must regard the best interests of the child as the paramount consideration'.

Changing perceptions of family are evident in how the courts take into account a range of factors in determining what is in the child's best interests. Section 60CC provides a detailed set of factors that must be considered to determine the child's best interests. As we saw in the previous chapter, a set of primary considerations was introduced in the *Family Law Amendment (Shared Parental Responsibility) Act 2006* (Cth) ('2006 amendments'). Simultaneously, the factors that were listed in the earlier legislation (s 68F(2)) are now listed as additional factors (s 60CC(3)). We examine these additional factors and primarily illustrate how these factors allow the court to be the final arbiter of what constitutes a normal childhood.

The discussion below focuses on selective case law involving the child's views (formerly the child's wishes), cases involving an Aboriginal or Torres Strait Islander child, parenting disputes involving a gay or lesbian parent, as well as disputes involving relocation of the primary child-caring parent. In our examination of these cases, we will revisit the question of the norm-setting function of family law raised in previous chapters. These cases also serve to illustrate the opposite pulls of paternalism, which informs the concept of the child's best interests, and liberalism, which treats the child as an autonomous being. In resolving these cases, the court inevitably functions as the conduit for channelling into family law certain values which reflect the nuclear family norm.

This discussion is followed by an examination of the provisions regulating cases involving child abduction and the enforcement of parenting orders. Our examination demonstrates how the regulatory aspects interact with considerations of the best interests principle. In the area of child abduction, the interests of the parents and children get enmeshed within the international law regime to normalise the concept of the nuclear family. Similar norm-setting functions are performed by the order enforcement regime of the FLA. It is designed to educate parents about their responsibilities arising from parenting orders and also to impose sanctions for breaches of such orders.

9.2   Jurisdiction of family courts under the FLA

As explained in the previous chapter, courts have historically assumed jurisdiction for the welfare of children and in the common law this power of the court can be traced to the *parens patriae* jurisdiction. The court's jurisdiction in Part VII of the FLA is more specific but includes a 'welfare power' (s 67ZC). Owing to constraints arising from the division of State and federal powers under the *Constitution*, the FLA initially applied only to the children of the marriage (see Chapter 2). Eventually the referral of powers by the States (except Western

Australia) to the Commonwealth resulted in the extension of the FLA to cover all children. The two major exceptions are in the areas of adoption and child welfare, where the States have retained their powers. With this proviso it can be said that the provisions of the FLA regulate the determination of issues related to the best interests of all children. However, despite the wide reach of the FLA and the discretion provided to the courts exercising jurisdiction under it, some children are excluded from this protection of the law. The FLA does not always assume exclusive jurisdiction over a child, as will be evident in the following discussion.

Children in immigration detention are among the most vulnerable children. The Family Court has tried to respond to their needs, but unsuccessfully. This is partly because of the legislative constraints, but it is also a manifestation of how family courts cannot change the broader legal culture as often manifested in the decisions of the High Court. For example, the facts in *AI and AA v Minister for Immigration and Multicultural and Indigenous Affairs* exposed the impact of long-term detention on adults and the resultant impact on children who were exposed for prolonged periods to their parents' distress and poor mental health.[1] The Family Court acknowledged that these children would remain at serious risk unless they were released into the community. However, the Court found that it lacked the authority or the power to release the children. Instead, it urged the Minister to give urgent and compassionate consideration to allow appropriate measures to be taken to release the children from detention.

B and B v Minister for Immigration & Multicultural and Indigenous Affairs concerned an application by a mother on behalf of her two sons (later joined by their three younger sisters and their father as intervenor) for the children's release from immigration detention where they were being held.[2] The applicant children sought orders from the Family Court in the exercise its welfare powers under s 67ZC for their release on the basis that detention was harmful to their welfare. The trial judge found that the Family Court lacked jurisdiction, as the welfare power was not completely unfettered or wide enough to bind the Minister. On appeal, the Full Court found the Family Court did have jurisdiction and, among other things, found that the welfare power to protect children was not confined to orders directed at parents or people *in loco parentis* where the orders sought were sufficiently connected to the relevant constitutional heads of power (in this case the marriage and divorce powers in the *Constitution*). The Court further held that the indefinite detention of the children was unlawful, but, even if that were not the case, the Court could still determine issues relating to the medical and educational facilities available to them while in detention. The Minister appealed to the High Court.[3] The High Court unanimously found that the Family Court did not have jurisdiction to order the Minister to release the children.[4] Inter alia it was held that s 67ZC, when considered in the context of Part VII, is concerned with parental responsibility: the Family Court jurisdiction is confined to these issues and could not be exercised to make orders binding third parties, even if it would advance the welfare of a child.[5] This is an apt

---

1   [2003] FamCA 943.
2   (2003) 199 ALR 604 (Nicholson CJ, Ellis and O'Ryan JJ).
3   In the meantime there were further proceedings relating to interim orders for the children's release from detention: *B and B v Minister for Immigration and Multicultural and Indigenous Affairs* [2003] FamCA 621.
4   *Minister for Immigration and Multicultural and Indigenous Affairs v B* (2004) 219 CLR 365.
5   Ibid 390 [52] (Gleeson CJ and McHugh J).

illustration of how the High Court can rely on the legal distinction between the private matter of parenting and the public matter of seeking refugee status, and thus confidently deny the protection of law to the most vulnerable children.

The Full Court in other instances has held that the Family Court is prevented by s 474 of the *Migration Act 1958* (Cth) from challenging or reviewing a decision made under that Act.[6] Cumulatively these decisions illustrate how technical arguments restrict the scope of the courts exercising jurisdiction under the FLA. It is understandable that the issue of jurisdiction can be used to restrict the family law's pursuit of the child's best interests, but it is more problematic to see a similar restriction on the welfare power that is supposed to be congruent with the *parens patriae* power. It is not unreasonable to compare the response of the High Court in cases involving children in immigration detention with cases involving non-therapeutic medical procedures to be carried out on children who cannot lawfully consent to these procedures (see Chapter 8). In both contexts the authority of the court is based on the welfare power. In the cases involving medical procedures, even when there is no indication that parents are incapable of making decisions for the benefit of the child, it has been held that only the Family Court can make the decision and authorise the procedures. In other words it is only the impartial and objective judgment of the court that provides sufficient safeguards for the protection of vulnerable children. Unfortunately, the same concern does not seem to extend to children in immigration detention. This is more problematic since the overall emphasis of the courts exercising jurisdiction under the FLA is to find solutions that will benefit the child.

Thus, in a case where the father lived in the United States and the child and mother lived in Australia, the mother instituted custody and child-maintenance proceedings in a court in California. The father in turn instituted his own proceedings with respect to these matters in the Family Court of Australia and also sought to restrain the mother's application in the Californian court.[7] A preliminary issue requiring determination by the Family Court of Australia was whether the welfare of the child as the paramount principle was applicable with respect to restraining the mother's application in a foreign court. At trial, the judge allowed the father's application and restrained the mother from pursuing her claim in the Californian court. On appeal the Full Court opined that it is important to distinguish between cases that are to be decided according to the strict principle that the child's welfare is paramount, and cases in which the child's welfare is relevant but not decisive.

The Full Court held that the 'paramount consideration' principle applies when an application can be characterised as proceedings in relation to the custody, guardianship or welfare of, or access to, a child. A further issue in this case was whether child-support proceedings were also covered by the paramountcy principle. The Full Court held that the mother could pursue child-support proceedings in California, as these proceedings were not subject to the paramountcy principle and, in any event, the child would be entitled to a higher award under that law. However, since the child was born in Australia and had lived here all her life it would be out of the question to suggest that her welfare would be served by having her custody determined in a Californian court.

6　See, eg, *HR and DR and Minister for Immigration & Multicultural & Indigenous Affairs* [2003] FLC 93-156. See also Tania Penovic and Adiva Sifris, 'Children's Rights Through the Lens of Immigration Detention' (2006) 20(1) *Australian Journal of Family Law* 12.

7　*Monticelli v McTiernan* [1995] FLC 92-617 (Nicholson CJ, Fogarty and Chisholm JJ).

It is undeniable that the Court is trying to ensure that the child gets the advantage of the Californian child-support laws, but the conclusion with respect to the custody application that her welfare will not be served in the Californian court is more of an assertion than an obvious conclusion. An element of arbitrariness and indeterminacy in the interpretations of what is in the child's best interests is a recurring theme in the cases and literature. For example, the same sentiment is present in the opinion of Brennan J in *Marion's* case, where he observed that 'in the absence of legal rules or a hierarchy of values, the best interests approach depends upon the value system of the decision-maker. Absent any rule or guideline, that approach simply creates an unexaminable discretion in the repository of the power'.[8] The critique of the 'best interests of the child' principle as an indeterminate standard is well known and not discussed here.[9] Instead, our approach is to identify the particular ways that indeterminacy is maintained.

We argue that the legislative design of the FLA, which provides a checklist of additional factors to the courts in determining the child's best interests, functions to make the courts the final arbiters of what is good for children. This is not a problem in itself, because when parents cannot decide, some other person or body has to step in. We are not critiquing the authority of the courts to decide per se, but *how* they decide. This brings into focus the legislative norms and other mechanisms of legal reasoning that the courts use. The following discussion explores the legislative provision of a non-hierarchical list of additional factors used in determining the child's best interests and how the courts exercise their wide discretion in applying these factors. We acknowledge the insights of Mnookin,[10] even though made some time ago, that in determining the child's best interests the courts are expected to make person-oriented determinations, while also trying to predict the future. It is thus not easy to determine whether the courts are providing the right answers or pragmatic answers. Moreover, it is difficult to ascertain whether the courts actually decide each case as a unique case or whether they are influenced by certain values – for example, two parents are preferable to one parent.[11] In identifying these issues the point is not to suggest that the courts are biased or less than objective, but to emphasise that we are the products of the contexts we inhabit. That the values of judges can find expression in their judicial pronouncements of what may constitute the best interests of a child is a consequence of the standard being an indeterminate standard.[12] The suggestion that the indeterminacy of family law is being reduced as indicated by the general trend towards more rights-based

---

8 *Secretary, Department of Health and Community Services v JWB and SMB* ('*Marion's* case') (1992) 175 CLR 218, 271. For an introduction to the literature and issues see Susan M Brady and Sonia Grover, *The Sterilisation of Girls and Young Women in Australia – A Legal, Medical and Social Context* (Human Rights and Equal Opportunity Commission, 1997).

9 Robert Mnookin, 'Child Custody Adjudication: Judicial Functions in the Face of Indeterminacy' (1975) 39(3) *Law and Contemporary Problems* 226. For a contemporary analysis of issues relating to the standard of the best interests of the child (hereafter 'BIC'), see articles in (2014) 77 *Law and Contemporary Problems*. See also Michael Freeman, 'Article 3: The Best Interests of the Child' in A Alen et al (eds), *A Commentary on the United Nations Convention on the Rights of the Child* (Martinus Nijhoff Publishers, 2007) 11.

10 Mnookin, above n 9.

11 David Bradley, 'Homosexuality and Child Custody in English Law' (1987) 1(2) *International Journal of Law and Family* 155, 186.

12 Helen Reece, 'Paramountcy Principle: Consensus or Construct?' (1996) 49(1) *Current Legal Problems* 267, 295–6.

family laws[13] may also apply to the FLA, especially since the 2006 amendments introduced more prescriptive rules on how to determine the child's best interests. However, we argue that the introduction of more prescriptive rules coexists with the very wide discretion still available to judges.

9.2.1   History of the 'best interests of the child' principle in the FLA

The *Family Law Reform Act 1995* (Cth) ('1995 amendments') introduced the 'best interests' principle and replaced the welfare principle that previously applied.[14] The 2006 amendments incorporate a number of objectives and principles that a court must use when making a parenting order.[15] Section 60CA provides that a court, when deciding to make a particular parenting order, must have regard to the best interests of the child as the paramount consideration. There are circumstances where the court does not have to use child's best interests as the paramount consideration, but even in those matters a child's interests are treated as an important matter.[16]

The main change introduced by the 2006 amendments was the rebuttable presumption that it is in the best interests of the child for both parents to have equal shared parental responsibility (s 61DA). This may be understood as an effort to give more definite legislative content to the concept of the child's best interests. Thus, there is a continuation from before that, whenever a court makes a parenting order, the best interests of the child is the paramount principle.[17] But it must be borne in mind that the legal presumption is that shared parental responsibility is in the best interests of the child, and this can only be rebutted on the basis of a few grounds.[18] The following discussion illustrates the norm-setting function of the presumption of equal shared parental responsibility and how this norm is filtered through the exercise of judicial discretion.

---

13   See John Dewar, 'Family Law and its Discontents' (2000) 14(1) *International Journal of Law, Policy and the Family* 59, 68.

14   The 1995 amendments to Part VII of the FLA were partly to discharge Australia's obligations under the *Convention on the Rights of the Child*, opened for signature 20 November 1989, 1577 UNTS 3 (entered into force 2 September 1990); when enacted originally the FLA did not contain a list of factors that would guide the court in determining the best interests of the child.

15   Parenting orders can deal with any of the matters in s 64B(2) and make an order allocating responsibility for long-term issues (s 64B(3)).

16   See *B v B* [2003] FLC 93-136, where it was held that the 'best interests of the child' principle does not govern various procedural and jurisdictional matters in parenting proceedings, though it may be a relevant and, in some cases, the most important matter.

17   This principle has existed in the FLA from its inception although in different sections and with minor linguistic modifications. Originally, the only specification was that the court must give effect to the wishes of a child 14 years of age or above. The 1983 amendments added detailed factors to be taken into account by the court. The 1995 amendments specified when the best interests of the child are to be a paramount consideration. The scope of the best interests of the child as the paramount consideration has been discussed in various cases.

18   See Chapter 8.

9.2.2   How a court determines what is in the child's best interests

In deciding what orders should be made in the child's best interests, the court must consider all the factors set out in s 60CC and the objects and principles in s 60B. The primary and additional considerations are included in s 60CC(2) and (3) respectively. The previous chapter discussed the primary considerations, which are the benefit of the child having a meaningful relationship with both parents,[19] and the need to protect the child from abuse, neglect or family violence. The primary considerations mirror the first two objectives in s 60B. In this chapter the discussion focuses on the additional considerations for determining the child's best interests.

It is often said that the relationship between the primary and additional considerations is not supposed to be hierarchical.[20] In the absence of clear guidance in the legislation, one option is to examine the relevant cases in order to determine how the courts have interpreted the relationship between the primary and additional considerations.[21] On the one hand, it has been observed that, for the purposes of applying the primary considerations, it is necessary to make findings of fact, which may involve making findings in relation to one or more of the discrete matters listed in the additional considerations.[22] On the other hand, it has been found that, although the legislation asks the court to consider all the factors mentioned in s 60CC, it does not mean each should be discussed.[23] So too in a recent decision related to the making of interim orders, the Full Family Court engaged in a 'discussion of the most relevant of the "additional considerations" in s 60CC(3) by reference to the proposals' of the parties.[24] Therefore, despite the legislation not specifying a hierarchical relation between the two sets of considerations, it is only to be expected that the judges will have to weigh different considerations differently. Thus, one function of the judicial discretion could be to privilege the two-parent family without having to say so.

The list of factors that are included as additional considerations is wide ranging. In the following discussion, we have not included all additional considerations. Instead, a few selected cases serve as examples of how the courts use the list of factors for making a decision about what is in the child's best interests. Moreover, these are decisions made in the exercise of discretion by the courts and their precedent value remains minimal. However, they provide a good illustration of how, despite the presence of wide-ranging additional factors, the two-parent family is privileged in the case law in the name of the best interests of the child.

---

19   See *Mazorski v Albright* (2007) 37 Fam LR 518 for the view that a meaningful relationship is one which is important, significant and valuable for the child.

20   See also *Slater v Light* (2011) 45 Fam LR 41 for the view that the primary considerations do not trump additional considerations.

21   See *Marsden v Winch (No 3)* [2007] FamCA 1364 for the observation that all considerations must be considered, but with special emphasis on primary considerations.

22   See *Nawaqaliva v Marshall* [2006] FLC 93-296.

23   *SCVG v KLD* (2014) 51 Fam LR 340. See also *Banks and Banks* [2015] FamCAFC 36, [49] (Thackray, Murphy and Kent JJ), where the Court found that the 'requirement to "consider" each factor does not mean each must be discussed'.

24   *Banks and Banks* [2015] FamCAFC 36, [61].

9.3   Determining the best interests of the child – particular issues

The additional considerations listed in s 60CC(3) can be summarised as follows to include the views of the child; the nature of the child's relationship with each parent, and others (including grandparents or other relatives); the level of cooperation between parents; the likely effect of any changes in the child's circumstances, including the likely effect on the child of any separation from either of their parents, or any other child or person (including grandparent or other relative) with whom the child has been living; the practical difficulty and expense of a child spending time and communicating with a parent; the capacity of each parent to provide for a child; the maturity, gender, lifestyle and background of the child and parents (including Aboriginal or Torres Strait Islander culture); the parental attitude towards child and parental responsibilities; family violence involving the child or a member of the child's family; and whether it would be preferable to make an order least likely to lead to the institution of further proceedings in relation to the child.[25]

We use cases discussing the relevance of the views of a child, the significance of a child's Aboriginal or Torres Strait Islander culture, the sexuality of a parent and the relocation of a primary caregiving parent as examples that illustrate how societal ideas about the ideal conditions for the upbringing of a child find their way into family law through the exercise

---

25   Section 60CC(3) Additional considerations are: '(a) any views expressed by the child and any factors (such as the child's maturity or level of understanding) that the court thinks are relevant to the weight it should give to the child's views; (b) the nature of the relationship of the child with: (i) each of the child's parents; and (ii) other persons (including any grandparent or other relative of the child); (c) the extent to which each of the child's parents has taken, or failed to take, the opportunity: (i) to participate in making decisions about major long-term issues in relation to the child; and (ii) to spend time with the child; and (iii) to communicate with the child; (ca) the extent to which each of the child's parents has fulfilled, or failed to fulfil, the parent's obligations to maintain the child; (d) the likely effect of any changes in the child's circumstances, including the likely effect on the child of any separation from: (i) either of his or her parents; or (ii) any other child, or other person (including any grandparent or other relative of the child), with whom he or she has been living; (e) the practical difficulty and expense of a child spending time with and communicating with a parent and whether that difficulty or expense will substantially affect the child's right to maintain personal relations and direct contact with both parents on a regular basis; (f) the capacity of: (i) each of the child's parents; and (ii) any other person (including any grandparent or other relative of the child); to provide for the needs of the child, including emotional and intellectual needs; (g) the maturity, sex, lifestyle and background (including lifestyle, culture and traditions) of the child and of either of the child's parents, and any other characteristics of the child that the court thinks are relevant; (h) if the child is an Aboriginal child or a Torres Strait Islander child: (i) the child's right to enjoy his or her Aboriginal or Torres Strait Islander culture (including the right to enjoy that culture with other people who share that culture); and (ii) the likely impact any proposed parenting order under this Part will have on that right; (i) the attitude to the child, and to the responsibilities of parenthood, demonstrated by each of the child's parents; (j) any family violence involving the child or a member of the child's family; (k) if a family violence order applies, or has applied, to the child or a member of the child's family – any relevant inferences that can be drawn from the order, taking into account the following: (i) the nature of the order; (ii) the circumstances in which the order was made; (iii) any evidence admitted in proceedings for the order; (iv) any findings made by the court in, or in proceedings for, the order; (v) any other relevant matter; (l) whether it would be preferable to make the order that would be least likely to lead to the institution of further proceedings in relation to the child; (m) any other fact or circumstance that the court thinks is relevant'.

of judicial discretion. It needs reiterating that the following discussion is focused on exposing the values underpinning the legislative rules and the mechanisms of legal reasoning that infuse the exercise of judicial discretion and shape judicial decision-making. In particular, our emphasis is on analysing the mechanism of legal reasoning rather than criticising judges for making particular choices.

9.3.1   Child's wishes/views

The views of the child have always been a relevant consideration in determining what is in the child's best interests.[26] This consideration is often seen as evidence that family law accords agency to the child. The FLA now provides that the court *must* consider any views that are expressed by the child and apply such weight as is appropriate in the circumstances, having regard to the child's age and degree of maturity (ss 60CC(3)(a) and 60CD(1)). Initially, this consideration was framed in terms of the 'wishes of the child'. However, the cumulative effect of the legislative design, the manner in which courts determine how much weight should be given to the child's views, and the mechanisms for ascertaining the child's views is that the court, and not the child, has the power to decide what weight to give to the child's views.

Significantly, when the FLA was first enacted it specified that a court should make an order in conformity with the wishes of a child who had attained 14 years of age. It was possible for the court to go against the wishes of such a child in exceptional circumstances if the court was satisfied that compelling special circumstances were present. The legislation was modified by the *Family Law Amendment Act 1983* (Cth) to remove the specific reference to the age of 14 years and further to provide that a child could not be compelled to express his or her wishes. Whether these changes represent recognition of the rights of the child, or a curtailment of them, is an open question.

On the one hand, it could be argued that, in the light of the *Gillick* principle,[27] it is more useful to not specify an age at which a child would be considered mature and able to make important decisions. On the other hand, it is also possible to interpret the effect of this change as operating to give the court a greater say than the child. That is, the courts are now free to disregard the wishes or views of the child even after he or she reaches 14 years of age. Thus, it is not the recognition of the rights of the child but more a way of giving greater control over children to the court and for a longer time. In all probability, individual judges would be reluctant to override the views of a 'mature' child, but the issue we wish to emphasise is how the legislative design seems to be moving in the direction of giving greater control to the judge than to the 'mature' child.

This change also goes against the global trend in criminal law to pin ever-greater responsibility on the child at an increasingly younger age.[28] Thus the contrary pulls of

---

26   There is extensive literature in this area. For an introduction, see Christine Hallett and Alan Prout, *Hearing the Voices of Children: Social Policy for a New Century* (Routledge, 2003). For the various mechanisms available to the court to ascertain the views of the child, see the discussion of court personnel in Chapter 8.

27   *Gillick v West Norfolk and Wisbech Area Health Authority* [1985] 3 All ER 402. For a discussion from a medical perspective, see Richard Griffith, 'What is Gillick Competence?' (2016) 12(1) *Human Vaccines and Immunotherapeutics* 244.

28   Discussed in Chapter 8. See also Australian Law Reform Commission, *Seen and Heard: Priority for Children in the Legal Process*, Report No 84 (1997) ch 18.

conceptualising the child as autonomous on the one hand, and in need of special/different treatment on the other, remain unresolved. The contrary pulls between child self-determination and protection are even more starkly evident in the context of determining the child's best interests in contested parenting cases.

In *H v W*, the Full Court, in explaining the significance of the 1995 amendments relating to the wishes of the child noted how various developments indicate that the concept of the rights of children is gaining acceptance in society.[29] It cited the history of relevant legislation in Australia, the *Convention on the Rights of the Child*, the judicial formulation of the *Gillick* competency test and general developments in society as some of the indicative factors. It further opined that since there has been a perceptible change in society with regard to the wishes of the child, it is appropriate that proper and realistic weight is given to any wishes expressed by the child.

The Court went on to acknowledge the practical difficulties involved in determining how the wishes of the child could be ascertained. Furthermore, the Court found difficulty in deciding how to interpret and assess such wishes, especially in the presence of conflicting claims. It was inevitable that the Court would attach different weight to the wishes of the child depending upon how strongly such wishes were held and for how long; whether the wishes were soundly based; the level of maturity of the child; and whether the child had any appreciation of the matters before the Court and their long-term implications. The Court ultimately decided the issues in the case on the basis of the welfare of the child.

This detail of the reasoning of the Full Court helps illustrate how the wishes of the child provide one source of information in the judicial decision-making process, but it would be overstating the case to say that the voice of the child is recognised as a determinative factor. Predictably, the objection to this observation would be that no single factor is determinative of the issue of what is in the child's best interests. The point we wish to make is that a decision has to be made and the legislation is designed in a manner that means the decision-maker is the court and not the child. Even when the child is sufficiently mature and the court considers him or her to be capable of making a right choice and accepts his or her capacity to form such views, it is the court's decision to accept or not accept those views.

This continues to be the approach after the 2006 amendments. Section 60CC(3)(a) provides 'any views expressed by the child and any factors (such as the child's maturity or level of understanding) that the court thinks are relevant to the weight it should give to the child's views'. The language used reflects closely the relevant article in the *Convention on the Rights of the Child*.[30] The decision-maker is the court, and it decides what weight should be attached to such wishes. Thus, even if the wishes of the child are upheld in the final determination of the court, it is less than giving the child a voice.

As noted previously, the FLA has moved away from treating the child as an agent even after attaining 14 years of age. This protectionism is also manifest in the FLA provision that

29   [1995] FLC 92-598 (Fogarty, Baker and Kay JJ).
30   *Convention on the Rights of the Child*, above n 14, art 12: '1. States Parties shall assure to the child who is capable of forming his or her own views the right to express those views freely in all matters affecting the child, the views of the child being given due weight in accordance with the age and maturity of the child. 2. For this purpose, the child shall in particular be provided the opportunity to be heard in any judicial and administrative proceedings affecting the child, either directly, or through a representative or an appropriate body, in a manner consistent with the procedural rules of national law.'

a child cannot be required to express his or her views in determining whether to make a particular parenting order (s 60CE). Thus, the discourse about the child as someone needing the protection of the law/court is reinforced. The same can be said about the mechanisms used to ascertain the views of the child and how the court may use those views in making an order.

The court may inform itself of the views of a child by taking note of the contents of a s 62G report prepared by a family consultant (s 60CD(2)), authorising the appointment of an independent representative of the child ('ICL') (s 68L), or any other means it may consider necessary.[31] The report by the family consultant would normally include the views of the child unless in the view of the consultant it would be inappropriate to ascertain such views of the child by reason of the child's age or maturity or any other special circumstances (ss 62G(3A) and 62G(3B)). If a private person (usually a social worker, psychologist or psychiatrist) prepares a report, it is desirable that the writer indicates whether the views of the child were specifically ascertained and what weight should be attached to such views. It has been recognised for a long time that children should not be compelled to express any views and this idea continues to find expression in the legislation (s 60CE).[32] The possibility of interviewing the child by the judge in chambers existed from the beginning, but is not followed very commonly now.[33] The emphases in the legislation, the mechanisms used in court practices to ascertain the child's views, and the legal scholarship on how best to ascertain the views of the child help create the impression that the views of the child are a significant factor in the decision-making process.

Yet it is accepted practice that the views of the children are to be assessed by the court and it is for the judge to decide what weight to attach to such views. Thus, the inclusion of this consideration in the list of factors does not create autonomy for the child, and it cannot be explained as evidence of increased recognition of the rights of the child because the decision-maker remains the court charged with protecting the interests of the child. Moreover, the courts have interpreted their role as the final arbiters, and not answerable to anyone else. For example, in the case of *R v R*,[34] the Full Court specifically stated that the trial judge was not obliged to make an order in conformity with the child's wishes. Moreover, in deciding to depart from the wishes of the child, the court is not required to show that the wishes were unsound, or based on improper considerations, or made under the influence of others, although the Court simultaneously found that it must advance good reasons for not accepting the child's views.

We use the judgment in *Dylan v Dylan* as an illustration of the difficulties faced by judges in exercising discretion in deciding what weight to give to the views of children who in this

---

31   See also the significant advances made in the procedural aspects of conducting child-related matters: *Less Adversarial Trial Handbook* (1 June 2009) Family Court of Australia <http://www .familycourt.gov.au/wps/wcm/connect/fcoaweb/reports-and-publications/reports/2009/LAT>.

32   See, eg, *In the Marriage of Ahmad* [1979] FLC 90-633 (Asche, Marshall SJJ and Tonge J), where the Full Court was particularly critical of the children being questioned in the open court and in the presence of both parents.

33   *ZN v YH* [2002] FLC 93-101. See also Michelle Fernando, 'What do Australian Family Law Judges Think about Meeting with Children?' (2012) 26(1) *Australian Journal of Family Law* 51; Kristin Natalier and Belinda Fehlberg, 'Children's Experiences of "Home" and "Homemaking" After Parents Separate: A New Conceptual Frame for Listening and Supporting Adjustment' (2015) 29(2) *Australian Journal of Family Law* 111.

34   [2000] FLC 93-000 (Nicholson CJ, Finn and Guest JJ).

case were aged 15 and 10 years.[35] The main contentious issue before the appeal court was that the trial judge, Carmody J, had decided against the views of the children in making an order that more time should be spent with the father. In reaching this decision, the Court had also disregarded the views of various experts. The trial judge held that the weight to be given to a child's views was dependent on a range of factors, which included the child's age and maturity; whether they had any protective needs; the views of siblings in situations where keeping them together appeared desirable; and the possibility of a long-term relationship with a parent towards whom the child at present seemed to be resentful.

The trial judge said among other things that his judgment and conscience told him that, despite what the children think or believe, they should be spending more time with their father than they currently do. This view was contrary to the recommendations of the ICL, the family reporter and the child psychiatrist, but in the opinion of the judge they were all influenced by the views of children, which had been expressed in the context of litigation. These personnel did not give adequate weight to the family dynamics (such as the conflict between parents and allegations of abuse against the father, which were later withdrawn), the non-contact between children and father after separation, its cause and effects, the function of contact, the father's long-term future presence in the lives of the children, or the 2006 changes to the law. The trial judge went on to say that in his opinion the above-mentioned personnel were overly concerned with highly speculative future risks.[36] The Court ordered increased time to be spent with the father. The mother appealed against this decision, but was unsuccessful.

On appeal, the mother argued that the trial judge did not give enough weight to the views of the children and, while he criticised aspects of the family report, he then used it as the primary means of communicating the children's wishes. The Full Court found that the Court is not bound to give effect to the expressed views of the child. Among other things the Full Court considered the use of extraneous materials by the trial judge in making the particular parenting orders and said the '[s]ources identified range across journal articles on legal and social work topics, Explanatory Memoranda, published research results and case law. It is not always clear whether a statement in his Honour's judgment is extracted from a source or from segments of his Honour's synthesis of it'.[37]

Even though the appeal was unsuccessful, a close reading of the judgment shows how the Full Court is inclined to agree with the trial judge's decision but not necessarily with the reasons for reaching the outcome. For instance, right at the beginning of its judgment the Full Court observed that a trial judge's primary function is to decide the issue before the court and explain the result. When the judge engages in discussion that is superfluous to such a task, the court opens itself to the charge that irrelevant considerations influenced the result. If the trial judgment were to survive an appeal, it would be necessary to show that this discussion did not influence the outcome because such a discussion would be better placed in a law journal.[38] In these comments, the Full Court is disapproving of the efforts made by the trial judge, trying hard to find in the 'extraneous literature' what constitutes a desirable parenting arrangement for the children.

---

35   [2008] FamCAFC 109 (Warnick, May and Boland JJ).
36   Ibid [23].
37   Ibid [75].
38   Ibid [2]–[4].

One of the more revealing aspects of this case is that the trial judge explicitly said that the reasons why he did not give effect to the wishes of the children was that they were not consistent with the requirements of the law or the children's overall long-term best interests. The Full Court interpreted this statement as the lower court saying that *the law is that the best interests of the child are to be the paramount consideration*. However, a closer reading of the lower court judgment makes it apparent that the trial judge was referring to the requirements of the law to promote shared parenting arrangements that had been introduced in 2006. The same context also helps explain the insistence of the trial judge that it is in the best interests of the children to spend more time with the father. Thus it becomes easier to comprehend why the lower court was willing to override the assessments of various experts in this regard.

The Full Court, however, interpreted these aspects of trial judge's reasoning differently. The Court observed that the trial judge was entitled to assess the expert evidence, including the views of the ICL, the child psychiatrist and the family report, and make an order different from that recommended by them. Furthermore, the trial judge's 'dissertation on the topic of methods by which children's views may be communicated to courts did not provide a reason for the result',[39] and thus the discussion could be treated as not relevant to the decision. In deciding to also go against the expressed views of the children, the trial judge was not obliged to show that such views were wrong or misplaced. An additional reason reiterated a couple of times in the Full Court judgment for accepting that the trial judge had given appropriate weight to the views of the children was that the mother's proposal for time share itself was different from the views of the children. However, it must be pointed out that the mother had proposed an increase in time to be spent with the father but the Court exceeded that. In the wider context, it is a matter of speculation whether the mother would be considered a 'mature' parent, if she had not done so.

In deciding what weight to attach to the views of the child, the Court said that giving excessive weight to a child's view could be potentially detrimental to the child's best interests, the expressed views of the child may not represent their own preferences and they may be a result of one parent manipulating the children. Thus, the Court has the responsibility to take into account the child's views, but they cannot always be the decisive factor. It is, however, necessary to point out that none of the reasons why the views of the child should not be decisive was present in this case. Both the lower and appeal courts were content to depart from the views of the children in the name of the best interests of the child. The point is that the 'reasons' for the decision remain subjective and to an extent speculative.

This analysis of the Full Court's decision illustrates how both courts managed to subordinate the views of children. Moreover, the Full Court delegitimised reliance on social science literature in decision-making; agreed with the decision of the trial judge but not his reasoning; and in interpreting the requirements of the legislation it denied the significance of the legislative preference for a two-parent family in the decision-making process. It also managed to justify increased time with the father against the views of the children, but at the same time portrayed this as an objective outcome of the application of the law. Both judgments construct a discourse which portrays the matter as a principled decision by the judges

---

39   Ibid [87].

who are remaining within the law by applying the law on the basis of the 'best interests of the child' principle.

In juxtaposing the two decisions, it becomes evident that judicial treatment of the child's views is unpredictable, if not inscrutable. Reluctance to change existing parental arrangements produces entirely different results. For example, in an earlier case, *In the Marriage of Wotherspoon and Cooper*,[40] the application was made by the father at the request of his 13-year-old son, who had expressed a wish to stay with his father many times over the last four or five years. The Court had to consider what weight to attach to the wishes of the child. The matters in favour of accepting the boy's wishes included the strength of the wish, his close association with his father, the personality and common sense of his stepmother, the better use and direction of his leisure-time pursuits, the opportunity of getting more expert guidance from his father for his choice of school and career, and the chance to further his relationship with his stepbrother at least temporarily. There was also evidence of the child developing some behavioural problems if his wishes were not granted. Nevertheless, his wishes to change the status quo were not acted on. The Court decided not to change the existing arrangements, saying that it had to consider not merely the child's desires but also his welfare.

In the relatively recent case of *Morton v Berry*,[41] the trial judge, Donald J, had refused the father's application to change existing parenting orders based on the views of a 10-year-old child who now wanted to live with the father. Among other things, the trial judge had found, according to the decision in *Rice v Asplund*, that it is not in the interests of the parents, the child or the community that every time a change of view is expressed the parenting arrangements can be subject to re-litigation.[42] The father appealed against this finding, and the Full Court found that the trial judge had erred in not determining the issue on the basis of the child's best interests and taking into account irrelevant matters like the interests of the parents or the community.

The trial judge had accepted the father's assertion that the child now expressed a different view and wanted to stay with the father. However, in the opinion of the trial judge this was not a sufficient reason to change the residence arrangements. In the Full Court the issue of the correct application of the so-called *Rice v Asplund* rule was explained as requiring the best interests of the child to remain the paramount consideration. It found that considerations acutely relevant to a child's best interest could change owing to the child's age or level of maturity. The Court held that the trial judge had erred in not finding a change of circumstances when the child had not expressed his views at the time the original consent orders had been made, and remitted the case for rehearing. This raises the question of how and on what basis the Court could now reach a different conclusion other than by making a subjective judgment as to whether it is in the child's best interests to give effect to the views of the child.

---

40   (1980) 7 Fam LR 71 (Wood SJ). See *C v C* [2003] FLC 93-159 for an example of the court giving effect to the child's wish to spend more time with his father. In *Barningham v Barningham* [2011] FamCAFC 12, the Full Court allowed the appeal on the basis that the trial judge had not adequately explained why such little weight was placed on the children's wishes.

41   [2014] FamCAFC 208 (May, Ainslie-Wallace and Watts JJ).

42   [1979] FLC 90-725, where it was held that, where final parenting orders have been made, before the court sets aside or varies those final orders the applicant must establish a significant change in circumstances. The Full Court accepted in *Morton v Berry* that subsequent to *Rice v Asplund* pt VII of the FLA has undergone significant amendment, but principles established in that case and subsequent authority applied.

These examples illustrate the difficulties the law faces in trying to bridge the gap between conceptualising a child as lacking legal capacity, and therefore in need of protection, and the increasing recognition of the child as a bearer of rights. Discretion given to the court operates as a primary mechanism in denying autonomy to the child despite the legislation appearing to take their views seriously.[43] We say this with full acknowledgement of the increasing recognition of the autonomy of the child in various aspects of the legal system and in legal scholarship. However, the point we wish to make is that the ultimate decision-making authority remains with the judiciary, and it is here that the paternalism of the law, rather than the autonomy or the full capacity of the child, is prioritised. Similar issues surface in the cases where one parent wishes to relocate after separation (discussed below).

9.3.2   Aboriginal or Torres Strait Islander culture

The significance of Aboriginal or Torres Strait Islander culture as a factor to be considered in determining a child's best interests was specifically included in the 2006 amendments, but it was present in the 1995 amendments and has engaged the attention of the courts from an even earlier time. The main issue discussed below is the tension between the wide discretion given to the courts to determine what is in the best interests of the child and the recognition of the importance of culture for the wellbeing of Aboriginal and Torres Strait Islander children, especially in light of the damaging effects of earlier colonial policies which authorised their removal from their families. Running parallel to the developments in Australian family law that have identified Aboriginal or Torres Strait Islander culture as a relevant consideration in determining the child's best interests has been the incorporation of the Aboriginal Child Placement Principle in State and Territory child protection laws and policies. One of the recommendations of the then Human Rights and Equal Opportunity Commission in its report, *Bringing Them Home*, was to apply the Aboriginal Child Placement Principle to Aboriginal and Torres Strait Islander children requiring out-of-home care so that a child would be placed in this order: with a member of the child's family according to local custom and in accordance with Aboriginal or Torres Strait Islander law; with a member of the child's community in a relationship of responsibility with the child according to local custom and practice; with another member of the child's community; or with another Indigenous carer. This list of preferred placement would be displaced where it was contrary to the child's best interests; the child objects to the placement; or no carer in the preferred category was available, meaning that the placement of a child in a non-Indigenous family should be of last resort.[44]

---

43   For a different argument, see Patrick Parkinson, 'The Values of Parliament and the Best Interests of the Children – A Response to Professor Chisholm' (2007) 21(3) *Australian Journal of Family Law* 213.

44   Human Rights and Equal Opportunity Commission ('HREOC'), *Bringing Them Home: Report of the National Inquiry into the Separation of Aboriginal and Torres Strait Islander Children from their Families* (1997) ('*Bringing Them Home*') rec 51a, 51b, 51c <https://www.humanrights.gov.au/publications/bringing-them-home-report-1997>. This approach makes a presumption in favour of placing the child with their immediate family. However, it is not exactly how the ACPP has been incorporated in every Australian jurisdiction, or applied in practice: see Chapter 11. For coverage of the application of the Aboriginal Child Placement Principles in 1997, see HREOC ch 20; and for the recommendations made by HREOC on Indigenous child welfare, see ch 26 <http://www.hreoc.gov.au>. See also Sonia Harris-Short, *Aboriginal Child Welfare, Self-Government and the Rights of Indigenous Children: Protecting the Vulnerable Under International Law* (Ashgate, 2013).

Section 60CC(3)(h) of the FLA recognises that Aboriginal or Torres Strait Islander children have the right to enjoy their culture (including the right to enjoy that culture with other people who share that culture), and the court must consider the likely impact any proposed parenting order will have on that right. Sections 60B(3) and 60CC(6) provide what it means to have a right to enjoy one's culture. This includes the right to maintain a connection with that culture, to have the necessary support, opportunity and encouragement to explore the full extent of the culture, and develop a positive appreciation of that culture. Section 61F(b) provides that, in identifying a person or people who have exercised, or who may exercise, parental responsibility for a child, the court must have regard to any kinship obligations, and child-rearing practices, of the child's Aboriginal or Torres Strait Islander culture.

These provisions are in part implementing Australia's international obligations according to the *Convention on the Rights of the Child*.[45] However, whether the FLA has managed to give greater statutory recognition to the 'rights' of Aboriginal and Torres Strait Islander children is a debatable matter. The overarching discussion in various reports and cases emphasises how under the FLA (and unlike the Aboriginal Child Placement Principle as envisaged in *Bringing Them Home*) there is no presumption in favour of the placement of an Aboriginal or Torres Strait Islander child within their Aboriginal or Torres Strait Islander families or communities.

The reluctance to make the placement of Aboriginal and Torres Strait Islander children with their Aboriginal or Torres Strait Islander parent or extended kin an enforceable right may be understood as endorsing the overarching design of the FLA which gives wide discretion to the judge in determining what is in the child's best interests. However, since the 2006 amendments and the introduction (for the first time) of a rebuttable presumption of shared parental responsibility, it is worth considering why a similar presumption was not also introduced. It provides an illustration of how the legal discourse manages to simultaneously recognise the importance of culture to Aboriginal and Torres Strait Islander children, only to deny its importance by making the protection of their cultural rights one among many other considerations that the court may take into account in deciding what parenting orders to make. This is an illustration of how beneficial legal concepts can nevertheless function to disadvantage sections of the community. This may be an inevitable outcome arising from a legislative framework where preference is given to shared parenting – that is, to the biological ties between children and their families – and not to the rights of Aboriginal and Torres Strait Islander children to their culture.

In the wider literature the concept of settler colonialism is used to argue that colonial domination continues through various policies and the use of specific concepts.[46] We suggest that, despite the valiant efforts of the FLA to protect the cultural rights of Aboriginal and Torres Strait Islander children, the inability of the family law system to consistently

---

45   *Convention on the Rights of the Child*, above n 14, art 30 states: '[i]n those States in which ethnic, religious or linguistic minorities or persons of indigenous origin exist, a child belonging to such a minority or who is indigenous shall not be denied the right, in community with other members of his or her group, to enjoy his or her own culture, to profess and practise his or her own religion, or to use his or her own language'.

46   Elizabeth Strakosch and Alissa Macoun, 'The Vanishing Endpoint of Settler Colonialism' (2012) 37/38 *Arena Journal* 40, 42–3 use three recent policy approaches of reconciliation, neoliberal contractualism and intervention to illustrate the continuation of settler colonialism.

uphold these rights forms part of the structures of settler colonialism in continuing a practice of denying the importance of culture to the wellbeing of Aboriginal and Torres Strait
Islander peoples. A notable illustration of this point is *Oscar v Acres*, where, in the context
of unstable parental care,[47] the trial judge accepted 'that there can be no criticism of the
maternal [Aboriginal] grandmother as a parent figure. I have no doubt she could care for
the child's physical needs more than adequately'.[48] The grandmother, who had intervened
in the proceedings, was concerned for the child's welfare if he was deprived cultural knowledge of his heritage, and if he was placed in her care, her intention was to raise him according to his Aboriginal heritage.[49] Nevertheless, in determining the child's best interests, the
judge placed more emphasis on the father–child relationship, given that the child had spent
more time with his non-Aboriginal father.[50] Ultimately, in this instance the Court found that
's 60CC(2)(a) heavily favours making an order in favour of the Father'; and, in taking into
account the child's right to his Aboriginal culture in s 60CC(3)(h), the Court found 'it is not
sufficient to gamble on removing a child from an environment he has been in for the past
three years where he is well settled'.[51]

The rightly celebrated report, *Bringing Them Home*, chronicled the devastation caused
by the state-sanctioned practice of separating part-Aboriginal children from their families,
purportedly to promote their 'best interests'.[52] The pertinent and highly contentious issue is
that, central to the policies underpinning the practice, was the understanding that Aboriginal
and Torres Strait Islander peoples did not have any meaningful cultures or organised societies and that, by forcibly removing their children, the Aboriginal race would come to an
end. The acknowledgement of the wrongfulness of the practice of removing children from
their families has happened in various ways, and has included an apology delivered by then
Prime Minister Kevin Rudd in 2008.[53] However, there seems to be continued resistance to
accepting the importance of Aboriginal and Torres Strait Islander cultures for their survival.
The various reports that have led to the inclusion of 60CC(3)(h)[54] reiterate that the inclusion
of the importance of Aboriginality of the child should not create a presumption in favour
of placing the child with the Aboriginal parent or family. For instance, *Out of the Maze* had
recommended that the language of s 68F(2)(f) (of the pre-2006 FLA) be changed from 'any
need' to 'the need of every indigenous child' to maintain their culture.[55] The Family Law
Council endorsed this recommendation (so that it would read 'the need of every indigenous
child to maintain a connection with the lifestyle, culture and traditions of Aboriginal peoples

47   *Oscar and Acres* [2007] Fam CA 1/04 (Barry J).
48   Ibid [72].
49   Ibid [74].
50   Ibid [162].
51   Ibid [144], [182]. The judge's view was that it was sufficient for the child to have some contact with
      his Aboriginal mother and grandmother and otherwise to rely on the education system in remote
      New South Wales, where he would be living with his father, for his inculturation in Aboriginal
      history, culture and community. For a comparative approach, see *Davis v Davis* (2007) 38 Fam
      LR 671.
52   HREOC, above n 44.
53   Commonwealth, *Parliamentary Debates*, House of Representatives, 13 February 2008, 167–71
      (Kevin Rudd, Prime Minister).
54   Also ss 60B(3), 60CC(6) and 61F(b).
55   Family Pathways Advisory Group, *Out of the Maze: Pathways to the Future for Families Experiencing
      Separation* (Commonwealth, 2001) recommendation 22.

or Torres Strait Islanders') with the assurance that it would not amount to a presumption that a Torres Strait Islander child needs to maintain a connection with a parent simply because they are an Aboriginal or a Torres Strait Islander person.[56]

One of the findings of *Bringing Them Home* was that Aboriginal and Torres Strait Islander children continue to be disproportionately removed from their families even now, and this is in part attributable to the practices of child-welfare authorities in not adhering to the children's right of self-determination (see Chapter 11). It is in this context that it needs to be asked whether it is sufficient that the FLA incorporates consideration of Aboriginal and Torres Strait Islander culture as one among many other considerations while retaining wide discretion for the courts to determine how much weight to give these considerations. The sacrosanct idea that determining the child's best interests is a discretionary matter thus functions to foreclose the possibility of even asking whether Aboriginal and Torres Strait Islander peoples' right of self-determination must be met before the 'best interests of the child' principle can be genuinely pursued. The understanding that the child's best interests is the paramount consideration, that these interests are to be determined by the exercise of judicial discretion, and that they can be determined independently of the claims, interests and rights of parents, as well as the difficulty of deciding what weight to give to social science literature in making these decisions,[57] all come together to support the discourse that the court is the most reliable guarantor of the child's best interests. The following cases illustrate the inevitable subjective decisions made by judges trying to balance the demands of recognising the unique circumstances facing Aboriginal and Torres Strait Islander peoples and the reticence of the legislation to acknowledge the primacy of the right of Aboriginal and Torres Strait Islander children to their culture.[58]

B and R and the Separate Representative involved a dispute between an Anglo-Australian father living in Tasmania and an Aboriginal Australian mother living in Victoria. The child had stayed with the father for 15 months after separation.[59] The mother appealed against the trial judge's (Walsh J) refusal to allow evidence presented by the child's separate representative that Aboriginal children raised in non-Aboriginal environments suffer damage to their self-esteem and identity. On appeal the Full Family Court said this evidence ought to have been admitted in determining the best interests of the child and that allowing the evidence would not amount to discriminatory treatment or preferential treatment. It also said that both the history of Aboriginal Australians and their current position in Australian life are unique. Evidence of their everyday struggles in a predominantly white culture addresses the reality of their experiences. The Court found that the evidence was as relevant as any other consideration in determining the welfare of the child in the present case, as it constitutes a deeper reality than the broad statements of principle made by the trial judge. However, as with any other consideration, it remains for the judge to decide how much weight ought to

---

56   Family Law Council, *Recognition of Traditional Aboriginal and Torres Strait Islander Child-rearing Practices Response to Recommendation 22: Pathways Report, Out of the Maze* (Commonwealth, 2004) 6.

57   For a discussion of how social science literature is used in judicial decision making, see Zoe Rathus, 'Role of Social Science in Australian Family Law: Collaborator, Usurper or Infiltrator?' (2014) 52(1) *Family Court Review* 69.

58   See also Sven R Silburn et al, 'The Intergenerational Effects of Forced Separation on the Social and Emotional Wellbeing of Aboriginal Children and Young People' (2006) 75 *Family Matters* 10; Philip Alston, 'The Best Interests Principle: Towards a Reconciliation of Culture and Human Rights' (1994) 8(1) *International Journal of Law and the Family* 1.

59   [1995] FLC 92-636 (Fogarty, Kay and O'Ryan JJ).

be given to evidence or information of this kind. Moreover, such observations notwithstanding, the difficulties of using social science information in making judicial decision-making persist. It is not very often that legal policy-makers acknowledge openly that social science knowledge itself needs to be interpreted.[60] The subjective nature of an assessment of the significance of Aboriginal culture becomes even more evident when the dispute is between two parents who belong to different Aboriginal communities.

For example, in *M and L (Aboriginal Culture)* the parents were from different Aboriginal communities: the father lived in a remote community and the mother lived on the fringe of an urban community.[61] At trial, parenting orders were made for the children to live with the father on the basis that 'these children would be best off if they were fully immersed in their father's culture living in a remote community rather than being brought up as fringe dwellers in an urban community'.[62] On appeal a Full Court majority agreed with the appellant that the federal magistrate, Brown FM, had made an error about the collectivist approach to parenting of the mother and had not given sufficient weight to allegations about the father's violence and drinking problems.[63] The significant error was that the federal magistrate, in discounting the attachment the children had to their mother, placed too much reliance on a journal article that purported to explain how in Aboriginal cultures child raising was a collective activity and many people were responsible for raising the children. Moreover, the Court said there was no anthropological evidence that had been brought before it that supported the mother raising the children in a collectivist manner.[64]

In *Donnell v Dovey* the parents were also from two different communities.[65] They separated in 2002 and the father went back to Torres Strait Island while the mother, from the Wakka Wakka tribe, continued to stay in Brisbane with the child, O, and his half-brother and sister from the mother's previous relationship. The mother died in a car accident in 2007. O's eldest half-sister, along with her husband, looked after O after the death of the mother. The federal magistrate, Howard FM, ordered that O should live with his father. On appeal the Full Court criticised the family report and also the federal magistrate for seemingly accepting the modern Anglo-European ideas of social and family organisation. It also claimed that the federal magistrate should have taken into account the 2006 amendments that were designed to ensure that cases involving Aboriginal and Torres Strait Islander children might require taking their culture into account.

However, what would constitute sufficient sensitivity to the differences in cultures of two or more communities remains a matter for the court to decide.[66] The Family Law Council

---

60   Martha Fineman, *The Illusion of Equality: The Rhetoric and Reality of Divorce Reform* (University of Chicago Press, 1991).

61   (2007) 37 Fam LR 317 (Kay, Warnick and Strickland JJ).

62   Ibid [63] quoted by Kay J.

63   Ibid [63]–[64] (Kay J).

64   Ibid [51]. See also *In Re CP* [1999] FLC 92-741, where the appeal court remitted the case for rehearing on the basis that the trial court had not taken sufficient notice of precise differences between the Tiwi Islander culture and other Aboriginal cultures.

65   (2010) 237 FLR 53 (Warnick, Thackray and O'Ryan JJ).

66   See *Bailey v Cabell* [2011] FMCAfam 1020, [89]; *Knightley v Brandon* [2013] FMCAfam 148, [32]; *Maples v Maples* [2011] FMCAfam 510, [15], where courts have consciously considered the cultural rights of Aboriginal and Torres Strait Islander children. Compare *Kane v Sackett* [2011] FMCAfam 468, [81] (Bender FM), where the Court refused to give priority to the children's Aboriginal heritage, stating that 'the children's Somalian, Australian, Indigenous and Islamic cultures' were all 'equally important'.

studied 55 cases under the FLA where Aboriginal or Torres Strait Islander culture was an issue.[67] Among other things, it found that the judicial attitudes to the relevance of Aboriginal and Torres Strait Islander cultures had changed; the cases showed that the courts took into consideration anthropological evidence more often; and the judges were more aware of the significance of immersion in culture for Aboriginal and Torres Strait Islander children. At the same time, however, it also found that there remained issues about how the cultural differences are taken into account. We suggest that such issues will always remain as long as the FLA does not prioritise the right of Aboriginal and Torres Strait Islander children to their culture over other considerations in determining the child's best interests.[68] The prevailing orthodoxy of the FLA – that only a judge exercising discretion can determine what might constitute the child's best interests – does not leave much scope for Aboriginal and Torres Strait Islander perspectives on this issue.[69] Similar issues are presented in cases where one parent has declared their sexual preference for a same-sex partner.

9.3.3   Sexuality of parents

The wider issue of whether the court, in determining the child's best interests, should consider the sexuality of a parent as a relevant factor does not find specific reference in the list of additional factors. However, it is accommodated in s 60CC(3)(m) as 'any other fact or circumstance that the court thinks is relevant'. This issue usually arises at the end of a heterosexual relationship when one parent discloses that their sexual orientation is towards people of the same sex, or enters into a same-sex relationship. The court then is to determine whether the parent's sexuality has a bearing on what constitutes the child's best interests.

In the early days of the FLA this was a debated issue, as illustrated in the case of *In the Marriage of L*.[70] This case was decided in 1983 and was considered a progressive judgment at the time. The judgment provided a list of principles for considering the suitability of homosexual parents:[71]

> (1) whether children raised by their homosexual parent may themselves become homosexual, or whether such an event is likely;
>
> (2) whether the child of a homosexual parent could be stigmatised by peer groups, particularly if the parent is known in the community as a homosexual;
>
> (3) whether a homosexual parent would show the same love and responsibility as a heterosexual parent;

---

67   Family Law Council, *Improving the Family Law System for Aboriginal and Torres Strait Islander Clients* (Commonwealth, 2012).

68   A similar argument has been advanced in Keryn Ruska and Zoe Rathus, 'The Place of Culture in Family Law Proceedings: Moving Beyond the Dominant Paradigm of the Nuclear Family' (2010) 7(20) *Indigenous Law Bulletin* 8.

69   Maureen Long and Rene Sephton, 'Rethinking the "Best Interests" of the Child: Voices from Aboriginal Child and Family Welfare Practitioners' (2011) 64(1) *Australian Social Work* 96. It is our contention that upholding the cultural rights of Aboriginal and Torres Strait Islander children would be linked to upholding the broader right of self-determination, which could be done through the devolution of jurisdiction to Aboriginal and Torres Strait Islander child-welfare organisations. For a synthesis of reform agendas along these lines, see Jennika Woerde, *Rights of the Child and the Clash of Cultures* (LLB Honours Thesis, Macquarie University, 2015) 31–4.

70   [1983] FLC 91-353 (Baker J).

71   Ibid 78 363–4.

(4) whether homosexual parents will give a balanced sex education to their children and take a balanced approach to sexual matters;

(5) whether or not children should be aware of their parents' sexual preferences;

(6) whether children need a parent of the same sex to model upon;

(7) whether children need both a male and a female parent figure; and

(8) the attitude of the homosexual parent to religion, particularly if the doctrines, tenets and beliefs of the parties' church are opposed to homosexuality.

The court, in awarding the custody of the child to the wife, went on to say that '[a]lthough the wife's homosexuality has given me a great deal of concern, I am firmly of the view that her proclivity in this regard is not and cannot be, per se, a disqualifying factor against her'.[72] In making this statement, the court is able to appear progressive and yet deflect attention from its function in problematising the homosexuality of a parent by providing a checklist that determines when such behaviour could be a danger to the child. There is no comparable known example of a court making similar statements about the heterosexual behaviour of either parent.[73]

In *In the Marriage of A and J* both parents were equally involved in the care of a four-year-old boy.[74] After separation the mother had formed a same-sex relationship with Ms R. At the time of separation the parents had agreed to share the care of the child, but then the father initiated proceedings and was granted sole custody. The mother appealed against this decision on 10 grounds, and the relevant issue for us is that she challenged certain observations made in the course of the judgment. The trial judge, Butler J, had decided to give custody to the father, and one of the considerations was the need to maintain a relationship with the father. The Full Court reviewed the reasons given by the trial judge and noted that the trial judge had accepted that the mother and father were equally placed in their claims for the custody of the child. However, in deciding to give sole custody to the father the trial judge had mentioned the principles set out in *In the Marriage of L*. In addition the trial judge had observed that the wife and Ms R accepted that it was inappropriate for children

---

72   Ibid 78 366.

73   For a different example of how homosexual conduct of a parent affects the court at an unarticulated level, see *In the Marriage of B and C* [1989] FLC 92-043 (Smithers J). In this case the father was homosexual and suffering from AIDS. The mother and father had separated when the child was two months old and when the child was older the mother told him that his father was dead. After some time of not engaging with the child, the father wished to have access to the child. Apart from the anxiety this would cause to the mother, and the potential social ostracism this could create for the child, the Court found that it was not in the child's welfare to spend time with his father as the child would have to deal with the death of the father in the near future. It is unlikely that the same assessment would have been made if the father had been suffering from cancer or any other terminal illness. However, in *W v G (No 2)* (2005) 35 Fam LR 439 (Carmody J) the father seeking contact with the child was a homosexual and had been diagnosed with the HIV virus. He had not contacted the child for approximately 10 years. It was found that the benefits of the child spending time with the father outweighed the disadvantages. The conventional explanation for the different outcomes would be that each case is determined on its own unique facts. This is not, however, an entirely convincing explanation. In the later case the judge noted that 'the court's attitude to parental misconduct and the like is less rigid now than formerly' (at 447 [60]). But it still remains that future cases will be determined according to the discretion of the court.

74   (1995) 19 Fam LR 260 (Fogarty, Lindenmayer and O'Ryan JJ).

to observe overt displays of affection between homosexual partners, but they did little to put this into practice. He had also observed that the wife and Ms R moved in homosexual circles, but also concluded that this was not an adverse factor.[75] The Full Court dismissed the appeal and said that the trial judge had given due consideration to various relevant factors and not made an appealable error.

The emphasis in both the trial and Full Court judgments is that the sexuality of the mother was not a negative factor. However, there is little else in the reasoning of the trial judge to explain why the father was given sole custody. Despite the fact that this decision uses pre-1995 amendments language of custody and access, it seems difficult to explain why the trial court considers that maintaining a relationship with the father is 'more' important for the child than maintaining a similar relationship with the mother. The repeated assertion that the sexuality of the mother is not an adverse factor constructs the apparently progressive discourse of the law. Simultaneously, it prevents the Full Court from revising the decision as no appealable error could be identified, because the sexuality of the mother was supposedly not a relevant consideration in making the order.

These cases can be read as examples of the liberal stance of the Family Court, for being homosexual did not disqualify a parent from obtaining a parenting order. In every instance it is said that the court must look to the parenting ability of such a person and judge what is in the child's best interests. Yet the judgments also manage to construct a discourse for judging the homosexual parent differently.[76] While it may be said that these cases were decided in earlier times and are no longer relevant,[77] we include them as illustrations of how the value preferences of the decision-makers inevitably inform the outcomes. Thus, the heteronormativity of family law is established and maintained with very little space for questioning something that is not even admitted openly.[78] Similarly, the emphasis on the continued involvement of both parents with the child finds validation in the cases and legislative changes since 1995. A significant avenue of constructing such normative discourse is in disputes that can arise when a primary caregiving parent is seeking to relocate with the child after separation.

9.3.4 Mobility of parents/relocation

In cases where the child is residing with a parent and the parent wants to relocate with the child some distance away from the other parent, the issue may come before a family court for determination. This is likely if the other parent opposes the move because it will mean

---

75 Ibid 263.
76 For a similar analysis of cases in the context of decisions made by the courts in the United States, see Kim H Pearson, 'Sexuality in Child Custody Decisions' (2012) 50 *Family Court Review* 280.
77 Attention has turned to parenting disputes between former same-sex partners and between people who have entered into agreements to create a child through artificial means, which could involve a lesbian mother and co-parent, and a gay father who had provided sperm. See *Flynn v Jaspar* [2008] FMCAfam 106; *Keaton v Aldridge* [2009] FMCAfam 92; *Snell v Bagley* [2009] FMCAfam 1144; and for a pre-2006 decision, see *Re Patrick* (2002) 28 Fam LR 579. See generally Jenni Millbank, 'The Limits of Functional Family: Lesbian Mother Litigation in the Era of the Eternal Biological Family' (2008) 22(2) *International Journal of Law, Policy and the Family* 149.
78 This is further substantiated with the court's reluctance to let a 'mature' young person decide to undergo irreversible medical treatment that will assist in the management of their gender identity disorder (see discussion in Chapter 8).

that they will lose contact with the child. There are no specific provisions in the FLA that address this matter directly, but the child's best interests principle does apply.[79] Ordinarily the courts are very reluctant to deny contact between the child and the parent. But prior to the 1995 changes to the FLA, there was no expectation that the parent with custody could be restricted from moving. The 1995 amendments changed the language of guardianship and custody to that of parental responsibility and contact. This change in language reflected the idea that it is children who have a 'right' of contact with both parents rather than the parents having control over their children.[80] The possible significance of these changes generated both scholarly and judicial discussion.[81] The following cases outline how the courts have interpreted the change in emphasis after the 1995 amendments.

B and B: Family Law Reform Act 1995 is a decision of the Full Family Court where the effect of the 1995 amendments to the FLA were examined in the context of a mother seeking to relocate interstate with the children of the marriage.[82] The Court stated with respect to the child's right of contact with both parents (then enshrined in s 60B) that the best interests of the child remained the paramount consideration and that relocation cases are also subject to this consideration. In this case the children were living with the mother and had regular contact with the father. Subsequently, the mother wished to move with the children from Cairns to Bendigo to marry a man living there. It was accepted that the man could not move to Cairns. The father opposed the mother's plan to move with the child inter alia on the basis that s 60B(2) 'entrenches' the right of the child to have contact with both parents. The trial judge, Jordan J, allowed the mother's application and the father appealed to the Full Court. At this stage the Commonwealth Attorney-General and the then Human Rights and Equal Opportunity Commission intervened in the proceedings. The Full Family Court declined to accept the father's contention and, among other things, found that s 60B represents a deliberate statement of the objects and principles the Court must apply, but is subject to s 65E (that is, the best interests of the child principle); the statement that the child has a right of contact with both parents does not by itself define what may be in the child's best interests; relocation cases are not a special category of cases; and they must be decided by reference to the best interests of the child as the paramount consideration. The Full Court also laid down guidelines for deciding the best interests of the child in the context of relocation.[83]

In the subsequent case of *A v A: Relocation Approach*, the Full Family Court emphasised the interconnections between issues of relocation, residence and the best interests of the

---

79   Although as explained by the High Court, in deciding a request for relocation, the best interests of the child are not the paramount consideration but are a relevant factor: see *AMS v AIF* (1999) CLR 160 (Gleeson CJ, Gaudron, McHugh, Gummow, Kirby, Hayne and Callinan JJ).

80   Pre-2006 amendment s 60B(2)(b) stated: 'children have a right of contact, on a regular basis, with both of their parents and other people significant to their care, welfare and development'.

81   See, eg, Helen Rhoades, Reg Graycar and Margaret Harrison, *The Family Law Reform Act: The First Three Years* (University of Sydney and Family Court of Australia, 2000); *B and B: Family Law Reform Act 1995* [1997] FLC 92-755 (Nicholson CJ, Fogarty and Lindenmayer JJ).

82   [1997] FLC 92-755.

83   Ibid 84 174; the guidelines: the degree and quality of the existing relationship between the child and the residence parent; the degree and quality of the existing contact between the child and the contact parent; the reason for relocating; the distance and permanency of the proposed change; and the effects on the child, both positive and negative, of the proposed relocation.

child.[84] It provided guidelines for determining 'relocation' cases. Among other things, the Court said that relocation disputes could not be determined by treating relocation, residence and the child's best interests as discrete issues. It was not required that compelling reasons be given for or against relocation. The legitimate interests of both parents are relevant in determining the child's best interests. Although the parent seeking to change the place of residence of a child does not bear an onus, they must be able to show that the change in the residence or contact arrangements of the child are in conformity with the best interests of the child. It also provided that the correct approach in deciding cases of relocation is to: (1) identify the competing proposals of the parties; (2) explain the advantages and disadvantages of each proposal by examining the s 68F(2) factors (now the s 60CC factors) with regard to the objects and principles of the parenting provisions of the Act, which includes an evaluation of the 'reasons for relocation as they bear upon the child's best interests' against other factors; and (3) explain why one proposal is to be preferred having regard to the best interests of the child as the paramount, but not sole, consideration.[85]

In the case of *U v U* the dispute went all the way to the High Court.[86] The decision is treated mainly as an authority for the proposition that a court can decide to make orders that have not been proposed by either parent. It was a case where the parents were of Indian origin and had settled in Australia. After separation the mother wished to move back to India with their young daughter, but the father opposed the move. The trial judge and the Full Family Court disallowed the mother's application to move with the child and she was required to stay in Sydney with the child. The High Court also rejected the mother's appeal. One ground of appeal was that the trial judge and the Full Court had not given due consideration to the alternative proposals of the mother and the father and instead focused on the question of whether the mother should be allowed to move to India with the child.

The High Court in response found that a court is not bound by the proposals presented by the two parties and is free to make an order that was not sought by either party if it is in the child's best interests. Justices Kirby and Gaudron in separate dissenting judgments observed that the burden of an order restricting the mother as the primary carer from moving with the child is unfair. In not giving due consideration to the possibility that the father could relocate to India to be with the child, the Court had made an inherently sexist assumption that the father's choice of where to live is beyond question in a way that the mother's decision is not. However, the High Court majority approached the issue by focusing on abstract technicalities and propositions related to the scope of judicial discretion. By focusing on these legal technicalities, the Court avoided considering how to determine the most appropriate method of assessing the relative merits of all proposals put forward. Here we see how the 'best interests of the child' principle and the broad scope of judicial discretion it allows obscure the choices the members of the High Court are making in determining what is in the child's best interests in this case. This is a function of judges being expected to address issues of law and in the process treat 'law' as not intrinsically related to the fairness of outcomes. But in view of the dissenting judgments, the unfairness of the outcome in this

---

84   [2000] FLC 93-035 (Nicholson CJ, Ellis and Coleman JJ). In doing so it relied on the principles enunciated in the earlier cases of *B and B: Family Law Reform Act 1995* and *AMS v AIF; AIF v AMS* S [1999] 199 CLR 160, which were decided by the Full Family Court and the High Court respectively.
85   Summarised in Family Law Council, *Relocation*, Discussion Paper (2006) 10–11.
86   (2002) 211 CLR 238 (Gleeson CJ, Gaudron, McHugh, Gummow, Kirby, Hayne and Callinan JJ).

case becomes apparent. In emphasising the authority of the Court to make a proposal not put forward by either parent, the High Court majority reinforced the autonomy of the Court and at the same time the autonomy of the parent/mother wanting to relocate was lessened.

Courts have repeatedly held that the 1995 amendments to the FLA did not displace the best interests of the child as the paramount consideration, but it is nevertheless true that they did set the stage for reinforcing the norm for children to have both parents involved in their lives after relationship breakdown. The same emphasis was reinforced in the 2006 amendments.

9.3.4.1   2006 amendments to the FLA

Sections 60B and 60CC(2) now provide that both parents should be involved in their children's lives and children should have meaningful relationships with both parents. These sections, combined with the introduction of a rebuttable presumption that it is in the child's best interests for both parents to share parental responsibility after separation, raises the issue of whether the relocation of a parent with the children could ever be permissible.[87] Examples of more recent relocation cases are used here to illustrate the normative force of the idea that two parents are necessary for a normal childhood.

PBC v LMC was a case concerning parenting arrangements for two girls aged 10 and eight years.[88] The children were living with the mother and seeing the father five out of 14 nights each fortnight. The mother wanted to relocate to Brisbane and, if permitted to do so, the children would see the father one weekend a month and half the school holidays. The federal magistrate declined the mother's application and held: 'The law provides that the benefit to the children of having a meaningful relationship with both parents is a primary consideration. In the event the children lived in Brisbane, they would not see their father on weekdays … there is a likelihood the children's relationship with the father will become less meaningful'.[89] The mother's application to move to Brisbane was thus refused and it was held that the father's proposal best promoted a meaningful relationship between the children and both parents.

However, in the case of *Hepburn v Noble* there was an equal-time arrangement in place but the mother wished to relocate with the children.[90] The mother had re-partnered and wanted to move from Wollongong to Melbourne. Her new partner could not move to Wollongong and the mother was not in paid employment. The father had also re-partnered. He was employed as a pilot and was not in a position to relocate. The mother provided evidence of the children's distress at being away from her. The federal magistrate, Brewster FM, held that it was not in the child's best interests to continue this arrangement and allowed the mother to relocate with the children. The father appealed, but the Full Family Court did not allow the appeal. It expressed a concern that *A and A: Relocation Approach* was still being

---

87   Patrick Parkinson, Judy Cashmore and Judi Single, 'The Need for Reality Testing in Relocation Cases' (2010) 44(1) *Family Law Quarterly* 1; Juliet Behrens and Bruce Smyth, 'Australian Family Law Court Decision on Relocation: Parents' Experiences and Some Implications for Law and Policy' (2010) 38(1) *Federal Law Review* 1. See also Chapter 8 for the academic commentary, judicial pronouncements and empirical studies generated by the 2006 amendments to the FLA.

88   [2006] FMCAfam 469 (Sexton FM).

89   Ibid [23].

90   [2010] FLC 93-438 (Coleman, Strickland and Crisford JJ).

quoted in cases. It said that pre-2006 cases ought to be treated with caution and the federal magistrate should have referred to relocation cases decided after the 2006 amendments.[91]

The inevitable consequence of the emphasis of the FLA on shared parental responsibility is that the parent wishing to relocate must establish that such a move is in the child's best interests. It also happens to be the case that most primary carers continue to be mothers. Thus, the placing of restrictions on the movement of mothers as primary carers of children is not surprising. It is rather the function of gender-neutrality underpinning the best interests principle that the law can deny that such outcomes are a consequence of men and women performing different functions in contemporary society. This becomes starkly evident in cases where the courts have had to deal with situations of compelling a parent to relocate or where the possible relocation of the parent's new partner's is being considered.

In *Sampson v Hartnett (No 10)*, the Full Court was dealing with an appeal by the mother against an order that she move back to Sydney with the two children, as the father lived there.[92] The mother argued that this was an order effectively ordering her to relocate. Significantly, the Full Court said that the court had never before considered whether it has the power to order a parent to move, as compared to restraining a primary carer parent from relocating. It nevertheless held that the Court does have this power, but it should be exercised rarely.[93]

In *Taylor v Barker* it was held that 'relocation' should not be considered a separate issue from the best interests of the child.[94] This case concerned an appeal by the father against orders made by the federal magistrate, Brewster FM, that allowed the mother's application to relocate to North Queensland, partly on the basis that otherwise her new partner would have to relocate to Canberra to be with her. The mother had a child with the new partner and wanted both children to live together. The majority in the Full Family Court did not accept the father's appeal. They held that after the 2006 amendments the Court must first consider whether it is in the child's best interests for the child to spend equal time or substantial and significant time with each parent, even when a relocation proposal may have to be given subsequent consideration. One of the grounds of appeal by the father was that the federal magistrate had not given due consideration to the possibility that the mother's new partner could relocate to Canberra. The majority judges did not accept this ground and agreed with the federal magistrate that the case would not be decided on this basis. It further found that there is no reported authority for a relocation case to be decided on the basis of what might be the response of the partner of the parent proposing relocation in the event that relocation with the child is not allowed by the court.

---

91   The Full Court referred to *Taylor v Barker* [2007] FLC 93-345; *Sealey v Archer* [2008] FamCAFC 142; *Starr v Duggan* [2009] FamCAFC 115; and *McCall v Clark* (2009) 41 Fam LR 483.

92   [2007] FLC 93-350 (Bryant CJ, Kay and Warnick JJ). After separation the mother, with the child, moved from Sydney to Geelong. The second child was born after she had moved. The father initiated proceedings and the court ordered that the best interests of the child required that the mother and children move back to Sydney. See also *Adamson v Adamson* (2014) 51 Fam LR 626, where the trial judge had ordered the mother to move in close proximity to the town that the father had moved to. The mother appealed and the full court allowed her application that there was no rare and exceptional circumstance that permitted such a coercive order.

93   Richard Chisholm, 'To What Extent Can the Court Make Orders that Inhibit a Parent's Right to Relocate?' (2008) 22(2) *Australian Journal of Family Law* 154.

94   (2007) 37 Fam LR 461 (Bryant CJ, Faulks DCJ and Finn J).

It is significant that in this case the federal magistrate had accepted that the child had lived his entire life in Canberra and, if the status quo were changed, the child would most likely lose contact with his paternal grandparents. The federal magistrate, however, was inclined to allow the mother to relocate with the child and the majority in the Full Court agreed with the decision. They accepted that it was a finely balanced case and the Court could decide to give more weight to one factor. In this case such a factor was the happiness of the mother in being allowed to move and marry the father of her second child. In dissent, Faulks DCJ also accepted that it was open for the Court to consider the happiness of the mother as the decisive factor. However, he disagreed with the majority judges on whether there was adequate proof that, if not allowed to relocate, the mother would suffer mental distress, as was her claim. The dissenting judge was particularly concerned that an inference was made about the mother being unhappy and the difficulty in this case was that an inference, not based on evidence, was elevated to the conclusive factor in determining that the proposal of the mother to relocate with the child was in the child's best interests. He also went on to say that in that case most relocation proposals would succeed, although he pointed out that the happiness of a parent is not prescribed as one of the factors in determining the child's best interests.

However, the obvious and in a sense unanswerable question is: why did the courts consider the child's relationship with the father of lesser significance than with the mother? Posing this question brings into stark focus the norm-setting function of the law that seeks to uphold the two-parent family norm.[95] When courts have to choose between proposals of two parents in order to allow relocation of one parent with the child or maintain the status quo, the insistence on two parents and shared parenting wears thin. Reasons such as those given in this case for allowing one parent's proposal over another are strained and could be described as not based on anything more than a value preference.[96] It is also evident from the reported cases that usually the mother is asked not to relocate as that is not in the child's best interests, while the father is not asked to move to the place where the mother is seeking to relocate with the child. This gendered outcome may not be intentional, but is a direct function of women being the primary carers in contemporary society.

9.4   Parental child abduction

Particularly difficult issues arise when one parent wants to relocate with the child to another country. Applicable international law principles can come into tension with aspects of domestic family law. In particular, the replacement of the 'best interests of the child' principle with the primacy of returning an abducted child to his or her place of habitual residence denies the extant social realities that primary carers of children are predominantly women, and after relationship breakdown they are caught in intolerable situations requiring ongoing interaction with the other parent of the child, often in a country where they have

---

95   For a review of judicial approaches, see Lisa Young, 'Resolving Relocation Disputes: The "Interventionist" Approach in Australia' (2011) 23 *Child and Family Law Quarterly* 203.

96   Gendered aspects of such value preferences are discussed in the literature. See, eg, Marilyn Freeman and Nicola Taylor, 'The Gender Agenda and Relocation Disputes' [2012] *International Family Law* 184.

no extended family support.[97] A survey of Australian lawyers dealing with cases arising under the *Hague Convention on the Civil Aspects of International Child Abduction* ('*Hague Convention on Child Abduction*')[98] found that a majority of abductors were mothers. In 2015 there were 52 applications from another country regarding a child brought to Australia and 82 applications related to children removed from Australia. The majority of applications (both for children brought to, and removed from, Australia) concerned New Zealand, the United Kingdom or the United States, while approximately 30% related to children in all other countries.[99]

In an age of international mobility and relative ease of travel it is often the case that one parent wants to move with the child to their country of origin. The international community's main response to this phenomenon has been the introduction of the *Hague Convention on Child Abduction*.[100] Australia has signed and ratified this convention, and thus the principles therein apply if a child is wrongfully taken to or from Australia, provided the other country is also a party to the convention (art 4). Before discussing these rules a few preliminary matters need to be mentioned.

Parental abduction of children can happen within Australia and the FLA makes specific provisions for children subject to parenting orders made in Australia and children subject to overseas child orders but present in Australia.[101] Thus, if there is a relevant parenting order in force, a party must not take or send the child out of Australia except with the written permission of all the parties in whose favour the order was made, or with the permission of the court (s 65Y). If, however, a child is taken in contravention of parenting orders (or abducted) within Australia s 67Q provides for a recovery order to be made.[102] Any person with whom the child is to live, spend time or communicate with, or a person who has parental responsibility for the child under a parenting order, or a grandparent or any other person concerned with the care, welfare or development of the child can apply for a recovery order (s 67T).

---

97   The dilemmas that can arise when a child is abducted to a non-convention country are well illustrated in a recent story involving reporters from the television program *60 Minutes* who tried to assist an Australian mother regain custody of her children, who had been abducted by their father in Australia and taken to Lebanon. See, eg, Julie Szego, '60 Minutes: Who are the Real Victims in the Abduction Story?', *The Age* (online), 20 April 2016 <http://www.theage.com.au/comment/the-kids-are-the-victims-in-the-60-minutes-story-20160419-goagex.html>.

98   Opened for signature 25 October 1980, 1343 UNTS 89 (entered into force 1 December 1983).

99   *Hague Convention Application Statistics* (July 2015) Attorney-General's Department <https://www.ag.gov.au/FamiliesAndMarriage/Families/InternationalFamilyLaw/Pages/Internationalparentalchildabduction.aspx>.

100   Danielle Bozin-Odhiambo, 'Re-examining Habitual Residence as the Sole Connecting Factor in the Hague Convention Child Abduction Cases' (2012) 3(1) *Family Law Review* 4. See also Michael Salter, 'Getting Hagued: The Impact of International Law on Child Abduction by Protective Mothers' (2014) 39(1) *Alternative Law Journal* 19.

101   See also the *Family Law (Child Protection Convention) Regulations 2003* (Cth), enacted to give domestic effect to Australia's obligations under the *Hague Convention on Jurisdiction, Applicable Law, Recognition, Enforcement and Cooperation in Respect of Parental Responsibility and Measures for the Protection of Children*, opened for signature 19 October 1996, 2204 UNTS 95 (entered into force 1 January 2002). This convention is designed to facilitate resolution of matters among different central authorities in convention countries. They provide uniform rules that determine which countries' laws are applicable; and facilitate communication and cooperation among various countries' central authorities. See also *Cape v Cape* [2013] FLC 93-549.

102   Judicial registrars make such orders in accordance with the *Family Law Rules 2004* (Cth) pt 21.3.

Other relevant provisions in Part VII Division 13 Subdivision C permit that an 'overseas child order'[103] from a prescribed overseas country can be registered and will have the effect of restricting the power of Australian courts to make an overriding order for the child.[104] This mechanism can assist where the child may not be covered by the *Hague Convention on Child Abduction*.

If a child is abducted to a place outside of the jurisdiction of the Australian courts or is brought into Australia illegally, the *Hague Convention on Child Abduction* may become relevant. This convention is designed to return a child (16 years or under) to his or her original place of habitual residence if the child is removed or abducted in contravention of existing custody/access orders. It is not designed to determine what orders would serve the welfare or best interests of the child. That issue remains to be decided by the law of the place where the child was habitually resident. If the other country is not a party to the convention,[105] the court will decide whether the welfare of the child as the paramount consideration allows it to hear and decide the case.

The *Family Law (Child Abduction Convention) Regulations 1986* (Cth) ('Regulations') were enacted to give effect to the *Hague Convention on Child Abduction* within Australia.[106] Article 1 articulates the main objects of the convention as securing the prompt return of children wrongfully removed to or retained in any contracting state; and to ensure that rights of custody and of access under the law of one contracting state are effectively respected in other contracting states. In each state, the institutional mechanism of a central authority is responsible to secure the return of the child. In Australia, the Commonwealth central

---

103   Defined in s 4(1) as an order made by a court of a prescribed overseas jurisdiction that, however it is expressed, has the effect of determining the person(s) with whom a child is to live, or that provides for a person(s) to have custody of a child; providing for contact or access between a child and another person(s); or varying or discharging such an order. The procedure for registering an overseas order is in *Family Law Regulations 1984* (Cth) reg 23.

104   See ss 70G–70L for further details. The court may make an order relating to a child if it is of the opinion that there exist substantial grounds for believing that the welfare of the child requires it. See, eg, *In the Marriage of Trnka* [1984] FLC 91-535.

105   For a list of *Hague Convention on Child Abduction* countries, see *Hague Convention on the Civil Aspects of International Child Abduction*, Attorney-General's Department <https://www.ag.gov.au/FamiliesAndMarriage/Families/InternationalFamilyLaw/Pages/HagueConventionontheCivilAspectsofInternationalChildAbduction.aspx>.

106   Authorised by s 111B FLA; the regulations came into operation on 1 January 1987. Section 111B provides: '(1) The regulations may make such provision as is necessary or convenient to enable the performance of the obligations of Australia, or to obtain for Australia any advantage or benefit, under the Convention … (1A) In relation to proceedings under regulations made for the purposes of subsection (1), the regulations may make provision: (a) relating to the onus of establishing that a child should not be returned under the Convention; and (b) establishing rebuttable presumptions in favour of returning a child under the Convention; and (c) relating to a Central Authority within the meaning of the regulations applying on behalf of another person for a parenting order that deals with the person or persons with whom a child is to spend time or communicate if the outcome of the proceedings is that the child is not to be returned under the Convention. (1B) The regulations made for the purposes of this section must not allow an objection by a child to return under the Convention to be taken into account in proceedings unless the objection imports a strength of feeling beyond the mere expression of a preference or of ordinary wishes. (1C) A Central Authority within the meaning of the regulations may arrange to place a child, who has been returned to Australia under the Convention, with an appropriate person, institution or other body to secure the child's welfare until a court exercising jurisdiction under this Act makes an order (including an interim order) for the child's care, welfare or development. (1D) A Central Authority may do so despite any orders made by a court before the child's return to Australia.'

authority is the Secretary to the Attorney-General's Department and ordinarily it will follow up an initial application regarding a child abducted from Australia with the counterpart in another convention country.[107] If a child is retained in Australia, the applicant would be the central authority or an individual with rights of custody/access to the child.

The courts in Australia typically need to decide whether they can entertain an application regarding a wrongfully removed or retained child. The initial issue is whether the *Hague Convention on Child Abduction* is applicable in the matter. If the convention does not govern the application, the court still exercises jurisdiction unless it is clearly an inappropriate forum.[108] The High Court in *ZP v PS* overturned the trial and Full Court's finding about Australia being a wholly inappropriate forum.[109] It held that the test of the 'clearly inappropriate forum' is not an alternative test to the welfare of the child in determining the order to be made. In cases not governed by the convention, the abduction is relevant only in determining what effect it may have on the welfare of the child.

9.4.1   When the *Hague Convention on Child Abduction* applies

If, however, the *Hague Convention on Child Abduction* applies, the following conditions must be met:[110] the child is wrongfully removed or retained (art 3); the child was habitually resident in a contracting state immediately before the wrongful removal or retention (art 4); and the child is under 16 years of age (art 4). Wrongful removal or retention is decided by reference to the circumstances mentioned in art 3 of the convention. Regulation 16(1A) explains that a child's removal to, or retention in, Australia is wrongful if the child is under 16; and habitually resided in a convention country immediately before; and the person, institution or other body seeking the child's return had rights of custody in relation to the child under the law of the country in which the child habitually resided, and such rights were actually being exercised at the time of the child's removal.

9.4.2   Habitual residence and rights of custody

The courts have had occasion to determine the interpretations of the concepts of habitual residence and rights of custody. Habitual residence usually has two elements: actual residence for an appreciable period in a country and a settled intention to reside there habitually

---

107   The States and Territories have their own central authority: *Family Law (Child Abduction Convention) Regulations 1986* (Cth) reg 8. The pathway to making an application is explained on the Attorney-General's web page: see *Hague Convention on the Civil Aspects of International Child Abduction*, above n 105.

108   See *In the Marriage of Scott* [1991] FLC 92-241 (Nicholson CJ, Barblett DCJ and Mushin J), where the Full Court held that Australia would be an inappropriate forum if the welfare of the child required that the proceedings be determined elsewhere, or if continuing the proceedings in an Australian court would be vexatious or oppressive.

109   (1994) 181 CLR 639 (Mason CJ, Brennan, Deane, Dawson, Toohey, Gaudron and McHugh JJ). In this case the child and his parents were Australian citizens, but the child had been brought up in Greece. The mother had a custody order from a Greek court in her favour, but brought him to Australia in breach of that order. She applied to the Family Court of Australia and was granted interim custody. In the meantime, the father applied and was given custody by a Greek court.

110   Unless the exceptions mentioned in art 13 (incorporated in *Family Law (Child Abduction Convention) Regulations 1986* (Cth) reg 16(3)(a)–(c)) apply.

(reg 4(1)(a)). It is a mechanism for establishing a connection between a person and a legal system, and the High Court in *LK v Director-General, Department of Community Services* reiterated that since this is the concept used,[111] other factors such as domicile or nationality are not relevant. It went on to explain that habitual residence is a question of fact, which allows consideration of a wide variety of circumstances. It is possible that individuals' intentions about habitual residence may be ambiguous or uncertain. Moreover, a child's place of habitual residence is to be determined in the context of both parents' intentions.

However, change of place of residence by one parent will not necessarily change the place of habitual residence for the child.[112] Whether the child will be returned to another country is dependent on the finding of his or her place of habitual residence.[113] For example, in the case of *Commonwealth Central Authority v Cavanaugh* the Full Court determined that, since the parents had decided to live in Finland for one year,[114] the children were not habitually resident in Australia, but in Finland, where the parents had established a home. The father had wrongfully retained them in Australia and therefore the Court ordered their return to Finland.

Rights of custody are defined in reg 4, though not exhaustively.[115] They include rights relating to the care of the person of the child and, in particular, the right to determine the place of residence of the child under a law in force in that convention country (reg 4(2)). Rights of custody may arise by operation of law, by judicial/administrative decision or by an agreement having legal effect (reg 4(3)).[116] Section 111B(4) of the FLA sets out who has rights of custody and rights of access for the purposes of the convention.[117] The convention concepts of rights of custody and access have been translated into the language as used in the FLA (for example, in terms of who has parental responsibility for the child or who the child spends time with), but the translation is somewhat at odds with the fact that the FLA no longer uses the concepts of custody and access and the implications these concepts have for parent–child relationships based on guardianship and control.

---

111   (2009) 237 CLR 582 (French CJ, Gummow, Hayne, Heydon and Kiefel JJ). See also Richard Chisholm, 'The High Court Rules on "Habitual Residence": LK v Director-General of Community Services' (2009) 23(1) *Australian Journal of Family Law* 71.

112   See, eg, *Laing v The Central Authority* [1996] FLC 92-709.

113   For a discussion of the need to define the concept of habitual residence in an international sense, see Linda Silberman, 'Interpreting The Hague Abduction Convention: In Search of a Global Jurisprudence' (2005) 38 *University of California Davis Law Review* 1049.

114   [2015] FLC 93-682 (May, Strickland and Aldridge JJ).

115   See also *State Central Authority v LJK* (2004) 33 Fam LR 307.

116   See, eg, *Director-General, Department of Family and Community Services v Radisson* [2012] FLC 93-500, 86 398.

117   Section 111B(4): '[f]or the purposes of the Convention: (a) each of the parents of a child should be regarded as having rights of custody in respect of the child unless the parent has no parental responsibility for the child because of any order of a court for the time being in force; and (b) subject to any order of a court for the time being in force, a person: (i) with whom a child is to live under a parenting order; or (ii) who has parental responsibility for a child under a parenting order; should be regarded as having rights of custody in respect of the child; and (c) subject to any order of a court for the time being in force, a person who has parental responsibility for a child because of the operation of this Act or another Australian law and is responsible for the day-to-day or long-term care, welfare and development of the child should be regarded as having rights of custody in respect of the child; and (d) subject to any order of a court for the time being in force, a person: (i) with whom a child is to spend time under a parenting order; or (ii) with whom a child is to communicate under a parenting order; should be regarded as having a right of access to the child'.

In *State Central Authority v LJK* the Family Court set out general principles in regard to an application brought under the Regulations.[118] The child was born in Australia but subsequently the mother and child moved to live with the father in the United States. The parents married and lived together, but after a couple of years the mother brought the child to Australia without notice to the father. Consent orders had been made in the Family Court of Australia soon after the child was born that the child would live with the mother, and the mother would be responsible for the child's short-term and long-term care, welfare and development. No orders had been be made with respect to the father's role in the child's life. Nevertheless, it was held in this case that the father was exercising rights of custody immediately prior to the removal of the child. The fact that the parties had subsequently married was a significant factor in this case.

It could be more difficult to ascertain what constitutes the rights of custody in another country. For example, in the case of *J v Director General, Department of Community Services* the father had the right to be consulted but, as the orders gave the mother the right to make the final decision if they disagreed,[119] it was held the father did not have the rights of custody. As a result the removal of the child by the mother was not wrongful.

9.4.3   Discretion to not return a wrongfully removed or retained child

In a few circumstances the court has discretion to not return a child even if the child was wrongfully removed. Regulation 16(3) enumerates these as where (1) the person, institution or other body seeking the child's return was not actually exercising rights of custody or had consented or subsequently acquiesced in the child being removed to, or retained in Australia; or (2) there is a grave risk that the return of the child would expose the child to physical or psychological harm or place the child in an intolerable situation; or (3) the child objects to being returned, such feelings are strong and the child has sufficient maturity; or (4) the return of the child would not be permitted by the fundamental principles of Australia relating to the protection of human rights and fundamental freedoms. In certain circumstances, if the application for the return of the child was made more than a year after such removal or retention, the court may not order the return of the child.[120]

9.4.4   Rights of custody and acquiescence

The interpretation of 'rights of custody' is discussed above. A person with the rights of custody does not need to be exercising them actively.[121] What may constitute 'acquiescence' in the removal of the child is a matter of fact. For example, in *Department of Community Services v*

---

118   (2004) 33 Fam LR 307 (Morgan J).

119   [2007] FLC 93-342.

120   Regulation 16(2) (application more than one year after removal: when court must order child's return): 'if: (a) an application for a return order for a child is made; and (b) the application is filed more than one year after the day on which the child was first removed to, or retained in, Australia; and (c) the court is satisfied that the person opposing the return has not established that the child has settled in his or her new environment; the court must, subject to subregulation (3), make the order'.

121   For example, in *In the Marriage of S S and D K Bassi* (1994) 17 Fam LR 571 (Johnston J) the Court did not accept the wife's argument that the father was not exercising rights of custody. Even though he had almost no contact with the children, was violent and did not pay child maintenance, the court found the father continued to have parental responsibility for the child.

Frampton it had been found by the trial judge that the father's refusal to help the mother obtain a visa to stay in the United Kingdom meant that she had to return to Kenya (her home country) with the child.[122] The father had responded to her request to assist in getting a divorce (which would enable her to marry another UK resident and obtain a visa) with the words, '[e]njoy your life in Kenya'. The mother stayed in Kenya with the child and subsequently came to Australia to work. The father initiated proceedings with the help of the central authority to return the child to Scotland. On appeal, the Full Court held that the father's actions did not constitute sufficient acquiescence in the child's removal from the United Kingdom. The Court ordered that the child should return to Scotland with the mother, provided financial assistance was assured.

9.4.5 Grave risk

Another exception to the return of the child is if there is grave risk that the return of the child will expose the child to harm, whether physical or psychological, or place him or her in an intolerable situation. The High Court majority in the case of *DP v Commonwealth Central Authority; JLM v Director-General, NSW Department of Community Services* held that the words 'grave risk' should be given their ordinary meaning and exposure to grave risk of harm is to be avoided.[123] The obvious issue here is the risk faced by mothers subjected to domestic violence who are removing the child to what they might consider a safer environment. The orders to return the child in such circumstances can raise issues of harm and safety for both the child and mother.[124]

In *Harris v Harris* the Full Court addressed the argument of the father that he was only asking for the return of the three-year-old child to Norway and not the return of the mother.[125] The evidence before the trial judge was mostly to do with violence against the mother. The Full Court emphasised that it agreed with the order made at trial not to return the child to Norway, but was critical of the trial judge's choice to not assess the exposure to violence and the risk of violence to the child separately from such risks to the mother. It agreed with the assessment by the trial judge that the child would be put in an intolerable situation if forced to return to Norway with the mother, for the mother would have no entitlement to social security, no other source of income, and no possibility of employment or emotional support from the family of the father. The Court thus acknowledged that the circumstances faced by the mother would also affect the child. At the same time, however, it found that the risk to the child and to the parent should be clearly distinguished.[126]

9.4.6 Child's views

The third situation where the court may refuse to return the child is included in reg 16(3)(c) and refers to the child's objection to being returned. The court must decide whether the child holds a strong view and has the requisite maturity and age to form such a view. In the

---

122   (2007) 37 Fam LR 583 (Kay, Warnick and Boland JJ).
123   (2001) 206 CLR 401 (Gleeson CJ, Gaudron, Gummow, Kirby, Hayne and Callinan JJ).
124   See also the dissenting judgment by Kirby J, who argues that the aim of the convention to protect the welfare of children by discouraging abduction will be frustrated if national courts do not uphold its letter and spirit.
125   [2010] FLC 93-454, 85 187 (Bryant CJ, Finn and Boland JJ).
126   For a different outcome, see *JMB, RWS & MMS v Secretary, Attorney-General's Department* [2006] FLC 93-252.

much-publicised case of four girls brought to Australia from Italy by their mother, the Court discussed, inter alia, the issue of whether the defence in reg 16(3)(c) was relevant.[127] This discussion illustrates most of the difficulties a court is likely to face in deciding what weight to give to the views of the child. In this case the Court had before it two reports, commissioned by the mother and the Court respectively.

It referred to the report by the family consultant, where the consultant recorded her views that the girls' objections to returning to Italy were predominantly related to their father, who had been violent to the mother and physically disciplined the girls. The girls had said that the father was not actively involved in their lives and they were fearful of the potential repercussions that could arise from their expression of negative views about him if they were to return to Italy. Moreover, if they were returned to Italy they did not wish to live with the father and they would accept returning to Italy if the mother accompanied them. However, the consultant went on to say that in her opinion neither the two youngest girls nor the two older girls had fully formed their ability for abstract thought and future forecasting. Accordingly, they lacked the capacity to decide how their decision would affect their future relationship with their father. The Court thus found that the views of the girls lacked the requisite maturity and they had not reached an age where it would be appropriate to take into account their views.

This case attracted wide media coverage that was sympathetic to the mother and girls,[128] but eventually the girls were returned to Italy. It brings into stark view that at its core the *Hague Convention on Child Abduction* deals with situations where national and international laws come into competition, and it tries to resolve the tension by giving priority to the procedural issues. While it is obvious that child abduction ought to be discouraged, it remains the case that in all other aspects the FLA is uncompromising in pursuing the best interests of the child. While it is widely accepted that international cooperation is required in these cases, and generally courts try to recognise the authority of the legal systems of other nations, it is surprising that the child's best interests are displaced by procedural rules as the deciding consideration in child abduction cases.

Interestingly, while the Family Court has mostly tried to give effect to Australia's obligation under the *Hague Convention on Child Abduction*, the High Court has more often decided that the child should remain in Australia. The Hon Michael Kirby has questioned the approach of the Australian High Court in declining to return the child to another country in all cases between 1996 and 2009.[129] His view is that if the *Hague Convention* is to succeed in deterring child abduction, the courts need to show reciprocity to other legal systems and have the confidence that, in courts of other states, cases will be determined in the interests of the child. However, it is also worth remembering that the national law of Australia itself

---

127   *Department of Communities (Child Safety Services) v Garning* [2011] FamCA 485 (Forrest J). See especially [117]–[121]. At the time of the first court decision the girls were 14, 12, 9 and 8 years old respectively. They were born in Italy and had lived there all their lives before the mother brought them to Australia.

128   See, eg, the *Sydney Morning Herald* report of the girls being removed and put on a plane to Dubai: Bridie Jabour, 'Mother of Daughters Sent Back to Italy "is Afraid to Visit Them"', *Sydney Morning Herald* (online), 5 October 2012 <http://www.smh.com.au/national/mother-of-daughters-sent-back-to-italy-is-afraid-to-visit-them-20121004-27230.html>.

129   Michael Kirby, 'Children Caught in Conflict: The Child Abduction Convention and Australia' (2010) 21(1) *Australian Family Lawyer* 3.

has been critiqued as less than fair to the returned child and parent,[130] and the same could be said of many other legal systems.

9.4.7 Human rights

It is thus with some concern that the ground for possibly refusing to return the child in reg 16(3)(d) needs to be considered. It allows a court to decide not to return a wrongfully removed/retained child if it is not permitted by 'the fundamental principles of Australia relating to the protection of human rights and fundamental freedoms'. The problem that arises is that the general practice of nations giving mutual recognition to the laws of other nations is the basic tenet that makes international cooperation possible. Moreover, this regulation is to be applied in relation to another convention country. Presumably Australia is willing to enter into international relations with such a country. It has been said by the Full Court that this regulation is designed to cover the rare situation where the return of the child would utterly shock the conscience of the court or offend all notions of due process.[131] In the same case the Full Court also observed that it is a somewhat startling proposition that returning the child to England would attract this objection. It was also said that there was no reported case of refusal to return a child on this ground. Similarly, in another case the Full Court declined to accept an argument that the return of a child of Aboriginal or Torres Strait Islander descent is per se a breach of Australian principles relating to the protection of human rights and fundamental freedoms.[132]

These are some examples of how the courts end up balancing the national and international principles in child abduction cases. The considerations of what may be good for the individual child are not even allowed any standing.[133] So, too, there is an argument that one of the functions of the *Hague Convention on Child Abduction* is to normalise the idea of a two-parent family in that it prioritises the claims of parents and in the process can downplay the significance of extended family.

9.5 Enforcement of orders

Disputes regarding children are very emotive and, not unexpectedly, court orders related to children are breached probably more often than other kinds of orders. Historically the enforcement of child-related orders has been treated with caution. The basic tension is between the need to reconcile the aims of promoting the child's best interests and the punitive enforcement of orders. Originally in family law regimes, maintenance orders were

---

130   See Danielle Bozin, 'Equal Shared Parental Responsibility and Shared Care Post-Return to Australia under the Hague Child Abduction Convention' (2014) 37(2) *UNSW Law Journal* 603.

131   *McCall and State Central Authority; Attorney General of the Commonwealth (Intervener)* [1995] FLC 92-551, 81 518–19 (Nicholson CJ, Ellis and Fogarty JJ).

132   *Director-General, Department of Families, Youth and Community Care v Bennett* [2000] FLC 93-011 (Barlow, Coleman and Kay JJ). For a discussion of the complex interaction of cultural rights and other issues, see Wibo Van Rossum, 'The Clash of Legal Cultures over the "BIC" Principle in Cases of International Parental Child Abduction' (2010) 6(2) *Utrecht Law Review* 33.

133   For an argument that the primary care setting defines the individual identity of a child and thus is a better connector to decide a stable situation for a child, see Danielle Bozin-Odhiambo, 'Re-examining Habitual Residence as the Sole Connecting Factor in Hague Convention Child Abduction Cases' (2012) 3(1) *Family Law Review* 4.

notoriously difficult to enforce and contact/access orders were breached often. The nexus between these two kinds of breaches was not acknowledged formally, but the social reality was that fathers commonly did not pay maintenance and mothers would deny them access to children.[134] Child-support obligations are now much more effectively enforceable while spousal maintenance is now awarded infrequently. However, informal ideas about mothers obstructing access to children have continued to circulate and inform legislative changes.[135]

This may be an explanation for the increasing emphasis on enforcement regimes in the FLA. In 1989 specific provisions for enforcement of orders were included in the FLA (Part XIIIA). Young et al explain how various reports over the years have grappled with the idea of punitive enforcement provisions.[136] In *D and C (Imprisonment for Breach of Contact Orders)*[137] Kay J explained that the primary purpose of enforcement proceedings for non-compliance with an order is to try to ensure compliance with the order. However, there are circumstances where it is important to uphold the authority of the court and impose a penalty as a specific or general deterrent.

The trend of imposing punitive measures for non-compliance with child-related orders is evident in the introduction in 2006 of 'Division 13A – Consequences of failure to comply with orders and other obligations that affect children'. It modified the provisions introduced in the *Family Law Amendment Act 2000* (Cth) and provides that with respect to child-related orders this division entirely supersedes Part XIIIA enforcement provisions. It includes provisions regarding the definition and meaning of a contravened order, and provides a gradation of responses to the contravention of parenting orders (from non-punitive to punitive responses): namely, if contravention is alleged but not established, there is the possibility of making cost orders against the person starting the proceedings; if contravention is established but a reasonable excuse is available, the court can make orders for compensation of time lost and costs; and, if contravention is established, it may be classified as a less serious or more serious contravention. In the case of a less serious (and/or first) contravention with no reasonable excuse, the court may order attendance at post-separation parenting programs, payment of bonds or award costs; in the case of a serious (or subsequent) contravention with no reasonable excuse, the court can order imprisonment and award costs.

134   Martha Fineman, 'Dominant Discourse, Professional Language and Legal Change in Child Custody Decision-making' (1988) 101 *Harvard Law Review* 727.
135   Helen Rhoades, 'The "No Contact Mother": Reconstructions of Motherhood in the Era of the "New Father"' (2002) 16(1) *International Journal of Law, Policy and the Family* 71.
136   Lisa Young et al, *Family Law in Australia* (LexisNexis, 8th ed, 2013) 468–9; they mention the Commonwealth Joint Select Committee on Certain Aspects of the Family Law Act, Parliament of Australia, *The Family Law Act 1975: Aspects of its Operation and Interpretation* (1992), which observed that the Family Court was not using the enforcement powers given to it; ALRC, *For the Sake of the Kids: Complex Contact Cases and the Family Court*, Report No 73 (1995); Family Law Council, *Child Contact Orders: Enforcement and Penalties* (Commonwealth of Australia, 1998); and Rhoades, Graycar and Harrison, above n 81.
137   [2004] FLC 93-193, 79 230. In this case the mother resisted the father's claim for contact with the child as she claimed the child was at a risk of sexual abuse by the father. This claim had been rejected in the initial seven-day hearing and subsequently the mother had contravened the contact orders repeatedly. The mother had been imprisoned for 12 days, and in this appeal the Court suspended the remaining sentence as the mother had shown a greater willingness to comply with the court orders.

Before discussing these provisions, it is worthwhile noting that, in addition to enforcement orders, it is also possible for a recovery or location order to be made with regard to a child. As explained above, any person with whom the child is to live, spend time or communicate, or a person who has parental responsibility for the child under a parenting order, or a grandparent or any other person concerned with the care, welfare or development of the child can apply for a recovery order (s 67T).[138] Commonly, there would be some urgency about such applications and the court can make any order that it considers necessary.[139] In addition, ss 65M, 65N, 65NA and 65P are relevant as they specify general obligations created by parenting orders.

For the purposes of Division 13A, contravention in the relevant sense is defined in s 70NAC to mean an intentional failure to comply with the order or failure to make a reasonable effort to comply with the order. An intentional prevention of compliance with an order or aiding or abetting contravention is also included in the definition. The note to the section explains that parenting plans made later than a parenting order take precedence and an action in conformity with such a parenting plan will not constitute contravention of the parenting order. 'Reasonable excuse' is defined in s 70NAE(2) as a contravention owing to the person not understanding the order and the court accepting that the person ought to be excused. In such a case the court has the obligation (s 70NAE(3)) to explain the order to the person and also explain the consequences of contravening the order again. The court may also vary the parenting order in such a case.

For example, *Ongal v Materns* was an appeal by the father against the trial judge's (Dawe J) orders that he pay a bond for contravening the parenting orders,[140] even though the trial judge had accepted that the father had misunderstood the orders. In allowing the appeal the Court said that the 'legislation is silent on the matters a court should consider in deciding whether someone ought to be excused from a contravention pursuant to s 70NAE(2)(b) for misunderstanding an order',[141] but the trial judge had misdirected herself by placing weight on the fact that the father's understanding was not logical.[142] Whether it was logical or not could be a relevant question in assessing whether the father truly misunderstood the order. However, the trial judge had already accepted that the father genuinely did not understand the orders.[143]

Furthermore, in cases where parenting orders that provide for the child to live with a person, spend time with a person, or communicate with a person have been contravened, it would only be a reasonable excuse if the person who contravened the orders believed on reasonable grounds that his or her actions were necessary to protect the health and safety of a person (including himself or herself or a child), and lasted only as long as necessary to protect the health or safety of the person (s 70NAE(4)–(6)). In the case of *Childers v Leslie* the father appealed against an order of the federal magistrate, Spelleken FM, dismissing his

---

138 Location orders can be made by such people, but grandparents are not mentioned in s 67K.
139 In *Tokely v Tokely* [2014] FLC 93-601 (Thackray, Ryan and Aldridge JJ), the Full Court allowed the mother's application and directed the trial judge to give urgent attention to her application for recovery of her child, retained by the father.
140 (2015) 54 Fam LR 86 (Thackray, Strickland and Aldridge JJ).
141 Ibid 94 [38].
142 Ibid 94 [41].
143 Ibid 94 [40].

contravention application.[144] The incident in question involved the mother not allowing the child, who was four years of age at the time, to spend time with the father on a weekend as was required according to previously made parenting orders. The mother explained that the child was sick and the doctor had advised bed rest. Moreover, the child had expressed the wish to be cared for by the mother.

On appeal the Family Court found that the federal magistrate had applied s 70NAE(2)(b) and that was not the right approach. The correct approach would have been to test the mother's explanation by reference to s 70NAE(5). This is because s 70NAE(2)(b) is relevant only if the explanation for contravention was that the respondent had misunderstood the order; this could be accepted under this subsection as a reasonable excuse. However, in this case the mother had explained that the child was sick and whether that was a reasonable excuse had to be understood in the context of the limitations mentioned in s 70NAE(5). It was not open to the Court to use some ill-defined concept of reasonableness or fairness. More specifically ss 60B, 60B(2) and 65N all support the proposition that the father was entitled under a court order to spend time with the child unless a relevant exception applied.

The appeal was allowed. Originally the father had asked for compensation of time, but, owing to the lapse in time of a year since the application had been made, this was not granted. We dwell on the details of this case for a couple of reasons. It demonstrates the use of court proceedings to 'make a point', and even the Court agreed that the case depicted features of very common complaints by applicants where the recourse to courts for a contravention order seems heavy handed, where the excuse offered by the respondent might seem reasonable enough and not the kind of behaviour that ought to attract punishment, and that in all likelihood the court's intervention would not reduce the conflict in that particular family. However, the Court went on to say that it was nevertheless important for the Court to ignore these nebulous factors, ascertain the facts and apply the law.[145]

It is this exhortation to 'apply the law' that requires a moment's reflection. The facts that the four-year-old child was ill and wanted to be looked after by the mother were interpreted differently by the federal magistrate and the Family Court. There is no way of saying that one was right and the other wrong. It is a subjective decision and, not surprisingly, the mother and father disagreed and the two courts disagreed. The issue, however, is whether a contravention order was required to enforce the original court order. It is evident that the father is proving a point, that the court is more interested in the 'correct' application of the law, and that the mother's plea that the child was ill and needed her was somehow not important enough. The repeated insistence that promoting the best interests of the child is the main goal thus becomes a formula employed in the service of the ideology of a child needing two parents. We say this because the Family Court itself quotes provisions like ss 60B(2) and 65N to support its stance that contravention of parenting orders should be taken seriously.

There is no way anyone can argue against this as a general proposition, but to say that in this particular case the court applied the law and this was the only interpretation available to it is more difficult to accept. The child was ill and vomiting, and the mother administered Panadol every four hours on the Friday night, stayed awake until 3 am because of this, and the next morning sent the child to the doctor with the paternal grandparents. The doctor

---

144   (2008) 39 Fam LR 379 (Warnick J).
145   Ibid 380 [2].

advised the child to rest, and the mother advised the father in the morning. Yet the Court ultimately found that the mother did not have a reasonable explanation for retaining the child. It could be argued that the Court is prioritising compliance with court orders to make contact with the father as the weightier issue than anything else. It may be the case that our interpretation of the facts and outcome is biased, but so too is the Family Court – that is the point of our analysis. The courts of necessity have to make subjective assessments, but then are compelled to clothe them in the garb of 'applying the law'. It is this function of legal reasoning as somehow able to reach an objective and presumably correct decision that needs to be examined at every step.

The legislative design of providing graded penalties for contraventions classified from less serious to more serious, as explained above, culminates in the power to imprison the person (s 70NFB(2)). This penalty is to be imposed only if the court considers and explains why it is that no other penalty would be adequate (s 70NFG(2)–(3)). However, the actual interpretation of the provision is more nuanced, as illustrated in the separate judgments in the case of *McClintock v Levier*.[146] At first instance, the trial court had imposed a six-month custodial sentence on the mother for six contraventions of prior orders. The mother appealed successfully to the Full Court, but each of the three appellant judges gave slightly different reasons in their judgments. They held respectively that the Court could pursue the general aim of deterrence but the federal magistrate had not considered a suspended sentence option (Finn J); that the Court was not entitled to make an order with the aim of ensuring that the mother was adequately punished for reasons such as to deter others, protect the community from the mother, or denounce her conduct to the community (Coleman J); and that to punish a person for contravening a prior parenting order for the purpose of making an example of them would be contrary to law (Cronin J).

9.6   Conclusion

The above discussion has considered various aspects of the 'best interests of the child' principle – how it is defined in the legislation, how it is interpreted by the courts, the priority accorded to international relations in the *Hague Convention on Child Abduction* and the emphases of the enforcement regime in Division 13A. These all come together to construct the dominant idea that, as far as possible, two parents must be involved in the lives of their children. What is left out of this narrative is that only a very small proportion of parents end up in the courts. For the great majority of children, the parenting arrangements are put in place in the privacy of agreements reached without the supervisory gaze of the legal system. It is thus the family law system that leaves the majority of children in the competent hands of their parents – or does it?

The FLA only becomes relevant after separation and when parents cannot agree about the parenting arrangements for their children. Nevertheless, the FLA provisions function discursively to convey messages about what post-separation parenting arrangements should look like. The function of the various aspects of the family law system has been to promote the role of fathers (especially after separation) in the lives of their children notwithstanding the introduction of a gender-neutral rebuttable presumption of shared parental responsibility

---

146   [2009] FLC 93-401.

in the 2006 amendments. Indeed, this rebuttable presumption functions to efface the role of the carer parent, usually the mother. It has been observed that the 're-instatement' of the 'biological father into potentially fatherless families has futher helped to contain social anxiety about the collapse of the family'.[147]

The construction of shared parenting as being in the best interests of the child serves a double function of promoting the interests of children while also promoting the two-parent family. But in treating the role of mothers and fathers equally at the end of relationships, the law cannot account for the unequal caring arrangements that usually existed when these relationships were intact. The message conveyed by the legislation is that the nuclear, two-parent family construct is best for children. In turn, this normative standard also enables the courts to construct ideas about 'good' parents.[148]

Corresponding to these developments has been the introduction of a separate set of provisions for the financial support of children. In the following chapter we examine how the responsibility of parents to provide financial support to children is enforced under the child-support legislation. Again, the approach is to distribute this responsibility equally between parents, which does not account for financial inequities between men and women. Moreover, while these provisions were supposedly introduced to encourage all fathers to support their children, the poorest fathers have attracted the most punitive attention, and their inability to pay has often left the poorest mothers to bear the greater cost of raising children.

---

147   Helen Reece, 'UK Women's Groups' Child Contact Campaign: "So Long as it is Safe"' (2006) 18(4) *Child and Family Law Quarterly* 538, 548. See also Fineman, above n 60, 119–21 for the argument that policy-makers oversimplify the available social science research to derive support for the importance of fathers for normal childhood.

148   Felicity Kaganas and Shelley Day Sclater, 'Contact Disputes: Narrative Constructions of "Good Parents"' (2004) 12(1) *Feminist Legal Studies* 1. See also Fineman, above n 60, 119–21 for the argument that policy-maker's oversimplify the social science research to derive support for the importance of fathers for a normal childhood.

10

CHILD MAINTENANCE AND SUPPORT AND THE WIDER SOCIAL CONTEXT OF AUSTRALIAN FAMILY LAW

PART ONE
10.1   Introduction

The chapter is in two parts. Part One begins by providing the historical background of child maintenance and the introduction of the contemporary child-support regime. The introduction of the Child Support Scheme ('CSS') (as opposed to court-ordered child maintenance) marks a significant move from a legal to an administrative model of regulation. The CSS particularly requires analysis in the way it was designed to help address child poverty by imposing financial obligations on parents (but in effect on fathers) for their offspring. The focus on key changes to the regime since its introduction allows us to demonstrate the development of family law in its broader social context and how the influence of the discourse of neo-liberalism has translated into the context of private responsibility for the child. The tensions that exist in this area and changes to the specific provisions of the Child Support Acts[1] are used to illustrate how the competing interests of parents (voiced most notably by fathers' groups), children and the state have informed developments in this area.

The analysis of these developments also allows us to revisit the opposing pulls of the public/private discourse in family law. In particular, the analysis of child-support agreements (like the analysis of financial agreements in Chapter 7) will reveal the stake that the state continues to maintain in minimising the costs of family breakdown in its capacity to reject agreements that would otherwise come at a cost to the public purse. Simultaneously, this analysis will also illustrate the function of family law and how, in adopting the discourse of individual autonomy, it manages to disengage the cost of caregiving within an ongoing relationship from the arrangements as they exist after relationship breakdown. In the process, it normalises the idea of shared parental responsibility and the primacy of the child's biological parents. Similar to the effect of the child dispute provisions discussed in chapters 8 and 9, the effect of the child support provisions is to normalise the idea of the nuclear family as the ideal form of family, but in a way that promotes parenting as a gender-neutral activity, which fails to account for the reality of the effects of the sexual division of labour. The child-maintenance provisions of the *Family Law Act 1975* (Cth) ('FLA') when juxtaposed with the Child Support Acts also demonstrate the problems in conceptualising the parents and the child as autonomous individuals.

The analysis of the legal provisions will include the *Child Support (Assessment) Act 1989* (Cth) (CSAA), *Child Support (Registration and Collection) Act 1988* (Cth) ('CSRCA') and the child-maintenance provisions in the FLA. Evident in Part One are the intersections between the CSS and the Australian welfare system. Part Two explores the intersections between family law and the social-welfare system further.

Social-welfare provisions are not usually incorporated in the study of family law. The significance of analysing these provisions is to illuminate not only the breadth of the issues of relevance to this area of law, but also the various sources of regulation of the family that are not immediately apparent from looking at the conventional family law legislation and case law.

---

1   *Child Support (Assessment) Act 1989* (Cth) and the *Child Support (Registration and Collection) Act 1988* (Cth).

Part Two begins by building on a theme of this book that relates to how family law legitimises financial dependencies in the family by treating it as a private institution in order to contain the costs of the breakup of relationships and the raising of children on the state. This is most evident in the area of spousal maintenance (Chapter 6) and child support (discussed in Part One). At the same time, it is evident that social-welfare laws informed by neoliberalism want individuals to be self-sufficient by engaging in gainful employment. The juxtaposition of the family law and welfare provisions will reveal how the contrary tensions between the discourses of dependency and autonomy entrench gendered hierarchies. An examination of more recent developments in social welfare will also reveal how social-welfare functions to reproduce other structural hierarchies based on class and race. The child subject has been instrumental in promoting this policy agenda.

10.2   Child support and spousal maintenance

In the previous chapters, we have seen how the construction of the 'private family' can produce different outcomes for individual family members. The treatment of the family as private when it is intact can result in the creation of dependencies between its members, arising from the sexual division of labour. In contrast, when a relationship breaks down the law expects the parties to settle outstanding family matters in ways that treat them as private autonomous beings who are subsequently required to start their lives again, independently of each other. This is the ideal, but in the event that the financial independence of the parties is not secured by property settlement – usually because there are children requiring ongoing care – the law makes it possible to continue to maintain the financial relationship between the parties through the payment of spousal maintenance and child support. Thus, the dependencies that existed during the relationship can continue even after the relationship has ended.

The idea that child support is needed represents an acknowledgement that the existence of dependencies within families is inevitable. Since children cannot look after themselves, someone else has to take care of them. The intuitive response, and one that is rooted in biology, is that the parents are the obvious choice. It follows that they are morally and, by extension, legally responsible for their children. Thus, the prevailing social and legal expectation is that parents will support their children. In family law the allocation of this responsibility usually becomes a legal issue when the parents separate and disputes arise about how the children will be financially supported.[2] As we saw in earlier chapters, at common law married women were not entitled to own property but with the possibility of divorce arose the need for specifying the property and maintenance rights of divorced spouses. Thus, the Married Women's Property Acts, child guardianship and custody laws, as well as maintenance laws, sought to address how provisions would be made for divorced women with children. However, more recent developments in family law have seen the

---

2   For the argument that the concepts of parent and parental responsibility should be separate, see Emily Jackson, 'What is a Parent?' in Alison Diduck and Katherine O'Donovan (eds), *Feminist Perspectives on Family Law* (Routledge-Cavendish 2006) 59.

separation of spousal maintenance and child support while, increasingly, parents have been treated as having equal capacity to financially support their children. These developments are highly problematic as they ignore the effects of the sexual division of labour, as we explain below.

As the preceding chapters have made clear, the core concerns in family law revolve around children and their care and support. For example, the financial provisions in family law are necessitated by the uneven impact that the performance of primary caregiving functions can have on the financial position of each parent. Child-related provisions of family law are a response of the law to the need to provide for the emotional and physical care of children at the end of the relationship between their parents. Child support is a more specific response to meet the material needs of children if the relationship between the parents has broken down and they cannot agree on how to provide for the children.

The canvassing of these provisions brings into focus the responses of the law when the relationship of the parents is ongoing and when it has ended acrimoniously. For instance, while a marriage/de facto relationship is intact it is assumed in family law that the parents are best suited to take care of the child and meet his or her emotional and financial needs. The law only sets minimum standards to protect children from maltreatment.[3] At the end of the relationship between parents, the law also encourages them to come to an amicable agreement about the care arrangements and financial support of their children. In other words, the law accepts that the parents can be trusted to look after the child and it is up to them to decide how to do so. With respect to the financial support of children, if parents cannot reach an agreement, family law in Australia, as in many other jurisdictions,[4] provides for maintenance to be paid for the upkeep of the child. The applicable rules are either in the FLA (in exceptional cases) or in the CSAA (in most cases). The assessment under the CSAA also represents a change from the judicial to the administrative model of regulation in the area of child support.

As noted above, the rationale of the parental child-support obligation is implied rather than articulated. It is useful to ask, as does Krause, whether this assumption needs to be revisited.[5] He explains that in earlier times the reciprocity between parents and child was both economic and social and, among other things, parents could expect their children to support them in old age. But the modern reality is different in many ways, including that the law does not impose any obligation on adult children to support their aged parents. Since marriages are no longer for life, and children may be born in different relationship circumstances, it is necessary for the law to acknowledge that not all families are organised in traditional nuclear family structures. However, the imposition of this model on all families can entrench social disadvantage on those who do not fit this structure. Krause is writing in the context of the United States and is critiquing the insistence of American family law

---

3   For a discussion of the definition of 'child maltreatment', see CFCA, *What is Child Abuse and Neglect* (Resource Sheet, AIFS, September 2015).

4   See Marygold S Melli and Patricia R Brown, 'Exploring a New Family Form – the Shared Time Family' (2008) 22(2) *International Journal of Law, Policy and the Family* 231 for an analysis of the increasing trend in many countries towards the twin developments of shared parenting laws and the privatisation of child-support responsibilities.

5   Harry D Krause, 'Child Support Reassessed: Limits of Private Responsibility and the Public Interest' (1990) 24 *Family Law Quarterly* 1, 13–17.

that child support must be recovered from absent fathers. The effect of this insistence is that it mostly targets poor fathers who are unable to meet their obligations, and results in a de facto delegation of the child-raising chore to the lower economic strata, especially unmarried, divorced and unemployed women who do not have adequate income to support their children. Forcing the poorest fathers to pay for child maintenance is not the only option.[6] Nor is the assumption that parents are primarily responsible for their children inevitable. Therefore, it is worthwhile asking whether the costs of raising children could be understood as a collective societal responsibility.

Krause argues that children have a direct claim on society in addition to a parallel claim on their parents.[7] It is plausible to explain societal responsibility for children in terms of, inter alia, debt, self-interest and funding of the social security system. In contemporary industrialised societies, social security systems provide a form of economic reciprocity between taxpayers and old-age support for all workers and their spouses irrespective of whether they 'invested' in having their own children. The non-parents are as entitled to pensions as parents who shared their earnings with their children. Therefore, sharing in childcare costs is considered to be payment of a debt, rather than charity.[8] Moreover, we already accept the two most burdensome aspects of child support – health care and education – as primarily social, rather than private, responsibilities.

Folbre makes a similar argument.[9] She argues that people think of children as pets – parents acquire them because they provide companionship and love. It follows that they should either take full responsibility for them or drop them off at the pound. The logic behind this reasoning is that those who care for them are the ones who get the fun out of them and therefore they should pay the costs associated with keeping them. Thus, there are no reasons to ask taxpayers for subsidies for people having children. Folbre juxtaposes this with a person acquiring pets. She explains that a person gets a lot of pleasure out of the company of his or her pets, but cannot seriously claim that the time and money spent on pets benefits anyone but the owner. The owner cannot and does not ask society to help pay for the expense of taking care of them. To illustrate the difference between pet owners and parents, she compares her situation as a pet owner to that of her neighbours, who are raising five children (and a few pets). Not surprisingly, both parents work full-time, splitting shifts so that one adult is always at home. Folbre believes that they probably get even more pleasure from their menagerie than she does from her pets. But a significant difference between the two is that the money, time and love they devote to their children will benefit the rest of society. She refers to a 1998 study that found that a middle-income family raising a typical child spends

6   Ibid 20–1. Krause uses the example of unwed fathers who may have never had a social relationship with the child, but are asked to support the child financially. Since marriages/relationships are no longer arrangements for life, it may be necessary to determine how to equalise the cost of relationship breakdown in a more realistic manner.

7   Ibid 24–8.

8   The wider idea is that the earlier reciprocity between parents and children is now replaced with parents relying not on their children in their old age, but on state healthcare services, aged-care institutions and other social provisions and services: ibid 25.

9   Nancy Folbre, 'Children as Pets' in Chiara Saraceno, Jane Lewis and Arnlaug Leira (eds), *Families and Family Policies* (Edward Elgar, 2012) 450. For Australian perspectives, see Australian Institute of Family Studies, *A Guide to Calculating the Costs of Children* (AIFS, 2000); Bruce Smyth, 'Modernising the Child Support Scheme; Some Reflections' (2005) 71 *Family Matters* 58.

about US$1.45 million over a 22-year period.[10] Childless individuals and non-paying fathers can put that money into investments that offer a much higher private rate of return.

Moreover, children (of other people) will take care of the rest of us in our old age. Child rearing provides important public benefits, yet as a society we give support indirectly and grudgingly and explain our reluctance as not wanting to encourage a situation where people have 'incentives "not to work"'.[11] In industrialised and affluent economies, family work is not rewarded in the labour market and very few programs apart from welfare support have provided family support. It came to be accepted that mothers living in poverty were the only ones who could afford to take time out of paid employment to stay home with their children and be supported by social welfare. However, social welfare is not enough to meet the costs of raising children. Thus, most families currently living in poverty are there because the private costs of raising children are so high. Yet it is the high cost of social welfare that is emphasised and not the tax benefits that more affluent families enjoy.[12]

Folbre argues that children are public goods, which does not mean that everyone should raise them or that we need a greater number of them; rather, it means that, once they are brought into the world, society as a whole has something to gain from fully developing their capabilities.[13] It is only right that parents should take responsibility for their own children but, by the same token, the public should accept responsibility for recognising, rewarding and supplementing parental efforts. She critiques economists who seldom examine the ways in which the costs of child rearing are distributed. They certainly do not account for the cost of the time that parents devote to child care, which substantially lowers lifetime earnings. In addition, the gendered nature of child care has very real significance for women with children after separation.

It is in this context that we need to assess the trend in the family laws of most industrialised countries to privatise the issue of child support. The trend is a manifestation of neo-liberal ideas that seek to reduce state expenditure on welfare measures. The introduction of the child-support program represents the search for private solutions to the poverty of women and children.[14] Graycar, in an early response to the proposal to introduce the CSS,

---

10   Folbre, above n 9, 450. For an Australian estimate, see Ben Phillips, 'Cost of Kids: The Cost of Raising Children in Australia' (2013) 33 *AMP.NATSEM Income and Wealth Report* <http://www.natsem.canberra.edu.au/storage/AMP_NATSEM_33.pdf>, where raising two children in a typical middle income family is reported as costing $812 000. It is important to be aware that the methods of computing the costs determine the estimates.

11   Folbre, above n 9, 451.

12   Ibid 457–61. Folbre's discussion relates to the United States. This is a live issue in Australia in view of more recent government attempts to roll back social-welfare payments. For an overview of the issues and a counterargument for the government's claims that welfare benefits recipients at the expense of taxpayers, see Greg Jericho, 'If You're Going to Compare Levels of Income and Welfare, do it Fairly', *The Drum* (online), 20 May 2015 <http://www.abc.net.au/news/2015–05–20/jericho-budget-2015-unfair-comparisons-of-income-and-welfare/6480576>.

13   Folbre, above n 9, 452.

14   Regina Graycar, 'Towards a Feminist Position of Maintenance' [1987] *Refractory Girl* 7. It is also significant that the child-support schemes are generally mandatory for the parents in the relatively lower socioeconomic brackets as the resident parent (usually the mother) would seek social-welfare payments if the father did not pay. A parallel situation, where the father does not pay but the mother has enough resources to not seek social-welfare payments, still exposes the reluctance of the law to ensure that the child shares the standard of living that the father enjoys. For an argument against privatising income support for single parents, see Anna Yeatman, *Bureaucrats, Technocrats, Femocrats: Essays on the Contemporary Australian State* (Allen & Unwin, 1990).

argued that the government is out looking for recalcitrant fathers, rather than formulating public policies around women's employment, child care and related services. Children (unlike the former spouse) do not have the alternative of economic independence and have to be provided for. Private maintenance payments by fathers should be encouraged, but only if they serve the purpose of increasing the child's standard of living, not for the purpose of saving the government money. Thus, the collection of child support cannot be done in a punitive way or it might well result in children already living in poverty being worse off.

Moreover, Graycar makes an important connection when she argues that spousal maintenance and child maintenance, despite being legally defined as separate matters, are inextricably linked. Childcare responsibilities are often the reason why women find themselves in need of spousal maintenance, as those responsibilities have far-reaching effects on the participation rate of women in the workforce. Similarly, the legal links between the concepts of maintenance and property distribution make it impossible to consider them in isolation from one another. Privatising the cost of children works against the best interests of children, as the evidence of child poverty shows. The use by policy-makers of the two-parent family as the basis of child-support law denies the social (and legal) reality that one-parent child rearing is an increasingly common experience. We agree with Graycar that to force the absent 'welfare' father to pay child support does not even begin to address the costs of child care.[15]

In addition, the more recent changes in the CSAA that make both parents equally liable to pay for child support assume that the effects of childcare responsibilities have somehow changed. These changes explicitly or indirectly invoke the fiction that men and women are equal financial actors in contemporary societies.[16] But this is a fiction as evidenced by the official figures on child-support users, which identified that in 2009 88% of receiving parents were mothers.[17] Furthermore, the receiving parent's average taxable income in 2013 was $28 500. In comparison, the paying parent's average taxable income was $46 100. Moreover, 58% of receiving parents and 24% of paying parents were eligible for an income-support payment (most commonly these were Newstart Allowance, Parenting Payment and the Disability Support Pension).[18] In the discussion below, we ask how policy-makers manage to justify this discourse of equal liability of both parents. There is a curious lack of engagement by family law reformers with the existing social science literature on the effects of childcare responsibilities on women's earning capacities. There is also no public

---

15   Graycar, above n 14. See also Margaret Harrison, 'Continuous Parenting and the Clean Break: The Aftermath of Marriage Breakdown' (1988) 23(3) *Australian Journal of Social Issues* 208 for the argument that the economic vulnerability of women is the result of their discontinuous work patterns caused by child raising. This is further exacerbated by the low-paid and low-status jobs they perform before marriage and after its breakdown. It has also been noted that the ways this issue is framed by policy-feminists and conservatives are not dissimilar, though their solutions to issues facing women and welfare are very different: see Joy Puls, 'Poor Women and Children' (2002) 17(37) *Australian Feminist Studies* 65, 73–4.

16   According to the Australian Government, Workplace Gender Equity Agency, *Gender Pay Gap Statistics* (2016) 3 <https://www.wgea.gov.au/sites/default/files/Gender_Pay_Gap_Factsheet.pdf>, there is a 17.3% gap between men and women's average full-time weekly earnings. The gap has hovered between 15% and 19% over the past two decades.

17   See Child Support Agency, *Facts and Figures 08–09* (Department of Human Services, 2009) 28 <https://www.humanservices.gov.au/sites/default/files/documents/facts-and-figures-2009.pdf>.

18   See Department of Social Services and Department of Human Services, *Inquiry into the Child Support Program*, Submission No 99 to House of Representatives (2014) 6.

debate about engendering more realistic state support of families. This in turn illustrates how the dominant discourse of economic rationalism functions to silence any dissent or alternative conceptions of responsibilities for children. Thus, the 'problem' of child maintenance is resolved in family law by making the parents pay. The issue is constructed as private and between the parents, but in a way that is oblivious to social realities, as the law remains unconcerned with how children are cared for and maintained in ongoing families.[19]

Cumulatively these developments demonstrate how family law privileges the nuclear family by pinning the primary responsibility for children on the biological parents in the first instance.

10.3   The FLA and child maintenance

Originally, child maintenance was covered exclusively under the FLA, but since the CSS was introduced, the FLA provisions have applied to very few cases. As a general rule an application can be made under the FLA (Part VII Division 7) only when a claim for child support falls outside of the CSAA (FLA s 66E). The FLA applies, for example, in cases when the child, a parent or a party to the proceedings has the necessary connection with Australia (s 69E(1)). An application for child maintenance can be made by either or both of the child's parents, the child, the grandparents or any person concerned with the care, welfare or development of the child (s 66F). Section 66G gives wide discretion to the court to make 'such child maintenance order as it thinks proper'. Applications in respect of 'children' over the age of 18 are possible primarily to support the child during higher education[20] or because of their physical or mental disabilities (s 66L). In certain circumstances, a step-parent can be asked to pay maintenance for a stepchild (s 66 M).

Some of the difficulties in seeking maintenance for a child under the FLA are illustrated in *Everett v Everett*.[21] The adult daughter in this case suffered from various health difficulties, including cystic fibrosis and diabetes. The mother was the full-time carer of the daughter and had not engaged in paid work since the child was born. The father, a medical practitioner, appealed against the order of Demack FM to pay adult child maintenance of $620 per week and other expenses. The father, among other things, wanted the mother's application for adult child maintenance to be dismissed in its entirety. Communication between the father and the child had broken down and the father sought to rely on this fact. The Court rejected his argument, but on other grounds remitted the case for rehearing. We detail these facts to underscore the point that the adult child with considerable health difficulties is being cared for on a full-time basis by the mother. The father is earning about $665 600 per annum, but is not a willing contributor to the ongoing needs of his adult child. The remedies available under the FLA are at best a stopgap arrangement and bring into focus the paucity of discussion about public or social support of the needs of children in general, and special-needs

---

19   If the child is at risk, State child-welfare/protection laws come into effect, but this in turn illustrates how child-welfare laws in Australia are dispersed in various jurisdictions and contain different interpretations of the 'best interests of the child' principle.

20   See *Masterson v Masterson* [2012] FMCAfam 913.

21   [2014] FamCAFC 152 (May, Strickland and Tree JJ). See also *Re AM (Adult Child Maintenance)* [2006] FamCA 351.

children in particular.[22] The provisions of the FLA for ongoing support of adult 'children' cannot be an adequate response, as illustrated in this case.[23] The introduction of the CSS has further obscured the need for considering whether parental responsibility is the only solution for providing adequate financial support of children.

10.4   The history of the CSS

In 1989 the Commonwealth government with bipartisan support passed the Child Support Acts, but prior to this the FLA regulated the matter and, as explained above, provided that both parties to a marriage were responsible for maintaining children under 18 years of age (Part VII Division 7). There were documented difficulties with the amounts of maintenance awarded by courts and it was notoriously difficult to enforce such orders.[24] For example, in a study it was reported that in the 1980s only a small proportion of parents paid child maintenance and the amounts paid did not correspond either to the needs of children or the ability of the parent to pay.[25] The Full Family Court had criticised the legislation for permitting child maintenance to be treated less seriously than the issue of primary parental responsibility.[26] The Commonwealth introduced the CSS in 1988–89 with the enactment of the Child Support Acts.[27] The stated aims of the government were to reduce child poverty in sole-parent families and social security costs.[28] It did this by reinforcing the idea that parents had the primary obligation of maintaining their children. The CSS was designed to ensure that more realistic amounts of maintenance were payable and that they were paid through an effective enforcement process. In parallel, the social security legislation was modified, linking the availability of social-welfare benefits with an obligation to seek child support under the CSS.[29]

The CSS was introduced in stages. In Stage 1 the Child Support Agency was created under the CSRCA. Stage 2 followed with the enactment of the CSAA, which provided for

---

22   Greg Shoebridge and Donna Cooper, 'Is there a Need for a Nexus of Disability and Dependence in Adult Child Maintenance Cases?' (2007) 28 *Queensland Lawyer* 70.

23   See also Bruce Smyth, 'Child Support for Young Adult Children in Australia' (2002) 16(1) *International Journal of Law, Policy and Family* 22.

24   See, eg, S Edwards, C Gould and A Halpern, 'The Continuing Saga of Maintaining the Family After Divorce' (1990) 20 *Family Law* 31.

25   M Edwards, P Harper and M Harrison, 'Child Support: Public or Private Duty?' (1985) 4 *Australian Society* 18.

26   *In the Marriage of Mee and Ferguson* (1986) 10 Fam LR 971. The 1987 amendments to the FLA introduced ss 66A–66N to emphasise the responsibility of parents for their children and removed the provision that child maintenance could be dependent on the pension received by the parent.

27   For a concise history, see Ministerial Taskforce on Child Support, 'In the Best Interests of Children – Reforming the Child Support Scheme' (2005) ch 2 <http://www.dss.gov.au/our-responsibilities/families-and-children/publications-articles>. Information about successive legislative amendments to the Child Support Acts is available at Department of Social Services, *Child Support Guide*, Australian Government <http://guides.dss.gov.au/child-support-guide/1/2>.

28   See Reg Graycar, 'Family Law and Social Security in Australia: The Child Support Connection' (1989) 3(1) *Australian Journal of Family Law* 70 for an argument that there is an inconsistency in the twin goals. Also, the CSS would only help families where a liable parent with a capacity to pay would be present. Thus children without fathers (dead, missing or unknown) or with fathers without money would not be helped.

29   For a short history of the lead up to the legislation, see Meredith Edwards, Cosmo Howard and Robin Miller, *Social Policy, Public Policy: From Problem to Practice* (Allen & Unwin, 2001) ch 3.

the calculation of child support by the Child Support Agency. Originally the Child Support Agency was part of the Taxation Office, but was later made a part of the Department of Social Services ('DSS'), and then the Department of Human Services ('DHS'). The initial proposal included the distinctive feature that enforcement of maintenance liability would be managed through the Australian Taxation Office. The level of maintenance payable, at least in non-exceptional cases, was to be calculated according to a formula. The formula was to be applied by the Child Support Agency, with a right of appeal to the courts.

The legislation covered children born after 1 October 1989 (with a few exceptions). As mentioned above, the CSS was designed to operate in tandem with the relevant social security laws. Thus, the payee parent seeking child support (usually the mother) was obliged to seek an assessment of maintenance liability of the payer parent (usually the father) under the CSAA. If this was not done, the mother would lose social security benefits, as it was assumed that she was receiving the assessable amount of child support. The original formula for assessment of the child support amount was uncomplicated, compared to the current formulae.

In the original formula, the calculation of child-support liability took into account the taxable income of the payer parent minus the 'exempted income amount'. The exempted income amount was to provide for the self-support of the payer parent. The child-support income amount was the most recent taxable income (including exempt foreign income and rental property losses). The child-support percentages were specified as: 1 child – 18%; 2 children – 27%; 3 children – 32%; 4 children – 34%; 5 children – 37%. The basic formula (where all the children lived with the payee, whose income was less than \$31 351 pa) could be stated as follows:

$$\text{child-support amount} = \text{child-support income amount} - \text{exempted income amount} \times \text{child support \%}^{30}$$

Pension rates and the number and ages of dependent children were relevant in determining the exempted income amount.

This scheme generated a lot of anger and dissatisfaction among payer parents (mostly fathers). The Child Support Agency not only calculated child support at a more realistic level (unlike the abysmally small amounts of child maintenance ordered by the family courts), but there were more effective mechanisms in place to enforce the payment of child support. However, fathers' groups lobbied successfully and the CSS was reviewed extensively. The 1992 parliamentary report identified a number of issues, but the main problem with the original CSAA was that the payer parents appeared to be liable for the full cost of supporting their children.[31] This issue related to the provisions that the payee parent could earn a significant income (average weekly earnings plus an additional amount for each child in that parent's care) before a corresponding reduction in the level of child support provided by the payer parent would occur. Moreover, it was considered

---

30   See ss 35 and 36 in the original *Child Support (Assessment) Act 1989* (Cth) <https://www.legislation.gov.au/Details/C2009C00272>.

31   Joint Select Committee on Certain Aspects of the Operation and Interpretation of the Family Law Act, Parliament of Australia, *The Family Law Act 1975: Aspects of its Operation and Interpretation* (1992) 363–7.

problematic that the formula did not take into account expenditure in the form of school fees, mortgage payments or other expenditure that would benefit the children directly. It was also argued that the payer parent would need to show significant shifts in income before being qualified to ask for a review of the amount paid as child support. The administrative practices of the Child Support Agency with regard to default assessments were also considered unfair, especially when the evidence indicated that 81% of the payer parents earned less than the average weekly income.[32] By contrast, the majority of payee parents under the scheme were sole-parent pensioners and by definition did not earn the average weekly income amounts. Therefore, their incomes would not affect the liability of the payer parent.

The Joint Select Committee in its report recommended that the objective of the CSS (that payer parents share in the cost of supporting their children according to their capacity to pay) be redrafted, so that the objective would be that both parents share in the cost of supporting their children according to their respective capacities to pay. The issue of the respective capacities of both parents to pay for the children has been the recurring theme in subsequent reviews of the CSS. Fathers, who are the main payers of child support, have argued that they are treated unfairly when compared to mothers who receive the child-support amount.

This fundamental issue is analysed well by Fehlberg and Smyth.[33] They were specifically responding to the proposed legislative changes that would allow a reduction in the payable child support if the child were residing with the payer parent for 10–30% of nights in a year.[34] Corresponding changes in tax law (Family Tax Benefit 2000) resulted in this benefit being apportioned between the two parents in proportion to their shared level of care. Prior to this the payer parent who had a minimum of 30% care of the child could apply for a proportion of the benefit, but after this amendment the apportionment became automatic.[35] For the purpose of apportioning the benefit, the information provided to Centrelink would be used.

Fehlberg and Smyth focus on the twin emphases in the amendments on the need to provide additional support to payer parents bearing the costs of contact and the nexus between contact and child support. These amendments demonstrate how the policy shift towards co-parenting after separation, as manifest in the 1995 amendments to the FLA (which replaced

---

32   If the Child Support Agency was unable to readily ascertain a person's taxable income for the relevant tax year, it could issue a default assessment. The Child Support Agency's general administrative practices showed that such default assessments used average weekly earnings or 2.5 times such earnings. The vast majority of custodial parents under the scheme were sole-parent pensioners who by definition earned less than the custodial parent disregarded income level. The exclusion of the custodial parent's disregarded income level from the definition of the basic child support formula was considered unfair: ibid 56–8.

33   Belinda Fehlberg and Bruce Smyth, 'Child Support and Parent Child Contact' (2000) 57 *Family Matters* 20.

34   The Child Support Legislation Amendment Bill (No 2) 2000 (Cth) was passed in the House of Representatives, but was defeated in the Senate.

35   The percentage of shared care of a child has since changed. Now, when parents have shared care of a child for 35–65% of the time they may be able to share the Family Tax Benefit ('FTB'): *Your Percentage of Care Affects Your Child Support Payments*, Department of Human Services ('DHS') <https://www.humanservices.gov.au/customer/enablers/your-percentage-care-affects-your-child-support-payments>.

the concepts of guardianship and custody with the concept of shared parental responsibility after separation), was being further pursued through the relationship between contact and child support. The reform process was informed primarily by the discourse on the increase in costs of contact for payer parents, who were usually the non-resident parent after relationship breakdown.

The authors point out that the research used to support the position that the cost of care for non-resident parents is high relies on research that looks at the issue of cost to the non-resident parent without situating it in comparison to the costs of care for the resident parent. Moreover, it does not take into account the differential reporting by resident and non-resident parents. That is, payers grossly overestimate their compliance with their child-support obligations and the resident parents marginally underestimate actual payments. Another issue that is not considered is whether the costs to the non-resident parent in any way reduce the costs incurred by the resident parent. It is obvious that two households are more expensive to run than one. Furthermore, the costs of contact were already taken into account when the original formula for child support was designed.

The authors go on to argue that the nexus between contact and paying child support is a complex matter, but it is necessary that the best interests of the child, and not other considerations, remain the guiding feature. Contrary to this, the proposals were supported by the rationale that they would encourage parents to maintain contact with their children; that is, if you pay you are more likely to maintain contact with the child. Not only is this idea contrary to the core tenet of family law that contact with the child should not be linked to payment of child support, but it also implies that contact will happen for reasons other than that it is in the best interests of the child. It is also important to note that the CSS is compulsory only for the parents receiving certain social-welfare benefits. A parent who is not in receipt of these benefits does not have to comply, but again any arrangements made between the parents regarding child support are not governed by consideration of the best interests of the child. The authors make the point that there is a need to consider not only the relative economic positions of the resident and non-resident parents, but also the role of the state in providing some post-separation support to children. Thus, the discourse of sole responsibility of the parents for the children should give way to a greater consideration of the possibilities of public support for the costs of bringing up children. This, however, did not happen.

10.5   The current CSS

The CSS has been subject to frequent inquiries and amendment, culminating in the establishment of the Ministerial Taskforce on Child Support in 2004, which published its report in 2005.[36] The Commonwealth accepted most of its recommendations, which resulted in changes to the CSS between 2006 and 2008 as summarised by the Department of Families,

---

36   Ministerial Taskforce on Child Support, 'In the Best Interests of Children – Reforming the Child Support Scheme' (2005). This taskforce was appointed in response to recommendations made in House of Representatives Standing Committee on Family and Community Affairs, House of Representatives, *Every Picture Tells a Story: Inquiry into Child Custody Arrangements in the Event of Family Separation* (2003) ('*Every Picture Tells a Story*').

Housing, Community Services and Indigenous Affairs.[37] The key elements of the new scheme are that it:

- calculates child-support payments based on the costs of raising children[38]
- uses the combined income of both parents to calculate child-support payments, treating both parents' incomes in the same way
- recognises both parents' contributions to the cost of their children through care and contact,[39] and
- treats children of first and second families more equally.[40]

The 2006–08 reforms to the CSS were implemented in three stages.[41] In Stage 1 – July 2006 the way child support is calculated was modified and parents were given access to services such as family relationship centres and the Family Relationship Advice Line so that they could negotiate child support privately; in Stage 2 – January 2007 changes in review procedures were made, including introducing reviews of child-support decisions in the Social Security Appeals Tribunal and broadening the powers of the courts to ensure child-support obligations were met; in Stage 3 – July 2008 the way that child support is calculated was further modified with the introduction of a new formula with the aims of promoting shared parenting and recognising the costs of contact, while also allowing for the needs of parents to re-establish themselves after separation and for the support they may provide to dependent step-children.[42] The cumulative aim of these changes is to ensure that both parents share the cost of raising their children. The amount payable by each parent is calculated by reference to one of the six formulae included in the CSAA (ss 35–40). In calculating child support, the income of each parent is treated in the same way (except that high-income earners can disregard certain income). The proportion of time children spend with each parent, how many children spend time with the parent and their ages are also relevant. Tables that provide information about the costs of children are also used in the calculation of child support.

In the discussion below, we first briefly explain the process of making an application for the assessment of child support and the related issues of enforcing the liability to pay. Next the assessment formula is explained and its underlying assumptions are analysed. The

---

37   Department of Families, Housing, Community Services and Indigenous Affairs, *Child Support Scheme Reforms: Fact Sheet One – An Overview of the Reforms*, Department of Social Services <https://www.dss.gov.au/sites/default/files/documents/01_child_support_scheme_reforms_factsheet.pdf>. For a more detailed account of the legislative changes, see *History of the Child Support Scheme*, Department of Social Services <https://www.dss.gov.au/our-responsibilities/families-and-children/programs-services/history-of-the-child-support-scheme>.

38   This has resulted in a reduction of the maximum amount of child support payable by higher income earners and was put into effect by the new child support system that was introduced in Stage 3 – July 2008.

39   For instance, the concept of 'regular' contact (where children spend 14–34% of nights in the care of the paying parent) reduces the child support payable in order to acknowledge the cost of providing regular overnight stay of the child. Moreover, payers with regular contact are not eligible for family assistance payments, but could be eligible to receive a higher rate of income support: *Your Percentage of Care Affects Your Child Support Payments*, DHS <https://www.humanservices.gov.au/customer/enablers/your-percentage-care-affects-your-child-support-payments>.

40   Department of Families, Housing, Community Services and Indigenous Affairs, above n 37, 1.

41   The changes were enacted in the *Child Support Legislation Amendment (Reform of the Child Support Scheme – New Formula and Other Measures) Act 2006* (Cth).

42   Department of Families, Housing, Community Services and Indigenous Affairs, above n 37.

connection between the CSS and social-welfare laws is linked to this analysis to demonstrate how private liabilities for child support are enforced selectively against the poorest members of society.[43]

10.5.1   CSS: assessment of child-support liability

For the purposes of the CSAA, child support is payable if there is an eligible child, an eligible carer and a liable parent. All children are covered by the CSS as it applies to children born after 1 October 1989 (s 19).[44] The child must be present in Australia on the day the application is made or must be a citizen or ordinarily resident in Australia (s 24(1)(b)).[45] The 'eligible carer' (s 7B) may be a 'parent', or a 'non-parent carer' (s 5) if they have shared care of the child 35–65% of the nights in a year.[46] If the non-parent carer is looking after the child under relevant child-welfare laws, they would be an eligible carer only if they are a relative of the child (s 26A). The eligible parent or another carer must not be living with the other parent of the child on a genuine domestic basis (ss 25 and 25A(c)). The liable parent is the legal parent within the provisions of the FLA and a resident in Australia (or resident in a prescribed overseas jurisdiction).[47]

The process of making an application for child support and enforcing the liability

The process of applying for child support commences with an application being made to the Child Support Registrar for an assessment.[48] If the applicant meets the proof

43   A list of relevant legislation is provided in *Family Assistance Law*, Department of Education and Training <https://www.education.gov.au/family-assistance-law>.

44   The few exceptions are that the child is not an Australian citizen, or has attained 18 years of age, or is married/living in a de facto relationship (CSAA s 24(1)(ii)–(iii)). Western Australia did not refer its powers with respect to ex-nuptial children to the Commonwealth, but the CSAA and its amendments apply to WA ex-nuptial cases to the extent that it has been adopted by the WA Parliament. It adopted the child-support scheme when it enacted the *Child Support (Adoption of Laws) Act 1990* (WA), and adopted the 2006 amendments to the CSAA when it enacted the *Child Support (Adoption of Laws) Amendment Act 2007* (WA).

45   An exception to this requirement is that the eligible parent or non-parent carer entitled to receive child support is resident in a reciprocating jurisdiction (CSAA s 24(2)).

46   Presumptions of parentage are contained in s 29(2): '(a) that the person was a party to a marriage and the child was born during the marriage; or (b) the person's name is entered in a register of births as a parent of the child; or (c) a relevant court has found expressly (or made an order assuming) that the person is a parent of the child; or (d) the person has executed an instrument acknowledging that he or she is a parent of the child; or (e) the child has been adopted by the person; or (f)–(h) that the person is the man who cohabited with the woman (in a marriage that was annulled; or, in a marriage where the parties separated, they resumed cohabitation and within three months separated again; or there was cohabitation without marriage) to whom the child was born in a period beginning 44 weeks before the birth and ending 22 weeks before the birth; or (i) that the person is a parent of the child under section 60H or section 60HB of the FLA.'

47   See *Peters v Peters* [2012] FLC 93–511 (Bryant CJ, Faulks DCJ and Thackray J) for the situation where the child was an Australian citizen, but both parents were resident in two prescribed overseas jurisdictions. The Full Court held that the trial judge made an error in accepting the application of the mother to assess the father's liability for child support.

48   This can be done online at <http://www.humanservices.gov.au>, by telephone, mail, fax or personally at a service centre providing child-support services. The relevant provisions of the CSAA are ss 23–24 and 64B–79.

of parentage and the application is made in the prescribed form, the Registrar must accept the application (ss 29 and 30). Once the application for assessment is accepted, the child-support period starts from the day of the application (s 31(1)(b) and *Child Support Assessment Regulations 1989* (Cth) reg 12).[49] The Registrar determines the percentages of care.[50] Once the assessment is made, the Registrar must give notice both to the carer who is entitled to child support and to the parent who is liable to pay, including their rights to appeal (ss 76(1) and (3)).[51] A parent can seek an internal review of a decision of the Registrar in the first instance.[52] Since 2015, appeals against child-support decisions can be made to the Social Support and Child Support Division of the Administrative Appeals Tribunal.[53] The Registrar has broad powers to amend a child-support assessment, ranging from an obligation to give effect to the provisions of the CSRCA (s 74), to variations that give effect to other specific purposes (s 75). These powers enable the Registrar to amend the assessment in accordance with the provisions of the CSAA (ss 98C and 117(2))).

The payer or payee can seek a departure from the administrative assessment of child support (Part 6A). After an assessment is made, there are two main methods of collection of child support – Private Collect and Child Support Collect. In Private Collect the transfer of payments takes place between the parents. In Child Support Collect the DHS collects and passes on the payments. The Registrar can collect child support as voluntary payments by the payer or has the authority to intercept other kinds of payments that are payable to the payer. For example, the Registrar can intercept a tax refund or the wages or salary from the payer's employer.[54]

Assessments are registered under the CSRCA and the amount of child support payable is treated as a debt to the Commonwealth.[55] It can be recovered by the Registrar or by the payee (after January 2007, when Stage 2 came into effect), provided he or she has given a notice to the Registrar (CSRCA s 113A(2)). In some instances where there is a registered child-support liability, direct payments by the payer to the payee are possible (CSRCA ss 71 and 71A). With this background context, we now examine how an assessment of child-support liability is made. As noted above, there are six formulae for assessing child-support liability; we use the basic formula as an illustration.

---

49   The child-support period will end at whichever of the times provided in s 7A(3) occurs soonest, but in any case the child-support period can be a maximum of 15 months' duration (s 7A(3)(a)).

50   The *Child Support and Family Assistance Legislation Amendment (Budget and Other Measures) Act 2010* (Cth) altered the rules relating to the determination of care percentages after 1 July 2010. Now a single care determination is made for the purposes of child support and FTB (CSAA s 54K and *A New Tax System (Family Assistance) Act 1999* (Cth) s 35T ('FA Act')).

51   Part VI of the CSRCA contains the provisions for review to the Administrative Appeals Tribunal.

52   CSRCA pt VII, s 42; CSAA s 75.

53   When the CSS was initially introduced appeals were heard by the Family Court. From January 2007, they were heard by the Social Security Appeals Tribunal.

54   *Payment Methods for Child Support*, DHS <https://www.humanservices.gov.au/customer/enablers/payment-methods-child-support>.

55   See ss 17 and 18 for liabilities that can be registered and s 19 for the liabilities that cannot be registered.

The formula for assessment of child-support liability

The basic child-support formula is set out in s 35 of the CSAA. It provides:

> **Formula 1: Method statement using incomes of both parents in single child support case with no non-parent carer**
>
> This is how to work out the annual rate of child support payable for a child for a day in a child support period if no non-parent carer has a percentage of care for the child for the day.
>
> *Method statement*
>
> Step 1. Work out each parent's child support income for the child for the day (see section 41).[56]
>
> Step 2. Work out the parents' combined child support income for the child for the day (see section 42).[57]
>
> Step 3. Work out each parent's income percentage for the child for the day (see section 55B).[58]
>
> Step 4. Work out each parent's percentage of care for the child for the day (see Subdivision B of Division 4 of Part 5).[59]
>
> Step 5. Work out each parent's cost percentage for the child for the day (see section 55C).[60]
>
> Step 6. Work out each parent's child support percentage for the child for the day (see section 55D).[61]
>
> Step 7. Work out the costs of the child for the day under sections 55G and 55H.[62]
>
> Step 8. If a parent has a positive child support percentage under step 6, the annual rate of child support payable by the parent for the child for the day is worked out using the formula:[63]

$$\text{Parent's child support percentage for the child for the day} \times \text{Costs of the child for the day}$$

---

56   Child-support income of each parent is their adjusted taxable income minus the self-support amount. In relevant cases the dependent child amount and multi-case allowance will also be subtracted. Adjusted taxable income is calculated by including the taxable income, reportable fringe benefits, target foreign income, the total of tax-free pensions or benefits, reportable superannuation contributions and the parents' total investment loss (s 43). Self-support amount is one-third of the Male Total Average Weekly Earnings as published by the Australian Bureau of Statistics (s 45).

57   The parents' combined child-support income is calculated by adding the child-support income of each parent together.

58   Each parent's income percentage is calculated by dividing each parent's child-support income by his or her combined income amount.

59   The parent's percentage of care is based on the number of nights the child spends with each parent.

60   Each parent's cost percentage is determined by the table in s 55C.

61   Each parent's child-support percentage is calculated by subtracting his or her cost percentage from his or her income percentage.

62   The costs of the children are determined by the parents' combined incomes, the number of children and the age of the children. The costs are calculated using the Costs of the Children Table (CSAA sch 1).

63   The parent with a negative percentage receives the child support payments. The child-support formulae determine how these costs will be met.

Note: If a parent's percentage of care for a child is more than 65%, the parent's annual rate of child support for the child is nil (see section 40C).[64]

The DSS website provides an example of how the basic formula works in practice. It is salutary to follow the example, to understand that the basic formula itself is complex and other variations further add to the complexity.

The following example demonstrates how the formula operates.

Example

M and F have 3 children, A aged 9, B aged 7, and C aged 5, who live mostly with M. The children spend 75 nights a year with F, who has regular care of the children. M has an adjusted taxable income of $35,000 and F has an adjusted taxable income of $55,000.

Step 1: *Work out each parent's child support income by deducting the self-support amount of $22,379 from their adjusted taxable income.*

M has a child support income of $12,621 ($35,000 less $22,379)

F has a child support income of $32,621 ($55,000 less $22,379)

Step 2: *Work out the parents' combined child support income.*

$12,621 + $32,621 = $45,242

Step 3: *Work out each parent's income percentage.*

M = $12,621 ÷ $45,242 × 100 = 27.90%

F = $32,621 ÷ $45,242 × 100 = 72.10%

Step 4: *Work out each parent's percentage of care for each child.*

M has care of all the children for 290 nights, 79.45% of the nights, rounded to a care percentage ... of 80%.[65]

F has care of all the children for 75 nights, 20.55% of the nights, rounded to a care percentage of 20%.

Step 5: *Work out each parent's cost percentage for each child by looking up the table in section 55C.*

M has a cost percentage of 76%

F has a cost percentage of 24%

(Note: a percentage of care is calculated for each child. As the care arrangements for these children are the same, the percentage is the same for all the children. If there are different care arrangements for different children, then they will have different percentages of care).

Step 6: *Work out each parent's child support percentage for each child by subtracting their cost percentage for that child from their income percentage. As the care arrangements are the same for all the children we will show the 1 percentage that is used for all the children.*

64   *Working Out Child Support Payments Using the Basic Formula*, DHS <https://www.humanservices .gov.au/customer/enablers/working-out-child-support-payments-using-basic-formula>.

65   A parent's or non-parent carer's care percentage is the percentage of care of the child the person is likely to have over the next 12 months (ss 49 and 50) and is rounded up if more than 50%, or rounded down if less than 50%, to ensure that shared care never exceeds 100% (s 54D).

$M = 27.90\% - 76\% = -48.10\%$

$F = 72.10\% - 24\% = 48.10\%$

(This means that F is responsible for 72.10% of the children's costs because they have 72.10% of the combined child support income. As F meets only 24% of the costs through care they need to transfer 48.10% of the costs to M through child support.)

Step 7: Work out the costs of each child.

The combined child support income is $45,242.

From the 2013 costs of children table the total costs of the children (3 children 12 or under) =

$9,064 + ($0.26 for every $ over $33,569)

$9,064 + ($45,242 − $33,569 = $11,673 × $0.26 = $3,035)

Therefore: $9,064 + $3,035 = $12,099

The cost of each child = $12,099 ÷ 3 = $4,033

Step 8: Work out the annual rate of child support payable by the parent with a positive child support percentage.

48.10% × $4,033 = $1,940

$1,940 × 3 (children) = $5,820

F is liable to pay M child support of $5,820 (annual rate).

If there is an annual rate payable by each parent (because they each care for a child) these rates are offset against each other to arrive at 1 overall rate of child support (section 67A).[66]

10.5.2   The social-welfare connection to the CSS

An issue we have not discussed in detail is whether compliance with the CSS is compulsory. The short answer is that if the claimant is in receipt of specific social security payments or family assistance payments such as the Family Tax Benefit, then compliance with the CSS is compulsory, but for everyone else it is an optional scheme. We will briefly explain the options available to parents who are not compelled to seek a child-support assessment before examining the connection between the CSS and social welfare.

10.5.2.1   Private child-support agreements

There are a number of private agreement options available to separating parents. For example, parenting plans and parenting orders can include child-support payment plans. Alternatively, a child-support agreement can be part of a financial agreement or can be a separate private arrangement for financial support (CSAA s 4(3)). Part 6 of the CSAA provides for the making of child-support agreements and since 2007 two types of agreements can be made. They are binding child-support agreements, and limited child-support agreements (s 81) that have been accepted by the Registrar (ss 92 or 98U).

---

66   See *2.4.7 The Basic Formula – a Single Case Assessment (Formula 1)*, Department of Social Services <http://guides.dss.gov.au/child-support-guide/2/4/7#example>.

Binding child-support agreement requirements (CSAA s 80C(2)) are very similar to the binding financial agreements under the FLA. Such an agreement must be in writing; it must be signed by each party; it must contain a statement that the required legal advice about the effect on the rights, and the advantages and disadvantages of entering the agreement, was obtained by each party; it must have a certificate by the legal advisers that such advice was given; the agreement must not have been terminated under s 80D; and a signed copy must be given to each party. Significantly, no administrative assessment is required before an agreement is made, and therefore it can be for an amount that may be less than a notional assessment under the CSAA. A binding child-support agreement cannot be varied (s 80CA), but may be terminated by a subsequent binding agreement (s 80D(1)) or set aside by a court order under specified circumstances (s 136). An agreement can be set aside in circumstances where the party's agreement was obtained by fraud or there was a failure to disclose material information; or the agreement was obtained by one person exerting undue influence or duress; or engaged in unconscionable conduct, to such an extent that it would be unjust not to set aside the agreement (s 136(2)(a) and (b)). The agreement can also be set aside if there are 'exceptional circumstances, relating to a party to the agreement or a child in respect of whom the agreement is made, that have arisen since the agreement was made, [and] the applicant or the child will suffer hardship if the agreement is not set aside' (s 136(2)(d)).

A limited child-support agreement must also be in writing and signed by each party, but it can only be made if there is an administrative assessment in force in respect of the child for whom the agreement is made (s 80E(1)). Similar to a binding agreement, it cannot be varied (s 80F), but it can be terminated (s 80G(1)(a) and (b)). It can be terminated by one party giving notice in writing to the Registrar if the assessment has changed by more than 15% or if the agreement was made three or more years earlier (s 80G(1)(d) and (e)). A court can also set aside an agreement if there has been a significant change in circumstances so that it would be unjust not to set aside the agreement; or the agreement provides for an annual rate of child support that is not proper or adequate (s 136(2)(c)). Both binding and limited agreements must include the children in relation to whom agreements may be made (s 82); the people who may be parties to agreements (the parents and any non-parent carer of the child) (s 83); and how the child support will be paid (whether periodic, lump sum or in kind), and can include other matters although they may not be enforceable (s 84).

Child-support agreement applications can be lodged with the DHS[67] and are accepted by the Registrar (s 88). The Registrar is not required to conduct an inquiry into the matter and can rely on the documents presented with the application (s 92). As a consequence of acceptance or registration of the child-support agreement, the periodic cash payments can be collected by the Child Support Agency.[68] The significant effect of a registered child-support agreement is that it will be assumed, for the purposes of the Family Tax Benefit Part A, that the assessment amount of child support is being paid under the agreement. Thus, the policy decision is that, if the eligible parent 'chooses' to accept a lesser amount of child support than he or she is entitled to under the CSAA, then they must bear the loss or the shortfall if they are in need of welfare payments.

---

67   *Child Agreement Form (CS1666)*, DHS <https://www.humanservices.gov.au/customer/forms/cs1666>.

68   The non-periodic payments can be registered at a court exercising jurisdiction under the FLA and will be enforced as a deemed order (CSRCA s 95(3)).

10.5.2.2   CSAA and welfare benefits

The Family Tax Benefit ('FTB') is available to help parents meet the costs of raising children and is available in the form of FTB Part A and FTB Part B.[69] An individual may apply for maintenance or child support for a child if he or she is not living with a parent of the child. However, to receive more than the basic rate of FTB Part A, they must take reasonable maintenance action.[70] For the purposes of the FTB, maintenance includes child support and spousal maintenance, but maintenance action is required only for child support.

The claimant of FTB has 13 weeks to take reasonable maintenance action and, if after 13 weeks the maintenance action test is not met, they will be paid only the base rate of FTB Part A.[71] In certain circumstances, exemptions from the maintenance action test are available.[72]

This information must be understood in the context of the statistical profile of the CSS participants: according to the 2009 CSS figures, 88% of receiving parents were female.[73] In 2014–15, 53% of cases used private collect arrangements (and the DHS assumes that 100% of this amount is collected). In the remaining Child Support Collect arrangements, approximately 24% of payers had debts owing.[74] Two relevant issues for us to consider are that for children who are not FTB children, neither the family law nor the social-welfare law sets an enforceable standard of child support; while children for whom FTB Part A assistance is available are mostly living with single mothers and in relatively constrained financial circumstances. These mothers are the ones who are compelled by the legal regime of family assistance and child support to apply for a child-support assessment, or it will be assumed that they are already receiving the assessment amount. But even for these children, about 25% of payer parents are not meeting their child-support obligations and the payee parent,

---

69   For a summary of the eligibility requirements of the FTP, see *Family Tax Benefit*, DHS <https://www.humanservices.gov.au/customer/services/centrelink/family-tax-benefit>. People in receipt of FTB Part A may be eligible for other assistance such as Rent Assistance, the Health Care Card, and the Extended Medicare Safety Net. Child support received above the Maintenance Income Free Area results in FTB Part A payment being reduced by 50 cents for each dollar of child support until the base rate of FTB Part A is reached: *Child Support and Your Family Tax Benefit Part A*, DHS <https://www.humanservices.gov.au/customer/enablers/child-support-and-your-family-tax-benefit-part#a3>.

70   For what constitutes maintenance action, see *Family Assistance Guide: 3.1.5.40 Maintenance Action in Progress*, Department of Social Services <http://guides.dss.gov.au/family-assistance-guide/3/1/5/40>.

71   *Family Assistance Guide: 3.1.5.30 Taking Reasonable Maintenance Action*, DSS <http://guides.dss.gov.au/family-assistance-guide/3/1/5/30>.

72   For example, exemptions may be available in the following circumstances: if they fear that if they take action for child support the payer will react violently towards them or their family; where seeking child support may have a harmful or disruptive effect on them or the payer; if the identity of the other parent of the child or children is unknown; if they have had legal advice that paternity could not be proven through a court; if they have been unsuccessful in proving paternity, such as failed attempts to locate the father, where the child was born as a result of a surrogacy arrangement which is not recognised under the FLA; if there are cultural considerations that adversely affect the individual's capacity to take reasonable maintenance action; where the payer in the child-support case is deceased; and where there are other exceptional circumstances: *Family Assistance Guide: 3.1.5.70 Exemptions from the Maintenance Action Test*, Department of Social Services <http://guides.dss.gov.au/family-assistance-guide/3/1/5/70>.

73   Child Support Agency, above n 17.

74   *Annual Report 2014–2015*, DHS <https://www.humanservices.gov.au/corporate/annual-reports>.

who in the majority of cases is the mother, must pursue the payment or be prepared to suffer the economic consequence that she will be entitled to only the base rate of FTB Part A.[75] The recipient mothers often report that the complexities of the system, and the need to engage repeatedly with the non-paying fathers, mean that they are willing to accept the financial penalties of getting lower benefits.[76]

McKenzie and Cook have identified various mechanisms used by payers (mostly fathers) to avoid child support.[77] They explain that these non-paying fathers use tactics like channelling income through the name of a business, or not declaring full income by working for cash in hand. Furthermore, Cook argues that, even though the successive modifications of the CSS have targeted non-compliant payers, they have not helped the most vulnerable mothers to receive the child support and family benefits owed to them.[78] For example, the budget measures in 2012–13 designed to strengthen compliance in fact functioned to diminish the financial autonomy of the recipient mothers while enhancing the autonomy of the non-compliant fathers. This is in part because, rather than compel the men to lodge tax returns, the budget measures assume a certain income. Cook points out that men would have an incentive to comply and file tax returns if their estimated income is more than their actual income. In contrast, the recipients, who are mostly low-income women, are assessed for their FTB Part A entitlement on the basis of the CSAA assessment of child support rather than the amount agreed upon by the parents or actually received by the payee.[79] Even though there is a policy in place that FTB Part A compensation is possible if the full amount of child support is not received, most recipient mothers face hurdles in seeking this compensation. For instance, they may not be aware that reporting underpayment can result in an increase in the FTB Part A payments as the DHS does not advertise this fact widely. Even so, if the child support arrears are subsequently paid, the possibility exists that Centrelink may institute action for debt recovery as a result of overpayment of FTB Part A. It is also the case that if the recipient reports underpayment she may fear violence from the payer.

Significantly, extracting the maximum amount payable from non-complying payers (mostly biological fathers) seems to be the main policy aim. Furthermore, most fathers who are compelled to pay are also relatively financially constrained with low incomes. It is not surprising that the primacy given to saving public money comes at the expense of the most vulnerable sections of society – men and women and their children who need welfare support.[80] How is it then that policy-makers make such laws?

---

75   It has been found that about half of liable parents paid either below the assessed rate or not at all: Belinda Fehlberg and Christine Millward, 'Post Separation Parenting and Financial Arrangements over Time: Recent Qualitative Findings' (2013) 92 *Family Matters* 29, 37.

76   See Hayley McKenzie, *Accepting the Unacceptable: Patriarchal Hegemony and Child Support Arrangements* (PhD Thesis, Deakin University, 2012). See also Kristin Natalier, Kay Cook and Torna Pitman, 'Payee Mothers' Interactions with the Department of Human Services-Child Support: A Summary of Recent Qualitative Findings' (2016) 97 *Family Matters* 30.

77   Hayley Mckenzie and Kay Cook, 'The Influence of Child Support and Welfare on Single Parent Families' (2007) 45 *Just Policy: A Journal of Australian Social Policy* 13, 15.

78   Kay Cook, 'Child Support Compliance and Tax Return Non-filing: A Feminist Analysis' (2013) 11(2) *Australian Review of Public Affairs* 43.

79   Ibid 54–5.

80   Rebecca Patrick, Kay Cook and Hayley McKenzie, 'Domestic Violence and the Exemption from Seeking Child Support: Providing Safety or Legitimizing Ongoing Poverty and Fear' (2008) 42(7) *Social Policy and Administration* 749.

10.6   Critique of the CSS

The reform process and the policy choices made in the 2006–08 changes to child-support laws have generated a substantial amount of literature. The critiques of these measures identify, among other things, problems with the process of reform, the eclectic and gendered use of evidence, and that the outcomes have resulted in benefits to fathers (especially with substantial financial resources) rather than achieving fair outcomes for children and mothers. It is not a coincidence that scholars in comparable common law jurisdictions have voiced parallel concerns.[81] These issues point to the necessity of examining how discourses about justice and fairness are framed in the processes of law, and differently at various sites. A brief overview of this literature is necessary, but we also wish to strongly emphasise that there is an urgent need to refocus the issue on the social responsibility for child support rather than making it the primary responsibility of the poorest mothers and fathers in our society.

Feminist legal scholars have argued consistently that the processes of law, including law reform, remain gendered, but the language of law is fiercely gender-neutral. In an article addressing the 1995 changes to custody laws in Australia and Canada, Rhoades and Boyd demonstrate how the move from a custody and access model to one emphasising shared parenting was not informed by empirical evidence of changes to parenting practices.[82] Rather, the reform processes in both jurisdictions were a response to fathers' groups seeking shared parenting after separation (and a corresponding reduction in child-support obligations). Fineman and Opie go further and question the implicit faith in the objectivity of social science literature itself. They explain that the 'legal uses of social science literature, designated as objective, neutral, and scientific facts, may "in fact" be inherently political and/or ideological statements, which are shielded and obscured by the scientific mantle in which they are wrapped'.[83] They argue that the use of sociological literature by legal policy-makers is fraught because it is treated as scientific, objective truth. It is necessary to be aware that social scientists start from essentially political and ideological positions and that when legal policy-makers use this literature they not only apply but also interpret it.

These issues are illustrated well in the successive reform processes of child custody laws in Australia. They have been instigated by fathers' groups and have pursued a normative preference for shared parenting. However, the claims that change was needed in order to promote a fairer system have not been supported by empirical evidence (though a problematic construct) of changes in parenting patterns, other than by unsubstantiated statements that families have

---

81   Although it is not the case that all jurisdictions treat the issue of child maintenance in the same manner, see Christine Skinner and Jacqueline Davidson, 'Recent Trends in Child Maintenance Schemes in 14 Countries' (2009) 23(1) *International Journal of Law, Policy and the Family* 25.

82   Helen Rhoades and Susan B Boyd, 'Reforming Custody Laws: A Comparative Study' (2004) 18(2) *International Journal of Law, Policy and the Family* 119. In support of this assertion, they cite Richard Chisholm, 'Assessing the Impact of the Family Law Reform Act 1995' (1996) 10(3) *Australian Journal of Family Law* 177, 185. See for discussion of the reforms Helen Rhoades, 'Posing as Reform: The Case of the Family Law Reform Act' (2000) 14(2) *Australian Journal of Family Law* 142. For a comparative analysis framed by the discourse of 'new fatherhood', see, eg, A Gregory and S Milner, 'What is "New" about Fatherhood? The Social Construction of Fatherhood in France and the UK' (2011) 14(5) *Men and Masculinities* 58.

83   Martha Fineman and Annie Opie, 'The Uses of Social Science Data in Legal Policy Making: Custody Determinations at Divorce' [1987] *Wisconsin Law Review* 107, 110.

changed.[84] Any suggestion that the legislative changes were designed to facilitate the involvement of fathers in the lives of their children, however, is spurious if the same fathers are not required by the law to be equally involved in caring for the children before separation. The reluctance of family law to give any attention to the 'primary carer' as the more suitable parent to care for the child after separation further negates the existing patterns of child rearing. The reform outcomes disadvantage women in various ways, but that is not surprising given that fathers' financial interests were central to setting up the inquiries that have led to these more recent reforms.

Cook and Natalier have analysed the 2003 Inquiry into Child Custody Arrangements that culminated in the report, *Every Picture Tells a Story*.[85] This report led to the 2006 amendments to the FLA, namely the introduction of the rebuttable presumption of shared parental responsibility (see Chapter 8). But it also led to the establishment of the 2004 Taskforce on Child Support, which subsequently led to the 2006–08 child-support reforms. In their analysis, Cook and Natalier ultimately demonstrate 'how different types and sources of data were regarded in child-support policy reform that, as a whole, buttressed fathers' interests and undermined those of mothers'.[86] Cook and Natalier examined the treatment of evidence gathered during the 2003 inquiry and the processes through which data was characterised as legitimate or illegitimate.[87] For instance, with respect to child support, the main issues raised by paying fathers related to how unfairly they were being treated in comparison to payee mothers with respect to amounts of child support they pay and how it is spent. In contrast, payee mothers primarily identified their concerns as relating to the low values of minimum payments, the minimisation of liability by manipulating payers' income, and non-compliance with regard to payment of child support. The way this evidence was treated in the inquiry was reflected in the 2006–08 reforms, where only marginal changes were made to minimum payments while all of the fathers' concerns were enacted in the legislation.

Thus, the eclectic and gendered use of evidence set the stage for the outcomes of the inquiry process; that is, the changes have to a larger extent benefitted fathers and disadvantaged mothers. Fehlberg et al report that prior to the amendments in 2006–08 incremental changes favoured payers (mostly fathers), including that there was a reduction in the amount of income that payees (mostly mothers) could earn before their child-support payments decreased; shared time changes favoured fathers by reducing their child-support liability when they had care of the child for 30%, when previously the threshold was 40%; allowance was made for the support of new children by the liable father; and fathers were given more control over how the child support they paid was to be spent.[88] These trends continued in the 2006–08 reforms, for example, with the liability to pay child support decreasing if the liable parent spent 14% of time with the child and also decreasing the liability of high-income earners by increasing the disregarded amount of income fathers could earn in child-support calculations. Nonetheless, in spite of the unequal effects of these

---

84   Rhoades and Boyd, above n 82. See also Susan B Boyd, 'Demonizing Mothers: Fathers' Rights Discourses and Child Custody Law Reform Processes' (2004) 6(1) *Journal of the Association for Research on Mothering* 52.

85   Kay Cook and Kristin Natalier, 'Selective Hearing: The Gendered Construction and Reception of Inquiry Evidence' (2014) 34(4) *Critical Social Policy* 515.

86   Ibid 518.

87   Ibid 521–8.

88   Belinda Fehlberg et al, *Australian Family Law: The Contemporary Context* (Oxford University Press, 2nd ed, 2015) 426.

changes, the rhetoric supporting them is to ensure that parents share the cost of raising their children equally: that is, each parent is treated as a nominal child-support payer and each of them is allowed the same amount of self-support amount.

The assumption that both parents are equal in their access to income and use of that income denies the well-known fact that care work limits women's participation in paid work.[89] Similarly, other authors state, with the help of relevant literature, that, even though the gendered division of labour is changing, men do not take up care work to the same extent that women take up paid work.[90] In a comparative study, Australia stood out as the country where formal equal opportunity in education and employment for men and women coexisted with social policies that tend to reinforce traditional gender roles in families with children.[91] Moreover, in Australia most mothers are employed part-time and perform the greater share of care work.[92] In an early study of the 2006–08 changes, it was anticipated that under the changes low-income families and resident parents (mostly mothers) with part-time or casual employment are most likely to face greater hardships.[93] In view of this kind of evidence it is surprising, to put it mildly, that the 2006–08 changes treat both parents' incomes in the same manner. In other words, the costs of caring for children have much broader effects than the financial costs of raising children, and mothers as primary carers who are also waged workers are disadvantaged on both counts.

One of the main arguments justifying the changes in the CSS was that the costs of children would be assessed more realistically with the help of a Costs of Children Table. Fehlberg et al, however, point out that, among other things, the research informing this data is based on the costs of children in intact families. It does not take into account the unpaid care work undertaken by women; and the costs for children in the age group 0–12 are less than for older children and do not take into account very substantial costs of child care, including the income foregone by the parent who might stay at home to care for very young children.[94] This is an illustration of how social knowledge is not simply translated into progressive social policy. We reiterate Jenson's conclusion that:

> There can be a very large amount of policy talk and even social knowledge about unequal gender relations as well as about the important contribution of women to social and economic life without there being any commitment to using public policy to promote equality in income, work and care.[95]

89   See, eg, Michelle Budig, Joya Misra and Irene Boeckmann, 'The Motherhood Penalty in Cross-National Perspective: The Importance of Work-Family Policies and Cultural Attitudes' (2012) 19(2) *Social Politics* 163, who argue that mothers' employment and earnings partly depend on social policies and cultural norms supporting women's paid and unpaid work.

90   See, eg, Lyn Craig et al, *Managing Work and Family*, SPRC Report 6/08 (Social Policy Research Centre, University of New South Wales, 2008); Elisa Rose Birch, Anh Le and Paul W Miller (eds), *Household Divisions of Labour: Teamwork, Gender and Time* (Palgrave Macmillan, 2009).

91   Lyn Craig and Killian Mullan, 'Parenthood, Gender and Work-Family Time in the United States, Australia, Italy, France, and Denmark' (2010) 72(5) *Journal of Marriage and Family* 1344, 1358.

92   Ibid.

93   Bruce Smyth and Paul Henman, 'The Distributional and Financial Impacts of the New Australian Child Support Scheme: A "Before and Day-After Reform" Comparison of Assessed Liability' (2010) 16(1) *Journal of Family Studies* 5, 26.

94   Fehlberg et al, above n 88, 442–3.

95   Jane Jenson, 'The Fading Goal of Gender Equality: Three Policy Directions that Underpin the Resilience of Gendered Socio-economic Inequalities' (2015) 22(4) *Social Politics* 539, 540.

Fehlberg et al argue that it is a matter of debate whether and to what extent child-support reform has achieved its twin goals of reducing child poverty and reducing the cost to the state of supporting children after relationship breakdown.[96] Specifically, they caution against reading and interpreting the DHS child-support compliance data as the Department makes the assumption that in Private Collect cases there is full compliance.[97] Smyth et al, in an evaluation of the child-support changes, have in fact found that the reforms have led to lower child-support payments to separated mothers,[98] who on average received $20–27 less per week. The payments increased slightly two years later, but three years after the reforms fathers reported paying slightly less child support than they were paying under the old formula. The authors also find that the child-support changes did not lead to any significant increases in child-support compliance, whether in Private Collect or in Agency Collect arrangements.[99] They conclude that the reforms have not made as much progress as was the aim. Yet the House Standing Committee on Social Policy and Legal Affairs in a recent report found that the CSS is generally functioning as it is intended and that in approximately 75–80% of child-support cases parents meet their child-support obligations.[100] The Standing Committee considered the merits of a child-support guarantee, but did not support it. Instead, it only recommended that the government should review the available information from other countries in order to consider whether to introduce a guaranteed child-support payment system to meet the shortfall when the paying parent does not fulfil their obligations.

In conclusion, the process of law reform of child support and parenting arrangements (in the preceding two chapters) illustrates graphically how discourse about parenting is constructed at various sites.[101] The issue extends beyond acknowledging how the reforms are buttressed by a gendered agenda and goes deeper, to illuminate how we as a society seem unable to acknowledge how the costs of child care are apportioned unfairly between men and women. The discourse of choices made by individual men and women does not even begin to identify the structural issues. Family law reform, even if well informed by appropriate social science knowledge, would not be adequate to change these structures. In this context, supplementing family law with social-welfare law is yet another mechanism for making the single mothers pay for the rest of us. As Daly has found in analysing social policy across countries, the notion of lone mothers is increasingly distinguished from that of other mothers, so that, unlike women who rely on male support, they are expected to be employed as well as to be 'good mothers'.[102] We turn to this and related issues in the next part of the chapter.

---

96   Fehlberg et al, above n 88, 424–5.

97   The two collection methods are Private Collect and Child Support Collect. In Private Collect the transfer of payments takes place between the parents. In Child Support Collect the DHS collects and passes on the payments.

98   Bruce Smyth et al, 'The Australian Child Support Reforms: A Critical Evaluation' (2015) 50(3) *Australian Journal of Social Issues* 217, 225.

99   Ibid 226.

100   House of Representatives Standing Committee on Social Policy and Legal Affairs, *From Conflict to Cooperation: Inquiry into the Child Support Program* (Parliament of Australia, 2015).

101   This is reason enough for legal analysts to take seriously the task of critical discourse analysis. See Siegfried Jäger, 'Discourse and Knowledge: Theoretical and Methodological Aspects of A Critical Discourse and Dispositive Analysis' in Ruth Wodak and Michael Meyer (eds), *Methods of Critical Discourse Analysis* (Sage Publications, 2001) 32.

102   Mary Daly, 'What Adult Worker Model? A Critical Look at Recent Social Policy Reform in Europe from a Gender and Family Perspective' (2011) 18(1) *Social Politics* 1, 10.

PART TWO

10.7 Financial relations and the wider social context

In this section we pause to consider the wider social context in which the family law provisions relating to property, maintenance, parenting and child support operate.

The preceding analysis shows how the role of law in creating dependencies is indisputable, but is obscured by the understanding of the family as natural and private. The presence of children in a relationship cements the understanding of family as the biological unit of society. The unequal financial relationship that usually exists at the end of a relationship between the child's parents is seen as a natural consequence of having children. The standard explanation is that family law is merely responding to the realities of family life, instead of actively engaged in constructing family relations and the hierarchies that exist within them. This approach gives only a limited view of family law in Australia by failing to acknowledge that there are many laws and policies that shape families and relations within them. Taxation laws, employment laws and social-welfare laws are just some examples of areas that have a direct impact on families and construct family relationships.[103]

In this section, we focus on the area of social welfare and its interface with family law in responding to and shaping family relationships. In keeping with the general thesis of the book, our focus is on how the provision of social-welfare payments also relies on the nuclear family construct and in doing so supports the gendered hierarchy present in the nuclear family. Of course, state welfare need not be set up this way and it could be used to alleviate social disadvantage. Nonetheless, with the rise of neoliberalism, more recent developments in social-welfare law have resulted in the retraction of welfare support for the most vulnerable members of society, who are now expected to help themselves. Simultaneously, there has been a growth in the provision of 'middle-class welfare', which seems to contradict the neoliberal agenda. These apparent contradictions can be reconciled by viewing them in terms of traditional values, among them being a concern for the welfare of children and helping families meet the costs of raising children. But the upholding of these values obscures how governments are reproducing gendered hierarchies as well as hierarchies based on race and class. This is illustrated well by the introduction of mutual obligation measures for single parents on the 'parenting payment' and for Aboriginal and Torres Strait Islander peoples subject to income management. We will further substantiate our analysis by contrasting these developments with payments such as the Baby Bonus and the Parental Leave Pay.

---

103   We cannot examine the interface between all the different areas of law and the family in Australia. But now that we have canvassed the areas related to financial relations and parenting arrangements in family law, it is important at this point of the discussion to illuminate how these provisions fit in with other areas. However, in focusing on welfare we will not be engaging with the issues of welfare or welfare policy at a broader level. Instead our focus is on how family law and welfare provisions respond to caregiving, mostly related to children in different socioeconomic groups.

10.8   Family law, social welfare and the nuclear family

There are various reasons why it is pertinent at this point to turn our focus to the relationship between family law and social welfare. Primarily, it is because there is a direct relationship between various provisions in the FLA and the social-welfare system. These provisions directly support our thesis that family law is actively engaged in the construction of the family as the private nuclear family. This is evident in the way that the law dictates that the costs of relationship breakdown are to be absorbed by the parties themselves – even if that means maintaining a financial relationship between the parties after relationship breakdown. This is explicitly evident with respect to spousal maintenance, where one of the grounds a court granting leave to a party to proceed out of time and seek an order for maintenance is when the court is satisfied that:

> at the end of the period within which the proceedings could have been instituted without the leave of the court, the circumstances of the applicant were such that the applicant would have been unable to support himself or herself without an income tested pension, allowance or benefit.[104]

It is again evident with respect to binding financial agreements, where power is vested in a court:

> to make an order in relation to the maintenance of a party to a marriage if … the court is satisfied that, when the agreement came into effect, the circumstances of the party were such that, taking into account the terms and effect of the agreement, the party was unable to support himself or herself without an income tested pension, allowance or benefit.[105]

These provisions can be read in at least two different ways: as the law recognising the obligations assumed by the parties in entering into a relationship, or as attempting to absorb the costs of relationship breakdown between the parties and minimise their impact on the rest of society. The first reading is consistent with the rationale for spousal maintenance based on a rehabilitative or a compensatory approach that acknowledges the sacrifices made by the parent (usually a woman) taking care of the children during the relationship – sacrifices that should be accounted for when the relationship breaks down. The second reading acknowledges the privatisation of the maintenance of dependent women as a cost-saving exercise of taxpayer dollars. This reading is supported by how maintenance payments (including child maintenance/support) form part of the assessable income in determining certain welfare payments in Australia (such as the FTB Part A) and have the effect of reducing those payments.[106] The original rationale for the CSS in Australia, as explained above, reflects similar privatisation logic – that parents should be the ones to support their children. The recent

---

104   *Family Law Act 1975* (Cth) s 44(4)(b).
105   Ibid s 90F(1)–(1A).
106   *A Guide to Australian Government Payments*, DHS <https://www.humanservices.gov.au/corporate/publications-and-resources/guide-australian-government-payments> 7. FLA s 77A engages the court in the administration of spousal maintenance payments by requiring it to specify in orders any payments for spousal maintenance.

changes to the CSS represent an even more explicit ideological stance on promoting shared parenting through entrenching the idea that children are the financial responsibility of their parents – and not the state.

These examples illustrate how the financial provisions of family law fit within the social-welfare regime. In doing so they challenge the assumptions that are made in family law about the nature of the family – particularly in this instance, the understanding that the family is in fact a private or natural institution functioning independently of the state. If we return to the discussion in Chapter 1 of the structural-functional view where the nuclear family is upheld as the ideal model for the upbringing of children and mediating between society and the market economy, these family law and social-welfare provisions reveal how the structural-functional view of the family does not arise naturally from familial relationships. The effect of these provisions is to impose financial dependency on family members and thereby create and maintain dependent relationships even when a relationship has broken down. The state thus continues to be actively engaged in averting dependency on the state by maintaining the semblance of the self-sufficient family in this conjunction of family and welfare laws.

Indeed, the history of social welfare in western societies shows how the rise of social welfare was centred on promoting and protecting the family unit of the male breadwinner, his stay-at-home wife and their dependent children.[107] In Australia this was entrenched in the 1907 *Harvester Judgment*, which set the adult male minimum wage at a standard that would support the nuclear family unit.[108] It was developments such as these that gave the impression that the nuclear family was the natural fundamental unit of society by creating the image of the self-reliant family unit. But it cannot be ignored that legal and socioeconomic developments of the time helped construct this unit, which ultimately benefitted working men and was at odds with the experienced realities of working women, who were paid less under this wage scheme.

10.9   Social welfare, citizenship rights and the reproduction of social hierarchies in Australia

Over the course of the 20th century, the growth of the welfare state proceeded through the introduction of other state welfare measures to support socially disadvantaged members of society.[109] The welfare state is commonly associated with the provision of pension payments for the aged, the unemployed, people with disabilities and single parents, and the provision

---

107   Lesley Chenoweth, 'Redefining Welfare: Australian Social Policy and Practice' (2008) 2(1) *Asian Social Work and Policy Review* 53, 54.

108   *Ex parte H V McKay* (1907) 2 CAR 1.

109   Christopher Pierson, Francis G Castles and Ingela K Naumann (eds), *The Welfare State Reader* (Polity Press, 3rd ed, 2014). Owing to space constraints, we cannot discuss the different welfare regimes and the underlying competing assumptions in different welfare models, but for a review of the literature see Emanuele Ferragina and Martin Seeleib-Kaiser, 'Thematic Review: Welfare Regime Debate: Past, Present, Futures?' (2011) 39(4) *Policy and Politics* 583.

of state services such as public education and health care.[110] The justification for these measures was aligned to upholding the social rights of citizens. However, it is important to point out that social-welfare payments have never been designed to serve as a substitute for a paid income, and it is to be remembered that living on social welfare often means living in a state of poverty.[111] In this respect, these developments incorporated elements of social democracy in the redistribution of wealth through the system of taxation, but in ways that did not ultimately undermine the established capitalist wage labour economy.

In this regard, it is notable how early feminists at the turn of the 20th century were adamant supporters of the family wage, as they saw its potential to protect women's roles as mothers and men's roles as providers;[112] however, by the late 20th century feminists were heavily critical of the family wage because it functioned on the assumption that men would financially support their wives, compounding women's dependence on men, and the corresponding economic inequalities created by the resulting sexual division of labour.[113] In Australia the continued influence of the breadwinner model is present in the assessment of welfare payments, which reflect an assumption that the more financial partner will support the more vulnerable financial partner.[114] Though the language is no longer couched in gender-specific terms, these provisions continue to assume that relationship partners will share their financial resources. They implicate state welfare in maintaining unequal relationships of dependency of women on men, particularly given the prevalence of the sexual division of labour.[115]

In the case of women as a social group, the role of the feminist movement in the 1960s and 1970s was vital in achieving unprecedented recognition and protection of women's interests within the discursive framework of protecting and upholding equal rights for women. The growth of the welfare state did to some extent provide increased autonomy and choice for women, especially when it came to marriage and divorce. For example, state

---

110   Chenoweth, above n 107, 54. In the literature, the former type of measures may be termed 'selective' and the latter 'universal'. For an analysis of these forms of welfare see Paul Spicker, *Social Policy: Theory and Practice* (Policy Press, 3rd ed, 2014).

111   Julia Perry, 'Women, Work and Families: Implications for Social Security' in Julian Disney and Lynelle Briggs (eds), *Social Security Policy: Issues And Options* (AGPS, 1994) 127, 137–8. According to more recent figures, 'people more likely to be found in the bottom of the income distribution are: over 65 year olds; sole parents; people from non-English speaking countries; and those reliant on government benefits as their main source of income': ACOSS, *Inequality in Australia: A Nation Divided* (ACOSS, 2015) 11.

112   For a discussion of the developments in the United States, see Eli Zaretsky, 'The Place of the Family in the Origins of the Welfare State' in Barrie Thorne and Marilyn Yalom (eds), *Rethinking the Family: Some Feminist Questions* (Longman, 1982) 188, 211–7.

113   See David Cheal, *Family and the State of Theory* (University of Toronto Press, 1991) 107–11.

114   For instance, as of July 2016 a person's partner's income reduces a person's Newstart Allowance by 60 cents for every dollar their partner earns over the partner income-free area. The partner income-free area is $937 per fortnight and may be higher if the partner is eligible for Pharmaceutical Allowance or Rent Assistance. Partner means husband or wife, or de facto partner – opposite or same-sex: *Income Test for Newstart Allowance, Partner Allowance, Sickness Allowance and Widow Allowance*, DHS <https://www.humanservices.gov.au/customer/enablers/income-test-newstart-allowance-partner-allowance-sickness-allowance-and-widow>. Similar observations can be made in relation to the FTB Part B: see below n 161.

115   See Mel Gray and Kylie Agllias, 'Australia: Contemporary Issues and Debates on the Social Welfare System' in Jason L Powell and Jon Hendricks (eds), *The Welfare State in Post-Industrial Society: A Global Perspective* (Springer, 2009) 271.

support of single motherhood reduced the stigma of being divorced or having children out-side of marriage, and thus gave women with children options other than dependency on a man. These changes coincided with the raising of awareness by the women's movement of the incidence of male violence in the family and the need for the state to protect women and children so that they did not have to live in fear of violence and abuse. At the same time the women's movement was instrumental in gaining recognition of women's reproductive freedom, particularly with respect to birth control (discussed in Chapter 11).

The growth of the welfare state also corresponded with increased educational oppor-tunities for girls in the 1960s and employment opportunities for women, reflected in devel-opments such as the abandonment in 1966 of the marriage bar in gaining employment in the Commonwealth Public Service (by 1974 all States had followed suit) and the equal pay for equal work case in 1969, which was followed by the equal pay for work of equal value case in 1972, and the sex-neutral minimum award in 1974.[116] These developments signalled acceptance that a woman as a mother was fit to be a parent in the absence of a man, and that the rights of women as workers should be accorded equal protection. In the context of our argument these developments demonstrate how the state can support diversity in fam-ily formation and it was thought that such support could extend not only to single female-headed households, but also to migrant and Aboriginal and Torres Strait Islander families.[117]

However, these developments did not escape criticism, which has often been levelled at the gains made by women, who are considered to have benefited most and at the expense of their children (and men).[118] Of course, the extent to which women have made consistent gains from these developments remains to be seen.[119] First, there is a question of whether all women benefited equally from these developments, particularly across all classes and ethnicities; and, second, even though women may now participate more in the workforce, it continues to be the case that their participation is shaped by the sexual division of labour.[120] In that regard it is important to acknowledge how increased protection of the rights of women has not achieved women's equality with men, even though this is apparently the assumption that currently informs the shared parenting regime in Australian family law. Moreover, it is also important to acknowledge how inequalities exist between individuals

---

116   Ailsa Burns, 'When is a Family?' in Kathleen Funder (ed), *Images of Australian Families* (Longman Cheshire, 1991) 23, 32–3. For a comparable argument, see Linda Gordon, 'What Does Welfare Regulate?' (1988) 55(4) *Social Research* 609.

117   See Robyn Hartley and Peter McDonald, 'The Many Faces of Families: Diversity Among Australian Families and its Implications' (1994) 37 *Family Matters* 6.

118   See generally Michael Flood, 'Backlash: Angry Men's Movements' in Stacey Elin Rossi (ed), *The Battle and Backlash Rage On: Why Feminism Cannot be Obsolete* (Xlibris, 2004) 261.

119   It is notable that the gains made when Gough Whitlam was Prime Minister were subsequently wound back by his successor, Malcolm Fraser. See Gisela Kaplan, *The Meagre Harvest: The Australian Women's Movement 1950s–1990s* (Allen & Unwin, 1996) 37.

120   This is evident not only in women continuing to be responsible for caring children at home, but is also evident in the gendered work market. See *Trends in Household Work* (Australian Bureau of Statistics, 2009) <http://www.abs.gov.au/AUSSTATS/abs@.nsf/Lookup/4102.0Main+Features40March%202009>; Glenda Strachan, 'Still Working for the Man? Women's Employment Experiences in Australia Since 1950' (2010) 45(1) *Australian Journal of Social Issues* 117, 125–6; and it has been found that migrant women are significantly worse off than Australian-born women: see Gillian Triggs, *The Economic Rights of Migrant and Refugee Women* (Australian Human Rights Commission, 2013) <https://www.humanrights.gov.au/news/speeches/economic-rights-migrant-and-refugee-women>.

(and between couples), which in the context of family law means that many of its provisions (especially the financial provisions) are irrelevant when the relationships of poorer couples break down because the means of the parties do not allow for property settlement or maintenance. The 'clean break' philosophy in family law is that the parties should fend for themselves after relationship breakdown. If that is not possible, the law provides for ongoing maintenance. The idea is to contain the cost of relationship breakdown between the parties. This approach treats social welfare as a last resort measure to be provided only to the most in need. However, as will be evident below, social-welfare provisions also play a significant role in legitimising gender inequalities, while also entrenching other social hierarchies of class and race. The point of raising these issues is to illuminate the underlying assumptions that need to be more closely scrutinised so that, through greater understanding, the impetus for a fairer system can be engendered.

10.9.1   Mutual obligations and sole parents/single mothers

Since the 1990s the effects of increased global market competition have led to the rise of neoliberal ideology, whose influence has, in turn, led to radical changes to the welfare system.[121] Changes to welfare policy have resulted in changes to the role of the state from redistributing wealth in efforts to support socially disadvantaged individuals and groups in society to the state retracting welfare support in efforts to encourage cost efficiency and self-sufficiency among individuals.[122] The shift in policy was marked by the adoption of the stance of the minimalist state evident in the privatisation of the delivery of welfare services. Encapsulating the practical and ideological changes to welfare provisions has been the adoption of the notion of mutual obligation, which entails imposing on individuals certain eligibility requirements that they must meet in order to receive their welfare payments. Underpinning the notion of mutual obligation is the understanding that social disadvantage is not a failing of the market economy, but of the individual and that individuals must do more, for example actively seek employment, to be entitled to unemployment benefits.

In Australia, the long-term unemployed were the first targets of the mutual obligation regime, but this has since been extended to other groups – notably to the principal carers of children under the age of 16. Mutual obligation for sole-parent pensioners began in 2006 with the coming into effect of the *Employment and Workplace Relations Legislation Amendment (Welfare to Work and Other Measures) Act 2005* (Cth).[123]

Currently, individuals receiving the Parenting Payment (as it is now called) are expected to fulfil their mutual obligations by seeking part-time work that is at least 30 hours per fortnight. The mutual obligation requirements start when the youngest child turns six years old. When that happens, partnered parents are also put on the Newstart Allowance. Single parents can stay on the Parenting Payment until the youngest child turns eight, but then they

---

121   Chenoweth, above n 107, 53, 55.
122   Ibid. See also Yvonne Hartman, 'In Bed With the Enemy: Some Ideas on the Connections Between Neoliberalism and the Welfare State' (2005) 53(1) *Current Sociology* 57.
123   The groundwork for change had been laid by the 'McClure Report'. See Reference Group on Welfare Reform, *Participation Support for a More Equitable Society: Final Report of the Reference Group on Welfare Reform* (Department of Family and Community Services, 2000).

must go on Newstart.[124] The gender-neutral language obscures the social reality that most women are primary carers and, even if they are not mothers, they face disadvantages in the labour market. The inequality between men and women is a result of a complex interaction of factors: women often attract lesser rates of pay, engage in part-time work and casual work, and are concentrated in lower paid occupations.[125] All these effects are further exacerbated when single mothers with children are expected to engage in paid work.[126] According to Australian Institute of Health and Welfare ('AIHW'), in 2015 in families with children under 17 years of age, 19% were one-parent families and most of these were headed by women.[127] Furthermore, in the lone-parent families, 40% of lone mothers did not participate in the labour force at all.[128] Not surprisingly, the cost of child care, and the increases in tax as hours of work increase and the corresponding need for child care increases, negate the financial benefits of returning to work.[129]

From the perspectives of the governments that have introduced these welfare changes, they are justifiable because the costs are considered unaffordable and inefficient in today's economic climate.[130] The assumption is that cutting welfare costs will increase profit margins through reduced taxation and generate more economic growth and employment. The trouble with this analysis is that it has not succeeded in alleviating the widening gaps in unemployment and poverty.[131] Indeed, a closer examination of these changes reveals deeper ideological forces at work. Coinciding with the rise of neoliberal ideology has been the rise of the New Right, whose members subscribe to neoliberal ideology *and* traditional family values and nationalistic sentiment.[132] When considered in terms of the rhetoric of the New Right, the introduction of measures based on the notion of mutual responsibility represents a rolling back of the rights of those individuals and groups that are perceived as posing a

---

124   *Parenting Payment, Eligibility Basics*, DHS <https://www.humanservices.gov.au/customer/services/centrelink/parenting-payment>. See also *Mutual Obligation Requirements and Exemptions for Principal Carers*, DHS <https://www.humanservices.gov.au/customer/enablers/mutual-obligation-requirements-and-exemptions-principal-carers>. See also Kay Cook and Andrew Noblet, 'Job Satisfaction and "Welfare-To-Work": Is Any Job a Good Job for Australian Single Mothers?' (2012) 47(2) *Australian Journal of Social Issues* 203.

125   *Women's Incomes* (Australian Bureau of Statistics, 2008) <http://www.abs.gov.au/AUSSTATS/abs@.nsf/Lookup/4102.0Chapter8002008>; Rebecca Cassells et al, *The Impact of a Sustained Gender Wage Gap on the Economy: Report to the Office for Women, Department of Families, Community Services, Housing and Indigenous Affairs* (FaHCSIA, 2009). See above n 16 for more recent statistics on the gender gap in men's and women's incomes.

126   Sara Charlesworth et al, 'Parents' Jobs in Australia: Work Hours, Polarisation and the Consequences for Job Quality and Gender Equality' (2011) 14(1) *Australian Journal of Labour Economics* 35.

127   Australian Institute of Health and Welfare, *Australia's Welfare 2015* (AIHW, 2015) 16.

128   Ibid 190. In comparison, 48% of all lone fathers are in full employment.

129   'Childcare Affordability in Australia' (2014) 35 *AMP.NATSEM Income and Wealth Report* <http://www.natsem.canberra.edu.au/storage/AMP_NATSEM_35.pdf>.

130   See, eg, Peter Costello, 'Budget Speech 2005–06' (Speech delivered on the Second Reading of the Appropriation Bill (No 1) 2005–06, Canberra, 10 May 2005) <http://www.budget.gov.au/2005-06/speech/download/speech.pdf>.

131   For instance, the poverty rate in lone-parent families in 2012 was 18.5% and for couples with children it was 5.4%. See Roger Wilkins, *The Household, Income and Labour Dynamics in Australia Survey: Selected Findings from Waves 1 to 12* (Melbourne Institute of Applied Economic and Social Research, 2015) Table 3.4, 28.

132   Ben Wadham, 'Differentiating Whiteness: White Australia, White Masculinities and Aboriginal Reconciliation' in Aileen Moreton-Robinson (ed), *Whitening Race: Essays in Social and Cultural Criticism* (Aboriginal Studies Press, 2004) 192, 198.

threat to the hegemonic order composed of the traditional nuclear family and the notion of white Australianness. Thus, for instance, while the changes to the sole-parent pension (now Parenting Payment) were couched in gender-neutral language, it remains true that women predominantly head sole-parent families.[133] Once that is accepted, then we can perceive these changes as an attack on these (non-nuclear) families.

It is no coincidence that the changes to the Parenting Payment coincided with the more recent changes to the CSS in 2006–08 and were influenced by concerns raised by fathers' rights groups about the effect past state policies have had in undermining the family unit and the need for the state to take a new direction to protect the family. However, these arguments thinly veiled the main concern of these groups, which was the demise of the traditional nuclear family unit headed by the father.[134] As Kaye and Tolmie found in their study of the attitudes of fathers' rights groups in the late 1990s, these groups expressed conflicting attitudes towards women and single motherhood – on the one hand, calling on government to abolish the sole-parent pension so as to force women into the paid workforce and, on the other hand, lamenting the growth in the number of women in the workforce and the impact this was having on the employment of men. Kaye and Tolmie found that the only way these arguments could be reconciled was by appealing to the traditional family and particularly the traditional place of women in society – that is, that 'women should be forced to be financially reliant on men, and that financial reliance should be linked to being contained within a traditional family unit'.[135] We can see how the government at the time, under conservative Prime Minister, John Howard, responded positively to these concerns,[136] not only in its changes to the Parenting Payment, but also in its refusal to introduce a maternity leave payment, and its introduction of the 'Baby Bonus' (discussed below).

10.9.2   The best interests of the child: a surrogate for regulation of 'different' families

It is equally evident from our analysis of the family law parenting provisions and the CSS that concerns over the fate of the traditional family – and the place of men in the family – came to be discursively articulated in law and policy as concerns for children and the need for children to be cared for by both parents. As demonstrated in chapters 8 and 9, the 'best interests of the child' principle has been the vehicle used to facilitate the entrenchment of these ideas in family law. Another major site where the concept of the child's best interests has been deployed is in relation to Aboriginal and Torres Strait Islander peoples. The following discussion illustrates how government policy has functioned in recent times to maintain traditional ideological values in trying to reconstruct not only the image of the nuclear family but that of the Australian nation as well. The idea of protecting the child subject has been instrumental in advancing this ideological agenda. In our view, this interpretation of the

---

133   See, eg, Australian Institute of Health and Welfare, above n 127, 16.

134   Miranda Kaye and Julie Tolmie, 'Fathers' Rights Groups in Australia and their Engagement with Issues in Family Law' (1998) 12(1) *Australian Journal of Family Law* 19.

135   Ibid.

136   Liz Van Acker, 'The Howard Government's Budgets: Stay-at-Home Mothers Good – Single Mothers Bad' (2005) 31(2) *Hecate* 90.

ideology driving government policy of social welfare seems more plausible than simply the ideological effects of neoliberalism in attempts to achieve economic efficiency.

The notion of mutual responsibility was also extended to Aboriginal and Torres Strait Islander peoples at the turn of the 21st century under the Howard government as part of the policy of practical reconciliation. This policy replaced self-determination as the official government policy for Aboriginal and Torres Strait Islander peoples. This approach was a direct undermining of rights recognition for Indigenous peoples, but was legitimised at the time on the basis that rights recognition would be divisive and undermine national unity.[137] One of the features of this policy was the introduction of shared responsibility agreements ('SRAs'), which required Aboriginal and Torres Strait Islander communities to enter into agreements with government (federal, State and/or Territory governments) in exchange for the provision of services to their communities. Though not exclusively, most agreements related to the education of Aboriginal and Torres Strait Islander children.[138]

One main focus of these agreements was children's absenteeism from school. Agreements provided for the provision or withdrawal of services to communities depending on whether children attended school or not. To the credit of a number of Aboriginal and Torres Strait Islander communities, they embraced the initiative despite its punitive undertones and despite the fact that the services being promised in the agreements were often services – like a basic education – that non-Indigenous peoples mostly take for granted. Nevertheless, the policy largely failed to produce positive outcomes for affected communities. A notable example occurred in the Northern Territory where the community in Wadeye implemented a 'no pool, no school' policy in 2005 and ran community-based workshops on the importance of education for children as part of their SRA obligations. As de Plevitz observes, the approach was successful and 600 students attended school in the first term of that year. However, the Northern Territory government was not prepared for such a response and had not provided enough desks, teachers or classrooms for the students. By the end of the year, student enrolments had fallen to 100. In 2006, 700 students attended school, and again the government was not in a position to meet its promises to the community.[139]

The adoption of the policy of practical reconciliation (which was renamed the 'Closing the Gap' policy when Howard was succeeded by Labor Prime Minister Kevin Rudd) is aimed at addressing social disadvantage among Aboriginal and Torres Strait Islander communities. In this regard, it is pertinent to point out how the introduction of this policy followed revelations of past violations of the rights of Indigenous peoples in cases such as *Mabo v Queensland [No 2]*,[140] which was a belated attempt to address unjust dispossession of their lands, and *Bringing Them Home*,[141] which was an attempt to provide a model for reparations for the negative impact that the forced removal of Aboriginal and Torres Strait

---

137   Commonwealth of Australia, *Commonwealth Government Response to the Council for Aboriginal Reconciliation Final Report – Reconciliation: Australia's Challenge* (AGPS, 2002) 1, 17.

138   Loretta de Plevitz, 'No School, No Funds: Shared Responsibility Agreements and Indigenous Education' (2006) 6(22) *Indigenous Law Bulletin* 16.

139   Ibid.

140   (1992) 175 CLR 1.

141   Human Rights and Equal Opportunity Commission, *Bringing Them Home: Report of the National Inquiry into the Separation of Aboriginal and Torres Strait Islander Children from their Families* (1997) ('*Bringing Them Home*') <https://www.humanrights.gov.au/publications/bringing-them-home-report-1997>.

Islander children has had on individuals, their families and communities. However, in neither context have the rights of Indigenous peoples been upheld and protected. Instead we
witnessed Howard during his term in office adopt a stance of denial that there was anything
wrong about their past treatment when considered within the historical context in which
the treatment occurred.[142] Although his government accepted that Aboriginal and Torres
Strait Islander peoples were now socially disadvantaged as a consequence of past policies
and laws (and Rudd offered an 'Apology to the Indigenous Peoples of Australia' for these
policies and laws),[143] this evidence provided the basis for the construction of Aboriginal and
Torres Strait Islander subjects as victims, which in social policy has functioned to reinforce
stereotypes of them as deficient and dysfunctional. Thus the legitimacy of state power was
reasserted, while the legitimacy of Aboriginal and Torres Strait Islander peoples' claims to
self-determination and cultural rights was undermined.

Indeed, it was not long before it became apparent that the changes to Indigenous
policy were a means by which the Howard government sought to reassert notions of
white supremacy and Indigenous inferiority through the expression of concern for the
well-being of Indigenous children. This was most starkly apparent when in 2007 the
government instituted the Northern Territory Emergency Response ('NTER') in the name
of protecting Indigenous children from violence and sexual abuse.[144] The government
initiated the NTER without any consultation with affected communities and in violation
of their rights, which was most evident at the time in the government's suspension of the
Racial Discrimination Act 1975 (Cth) as part of the NTER. Among the extensive measures
of control and surveillance imposed on these communities has been the quarantining of
welfare payments.[145]

This practice is commonly referred to as income management and applies to payments
such as Newstart, the Parenting Payment and the Disability Support pension. Payments are
made on what is called a 'BasicsCard' and individuals are prohibited from using it to purchase things such as alcohol, tobacco, pornography or lottery tickets. The aims of income
management include the end of welfare dependency; to foster self-sufficiency; to ensure the
needs of children are met; to reduce harassment for money; and to improve money management.[146] These provisions are not only paternalistic in approach and humiliating for recipients, but from an Indigenous cultural perspective they are evidently informed by traditional
western notions of family in ensuring that recipients uphold their responsibilities to maintain
their children, and with the corresponding effect of undermining the cultural obligations the
recipient may owe to extended family members.[147] This practice has since spread to other

142   Stuart Macintyre and Anna Clark, *The History Wars* (Melbourne University Press, 2004).
143   Commonwealth, *Parliamentary Debates*, House of Representatives, 13 February 2008 (Kevin Rudd,
       Prime Minister) 167–71.
144   The NTER was a reaction to the Northern Territory Board of Inquiry into the Protection of
       Aboriginal Children from Sexual Abuse, *Ampe Akelyernemane Meke Mekarle ('Little Children are
       Sacred') Report* (Northern Territory Government, 2007).
145   First introduced in the *Social Security and Other Legislation Amendment* (*Welfare Payment Reform*)
       Act 2007 (Cth).
146   ACOSS, *Compulsory Income Management* <http://www.acoss.org.au/images/uploads/Income_
       management_policy_analysis_September_2014.pdf>.
147   Shelley Bielefeld, 'Compulsory Income Management and Indigenous Peoples – Exploring Counter
       Narratives Amidst Colonial Constructions of "Vulnerability"' (2014) 36(4) *Sydney Law Review* 695,
       706–8.

parts of Australia, and both Indigenous and non-Indigenous peoples in certain areas can be subject to income management. However, Indigenous peoples continue to be most affected by the scheme.[148]

These initiatives are apt illustrations of how social-welfare laws function to entrench ideas of 'normal' families with 'normal' children with appropriate gender and racial scripts. This seems a more plausible explanation than simply the workings of neoliberalism, particularly considering that the cost of administering income management significantly outstrips the usual cost of administering welfare payments and that the overall effectiveness of income management remains uncertain.[149]

These deeper ideological concerns are also evident in other more recent developments in the welfare sector, namely the introduction of payments such as the FTB, the Baby Bonus (which is now called the Newborn Upfront Payment and Newborn Supplement), the Child Care Benefit, the Child Care Rebate and Parental Leave Pay. All of these payments share the same rationale: that they are to help Australian families with the cost of raising children.[150] Currently, only the Child Care Rebate is not income tested and it serves to cover the cost of commercial child care – 50% of childcare costs for a child, up to $7500 per year. Moreover, the income threshold for these payments is significantly higher than for other welfare payments (such as the Parenting Payment), suggesting that these payments function as 'middle-class welfare'.[151] For instance, a single mother on the Parenting Payment with a dependent child under eight years of age is currently paid $737.10 per fortnight (with the Pension Supplement) and her payment is reduced by 40 cents in the dollar for every dollar she earns more than $186.60 per fortnight.[152] In contrast, the mother of a newborn or an adopted child on Parental Leave Pay could have earned an individual adjusted tax income of $150 000 or less and still be eligible for the Parental Leave Pay. Parental Leave Pay is paid for 18 weeks to women with new babies who meet the work test and at the rate of the national minimum wage, which is currently $672.60 ($1345.20 per fortnight).[153] It is also payable when

---

148   Ibid.

149   Ibid.

150   For an overview of family payments, see *Payments for Families*, DHS <https://www.humanservices .gov.au/customer/subjects/payments-families>.

151   This is most evident with respect to the Child Care Rebate, which is not subject to an income test at all. But it is also evident with respect to the Parental Leave Pay, which has an income threshold of $150 000, and the FTB Part B, which has an income threshold of $100 000. These payments follow a past tradition in Australian welfare policy of providing payments to families, the most well known of which was the child endowment payment introduced in the mid-20th century.

152   Note that she may also be eligible for FTB (and the Newborn Upfront Payment and Newborn Supplement). As of July 2016 the maximum amount per year for FTB Part A is $5493.25 for each child aged 0–12 years: *Payment Rates for Family Tax Benefit Part A*, DHS <https://www .humanservices.gov.au/customer/enablers/payment-rates-family-tax-benefit-part>, while the maximum amount for Part B is $4409.20 per year when the youngest child is under five years old: *Payment Rates for Family Tax Benefit Part B*, DHS <https://www.humanservices.gov.au/customer/ enablers/payment-rates-family-tax-benefit-part-b>.

153   This is the rate as of July 2016. Eligible 'dads' and 'partners' may claim the Dad and Partner Pay, which is paid for two weeks on the basis of the minimum wage: *Dad and Partner Pay*, DHS <https://www.humanservices.gov.au/customer/services/centrelink/dad-and-partner-pay>. For an analysis of the underlying assumptions of these payments, see Marian Baird and Margaret O'Brien, 'Dynamics of Parental Leave in Anglophone Countries: The Paradox of State Expansion in Liberal Welfare Regimes' (2015) 18(2) *Community, Work and Family* 198.

the employer has a paid parental leave scheme.[154] Although the Parental Leave Pay may work out to cost less than the Parenting Payment for individual women in the long term, in the short term it is evident that the interests of women with working histories are being given greater state support than those who do not work at the time of the birth of a child. Although all women with new babies who have earned below the threshold and meet the work test are eligible for Parental Leave Pay,[155] the fact is that the Parenting Payment is less than Parental Leave Pay; this raises the question 'why?', considering that there is an expectation that women, whether in receipt of the Parenting Payment or Parental Leave Pay, will re-enter the workforce at some point in the future. Notably, for single parents on the Parenting Payment, this means that when their youngest child turns eight years old they are moved onto the Newstart Allowance, which is significantly less than the Parenting Payment and is currently $570.80 per fortnight for single parents.

Thus, broadly speaking, payments such as Parental Leave Pay can be seen as functioning to support employed families. But at the same time they can also be seen as contradicting the neoliberal stance on promoting economic efficiency and individual self-sufficiency. Evidently, other ideological forces are underpinning these payments. One way to rationalise the introduction of the Parental Leave Pay[156] is to consider it in its historical context as a long-awaited recognition of women's connection to the workforce and a step towards achieving greater gender equality between men and women in workforce participation. In that respect, the Parental Leave Pay is a measure that functions to ensure women's continuing attachment to the workforce in response to the effects that child care has had on women's long-term job prospects in the past. But it is also evident that state support of the employment of women (and men) is inconsistent when payments such as the Parenting Payment (and Newstart Allowance) remain below the minimum wage, despite recipients fulfilling their obligations to find work. And although the Parental Leave Pay is equivalent to the minimum wage, it does not bridge the gap that continues to exist between men and women's average weekly earnings. Currently, the national average full-time weekly earnings for men is $1602.80, which is 17.3% more than women's full-time weekly earnings, currently $1325.10.[157]

However, there are also some ideological tensions between the various payments, particularly evident with respect to the Parenting Payment, the Baby Bonus and Parental Leave

---

154   Recipients of the Parental Leave Pay cannot also receive the FTB or the Newborn Upfront Payment and Newborn Supplement at the same time. However, after their Parental Leave Pay ends, they can be eligible for the FTB. The FTB Part A is subject to two tests. As of July 2016, the first test reduces the maximum rate of FTB Part A by 20 cents for each dollar earned above $51 903 until the payment reaches the base rate of FTB Part A. The second test reduces the base rate of FTB Part A by 30 cents for each dollar earned above $94 316 until the payment is nil: *Income Test for Family Tax Benefit Part A*, DHS <https://www.humanservices.gov.au/customer/enablers/income-test-family-tax-benefit-part>. They may also be eligible for the FTB Part B, which is payable to single parents and couples where the primary earner has an adjusted taxable income of $100 000 or less per year: *Family Tax Benefit*, DHS <https://www.humanservices.gov.au/customer/services/centrelink/family-tax-benefit>.

155   To meet the work test for Parental Leave Pay, a new mother must have worked for at least 10 of the 13 months before the birth or adoption of her child, and 330 hours in that 10-month period (which is just over one day a week) and had no more than an eight-week gap between two consecutive working days: *Work Test for Parental Leave Pay*, DHS <https://www.humanservices.gov.au/customer/enablers/work-test-parental-leave-pay>.

156   For a brief history, see Baird and O'Brien, above n 153.

157   Workplace Gender Equity Agency, *Gender Pay Gap Statistics* (Australian Government, 2016) 2 <https://www.wgea.gov.au/sites/default/files/Gender_Pay_Gap_Factsheet.pdf>.

Pay. As discussed above, the changes to the Parenting Payment appeared to be responding to renewed attempts of fathers' rights groups to stigmatise single motherhood and reinforce dependent family relationships based on the sexual division of labour. At the time these changes were introduced, in 2006, the Howard government had already introduced the Baby Bonus (in 2004). This was a pronatalist policy aimed at addressing fears that Australia's fertility rate was decreasing and that the economy would not be able to afford the long-term costs of an increasing ageing population. Whether these fears were real or not was debatable.[158] Notably, when Treasurer Peter Costello introduced the Baby Bonus he echoed traditional values in urging Australian families to have 'one [baby] for your husband and one for your wife and one for the country'.[159] When considered within the ideological context in which it was introduced, the Baby Bonus appeared to straddle upholding traditional notions of the family and maintaining the capitalist system by topping up the income of these families in the name of meeting the financial demands of bringing up children. This seemed to be particularly true while the Baby Bonus was paid as a one-off, non-means-tested payment made at the time of the birth of a child and could be spent however the recipient of the payment desired. In 2004 the payment was $3000 per child and by 2012 the payment was in excess of $5000 per child. This was slashed by more than half in 2014 by the Labor government[160] and is now an income-tested payment, which is paid with the FTB Part A.

The changes to the Parenting Payment and the introduction of the Baby Bonus do not directly conflict in so far as both are ideologically oriented towards upholding the traditional family. However, they subscribe to the traditional family in conflicting ways. In this regard, the Baby Bonus was more direct in rewarding parents for reproducing children, and if Costello's comment is accepted at face value it was directed at white, middle-class, heterosexual Australian families. In contrast, the Parenting Payment has been more indirect in suggesting that single mothers do not add anything of value to society – in fact, they are a burden, and should earn their keep in maintaining mutual obligation requirements and become responsible members of society. Of course, single mothers were also eligible for the Baby Bonus and, as a seemingly generous payment, it could have been an incentive for women to have babies only to then find themselves on the Parenting Payment.

Ultimately, the Baby Bonus proved too costly to maintain in its original form. Over time, it has also become evident that the changes to the Parenting Payment have only contributed to growing numbers of single mothers living in poverty with their children.[161] Cutting across these developments has been the introduction of Parental Leave Pay, which, as noted above, seeks to maintain the connection working mothers have to the paid workforce. All of these measures are responding in one way or another to the costs of raising children and in that sense they each reinforce the role of women as mothers. However, when the differences

---

158   Ross Guest, 'The Baby Bonus: A Dubious Initiative' (2007) 23(1) *Policy* 11.

159   Ibid.

160   Michael Klapdor, *Abolishing the Baby Bonus* (Parliament of Australia, 2013–14) <http://www
       .aph.gov.au/About_Parliament/Parliamentary_Departments/Parliamentary_Library/pubs/rp/
       BudgetReview201314/BabyBonus>.

161   *One in Four Children from Single-parent Families Live in Poverty* (12 June 2013) *The Conversation*
       <http://theconversation.com/one-in-four-children-from-single-parent-families-live-in-poverty-15097>
       citing the *Household, Income and Labour Dynamics in Australia (HILDA) Survey Annual Report
       2013*, Faculty of Business and Economics, University of Melbourne <http://www
       .melbourneinstitute.com/downloads/hilda/annual_report/a_report_2013.pdf>.

in payment rates and eligibility criteria come under scrutiny, it is clearly evident that some women are being valued more than others in fulfilling this role. At this point in time, working mothers are evidently being valued the most, arguably because of their past and future contributions to the market economy.[162] With respect to the Parental Leave Pay, this may reflect the ideological stance of the Gillard Labor government which introduced this measure in 2011, and although the conservative Abbott government, and now Turnbull government have sought to roll back these family payments, at the time of writing they remain in place. Of course, if these family payments were not available the disparity between rich and poor would increase even further. Nonetheless, even in their current form their effect is to entrench social hierarchies, not only between men and women but also between classes and cultures. If the effect of these payments is to address the costs associated with bringing up children, evidently some children are faring better than others.

10.10   Conclusion

In this section, we have examined how the intersections between family law and social welfare manage to reproduce social hierarchies based on sex, race and class through the social-welfare system. As basic rights are being stripped from the poorest recipients of welfare, we need to question their ideological rationale, especially as at present they are failing to achieve their stated goals of promoting economic self-sufficiency among the recipients of these payments. Indeed, if the government's concern is to promote the wellbeing of children, much more serious attention needs to be given to the unequal treatment of adults in the welfare system and the impacts this has on the welfare of their children. These issues will be explored further in the following two chapters, where we consider the laws regulating abortion, child protection, adoption and assisted reproductive technologies, and how they too reproduce social hierarchies based on sex, race and class.

---

162   But again not as much as men. Apart from disparity in pay, we can see how women are not being treated equally with respect to social-welfare payments. For example (and as noted above), the FTB Part B is payable to families where the primary earner has an adjusted taxable income of $100 000 or less per year. In cases of two-parent families, if the primary earner earns less than this amount, then the FTB is assessed on the basis of the secondary earner's income. As of July 2016 the secondary earner can earn up to $5475 each year before it affects the rate of FTB Part B. Payments are reduced by 20 cents for each dollar of income earned over $5475. The maximum that the secondary earner can earn is $27 886 a year (if the youngest child is under five years of age), or $21 663 a year (if the youngest child is five to 18 years of age) before the FTB Part B is nil: *Income Test for Family Tax Benefit Part B*, DHS <https://www.humanservices.gov.au/customer/enablers/income-test-family-tax-benefit-part-b>. Though gender-neutral language is used, given the disparity in income between men and women, it would be usual to find that men are the primary earners and women are the secondary earners. If that is accepted, then the whole setup is designed to encourage full-time paid employment for men and part-time paid employment for women (or no paid employment for women, depending on the man's income).

FAMILY REGULATION: ABORTION AND CHILD PROTECTION

11.1   Introduction

Throughout this book, we have demonstrated how the nuclear family is upheld as the ideal family model in law. Generally, the nuclear family is treated as a private family. In family law this understanding has been translated to mean that the state has a role in regulating the family only in specific circumstances. This is usually when the family is not functioning as normal – that is, like a nuclear family – and the state needs to step in and normalise the family situation. In the financial relations chapters, we saw how family law in Australia generally will only intervene at the time the relationship breaks down to make an order for property distribution or spousal maintenance.[1]

Similarly, we have seen how the law functions to reconstruct the nuclear family for the child when the relationship between the parents has broken down. As discussed in the chapters on children's matters, there has been a rise in the protection of children's rights. In family law these rights are inextricably linked to the rights of their parents. For example, the *Family Law Act 1975* (Cth) (FLA) identifies the right of children 'to know and be cared for by both their parents' (s 60B(2)(a)). This example illustrates how a right of the child is being upheld, but at the same time the right relates to their immediate familial relationship. It is through the upholding of these rights that the nuclear family structure is upheld in law.

Moreover, when the discussions in the chapters on financial relations and children are considered together, we can see how family law operates to naturalise the sexual division of labour. It does this by maintaining a non-interventionist stance when a relationship is intact. But when the relationship breaks down, its methods of intervention impose an autonomy model upon families that does not adequately account for any dependencies that can (and do) exist within them. This creates unequal outcomes especially for women, as they are usually the more financially dependent partners. This approach does not adequately account for women's caring role, either in the distribution of property or in determining parental responsibility in child-related disputes.

The legal regulation of abortion, child protection, adoption and assisted reproductive technologies also provides illustrations of the law playing a normative role in defining and constructing the family. Each of these is an example where the circumstances of the individuals involved deviate from the standard nuclear family model, allowing the law to claim that it has a legitimate role in regulating their behaviour. In these cases the law decides who is allowed to be a parent (or not) and under what circumstances. The conventional explanation is that these issues are resolved by reference to the principle of the best interests of the child. We will deconstruct this argument in our analysis of the relevant legal provisions and the wider sociological literature to illustrate how this principle serves to maintain and privilege the nuclear family form. In the previous chapters, we saw how the privileging of the nuclear family has largely disadvantaged women as mothers. In this and the following chapter, we will see how the nuclear family functions to maintain broader social hierarchies – not only those that exist between men and women, but also inequalities based on class and race.

This chapter focuses on the legal regulation of abortion and the protection of children. Chapter 12 focuses on the regulation of family formation through the techniques of adoption and reproductive technologies. In each section the relevant overseas and domestic laws are

---

1   The case of *Stanford v Stanford* (2012) 247 CLR 108 illustrates this point.

outlined. In focusing on particular factors, including the rights of women to an abortion, the over-representation of Aboriginal and Torres Strait Islander children in out-of-home care, the move towards easing the availability of adoption in Australia, and the increased use of assisted reproductive technologies to create parent–child relationships, we will illuminate the uneven impact of the law on different sections of society as it continues to uphold the nuclear family model as the ideal model for the upbringing of children.

Both of these chapters pull together the illustrations throughout the book of the normative functions performed by family law. In appealing to the 'best interests of the child' principle, law-makers are able to dictate who is a suitable parent and who is not and, as will be evident, these decisions are largely informed by traditional parenting roles in the nuclear family.

These chapters also return us to the discussion in Chapter 1, where we considered the issue of family justice. In the discussion it will be evident that family justice involves questioning the legal treatment of everyone in society who is affected by laws regulating familial relationships. Once that is accepted, the privileging of the nuclear family can be further questioned as just one ideological position among a variety of others.

11.2 Abortion

Abortion is a topic in which many sections in society have a vested interest. However, it cannot be forgotten that the person most affected by the decision to have an abortion, or not, is the pregnant woman. While feminists are cognisant of this fact and focus on the need to promote the rights of women to equality by providing them with safe access to abortion, this is not the mainstream position, where abortion is treated as part of the broader issue of population control, or is framed as concerned with upholding the rights of the unborn child – an argument that serves to trump the rights of women completely. In the legal arena as well, the rights of women have been marginalised. Historically, abortion was a criminal offence in English law and it continues to be a criminal offence in some jurisdictions. Though abortion has been decriminalised in a number of jurisdictions in nations such as Australia, the United Kingdom and the United States, it continues to be largely regulated using the criminal law. Moreover, even though prosecutions pursuant to these laws are extremely rare, in none of these jurisdictions has the right of women to an abortion been recognised. Instead, the issue is framed as a private health issue, whether for the woman, her unborn child, or society more broadly. In these arguments, we will see how the nuclear family model informs these views, particularly the understanding of the family as a private unit and the role of women within this unit as mothers and caregivers. Moreover, none of these regulatory regimes acknowledges that the autonomy to have a child, or not, is available differentially to differently situated women.

In this section, the sociological arguments in favour of birth control are examined first, followed by the central moral arguments in favour of and against abortion that focus on balancing the rights of the pregnant woman to self-determination with the rights of her unborn child. This will then lead to an overview of the legal position on abortion as it currently stands in the various Australian States and Territories. The final section discusses legal actions for compensation in wrongful birth cases and examines how the discourses supporting the nuclear family also infuse these cases.

In this discussion, we will flesh out the key arguments that support birth control and those that do not and consider how these arguments are tempered in the legal regulation of abortion. The discussion will focus on addressing the question: who has the right to decide whether a woman can have an abortion or not? This will help to identify the different rationales used to deny women the right to choose whether to carry a pregnancy to full term.

11.2.1   Birth control: individual autonomy versus state control of fertility

Sociologist Victoria Greenwood,[2] in a seminal work on abortion and population control, discusses the two main positions that support the use of birth control: the feminist and socialist movements aimed at individual/couple reproductive self-determination; and the eugenics movement based in neo-Malthusianism, which is directed at controlling population growth of entire communities, usually in places where there is poverty and civil unrest.

These two streams of thought coincide to support birth control, but appear to provide very different answers to the question of who has the right to decide on birth control (for example, abortion) and why. Their differences are explicable in terms of their ideological points of view.

The feminist/socialist perspectives are focused on the individual woman or couple. They are identified as the people who should decide whether to use birth control or not. Feminists rationalise this by promoting the idea that birth control should allow women to control their own fertility. This is aligned with the feminist stance on achieving sexual equality by separating sexuality from procreation. From a socialist stance, birth control is considered necessary at the individual level to prevent poverty and financial dependency. At the social level, birth control is identified as a necessary measure to ensure against immiseration and brutalisation. Overall, the feminist and socialist positions coincide in their stance on birth control as contributing to the larger movement towards economic and sexual liberation of women. It is treated as one step within a general program of fundamental change for women.

In contrast, the neo-Malthusianism movement is concerned with population control. It supports population reduction through birth-control measures. It believes that population reduction can be beneficial to society in alleviating social ills such as poverty and starvation, and thereby promoting economic development and advancement. But in seeking to achieve these things, it appears to be a distinctly conservative movement in how it ascribes power to elite experts to determine when and where population control is appropriate, which is usually with respect to socially disadvantaged groups who are living in the developing world or where there is urban unrest and political dissatisfaction. In these respects, as a movement for population control, it is related to the eugenics movement, which aimed to eliminate the unfit. The focus is on the unruly population as the source of the problem that needs controlling. From a socialist perspective, presenting the problem in this way averts attention from the capitalist system as creating many of the social problems that population control seeks to

---

2   The following discussion is based on Victoria Greenwood, 'The Politics of Population Control' in Victoria Greenwood and Jock Young (eds), *Abortion in Demand* (Pluto Press, 1976) 103, 103–16; see also Donald T Critchlow (ed), *The Politics of Abortion and Birth Control in Historical Perspective* (Pennsylvania State University Press, 1996).

address. Ultimately, population control is advanced as the solution to social problems without any fundamental change in the system.

Evidently, while the feminist movement presents birth control as a means by which to advance women's liberation, the population-control movement uses birth control as a means of social regulation at the expense of the poor and underprivileged. However, despite the apparent ideological differences in these two perspectives on birth control, Greenwood identifies how the two coincide, particularly with respect to arguments in favour of birth control, to prevent unwanted births among poor women because of the burden this can create for these women and for the state. In this regard, the feminist position on abortion, based on the concept of rights and self-determination, can play into the hands of the population-control movement. In both movements, birth control is presented as best for the individuals involved and the system as a whole. Promoting women's freedom to choose coincides with the need for population control as a social good. However, this does not reflect the experiences of women whose capacities to make informed choices can be undermined by their social circumstances. This discussion illuminates an unresolved tension within the pro-birth control movements: the need to promote reproductive freedom for women in a way that does not compound other forms of inequality in society based on race and class.

Greenwood's discussion raises important issues about protecting the rights of the more vulnerable in society and about the need to create the conditions in society where people's rights are not violated, but can be exercised freely and not under economic duress.[3] This is a theme we will return to in Chapter 12.

However, her discussion does not account for the fact that abortion is not and has never been freely available. Surely, if abortion is seen as a social good, then it would not be the subject of legal regulation – and especially not the subject of criminal sanction as historically has been the case. One explanation may be that eugenics arguments were largely debunked in response to the atrocities committed by the Nazis during World War II. Another could lie in attitudes towards abortion that consider it to be a violation of the natural role of women as mothers.

Interestingly, more recent scholarship in the area has shown how the criminalisation of abortion was historically tied to the eugenics movement, but not in the sense of breeding out the unfit.[4] Rather, the anti-abortionist stance reflected a concern, based in eugenic logic, to ensure that those who were fit would continue to reproduce. Making abortion a criminal offence was the means by which to achieve this end,[5] and in adopting this approach traditional values about the role of women as mothers were entrenched.[6]

Although, as mentioned, eugenics arguments are now generally viewed suspiciously, anti-abortion arguments continue to be articulated in terms of traditional family values and

---

3   See also Matthew Connelly, *Fatal Misconception: The Struggle to Control World Population* (Harvard University Press, 2008).
4   Karen Weingarten, 'Bad Girls and Biopolitics: Abortion, Popular Fiction and Population Control' (2011) 29(1) *Literature and Medicine* 81. For a more detailed introduction to the issues, see Leslie J Reagan, *When Abortion Was a Crime: Women, Medicine, and Law in the United States, 1867–1973* (University of California Press, 1997).
5   The argument changed from criminal regulation to medical regulation. See, eg, Melanie Latham, *Reproduction: A Century of Conflict in Britain and France* (Manchester University Press, 2002) ch 4.
6   More specifically, it has been argued that the aim was to promote white middle-class motherhood. See Weingarten, above n 4, 83.

the need to protect vulnerable unborn babies.[7] Challenging these anti-abortion laws are the feminist arguments that support giving women access to safe abortion as part of the process of achieving women's equality in society.[8] This has led to moral debates on protecting the rights of women as opposed to the rights of the unborn child.

Eisenstein assesses the arguments for and against abortion in the United States that reflect the usual moral arguments about abortion in the western world.[9] In the following discussion, we will see how the opposing positions have been reconciled in the United States by framing the issue as a private matter to be determined by the individual woman in consultation with her doctor. On the one hand, this approach demonstrates how the eugenics logic continues to inform abortion laws, evident in how the availability of abortion is framed as a health issue to be determined by a medical practitioner. On the other hand, this approach fits the usual legal framing of family issues as private matters in which the state has no role.

11.2.2   The pro-abortion arguments: the intersection between the right to equality and sexual freedom for women

The pro-abortion argument usually centres on women's right to equality, particularly with respect to women's 'difference', namely her pregnant body. This right has been asserted by combining different feminist thinking: within the liberal feminist framework that seeks equality for women in public life, and within the framework of radical feminism that seeks equality for women with respect to their sexuality and sexual reproduction.[10]

It was in the late 1960s that the demand for abortion came to include the issue of sex equality and the right to abortion was seen as essential to women's right to equality as 'individuals'; that is, equality was equated with equal participation of women in public life. The demand for abortion as a right was particularly tied up with women's demand for equality at work and was seen as a means by which women could determine their own futures. As Eisenstein explains:

> The demand to legalize abortion was an attack on both the segregated labor market and the cultural expectations about women's roles. It allowed women to argue (and symbolically demonstrate) that although childbearing was important, it was not the single most important thing in a woman's life.[11]

---

7   See, eg, the policy statement of the Australian Christians that they 'will definitely not support funding of politically contentious aid programs such as those that foster abortion, sterilisation, normalising of same sex attraction etc., which are incompatible with our values': *Policies*, Australian Christians <http://australianchristians.com.au/values/>.

8   A further connection between the availability of abortion and safe contraception is an issue discussed in the context of aid provided to developing nations. See, eg, Grant Miller and Christine Valente, 'Population Policy: Abortion and Modern Contraception are Substitutes' (Working Paper No 426, Stanford Center for International Development, 2016).

9   The following discussion is based on Zillah R Eisenstein, *The Female Body and the Law* (University of California Press, 1988) ch 5.

10   Feminism is by no means a monolithic phenomenon. See generally Alison M Jaggar and Paula S Rothenberg, *Feminist Frameworks: Alternative Theoretical Accounts of the Relations between Men and Women* (McGraw-Hill, 3rd ed, 1993), where various theories of women's subordination are discussed, including radical feminism, liberal feminism, Marxist and socialist feminism and other schools of thought.

11   Eisenstein, above n 9, 184.

However, abortion as an issue of equality is understandable only if it is recognised that it is also tied up with the issues of sexual freedom and sex 'difference'.

Abortion developed as a demand not only in relation to women's entrance into the labour market, but also as a part of changing morality about women's sexuality and sexual activity that was taking place during the 1960s and 1970s. Abortion formed part of the sexual revolution of the time and reflected growing social acceptance of women engaging in heterosexual sex more the way men do. Making abortion freely available to women would increase women's freedom from the risk of having an unwanted baby so that their sexual experiences would be more like those of men, who cannot fall pregnant.[12] Thus, abortion simultaneously creates greater freedom to engage in sexual activity, and focuses attention on women's sexual 'differences' from men, but lessens the effect of these 'differences' for women so that women can attain equality in all areas of life.

Central to the pro-abortion argument are the sexual differences between men and women, evidently portrayed by the pregnant body, which is invariably a woman's body. Difference and sameness are both at issue in abortion. At the other end of the spectrum is the conservative New Right movement, which sidelines the feminist arguments for women's equality by treating the foetus as the individual whose rights need protecting.

11.2.3   The pro-life message on abortion

It is usual for members of the pro-life movement to link abortion with religious views on the sanctity of human life, which in turn obscures its anti-equality agenda.[13] The imagery they have used in their campaigns puts forth an autonomous foetus (as person) and an absent and peripheral woman: '[i]t is this abstract individualism, effacing the pregnant woman and the fetus' dependence on her'[14] that leaves the viewer with images of the foetus or baby 'as if it were outside a woman's body, because it can be viewed'.[15] When these images are fused with anti-abortion rhetoric, this kind of 'politics as imagery' blurs the lines between the real and the ideal. The New Right likens abortion to murder of the unborn and creates a discourse where the woman is considered as an incubator rather than as an individual in her own right. The dehumanisation of the woman is an effective strategy by which to control her sexual and reproductive freedom and thereby maintain male privilege that the feminist pro-choice movement has sought to dismantle. As we will see in the following section, more recent shifts in the legal discourse on abortion, which frame its availability in terms of protecting the health of women, have been embraced by pro-life proponents who emphasise

---

12   See Laura Kaplan, *The Story of Jane: The Legendary Underground Feminist Abortion Service* (University of Chicago Press, 1995); Boston Women's Health Book Collective and Judy Norsigian, *Our Bodies, Ourselves* (Touchstone, 9th ed, 2011) chs 9 and 13.

13   It is not our intention to deny the moral convictions of the pro-life campaigners, but it is certainly our aim to point out that in liberal democratic systems the moral preferences of one group should not restrict the autonomy of other individuals.

14   Rosalind Pollack Petchesky, 'Fetal Images: The Power of Visual Culture in the Politics of Reproduction' (1987) 13(2) *Feminist Studies* 263, 270. A recent attempt to recognise the personhood of a foetus was made in New South Wales with the introduction by the Liberal and Christian Democratic Party of the Crimes Amendment ('Zoe's Law') Bill 2013 (No 2), but it has since lapsed in Parliament.

15   Petchesky, above n 14.

the possible risks of abortion to women's health as a rationale for imposing more stringent regulation on its availability and thereby making it more difficult for women to obtain an abortion.

11.2.4   Abortion law: the United States and Australia compared

In the United States, the Supreme Court's landmark decision in *Roe v Wade*[16] was a breakthrough in upholding that a right to privacy under the Due Process Clause of the 14th Amendment of the US *Constitution* extended to a woman's decision to have an abortion.[17] The significance of the decision was to place limits on the criminalisation of abortion by separate State laws. However, framing the woman's right to an abortion on the basis of a right to privacy rather than on the right to equality has severe limitations.

Privacy doctrine does not argue for abortion on the basis of a woman's right to reproductive control, or her right to equality, or her right to freedom of sexual expression. Nor does it challenge the patriarchal/phallocratic dimension of privacy. Instead, it works within the confines of the opposition of public and private, which obfuscates the political nature of the private realm. As we have argued in earlier chapters, the concept of public and private as distinct spheres of existence is one way that the nuclear family is normalised.

Feminists have long argued that the private realm – the realm of sex and sexual decision-making – is at least as political as the public realm. The right to an abortion, based solely on the right to privacy, therefore remains tenuous. Instead of discussing abortion as an issue of reproductive freedom, privacy doctrine makes it a debate about the constitutional protection of a 'medically assisted right to choose abortion freed from unwarranted governmental interference'.[18]

The effect of the decision in *Roe v Wade* is that a woman's decision to have an abortion is one that she would make in consultation with her physician. Indeed, in this respect the Court held that the primary right being protected was the physician's: to practise medicine freely without interference by the state.[19] But this was qualified by the Court, which held that the right to an abortion must be balanced against the state's legitimate interest 'in preserving and protecting the health of the pregnant woman' and the other 'important and legitimate interest in protecting the potentiality of human life'.[20] The Court resolved this balancing test by continuing to allow for the States to regulate pregnancy in the third trimester. This has since been modified by the Supreme Court decision in *Planned Parenthood of Southeastern Pennsylvania v Casey* ('*Casey*').[21] Although the Court in this case made it clear that it was the woman's constitutional right being protected, it also held that a woman's right to abortion was limited to when the foetus became viable. Considering advances in medical science,

---

16   410 US 113 (1973).
17   *United States Constitution* amend XIV.
18   Kristin Booth Glen, 'Understanding the Abortion Debate' (1986) 16(5) *Socialist Review* 51, 67 quoted in Eisenstein, above n 9, 187.
19   Linda Greenhouse, *Becoming Justice Blackmun: Harry Blackmun's Supreme Court Journey* (Times Books, 2005) 98–9.
20   *Roe v Wade* 410 US 113, 162 (1973).
21   505 US 833 (1992).

the effect of this decision has been to encroach on the right to an abortion first recognised in the *Roe v Wade* decision.[22]

From a feminist perspective, the right to privacy upheld in *Roe v Wade* has continued to sideline women's right to equality and reproductive freedom. The construction of abortion as a right to privacy is linked to abortion as a therapeutic treatment aimed at promoting the health of women. This has allowed States to continue to regulate abortion in determining what constitutes the necessary treatment to promote women's health, which can place onerous requirements on doctors and make it difficult, if not impossible, for women to access abortion services.[23] By contrast, constructing abortion as necessary for the attainment of equality in society would bring into focus the inequalities of women in society that stem from their sexual differences from men. Framing abortion in the language of equality would provide the rationale to provide affordable, accessible and safe abortion for women seeking an abortion. As it is, the right to an abortion is only a partial right that continues to be encroached upon by the separate States in the United States under the guise of protecting the health of women.[24]

By comparison, in Australia, abortion continues to be largely regulated through the criminal laws of the different States and Territories. Historically these laws are based on the *Offences Against the Persons Act 1861* (UK). However, some jurisdictions have decriminalised abortion to some extent, consistent with developments in the United States and elsewhere.[25]

The details of these laws follow. The laws have been ordered starting with the jurisdictions that continue to criminalise abortion and going on to the jurisdictions that have decriminalised abortion to varying degrees.[26] Although the Australian jurisdictions do not construct abortion as a right to privacy, it is evident that abortion is treated as a health issue, as is the case in the United States.

---

22   Separate State laws have also limited the right to an abortion through regulation. These include requiring women seeking an abortion to undergo intensive counselling, and the imposition of a 24-hour waiting period before the procedure can be performed. Apart from the gestational limits imposed by *Casey*, most States require the involvement of at least one parent in cases involving women under the age of 18 years. State funding and private healthcare subsidy of abortions is limited. There is also a growing number of States that have introduced laws that require the woman seeking an abortion to view or hear the foetus through an ultrasound before having the abortion: Find Law, *Abortion Laws*, Find Law <http://family.findlaw.com/reproductive-rights/abortion.html>.

23   Similar issues have arisen in the Northern Territory, where, for example, abortions are required to be performed in a hospital, unlike in other States, which have stand-alone abortion clinics. In 2015 it was reported that there were only two hospitals – a private hospital in Darwin with few doctors who could perform surgical abortions and a public hospital in Alice Springs – where women could access an abortion: Allyssa Betts, 'Push to improve Access to Abortion Services by Northern Territory Doctors', *ABC News* (online), 27 January 2015 <http://www.abc.net.au/news/2015-01-27/nt-doctors-call-for-abortion-law-reform-to-improve-access/6048070>.

24   The position in the United States may be set to change now that the US Supreme Court (5:3) struck down the Texan House Bill 2 (HB 2) that imposed an 'admitting privileges requirement' on physicians and an 'ambulatory surgical center' requirement on clinics. The Court found both of these provisions 'place a substantial obstacle in the path of women seeking a previability abortion, constitute an undue burden on abortion access, and thus violate the Constitution': *Whole Woman's Health v Hellerstedt* 579 US __ (2016) 19–39.

25   See, eg, *Abortion Act 1967* (UK).

26   The content of this summary is based on the summary provided by Children by Choice, *Australian Abortion Law and Practice* (26 November 2015) <https://www.childrenbychoice.org.au/factsandfigures/australianabortionlawandpractice>.

11.2.4.1   New South Wales and Queensland

Abortion is a crime in New South Wales[27] and Queensland.[28] Only the legislation in Queensland defines when an abortion would be considered lawful or unlawful.[29]

In the leading NSW case on abortion, *R v Wald*, it was held that an abortion would be lawful if there was 'any economic, social or medical ground or reason' upon which a doctor could base an honest and reasonable belief that an abortion was required to avoid a 'serious danger to the pregnant woman's life or to her physical or mental health'.[30] The doctor need not have believed that the woman's health was in 'serious danger' at the time of consultation, merely that her health 'could reasonably be expected to be seriously endangered at some time during the currency of the pregnancy, if uninterrupted'.[31] It was evident in the Court's reasons that the termination procedure was required to be performed by a 'duly qualified medical practitioner' in order to be lawful.[32] Also evident was the requirement for health reasons in order for the doctor to base his or her decision to perform an abortion on a woman. In this respect, the decision fell short of allowing a doctor to perform an abortion on a woman on the basis of her request and informed consent, which had been the argument put forward by counsel for the accused in this case.[33]

In Queensland it was held in *R v Bayliss and Cullen* that an abortion is lawful if carried out to prevent serious danger to the woman's physical and mental health in continuing

---

27   *Crimes Act 1900* (NSW) ss 82–84. Section 82 provides that '[w]hosoever, being a woman with child, unlawfully administers to herself any drug or noxious thing, or unlawfully uses any instrument or other means ... to procure her miscarriage, shall be liable to imprisonment for ten years'. Section 83 provides that '[w]hosoever: unlawfully administers to, or causes to be taken by, any woman, whether with child or not, any drug or noxious thing, or unlawfully uses any instrument or other means, with intent in any such case to procure her miscarriage, shall be liable to imprisonment for ten years'. Section 84 provides that '[w]hosoever unlawfully supplies or procures any drug or noxious thing, or any instrument or thing whatsoever, knowing that the same is intended to be unlawfully used with intent to procure the miscarriage of any woman, whether with child or not, shall be liable to imprisonment for five years'. In August 2016, Greens MP Mehreen Faruqi introduced the Abortion Law Reform (Miscellaneous Acts Amendment) Bill 2016 (NSW), which is designed to decriminalise abortion in New South Wales. At the time of writing, the Bill is still before Parliament.

28   *Criminal Code Act 1899* (Qld) ss 224–226. Section 224 provides that '[a]ny person who, with intent to procure the miscarriage of a woman, whether she is or is not with child, unlawfully administers to her or causes her to take any poison or other noxious thing, or uses any force of any kind, or uses any other means whatever, is guilty of a crime, and is liable to imprisonment for 14 years'. Section 225 provides that '[a]ny woman who, with intent to procure her own miscarriage, whether she is or is not with child, unlawfully administers to herself any poison or other noxious thing, or uses any force of any kind, or uses any other means whatever, or permits any such thing or means to be administered or used to her, is guilty of a crime, and is liable to imprisonment for 7 years'. Section 226 provides that '[a]ny person who unlawfully supplies to or procures for any person anything whatever, knowing that it is intended to be unlawfully used to procure the miscarriage of a woman, whether she is or is not with child, is guilty of a misdemeanour, and is liable to imprisonment for 3 years'. In May 2016, former ALP and now independent State Parliament member Rob Pyne introduced the Abortion Law Reform (Woman's Right to Choose) Amendment Bill 2016 (Qld). It was designed to decriminalise abortion in Queensland, but was rejected by Parliament in August 2016.

29   *Criminal Code Act 1899* (Qld) s 282.

30   (1971) 3 DCR (NSW) 25, 29 (Levine DCJ).

31   Ibid.

32   Ibid.

33   Ibid 28. See Catherine Henry, 'Abortion Retried' (1995) 20(5) *Alternative Law Journal* 239, 240.

the pregnancy.[34] Unlike the NSW decision *R v Wald*, economic and social issues were not included in this decision in determining legality.

Notably, in this case, the Court was clear in pointing out that the woman's desire to be relieved of her pregnancy was not, of itself, justification for an abortion. It reiterated that the State continues to be 'the guardian of the silent innocence of the unborn'. Thus, abortion on demand has no legal justification and the State should use its authority to ensure that abortion is not permitted on whim or capricious grounds.[35]

11.2.4.2   South Australia

South Australia was the first Australian State to liberalise access to abortion through legislation.[36] An abortion is lawful under the *Criminal Law Consolidation Act 1935* (SA) if it is carried out within 28 weeks of conception in a prescribed hospital by a legally qualified medical practitioner, provided he or she is of the opinion, formed in good faith, that either the 'maternal health' ground or the 'foetal disability' ground is satisfied.[37]

The 'maternal health' ground permits abortion if continuing rather than terminating the pregnancy would pose more risk to the pregnant woman's life, or to her physical or mental health (taking into account her actual or reasonably foreseeable environment).[38] The 'foetal disability' ground permits abortion if there is a substantial risk that the child would be seriously physically or mentally handicapped.[39]

A second qualified medical practitioner must share the medical practitioner's opinion that either of these grounds is satisfied.[40]

11.2.4.3   Northern Territory

The provisions for abortion in the Northern Territory are contained in the *Medical Services Act* (NT). Services for termination of pregnancy are legally available in the Northern Territory up to 14 weeks' gestation if either the 'maternal health ground' or the 'foetal disability ground' is satisfied (s 11(1)(b)).

Section 11(a) and (b) provides that abortions are lawful up to 14 weeks of gestation, but only if performed in a hospital by an obstetrician or gynaecologist, and where that practitioner and another form the opinion that the continuance of the pregnancy would be a greater risk to a woman's life, or a greater risk of physical or mental health injury, than if the pregnancy were terminated; or if the pregnancy were not terminated there was a substantial risk that the child would suffer from physical or mental abnormalities and be seriously handicapped. Section 11(3) provides that abortion up to 23 weeks of gestation is legal if a medical practitioner is of the opinion that the termination of pregnancy is necessary to prevent grave injury to a woman's physical or mental health. Abortion is legal at any stage

---

34   (1986) 9 Qld Lawyer Reports 8 (McGuire DCJ).

35   Ibid 45.

36   The legislation in South Australia and Northern Territory discussed below is based on the *Abortion Act 1967* (UK).

37   *Criminal Law Consolidation Act 1935* (SA) s 82A(7)–(8). The legislation in the Northern Territory or elsewhere in Australia does not use the terms 'maternal health ground' and 'foetal disability ground', but we use them here and below as shorthand for the legislative language.

38   s 82A(1), (3).

39   s 82A(1)(a)(ii).

40   s 82A(1)(a).

of the pregnancy if the treatment is given in good faith, with the sole purpose of saving the woman's life (s 11(4)).

11.2.4.4 Western Australia

In Western Australia, provisions relating to abortion are found in the *Criminal Code Act 1913* (WA) ('*Criminal Code*') and in the *Health Act 1911* (WA) ('*Health Act*') (amended by the *Acts Amendment (Abortion) Act* 1998 (WA)).

Pursuant to the *Criminal Code*, the new s 199(1) provides that it is unlawful to perform an abortion unless it is performed by a medical practitioner, in good faith and the performance is justified under s 334 of the *Health Act*.

An unlawful abortion can attract a $50 000 fine.[41] Subject to s 259, if a person who is not a medical practitioner performs an abortion, that person is guilty of a crime and is liable to imprisonment for five years.[42]

Unlike in New South Wales and Queensland,[43] in Western Australia the people involved in performing the abortion may only commit the offence of 'unlawful' abortion.[44] The patient herself is not subject to any legal sanction in Western Australia.

The new *Criminal Code* s 259(1) is a defence for unlawful abortion if the person has performed the surgical or medical procedure in good faith, with reasonable care and skill, for the benefit of the other person, or to an unborn child in order to preserve the life of the mother. The administration of treatment should be reasonable having regard to the patient's state and all the circumstances of the case.

Section 334(3) of the new *Health Act* provides that the performance of abortion is justified when the woman concerned has given informed consent; or if the abortion is not performed she will suffer serious personal, family or social consequences, or serious danger to her physical or mental health would result; or the pregnancy is causing serious danger to the woman's physical or mental health.

Informed consent is defined under the *Health Act* as when a medical practitioner, other than one performing or assisting with the abortion, has provided counselling to the woman about the medical risk of continuing the pregnancy, and offered her an opportunity of referral for counselling prior to and following a pregnancy termination or carrying a pregnancy to term.[45]

After 20 weeks of pregnancy, two medical practitioners from a panel of six appointed by the Minister have to agree that the mother or unborn baby has a severe medical condition. These abortions can only be performed at a facility approved by the Minister.[46]

11.2.4.5 Victoria, Tasmania and the Australian Capital Territory

Abortion was legalised in Victoria with the enactment of the *Abortion Law Reform Act 2008* (Vic). Before this enactment, Victorian abortion law was almost identical to the law in New South Wales and Queensland.[47]

---

41   *Criminal Code Act 1913* (WA) s 199(2).
42   s 199(3).
43   See *Crimes Act 1900* (NSW) s 82; *Criminal Code 1899* (Qld) s 225.
44   *Criminal Code Act 1913* (WA) s 199(2).
45   *Health Act 1911* (WA) s 334(5).
46   s 334(7).
47   See *Crimes Act 1958* (Vic) ss 65, 66; *R v Davidson* [1969] VR 667 (Menhennitt J).

If a woman is less than 24 weeks pregnant, the 2008 Act allows for the provision of abortion on request by a qualified medical practitioner, nurse or pharmacist;[48] after 24 weeks' pregnancy, a second practitioner must agree that the termination is in the patient's best interests for an abortion to be lawfully performed.[49] Abortion by an unqualified person remains a crime.[50]

In Tasmania, abortion was decriminalised with the enactment of the *Reproductive Health (Access to Terminations) Act 2013* (Tas). Under this law, abortion is lawful on request up to 16 weeks' gestation, and beyond that point with the agreement of two doctors.[51]

The provisions for abortion in the Australian Capital Territory are contained in the *Medical Practitioners (Maternal Health) Amendment Act 2002* (ACT).

Unlike most of the other jurisdiction, the ACT legislation does not prescribe a period of time when an abortion can be lawfully administered. However, like most other jurisdictions it requires a registered medical practitioner to carry out an abortion;[52] and like some other jurisdictions an abortion is to be carried out in, or in part of, a medical facility;[53] and the Minister's approval is required for the medical facility, or part of, to perform abortions.[54]

11.2.4.6   Provisions for conscientious objections and access zones

The availability of abortion is also affected by the willingness of a medical practitioner to perform the procedure.

Some jurisdictions contain conscientious objection clauses. In South Australia, a conscience clause allows medical practitioners to elect not to participate in an abortion.[55] In the Northern Territory, any person with a conscientious objection to abortion is not under a duty to assist in the operation or disposal of an aborted foetus.[56] In Western Australia, no person, hospital, health institution, or other institution or service is under a duty, whether by contract or by statutory or other legal requirement, to participate in the performance of an abortion.[57] In the Australian Capital Territory, no person is required to carry out or assist in the carrying out of an abortion.[58]

In Tasmania, medical practitioners with a conscientious objection to abortion are not obliged to participate in termination of pregnancy procedures except in an emergency to save the woman's life or prevent serious physical injury.[59] However, medical practitioners who hold a conscientious objection to abortion have an obligation to refer pregnant women seeking information about pregnancy options to another medical practitioner without a conscientious objection.[60]

---

48   *Abortion Law Reform Act 2008* (Vic) ss 4, 6.
49   ss 5, 7.
50   *Crimes Act 1958* (Vic) s 65(1).
51   *Reproductive Health (Access to Terminations) Act 2013* (Tas) s 5.
52   *Medical Practitioners (Maternal Health) Amendment Act 2002* (ACT) s 55B (maximum penalty: five years' imprisonment).
53   s 55C (maximum penalty: 50 penalty points, six months' imprisonment or both).
54   s 55D.
55   *Criminal Law Consolidation Act 1935* (SA) s 82A(5).
56   *Medical Services Act* (NT) s 11(6).
57   *Health Act 1911* (WA) s 334(2).
58   *Medical Practitioners (Maternal Health) Amendment Act 2002* (ACT) s 55E.
59   *Reproductive Health (Access to Terminations) Act 2013* (Tas) s 6.
60   s 7.

Tasmania is the only jurisdiction that prohibits threatening or harassing behaviour, protesting, footpath interference, and the recording of people entering an abortion facility, within an 'access zone' of 150 metres from premises at which abortions are provided.[61]

11.2.5   Who decides whether a woman can have an abortion?

It is evident from the above overview of abortion law in the United States and Australia that in law it has been more or less accepted that abortion is legally permissible, but only in certain circumstances and when certain requirements are met, as prescribed by the law of the particular jurisdiction. Of most interest to us is how, through legal regulation, the law conveys its own views on who should decide on an abortion and why. In light of the overview of the law in the previous section, it is evident that a woman cannot have a lawful abortion unless it is also supported by a health professional, usually a medical practitioner. In this respect, medical practitioners are expected to administer the law in determining whether an abortion is lawful or not, and are subject to a criminal penalty if they do not operate within the legal framework. In Australia, this became glaringly apparent when a couple in Queensland were unsuccessfully prosecuted for attempting to procure an abortion, in *R v Brennan and Leech*.[62] At the time, medical practitioners offering abortion services became reluctant to do so for fear that they too would be prosecuted. This was because s 282 of the *Criminal Code Act 1899* (Qld), which sets out the legal duties and standards for performing an abortion, referred to it as a 'surgical operation', but a medical abortion could not really be defined as a surgical operation.[63] The legislature subsequently amended the section so it now reads:

> A person is not criminally responsible for performing or providing, in good faith and with reasonable care and skill a surgical operation on or medical treatment of:
>
> (a) a person or unborn child for the patient's benefit; or
>
> (b) a person or unborn child to preserve the mother's life;
>
> if performing the operation or providing the medical treatment is reasonable, having regard to the patient's state at the time and to all circumstances of the case.

It is clear from the legislation that the Australian position, although not framed as a right to privacy (as it is in the United States) still approaches abortion as a health issue that completely obscures the politics that surrounds the abortion debate.[64] It is indeed rare to find within the law justification for an abortion based on meeting the 'social' or 'economic' needs of the woman involved, let alone provision for the realisation of women's reproductive freedom. We raise this point to illuminate the paternalistic treatment of women in abortion

---

61   s 9.
62   [2010] QDC 329 (Everson DCJ).
63   Children by Choice, above n 26.
64   For an overview of the contemporary debates in Australia, see Barbara Baird, 'Abortion Politics During the Howard Years: Beyond Liberalisation' (2013) 44(2) *Australian Historical Studies* 245; Kate Gleeson, 'Tony Abbott and Abortion: Miscalculating the Strength of the Religious Right' (2011) 46(3) *Australian Journal of Political Science* 473.

law and how concern for their wellbeing continues to be pitted against the wellbeing of their unborn children. The message that is being sent by these laws is that a woman cannot make decisions for herself, let alone be trusted to make decisions about her unborn child.[65] Someone else must make these decisions for her and it appears that the medical profession has been assigned this responsibility. This is so even though the social expectation continues to assign women the role of primary carers of their biological children.

Moreover, while it appears that women seeking abortions must rely on the medical profession to support their decisions, this has obscured the role of the state in regulating abortion: not only in making laws that regulate medical practitioners' treatment of women seeking an abortion, but also in providing the facilities and funding so that women can access safe and affordable abortions. As long as abortion is treated as a private issue (in the United States) or as a health issue (in Australia), the politics of the area can be obscured by the invisible hand of the state, enabling it to pursue its own political agenda through the regulation of the medical profession on what is lawful and unlawful treatment, and thereby control the availability of abortion services to women.[66]

In this respect, it is also important to acknowledge how medical science, more broadly, is implicated in the regulation of abortion by providing the basis for its legitimacy. If we return to the discussion of *Roe v Wade* above, it is evident that the period for a woman to have a legal abortion was reduced in the later case of *Casey*. As we see from the discussion of the Australian laws, the period for women to have an abortion varies. The differences can be explained by developments in medical science, particularly with respect to obstetrics and paediatrics, where more babies are being born prematurely and survive. However, considering the variations in the law on this issue, the question of whether this balance is grounded in medical knowledge remains to be seen. These developments help support claims that the rights of the unborn child should be protected. Even so, one interesting development in the area is how some jurisdictions legalise abortion on the 'maternal health ground' or the 'foetal disability ground'.[67] Evidently the law is concerned with promoting healthy individuals, but it seems that not all unborn babies are accorded the same protection of the law. These sorts of provisions have raised questions about whether the law is protecting the rights of the unborn child, or whether it is engaging in a much grander project of social engineering and control reminiscent of the eugenics movement.[68]

---

65   See also Anne O'Rourke, 'The Discourse of Abortion Law Debate in Australia: Caring Mother or Mother of Convenience' (2016) 56 *Women's Studies International Forum* 37 for the argument that the political discourse in the federal and Victorian parliaments when discussing abortion laws managed to stigmatise women seeking abortion and maintain ongoing state control.

66   As recently as 2006, a doctor in Sydney was convicted for performing an unlawful abortion. See the details in Kate Gleeson, 'The Other Abortion Myth: The Failure of the Common Law' (2009) 6(1) *Journal of Bioethical Inquiry* 69.

67   Sheelagh Mcguinness, 'Law, Reproduction and Disability: Fatally "Handicapped"?' (2013) 21(2) *Medical Law Review* 213; John F Muller, 'Disability, Ambivalence, and the Law' (2011) 37(4) *American Journal of Law & Medicine* 469.

68   This is a debated issue in the literature. For an overview of the main arguments, see Tom Shakespeare, 'Choices and Rights: Eugenics, Genetics and Disability Equality' (1998) 13(5) *Disability and Society* 665. Compare Ann Furedi, *Abortion for Fetal Abnormality: Ethical Issues*, Pro Choice Forum <http://www.prochoiceforum.org.uk/aad4.php>.

It is apparent that the law is not upholding the right to equality of women in the area of abortion, but neither does the law (at least in Australia) uphold the father's claims to equality to have a say in the decision to have an abortion. The legal control of women's sexuality and reproduction in this context is thus diffused within the broader systems of law, society and the economy, and not placed under the direct control of individual men.

In the English case *Paton v Trustees of British Pregnancy Advisory Service Trustees*, a father sought to prevent his former wife from terminating a pregnancy.[69] It was held that the father's right does not arise from the protection of the rights of the foetus. The common law position is that the foetus does not have any rights of its own until it is born and has a separate existence from its mother. The father had to establish his own right to prevent the abortion, which he could not do because the Court found that it was not a matrimonial obligation that he could rely on and enforce by injunction; the *Abortion Act 1967* (UK) did not provide for such a right and, in any case, the woman's circumstances met the requirements of the Act. This decision was followed by the High Court in *Attorney General (Qld) (Ex rel Kerr) v T*.[70] In that case the Queensland Attorney-General intervened in support of the application of the father of an unborn child to prevent the woman from having an abortion. The Attorney-General first argued that the civil courts should come to the aid of preventing a breach of the criminal law. In this case the mother would be contravening the criminal law in Queensland if she had an abortion. Second, he argued that an unborn child is a person whose life should be protected by the Court in its delegated role as *parens patriae*. Chief Justice Gibbs rejected these arguments. He found that it was wrong to assume that the woman would be convicted of a criminal offence under the *Criminal Code Act 1899* (Qld) and on that assumption to interfere in the most serious way with her liberty of action. In response to the second argument, Gibbs CJ upheld the decision in *Paton* that a foetus has no rights of its own until it is born and has a separate existence from its mother.[71]

A similar issue arose in *In the Marriage of F*, where the husband sought orders in the Family Court to prevent the wife from having an abortion.[72] In responding to his arguments, the Court held that the husband's right to procreate did not extend to preventing the wife from having an abortion;[73] that the unborn child did not have any common law rights because it had no legal personality or rights of its own until it is born;[74] nor did the unborn child have any rights under the FLA because the relevant provisions did not extend to an unborn child.[75]

However, the Court held that it did have jurisdiction in this case because the proceedings sought an injunction pursuant to s 114 of the FLA in circumstances arising out of the

---

69   [1979] QB 276 ('*Paton*') (Sir George Baker P).
70   (1983) 46 ALR 275.
71   Ibid 277.
72   (1989) 13 Fam LR 189 (Lindenmayer J).
73   Ibid 193.
74   Ibid 194.
75   Ibid 194–5.

marital relationship.[76] Nevertheless, the Court found that the jurisdiction under s 114(1) was discretionary and in the particular circumstances of the case it was not 'proper' to grant the injunction.[77] The Court offered three reasons:

- First, that the marriage had broken down and therefore the underlying and fundamental basis for having the child, namely a continuing marriage and 'the nurturing of that child within that relationship', had disappeared.
- Second, to grant the injunction would force the wife, 'under threat of proceedings for contempt of court, to carry to the end a foetus which she clearly does not want and, barring unforeseen events, to give birth to a child which she clearly does not want and which she may very well resent in those circumstances'.
- Third, it was the fact that the foetus must grow within the wife's body, not that of the husband. To 'grant the injunction would be to compel the wife to do something in relation to her own body which she does not wish to do. That would be an interference with her freedom to decide her own destiny'.[78]

However, this very freedom to decide her own destiny comes into serious question in actions for wrongful birth, as discussed below.

11.2.6   Actions for wrongful birth

Actions for wrongful birth or wrongful life arise in cases where an allegation of medical negligence is made with respect to the birth of a child. In this discussion, we are interested in cases where an adult (usually a woman is the principal plaintiff) has been the subject to negligent advice or medical treatment that has deprived her of reproductive freedom and has resulted in the birth of a child. The adults in these cases are claiming that the practitioners involved in their treatment failed in their duty of care. Owing to the negligence of the medical practitioners, a child has been born. The parents are, accordingly, seeking damages. Where these cases have been most controversial has been with respect to claims for damages for the cost of raising the child. Although these cases are not family law cases in the

---

76   Ibid 195–6. Section 114 provides: 'In proceedings of the kind referred to in paragraph (e) of the definition of 'matrimonial cause' in subsection 4(1), the court may make such order or grant such injunction as it considers proper with respect to the matter to which the proceedings relate, including: (a) an injunction for the personal protection of a party to the marriage; (b) an injunction restraining a party to the marriage from entering or remaining in the matrimonial home or the premises in which the other party to the marriage resides, or restraining a party to the marriage from entering or remaining in a specified area, being an area in which the matrimonial home is, or the premises in which the other party to the marriage resides are, situated; (c) an injunction restraining a party to the marriage from entering the place of work of the other party to the marriage; (d) an injunction for the protection of the marital relationship; (e) an injunction in relation to the property of a party to the marriage; or (f) an injunction relating to the use or occupancy of the matrimonial home'.

Cf *K v T* (1983) 1 Qd R 396 (Williams J); *Talbot v Norman* [2012] FamCA 96 (Murphy J). In both cases, the Court confirmed that an unborn child has no legal personality. In the latter case, the father of the unborn child sought an injunction under s 68B(1)(a) of the FLA for the personal protection of the child. He could not seek an injunction under s 114 as the parties were not married.

77   *In the Marriage of F* (1989) 13 Fam LR 189, 197.

78   Ibid 198.

conventional sense, they provide good illustrations of how conceptions of the ideal mother that reflect traditional maternal roles are constructed in judicial discourses.

In *CES v Superclinics Australia Pty Ltd* ('*CES v Superclinics*') the first plaintiff alleged that the defendants (whether personally or vicariously) had breached their duty of care in failing to either diagnose her pregnancy or communicate a positive diagnosis of pregnancy to her.[79] The plaintiff had sought the medical services of the defendant's clinic and medical staff on a number of occasions to determine whether she was pregnant or not. By the time her pregnancy was finally confirmed, it was too late for her to have an abortion. The plaintiff sought damages for being denied the opportunity to have an abortion performed at a time when it was safe so to do. As a result of the defendants' negligence, the plaintiff gave birth to a child whom she did not want to have.

The defendants' main argument was that what the plaintiff was claiming was the loss of an opportunity to perform an illegal act contrary to s 82 or 83 of the *Crimes Act 1900* (NSW).

At first instance, the Court found that the defendants were in breach of their duty of care, but it refused to award damages. Basically, the Court relied on precedent that maintains that common law damages are unavailable to the plaintiff who has committed (or intends to commit) an illegal act.[80] The Court found that if the plaintiff had been given the opportunity to have an abortion, she would have committed an illegal act. According to the Court, a lawful abortion under the Act would only have been possible if the pregnancy posed a serious danger to either her physical or mental wellbeing. On the evidence the plaintiff had failed to prove that the pregnancy had posed a serious danger to her health. However, the evidence did indicate that, while the plaintiff's health was not put in danger during the pregnancy, after the birth she did show symptoms of depression and anxiety and was referred to a psychiatrist.

The plaintiffs appealed to the Court of Appeal and were successful.[81] It was held that negligent advice resulting in loss of the chance to have a lawful abortion could give rise to a claim for damages. However, the damages recoverable were limited to those flowing from that advice, and did not include the expenses of a child born of the pregnancy, as those expenses were incurred by the mother's own choice (for example, she could have put the child out for adoption). In finding for the appellants, the Court provided a more liberal definition of a lawful abortion. President Kirby was of the view that the question of whether the pregnancy posed a serious danger to the health of the mother extended to after the birth of the child:

> There seems to be no logical basis for limiting the honest and reasonable expectation of such a danger to the mother's psychological health to the period of the currency of the pregnancy alone. Having acknowledged the relevance of other economic or social grounds which may give rise to such a belief, it is illogical to exclude from consideration, as a relevant factor, the possibility that the patient's psychological state might be threatened after the birth of the child, for example, due to the very economic and social circumstances in which she will then probably find herself. Such

79   (Unreported, Supreme Court of New South Wales, Newman J, 18 April 1994).
80   See especially *Gala v Preston* (1991) 172 CLR 243; *Smith v Jenkins* (1970) 119 CLR 397 cited in *CES v Superclinics*.
81   *CES v Superclinics (Australia) Pty Ltd* (1995) 38 NSWLR 47 ('*CES v Superclinics (Appeal)*').

considerations, when combined with an unexpected and unwanted pregnancy, would, in fact, be most likely to result in a threat to a mother's psychological health after the child was born when those circumstances might be expected to take their toll.[82]

Justice Meagher delivered a powerful dissent:

> The case is not about the morality of abortion; nor is it really about whether the plaintiff would or would not be legally entitled to have an abortion. It is about the question whether a woman may in our courts sue a defendant because he allegedly deprived her of the opportunity of having an operation, with the result that she involuntarily gave birth to a child. Having given birth to a healthy child in August 1987, the plaintiff claimed at a Court hearing in December 1993 that the child, then over six years old, was unwelcome, a misfortune, perhaps a disaster, certainly a head of damages. For all I know the child was in court to witness her mother's rejection of her. Perhaps, on the other hand, the plaintiff had the taste to keep her child out of court. Even if that be so, it does not mean the unfortunate infant will never know that her mother has publicly declared her to be unwanted. When she is at school some ame [sic] charitable – perhaps the mother of one of her 'friends' – can be trusted to direct her attention to the point. That a court of law should sanction such an action seems to me improper to the point of obscenity.
>
> It seems to me that our law has always proceeded on the premise that human life is sacred. That is so despite an occasional acknowledgement that existence is a 'vale of tears'.[83]

On the question of assessment of damages, Meagher JA scoffed at the effect that discounting for contingencies would have on the award and found that it could lead to the absurd situation that if the mother said she loved the child, 'heavy discount' would apply, but if she said she loathed the child, no discount would apply. This would amount to a significant bonus for unnatural motherhood and indicated to him that the law had strayed into an area that was not in its domain. Furthermore, he said that law expects the plaintiff to mitigate her damages and asked why the mother did not put the child that she so 'vociferously complains' out for adoption.[84]

In 1996 Superclinics was granted leave to appeal to the High Court against the Court of Appeal's decision. At this stage the Catholic Bishops and the Catholic Hospitals Association sought and were given permission to be heard on the matter as it was a matter of public importance. They sought permission to argue that termination of pregnancy is an unlawful act and the decision of the NSW Court of Appeal was an incorrect statement of law. The appeal was never determined by the High Court. The parties entered into a private agreement and the case was withdrawn. As a consequence the issue of when an abortion in New South Wales is lawful was left undecided.

---

82   Ibid 60.
83   Ibid 86.
84   Ibid 87. On this point Meagher J preferred the judgment of Priestley J, who had found that the plaintiff's decision to keep the child had severed the chain of causation, the effect of which was that the defendants were not held liable for damages for the cost of rearing the child (at 84).

In *Cattanach v Melchior* the issue of the costs of raising a child in a wrongful birth case came before the High Court for determination.[85] In that case Dr Cattanach had performed a tubal ligation operation on Mrs Melchoir at a public hospital. She subsequently gave birth to a child. At trial, Holmes J found Dr Cattanach had been negligent and was in breach of the duty of care he owed to his patient. He was not negligent in the way in which he had performed the operation but in his failure properly to investigate Mrs Melchior's information that her right ovary and fallopian tube had been removed when she was 15 years old.

Mrs Melchior was awarded damages for various economic and non-economic heads of loss. Her husband was awarded modest damages for loss of consortium. Jointly they received awards of $20 353.80 for the past costs of raising the child (Jordan) and $105 249.33 for the cost of rearing him to adulthood.[86]

The doctor's appeal to the Queensland Court of Appeal was dismissed.

On further appeal to the High Court, the sole issue was whether or not the Court of Appeal had erred in holding that the couple were entitled to recover the costs of raising and maintaining Jordan to 18 years of age. A majority of the High Court dismissed the appeal.

In dissent Gleeson CJ stressed that in essence the actionable wrong in this case was the creation of the parent–child relationship, but this gave rise to the legal coherency argument. He observed that the family is recognised as the fundamental unit of society in various international instruments and so too is the need to provide for the care and protection of children. This recognition is not easy to reconcile with the idea that the parent–child relationship can be an element of actionable damage.[87]

Further, in assessing damages for the creation of this relationship, he questioned whether any limits could be placed on this assessment. He asked whether the costs of birthday and Christmas presents would be included and also the expense of a wedding. Similarly, he said, if the cost of schooling is permissible, then why not of tertiary education? He also observed that there seemed to be no principle to distinguish between child-rearing costs and the adverse effects on the career prospects of the parents, which might even exceed the costs of raising the child.[88]

At the same time, the assessment would also require making allowance for any benefits the parents may derive from having had the child. The parents may be caring for the child now, but what of the benefits they could derive from him in their old age? More importantly, it seemed, in Gleeson CJ's view: 'Mr and Mrs Melchior have spent the money itemised in their claim on food, clothing, education, maintenance and entertainment, what will they have to show for it? An adult son. No allowance has been, or can be, made for that.'[89]

Justices Hayne and Heydon also delivered separate dissenting judgments. Their judgments too were infused by arguments about the value of human life. Justice Hayne opined that the public policy considerations inform the development of the law, and in this case 'the

---

85   (2003) 215 CLR 1.

86   The costs of raising a healthy child born in similar circumstances are no longer available in New South Wales: *Civil Liability Act 2002* (NSW) s 70(1), (2). See also *Civil Liability Act 1936* (SA) s 67(2) and *Civil Liability Act 2003* (Qld) s 49A. See also Sonia Allan, *Wrongful Birth* (Health Law Central, 2016) <http://www.healthlawcentral.com/pregnancy-birth/wrongful-birth/>.

87   *Cattanach v Melchior* (2003) 215 CLR 1, 22 [35].

88   Ibid 20 [32].

89   Ibid 23 [36].

parent should not be permitted to attempt to demonstrate that the net worth of the consequences of being obliged to rear a healthy child is a financial detriment'.[90] Justice Heydon
warned against the commodification of the child and said that a child is not an object of
gratification for its parents like a pet or a car. Therefore, it is wrong to attempt to place a
monetary value on human life as it is invaluable.[91]

By contrast, McHugh and Gummow JJ, in their joint judgment in favour of awarding damages, refused to endorse the appeal made to public policy that effectively cut off a plaintiff's
access to future economic loss damages. While they recognised 'the importance of human
life, the stability of the family unit and the nurture of infant children',[92] they questioned
whether these values meant that no damages should be awarded for the cost of bringing
up a child born after a failed sterilisation procedure. They commented: '[i]t is a beguiling
but misleading simplicity to invoke the broad values which few would deny and then glide
to the conclusion that they operate to shield the appellants from the full consequences in
law of Dr Cattanach's negligence'.[93] With respect to discounting of damage by the value of
benefits derived from the birth of the child, McHugh and Gummow JJ disapproved of such
a notion, noting that the law did not apply discounts in any comparable circumstances.[94]

Justices Kirby and Callinan, in their separate judgments in favour of a damages award,
took the view that judges in developing and applying legal principle should not engage in
public policy arguments that involve emotional and moral values. Justice Callinan opined:
'That a judge might find a task distasteful is not a reason for the judge not to do it'.[95]

In summary, the dissenting judgments in *CES v Superclinics (Appeal)* and *Cattanach v
Melchior* share common concerns about the law undermining the value of the human life
of the child. The negligent circumstances that brought about the child's life should not outweigh the value of the child's life. Indeed, the dissenting judges virtually treat the negligent
behaviour as a positive, for if it were not for the breach of the duty of care the child would
never have been born. In contrast, the judges deciding in favour of the plaintiffs in these
cases are upholding general principles of the law in finding that the defendants should
pay damages for breaching their duty of care. Nevertheless, neither approach engages with
the issue that the reproductive freedom of the women involved in these cases had been
infringed by the negligence, or with the implications this has for women's claims for equality. The conventions of legal reasoning allow this outcome, but in the process the interests
or rights of women are effaced.

Implicit in the arguments about the value of the child's life is the belief that motherhood
is the natural role of women.[96] This outcome, however, reflects the limitations present in the
law itself. If the focus of the Court in *CES v Superclinics (Appeal)* was on whether the plaintiff's intention to have an abortion was lawful or not, it is because the way the *Crimes Act
1900* (NSW) is framed invites such an approach. If the legislation were framed in terms of

---

90   Ibid 90 [247].
91   Ibid 128 [353].
92   Ibid 35 [76].
93   Ibid 35 [77].
94   Ibid 39 [90].
95   Ibid 107 [296] citing *De Sales v Ingrilli* (2002) 211 CLR 338, 404–5 [189].
96   See generally Janice Richardson, 'The Concept of Harm in Actions for Wrongful Birth: Nature and
        Pre-Modern Views of Women' (2011) 35 *Australian Feminist Law Journal* 127.

protecting the rights of women to safe reproductive care, the Court's line of reasoning could have been completely different and focused on the negligence of the medical staff in failing to properly diagnose her pregnancy. A similar conclusion can be reached with respect to the judgments in *Cattanach v Melchoir*, where the majority judges appeared to share the same moral values of the dissenting judges; but, in determining the case according to the general principles of tort law, the judges were limited by these principles as the principles are yet to fully recognise the rights of women to equality.[97] Therefore, the judicial determinations in themselves are not the sole problematic element of the legal system, but at the same time the fact that the majority and dissenting judges can reach different conclusions demonstrates the element of choice involved in judicial interpretation. While they claim to 'apply' the law, they also construct the legal discourse of motherhood and, by making it a revered and natural state that every woman should naturally aspire to, the courts participate in translating prevailing social and cultural attitudes into legal ideas. The same expectation that mothers (and fathers) are the natural protectors of children finds expression in child protection laws, as discussed below. The normative standards of good parenting are used to protect children, this time against the parents' failure to meet those expected standards of behaviour.

11.3   Child protection

In this section we focus on the area of child protection (see also the section on adoption in Chapter 12). The developments in this area follow the same contours as the other areas canvassed in the book. This area is governed by State and Territory legislation, but, similar to the federal family law system, the focus of the area is on promoting the best interests of the child. Moreover, and similar to the federal jurisdiction, ensuring the best interests of the child continues to be interconnected with maintaining the family unit. In this context, the ideal is for the family to remain intact and children are only to be removed from their families as a last resort, usually in cases of child maltreatment, namely where the child is subject to physical abuse; emotional maltreatment; neglect; sexual abuse; and exposure to family violence.[98] In these respects, the law relies on the family unit as a private unit and the approach, like the approach in family law more generally, is ostensibly therapeutic in nature. Nevertheless, despite the apparent aims of child protection to support families and

---

97   In determining claims for compensation by women for loss of earning capacity, the High Court has had to turn its mind to consider issues of formal equality with respect to women's participation in the workforce. In *Sharman v Evans* (1977) 138 CLR 563 (Barwick CJ, Gibbs, Stephen, Jacobs and Murphy JJ), the High Court was required to consider whether the plaintiff's marriage prospects should reduce her award for damages under this head of loss. The argument put to the Court was that if the plaintiff had not been injured she would have married and left the workforce and this should be factored into the assessment of damages. The Court did not reduce damages on this basis, but only Murphy J acknowledged that it was wrong to assume that women leave the workforce when they get married (at 598–9). In *Wynn v NSW Insurance Ministerial Corporation* (1995) 184 CLR 485 (Brennan CJ, Dawson, Toohey, Gaudron and Gummow JJ), the High Court considered whether the cost of child care the plaintiff is now saving as a result of her injuries should reduce her damages for loss of earning capacity. Among the reasons it gave for rejecting this argument, the majority found that '[c]hild care is a cost that may be incurred by men or women' (Dawson, Toohey, Gaudron and Gummow JJ at 495). See also *De Sales v Ingrilli* (2002) 211 CLR 338.

98   For a discussion of the definition of 'child maltreatment', see Child Family Community Australia ('CFCA'), *What is Child Abuse and Neglect* (AIFS, 2015).

protect children, the increasing number of children, and particularly the over-representation of Aboriginal and Torres Strait Islander children, in the child protection system brings the effectiveness of the system into question.

The area of child protection is quite extensive and closely intersects with youth justice, which is also an extensive topic.[99] It will not be possible to delve into the details of the legislative and administrative aspects of the various regimes in Australia.[100] The discussion will provide an overview of the history of child protection law in Australia where the history is presented as a history of progress in the protection of children's safety and wellbeing. This history will then be contrasted with the shortcomings of more recent attempts to overcome the negative impact that the history of policies of 'protection' and 'assimilation' has had on Aboriginal and Torres Strait Islander children, exemplified by their disproportionate over-representation in the child protection system.

What is at issue in this area is that, despite efforts to uphold and protect Indigenous self-determination and cultural rights through the adoption of the Aboriginal Child Placement Principle (ACPP) in law and policy (see Chapter 9), the mainstream child protection system is inadequately acknowledging the importance of Aboriginal and Torres Strait Islander culture for the future safety and wellbeing of these children. Thus, the child protection regime itself is implicated in the over-representation of Aboriginal and Torres Strait Islander children in care. Embedded in the shortcomings of the system is the ongoing history of colonialism in Australia, where non-Indigenous values and family practices are given preference over the values and child-rearing practices of Aboriginal and Torres Strait Islander peoples. In the discussion, it will be evident that more attention needs to be given to how child protection services determine when an Indigenous child is at risk; how they approach the placement of a child at risk; and what role negative cultural assumptions play in the making of these decisions.

11.3.1   Historical overview of child protection laws in Australia

On one view, the history of child protection can be appreciated as a history of progress. Whereas children were at one time treated in law as the property of their fathers, who were legally permitted to treat their children in any way they saw fit, the situation now is one

---

99   It has been found that in States and Territories where child protection and youth justice data are linked (ie, Victoria, South Australia, Tasmania and the Australian Capital Territory) young people (aged 10–17 years) receiving child protection services in 2013–14 were between 13 and 27 times more likely at some time to be under youth justice supervision than the general population: Australian Institute of Health and Welfare, *Young People in Child Protection and Under Youth Justice Supervision 2013–14* (AIHW, 2016) 7. The study also found that youth justice supervision 'was most likely for Indigenous young people: Indigenous males were 1.7 times as likely to be under supervision as non-Indigenous males, and Indigenous females were 2.2 times as likely' (at vi). These statistics suggest that the aims of child protection are not being achieved for younger children who from the age of 10 years old can be subject to youth justice supervision. They also suggest that the approach to youth justice is inconsistent with the aims of child protection and that this is particularly problematic for Indigenous young people. This seems clearly evident when children as young as 10 years old can be put in to juvenile detention (in all States and Territories) and 17-year-old youths can be placed in adult prison facilities (in Queensland): 'Queensland to remove 17-year-olds from adult prisons' *Brisbane Times* (online), 7 September 2016 <http://www.brisbanetimes .com.au/queensland/queensland-to-remove-17yearolds-from-adult-prisons-20160907-graizx.html>.

100   For a detailed coverage of child protection and juvenile justice in Australia, see Chris Cunneen, Rob White and Kelly Richards, *Juvenile Justice: Youth and Crime in Australia* (Oxford University Press, 5th ed, 2015).

where 'protecting children is everyone's business and … parents, communities, governments, non-government organisations and businesses all have a role to play'.[101]

The Australian Institute of Family Studies ('AIFS') has provided an overview of the history of child protection services that we summarise briefly as follows.[102] Prior to the late 19th century, western society was characterised by particularly brutal attitudes towards children.[103]

Concern for the brutalisation of children in the late 19th century grew in response to the revelation of shocking cases of child neglect and abuse. Awareness of these cases was first raised in the United States and then in England and Australia. This led to the creation of the first child protection services in each respective nation. At first, non-government organisations were established for the prevention of cruelty to children. In Australia, legislation and specialist children's courts were eventually established to protect children from more serious forms of neglect and abuse. At the time of federation in Australia, in 1901, responsibility for child protection became a State issue. Since that time, different regimes have been established across Australia to meet the local needs of each State and Territory.[104]

Over the course of the first half of the 20th century, concern for the protection of children was not something in which the general public invested a lot of interest. It was not until the 1960s that a new wave of 'child rescue' emerged. This was largely owing to research that revealed the negative effects of abuse on children. This research, and the media attention it garnered, would result in changes to government approaches over the course of the next few decades.

Thus, over the course of the second half of the 20th century there were a number of changes to the provision of out-of-home care aimed at providing better protection to children.[105] For example, instead of institutionalised care, preference was given to returning children to their homes, or placing them in foster care or smaller group care. Mandatory reporting laws were also introduced.[106] During this time, there were also changes to the understanding of what constitutes child maltreatment. The definition originally included severe physical abuse and severe neglect and now includes child sexual abuse, emotional abuse and exposure to family violence.

In the last few decades, the approach to child protection and its administration has also changed. Notably, in the 1980s and 1990s there was a rise of a legalistic approach, which was reliant on forensic investigation of child maltreatment allegations to determine

---

101   CFCA, *History of Child Protection Services* (AIFS, 2015). But this is a superficial view of history, considering recent revelations of child maltreatment in care (see chapter 12). See also *Broken Homes* (reported by Linton Besser and presented by Sarah Ferguson, ABC, *Four Corners*, 2016).

102   Ibid. See also Shurlee Swain, *History of Child Protection Legislation* (Royal Commission into Institutional Responses to Child Sexual Abuse, 2014) 5–9.

103   At common law, fathers had complete control over their children and the main concern of family law was to protect the property interests of the upper and middle classes. The law generally was not concerned with saving children, but instead ensuring the protection of property from the actions of destitute children. See John F Fogarty, 'Some Aspects of the Early History of Child Protection in Australia' (2008) 78 *Family Matters* 52, 54.

104   Broadly, the official response changed from viewing destitute children as in need of control (which attracted criminal sanction and institutionalisation) to viewing them as in need of care (and protection from the neglect of their parents): Swain, above n 102, 6–7.

105   There was a discursive shift from constructing child neglect in terms of criminality and the child requiring institutionalisation to child neglect as requiring prevention and ensuring that the child's best interests were met: Swain, above n 102, 9.

106   For a summary of current provisions, see CFCA, *Mandatory Reporting of Child Abuse and Neglect* (AIFS, 2016).

whether they were serious enough to warrant protective intervention. However, by the 1990s this system had proven inefficient to meet the needs of families at risk of abuse and neglect. Reduction in funding of child protection services and non-government family-support services meant that support for families at risk was limited. As child-support services were the only point of call for families at risk, it became increasingly difficult to meet demand.

In the 21st century, a new model for child protection was adopted in various Australian jurisdictions, one that sought to achieve a balance between child protection statutory services and family-support services. The development of this model reflected recognition of the importance of prevention of child maltreatment in the overall process of child protection. The identified benefits of this regime are that child protection services and family-support services can work collaboratively to tailor solutions to meet the needs of the family, instead of narrowly focusing on the risks to the child of abuse. This is considered appropriate in low-risk cases to avoid further trauma to the family through departmental investigations.

Thus, over the course of the past decades there has been a shift from statutory child protection services based on an intervention model that responded to child maltreatment when it had occurred, to a public health model that takes a preventative approach. In a public health model approach:

> priority is placed on having universal services available to all families, such as health and education. Secondary prevention interventions are provided to families that are deemed to be at risk of child maltreatment, while tertiary child protection services are deemed to be a last resort for families where child abuse and neglect has occurred.[107]

11.3.2   The main features of the child protection schemes in Australia

Currently there is no uniform national protection scheme in Australia although the development of a national approach was adopted in principle in 2009.[108] Child protection is a matter for the States and Territories.[109] While there are variations in each scheme, they share common aspects.

They can be summarised as follows:[110]

---

107   CFCA, *Defining the Public Health Model for the Child Welfare Services Context Services* (AIFS, 2014).

108   Department of Social Services, *Protecting Children is Everyone's Business: National Framework for Protecting Australia's Children 2009–2020* (Department of Families, Housing, Community Services and Indigenous Affairs, 2009).

109   The main pieces of legislation are the *Children and Young People Act 2008* (ACT); *Children and Young Persons (Care and Protection) Act 1998* (NSW); *Care and Protection of Children Act 2007* (NT); *Child Protection Act 1999* (Qld); *Children's Protection Act 1993* (SA); *Children, Youth and Families Act 2005* (Vic); *Children and Community Services Act 2004* (WA).

110   The following is a summary of Leah Bromfield and Prue Holzer, *A National Approach for Child Protection: Project Report* (2008) Department of Communities, Child Safety and Disability Services, Queensland Government <https://aifs.gov.au/cfca/sites/default/files/publication-documents/cdsmac.pdf> ch 4. Due to constraints of space, examples of the common aspects of the State and Territory child protection regimes only will be provided.

- **The 'best interests' principle:**

  All jurisdictions uphold the paramount importance of the principle of the 'best interests of the child'.[111] This principle comes into play in determining whether to support children to stay with their families or to place them in care. Legislative and/or policy provisions exist in each jurisdiction to provide guidance as to how such critical decisions are to be made. Where a conflict exists, it should be resolved in favour of protecting the child's interests.

- **Whole-of-government and community responsibility for child protection and child welfare:**

  This approach has been accepted by each jurisdiction.[112] Generally, this approach reflects the belief that a collaborative approach is required (as evident in Western Australia) between public authorities, non-government agencies and families in the provision of social services directed towards strengthening families and communities and maximising the wellbeing of children and other individuals, and in responding to child abuse and neglect.[113]

- **Early intervention:**

  Each jurisdiction subscribes to the belief that early intervention is necessary to promote the wellbeing of a child and they each have their legislation or policies to guide the process.[114] Generally, early intervention is based on the understanding that 'parents, family and the community of a child have the primary role in safeguarding and promoting a child's wellbeing, [and] ... the preferred way of safeguarding and promoting a child's wellbeing is to do so by supporting the child's parents, family and community to provide that care'.[115] Government officers may also be empowered to initiate or assist in the provision of services, and to take, or cause to be taken, any action considered reasonably necessary to promote the wellbeing of a child/children for whom there are concerns.[116]

- **The participation of children and young people in decision-making:**

  In line with international recognition of the importance of children's views (for example, art 12 of the *Convention on the Rights of the Child*,[117] which expressly stipulates a child's right to participation and to be heard), legislation in all Australian jurisdictions endorses the importance of involving children and young people in decision-making (to the extent that their age and maturity enables) and to consult and seek the views of children on issues affecting their lives.[118]

---

111   *Children and Young People Act 2008* (ACT) s 8; *Children and Young Persons (Care and Protection) Act 1998* (NSW) s 9(1); *Care and Protection of Children Act 2007* (NT) s 10; *Child Protection Act 1999* (Qld) s 5A; *Children's Protection Act 1993* (SA) s 4(3), (4); *Children, Young Persons and Their Families Act 1997* (Tas) s 10E; *Children, Youth and Families Act 2005* (Vic) s 10(1); *Children and Community Services Act 2004* (WA) s 7.

112   See, eg, the objects of the *Children and Young People Act 2008* (ACT) s 7(a)–(d).

113   *Children and Community Services Act 2004* (WA) s 21(2)(b).

114   See, eg, *Children, Youth and Families Act 2005* (Vic) ss 16, 21, 22.

115   *Children and Community Services Act 2004* (WA) s 9(a)–(b).

116   *Children and Community Services Act 2004* (WA) s 21(1)(a)–(b).

117   Opened for signature 20 November 1989, 1577 UNTS 3 (entered into force 2 September 1990).

118   See, eg, *Children and Young Persons (Care and Protection) Act 1998* (NSW) ss 9(2), 10.

- **Culturally specific responses to Aboriginal and Torres Strait Islander peoples:**
  The impact of past Indigenous child removal policies and laws has resulted in the adoption of the ACPP by all jurisdictions either in legislation, and/or policy, or other forms of delegated legislation such as regulations.[119] Sections 13 and 14 of the *Children, Youth and Families Act 2005* (Vic) provide an example of the legislative approach to the placement of an Aboriginal child in out-of-home care according to the ACPP.[120] Of note is how these particular provisions give priority to the placement of an Aboriginal child with his or her Aboriginal extended family members, but, in cases where the child has an Aboriginal and a non-Aboriginal parent, the child is to be placed according to the best interests of the child principle (see Chapter 9).

  These principles also provide for advice from, and consultation with Aboriginal and Torres Strait Islander organisations and community members when developing cultural care plans for Indigenous children.[121]

- **Diversion from the court system:**
  In line with the overall collaborative approach of protective services, diversionary approaches that seek to reach agreement on matters before going to court have been adopted. There are principles in each jurisdiction used to guide this approach.[122]

---

119   See, eg, *Children's Protection Act 1993* (SA) s 4(5); *Children's Protection Regulations 2010* (SA).

120   Section 13 sets out the criteria for the placement of a child: '(1) For the purposes of this Act the Aboriginal Child Placement Principle is that if it is in the best interests of an Aboriginal child to be placed in out of home care, in making that placement, regard must be had – (a) to the advice of the relevant Aboriginal agency; and (b) to the criteria in subsection (2); and (c) to the principles in section 14. (2) The criteria are – (a) as a priority, wherever possible, the child must be placed within the Aboriginal extended family or relatives and where this is not possible other extended family or relatives; (b) if, after consultation with the relevant Aboriginal agency, placement with extended family or relatives is not feasible or possible, the child may be placed with – (i) an Aboriginal family from the local community and within close geographical proximity to the child's natural family; (ii) an Aboriginal family from another Aboriginal community; (iii) as a last resort, a non-Aboriginal family living in close proximity to the child's natural family; (c) any non-Aboriginal placement must ensure the maintenance of the child's culture and identity through contact with the child's community'.

Section 14 provides further principles for the placement of an Aboriginal child:
'*Self-identification and expressed wishes of child*
(1) In determining where a child is to be placed, account is to be taken of whether the child identifies as Aboriginal and the expressed wishes of the child.
Child with parents from different Aboriginal communities
(2) If a child has parents from different Aboriginal communities, the order of placement set out in sections 13(2)(b)(i) and 13(2)(b)(ii) applies but consideration should also be given to the child's own sense of belonging.
(3) If a child with parents from different Aboriginal communities is placed with one parent's family or community, arrangements must be made to ensure that the child has the opportunity for continuing contact with his or her other parent's family, community and culture.
Child with one Aboriginal parent and one non-Aboriginal parent
(4) If a child has one Aboriginal parent and one non-Aboriginal parent, the child must be placed with the parent with whom it is in the best interests of the child to be placed.
Placement of child in care of a non-Aboriginal person
(5) If an Aboriginal child is placed with a person who is not within an Aboriginal family or community, arrangements must be made to ensure that the child has the opportunity for continuing contact with his or her Aboriginal family, community and culture.'

121   See, eg, *Children, Youth and Families Act 2005* (Vic) ss 13(1)(a), 13(2)(b).

122   See, eg, *Children and Young People Act 2008* (ACT) chs 3, 12; *Care and Protection of Children Act 2007* (NT) div 6; *Children, Young Persons and Their Families Act 1997* (Tas) pt 2, pt 5 div 1, s 52.

- **Out-of-home care:**[123]

  Out-of-home care is at the extreme end of the statutory child protection continuum and should typically only be used when all other care arrangements have been pursued and exhausted with respect to children deemed to be at risk of maltreatment. Children can be placed in out-of-home care voluntarily, but usually it involves the making of a court order. The Minister, as an authorised person, or the police, have powers to take children into custody where there are reasonable grounds to believe that a child is in need of care and that no other action would ensure the adequate care of the child.[124]

- **Permanency planning and stability of care:**

  Child protection regimes usually seek to maintain the child's relationship with his or her biological family so that even when a child has been placed in out-of-home care the goal has been to reunite children with their biological parents. A relatively new development in this area relates to the introduction of permanency planning. This approach is supported by research that has shown that children require stability and continuity for optimum development. The idea is that permanency planning is to be pursued after attempts at reunification have failed and involves finding more permanent, consistent and stable alternative care to support and provide for the child's safety, and developmental, emotional and physical needs.[125]

- **After care:**

  Reactions of young people leaving care have been mixed, ranging from those who feel positive about their futures to others who have expressed concern for their future wellbeing, economic prospects and relationships. Legislative provisions have been introduced to provide after-care support to these young people to make the transition from care to independent living.[126]

11.3.3   The over-representation of Aboriginal and Torres Strait Islander children in care

The details of the Australian child protection scheme set out above mirror the same sort of developments we have seen in other areas of family law, where the regulation of the family is through the adoption of a therapeutic model aimed at preserving the family unit. The understanding of the family as a private unit is essential in maintaining this system.

However, the system is far from perfect. Indeed, despite what seems to be the strong commitment of governments across jurisdictions to enhance the protection of children, improve the quality of out-of-home care, and enhance the success of young people leaving

---

123   There are legislative provisions that mandate state intervention to protect children. For an overview of the definitions of when a child is in need of protection, see CFCA, *Australian Legal Definitions: When is a Child in Need of Protection?* (AIFS, 2016).

124   See, eg, *Children and Young People Act 2008* (ACT) ch 15 pt 15.4.

125   See, eg, *Children, Youth and Families Act 2005* (Vic) s 167. See also Chapter 12.

126   See, eg, *Children and Young People Act 2008* (ACT) ch 15 pt 15.5; *Care and Protection of Children Act 2007* (NT) ss 68, 86.

care, none of these things has been achieved.[127] Recent statistics show that the number of children in care increases every year. Most significantly, these statistics show that the number of Aboriginal and Torres Strait Islander children in out-of-home care is increasing. They are over-represented across all age groups and are 10 times more likely than non-Indigenous children to be in out-of-home care.[128] In light of these statistics, our focus is on the over-representation of Indigenous children in care and how the child protection system, despite efforts to address this issue, is contributing to it.

As noted above, the ACPP has been adopted in each jurisdiction. Its adoption across jurisdictions was a response to the findings made in *Bringing Them Home* in 1997.[129] In that report, it was found that the past state-sanctioned practice of forcibly removing Indigenous children from their families pursuant to policies of 'protection' and 'assimilation' was in violation of international human rights laws on genocide and race discrimination, and had deprived children of their liberty, their parents of their parental rights, and involved abuses of power and breaches of guardianship duties.[130] These findings reflected how the practice was informed by perceptions of Indigenous peoples as an inferior race, and was administered with complete disregard for the humanity and cultures of Aboriginal and Torres Strait Islander peoples. The removal of children has had horrendous consequences for the children who were removed, their families and their communities.[131]

The recommendations in *Bringing Them Home* on child welfare were centred on making reparation based on the right of self-determination of Indigenous peoples;[132] this came to be understood to mean that the rights of the child would find protection across all domestic jurisdictions in provisions that would promote cultural safety, community identity and would, incrementally, lead to the transfer of jurisdiction, albeit in the form of delegated authority, to Indigenous children's organisations.[133] In broad terms, the pursuit of the right of self-determination is a direct response to the colonial legacy of the acquisition of British sovereignty, which has resulted in the complete subordination of Aboriginal and Torres Strait Islander peoples to Australian law. In the context of child welfare, the right of self-determination underpins measures such as the adoption of the ACPP, which aims to strengthen the capacity of Aboriginal and Torres Strait Islander families and communities to care for their children and maintain cultural connections for children in out-of-home care when the need arises. This approach is based on evidence of the cultural strengths of

---

127   Bromfield and Holzer, above n 110, ch 11.
128   As of 30 June 2014, there were 43 009 Australian children living in out-of-home care. This has increased from 7.7/1000 children at 30 June 2013 to 8.1/1 000 children at 30 June 2014. As of 30 June 2014, there were 14 991 Aboriginal and Torres Strait Islander children in out-of-home care in Australia – a placement rate of 51.4 per 1000 children. In contrast, the rate for non-Indigenous children was 5.6 per 1000: CFCA, *Children in Care* (AIFS, 2015).
129   Human Rights and Equal Opportunity Commission, *Bringing Them Home: Report of the National Inquiry into the Separation of Aboriginal and Torres Strait Islander Children from their Families* (1997) ('*Bringing Them Home*') <https://www.humanrights.gov.au/publications/bringing-them-home-report-1997>.
130   Ibid ch 13.
131   Ibid ch 11 provides a detailed account of the devastating personal and cultural effects of the practice on individuals, their families and communities.
132   Ibid ch 26.
133   Terri Libesman, 'Indigenous Child Welfare Post Bringing Them Home: From Aspirations for Self-determination to Neo-liberal Assimilation' (2016) 19 *Australian Indigenous Law Review* 42.

Indigenous child-rearing practices; the importance of Indigenous culture for the wellbeing of Indigenous children; that better outcomes are achieved through Indigenous-led solutions; and the importance of cultural knowledge to making decisions in children's best interests.[134] The ACPP is supposed to reflect the understanding that Aboriginal and Torres Strait Islander cultures are an intrinsic and indivisible part of their children's lives – and not an optional lifestyle choice that they can do without.

The ACPP is one of only a few recommendations in *Bringing Them Home* where implementation has been attempted, but this has taken place within a broader political and legal context where the finding of genocide has been rejected, and the rights of Indigenous peoples have been further violated.[135] Moreover, the implementation of the ACPP in practice has been far from complete.[136] Notably, the implementation of the ACPP has been extended in all jurisdictions, and some Indigenous child welfare organisations have authority to participate in the making of decisions concerning Indigenous children, and in some jurisdictions families can participate in this decision-making.[137] However, research shows that procedures for facilitating the participation of Indigenous organisations and families in decision-making have not been adequately put in place, meaning that the provisions designed for Indigenous children are often ignored.[138] The more recent introduction of permanency planning across all jurisdictions, although intended to promote stability in children's lives, in the absence of Indigenous institutional oversight has the potential to further undermine the implementation of the ACPP and put children at risk of abuse and/or substantial loss of culture (further discussed in Chapter 12).

Overall, the research suggests that there is uneven adherence to the ACPP at every stage of the process, including (but not limited to) lack of culturally appropriate early intervention

---

134   Family Matters, *An Evidence-based Approach to Address the Over-representation of Aboriginal and Torres Strait Islander Children in Out-of-Home Care* (Discussion Paper No 10, Family Matters, 2016) 3.

135   Notable examples are the amendments to the *Native Title Act 1993* (Cth) in 1998 and the introduction of the Northern Territory Emergency Response ('NTER') in 2007. In Committee on the Elimination of All Forms of Racial Discrimination (CERD Committee), Decision 2(54), 1331st Session, 18 March 1999, concern was expressed about 'the compatibility of the *Native Title Act*, as currently amended' with Australia's obligations under the *International Convention on the Elimination of All Forms of Racial Discrimination*, opened for signature 21 December 1965, 660 UNTS 195 (entered into force 4 January 1969). Similar conclusions were reached by the United Nations Special Rapporteur, James Anaya, with respect to the NTER, which was found to be incompatible with Australia's human rights obligations: James Anaya, *Report of the Special Rapporteur on the Situation of Human Rights and Fundamental Freedoms of Indigenous People*, UN Doc A/HRC/15 (4 March 2010). Most recently, UN High Commissioner for Human Rights Zeid Ra'ad Al Hussein has condemned the treatment of Indigenous children in juvenile detention in the Northern Territory as potential breaches of the *Convention on the Rights of the Child* and the *Convention Against Torture*: Michael Koziol, '"Shocked" United Nations Slams Australia on Child Abuse, Calls for Compensation', *Sydney Morning Herald* (online), 30 July 2016 <http://www.smh.com.au/federal-politics/political-news/shocked-united-nations-slams-australia-on-child-abuse-calls-for-compensation-20160730-gqh74x.html>.

136   Australia's failure to fully implement the *Bringing Them Home* recommendations on child welfare has also been commented on by the Committee on the Rights of the Child. See CRC/C, 40th sess, UN Doc CRC/C/15/Add.268 (20 October 2005) CRC/C/15/Add.268 ('*Concluding Observations: Australia*'); CRC/C, 60th sess, UN Doc CRC/C/AUS/CO/4 (28 August 2012) ('*Concluding Observations: Australia*').

137   Libesman, above n 133, 51.

138   Ibid.

and support/healing services that are crucial to the prevention of out-of-home care; uneven involvement and resourcing of Indigenous agencies in the early intervention stages and decision-making processes; poor knowledge among mainstream services of Indigenous communities and kinship structures, which can mean that suitable carers are not contacted and resulting in the placement of children in non-Indigenous care; failure of carer assessment procedures undertaken by mainstream child protection services to account for cultural differences in Indigenous family structures, living arrangements and parenting practices; and insufficient support available to staff (especially non-Indigenous staff) in devising meaningful cultural care plans for children to maintain their connection to culture when placed in non-Indigenous care.[139] The situation is further exacerbated by evidence of racist treatment of Indigenous children through abuse and neglect when placed in non-Indigenous care.[140]

However, it is not usual to find lack of compliance with the ACCP listed as a reason for the over-representation of Aboriginal and Torres Strait Islander children in care. The statistical data available depends on the reporting mechanisms followed by the child protection services themselves. Whether it is intentional or not, the impression that some data-collection surveys give supports the image of Aboriginal and Torres Strait Islander families as dysfunctional and unable to take care of their children at all.[141] This evidence is also used to explain any departures in the application of the ACPP. One of the main reasons given for States and Territories departing from applying the ACPP is that there is a shortage of carers available to care for Indigenous children owing to their own trauma and disadvantage.[142]

It is notable how this research acknowledges the legacies of past wrongs as the source of the problems Aboriginal and Torres Strait Islander communities are facing, but the focus is also on their families as the source of the problem of the over-representation of their children in care in present times.[143] It cannot be denied that the impact of colonisation on Indigenous peoples has been a significant contributing factor to the over-representation of children in out-of-home care. Yet, the emphasis on these facts of history construct the problems now facing Indigenous peoples as the product of past wrongs and diverts attention from the state's role in the commission of injustices in the present.[144] In the context of child welfare, this approach diverts focus from the failings of the current child protection

---

139   Fiona Arney et al, *Enhancing the Implementation of the Aboriginal and Torres Strait Islander Child Placement Principle* (CFCA Paper No 34, AIFS, 2015).

140   Andrew Jackomos (Victoria's Commissioner for Aboriginal Children and Young People), 'The Imperative for Change' (Speech delivered at the Family Matters Strategic Forum, Canberra, 10 February 2016).

141   CFCA, *Child Protection and Aboriginal and Torres Strait Islander Children* (AIFS, 2015). The reasons cited for the heightened rates of child abuse and neglect in Aboriginal and Torres Strait Islander communities are alcohol and drug abuse, family violence, pornography, overcrowded and inadequate housing, gambling.

142   Ibid.

143   See, eg, *Abuse and Neglect*, Find Legal Answers <http://www.legalanswers.sl.nsw.gov.au/guides/hot_topics/child_care_and_protection/abuse_and_neglect.html>.

144   Notably, in 2008 then Prime Minister Kevin Rudd delivered the 'Apology to Australia's Indigenous Peoples', where he accepted responsibility for the forced removal of Indigenous children from 1910 to 1975. Relegating the removal of children to the past meant that he could elide the disproportionate numbers of children in out-of-home care in present times and the complicity of current government laws, policies and practices in their removal: Commonwealth, *Parliamentary Debates*, House of Representatives, 13 February 2008, 167–71 (Kevin Rudd, Prime Minister).

regime in perpetuating the over-representation of Aboriginal and Torres Strait Islander children in care.[145]

It is important to acknowledge that, despite the history of past injustices, most Aboriginal and Torres Strait Islander children continue to be cared for by their families of origin, and that the strength of their wellbeing and safety lies with their families and communities. Using this as the starting point, we are in better position to ask whether the rate at which Aboriginal and Torres Strait Islander children are being removed is because they are at risk or because of institutional racism that still exists in child-welfare services.[146] But even when a child is at risk, the disproportionate levels at which Aboriginal and Torres Strait Islander children are being removed suggests that their families are not getting the cultural support they need to care for their children. Indeed, the fact that Indigenous children are being disproportionately removed in comparison to non-Indigenous children indicates how the strength of Indigenous communities – their culture – is continuing to be undermined by the removal of Indigenous children.[147] This then can lead us to reconsider the lack of compliance with the ACPP and to recognise how non-compliance is undermining Aboriginal and Torres Strait Islander cultures and contributing to the over-representation of Indigenous children in care.

When the issues are viewed in this way, it becomes clearer how non-compliance with the ACPP is exacerbating the problems facing Indigenous communities, creating a cycle where lack of adherence to the cultural rights of children is contributing to the over-representation of Aboriginal and Torres Strait Islander children in care. Evidently Indigenous peoples are living not only with the legacies of past injustices, but also with injustices in the present. As long as Indigenous child protection is administered within the mainstream (and under-resourced) child protection regime, it will be difficult for Indigenous peoples to meaningfully assert their right to self-determination and prevent the removal of their children. Indigenous child protection is in much need of reform in Australia.[148] However, this will require resources, and a commitment to change the system from one based on 'power over'

---

145   It also diverts attention from government failures to address the worsening poverty and disadvantage of Indigenous peoples caused by past and present injustices (eg, significant budget cuts) that are also contributing to the crises experienced by Indigenous children and their families. Indeed it is evident that a 'whole-of-government' approach to Indigenous child protection resulted in the NTER (now Stronger Futures), where punitive measures such as income management have been introduced in the name of protecting the child which, among other things, have not in practice improved women's safety and have undermined their perception as competent parents: Equality Rights Alliance, *Women's Experience of Income Management in the Northern Territory* (Equality Rights Alliance, 2011) 6.

146   Claire Moodie, '"Nothing Changed": Martu Elders Fight Against Removal of Aboriginal Children', *ABC News* (online), 20 December 2015 <http://www.abc.net.au/news/2015-12-20/martu-elders-fight-against-removal-of-aboriginal-children/7043798>.

147   Family Matters, above n 134, 1.

148   There is commitment in the community sector for reform, with the Secretariat of National Aboriginal and Islander Child Care (SNAICC), the national peak body representing the interests of Aboriginal and Torres Strait Islander children and families, leading a new initiative – 'Family Matters – Kids Safe in Culture, Not in Care' – that aims to eliminate the over-representation of Indigenous children in child protection systems by 2030. A grassroots movement, Grandmothers Against Removals, has also been established: Grandmothers Against Removals <http://stopstolengenerations.com.au>. However, in the most recent *Close the Gap* report there was no commitment made by the Commonwealth government under Prime Minister Malcolm Turnbull to close the gap on the over-representation of Aboriginal and Torres Strait Islander children in out-of-home care: Christopher Holland, *Close the Gap: Progress and Priorities Report 2016* (Australian Human Rights Commission, 2016) <https://www.humanrights.gov.au/sites/default/files/document/publication/Progress_priorities_report_CTG_2016_0.pdf>.

to one based on 'power sharing'.[149] Historically, the injustices experienced by Aboriginal and Torres Strait Islander peoples stem from perceptions of their inferiority, and it would seem much still needs to be done to change these perceptions.[150] In this context, it will mean no longer associating Indigeneity as a 'risk' factor but instead as a 'safety' factor to ensure that the wellbeing of Indigenous children and their families is secured in the future. When considered in terms of the broader claims of this book, we can understand the approach to Indigenous child protection as continuing to promote western family values. This is done by perpetuating the erroneous understanding that Indigenous families are too dysfunctional to have any values worth upholding.

---

149   Arney et al, above n 139, 13–7.
150   For an examination of official discourses constructing Indigenous stereotypes in present times, see Melissa Lovell, 'Languages of Neoliberal Critique: The Production of Coercive Government in the Northern Territory Intervention' in John Uhr and Ryan Walter (eds), *Studies in Australian Political Rhetoric* (ANU E Press, 2014) 221.

CHILDREN AND FAMILY FORMATION: ADOPTION AND REPRODUCTIVE TECHNOLOGIES

12.1   Introduction

Adoption and assisted reproduction treatment are practices usually associated with the creation of new families, especially for couples who cannot produce their own biological children.

These practices, however, are not without their critics. In this chapter, our focus is to identify how the nuclear family structure features in the regulation of these practices. The 'best interests of the child' continues to be the guiding principle, but, as we have seen in previous chapters, it is a much-contested concept. The debates in the areas of adoption and assisted reproduction treatment also highlight that there is no fixed understanding of what *is* best for the child. The discussion below shows how the principle serves to advance different ideological positions on the family. At the same time, this discussion demonstrates the potential for the family to be reconceptualised. Nevertheless, it will be evident that at present the legal approach functions to use the best interests principle to uphold the nuclear family and the social hierarchies that it supports.

12.2   Adoption

The area of adoption is a vast topic and we are unable to canvass all of the pertinent issues.[1] We will focus primarily on how adoption is a mechanism of maintaining the salience of children having a single set of parents as the quintessential family. Adoption as a legal device permanently transfers all the legal rights and responsibilities of being a parent from the child's birth parents (or anyone with parental responsibility for the child) to the adoptive parents.[2] However, and consistent with the approach adopted in this book, it is important to note that developments in the area of adoption also demonstrate how the state is involved in regulating behaviour related to forming a family (evident also in the area of abortion) and in determining who can maintain a family once a child is born (evident also in child protection),[3] and that this regulation is paradoxical in simultaneously privileging the private nuclear family unit. Moreover, the concept of the child's best interests is instrumental, whether in supporting adoption or disapproving of it; but, in either case, law- and policy-makers maintain that the nuclear family is the best family model for bringing up children.

The discussion will begin by providing an overview of the history and current practice of adoption in Australia.[4] Child protection and adoption are related areas. In Australia (and as noted in Chapter 11), it has been common policy in child protection to maintain the

---

1   For a brief history of adoption in Europe, see Bruno Perreau, *The Politics of Adoption: Gender and the Making of French Citizenship* (Deke Dusinberre trans, MIT Press, 2014) ch 1.

2   *Adoption*, Family and Community Services ('FACS'), NSW Government <http://www.community.nsw.gov.au/parents,-carers-and-families/fostering,-guardianship-and-adoption/adoption>.

3   For an analysis of different models of regulating adoption, see Amanda C Pustilnik, 'Private Ordering, Legal Ordering, and the Getting of Children: A Counterhistory of Adoption Law' (2002) 20(1) *Yale Law and Policy Review* 263.

4   The main pieces of legislation are the *Adoption Act 2000* (NSW); *Adoption Regulation 2015* (NSW); *Adoption Act 1993* (ACT); *Adoption Regulation 1993* (ACT); *Adoption of Children Act 1994* (NT); *Adoption of Children Regulations 1994* (NT); *Adoption Act 2009* (Qld); *Adoption Regulation 2009* (Qld); *Adoption Act 1988* (SA); *Adoption Regulations 2004* (SA); *Adoption Act 1988* (Tas); *Adoption Regulations 2006* (Tas); *Adoption Act 1984* (Vic); *Adoption Regulations 2008* (Vic); *Adoption Act 1994* (WA); *Adoption Regulations 1995* (WA).

biological family unit and place children who are at risk of maltreatment in out-of-home care as a last resort measure. However, the approach to child protection in Australia seems to be changing direction, with less emphasis being placed on the importance of maintaining biological ties of children with their families, and greater emphasis being placed on creating future stability for children. A similar shift seems to be occurring with respect to intercountry adoption. As the emphasis is changing, we are witnessing renewed interest in adoption as the stable family alternative to out-of-home care.

These changes are in part influenced by the cost of child protection to the state and the demand for easier access to adoption by adult carers. In the discussion below, we will also consider same-sex couples' claims for equality in the adoption area. This will illuminate the need for the development of an adoption process that is fair for everyone affected by the process. However, that may only become possible if we reconsider the nuclear family as serving the best interests of the child.

12.2.1   Adoption in Australia: past and present

Legal regulation of adoption in Australia can be divided into three periods.[5]

The first phase relates to a period from the late 19th to the early 20th century, where adoption was not regulated at all by law. At this time, adoption was facilitated through the placement of advertisements in newspapers. Adoption from the point of view of 'buyers' was an economic transaction. They sought to adopt children whom they could then put into service. This was in contrast to 'sellers', who sought substitute families for children in their care by appealing to the sentiment of a loving family. Adoption was also facilitated at no cost through the various State children's departments, which developed boarding-out programs that would result in the adoption of children by their former foster parents.[6]

The second phase relates to when the Australian States began to regulate adoption through legislation, in the 1920s. The rationale was that children would benefit from 'happy homes' unburdened by 'the misfortunes of their births';[7] adoptive families would benefit from certainty in not having the adoptions challenged by birth parents; and birth parents were presented as either lacking parental love or desirous to be rid of their unwanted children.[8]

However, it was not until the 1940s that the demand for children for adoption began to outstrip the supply of children available. It was at this time that birth mothers, who were usually unwed, became vulnerable to the forced relinquishment of their children for adoption. Notable court challenges by birth mothers to this practice eventually resulted in changes to the law to strengthen the rights of adoptive parents.[9] By the 1960s, amendments to adoption laws across the country had strengthened secrecy provisions to ensure that

---

5   The discussion is based on Shurlee Swain, 'Snapshots from the Long History of Adoption in Australia' (2012) 6(1) *Australian Journal of Adoption* 1. Cf Denise Cuthbert, Kate Murphy and Marian Quartly, 'Adoption and Feminism: Towards Framing a Feminist Response to Contemporary Developments in Adoption' (2009) 24(62) *Australian Feminist Studies* 395.

6   Ibid 2.

7   Ibid 6.

8   Ibid.

9   Ibid. See also, for a socio-legal analysis of adoption, Josephine Reeves, 'The Deviant Mother and Child: The Development of Adoption as an Instrument of Social Control' (1993) 20(4) *Journal of Law and Society* 412.

none of the parties knew each other's names. This was done by issuing new birth certificates that established the child's new identity and relationship with its adoptive parents to create the 'legal fiction' that the adoptive parents were the biological parents of the child.[10]

The third phase started in the 1970s through to the 1980s when some States introduced registers to assist adopted children and their birth parents to make contact with one another. This phase saw a move towards 'open' forms of permanent child placement and this continues to be the approach to adoption in Australia.[11] This approach was a response to agitation from birth parents and adoptees seeking to assert their rights and raise awareness of their negative experiences of forced adoptions.[12] These developments also coincided with revelations of child maltreatment at an institutional level that created, for example, what is now commonly referred to as the Stolen Generations, the Forgotten Australians and Former Child Migrants, who had suffered institutional abuse and neglect in out-of-home care (eg, children's homes and orphanages) during the 20th century.[13]

12.2.2   Overview of current legal provisions and adoption practice

Currently there are three main types of adoption in Australia:

1. Intercountry adoptions – adoptions of children from countries other than Australia who are legally able to be placed for adoption, but who generally have had no previous contact or relationship with the adoptive parent(s). Expatriate adoptions are not included in the numbers for intercountry adoptions.

---

10   Cuthbert, Murphy and Quartly, above n 5, 397.

11   Ibid 400.

12   The Commonwealth's role in the policies and practices of forced adoption was the subject of an inquiry of the Senate Community Affairs References Committee, which released its report, *Commonwealth Contribution to Former Forced Adoption Policies and Practices*, in 2012: see Senate Community Affairs References Committee, Parliament of Australia, *Commonwealth Contribution to Former Forced Adoption Policies and Practices* (2012). The following year, then Prime Minister Julia Gillard offered a national apology for forced adoptions: *National Apology for Forced Adoptions*, Attorney-General's Department, Australian Government <https://www.ag.gov.au/About/ForcedAdoptionsApology/Pages/default.aspx>.

13   In addition to the inquiry into the forced removal of Aboriginal and Torres Strait Islander children from their families (Human Rights and Equal Opportunity Commission, *Bringing Them Home: Report of the National Inquiry into the Separation of Aboriginal and Torres Strait Islander Children from their Families* (1997) ('*Bringing Them Home*') <https://www.humanrights.gov.au/publications/bringing-them-home-report-1997>), other inquiries include the Parliament of Australia's Senate Community Affairs Reference Committee's inquiry into Australians who experienced institutional or out-of-home care as children, the first report of which is entitled *Forgotten Australians: A Report on Australians Who Experienced Institutional or Out-of-Home Care as Children* (2004) and the second, *Protecting Vulnerable Children: A National Challenge* (2005); and the inquiry of the NSW Legislative Council's Standing Committee on Social Issues into adoption practices of the past, *Releasing the Past: Adoption Practice 1950–1998, Final Report* (2000). Revelations about the suffering of children who migrated to Australia under imperial migration schemes include work by Philip Bean and Joy Melville, *Lost Children of the Empire* (Unwin Hyman, 1989); Alan Gill, *Orphans of the Empire: the Shocking Story of Child Migration to Australia* (Random House, 1998); and the autobiographical work by David Hill, *The Forgotten Children: Fairbridge Farm School and its Betrayal of Australia's Child Migrants* (Random House, 2007). Child migration was the subject of an inquiry by the Senate Community Affairs Reference Committee that reported in 2001 (see Senate Community Affairs Reference Committee, *Lost Innocents: Righting the Record – Report on Child Migration* (Parliament of Australia, 2001)).

2. Local adoptions – adoptions of children who were born or permanently residing in Australia before the adoption, who are legally able to be placed for adoption, but who generally have had no previous contact or relationship with the adoptive parent(s).

3. 'Known' child adoptions – adoptions of children who were born or permanently residing in Australia before the adoption, who have a pre-existing relationship with the adoptive parent(s) and who are generally unable to be adopted by anyone other than the adoptive parent(s). Known child adoptions include adoptions by step-parents, other relatives and carers.[14]

Adults eligible to apply for adoption in Australia include opposite-sex couples, who can register to adopt an unrelated child under most State and Territory laws.[15] Same-sex couples can register to adopt an unrelated child in Western Australia, New South Wales, Tasmania, Victoria and the Australian Capital Territory.[16] Provisions for same-sex step-parent adoptions are available in Western Australia, New South Wales, Victoria and the Australian Capital Territory.[17] All States and Territories, except South Australia, permit a single person to adopt, including an individual applicant who is in a committed same-sex relationship.[18] Couples who are in traditional Aboriginal customary marriages can apply to adopt a child.[19] Intercountry adoption depends on meeting the eligibility criteria of the State or Territory in which expressions of interests are made and meeting the eligibility criteria specified by the relevant overseas countries with whom Australia has adoption agreements. Eligibility criteria of the overseas country may be more restrictive than the State or Territory criteria. For instance, none of the countries Australia has intercountry agreements with same-sex adoption.[20]

Adoption law varies between jurisdictions. The *Adoption Act 2000* (NSW) is an example of an attempt to reflect an open adoption approach in contrast to past adoptive practices.

---

14   Australian Institute of Health and Welfare, *Adoptions* (Australian Government) <http://www.aihw
      .gov.au/adoptions/>. In 2014–15 there were 292 adoptions in Australia: 83 (28%) intercountry
      adoptions and 209 (72%) Australian child adoptions. Of the 83 intercountry adoptions, 49 (17%)
      were *Hague Convention* adoptions and 34 (12%) were non-*Hague Convention* adoptions. Of
      the 209 Australian child adoptions, 56 (19%) were local adoptions and 153 (52%) known child
      adoptions. Of the 153 known child adoptions, 52 were step-parent adoptions, four were relative
      adoptions, 94 were carer adoptions, and three were other adoptions.

15   In the Northern Territory, adoption is limited to married couples: *Adoption of Children Act 1994*
      (NT) s 13(1)(a).

16   *Adoption Act 1994* (WA) ss 38–39; *Adoption Act 2000* (NSW) ss 23, 28; *Adoption Act 1988* (Tas)
      s 20(1); *Adoption Act 1984* (Vic) ss 10A–13A; *Adoption Act 1993* (ACT) s 14.

17   *Adoption Act 1994* (WA) ss 7, 55; *Adoption Act 2000* (NSW) s 30; *Adoption Act 1984* (Vic) s 11(5);
      Adoption Act 1993 (ACT) s 15. The lesbian co-mother or gay co-father(s) can also apply to the
      Family Court of Australia for a parenting order, as 'any other person concerned with the care,
      welfare or development of the child': *Family Law Act 1975* (Cth) ('FLA') s 65C(c). But the lesbian
      co-mother and gay co-father(s) will be treated in the same way as a social parent is treated under
      the law; they will not be treated in the same way as a birth parent.

18   *Adoption Act 1994* (WA) ss 38–39; *Adoption Act 2000* (NSW) s 27; *Adoption Act 1988* (Tas) s 20(4)–(5);
      Adoption Act 1984 (Vic) s 11(3); *Adoption Act 2009* (Qld) s 152(3); *Adoption Act 1993* (ACT) s 16;
      Adoption of Children Act 1994 (NT) s 14.

19   *Adoption Act 1984* (Vic) s 11(1)(b); *Adoption of Children Act 1994* (NT) s 13(1)(b).

20   See, eg, *Adopting a Child from Overseas*, Queensland Government <https://www.qld.gov.au/
      community/caring-child/adopting-child-overseas/>; *Intercountry Adoption*, Department for Child
      Protection and Family Support, Government of Western Australia <https://www.dcp.wa.gov.au/
      FosteringandAdoption/AdoptionAndHomeForLife/Pages/OverseasAdoption.aspx>.

Sections 7 and 8 respectively set out the objects and principles of this Act. The objects in s 7 include that adoption law and practice should pursue the best interests of the child and that adoption is a service for the concerned child.[21] The principles in s 8(1) provide that, when making a decision about the adoption of a child, a decision-maker is to have regard (as far as is practicable or appropriate)[22] that the best interests of the child are the paramount consideration and best interests are determined by having regard to a number of factors mentioned in sub-s (2). This list of factors makes it evident that the views or attitudes of parents are relevant, as well as any wishes expressed by the child, and his or her relationship to the parents and siblings. In addition, the attitudes and capacities of the adoptive parents are relevant, but how all or some of these factors are to be given any weight remains a decision of the court.

The contemporary reality, however, is that the number of adoptions has been declining over the last two decades, and has decreased considerably from the 1960s and 1970s.

---

21   Section 7: 'The objects of this Act are as follows: (a) to emphasise that the best interests of the child concerned, both in childhood and later life, must be the paramount consideration in adoption law and practice, (b) to make it clear that adoption is to be regarded as a service for the child concerned, (c) to ensure that adoption law and practice assist a child to know and have access to his or her birth family and cultural heritage, (d) to recognise the changing nature of practices of adoption, (e) to ensure that equivalent safeguards and standards to those that apply to children from New South Wales apply to children adopted from overseas, (f) to ensure that adoption law and practice complies with Australia's obligations under treaties and other international agreements, (g) to encourage openness in adoption, (h) to allow access to certain information relating to adoptions, (i) to provide for the giving in certain circumstances of post-adoption financial and other assistance to adopted children and their birth and adoptive parents'.

22   '(1) In making a decision about the adoption of a child, a decision maker is to have regard (as far as is practicable or appropriate) to the following principles: (a) the best interests of the child, both in childhood and in later life, must be the paramount consideration, (b) adoption is to be regarded as a service for the child, (c) no adult has a right to adopt the child, (d) if the child is able to form his or her own views on a matter concerning his or her adoption, he or she must be given an opportunity to express those views freely and those views are to be given due weight in accordance with the developmental capacity of the child and the circumstances, (e) the child's given name or names, identity, language and cultural and religious ties should, as far as possible, be identified and preserved, (e1) undue delay in making a decision in relation to the adoption of a child is likely to prejudice the child's welfare, (f) if the child is Aboriginal – the Aboriginal child placement principles are to be applied, (g) if the child is a Torres Strait Islander – the Torres Strait Islander child placement principles are to be applied. (2) In determining the best interests of the child, the decision maker is to have regard to the following: (a) any wishes expressed by the child, (b) the child's age, maturity, level of understanding, gender, background and family relationships and any other characteristics of the child that the decision maker thinks are relevant, (c) the child's physical, emotional and educational needs, including the child's sense of personal, family and cultural identity, (d) any disability that the child has, (e) any wishes expressed by either or both of the parents of the child, (f) the relationship that the child has with his or her parents and siblings (if any) and any significant other people (including relatives) in relation to whom the decision maker considers the question to be relevant, (g) the attitude of each proposed adoptive parent to the child and to the responsibilities of parenthood, (h) the nature of the relationship of the child with each proposed adoptive parent, (i) the suitability and capacity of each proposed adoptive parent, or any other person, to provide for the needs of the child, including the emotional and intellectual needs of the child, (j) the need to protect the child from physical or psychological harm caused, or that may be caused, by being subjected or exposed to abuse, ill-treatment, violence or other behaviour, or being present while a third person is subjected or exposed to abuse, ill-treatment, violence or other behaviour, (k) the alternatives to the making of an adoption order and the likely effect on the child in both the short and longer term of changes in the child's circumstances caused by an adoption, so that adoption is determined among all alternative forms of care to best meet the needs of the child.'

In 1972–73 there were close to 10 000 adoptions.[23] In 2014–15 there were 292 adoptions in total in Australia.[24] A combination of factors, including the increased use of contraceptives, changes to policies and mores around single motherhood, and the negative experiences that children and birth mothers have had of adoption, has resulted in changes to adoption practices and the development of child protection systems where out-of-home care is the preferred option for children in need of alternative care arrangements. The overall effect has been a drastic reduction in the number of children available for adoption. Currently across Australia, the demand drastically outstrips supply. There are many facets to the legal regulation and availability of adoption as a means of creating families for those otherwise unable to do so.[25] But in keeping with our theme throughout, that family law constructs or upholds the nuclear family, we focus on the mechanisms of excluding the effects of adoption on the birth mother.[26] The paradox is that this exclusion is carried out while extolling the virtues of a two-parent family for the child concerned.

According to a website managed by the Victorian Government's Department of Human Services, there are few local children available for adoption in that State. Most adoptions are usually through the State's intercountry adoption process. These children are usually 'over the age of four years and they have a range of emotional, psychological and medical special needs'.[27] It is notable that while there are many inquiries about intercountry adoption, few 'remain interested in pursuing an application to have an older child with special needs placed with them'.[28] The website goes on to explain why few 'healthy' children are available, including that most children in orphanages around the world are not free to be adopted. It says further that adoption is about finding families for children and not the reverse. A child can be considered for overseas adoption only after the relevant responsible authority is satisfied that all possible measures have been taken to find an in-country option for the child. In Australia, overseas adoption is usually possible from country signatories to the *Hague Convention on the Protection of Children and Cooperation in Respect of Intercountry Adoption*[29] ('*Hague Convention on Intercountry Adoption*') or under separate agreements between Australia and other countries. This is necessary to prevent trafficking of children, and since many countries are not signatories to the *Hague Convention on Intercountry Adoption* or do not have agreements with Australia, children from these countries cannot be adopted. Moreover, a majority of overseas countries do not have a need to adopt out very young children (0–2 years), as families within their countries are adopting them and that is the best outcome for

23   Daryl Higgins, *Past and Present Adoptions in Australia* (AIFS, 2012).

24   Australian Institute of Health and Welfare, *Adoptions*, Australian Government <http://www.aihw .gov.au/adoptions/>.

25   Notably in non-traditional arrangements involving same-sex couples or single people, allowing men to adopt a child is portrayed as a positive of this practice. However, we argue that the relinquishing or biological mother is still the absent figure in this discourse: see Amanda K Baumle and D'Lane R Compton, *Legalizing LGBT Families: How the Law Shapes Parenthood* (New York University Press, 2015).

26   For useful information for the birth parents, see *Impact of Adoption on Birth Parents* (Child Welfare Information Gateway, 2013) <https://www.childwelfare.gov/pubpdfs/f_impact.pdf>.

27   Department of Human Services, *About Intercountry Adoption in Victoria*, Victorian State Government <http://www.dhs.vic.gov.au/for-individuals/children,-families-and-young-people/ adoption-and-permanent-care/intercountry-adoption/about-intercountry-adoption-in-victoria>.

28   Ibid.

29   Opened for signature 29 May 1993, [1998] ATS 21 (entered into force 1 May 1995).

the children. Thus, the difficulties faced by Australians wishing to adopt from overseas are not obstacles put in the path of families, but measures to keep children safe and to make available processes that would protect them and the families adopting them.[30]

We have referred to this website at length because implicit in the information it is providing to members of the public interested in adoption are some of the key arguments in the literature on adoption, particularly transracial adoption.[31] Central to any discussion on adoption are the best interests of the child, and in this website it is repeatedly stressed that the interests of the child will be met if the child remains in his or her country of birth. Adoption may only be possible for special needs children and only if they cannot be placed in their countries of birth. The fact that this government department had to clarify these aspects of the adoption process is telling, and reads as though its aim is to counter standard discourses about adoption in mainstream society: that there are many children in poor underdeveloped countries in desperate need of adoption and that western families will provide better environments for these children to grow and thrive. It is notable that the website does not complicate things by bringing the birth mother of these children into the equation. It only refers to orphaned children and that it is desirable for their adoption to take place in their own country of birth.[32]

However, it cannot be so easily assumed that the need for adoption only arises when the birth parents have died. But bringing the birth parent – who is usually the mother – into the equation raises another set of issues.[33] Indeed, it can bring the whole adoption process into question. If the biological ties between mother and children are essential for the child's emotional development (as is claimed by the traditional proponents of the family), then adoption cannot so easily be constructed as in the best interests of the child.[34] In fact, adoption is the legal means through which the mother–child bond is severed completely.[35]

To get around this argument, conservative proponents reconcile their traditional values about the family and adoption by upholding adoption as the moral alternative to abortion: the mother has no intention to parent so why not give the child a better life through adoption?[36] In contrast, the liberal stance focuses on the choices adoption can give

30   Department of Human Services, *About Intercountry Adoption in Victoria*, Victorian State Government <http://www.dhs.vic.gov.au/for-individuals/children,-families-and-young-people/adoption-and-permanent-care/intercountry-adoption/about-intercountry-adoption-in-victoria>.

31   See generally Twila L Perry, 'Transracial and International Adoption: Mothers, Hierarchy, Race and Feminist Legal Theory' (1998) 10(1) *Yale Journal of Law and Feminism* 101.

32   For reasons of space, we will not discuss the very significant issues raised by interracial adoption, but for an introduction see Rowena Fong and Ruth McRoy (eds), *Transracial and Intercountry Adoptions: Cultural Guidance for Professionals* (Columbia University Press, 2016).

33   The following discussion draws on Elizabeth Bartholet, *Family Bonds: Adoption and the Politics of Parenting* (Houghton Mifflin Company, 1993) xiv–xxii.

34   Jacqueline Bhabha, *Child Migration and Human Rights in a Global Age* (Princeton University Press, 2014) 19.

35   Audra Behne, 'Balancing The Adoption Triangle: The State, the Adoptive Parents and the Birth Parents – Where Does the Adoptee Fit In?' (1996–97) 15 *Buffalo Journal of Public International Law* 49.

36   See the discussion in Nancy Felipe Russo, 'Psychological Aspects of Unwanted Pregnancy and its Resolution' in J Douglas Butler and David F Walbert (eds), *Abortion, Medicine, and the Law* (Fideli Publishing, 5th ed, 2011) ch 25. Moreover, the reform of legal provisions for abortion is itself influenced by interdisciplinary contests. See, eg, Sheelagh Mcguinness and Michael Thomson, 'Medicine and Abortion Law: Complicating the Reforming Profession' (2015) 23(2) *Medical Law Review* 177.

to the parties[37]: it gives the birth mother a choice in deciding whether to be a parent or not, and gives the adoptive parents – especially the adoptive mother – an opportunity to parent a child which she would not otherwise have. For conservatives, the adoptive family ultimately provides the child with a family that mirrors the traditional nuclear family; for liberals, adoption creates a positive alternative to the standard blood-based family model.

At the other end of the spectrum, there are the critics of adoption who question whether the process allows for any real choices to be made, especially considering the disparity in power and resources that would exist between birth and adoptive parents. These critics question whether adoption is another means of exploiting poor single women.[38] Their concerns seem pertinent, especially when adoption proponents tend to hold up the adoptive arrangement as superior when compared to the alternative situation of the child remaining with the birth mother whose parenting abilities are usually referred to in inferior terms by comparison to the adoptive mother.[39]

Notably, the change in policy on child protection in Australia (and concern to protect the rights of the child in international law) has, since the late 20th century, seemed to favour the importance of maintaining biological links between children and their birth families (and cultural ties in the case of intercountry adoptions); this has resulted in a rather cautious approach to adoption – evident in the very low number of adoptions in Australia. However, not everyone has been convinced that this has been a positive development and in some government circles we have seen attempts to revive adoption. During conservative Prime Minister John Howard's term in office, there were two inquiries conducted by the Australian House of Representatives Standing Committee on Family and Human Services. Both reports advocated a change in attitude to adoption, particularly with respect to intercountry adoptions and domestic adoptions where birth parents suffer from substance abuse.[40] It is notable in these reports that biological ties were devalued and constructed as standing in the way of

37   See, eg, Kathy Shepherd Stolley and Elaine J Hall, 'The Presentation of Abortion and Adoption in Marriage and Family Textbooks' (1994) 43(3) *Family Relations* 267; Steven L Nock, 'Abortion, Adoption, and Marriage: Alternative Resolutions of an Unwanted Pregnancy' (1994) 43(3) *Family Relations* 277.

38   See Christine Ward Gailey, *Blue-Ribbon Babies and Labors of Love* (University of Texas Press, 2010) especially ch 1.

39   See the discussion of the film *Losing Isaiah* (Directed by Stephen Gyllenhaal, Paramount pictures, 1995) in Perry, above n 31, 123–4; cf Susan Bordo, 'Adoption' (2005) 20(1) *Hypatia* 230 and the more recent discussion of this essay in Cuthbert, Murphy and Quartly et al, above n 5, 403–12.

40   The first on intercountry adoption (*Overseas Adoption in Australia: Report on the Inquiry into the Adoption of Children from Overseas* (2005)) and the second on the impact of illicit drug use on families (*The Winnable War on Drugs: The Impact of Illicit Drug Use on Families* (2007)). The approaches in these reports mirror the measures that are already in place in the United Kingdom and the United States. In the United Kingdom, 'new adoption' was recommended in the Department of Health, UK Government, *Adoption: A New Approach, A White Paper* (2000), endorsed by the Labour government led by Prime Minister Tony Blair in 2000. *A New Approach* provided the master plan and rationale for the major legislative overhaul of adoption law embodied in the *Adoption of Children Act 2002* (UK). In the United States, 'new adoption' formally emerged through policy and legislative changes, namely the *Adoption and Safe Families Act*, Pub L No 105–89, which was signed into law by President Bill Clinton in November 1997. See also Andrew C Brown, 'International Adoption Law: A Comparative Analysis' (2009) 43(3) *International Lawyer* 1337 for the interface between the federal law in the United States and international laws.

a child's future stability. Meeting the child's best interests was framed as achievable only by the permanency that adoption could give the child.[41]

Evidently, and specifically with respect to domestic child protection schemes, the cost, both financial (for the state) and emotional (for children who have be placed in care waiting for their birth parents to rehabilitate themselves), has led to some reconsideration of the virtues of adoption.[42]

However, the political response has been mixed. While the government under then Prime Minister Tony Abbott did make changes to the intercountry adoptions process 'to reduce the barriers facing Australian families wanting to adopt from overseas',[43] these changes have not been matched (at least not universally) by similar reforms to the domestic adoption process. When Kevin Rudd succeeded John Howard as Prime Minister, the Council of Australian Governments initiated a National Framework for Protecting Australia's Children 2009–2020.[44] The emphasis of this framework is on developing a 'public health model … with a greater emphasis on assisting families early enough to prevent abuse and neglect occurring'.[45]

In this respect, the emphasis is on reform to the front end of the protection system, and not the back end. Notably, there is no mention of adoption as a possible solution to overcoming the growing number of children currently in out-of-home care in Australia. The framework continues to maintain the child's relationship with its biological family as being in the child's best interests. However, it does mention the importance 'for children to have stable and secure placements, whether that be with their natural parents or in out-of-home care. The quality of relationships with carers is also critical. A sense of security, stability, continuity and social support are strong predictors of better outcomes for young people's long-term outcomes after leaving care'.[46]

As noted with regard to the child protection system, there have already been moves towards permanent care placements for the purpose of securing stability for children in cases where reunification with their birth family is considered not to be in their best interests (see Chapter 11). Higgins summarises the position in most jurisdictions, which 'have provisions to (a) make permanent care orders (which provide security of placement with a foster/ kinship carer); and/or (b) have policies relating to the creation of permanency plans when there is no foreseeable likelihood of children being able to safely return to the care of their parents'.[47] A notable difference between these care arrangements and adoption is that they do not legally extend past a child turning 18 years of age.

In Victoria, for example, the effect of a permanent care order is to transfer parental responsibility for the child to the permanent carer; however, the birth parents remain the child's legal

41   Cuthbert, Murphy and Quartly, above n 5, 400–1; see also Marit Skivenes, 'Judging the Child's Best Interests: Rational Reasoning or Subjective Presumptions?' (2010) 53(4) *Acta Sociologica* 339 for a non-legal interpretation of the best interests of the child in three adoption cases in the Netherlands.

42   Cuthbert, Murphy and Quartly, above n 5, 400–1.

43   *Intercountry Adoption Changes*, Attorney-General's Department, Australian Government <https:// www.ag.gov.au/FamiliesAndMarriage/IntercountryAdoption/Pages/changes>.

44   Department of Social Services, Australian Government, *Protecting Children is Everyone's Business: National Framework for Protecting Australia's Children 2009–2020* (Department of Families, Housing, Community Services and Indigenous Affairs, Australian Government, 2009).

45   Ibid.

46   Ibid.

47   Higgins, above n 23.

parents.[48] This approach is aimed at ensuring that a child can continue to have contact with his or her birth parent(s) while the permanent carer makes decisions about the child.[49] It has been argued that a permanent care order is better able to facilitate contact than adoption – even open adoption,[50] but it has also been criticised for not extending the same legal rights – such as rights of inheritance – that adoption would give the child.[51] Birth parents can also seek to revoke the order, which can disrupt the permanency of the arrangement.[52] Dissatisfaction among permanent carers with the 'impermanent' aspects of permanency orders has led to some suggestions for reform that would bring permanency orders closer in line with adoption orders.[53]

New South Wales has been at the forefront in making changes in this direction by introducing amendments to the *Adoption Act 2000* (NSW) and the *Children and Young Persons (Care and Protection) Act 1998* (NSW) to facilitate the adoption of children in out-of-home care. In 2006 an amendment to s 67 of the *Adoption Act* was enacted, enabling the Supreme Court of New South Wales to dispense with the consent of any person (other than the child) 'in the case of an application made by an authorised carer if the Supreme Court is satisfied that the child has established a stable relationship with the authorised carer and the adoption of the child by the authorised carer will promote the child's interests and welfare'.[54]

More recently, in 2014, New South Wales amended the *Children and Young Persons (Care and Protection) Act 1998* (NSW) to provide for the adoption of children in out-of-home care.[55] Section 10A of the Act sets outs 'permanent placement principles'. 'Permanent

---

48   Dan Barron, 'A "Carer's" Perspective on Permanent Care: Is there a Third Way between Permanent Care and Adoption?' (2014) 8(1) *Australian Journal of Adoption* 1, 3 <http://pandora.nla.gov.au/pan/98265/20150416-0016/www.nla.gov.au/openpublish/index.php/aja/article/view/3356/3927.html>.
49   Ibid.
50   Ibid 2.
51   Ibid 4–5.
52   Ibid.
53   Ibid 6–7. See also Jeremy Sammut, *The Madness of Australian Child Protection: Why Adoption Will Rescue Australia's Underclass Children* (Connor Court Publishing, 2015).
54   Explanatory Notes, Adoption Amendment Bill 2006 (NSW); *Adoption Act 2000* (NSW) s 67(1)(d). The Act was further amended in 2008 enabling a child aged 12 or more years of age to consent to their adoption if they had been cared for by the proposed adoptive parent or parents for at least two years. Originally the Act provided for at least five years: *Adoption Act 2000* (NSW) s 54(2).
55   *Children and Young Persons (Care and Protection) Act 1998* (NSW) ss 7–10A. The Act also amended provisions relating to parent responsibility contracts and introduced new parenting capacity orders: Family and Community Services, *Safe Home for Life: Parenting Resources* (2014), NSW Government <http://www.facs.nsw.gov.au/__data/assets/file/0013/302431/3355_FACS-_SafeHomeForLife_ParentingResources.pdf>. Parent responsibility contracts give parents up to 12 months to reduce risk of harm to their children, including unborn children. If a contract is breached, the Children's Court can make a supervision order; an order requiring the parent or primary caregiver to make undertakings to the court; or an order reallocating parental responsibility to another person for the child or young person. The timeframes for complying with the contract (six months for children under two years and 12 months for older children) are very strict, especially for women experiencing domestic violence: Lindy Kerin, 'Child Protection Measures too Strict for Domestic Violence Women', *Australian Broadcasting Corporation News* (online), 20 March 2014 <www.abc.net.au/news/2014-03-20/child-protection-measures-too-strict-for-domestic/5334162>. A parenting capacity order is the other measure that has been introduced. This is a new order that can be made by the Children's Court. It requires a parent to participate in a parent capacity program, service, course, therapy or treatment aimed at enhancing their parenting skills to reduce the risk of harm to their child and prevent the child's removal. These orders decontextualise the parents' social circumstances and enable the state to retreat from having a role in overcoming social disadvantage and poverty. Responsibility for the life circumstances of socially disadvantaged parents is clearly being placed in their hands and no one else's.

placement' is defined as the 'long-term placement following the removal of a child or young person from the care of a parent or parents pursuant to this Act that provides a safe, nurturing, stable and secure environment for the child or young person'.[56] The permanent placement principles list, in order, the preferences for the placement of a child: the first preference is with their parent/parents, and the second preference is with a relative, kin or other suitable person. But if neither of these options is in the best interests of the child, then the third preference is for the child to be adopted. If adoption is not in their best interests, then the last preference is for the child to be placed under the parental responsibility of the Minister under the Act.[57]

Aboriginal and Torres Strait Islander children can also be adopted according to these provisions. However, of the options available (including the exhaustion of the Aboriginal Child Placement Principle or being placed under the parental responsibility of the Minister), adoption is considered the least preferable.[58]

In these changes to the NSW legislation, we can see how the discourses on what is in the best interests of the child have shifted. While there continues to be a role for birth parents in a child's life, they can be dispensed with if that means creating a more stable environment for the child in another setting. Although the provisions promoting 'open adoptions' remain in place, how they will continue to work in circumstances where the consent of parents has been dispensed with remains to be seen.[59] Indeed, in many respects the discourses around adoption in New South Wales are not unlike those that legitimised closed adoptions during the 20th century, where the focus is on securing stability for children in a caring family environment in a context where birth parents are deemed incapable of caring for their children themselves. It is a neat picture painted by law- and policy-makers who throughout adoption legal history have indulged in the making and the unmaking of families and in determining who can be a parent and who cannot. In creating new and intact families in this 'new adoption' era,[60] the state maintains the family as a private unit, which has primary responsibility for the child's care and financial support – and can ultimately relieve itself of these responsibilities.

12.2.3 Adoption and same-sex couples

Evidently, while the list of eligible people who can apply to adopt children has expanded (namely, to include same-sex couples and single people), there has been a dramatic decrease in the number of children available for adoption. These developments raise pertinent issues. Our focus is on the same-sex adoption debate, as it illustrates how acceptance of non-traditional parenting arrangements for children has not been universal. At the same

---

56   *Children and Young Persons (Care and Protection) Act 1998* (NSW) s 10A(1).
57   s 10A(3)(a)–(d).
58   s 10A(3)(e).
59   See also Frank Ainsworth and Patricia Hansen, 'Babies for the Deserving: Developments in Foster Care and Adoption in One Australian State – Others to Follow?' [2009] (50) *Just Policy: A Journal of Australian Social Policy* 23. For a news story of the challenges a single mother could face in this new era of adoption, see Kirsty Needham, 'One Mother's View on Fast-track Adoption: "I Want My Children Back"', *Sydney Morning Herald* (online), 10 July 2016 <http://www.smh.com.au/nsw/one-mothers-view-on-fasttrack-adoption-i-want-my-children-back-20160709-gq2466.html>.
60   See generally Cuthbert, Murphy and Quartly, above n 5.

time, these debates are based on a pro-adoption platform which perpetuates the under-standing that the nuclear family serves the interests of adopted children. This discussion provides a strong rationale for engaging with the law at various sites. The developments in the area illustrate how legal discourse is not homogenous, but is constructed in differ-ent ways and can change over time to reveal how the construction of legal meaning is an ongoing process.[61]

The arguments for and against same-sex adoption, as in other instances of adoption, appeal to what is in the best interests of the child. The most common arguments against same-sex adoption are that a homosexual family is a violation of the rights of the child to a mother and a father; the complementary roles of mother and father are essential for the healthy development of the child; a mother and a father create the best conditions for the development of a safe, congruent gender identity; the promiscuity of gay men living together is much higher than in a normal father–mother relationship and would have a destructive effect on children; the majority of lesbian women do not have and do not desire to have a man/men in any close relationship, inhibiting the development of a male identity in boys; adolescent girls who have grown up without a father have greater difficulty relating to peers and boys and more often become unintentionally pregnant; to allow a homosexual couple to adopt a child would be deceiving the child about his or her sexual origin in two genders – a man and a woman; and the studies alleging that equality exists between heterosexual and homosexual parenthood have been found to be flawed.[62]

In response, supporters of same-sex adoption refer to the research that shows that there are no discernible differences in parenting styles between same-sex and heterosexual couples; there are no significant differences in the psychological health of children; children develop similarly to children raised by heterosexual parents with respect to sexual identity, psychological development and relationships with peers and adults; being raised by a gay or lesbian couple does not increase the likelihood that the child will be gay; there is some evidence that lesbian mothers are more likely than divorced mothers to encourage relation-ships with men; social stigma of children with same-sex adoptive parents does not have long-term effects; and opponents of same-sex adoptions often try to discredit the social science literature as flawed.[63]

However, in reviewing these arguments it is evident that more than the best interests of the child is at stake in permitting same-sex couples to adopt. Indeed, it would appear that what is fundamentally at stake is the privileging of heteronormativity in standard adop-tion practices. This challenge comes from the demands of same-sex couples to equality of treatment with heterosexual couples in accessing adoption services. Once it is accepted

---

61   For a brief overview of literature on adoption and parenting by sexual minorities, see David Brodzinsky and Abbie Goldberg, *Practice Guidelines Supporting Open Adoption in Families Headed by Lesbian And Gay Male Parents: Lessons Learned from the Modern Adoptive Families Study* (Donaldson Adoption Institute, 2016).

62   Christl R Vonholdt, *The Child's Right to a Mother and a Father: Ten Reasons Against Adoption Rights for Homosexual Couples*, German Institute for Youth and Society <http://www.dijg.de/english/ten-reasons-against-adoption-rights-for-homosexual-couples/>.

63   Marc E Elovitz, 'Adoption by Lesbian and Gay People: The Use and Mis-use of Social Science Research' (1995) 2(1) *Duke Journal of Gender Law and Policy* 207, 211–7.

that children fare as well (if not better) in same-sex-headed families, then it would seem there are no compelling reasons to exclude same-sex couples from the adoption process. Indeed, in not subscribing to strict gendered assumptions about the roles of men and women in society, same-sex parents could serve as role models to their children in contributing to the creation of a more egalitarian society. Furthermore, their own experiences of discrimination could be helpful to their children in overcoming any stigma they might face, instilling in the children a sense of justice and enabling these children to search out their own standards of right and wrong. They would better understand the importance of conforming their beliefs to reason and tested knowledge rather than popular sentiment or prejudice.[64]

These arguments are important in questioning whether the privileging of heteronormativity in society has a rational basis. Nevertheless, despite the disparate views on same-sex adoption, there seems to be agreement on adoption as being in the best interests of the child.[65] Moreover, in the process of debating what is in the child's best interests, the interests of the biological parents – usually the birth mother of the child – have been ignored.[66] Both camps treat the child as though it is freely available for adoption with no other attachments. The birth mother does not feature at all in standard debates on same-sex couple adoption. This seems troubling with respect to both sides of the debate, particularly as they are both concerned with preventing disadvantage and discrimination in one form or another; and yet they seem completely oblivious to the disadvantaged circumstances which the child could have come from, which would also have impacted on the birth mother, and which could worsen for her after the child is adopted.[67]

Now that New South Wales has taken a pro-adoption approach to out-of-home care (and the trend appears to be spreading to other States),[68] these are issues that we as a society need to address. Of course, there are any number of ways to rationalise the birth mother's exclusion from the adoption equation. The most obvious is to use the conceptual device of the 'best interests of the child' principle and focus on the argument that adoption is the best option for the child. It follows that the concern of the law is the child and it is irrelevant to focus on the child's birth mother. However, if we are committed to creating a more egalitarian society we need to demonstrate greater awareness of the effects that a practice like

---

64   Ibid 215, citing *M.P. v. S.P.*, 404 A.2d 1256, 1263 (NJ Super. Ct. App. Div. 1979).

65   For an example of practices in the United States, see Elizabeth Raleigh, 'Are Same-Sex and Single Adoptive Parents More Likely to Adopt Transracially? A National Analysis of Race, Family Structure, and the Adoption Marketplace' (2012) 55(3) *Sociological Perspectives* 449.

66   Susan M Henney et al, 'Evolution and Resolution: Birthmothers' Experience of Grief and Loss at Different Levels of Openness' (2007) 24(6) *Journal of Social and Personal Relationships* 875.

67   See Needham, above n 59.

68   See, eg, Western Australia, which also provides for carer adoptions: *Permanency Planning Policy*, Department for Child Protection and Family Support, Government of Western Australia, 6 <https://www.dcp.wa.gov.au/Resources/Documents/Policies%20and%20Frameworks/Permanency%20Planning%20Policy.pdf>. Permitting adoption in cases of permanent care also appears to have driven the political agenda to extend adoption services to same-sex couples in Victoria. See Farrah Tomazin, 'Gay Couples in Victoria Fighting for Right to Adopt Their Own Children', *The Age* (online), 6 September 2015 <http://www.theage.com.au/victoria/gay-adoption-feature–seo-here-20150903-gjehwb.html>.

adoption has on the relinquishing mothers, on the children involved, and on our society as a whole. We need not look further than the ongoing history of Aboriginal and Torres Strait Islander child removals to realise how this practice compounds injustice, social disadvantage and discrimination (see Chapter 11).

We argue that the fact that discussions about adoption tend to collapse into debates between groups about what is in the best interests of the child serves to privilege the family unit, while marginalising the needs of adults and their children who are socially disadvantaged. Even if we accept that adoption could save children from poverty and abuse, it is still valid to ask: what happens to their parents who are left behind? This is not to deny the seriousness of child abuse and neglect and the importance of protecting children from maltreatment. The mere fact of being the biological parent is never an adequate reason to avoid sanctioning adults who abuse and mistreat children. Our point is to question the neat picture of adoption (noted previously) and how, through the re-creation of the nuclear family (through adoption) as the answer to child maltreatment, the underlying social and economic conditions that have contributed to children requiring alternative care remain unaddressed. In these scenarios the 'best interests of the child' principle serves to legitimise the nuclear family as the child is moved from an unsatisfactory situation to a 'better' (usually two-parent) family. Once we acknowledge that, we are better able to understand how the nuclear family is used as an instrument of exclusion to privilege some and not others. It is only then that we can begin to imagine other ways of being in a family that do not privilege coupledom – whether same-sex or heterosexual – as the centre of the parent–child relationship.[69] We will explore these issues further in the next section on assisted reproductive technologies.

12.3   Assisted reproductive technologies

In this section, we discuss assisted reproductive technologies ('ART') in their role in shaping the family. We start the discussion by considering the potential of these technologies to help us rethink the family. Despite this potential, we argue that their regulation has in fact done the opposite and has reinforced the nuclear family concept as the basis for familial

---

69   We note that while single persons and same-sex couples may now be eligible to adopt, that does not necessarily mean they will be accorded equal treatment in the adoption process. The experience in the United States demonstrates that the privileging of heterosexual couples continues to be the norm in the placement of children for adoption: National Clearinghouse on Child Abuse and Neglect Information and National Adoption Information Clearinghouse, *Gay and Lesbian Adoptive Parents: Resources for Professionals and Parents* (2000) Child Welfare Information Gateway, 6–9 <https://www.childwelfare.gov/pubPDFs/f_gay.pdf>. In Australia, one way of limiting same-sex couples' equal right to be considered suitable to adopt a child has been to exempt religious adoption agencies from complying with the legislation allowing same-sex couples to adopt: Matthew Wade, 'Bill Allowing Victorian Same-Sex Couples to Adopt Passed, Will Become Law', *Star Observer* (online), 10 December 2015 <http://www.starobserver.com.au/news/local-news/victoria-news/bill-allowing-victorian-same-sex-couples-to-adopt-passed-will-become-law/143785>. With respect to single people, we note how legislation may give priority to couples in the adoption selection process: see, eg, *Adoption Act 2009* (Qld) s 153(2).

relationships.[70] Our focus is on the issues that arise in surrogacy arrangements when an individual or couple cannot produce their own biological children either through sexual intercourse or through ART treatment, and require other people's genetic materials to assist them to have a child (ie, using the womb of another woman and/or donated semen or eggs). These procedures usually involve in-vitro fertilisation ('IVF') treatment. In Australia ART is regulated at the State level, which makes it another complex area, and we can only discuss the more pertinent issues.[71]

12.3.1   ART and the biological family unit

Surrogacy is an ancient practice. The Bible tells the classic tale of Sarah, who, unable to conceive, offers her handmaiden to her husband Abraham, so that they could have a child.[72] In modern times, surrogacy is usually associated with an arrangement involving a surrogate mother who, through artificial means, becomes pregnant with a man's sperm (usually that of the intended father) and who subsequently relinquishes the child to the intended parents (usually a heterosexual or gay couple) when the child is born. In these arrangements, the embryo may be created by using the ovum of the surrogate mother or the intended mother.

However, developments in medical science, particularly ART, have made it so that a number of people can be involved in the life of a child – the woman who donates her eggs ('the genetic mother'), the man who donates his sperm ('the sperm donor'), the woman who carries the fertilised egg ('the gestational mother'), and 'the intended parents' of the child. Providing legal access to ART services to same-sex couples and single people has further

---

70   The fact that individuals and couples may need ART treatment can expose them to a level of scrutiny unknown to heterosexual fertile couples. The rationale for this scrutiny is that it is in the best interests of the child. A notable feature of the Victorian legislation is that it requires all people seeking treatment to submit a 'criminal [police] record check' and 'child protection order check': Victorian Assisted Reproductive Treatment Authority, *Criminal Record Check and a Child Protection Order Check* <https://www.varta.org.au/regulation/regulation-art-victoria/criminal-record-check-and-child-protection-order-check>. A key objective of NSW legislation is to ensure that children born from donated gametes (semen or eggs) or embryos will be able, once they turn 18, to learn the identity of their biological parents. The NSW Act establishes a Central ART Donor Register, which will hold identifying information about donors, recipients and their children, and make this information available to certain limited classes of people in accordance with the legislation. The register is also intended to allow the adult offspring of a donor to learn the identity of other children of the donor, provided those children also consent. The Act also contains a limit to the number of families that can be created from the gametes of a single donor (up to five different women): *Assisted Reproductive Technology* (19 June 2015) NSW Health, NSW Government <http://www.health.nsw.gov.au/art/pages/default.aspx>. For a broader overview of the legal limits on ART, see Sonia Allan, *Family Limits* (Health Law Central, 2016) <http://www.healthlawcentral.com/donorconception/family-limits/>.

71   For an overview of ART regulation, see *Assisted Reproductive Technology (ART)* (11 August 2016) National Health and Medical Research Council, Australian Government <https://www.nhmrc.gov.au/health-ethics/ethical-issues/assisted-reproductive-technology-art>. Legislation in four States regulates ART: *Assisted Reproductive Treatment Act 2008* (Vic); *Assisted Reproductive Technology Act 2007* (NSW); *Assisted Reproductive Treatment Act 1988* (SA); and *Human Reproductive Technology Act 1991* (WA). Each of these pieces of legislation established a State regulatory body which issues licences to clinics that provide ART services. When there are anomalies between the State Acts and the ART guidelines, the legislation takes precedence.

72   *Genesis* (Oxford University Press and Cambridge University Press, revised English version, 1989 ed) 16:1–16.

liberalised the family. Currently, South Australia is the only jurisdiction in Australia that does not permit fertile single women and lesbians to access IVF treatment,[73] while Western Australia and South Australia are the only two remaining States that do not permit single people or same-sex couples to engage in altruistic surrogacy arrangements.[74]

Evidently, the reproductive technologies available today (and the range of people who can access them)[75] have the potential to disrupt the monopoly of the nuclear family by providing the means by which a number of adults can participate in the birth and rearing of children. According to Macklin,[76] reproductive technologies illuminate how the family is more than a biological concept and can force us to rethink the concepts 'mother', 'father' and 'family'. Her argument returns us to Chapter 1, where we discussed how the way we understand 'family' can depend on the social, cultural and legal contexts in which we are discussing the family. This suggests we have a degree of freedom of choice in who we consider to be family and who is not, and that in making these choices we are not necessarily bound by biology in forming families or maintaining familial relations. When it comes to reproductive technologies, this could mean that a woman who gives birth to a child as a result of a surrogacy arrangement is the child's gestational mother as well as the child's grandmother; or that, as a result of the donation of semen to a lesbian couple in IVF treatment, a child can have two mothers and a father.

While Macklin's observations are important in illuminating how reproductive technologies can shape and change our understanding of family, this is not how they necessarily function in practice. Individuals who seek ART treatment might want to create their own families to the exclusion of the other people who were involved in the creation of the child. Individuals who have been involved in the process whether as sperm or egg donors, or as gestational mothers, might want to have a parenting role in the child's life, or they might not. The partners of the individuals who undergo this treatment may also want to take on a parenting role even though they have no biological link to the child. The law also has its own ideas about who the parents of the child born through assisted means are. This is an area of

---

73   South Australia requires single women and lesbians to be 'medically infertile' in order to receive IVF treatment: *Pearce v South Australian Health Commission* (1996) 66 SASR 486 (Bollen, Millhouse and Williams JJ). A similar decision was made in Victoria in *McBain v State of Victoria* [2000] FCA 1009 (Sundberg J). In both cases, it was held that the relevant State legislation that limited access to IVF treatment to heterosexual couples was inconsistent with the *Sex Discrimination Act 1984* (Cth). In both cases, the Court found that the State legislation could not discriminate against women on the basis of their marital status. However, the Court left it open for States to preclude women from accessing IVF if they were not 'medically infertile'. Thus, social reasons (single or lesbian status) could still be used to refuse IVF treatment. The Howard government introduced an amendment to the *Sex Discrimination Act 1984* (Cth) that would have allowed States to restrict access to IVF to heterosexual couples in line with the government policy to ensure that children have access to the care and affection of both a mother and a father: Commonwealth, *Parliamentary Debates*, House of Representatives, 17 August 2000, 17 538 (Daryl Williams).
        However, the Sex Discrimination Amendment Bill 2002 (Cth) lapsed in Parliament. In Victoria, the position changed in favour of lesbian and single women with the enactment of the *Assisted Reproductive Treatment Act 2008* (Vic).

74   *Surrogacy Act 2008* (WA); *Family Relationships Act 1975* (SA).

75   See, eg, Dean A Murphy, *Gay Men Pursuing Parenthood via Surrogacy: Reconfiguring Kinship* (UNSW Press, 2015).

76   Ruth Macklin, 'Artificial Means of Reproduction and Our Understanding of the Family' (1991) 21(1) *Hastings Center Report* 5, 9.

law that has been subject to substantial change in the last two decades.[77] Nevertheless, it is apparent in these changes that reproductive technologies, and the laws that regulate them, have functioned to reproduce new forms of nuclear families (as well as the traditional form) and may not be satisfactory for everyone involved.[78]

Ultimately, the success of creating a family in this way may depend on whether everyone involved is committed to the role they have accepted in the process of creating the child and they stick to the script after the child is born. Once the child is born, things can radically change if conflict arises between the adults over their role in the child's life. At this point, legal regulation of ART has a vital role to play. Indeed, once the parties seek legal redress to resolve the conflict between them, the law could override their original intentions and come up with solutions that no one intended. This could lead to very unhappy situations for everyone involved. This is particularly concerning, as the child will inevitably be caught in the cross-fire of the dispute between the adults.

In Australia, these issues are well illustrated in the case of *Re Evelyn*.[79] In that case, a dispute arose over the parenting arrangements for a child born as a result of an altruistic surrogacy arrangement. Mr and Mrs S and Mr and Mrs Q were friends. Mrs S agreed to act as the surrogate mother for Mrs Q, who was unable to have children. They agreed that when the child was born it would go and live with Mr and Mrs Q on a permanent basis.

Evelyn was the child born out of this arrangement. She was the biological child of Mrs S and Mr Q. Soon after she was born, Evelyn went to live with Mr and Mrs Q. Mrs S regretted her decision to give her to the Qs and took her back. Proceedings were initiated by both couples, and were heard in Brisbane, where the Qs resided. Leading up to the trial, Evelyn was placed in the care of Mr and Mrs Q, and Mr and Mrs S were granted contact. At the trial, both parties sought an order for Evelyn to reside with them and in the alternative they sought orders for contact. The trial judge (Hilton J) made orders that Evelyn was to live with Mr and Mrs S and they would have responsibility for her day-to-day care and development. He also ordered that Evelyn should have specified contact with Mr and Mrs Q, and that Mr and Mrs S and Mr and Mrs Q together share responsibility for her long-term care, welfare and development.

----

77   See Jenni Millbank, 'The New Surrogacy Parentage Laws in Australia: Cautious Regulation or "25 Brick Walls"?' (2011) 35(1) *Melbourne University Law Review* 165.

78   In *AA v Registrar of Births, Death and Marriages and BB* [2011] NSWDC 100, the ex-partner of a lesbian mother sought to be named on the birth certificate of a child born during their relationship. The application was sought on the basis of the enactment of the *Miscellaneous Acts Amendment (Same Sex Relationships) Act 2008* (NSW), which amended the *Status of Children Act 1996* (NSW) to permit both names of a lesbian couple to be included on the birth certificate of a child born to either of them using fertilisation treatment while they are in a de facto relationship. These amendments came into force after the names of the donor father and birth mother had been recorded on the child's birth certificate. The co-mother was successful in her application because the amendments had retrospective effect, and the donor father's name was removed. See also FLA s 60H, which sets out the status of parents of children born as a result of artificial conception procedures and in effect excludes donors of genetic materials who were not in a married or de facto relationship with one of the intended parents at the time of conception from claiming parentage of the child. The added effect of this provision is that genetic donors are not liable for child maintenance or child support for the child.

79   (1998) 145 FLR 90 (Nicholson CJ, Ellis and Lindenmayer JJ). See the discussion in Anita Stuhmcke, 'Re Evelyn: Surrogacy, Custody and the Family Court' (1998) 12(3) *Australian Journal of Family Law* 297.

Mr and Mrs Q's appeal to the Full Court failed on all grounds. They applied to the High Court for special leave to appeal, which was rejected. In its reasons for dismissing the appeal, the Full Court held that the child's best interests are the paramount consideration. This in effect meant that the Court could override the subjective intentions of the parties (eg, surrogacy agreements or contracts) in determining what is in the interests of the child. The Court further found that there is no presumption in favour of a biological parent or, where the child is female, in favour of the biological mother. This is important, but also reflects the accepted view in family law in Australia that the court determines the best interests of the child in every individual case and without relying on any presumption that the biological parent is the preferred parent (see also chapters 8 and 9). The decision in *Re Evelyn* therefore means that the biological parents of the child in such cases will not have special claims over the child.[80]

However, this approach did not prevent the Court in this case from emphasising the role of Mrs S and Mrs Q – Evelyn's 'mothers' – in making its decision. The same emphasis was not attached to Mr S and Mr Q – Evelyn's 'fathers' – even though Mr Q was her biological father. But in emphasising the role of the mothers, the Court particularly emphasised the role of Mrs S – Evelyn's biological mother. Mrs S was found to be the parent best able to answer any questions Evelyn would have about her birth in the future. The Court also recognised the importance for Evelyn to be with her biological siblings. Mr and Mrs S had three biological children aged from three to seven years while Mr and Mrs Q had a three-year-old adopted son. The Court found this 'equation' also favoured Evelyn's placement with Mrs S.

Thus, despite the Court's finding that there was no presumption in favour of biology, the Court found in favour of Evelyn's birth mother – Mrs S – for biological reasons. The overall outcome of this decision functions to give priority to the biological family even though it explicitly denies that biology matters, but as a discretionary judgment it does not constitute a binding precedent. However, this is not the complete picture. In giving partial effect to the agreement between the adult couples, the Court created a kind of blended familial arrangement for Evelyn, even though by the end of the matter the friendship between the couples appeared to have completely broken down.

12.3.2   Reproductive technologies in the global context

Another important issue that arises in the context of surrogacy arrangements is the issue of consent. If we return to the argument advanced by Macklin above, that reproductive technologies can help change the meaning of 'family', this would require each of the parties to make choices in the process of forming new family structures. Indeed, Macklin seemingly assumes that there can be equality of agency among the adults involved in the decisions that are made about a child's future parenting and care arrangements before the child is born. However, considering the inequality that exists in our contemporary society across sex, race and class hierarchies, it would be problematic to assume that each person has equality of agency in making these decisions. In the area of surrogacy, this issue is particularly pronounced where commissioning parents in western nations seek surrogacy services available

---

80   See also Julie Wallbank, 'Too Many Mothers? Surrogacy, Kinship and the Welfare of the Child' (2002) 10(3) *Medical Law Review* 271, 284–9.

in poorer countries, usually because surrogacy is illegal and/or unaffordable in their own countries.[81]

The fact that surrogacy is illegal in many western countries can be explained in terms of the claims advanced by religious conservatives that surrogacy arrangements undermine the family – based on ties between husband and wife and their biological children.[82] Feminists also have been critical of surrogacy.[83] They point to the unequal relations that exist between men and women in society arising from the sexual division of labour, which has resulted in financial inequality for women, and how the surrogacy arrangement can further devalue the reproductive work that women do. According to this line of thinking, surrogacy reduces the pregnancy of the surrogate mother to a form of medical treatment for infertile couples. Women involved in this work must alienate themselves from their mothering role in order to prepare themselves for the relinquishment of the child to the intended parents.[84]

With respect to altruistic surrogacy, feminists argue that it reinforces women's role as wives and mothers and the social expectations for women to be self-sacrificing and live in denial of their own desires and needs. Unlike abortion, which serves to promote the reproductive freedom of women, surrogacy arrangements hold women captive in their biologically determined social roles. Feminists contrast abortion and surrogacy, claiming that, while abortion is a socially responsible act aimed at preventing personal hardship and/or a socially stressed out (usually single-female-headed) family, surrogacy is a socially irresponsible act, more consistent with the consumer economy that undermines the mother–child bond, and where freedom, control and rights are treated as secondary considerations.[85]

Those who are critical of surrogacy generally agree that it is a practice that is harmful to society.[86] However, commercial surrogacy arrangements have attracted the most criticism.[87] Commercial surrogacy has been criticised because it means treating women and children like market commodities. The engagement of women in surrogacy services for a fee means that the product of their services – the child – is little more than any other market commodity[88] – like a car or pedigreed pet – and can be subject to a discount if it does not

---

81   For an overview of the legal position on surrogacy across the globe, see *Surrogacy Laws by Country*, Wikipedia <https://en.wikipedia.org/wiki/Surrogacy_laws_by_country>.

82   Radhika Rao, 'Assisted Reproductive Technology and the Threat to the Traditional Family' (1996) 47 *Hastings Law Journal* 951, 959–60.

83   The following discussion draws on Katherine B Lieber, 'Selling the Womb: Can the Feminist Critique of Surrogacy Be Answered?' (1992) 68(1) *Indiana Law Journal* 205, 212–7. See also Heather Dietrich, 'Dissenting View' in National Bioethics Consultative Committee, *Surrogacy Report 1* (National Bioethics Consultative Committee, 1990).

84   Heather Jacobson, *Labor of Love: Gestational Surrogacy and the Work of Making Babies* (Rutgers University Press, 2016); Anne Phillips, *Our Bodies, Whose Property?* (Princeton University Press, 2013) especially ch 3.

85   Gena Corea, *The Mother Machine* (Harper and Row, 1985); Kelly Oliver, 'Marxism and Surrogacy' (1989) 4(3) *Hypatia* 95.

86   The right to ART treatment is linked to the right to procreate: John Robertson, *Children of Choice* (Princeton University Press, 1994); John Robertson, 'Gay and Lesbian Access to Assisted Reproductive Technology' (2004–05) 55(2) *Case Western Reserve Law Review* 323. But no right is absolute and it can be limited by the prevention of harm to others.

87   Kalindi Vora, *Life Support: Biocapital and the New History of Outsourced Labor* (University of Minnesota Press, 2015) especially ch 4.

88   See also David Smolin, 'Surrogacy as the Sale of Children: Applying Lessons Learned from Adoption to the Regulation of the Surrogacy Industry's Global Marketing of Children' (2015–16) 43 *Pepperdine Law Review* 265.

meet the intended parents' expectations.[89] Indeed, the intended parents may reject the child completely because the child has a disability or simply because they have changed their minds. Recent cases of children abandoned by their intended parents illuminate the risk to children born through surrogacy arrangements.[90] But even when the surrogacy arrangement is executed as planned, it can be an alienating process for the child because it denies the child knowledge of his or her biological heritage; and even if the child learns of his or her origins this could be equally alienating.[91]

Similarly, treating a woman's womb as a commodity has been criticised for undermining the integrity of women. Surrogacy has been likened to prostitution, whereby the womb is treated as extractable from 'the woman as a whole person in the same way the vagina (or sex) is now'.[92] Lieber sums up the broader social concerns that, as a result of accepting surrogacy, women will once again be valued only for their reproductive capacities. Moreover, because surrogates are usually poorer women, this will create the conditions for their exploitation by the rich. They will be turned into a class of breeders and reproductive brothels will emerge.[93]

We need only consider the situation of the surrogacy market in Asia (the most popular (and cheapest) destination for Australians seeking to enter a surrogacy arrangement) to see that many of the fears expressed by feminists have come to pass in recent years.[94] Saxena et al have described the surrogacy experience of Indian women as an oppressive situation where they are persuaded into surrogacy arrangements by their spouses or middlemen to earn 'easy money', but are not afforded the same protections and social services as women performing the same work in countries such as the United States. The women are recruited by commercial agencies and, to protect them from social stigma, they are shifted into hostels

---

89 For a counter-narrative and a spirited defence of the women engaged in commercial surrogacy in India, see Sharmila Rudrappa, *Discounted Life: The Price of Global Surrogacy in India* (NYU Press, 2015).

90 In the recent case of baby 'Gammy', the child had been conceived as a result of a commercial surrogacy arrangement entered into by an Australian couple and his birth mother in Thailand. The child was abandoned by his Australian intended parents when they learned he had Down syndrome. Baby Gammy remained in the care of his birth mother. The intended parents did accept his twin sister and returned with her to Australia. It was later revealed that the intended father was a convicted child sex offender. A similar situation arose in India when an Australian couple abandoned one child of a set of twins. Their decision was based on the sex of the child. Even though consular officials were aware of the situation, the couple were granted a visa for the child to return to Australia. It was reported that money changed hands for a person known to the surrogate family to take the abandoned child. This implicates the Australian couple and the Australian government in child trafficking: Samantha Hawley and Suzanne Smith, 'Australian High Commission Knew of Disturbing Indian Surrogacy Case, Chief Justice of Family Court Says', *Australian Broadcasting Corporation News* (online), 9 October 2014 <http://www.abc.net.au/news/2014-10-08/high-commission-knew-of-surrogacy-case-in-india/5799438>.

91 See Anton van Niekerk and Liezl van Zyl, 'Commercial Surrogacy and the Commodification of Children: An Ethical Perspective' (1995) 14(3–4) *Medicine and Law* 163 for a discussion of whether surrogacy amounts to a wrongful commodification or transfer of children. For the legal complexities of surrogacy and the status of the child, see Tina Lin, 'Born Lost: Stateless Children in International Surrogacy Arrangements' (2012–13) 21 *Cardozo Journal of International and Comparative Law* 545.

92 Andrea Dworkin, *Right-Wing Women* (Perigee Books, 1983) 187.

93 Lieber, above n 83.

94 Pikee Saxena, Archana Mishra and Sonia Malik, 'Surrogacy: Ethical and Legal Issues' (2012) 37(4) *Indian Journal of Community Medicine* 211; Amrita Pande, 'Commercial Surrogacy in India: Manufacturing a Perfect Mother-Worker' (2010) 35(4) *Signs: Journal of Women in Culture and Society* 970.

for the duration of the pregnancy and are typically allowed to go home only over the weekends. Rich career women are resorting to hiring these women to act as surrogate mothers and if the outcome of pregnancy is unfavourable they are unlikely to be paid.[95]

It is an uncomfortable truth that accounts such as these reveal the dilemmas created by capitalist societies where individuals, in seeking to fulfil their desire to have a child, have become caught up in the production of new capitalist markets engaged in the exploitation of underprivileged women. However, it is these sorts of accounts that make the use of the concepts of agency and choice in surrogacy arrangements a contentious issue.

From the point of view of proponents of surrogacy, commercial surrogacy could be the last chance for a couple to have a baby, and it is a way for women who would otherwise remain in poverty, because there are no other viable alternatives available to them, to earn money.[96] Implicit in these arguments is a particular understanding of the notion of making 'choices'. On the one hand, surrogate mothers are considered to be making responsible choices, which will help them and their families overcome poverty; on the other hand, intended parents are regarded as having no other choice but to seek a surrogate arrangement so they can have 'a child of their own'. But the issue framed as individuals 'making choices' obscures the broader social issues.

We are mindful that from a feminist perspective it is important to avoid undermining the agency of surrogate mothers and their capacity to make decisions about their lives and futures, as this will only feed into another set of sexist stereotypes relating to women's incapacity to reason and make rational decisions. The concept of agency itself is a complex construct[97] and we do not wish to cast surrogate mothers in the binary classification of agents/victims. We accept the feminist view that it is important to recognise 'the subtleties of intra-class social divisions transnational surrogacy engenders and illustrate how women both exert power and are subject to it'.[98] However, these feminist arguments may emphasise the choices available to women too much, especially in circumstances where intersectional structural realities that limit agency and human relatedness exist.[99] Thus, women who 'choose' to act as surrogates may not be agency-less victims; but neither are they autonomous and free agents in relation to the commissioning parents or agencies.[100]

---

95   Saxena, Mishra and Malik, above n 94.

96   Agence France-Presse, 'India Bans Foreigners from Hiring Surrogate Mothers', *The Guardian* (online), 29 October 2015 <https://www.theguardian.com/world/2015/oct/28/india-bans-foreigners-from-hiring-surrogate-mothers>. For insight into how mainstream media portray the issues in Australia, see Sam Everingham, 'Australia's Outdated Surrogacy Laws Force Couples to Take Risks Overseas', *The Age* (online), 5 October 2015 <http://www.theage.com.au/comment/australias-outdated-surrogacy-laws-force-couples-to-take-risks-overseas-20151005-gk1avc.html>.

97   Catriona Mackenzie and Natalie Stoljar (eds), *Relational Autonomy: Feminist Perspectives on Autonomy, Agency, and the Social Self* (Oxford University Press, 2000).

98   Daisy Deomampo, 'Transnational Surrogacy in India: Interrogating Power and Women's Agency' (2013) 34(3) *Frontiers: A Journal of Women's Studies* 167, 169.

99   See Amrita Nandy, 'Natural Mother = Real Mother? Choice and Agency Among Un/natural "Mothers" in India' (2015) 53 *Women's Studies International Forum* 129. For a philosophical argument, see also Catriona Mackenzie, 'Embodied Agents, Narrative Selves' (2014) 17(2) *Philosophical Explorations* 154.

100   See, eg, the argument that in Thailand the local moral economy of surrogacy describes it as a form of merit-making within Buddhism as it is a way of providing for one's children: Andrea Whittaker, 'Merit and Money: The Situated Ethics of Transnational Commercial Surrogacy in Thailand' (2014) 7(2) *International Journal of Feminist Approaches to Bioethics* 100.

In making this observation, we wish to point out that the feminist arguments we referred to earlier are not suggesting that women are incapable of making decisions, but that the decision to be a surrogate is not one that can contribute to achieving women's equality.[101] Indeed, the decision to act as a surrogate usually arises because of the woman's (and women's universally) social and economic inequalities, not in spite of them. This seems evident in the few women who engage in altruistic surrogacy, in comparison to the number of women who participate in commercial surrogacy.

It is also important to acknowledge how surrogacy is tied not only to the inequalities that exist between men and women, but also to inequalities based on race and class. These intersections reveal the depth of the vulnerability of women, especially in underdeveloped countries, where poverty causes them to enter surrogacy arrangements, making them dependent on a market that has been created to serve not their interests but the interests of foreigners, and which is the subject of inconsistent regulation and is therefore unreliable and susceptible to change.[102] Furthermore, while it is true that intended parents can face uncertainty, hardship and even exploitation in seeking to have a child through a surrogacy arrangement, it is also true that they have more choices available to them, especially when compared to the means and resources available to the surrogate mother.[103]

It is at this point that we can identify how social hierarchies are reinforced in the surrogacy arrangement. Indeed, clinically – and it is to be remembered that service providers profit most from reproductive technologies – commercial surrogacy, like other reproductive technologies, is invested with notions of what is healthy womanhood and what is not; these promote the understanding that giving birth is healthy while the inability to give birth is a sickness in need of treatment.[104] By contrast, access to surrogacy services for single people and same-sex couples is usually framed in terms of promoting the principle of

---

101   Cf Jenni Millbank, 'Rethinking "Commercial" Surrogacy in Australia' (2015) 12(3) *Journal of Bioethical Inquiry* 477, 477–8.

102   This is evident in what is currently happening in Asia. In response to the Baby Gammy case and a case involving a Japanese man acquiring more than a dozen babies through surrogacy, Thailand has banned access to surrogacy services to foreigners. Only married Thai couples or couples with one Thai partner who have been married at least three years can seek surrogacy, and commercial surrogacy is banned. Anyone caught hiring a surrogate mother, or agents touting for surrogate mothers, could face imprisonment. Similar bans have been introduced in India. It has been reported that, as a result of these changes, surrogacy services in India and Thailand moved into Nepal, taking surrogates and embryos with them. In response to an action brought by human rights advocates, the Nepalese Supreme Court issued a halt on all commercial surrogacy in Nepal. It has been reported that these surrogacy services are now looking to move into Cambodia: Everingham, above n 96.

103   The main reason why intended parents seek surrogacy services is usually an unfulfilled desire to have a child of their own – usually felt among infertile couples, singles and partnered gay males. In Australia a number of factors have been listed as driving surrogacy as a means of family formation: the few children available for adoption in Australia; restrictions on intercountry adoptions; age-based infertility among women; technological advancements so the surrogate mother 'has no genetic relationship to the child(ren) she carries'; and increased community awareness of surrogacy as a family formation option: see Sam Everingham, 'Use of Surrogacy by Australians: Implications for Policy and Law Reform' in Alan Hayes and Daryl J Higgins (eds), *Families, Policy and Law: Selected Essays on Contemporary Issues For Australia* (AIFS, 2014) 67.

104   Deborah Porter, 'The Regulation of In-Vitro Fertilisation: Social Norms and Discrimination' (1997) 4(3) *Murdoch University Electronic Journal of Law* 18.

non-discrimination. Either way, these arguments sanitise the process by constructing it as 'a treatment for infertility' (whether medical or social) with the legitimate end of creating a family for the intended parents. This understanding makes the process primarily about the intended parents: the image of the self-sacrificing surrogate mother and the fact that the genetic material used to create the child usually 'belongs' to at least one intended parent – usually the father – erases the active role the surrogate mother plays in the process of creating a family, and subordinates her needs to the needs of the intended (paying) customers.[105]

These issues raise pertinent questions about how surrogacy arrangements should be regulated. Is banning (altruistic and commercial) surrogacy the only ethical solution available?

12.3.3 Reproductive technologies: the local context

Currently, the laws regulating surrogacy arrangements in Australia permit altruistic surrogacy, but criminalise commercial surrogacy arrangements.[106] On the one hand, this approach seems designed to protect the parties to surrogacy arrangements and the children born from them; on the other hand, it is designed to prevent evasion of the legislation and exploitation of women in developing countries.[107] Nonetheless, and in line with standard family law

---

105 If donor eggs are used, it is even rarer for the woman who donated the eggs, and the circumstances in which the eggs were acquired, to be seen as part of the process, notwithstanding the biological ties between the donor mother and the child.

106 The relevant provisions are contained in the *Parentage Act 2004* (ACT); *Assisted Reproductive Treatment Act 2008* (Vic); *Surrogacy Act 2010* (Qld); *Surrogacy Act 2010* (NSW); *Surrogacy Act 2012* (Tas); *Surrogacy (Consequential Amendments) Act 2012* (Tas); *Surrogacy Act 2008* (WA); and *Family Relationships Act 1975* (SA). The Northern Territory has no legislation governing surrogacy. Most of these laws make it a crime to enter into a commercial surrogacy agreement, advertise for surrogacy arrangements, and procure surrogacy arrangements: see Mary Keyes, 'Cross-border Surrogacy Agreements' (2012) 26(1) *Australian Journal of Family Law* 28, 40–1. However, there are exceptions. The SA legislation does not criminalise the commissioning parents' or birth mothers' actions in entering into the surrogacy agreement. In Victoria, the relevant offence is the receipt by the birth mother of payment in excess of reimbursement of her expenses pursuant to the *Assisted Reproductive Treatment Act 2008* (Vic) s 44(1): Mary Keyes and Richard Chisholm, 'Commercial Surrogacy – Some Troubling Family Law Issues' (2013) 27(2) *Australian Journal of Family Law* 105, 106 fn 8. In New South Wales, Queensland and the Australian Capital Territory the offences are expressly stated to apply with extraterritorial effect. For a summary of these provisions, see Keyes and Chisholm at 106 fn 9.
 Keyes and Chisholm have also summarised the penalties for entering into a commercial surrogacy agreement. In every jurisdiction except Tasmania, this offence may be penalised with imprisonment. In New South Wales, the maximum penalty for entering into, or offering to enter into, a commercial surrogacy arrangement is 1000 penalty units (or 2500 penalty units for a corporation) or imprisonment for two years, or both: *Surrogacy Act 2010* (NSW) s 8. In Queensland, the maximum penalty for the same offence is 100 penalty units or three years' imprisonment: *Surrogacy Act 2010* (Qld) s 56. In Western Australia, the maximum penalty for entering into a commercial surrogacy arrangement is $24 000 or two years' imprisonment: *Surrogacy Act 2008* (WA) s 8. In the Australian Capital Territory, the maximum penalty for intentionally entering into a commercial surrogacy agreement is 100 penalty units, one years' imprisonment or both: *Parentage Act 2004* (ACT) s 41. In Victoria, the receipt by the birth mother of 'any material benefit or advantage' is the relevant crime, and the maximum penalty is 240 penalty units or two years' imprisonment or both: *Assisted Reproductive Treatment Act 2008* (Vic) s 44(1). In Tasmania, the maximum penalty for entering into or offering to enter into a commercial surrogacy agreement is a fine not exceeding 100 penalty units: *Surrogacy Act 2012* (Tas) s 40.

107 Keyes and Chisholm, above n 106, 105–6.

philosophy, the best interests of the child is the overarching principle of these laws. The discussion below identifies the ideas underpinning the legalisation of altruistic and criminalisation of commercial surrogacy. Next, the complexities of federal and State laws in determining parentage are analysed, followed by a discussion of the constraints the family courts face in determining the best interests of the child born through surrogacy arrangements.

The legal position on surrogacy in Australia reflects particular ideas about the family.[108] The legalisation of altruistic surrogacy deflects attention from the importance of the birth mother–child bond and instead valorises the creation of a new family for the child with the intended parents. However, this approach continues to invest in traditional views of women's roles as wives and mothers and the view of the family unit as comprising a couple and a child. It reflects the image of the self-sacrificing mother willing to give the gift of the life of a child to a 'less fortunate' couple unable to conceive a child of their own. Moreover, altruistic surrogacy arrangements rely on the construction of the family as a private social institution. Even though the arrangement ultimately requires state intervention to sanction the arrangement, namely a court making orders to transfer legal parentage from the birth parent to the intended parents,[109] the fact that the arrangement is constructed as a gift aligns the actions of the birth mother with the traditional views of the family as the site of love and sacrifice and reinforces feminine altruism in the family. Thus, altruistic surrogacy can be constructed as in the best interests of the child because it is aligned to these traditional views of the family.

In contrast, the criminalisation of commercial surrogacy appears more aligned to the feminist arguments, outlined earlier, that construct such arrangements as treating the child and the surrogate mother as commodities, and risks the exploitation of poor families for the benefit of rich ones.[110] However, the official approach to criminalising commercial surrogacy is different from this feminist approach in one important respect. This feminist view of surrogacy is that it compounds women's social and economic inequalities through the exploitation of the mother–child bond. In this regard, feminists frame the issue as a public issue – that is, surrogacy creates injustice for women – whereas in official circles concerns about commercial surrogacy reflect attitudes about the damage that applying market values can have on the fundamental aspects of family life – mothering and childbirth.[111] The criminalisation of commercial surrogacy functions within the paradigm of preserving the traditional private family for the sake of the child's best interests.

Nevertheless, the new laws are not without their own shortcomings. In particular, they have been ineffective in deterring Australians from seeking surrogacy services overseas. This demonstrates how the effective regulation of overseas surrogacy arrangements depends on

---

108 See generally Anita Stuhmcke, 'For Love or Money: The Legal Regulation of Surrogate Motherhood' (1996) 3(1) *Murdoch University Electronic Journal of Law* 5, [78], [81].

109 *Parentage Act 2004* (ACT) s 24(c); *Surrogacy Act 2010* (NSW) s 34(1); *Surrogacy Act 2010* (Qld) s 20; *Family Relationships Act 1975* (SA) s 10HB(2)(a); *Status of Children Act 1974* (Vic) s 20(1)(a); *Surrogacy Act 2008* (WA) s 12. FLA s 60HB recognises State and Territory parentage orders made with respect to children born under surrogacy arrangements.

110 Standing Committee of Attorneys-General Australian Health Ministers' Conference Community and Disability Services Ministers' Conference, Joint Working Group, *A Proposal for a National Model to Harmonise Regulation of Surrogacy* (January 2009) 4–5.

111 Legislative Council Standing Committee on Law and Justice, *Legislation on Altruistic Surrogacy in New South Wales* (Parliament of New South Wales, 2009) 3.

the laws of the nations in which they take place. Where Australians have been permitted to enter these arrangements overseas, Australian law is left to deal with the reality of the situation that a child whose interests require protection has been born. But whether current Australian law is adequately designed to protect the interests of children born in commercial surrogacy arrangements overseas remains to be seen.

First of all, there are issues with parentage. State and Territory legislation provides for the transferral of parentage from the surrogate mother to the intended parents. However, these provisions have proven to be quite complex and impose onerous requirements, which intended parents must meet to obtain a parentage order.[112] The law's approach to determining parentage is quite an artificial exercise, as is evident in the NSW case of *Re Michael (Surrogacy Arrangements)*[113] (which pre-dated the *Surrogacy Act 2010* (NSW)). In this case, a married couple sought leave to commence adoption proceedings in the Family Court. The FLA provides that in certain circumstances a married couple can adopt a child of one party to the marriage (s 60G). The child in this case had been born through a surrogacy arrangement in which the mother of the wife had acted as the surrogate for a baby, produced using the sperm of the husband and the ovum of the wife's mother. After the child was born, the husband was registered as the father of the child on the birth certificate. Despite this fact, the Court found that the husband and wife were not the legal parents of the child. Instead, the wife's mother (the surrogate) and her partner were the legal parents of the child. Moreover, since neither the husband nor the wife was the 'prescribed adopting parent', they could not make the application.[114]

If the parties seeking a parentage order cannot meet the legal requirements now provided in the new surrogacy laws, they could establish the legal status of their relationship by adoption under State laws or they could seek a parenting order under the FLA. This latter is the avenue usually pursued by parties who have obtained a child through a commercial surrogacy agreement made in an overseas jurisdiction when they have been unable to legalise their relationship with the child through immigration law.[115] It appears from the case law that parenting orders sought in these cases involving overseas surrogacy arrangements are usually granted.[116] However, the effects of these orders last only until the child reaches 18

---

112   See, eg, the precondition requirements to making a parentage order in the *Surrogacy Act 2010* (NSW) pt 3, div 4. For a detailed comparative analysis of the surrogacy laws in Australia, see Stephen Page and Alexandra Harland, 'Tiptoe Through the Minefield: A State by State Comparison of Surrogacy Laws in Australia' (2011) 1(4) *Family Law Review* 198.

113   (2009) 41 Fam LR 694.

114   Section 60G(1) of the FLA provides: '(1) Subject to subsection (2), the Family Court, the Supreme Court of the Northern Territory or the Family Court of a State may grant leave for proceedings to be commenced for the adoption of a child by a prescribed adopting parent'; s 4(1) of the FLA defines 'prescribed adopting parent' as '(a) a parent of the child; or (b) the spouse of, or a person in a de facto relationship with, a parent of the child; or (c) a parent of the child and either his or her spouse or a person in a de facto relationship with the parent'.

115   There is a danger that children born through international surrogacy arrangement can find themselves stateless because of conflict between the laws of the country in which they were born and the laws of their intended country. The Baby Manji case is instructive in this regard: *Baby Manji Yamada v Union of India* [2008] INSC 1656.

116   See, eg, *Dennis v Pradchaphet* [2011] FamCA 123 and *Dudley v Chedi* [2011] FamCA 502. Both of these cases involved the same adult parties seeking separate orders with respect to a child and a set of twins born on the same day to two different surrogate mothers in Thailand.

years of age. For this reason, a parentage order would be more appropriate to secure and protect the legal rights of the children.

However, in the cases decided by the Family Court on the issue of parentage, there have been inconsistent outcomes. In *Ellison v Karnchanit* (relating to twins born in Thailand), Ryan J found that the Family Court had jurisdiction to make a parentage order under s 69VA of the FLA that enables the Court to make a declaration of parentage after receiving evidence about the parentage of the child.[117] However, when the issue arose again in *Mason v Mason*, Ryan J reconsidered her judgment in *Ellison* and found that the Family Court did not have jurisdiction to make a parentage order in this case.[118] In *Mason* (relating to twins born in India), the applicants were residents of New South Wales. In this case, Ryan J was of the view that parentage orders could only be made pursuant to the *Surrogacy Act 2010* (NSW). She came to this conclusion on the basis of her interpretation of ss 60H and 60HB of the FLA. Section 60H of the FLA provides for 'children born as a result of artificial conception procedures' and s 60HB provides for 'children born under a surrogacy arrangement'. She found that s 60HB was the relevant provision.[119] According to her reading of the FLA, if the State or Territory provides for the making of parentage orders, then that precludes the Family Court from making those orders.

Justice Johns distinguished the decision in *Mason* in *Green-Wilson & Bishop* (another surrogacy arrangement in India).[120] In this case, the intended parents were residents of Victoria. Justice Johns made a parentage order in their favour on the basis that the Court had jurisdiction in this case because the *Assisted Reproductive Treatment Act 2008* (Vic) did not make entering into a commercial surrogacy arrangement a criminal offence and the Act was silent about parentage.

These cases reveal how the inconsistencies in State and Territory laws can lead to different judicial interpretations, and highlight the need for national reform in order to provide uniform protection of the legal rights of children born through these surrogacy arrangements.

The second issue in these cases is that, when the applicants are seeking parenting orders in a court exercising family law jurisdiction, the court is required to make an order that is in the best interests of the child. However, judges are very often making decisions in the absence of the full disclosure of the facts. There is often little information about the surrogate mother or the surrogacy arrangement, and when that information is available it can be quite concerning. In *Mason*, for example, the Court referred to the surrogacy agreement that was 29 pages long, written in English and marked by the thumbprint of the surrogate mother, attesting that she was illiterate in Hindi and English. The agreement also placed restrictions on her autonomy in managing her health during the pregnancy.

Parenting orders made by a family court are also being sought against a backdrop of state and territory laws that generally prohibit commercial surrogacy. However, there has

---

117   (2012) 48 Fam LR 33 [hereafter '*Ellison*'].
118   [2013] FamCA 424 [hereafter '*Mason*'].
119   Section 60HB provides: '[i]f a court has made an order under a prescribed *law of a State or Territory* to the effect that: (a) a child is the child of one or more persons; or (b) each of one or more persons is a parent of a child; then, for the purposes of this Act, the child is the child of each of those persons' (emphasis added).
120   [2014] FamCA 1031.

only been one referral to the Director of Public Prosecutions (DPP) in the Queensland case, *Dudley v Chedi*.[121] Notably, a different judge decided the related case, *Dennis v Pradchaphet*,[122] but did not refer that case to the DPP.

These cases give rise to ethical and policy considerations about commercial surrogacy and how it can lead to the trafficking of babies; the exploitation of poor women; and concerns whether the child's interests are being served in the absence of all the available evidence – especially proof of informed consent by the relinquishing birth mother.[123] While the judges deciding these cases seem attuned to these issues, they have consistently held that making parenting orders in favour of the intended parents is in the best interests of the child. Considering the circumstances where there are no other adults before the court contesting the orders sought, it does seem as though these judges have no other choice but to make an order in favour of the intended parents.

Nevertheless, from a legal perspective these outcomes seem unsatisfactory considering the dubiousness of the intended parents' actions and their flagrant disregard of the law. Indeed, we may question the quality of their parenting skills and whether they can instil a sense of justice in the child in view of the lengths to which they went to obtain a child. In making parenting orders, judges may now be dealing with the reality that exists – a child who is in need of care and support has been born, and in making parenting orders in favour of the intended parents they may claim to be making an order that is in the child's best interests. But when examined against the backdrop in which the child was born, it appears that in making these orders judges have not moved far from the traditional view that children are the property of their parents.[124]

In view of the global and local scene, it is evident that the area is in need of reform.[125] The fact that commercial surrogacy is readily and relatively cheaply available in some parts of the world has undermined Australian attempts to criminalise this activity. In fact where attempts to criminalise surrogacy have been made, this seems only to have resulted in the increase in demand for surrogacy services in poorly regulated markets (like those that exist in Asia) and increased risk of exploitation. Thus, local bans on commercial surrogacy do not provide a solution, because that would not mean the practice would come to an end; as experience shows, it would continue.

Thus, in our view, banning surrogacy is not the solution at the present time. In so far as commercial surrogacy is a global phenomenon and is thriving in some of the poorest regions in the world, it requires the adoption of an approach that would maximise social

---

121   [2011] FamCA 502 (Watts J).

122   [2011] FamCA 123 (Stevenson J).

123   Justice Cronin considered similar issues in *Fisher-Oakley v Kittur* [2014] FamCA 123.

124   In this respect, surrogacy arrangements serve to resurrect the common law property right of the father to the child; this is especially true in cases where the father is the only intended parent who has a biological link to the child.

125   The House of Representatives Standing Committee on Social Policy and Legal Affairs (the 'Committee') recently held a roundtable on surrogacy to investigate the complexities of regulation of surrogacy and the issues faced by the increasing number of Australians who seek and use surrogacy arrangements. The Committee tabled its report, *Roundtable on Surrogacy*, on 24 March 2015. See House of Representatives Standing Committee on Social Policy and Legal Affairs, *Roundtable on Surrogacy* (Parliament of Australia, 2015) ch 1. To date, the federal government has not acted on the Committee's report.

responsibility, and minimise harm, to the most vulnerable participants of the surrogacy arrangement – the birth (and donor) mothers and the child.[126]

In developing regulatory standards, the aim would be to devise strategies aimed at preventing the exploitation of women and children engaged in surrogacy arrangements, while also implementing strategies to address the conditions of poverty that foster these arrangements.[127] In western nations like Australia, any reforms to surrogacy laws should form part of a broader process that would involve rethinking the family, addressing the subordinate role of women in society, and considering attitudes towards children that tend to conflate the child's best interests and the child as the property of the intended parents. These are long-term strategies that primarily would be concerned with overcoming women's economic inequalities and thereby removing the incentive for women to act as surrogates for economic reasons.[128] This strategy would also be aimed at explicitly articulating the role of 'heterosexual fertility' in supporting reproductive technologies. In our view, social norms that continue to associate the family in nuclear family terms are fuelling developments in reproductive technologies. Our strategy would involve inverting the role of 'heterosexual fertility' in providing the justification for treating infertility using reproductive technologies, with a view to considering alternative family arrangements that can disrupt the fertile/infertile dichotomy that exists in society, and which seems to have become increasingly pronounced with the growth of fertility treatments available via the reproductive technology industry.

12.4   Conclusion

In approaching the topics in this chapter, and throughout the book, we have analysed how family law manages to uphold the nuclear family as its preferred family. This is significant for many reasons; among them is that it fundamentally challenges the claim that the nuclear family is in decline. We started this book with Bittman and Pixley's insight that the claim that the

126   There have been recent investigations into surrogacy at the international level, particularly with respect to the recognition of the legal parentage of children and issues related to children's nationality, immigration status and parental responsibility: Hague Conference on Private International Law ('HCCH'), *Private International Law Issues surrounding the Status of Children, Including Issues Arising from International Surrogacy Arrangements* (Preliminary Document No 11, March 2011) 4 [3] <https://assets.hcch.net/docs/f5991e3e-0f8b-430c-b030-ca93c8ef1c0a.pdf>. See also Hague Conference on Private International Law, *A Preliminary Report on the Issues Arising from International Surrogacy Arrangements* (Preliminary Document No 10, March 2012) 30 [66] <https://assets.hcch.net/docs/d4ff8ecd-f747-46da-86c3-61074e9b17fe.pdf>.

127   Again, the focus has been on the rights of children where the HCCH believes that a multinational agreement is required for the prevention of child statelessness: Hague Conference on Private International Law (2011), above n 126, 23 [48]. However, with respect to the rights of surrogate mothers, concern has been expressed over whether agreement can be reached at the international level on whether a woman acting as a surrogate should be permitted to surrender her parental rights, whether she should be entitled to payment, and whether surrogacy should be permitted at all. See Natalie Gamble, 'In Practice: International Surrogacy Law Conference in Las Vegas' [2012] *Family Law* 198, 200.

128   This is not the direction of current reform proposals. See Keyes and Chisholm, above n 106, 46–9, where a 'choice of law' approach that would allow the parties to a surrogacy agreement to decide which laws would apply if a conflict of laws situation arises and thus indirectly permit commercial surrogacy in Australia is advanced; Millbank, above n 101, where an argument in favour of commercial surrogacy in the form of a compensation payment is advanced.

nuclear family is in decline is a myth.[129] At the conclusion of this chapter and of the book, we can claim that we have demonstrated not only that the nuclear family is not in decline, but that the law continues to rely on the nuclear family model in constructing what is the family in law. Most importantly, we have demonstrated why it is important to identify how the law relies on the nuclear family to maintain structural social inequalities. By framing our critique of family law on this basis, we have drawn on other disciplinary knowledges. In emphasising the point that law is constructed knowledge, our aim is to create the possibility for each one of us to consider whether family law could be different from its present form and content.

Adopting this approach stands in contrast with other approaches to the study of family law that present the law as either a neutral arbiter of family disputes or interacting with society and merely reflecting and responding to changing values. As we have traversed the various areas of family law, we have found how the law is involved in constructing ideas about the ideal family. In family law, the effects of the nuclear family construct are most evident at the time when relationships break down and individuals must reach agreement on how family property is to be divided and arrangements about children are to be made. We accept that the FLA does offer some protection to the interests of the more financially vulnerable party (usually the mother) in resolving disputes about property. However, the introduction of a regime that promotes shared parenting and the wholesale shift towards resolving disputes privately between the parties has not accorded with the reality of relationships that are organised according to the sexual division of labour. Nor are they an adequate response to family breakdowns where family violence and abuse may also be present.

The justification for these developments may lie in the conception of the liberal or egalitarian family, but in our analysis of family law and related fields it is evident that we are far from attaining this ideal as the normal family. The result has been to compound social inequality, most evidently in the disparate economic position that continues to exist between men and women in our society. In the process, these developments have reinforced the conception of the family as private and nuclear. Two significant effects of this are that the nuclear two-parent family construct can continue to be upheld as serving the best interests of the child while it can also be used to contain the costs of relationship breakdown between the parties, including any financial obligations for the children, so that the state can avoid having to meet these costs.

In illuminating these issues, our aim has been to see past the law's own appeals to neutrality and objectivity and to demonstrate how law-makers are engaged in the construction of law, an enterprise in which the nuclear family is a significant feature. The wide discretion given to judges in this area facilitates this process, but it also gives them choices. Similarly, we as legal thinkers have the choice and the responsibility to analyse how legal constructs are deployed, which categories of analysis are used, the issues that are chosen for analysis, and the way they are analysed. Undoubtedly, our perspectives will inform our choices, but this is not relativism if we can also be held responsible for justifying the outcomes as fair and non-oppressive to everyone involved. As we have seen, the choices we make can be constrained by contextual factors, but they can also mean the difference between contributing to oppressive practices and promoting fairer laws and policies that are responsive to the needs of disadvantaged groups in our society. This is self-reflexive of our views and the necessary responsibility of every legal thinker.

---

129   Michael Bittman and Jocelyn Pixley, *The Double Life of the Family: Myth, Hope and Experience* (Allen & Unwin, 1997).

INDEX